Population and Society

Written in an engaging, accessible style, the third edition has been extensively updated to include the most recent round of international censuses and emerging trends. There are new chapters on epidemics and the labor force and expanded empirical discussions of race/ethnicity, sexual orientation, sex structure and gender identity. Featuring plentiful recent examples and data from the United States, Europe, Asia, and Africa, this book explains the demographic processes of fertility, mortality, and migration, elucidating how these concepts can be applied to understand topics such as contraception and birth control, pandemics, and public immigration policy. Introducing students to the major sources and applications of demographic data, it demonstrates how demography forms a useful lens for understanding many aspects of society, including our most pressing global challenges. A comprehensive instructor manual, chapter outline PowerPoints, and figures and tables from the book are available.

Dudley L. Poston, Jr., Emeritus Professor of Sociology, held positions at the University of Texas at Austin, Cornell University, and, most recently, Texas A&M University. where he held the position of Abell Endowed Professor of Liberal Arts. He was also an adjunct professor at three universities in China. He has coauthored or edited twenty-four books and has authored or coauthored more than 400 journal articles, book chapters, and opinion pieces on various sociological and demographic topics.

Teresa A. Sullivan taught demography courses at the University of Chicago, the University of Texas-Austin, the University of Michigan, and the University of Virginia. She was President of the University of Virginia, Provost of the University of Michigan, and Vice President and Graduate Dean at the University of Texas-Austin. She chaired the National Academies panel on the accuracy of the 2020 census, publishing a separate book on the 2020 census. Her demographic specialty is labor force and related issues, and she has applied her knowledge in books analyzing consumer bankruptcy, work and labor force, and underemployment.

"An excellent introduction to the scientific study of human populations. Poston and Sullivan are eminent scholars who know how to communicate big ideas and the intricacies of measurement with clear logic and style. Students will learn that the headlines of today – the impact of immigration, sexual orientation and gender identity, partnering and parenting, ethnic and racial blending, pandemics, and the future of work – can be measured and studied with demographic data and analysis. The book addresses the policy implications of demographic research, but cautions against simple-minded policies designed to affect demographic behavior that have been tried in the past and have failed. Students and instructors will be informed by the rich review of classical topics and up-to-date research findings in an unusually comprehensive bibliography. Although primarily focused on social demography, it would be an excellent introduction to demography in any social or biological science course."

Charles Hirschman, *University of Washington*

"A valuable resource for those seeking to understand the importance of a demographic perspective. Writing in an engaging, accessible style, Poston and Sullivan cover the usual subfields (fertility, mortality, migration) but also include a broader range of topics (gender identity, sexual orientation, epidemics, aging), making it clear just how extensive and influential the field of demography and demographic processes are."

Nancy Riley, *Bowdoin College*

"An engaging, comprehensive, and updated introductory demography text. Poston and Sullivan present a highly understandable, and even conversational, approach to introducing and explaining theories, data sources, demographic processes, demographic characteristics, and more. They make demography accessible to today's students."

Carla Alphonso, *Presbyterian College*

"The much-awaited third edition of *Population and Society* is here! What a treat! Poston and Sullivan, two of the most prominent demographers in the field, have put together an exceptional book. The book features new chapters, data, and countries. Written in an engaging style, students will surely experience many 'aha' and eye-popping moments reading this fountain of demographic knowledge."

Rogelio Sáenz, *University of Texas at San Antonio*

"An outstanding introduction to demographic analysis. This book is ideal for introducing students to the discipline of demography. From theory to data to real-life examples, it covers the field comprehensively and helps students understand the application of demographic concepts to their everyday lives."

Fizza Raza, *Georgia State University*

"An exemplary textbook for learning the fundamentals of demography, and a user-friendly handbook for lay audiences interested in the myriad social and economic determinants and consequences of population dynamics. Drawing on their vast teaching and research experiences, veteran demographers Poston and Sullivan feature their expansive command of demography as an interdiscipline, providing broad-ranging historical, contemporary, domestic, and international accounts that illustrate how demography shapes social destinies. Five stars!"

Marta Tienda, *Princeton University*

Population and Society

An Introduction to Demography

THIRD EDITION

DUDLEY L. POSTON JR.
Texas A & M University

TERESA A. SULLIVAN
University of Virginia

CAMBRIDGE
UNIVERSITY PRESS

CAMBRIDGE
UNIVERSITY PRESS

Shaftesbury Road, Cambridge CB2 8EA, United Kingdom

One Liberty Plaza, 20th Floor, New York, NY 10006, USA

477 Williamstown Road, Port Melbourne, VIC 3207, Australia

314–321, 3rd Floor, Plot 3, Splendor Forum, Jasola District Centre, New Delhi – 110025, India

Cambridge University Press is part of Cambridge University Press & Assessment, a department of the University of Cambridge.

We share the University's mission to contribute to society through the pursuit of education, learning and research at the highest international levels of excellence.

www.cambridge.org
Information on this title: www.cambridge.org/highereducation/isbn/9781009696951

DOI: 10.1017/9781009696920

When citing this work, please include a reference to the DOI 10.1017/9781009696920

First published 2010

Second edition 2016

Third edition 2026

Cover image: Credit: Westend 61 / Getty Images

A catalogue record for this publication is available from the British Library

Library of Congress Cataloging-in-Publication Data
NAMES: Poston, Dudley L., 1940- author | Sullivan, Teresa A., 1949- author
TITLE: Population and society : an introduction to demography / Dudley L. Poston Jr., Texas A&M University, Teresa A. Sullivan, University of Virginia.
DESCRIPTION: Third edition. | Cambridge, United Kingdom ; New York, NY : Cambridge University Press, 2027. | Includes bibliographical references and index.
IDENTIFIERS: LCCN 2025048519 (print) | LCCN 2025048520 (ebook) | ISBN 9781009696951 hardback | ISBN 9781009696913 paperback | ISBN 9781009696920 epub
SUBJECTS: LCSH: Population | Demography | LCGFT: Textbooks
CLASSIFICATION: LCC HB849.4 .P678 2027 (print) | LCC HB849.4 (ebook) | DDC 304.6–dc23/eng/20260220
LC record available at https://lccn.loc.gov/2025048519
LC ebook record available at https://lccn.loc.gov/2025048520

ISBN 978-1-009-69695-1 Hardback
ISBN 978-1-009-69691-3 Paperback

Additional resources for this publication at www.cambridge.org/PostonJrSullivan

Contents

Detailed Contents

Preface

Why study demography? Demography is the scientific study of the size, composition, and distribution of human populations and their changes resulting from fertility, mortality, and migration. Because you are a human, demography is about *you*, and demography is also about individuals in far-flung parts of the world who also face demographic changes. Our aim in writing this textbook is to excite you about demography and, most importantly, to provide you with fundamental demographic literacy. In the process, you will find that understanding the dynamics of population is a practical skill. Urban planners, marketers, public policy analysts, school officials, public health and healthcare workers, and political and government workers at all levels use demographic data. By learning the fundamentals of demography, you will acquire useful knowledge and skills for your future positions.

Demographers use sophisticated statistical and mathematical models in their studies. In this textbook, however, we emphasize only the necessary information for you to understand demographic measures and population dynamics. If measurement and methods interest you, you should later pursue a course in demographic techniques. Depending on your interests, you might also find it interesting to take a course on population and development, or one on population economics, or one on population and the environment.

STRUCTURE AND SYNOPSIS

This book is organized into twenty chapters. The first three chapters are a general overview of demography, major demographic theories, and the sources of demographic data. In Chapter 1, you will learn the most basic equation, the population equation. Expressed in words, this equation says that the size of the population for a given geographic area at time 2 is equal to its size at time 1, plus the births that occurred between time 1 and time 2, minus the deaths that occurred between time 1 and time 2, plus the number of people who moved into the area between times 1 and 2, minus the number of people who moved out of the area between times 1 and 2. We will return to this equation again and again in the book to show you its many uses.

Chapters 4 through 7 present more details on fertility, mortality, and migration, which are the three demographic processes in the above population equation. Each chapter introduces the measurements used to analyze the demographic process and the major theories dealing with the process. In Chapter 5 on mortality, for example, we introduce the life table, one of the most important tools demographers use. You will get an overview of the range of values for these processes in different countries and in the United States.

Chapters 8 through 12 provide a deeper dive into the context for understanding the demographic processes. Most fertility takes place in the family, for example, so Chapter 8 discusses the family from a demographic perspective. Sexual orientation, sex structure and gender identity, and contraception and birth control are also relevant for fertility and are the subjects of Chapters 9 through 11. Chapter 12, on epidemics and pandemics, discusses how very large mortality events affect the society and the economy.

The three demographic processes also determine the composition of the population. Chapters 13 through 15 discuss important aspects of population composition: age composition, the labor force, and race and ethnicity.

Chapters 16 through 18 discuss large-scale changes in human populations. Chapter 16 focuses on population change and growth in the world, and Chapter 17 discusses these issues in the United States. Chapter 18 analyzes the distribution of human populations across the world and in the United States.

Not everyone agrees that human populations should be subject to public policy, and yet most countries have developed laws and regulations for immigration, and to a lesser extent, also for fertility and mortality. Population policy is the topic of Chapter 19. The concluding Chapter 20 talks about the future of the human population in the twenty-first and twenty-second centuries, and the mutual interactions of population and the environment.

NEW TO THIS EDITION

This is the third edition of *Population and Society: An Introduction to Demography*. There are two new chapters, which deal with epidemics and pandemics (including COVID-19), and with the labor force. In addition, there are now separate chapters on age composition and sex composition, and a greatly expanded chapter on gender identity. The data in the charts and tables have been updated, and in many of our discussions of US demography, we have included data from the 2020 US census. In this edition there is also more information about and more discussion of the demographic situation in countries outside North America.

Online Resources

We have prepared a new Instructor Manual to accompany this edition. It is available at www.cambridge.org/PostonJrSullivan and is complimentary for instructors who adopt the textbook. The manual has a chapter that corresponds with every chapter in the textbook. Instructors will find a list of key words, possible learning objectives for the textbook chapter, suggested classroom activities for both less advanced and more advanced students, and two sets of quiz or examination questions. The first set of questions includes multiple-choice, short answer, and essay questions that require only knowledge and comprehension of the chapter. The second set of questions is more challenging because its multiple-choice, short answer, and essay questions require analysis, application, synthesis, or evaluation. Chapter 21, the final chapter of the manual, covers some additional resources for the class such as videos and collateral demography books suitable for supplementary reading. It also contains a detailed description of a term project that instructors may wish to assign in their course in which each student prepares a demographic analysis of their home county.

Instructors will also find PowerPoint slides and jpeg files for all figures and tables in the book, suitable for classroom use. These files are available at www.cambridge.org/PostonJrSullivan and are complimentary for instructors who adopt the textbook.

HOW TO USE THIS BOOK

Here are some suggestions for both instructors and students about how they can best use this book in their teaching and learning.

For Instructors

The textbook contains twenty chapters, but unless you teach a two-quarter sequence, your semester is probably limited to fourteen or fifteen weeks. If you prefer to use just one chapter a week, then you have some choices to make about whether to use the "extra" chapters. We suggest that at a minimum you assign Chapters 1 through 8, 13, 15, 17, 19, and 20. You may use the remaining chapters for extra credit or let students choose an additional chapter to study. Depending on their majors, students may be interested in particular chapters. A student preparing for a health profession, for example, might want to study Chapter 12 on epidemics and pandemics.

The Instructor Manual, available at www.cambridge.org/PostonJrSullivan, can provide valuable help in organizing your class sessions. In addition, the files of PowerPoint slides can greatly shorten your classroom preparation time.

For Students

When they are studying a chapter, we recommend that students begin by reviewing the outline to see what the chapter covers. Then it can be helpful to read the introduction and the summary of the chapter, again to get a good overview of the chapter. Then it is time to read the chapter, paying close attention to the **boldfaced** key terms and phrases. There is a glossary at the back of the textbook with a short definition of each of these key terms. Be sure to look up words you don't understand. And do not skip the graphs and other illustrations! A valuable skill you will learn in a demography course is how to extract the maximum information from information in a table or graph. Finally, read the discussion questions at the end of the chapter. Your instructor may use these questions for class discussions or perhaps assign one for homework.

THE TEXTBOOK'S HISTORY

The first edition was written by Poston and his long-time demographer friend Leon Bouvier. Poston and Bouvier had been friends since 1974, and they would often talk about the teaching of demography, the topics they were covering in their classes, the teaching tools and techniques they were using, and the importance and relevance of demography to society. In 2005 they received a contract from Cambridge University Press to write *Population and Society: An Introduction to Demography*. The first edition of *Population and Society* was published in late spring of 2010. In late January 2011, several months after the book was published, Leon Bouvier died of heart failure in Norfolk, Virginia. He was 88 years old.

In early 2014, Robert Dreesen of Cambridge University Press asked Poston to consider writing a second edition of *Population and Society*. Poston knew that the book needed an update, but he wondered how he could write a new edition without Bouvier. Several months later he finally decided to take on the task of writing the new edition by himself. He delivered final drafts to Dreesen in 2016, and the second edition of *Population and Society* was published in 2017. But because several chapters contained parts of the text previously drafted by Bouvier, Poston retained Bouvier as a co-author of the second edition.

Six years later in 2022, Poston had a discussion with Robert Dreesen about writing a third edition of *Population and Society*. But Poston knew well that to be able to write a third edition of the book, he needed a co-author to help him and to write some of the chapter drafts. He decided to ask his long-time very dear friend and former colleague Teresa Sullivan to be his co-author. Poston's first academic job was at the University of Texas at Austin, starting in 1970. Sullivan joined the sociology faculty at UT in 1975, and she and Poston fast became good friends and colleagues. They team-taught a demography class at UT in the late 1970s; they later published two articles together, one in 1986 on the topic of teaching undergraduate demography, and another in 2020 on US Congressional apportionment. They have maintained their close friendship for decades even though they have not been colleagues on the same university faculty since 1988. They respect each other's research and students and professional contributions; their families and children know and respect one another. In April 2023, Poston and Sullivan delivered a proposal to Dreesen for the two of them to write a third edition of *Population and Society*. A final draft of the third edition was submitted in the summer of 2025.

ACKNOWLEDGMENTS

The writing of the third edition of *Population and Society* would not have been possible without the help and patience of many people, particularly our commissioning editor at Cambridge University Press, Robert Dreesen; we are indebted to Robert for his many suggestions and encouragement and patience. Rowan Groat, our development editor, provided us with much practical guidance.

We also thank many of our former faculty colleagues and graduate and undergraduate students. Our students have used earlier editions of *Population and Society* in demography classes they completed under our direction; we thank them for their suggestions and recommendations.

We also thank friends and colleagues who read one or more chapters and provided feedback, suggested improvements, and alerted us to the work of others. We appreciate their answering questions we sometimes raised about chapter topics.

Our long and time-consuming efforts in writing this third edition of *Population and Society* were assisted by the support, understanding, patience, and love of our spouses and our children and their families. We especially thank and are deeply indebted to our spouses Patricia Poston and Douglas Laycock, neither of whom has ever completed an undergraduate demography course, but both of whom know more about demography and demographers than most people. We dedicate this third edition of *Population and Society* to Pat and to Doug.

Introduction

The media these days are rediscovering population dynamics and the subject of demography. The first real heyday for demography was likely in the 1960s and 1970s with the "discovery" of rapid global population growth. In recent decades, demographic behavior and demographic characteristics have received increased attention from the popular media. And the term *demographics* has seeped into our vocabulary. More than half a century ago when Poston and Sullivan, the authors of this text, first began studying and teaching demography, the subject was not nearly as recognizable and discussed as it is today. Now, the importance of population change, in terms of size, composition, and distribution, has become increasingly relevant in policymaking at the local, state, national, and international levels. There is an increasing awareness not only of population growth and decline but also of compositional change in age, sex, and racial identity.

Care must be taken, however, to evaluate the works of journalists and others who use, or fail to use, demographic data, and nevertheless comment about populations and their dynamics. It is very easy to make errors when reporting on and interpreting population behavior. We hope that the readers of this book will become attuned to these errors that seem to appear every so often in the popular media.

Population and Society: An Introduction to Demography is intended for both undergraduate students and graduate students taking their first course in demography. It is sociologically oriented, although economics, political science, geography, history, and the other social sciences are also used to inform some of the materials we cover and discuss. Although the emphasis is on demography, we well recognize that at the individual level, population change is related to private decisions, especially in relation to fertility, but also to migration and even to mortality. We thus consider in some detail, early in the book, the role of individuals in population decision making. At the level of countries, and even the world, changes in population size have an important effect on environmental and related challenges facing all of the world's inhabitants. Despite a renewed interest in demography, journalists discussing issues such as global warming or immigration tend sometimes to overlook demographic data and patterns.

A significant and very necessary component of demography is its techniques. The study of demography involves much more than theories, concepts, and data. Demography, more so than any of the other social sciences, has a body of methods and approaches uniquely suited for the analysis of its concepts and events. In this book, we present some of the basic techniques that are needed to better understand demographic behavior. But our methodological discussions in the chapters are necessarily introductory. Students interested in pursuing the techniques in more detail will need to take a course or two dealing with demographic methods and/or consult any of a number of excellent texts focusing on demographic methods (e.g., Keyfitz and Flieger, 1971; Hinde, 1998; Pollard, Yusuf, and Pollard, 1990; Preston, Heuveline, and Guillot, 2001; Rowland, 2003; Siegel and Swanson, 2004; Smith, 1992; Yusuf, Martins, and Swanson, 2014).

We also hold that students of demography should be conversant with the basic sources of demographic data. Thus, on the Cambridge University Press webpage that is maintained for this book, we have placed detailed instructions on how to locate population data through the Internet and other sources. We are hopeful that in addition to learning about the relevance and importance of demography and its concepts, theories, and methods, students will also gain some knowledge about the richness of data available from a wide variety of governmental sources. This knowledge should come in handy in many future endeavors.

In sum, we have tried in this book to provide students and others interested in this exciting and relevant field with as much information as possible in a readable manner mostly free from professional jargon. The experience of our former students is that they have found this course useful in many fields of study, including data science, public health, medicine, public policy, and marketing, in addition to the social sciences.

1

An Introduction to Demography

WHAT IS DEMOGRAPHY?

This book is an introduction to **demography**. A short definition of demography is the systematic and scientific study of human populations. The word *demography* comes from the Greek words δημοσ (*demos*) for **population** and γραφια (*graphia*) for "description" or "writing," thus the phrase, "writings about population." The term *demography* was first used in 1855 by the Belgian statistician Achille Guillard in his book *Éléments de statistique humaine ou démographie comparée* (*Elements of Human Statistics or Comparative Demography*) (Borrie, 1973: 75; Rowland, 2003: 16). In the *Oxford English Dictionary* (2000: 444) it is noted that one of the earliest English language publications using the word demography was in 1880 when the *Library of Universal Knowledge* stated that demography is concerned with the statistics of health and disease. Most demographers (Hauser and Duncan, 1959; McFalls, 2007; Poston and Micklin, 2019) agree about the objectives and definition of demography.

Demography is the social science that studies (1) the size, composition, and distribution of the human population of a given area at a specific point in time; (2) the changes in population size and composition; (3) the components of these changes (**fertility**, **mortality**, and **migration**); (4) the factors that affect these components; and (5) the consequences of changes in population size, composition, and distribution, or in the components themselves. Hence, demography may be more broadly defined as the scientific study of the size, composition, and distribution of human populations and their changes resulting from fertility, mortality, and migration. Demography is concerned with how large, or how small, are the populations; how the populations are composed according to age, sex, race, marital status, and other characteristics; and how the populations are distributed in physical space, for example, how urban and rural they are (Bogue, 1969). Demography is also interested in the changes over time in the size, composition, and distribution of human populations, and how these result from the processes of fertility, mortality, and migration. The chapters of this book discuss these topics in much more depth and detail and will provide you with a thorough introduction to demography.

We begin this first chapter with the following point: Every one of us, whether we are aware of it or not, has already contributed, and will continue to contribute throughout our lives, to the subject matter of demography. We elaborate on the definition of demography introduced above. We then consider the so-called demographic equation. Two of the most important variables used by demographers are age and sex; hence, we give some examples of the relevance of age and sex to demography and to society. Next, we move to a discussion of the issue of population distribution and review briefly some of the major sources of demographic data. We conclude this first chapter by discussing the phrase "Demography is destiny."

WE ARE ALL POPULATION ACTORS

We are all population actors. This is a major theme of this book. Think about it: Your parents performed a demographic act when you were conceived. You, in turn, perform similar demographic acts when you decide to have, or not to have, children. Sometime during your lifetime you will move – once or perhaps numerous times. These, too, are demographic acts. Finally, you will die.

Now, you may think that your dying is not the same kind of demographic act as the decision-making of your parents when you were conceived because you yourself do not really decide how long you will live and when you will die. However, we do indeed have a lot to say about how old we will be when we die. That is, we have many options that may, or may not, extend our lives. These include such behaviors as stopping or never beginning smoking, limiting alcohol intake, eating a healthy diet, and exercising. Education is another very important behavior associated with longer lives, especially if you obtain a college degree.

As an example, let us compare women and men at age 25 with and without a college degree. On average, women in the United States with a college degree will live 62 additional years (beyond age 25) compared to those with just a high school degree who will live around 56 more years, a difference of six years. At age 25, men in the United States with a college degree are expected to live another 57 years compared to another 51 years for men who have only completed high school, again a difference of six years (Hummer and Hernandez, 2013; Rostron, Boies, and Arias, 2010).

So, one of the first pieces of important and relevant information for your life and livelihood that you have learned just by reading the first pages of this book is the following: Stay in school, graduate from college, and, on average, you will add several years to your life. In summary, we are all population actors. We are all very much involved in demography in our day-to-day lives, even though we may not always realize it.

Demography is the study of some of the most important events in our lives, and we are very much involved in them. Ask yourself: What are the only two times in your life when you will have a good chance of being identified by name and listed in your local newspapers? When you are born and when you die. These are two of the events that demographers study. Other very important events in the lives of many of us include getting married and, also for some of us, getting divorced. These are two more behaviors studied by demographers. Another really important event that almost every one of us will do at least once, if not many times, in our lives is moving from one residence to another. Demographers also study residential changes. So, as we would often tell our students in the undergraduate demography courses that we taught at Texas A&M University and at the University of Virginia, it is not at all an overstatement to say that demographers study the beginning and the end of our lives, as well as many, if not most of the really important events that occur in between. Or as the eminent demographer Samuel Preston (1987: 620–621) once stated, "The study of population offers something for everyone: the daily dramas of sex and death, politics and war; the interlacing of individuals in all their ... [groups]; and the confrontations of nature and civilization." In the next chapter, we will begin elaborating on these and related points.

DEFINITION OF DEMOGRAPHY

We have already defined demography at the start of this chapter as the systematic and scientific study of human populations. We turn now to a fuller consideration. Demography is the study of three basic processes: fertility, migration, and mortality. These are referred to as the **demographic processes.** In an important sense, that is really all there is to demography. When populations change in size, composition, or distribution, the changes depend solely on one or more of these three demographic processes. Hence, a discussion of the three demographic processes will comprise a major portion of this text.

THE DEMOGRAPHIC EQUATION

It should be clear to you that the size of a population can change only through the processes of fertility, mortality, and migration. There are only two ways of entering a population – being born or moving into it. There are also two, and only two, ways of leaving a population – dying or moving out of it. One of the fundamental facts about population change, therefore, is that populations can only change by way of a limited, countable number of events.

For example, consider the population size of a country. Suppose that this country at time t contains P_t persons, and that one year later it contains P_{t+1} persons. We may write this as the following equation:

$$P_{t+1} = P_t + B_{t\,to\,t+1} - D_{t\,to\,t+1} + I_{t\,to\,t+1} - E_{t\,to\,t+1} \tag{1.1}$$

where $B_{t\,to\,t+1}$ and $D_{t\,to\,t+1}$ are, respectively, the number of births and deaths occurring in the population between times t and $t+1$; and $I_{t\,to\,t+1}$ and $E_{t\,to\,t+1}$ are, respectively, the number of immigrants (or in-migrants) to, and emigrants (or out-migrants) from, the population between times t and $t+1$.

Equation (1.1) is known as the basic **demographic equation**, or sometimes as the demographic balancing or accounting equation. It states that the size of an area's population can change because of only three types of events: births, deaths, and migrations. These three events are known as the components of demographic change and also as the three demographic processes.

The quantity $(B_{t\,to\,t+1} - D_{t\,to\,t+1})$ is the difference between the number of births and the number of deaths that occurred during the time period t to $t+1$; if $B_{t\,to\,t+1} > D_{t\,to\,t+1}$, then the number of births exceeds the number of deaths during the interval ***t to t + 1***, and is known as **natural increase**; if $B_{t\ to\ t+1} < D_{t\ to\ t+1}$, then the number of deaths exceeds the number of births during the interval ***t to t + 1***, meaning negative natural increase, that is, **natural decrease**. The quantity $(I_{t\ to\ t+1} - E_{t\ to\ t+1})$ refers to the difference between the number of immigrants (persons who enter a country) and the number of emigrants (persons who leave a country) during the time period and is known as net international migration (or, in the case of **in-migration** minus **out-migration**, net internal migration). If $I_{t\ to\ t+1} < E_{t\ to\ t+1}$, then more persons leave (emigrate from) the area than enter (immigrate into) the area, and the quantity is known as negative net international migration. Finally, if the quantity $I_{t\ to\ t+1} > E_{t\ to\ t+1}$, then we have positive net international migration.

In the United States, we almost always have positive net international migration because it is the situation in the United States and in most developed countries that $I_{t\ to\ t+1} > E_{t\ to\ t+1}$; in 2022 nearly 14 percent of the US population was born in another country (www.census.gov/newsroom/press-releases/2024/foreign-born-population.html). The United States is, thus, a receiving country when it comes to international migration. In many developing countries, there is very frequently negative net international migration because $I_{t\ to\ t+1} < E_{t\ to\ t+1}$. Countries such as Mexico, China, India, and the Philippines are referred to as sending countries; they usually have more people leave their countries than enter and are hence characterized by negative net international migration. The Philippines sends around 1.5 million persons abroad every year, including 300,000 who work on ships around the world. Around 10 percent of the country's population lives abroad (Martin, 2013).

Within countries, however, there is usually a lot of variation in the demographic equation. The two authors of your textbook, Poston and Sullivan, live in the San Antonio-New Braunfels metropolitan area and in the Austin-Round Rock-San Marcos metropolitan area, respectively. Both these large metro areas have more births than deaths, and they also have more people moving in than moving out. Census data for the period of April 1, 2020 to July 1, 2023 (US Bureau of the Census, 2024a) indicate that in the San Antonio metro area there were 28,680 more births than deaths, and in the Austin metro area 47,227 more births than deaths. Moreover, San Antonio had almost 116,000 more people moving into the area than leaving it; and Austin had over 143,000 more people coming in than going out. In the 2020–2023 period, as a consequence, the San Antonio metro area grew in size by almost 145,000 people, and the Austin area grew by around 190,000 persons. In 2023, the cities of San Antonio and Austin were the seventh and tenth largest cities in the United States.

Unlike San Antonio and Austin, some cities – especially older ones – have more births than deaths, but have more people moving away than moving in. Large older cities often have net out-migration. If the extent of natural increase does not surpass the level of out-migration, then the city loses population. The Boston-Cambridge-Newton metropolitan area is an example with such a demographic pattern. Between 2020 and 2023, its total population declined by over 25,000 inhabitants. However, during the same period, over 24,000 more people were born in the Boston metro area than died there. But over 49,000 more people moved out of the metro area than moved in. Hence, the net out-migration more than offset the natural increase, resulting in the decline of the overall population of the Boston metropolitan area.

Some places have natural decrease, that is, more deaths than births, because elderly residents comprise a large share of their populations. A Census-designated Place (CDP) in Florida, The Villages – located in central Florida midway between the Gulf and Atlantic coasts, about one hour north of Orlando – had a total population in 2021 of 135,638 thousand persons. A CDP is defined by the US Bureau of the Census as "a statistical geography representing closely settled, unincorporated communities that are locally recognized and identified by name" (www.census.gov/programs-surveys/bas/information/cdp.html).

Between 2020 and 2021 The Villages was one of the fastest growing areas in the United States. In that one year between 2020 and 2021, The Villages grew by over 4,800 persons. But there were 2,250 more deaths in The Villages that year than births. To offset the loss, there was a net migration gain of 7,110. Why the high number of deaths? The Villages primarily consists of people over the age of 55, resulting in a very large elderly population. Many more people die in The Villages each year than are born there. Also, most of the residents of The Villages move there to retire. The Villages is said to be the largest gated retirement community in the United States (Cohen, 2009). There are many of these so-called retirement areas in Arizona, California, Florida, North Carolina, and Texas.

Some populations have both natural decrease and negative net migration. For example, in the Charleston, West Virginia, metropolitan area, between April 1, 2020 and July 1, 2023, there were 4,730 more deaths than births; and there were 2,717 more residents migrating away from Charleston than migrating into Charleston; so more people died than were born in Charleston, and more people left than entered Charleston. These losses in both natural change and migration change resulted in Charleston's loss in the period of over 7,440 people.

This phenomenon of natural decrease, that is, more deaths than births, is of increasing importance and relevance in the United States, in Europe, and in East Asia. Here are three examples. First, during the 2020–2023 period, of the 387 metropolitan areas in the United States, 178 of them had more deaths than births. For example, in the Pittsburgh, Pennsylvania, metro area, there were more than 31,000 more deaths than births; in the Tampa-St. Petersburgh-Clearwater, Florida, metro area, there were more than 20,000 more deaths than births; in the Cleveland, Ohio, metro area, there were more than 15,000 more deaths than births; and in the St. Louis, Missouri-Illinois, metro area, there were more than 9,000 more deaths than births.

Second, in the year 2008, more than half of the countries in Europe had more deaths than births. These include Germany, Hungary, Croatia, Romania, Bulgaria, the Baltic States, Greece, and Italy. Third, in recent years, more people died in South Korea than were born there (Poston, 2023b). The Korean Statistical Office reported that the country had 32.6 thousand more deaths than births in 2020, 57.1 thousand more deaths than births in 2021, and 123.8 thousand more deaths than births in 2022; and this trend is expected to continue into the future. Natural decrease has also been occurring in China in recent years. In 2022 in China, there were almost 10.41 million deaths and 9.56 million births; and in 2023, there were 11.1 million deaths and 9 million births (Poston,

2023a). This birth–death imbalance is also expected to continue in China in the years to come.

> A long-term continuation of natural decrease will result in the continual diminution of the population, and eventually lead to its disappearance, unless the excess of deaths over births is offset by population increase due to net migration. (Field and Poston, 2013: 2; Johnson, Field, and Poston, 2015)

From these examples, we can see that all three of the demographic processes play important roles in determining not only the size but also the composition of any population. Changes in the variables themselves are the result of our behavior as population actors. This is the heart of demography: Understanding how the many factors that cause changes in demographic behavior and that are the consequences of this behavior are all interrelated.

AGE AND SEX

Changes in any one of the demographic processes yield equally important information about how populations are composed, that is, their structure. The most important characteristics that tell us about population structure are age and sex. These two characteristics are so important to the study of demography and the demographic processes that they are referred to as *the* demographic characteristics.

Let us show you how closely age and sex are tied in with the three demographic processes. With regard to fertility, defined by demographers as the actual production of children, more males are born than females, usually around 105–106 males for every 100 females. **Fecundity**, that is, the ability to produce children, varies by sex; specifically, the childbearing years of females are, for the most part, between the ages of 15 and 49, and for males the fecundity years are generally between the ages of around 15 and 79 (Poston, 2019; Zhang, Poston and Chang, 2014).

Regarding mortality, that is, the frequency with which death occurs in a population, females have lower death rates than males at every age of life. Death rates are high in the first year of life and then drop to very low levels. In modern populations, the death rates do not again reach the level of the first year of life for another five to six decades. Also, cause-specific mortality is often age related. For instance, causes of "mortality such as infanticide, parricide and suicide are ... age (and sex) related" (Goldscheider 1971: 227; MacKellar, 2003). Two renowned demographers, both now deceased, Jacob Siegel and Henry Shryock, wrote that "in view of the very close relation between age and the risk of death, age may be considered the most important demographic variable in the analysis of mortality" (Shryock, Siegel, and Associates, 1976: 224; McGehee, 2004).

Migration also differs by age and sex. Traditionally, males and females have not migrated to the same places in equal numbers. Long-distance migration has tended to favor males, and short-distance migration, females, and this has been especially the case in developing countries. However, with increases in gender equity and with the lower costs of transportation, the migration of females now tends to approximate that of males. In fact, in 2020 over 48 percent of all the international migrants worldwide were women (www.migrationdataportal.org/themes/international-migrant-stocks). Internal migration is also age selective, with the largest numbers of migrants found among young adults (Bernard, Bell, and Charles-Edwards, 2014).

Age and sex are not the only important compositional variables in demography. Other variables are also related to the three demographic processes. Knowing something about marital status, for example, is important when studying fertility. Race is strongly associated with socioeconomic status, and socioeconomic status in turn affects fertility, mortality, and migration. On average, Blacks, Whites, Asians, and Hispanics all have somewhat different lifestyles, and these are related to the basic demographic processes. Education is an especially important variable to consider. In general, the higher the education attained, the lower the fertility and the lower the mortality.

These are just hints of the many compositional variables that demographers consider. The number is large, giving demographers a wide field to study. They are interested in most everything that is related to demographic behavior.

Finally, compositional variables are both the cause and the effect of population change. In turn, demographic changes can affect the compositional variables. We will have much more to say about this issue later.

AGE COMPOSITION: AN EXAMPLE

We now discuss an example that illustrates well the central importance in demography of **age composition**. It is an example that will be mentioned and discussed later in our book. It is the famous **baby boom** which began in the United States and in some other Western countries around 1946 at the conclusion of World War II and, in the United States, lasted until about 1964. Right after the end of World War II, the young adults of that period decided to have more children than those in previous generations. This resulted in a "bulge" in the age composition – a bulge, as we will later note, that resulted in numerous challenges for every institution in the US society. The bulge is easy to see in Figure 1.1, which is an age and sex population pyramid for the United States in 2010. A **population pyramid** is a graph showing the numbers of males and females according to their ages. We will cover these in greater detail in Chapter 13.

Have a look at the pyramid in Figure 1.1. The baby boom bulge is most evident in the 45–54-year age groups; and many of the babies of the baby boom babies, that is, the children of the Baby Boomers, are evident in the 15–24-year age groups. In future decades, the baby boom bulge moves higher up in the country's pyramid, but mortality will begin to shrink its numbers. McFalls, Gallagher, and Jones (1986) have noted that we can think, figuratively, of the people born during the baby boom period as a group, that is, a **cohort** that passes through the population from the youngest ages to the oldest ages, as a pig that has been swallowed by a python.

Those people born from the mid-1940s to the mid-1960s are known as baby boom babies, or Baby Boomers, because there were so many of them compared to the numbers of babies born before them and after them. The Baby Boomers have experienced problems throughout their lives. Their attendance at elementary and secondary school and at college was often marked by overcrowded classrooms and a shortage of teachers. When they entered the labor market, many of them discovered there were not

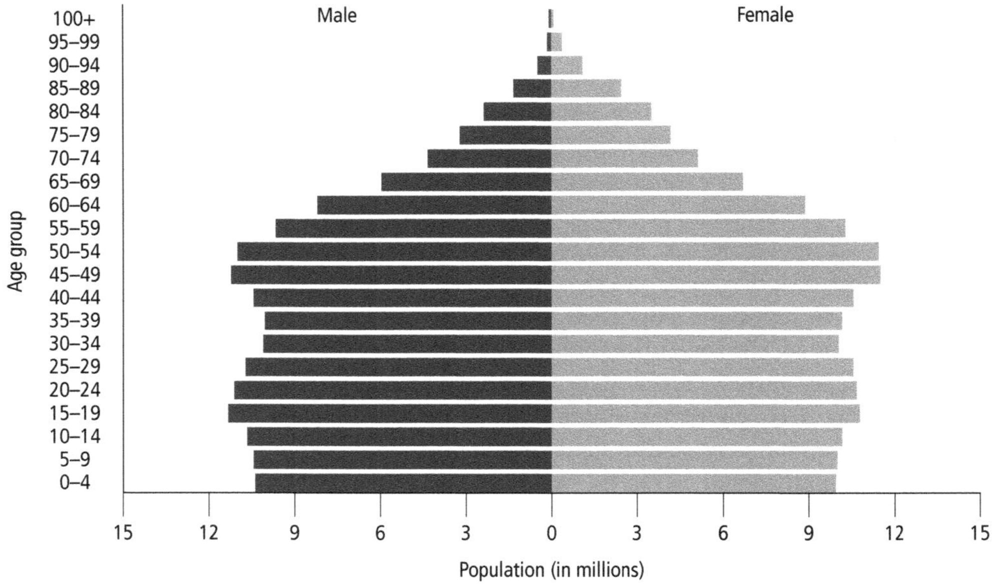

FIGURE 1.1 US population by age and sex, 2010
Data source: US Census Bureau, International Database.

enough jobs to go around. Housing for many of them was scarce. Most Baby Boomers have now reached retirement age and are finding that their demands on the US Social Security system are producing and will continue to produce strains between the financial demands of their large cohort and the smaller number of younger workers who must finance the system. These are examples of some of the problems that are likely to occur when one age group is considerably larger than groups before it or after it (Carlson, 2008).

In contrast, the babies born in the cohort after the Baby Boomers, say, those born in the 1970s, have had a much easier time during their lives. In the 1970s, there were 33 million babies born in the United States, 10 million fewer than the number born in the ten years between 1955 and 1964, the latter part of the period when most of the baby boom babies were born. The babies born after the baby boom, starting in the mid-1960s through the early 1980s, are referred to as the **baby bust** cohort, and also as the "Generation X" cohort (Carlson, 2008). They followed the enormously large group of Baby Boomers and have been in a relatively more favored position during their lives. Education facilities were more than adequate for them, and many more jobs were available for them than for the Baby Boomers who preceded them. But the Generation X babies have a big responsibility financing the retirement of the Baby Boomers.

The two authors of this book, Poston and Sullivan, were born in 1940 and in 1949, respectively. Sullivan is a Baby Boomer. But Poston was born before the start of the baby boom. His cohort, referred to as the **Lucky Few** cohort, extends from around 1929 through 1945. There were many fewer Lucky Few babies compared to the large number of Baby Boomers, around 41 million "Lucky Few" versus 78 million Baby Boomers (Carlson, 2008). Poston and the babies born in his cohort enjoyed higher employment rates and a greater variety of social opportunities than Americans in the preceding or in the following generations; and much of this was due to their small population size.

Clearly, being a member of the Lucky Few, or the baby boom, or Generation X, can have a significant impact on one's chances of success in life. We are not suggesting a form of demographic determinism. Indeed, individuals can and do succeed on their own. But it goes without saying that being born as a member of a large or a small cohort does in fact alter one's odds for later success in life (Carlson, 2008). Our generational location has a big influence on our life and our life chances. We will discuss this issue in greater detail in Chapter 13.

We have noted here the importance of age and age composition in demography and also some of the ways in which the size of one's age cohort can influence many aspects of one's life and livelihood. We turn next to a consideration of sex and **sex composition**.

SEX COMPOSITION: AN EXAMPLE

We mentioned earlier that most societies in the world have **sex ratios at birth** (SRBs) of around 105–106, that is, around 105–106 boys are born for every 100 girls. (And around 110 or so males are conceived for every 100 females.) The so-called biologically normal SRB level of about 105–106 is likely an evolutionary adaptation to the fact that females have higher survival probabilities at every age than do males. Since at every year of life more males die than females, around 105 to 106 or so males are required at birth per every 100 females for there to be approximately equal numbers of males and females when the two groups reach the reproductive ages (although there are often slightly more males than females at the beginning of the reproductive ages). Biology thus dictates that the age-specific sex ratio (SR) will be highest among the very young, and should then decline with age, attaining a value of around 100 for persons in their late twenties. SRs continue to decline to levels of around 50 or 60 among the oldest people. These SR patterns occur in most populations, barring extreme forms of disturbance or human intervention.

Later in this book, we will discuss in more detail the sex ratio at birth. But we note here that since the mid-1980s and the 1990s, several countries – for example, China, South Korea, Taiwan, India, and a few others – have been having sex ratios at birth (i.e., the number of male births per 100 female births) that are much higher than the biological average of around 105–106 (Hudson and Den Boer, 2004; Jha et al., 2006; Poston and Glover, 2005; Poston and Morrison, 2005; Poston, Conde, and DeSalvo, 2011). Indeed, in 2012, China had an SRB of 119; this means that in 2012 in China, there were 119 baby boys born for every 100 baby girls. The SRBs in China between 2005 and 2011 hovered around 119. In the past decade the SRB has dropped, and in 2020 it was just slightly above 108, still higher than the so-called biologically normal level of 105 (Tang and Hou, 2024).

These unbalanced SRBs occur because four events or phenomena have been present: (1) a rapid fertility decline in a 20–30-year period from high to low levels, starting in around the 1970s; (2) the presence of a strong preference for sons in the society's culture; (3) the availability and relative ease of access to technologies allowing the determination of the sex of the fetus; and (4) the availability and relative ease of access to abortion, both physically and normatively. These four phenomena/events are all present now in China and in several other countries in East Asia and South Asia.

Why would a country such as China resort to human interventions that would produce higher than biologically normal SRBs, of as high as 119 but a few decades ago? The answer lies in China's dramatic fertility decline. China's fertility rate declined from nearly 7 children per woman in the 1960s to 1 child per woman in 2024. China's extremely rapid fertility decline occurred in a culture that has been influenced by a Confucian patriarchal tradition for thousands of years, where son preference was strong and pervasive.

When the birth rate in a country is high, as it was in China for thousands of years up to the early 1980s, the chances that a boy will be born to a family are very good. When Chinese women were having six children on average, the probability was less than 2 percent that none of the six children would be male. By comparison, when women have two children, the probability that neither will be a son is around 25 percent, and when women have only one child, the probability of not having a son is a little less than 50 percent. Chinese parents are today having far fewer children than they had several decades ago, but the deeply rooted Confucian cultural influences of son preference have been, and are still influential in China, especially up through the early years of this new century, making it important for many families to have at least one son. Therefore, Chinese parents implemented strategies and interventions to ensure that they would have a son. The two major mechanisms are prenatal sex identification and abortion.

Ultrasound technology that enables prenatal determination of sex has been widely available in China since the 1980s. Many Chinese couples use this technology to identify the sex of the fetus, and some couples then choose to undergo an abortion if the fetus is female

In China, therefore, beginning around 1980, many more extra boys were born than girls. When these extra boys reach marriage age and start looking for Chinese girls to marry, most will be unsuccessful in their courtship pursuits. The extra boys born in the 1980s are now of marriage age and are looking for girls to marry. And many more of them will be reaching marriage age in the next two decades.

Approximately how many excess Chinese boys were produced starting in the early 1980s when China's sex ratio at birth has been so out of balance? We have estimated that there have born in China as many as around 40 million – likely more – extra boys who will not be able to find Chinese girls to marry (Poston, Conde, and DeSalvo, 2011). Some of these extra boys started to reach marriage age as recently as 2010 or earlier, and there will be lots more extra boys in China for another few decades.

The Chinese government could well turn to a more authoritarian form of government to be better able to control these millions of excess bachelors. Sociological research has shown that when large numbers of men do not marry, they are often more prone to crime than if they were married (Sampson and Laub, 1990; Laub and Sampson, 2006); banditry, violence, and revolutions could occur in areas with large numbers of excess males.

Another implication of this unbalanced sex ratio at birth is the potential for an HIV/AIDS epidemic of a scale previously unimagined. This will occur if many of the excess Chinese bachelors move to the big cities in China, and if China's commercial sex markets in the cities expand to accommodate the many millions of surplus males (Parish et al., 2003; Tucker et al., 2005; Tucker et al., 2009). The numbers of HIV cases in China in the next decades and later, owing to the bachelors and other factors (e.g., China's extremely large floating population – a topic we will cover in Chapter 6) could well rival the HIV numbers in sub-Saharan Africa. These are the kinds of societal impacts that could occur when the sex ratio becomes significantly unbalanced.

POPULATION DISTRIBUTION

We wrote the draft of this chapter in the late summer of 2024. The "World Population Clock" at the US Census Bureau (US Bureau of the Census, 2024e) estimated that the size then of the population of the world was nearly 8.1 billion people, and the population of the United States was 336.8 million. But these billions of inhabitants are not equally distributed across the planet or across the United States. Some areas are densely populated; others are not. Some areas are deserts; others are mountains. Consider, for instance, the population distribution of the United States. Figure 1.2 is a map of the United States produced by the US Census Bureau showing the distribution of the population using data from the 2020 census. Land area is shown in black and population locations are shown with white dots. Each white dot represents around 7,500 people.

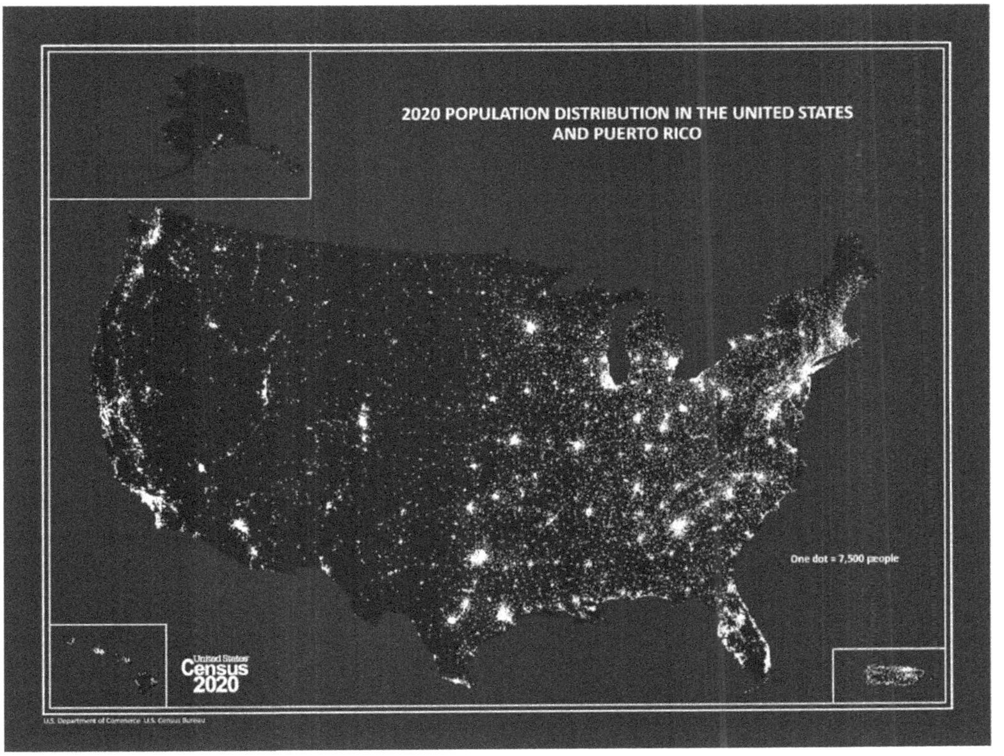

FIGURE 1.2 2020 population distribution in the United States and Puerto Rico
Source: US Bureau of the Census.

Look at the map and you will notice that the northeastern region of the country has the highest population density of population per square mile, but the southern region has the most people.

Population distribution reflects levels of fertility, mortality, and migration. Earlier in this chapter, we noted that the Boston metropolitan area was losing population mainly through out-migration. The same is true of many older large cities in the United States. Other, often newer, cities tend to grow quite rapidly. We mentioned Florida's The Villages, a CDP whose growth is due solely to in-migration, even though the area has many more deaths than births. We commented on other places where deaths outnumbered births and where the number of out-migrants exceeded the number of in-migrants.

Humans are constantly moving from place to place. We are indeed peripatetic. We always have been and always will be. The interesting point for demographers is that all three demographic processes are involved in this ongoing shift by the residents of our planet.

DEMOGRAPHIC DATA

We need to address another topic in this introductory chapter: the data that are used to study demography. Where do we find these data? We demographers are more fortunate than many of our social science colleagues who oftentimes must gather and develop their own data. Generally speaking, most of the data that demographers use have already been gathered for us. We will cover this topic in more detail in Chapter 3.

The US Bureau of the Census is an incredible source of demographic data. The data that the Census Bureau makes available and easily accessible to everyone on its webpage pertain not only to the United States. The international database of the US Census Bureau is especially thorough and of great relevance.

Another important source of data is the US National Center for Health Statistics (NCHS), particularly data dealing with fertility, **morbidity** (the prevalence of sickness in a population), causes of death, and mortality. The US Citizenship and Immigration Services (USCIS), a branch of the Department of Homeland Security, makes available extensive data on immigration. In addition, most of the US states have their own demographic data centers, and much valuable information can be gleaned from their webpages (see for example the webpage of the Texas State Data Center at https://demographics.texas.gov/).

The United Nations (UN) Population Division also publishes extensive demographic information for every country in the world, as does the US Central Intelligence Agency. The Population Reference Bureau (PRB) is a private nonprofit organization in Washington, DC, that focuses on population, health and the environment. The PRB provides a great amount of demographic information on its webpage, much of which we will use in this book.

At one time, finding and gathering data from these monumental sources were torturous. When Poston was an undergraduate student studying for his BA degree in sociology at the University of San Francisco in the late 1950s and early 1960s, he had to go to a library and find the different locations of all the various government publications. Then he had to find the actual books and census volumes. And then he had to code the data by hand. But today, almost all these sources are available on the Internet. On the Cambridge University Press webpage that is maintained for this book, we have placed specific sources for the various kinds of demographic data discussed in the chapters, with detailed directions about accessing them.

DEMOGRAPHY IS DESTINY

We often hear the expression, "Demography is destiny." Indeed, the founding father of sociology, August Comte, is believed to have been the first person to make such a statement (Thompson, 1975: 156–157). Today, commentators and news analysts often use the phrase as an explanation of how things are, and how they got that way, and how they will be. Some demographers, however, tend to shy away from the expression. While there is some validity to the phrase, there are far too many other variables that intervene in determining where an individual or a society stands at any given point in time. Nevertheless, there are instances in the study of demography, particularly with respect to population behavior occurring in relatively short periods of time, when it can indeed be argued that demography is destiny.

For instance, and again citing the baby boom example we introduced earlier, we have known for many years that by the year 2030 or so, there will have occurred a very large population increase in the numbers of elderly people in the United States and in most countries of the developed world. Why? Because we know how many people were born during the baby boom period, and we can be fairly accurate as to how many have survived into the elderly years of life. A similar statement can be made regarding the many, many millions of baby boys already born in China, Taiwan, South Korea, and India who, when it is time for them to marry, will not be able to find Chinese or Taiwanese or South Korean or Indian brides. These boys have already been born, and we know that they far outnumber the women who will be there for them to marry.

In these two cases someone could very well argue that demography is destiny. But we should not generalize too far. Nevertheless, we hold and will proclaim throughout this book that an educated person should have at least a basic knowledge of demography and how it affects almost every aspect of our lives and our institutions. We hope that the following chapters in our book will convince you of this argument.

SUMMARY

Demography is the systematic and scientific study of human populations, including their size, composition, and distribution, and changes resulting from fertility, mortality, and migration. Demographers study the changes over time in the size, composition, and distribution of human populations, and how these changes have resulted from changes in the processes of fertility, mortality, and migration.

The basic demographic equation states that the size of an area's population can change because of only three types of events: births, deaths, and migrations. These three events are known as the components of demographic change and also as the three demographic processes. Every person is a demographic actor by virtue of their birth, possible geographic moves, and eventual death.

Changes in any of the demographic processes change the population's composition or structure. Age and sex are the most important characteristics that tell us about population structure. Within a given population, the demographic processes vary depending on age and sex, but also on other characteristics such as marital status, education, and socioeconomic status.

Demographic data may come from many sources, including censuses, surveys, and the registration of births and deaths. Demographers pay close attention to the validity and reliability of the data they use.

These topics are explored in greater detail in the chapters to follow.

DISCUSSION QUESTIONS

1. Begin with a discussion of your birth, and carry your life through until the end when you die. Discuss the major demographic events that occurred/will occur in your life between the dates of your birth and your death. Reread the section in this chapter titled "We Are All Population Actors." Go over the demographic events that have occurred/will occur in your life and tell us how you have been or will be an actor in each of these events. You are/will be a population actor throughout your life, from its beginning to its end; write up short statements about each of these events and how you participated in them.
2. Imagine that it is sometime in the future and humans have colonized the Moon and the planet Mars. As it happens, the colonists are able to return to Earth from the Moon, but not from Mars. How would these developments affect how demographers construct the demographic equation?
3. August Comte is thought to be the first person to have stated that "Demography is destiny." Think about this phrase. It means that characteristics of a population, such as its age distribution, its size, its birth rate, and its geographic distribution, may well significantly influence its societal development and end up predicting its social trajectory. Select a country in Europe and one in Africa, learn something about their demography, and suggest how and why their demographic characteristics might well impact their destiny and the future daily lives of their populations.

2

Theories of Demography

INTRODUCTION

Demographers have developed several theories or explanations about why and how populations change their size. Many have written about world population growth and decline. In this chapter we consider first the general meaning of the term "population." Then we review the works of some of the early writers who discussed population and population change. Malthus is the most well known of the early scholars, and so we discuss him and his writings in some detail. Our discussion of Malthus is contrasted with shorter discussions of Karl Marx and Ester Boserup. We then turn to a detailed discussion of **demographic transition theory** and its major extensions. Finally, we discuss some of the principal theories and perspectives that demographers have developed that focus specifically and separately on fertility, mortality, and migration. These theories are discussed in greater detail in the chapters devoted to these topics.

WHAT IS A POPULATION?

Demography is the study of human populations. The word *population* is from the Latin *populare*, to populate, and the Latin noun, *populatio*. McNicoll has written that in ancient times, the verb *populare* "commonly meant to lay waste, plunder, or ravage," and the noun *populatio* "was a plundering or despoliation" (2003: 730). These usages became obsolete by the eighteenth century. According to Landry (1945), the modern use of the word *population* first appeared in 1597 in an essay by Francis Bacon (McNicoll, 2003).

Strictly speaking, a population is a group or collection of items. Biologists speak of a population of a particular species of plants or animals. To a demographer, a population is a group or collection of people. Preston, Heuveline, and Guillot (2001: 1) distinguish between a specific population or group of actual people alive at a given period of time, for example, the population of China as of November 1, 2025, and the population that persists over time even though its actual members may change, for example, the population of China during the past 4,000 years. But as McNicoll has noted, the more common use of the term *population* by demographers and in modern English usage is with regard to a "well-defined set, with clear-cut membership criteria" (2003: 731), such as the population of the United States as identified and enumerated in its 2020 census on April 1, 2020.

In a similar vein, Ryder (1964: 448) considered a population to be an aggregate of individuals defined in *spatial* and *temporal* terms. An aggregate is a collection of individuals who do not necessarily interact with one another; it is not the same as a group, which in sociological terms requires some form of interpersonal interaction and the development of a sense of community. The population then is a special type of aggregate defined in terms of a specific place and time. The analysis of human populations is inherently dynamic because attention is focused on changes in the population over time.

Ryder also stated that the population model is both microdynamic and macrodynamic. This means that processes of change in fertility, mortality, and migration can be identified at both the individual (micro) and the aggregate (macro) levels. Alfred J. Lotka (1880–1949) was a Polish-American mathematician and statistician who developed the important distinction between the persistence of the individual and the persistence of the aggregate (Lotka [1934], 1998). All human beings are born, live for some period of time, and then die. But a population aggregate is not temporally limited, provided that enough individuals continue to enter the population, usually through births, to replace those exiting. The population aggregate in this sense is immortal.

Population aggregates, both in terms of the changes in numbers and the characteristics of those entering and exiting, can experience changes not reducible to individuals who constitute the population (Haaga, 2000; Kingsland, 2015). For instance, when individuals enter a population through birth or through in-migration, they will "age" by becoming older. But the population aggregate cannot only become older; it can also become younger, provided that births exceed deaths and that the in-migrants are younger than the out-migrants. Indeed, all human institutions and organizations may be thought of in these terms. One way that social change may be studied is by monitoring the compositional change caused by entrances and exits (Ryder, 1964).

EARLY WRITINGS ABOUT POPULATION

Interest in and concern about population change have not been limited to demographers. In Genesis 1:28, humans were encouraged to "be fruitful and multiply and fill the earth." The philosopher Plato (428–348 BC) had his own ideas about population size. He believed that a community should not be larger than 5,040 citizens; otherwise, too many people would lead to anonymity. (By comparison, ten American high schools in 2024 were larger than 5,040 students [College Transitions, 2024].) The farsightedness of Plato and some of the other Greek philosophers of that time remains amazing to us today. A major concern of sociologists in the twenty-first century is the lack of face-to-face communication because of the Internet, the iPhone, the smart watch, social media, and other inventions. We can only speculate as to how Plato would react to these decreasing levels of face-to-face communication were he alive today!

Plato's ideas resonate well with the writings of the nineteenth-century sociologist Emile Durkheim (1858–1917), who visualized two types of societies: mechanical and organic. The former was small, with a simple **division of labor**, whereas the latter was considerably larger, with an extensive division of labor as well as increasing anonymity (Durkheim, [1893] 1984).

The fourteenth-century Arab historian Ibn Khaldun (1332–1406) was also concerned with population growth. He posited that societies pass through stages of population growth as they mature – much like individuals do: "The inhabitants of a more populous city are more prosperous than their counterparts in a less populous one . . .The fundamental cause of this is the difference in the nature of the occupations carried on in different places" (Issawi, 1987: 93).

In 1848, the great English philosopher John Stuart Mill (1806–1873) wrote the following:

> If the earth must lose that great portion of its pleasantness which it owes to things that the unlimited growth of wealth and population would extirpate from it, for the mere purpose of enabling it to support a larger, but not a happier or a better population, I sincerely hope, for the sake of posterity, that they will be content to be stationary, long before necessity compels them to it. ([1848] 1965, Book 4: 756–757)

What that necessity might be was explored in the work of Malthus.

MALTHUS

The most well-known early scholar who wrote about population growth is the English political economist Thomas Robert Malthus (1766–1834). He did not use the name "Thomas," but instead either "T. R. Malthus" or "T. Robt. Malthus." He was educated at Jesus College in Cambridge. At the age of 22 he became a curate near his family home in Surrey and later in Lincolnshire. In 1805, he was appointed a professor of history and political economy at East India College, Hailerbury, a position he occupied until his death in 1834. In his early years, at age 32 when he was a rural clergyman, he published anonymously the first edition of his famous work, *An Essay on the Principle of Population as it Affects the Future Improvement of Society, with Remarks on the Speculations of Mr. Goodwin, M. Condorcet, and Other Writers.*

According to demographer William Petersen, this publication right away made Malthus a very controversial figure. This first edition was mainly a "deductive book" of around 55,000 words, whereas the second edition (see below) expanded the theory and provided a great deal of illustrative data, resulting in around 200,000 words (Petersen, 1979: 52–53). Subsequent editions, ending in the seventh edition published posthumously in 1872, included relatively minor changes. The best edition is the second, with revisions, contained in two volumes and edited by Patricia James (Malthus, [1803] 1989).

Malthus's main argument was that the growth of a population is fueled by people's natural urge to reproduce. He claimed that material resources such as food and shelter can only grow at an arithmetic rate, while populations grow at a geometric rate. The potential rate of increase for population, in each generation, is geometric, that is, 1-2-4-8-16-32-64, while that for subsistence, in each generation, is arithmetic, that is, 1-2-3-4-5-6-7. If unchecked, population levels would double in size about every twenty-five years. In 225 years, the population would be at 512 billion – 511 billion more than at time 1. Yet in that same time period, the means of subsistence would only have increased by 10. Because productive capacity can never match the rate of population growth, the growth in population must be continually checked.

Malthus argued that population growth was held in check in two ways, by preventive checks and by positive checks. The major preventive check was "moral restraint," or the postponement of marriage (see below). The positive checks included wars, famine, pestilence, and other forms of misery. If population was left unchecked, it would grow much faster than material resources and lead to human misery, ultimately resulting in poverty. (It should be noted here that Malthus's term "positive" is not being used in the sense of affirmation, but rather in the sense of being definite. We still use this second meaning when we declare we are positive about something.)

Malthus's second edition of his essay was written following his travels to find ethnographic and statistical evidence to support the principle of population. In this edition, he focused more on moral restraint to limit the number of births. It referred to the postponement of marriage until an individual had prospects for supporting a family. Under the assumption that the "principle of population" was thought to be a natural law, Malthus wanted to see if human action could remove or limit the evil effects of this law.

Malthus's essay needs to be placed and considered in historical context. It opposed two very influential schools of thought, **mercantilism** and **utopianism**, and cast doubt on the hope of human perfectibility. Winch has written that "Malthus showed that any attempt to create an ideal society in which altruism and common property rights prevailed would be undermined by its inability to cope with the resulting population pressure" (2003: 169).

Eversley (1959) has noted that Malthus is sometimes misunderstood by people who have never read him or is misquoted by those who claim to have read him. He observed that Malthus was a good sociologist and his population theory important, although unsystematic and poorly written, but it is impossible to ignore the "Malthusian problem."

Glass (1953) has observed that when Malthus wrote his first essay, it was to attack the belief in the ideals of William Godwin and the Marquis de Condorcet regarding the perfectibility of man and society; indeed, the names of Godwin and Condorcet are in the book's subtitle. Glass has contrasted Malthusian theory with historical problems. He noted that Malthus's precepts of conduct are no longer relevant for preventing conflict between population and subsistence. Malthus was a poor prophet because the only nation that followed the Malthusian way was Ireland. Glass urged readers to respect Malthus as an important economist but to be wary of many of his ideas.

Malthus's essays have sparked much debate from the time the first edition was published. However, it is likely that many more people talk about Malthus's views than truly understand them. Today, scholars are still debating Malthus's ideas regarding population. Many non-believers note that Malthus's arithmetic analysis has faults, an argument with which Malthus may not have disagreed. According to Thompson and Lewis, Malthus actually noted that he used the geometrical ratio for population and an arithmetical ratio for subsistence mostly to illustrate his point (Thompson and Lewis, 1965). However, Malthus always held that population growth was faster than subsistence. Some of the other arguments attributed to Malthus are that he ignored the impact of contraception on controlling population growth. As a clergyman he was not able to recognize birth control within marriage as a check. Winch wrote that Malthus was "opposed to birth control on the grounds that such 'unnatural' experiments ran contrary to God's design in placing humankind under the right degree of pressure to ensure its development" (Winch, 2003: 620). Thompson and Lewis also stated that Malthus never clearly defined subsistence as either food or means of subsistence, which is synonymous with standard of life (Thompson and Lewis, 1965).

Bogue (1969) may have written one of the better appraisals of Malthus. He believed that Malthus's contribution to the development of demography, at best, was modest. He stated that Malthus's defenders often find solace in stating that those who do not accept him have not read him; however, Bogue disagrees. He wrote a detailed examination of Malthus's work, pointing out that he was not methodologically or substantively original. He observed that Malthusian principles were not valid for Europe or for North America because the Industrial Revolution has shown that increases in subsistence have far exceeded the human tendency to reproduce (Poston, 2006b).

The Danish economist Ester Boserup (1910–1999) posed an interesting challenge to Malthus's suppositions about the rate of growth of subsistence. She argued that population growth stimulated agricultural intensification such that new techniques increased the available sustenance. She also argued that women led this move to intensification (Boserup, 2005). There is substantial empirical evidence that agricultural productivity did indeed increase rapidly, and innovations such as new grain hybrids continue to increase yield (Soby, 2017).

The writings of Malthus are said to have influenced the work of Charles Darwin, Herbert Spencer, David Ricardo, John Maynard Keynes, and many others. For instance, Darwin wrote in his *Autobiography* ([1887] 1958: 42–43):

> Fifteen months after I had begun my systematic enquiry, I happened to read for amusement Malthus on population, and being well prepared to appreciate the struggle for existence which everywhere goes on from long-continued observation of the habits of animals and plants, it at once struck me that under these circumstances favorable variations would tend to be preserved and unfavorable ones be destroyed. The result of this would be a new species. Here, then, I had at last got a theory by which to work.

MARX

Karl Marx (1818–1883), the German-born economist and philosopher, disagreed with Malthus about the universal nature of the problem of overpopulation. Marx was writing at a time when the Industrial Revolution was reaching its apex. He argued that there were two classes of people, namely, the bourgeoisie (capitalists) and the proletariat (the workers) (Marx and Engels, [1848] 1935: 32). It was to the advantage of the bourgeoisie to encourage high fertility because this would result in a surplus of workers. Such a surplus would lead to more profits, the goal of the capitalists. According to Malthus, population was an **independent variable** and was the cause of much distress, such as poverty. In contrast, Marx argued that population was the **dependent variable**: "Whenever the reserve army of labor is relatively depleted and the level of wages tends to rise reducing the rate of surplus value, the capitalist class will adopt measures, i.e., technological improvements, foreign investments, and so forth, which, while increasing the productivity of labor and the rate of profit, will render obsolete the number of jobs" (Gimenez, 1971: 4). In other words, Marx believed that capitalism was the culprit that ended up causing poverty, whereas Malthus believed that population growth itself was the main cause of poverty.

Marx was aware that population growth could be a problem. Indeed, the German philosopher Friedrich Engels (1820–1895), his longtime friend and collaborator, wrote:

> [T]here is, of course, the abstract possibility that the number of people will become so great that limits will have to be set to their increase. But if at some time communist society finds itself obligated to regulate the production of human beings, just as it has already come to regulate the production of things, it will be precisely this society and this society alone which will carry this out without difficulty. (cited in Gimenez, 1971: 4)

DEMOGRAPHIC TRANSITION THEORY

The most prominent explanation for the growth of human populations is demographic transition theory (DTT). Changes in the size of the world's population over a certain period of time are due entirely to changes during the same time period in fertility and mortality (migration, obviously, does not figure into the equation when the focus is on the world). The world changes its size over a given time interval by adding persons born during the period and subtracting persons dying.

Demographic transition theory was first developed by Warren S. Thompson (1929) and Frank W. Notestein (1945) and extended by Kingsley Davis (1963). The original theory proposes four stages of mortality and fertility change that occur in the process of societal modernization (see Figure 2.1). The first stage is the pretransitional or preindus trialization stage. It lasted for thousands and thousands of years when the world was characterized by high birth and death rates and stable population growth. It shows high rates of fluctuating mortality and high fertility. The relative instability of the mortality rates means that during this stage, there were some periods of natural increase and some of natural decrease, but that over the longer period, there was very little change in population size.

This pretransitional stage was followed by a transition to the second stage. For numerous reasons, mortality began to decline in many countries of the world. (We discuss these reasons in more detail in Chapters 5 and 12.) With the onset of industrialization and modernization, many societies transitioned to lower death rates, especially lower infant and maternal mortality rates, but maintained high birth rates; rapid population growth was the result. It would take much longer before fertility would begin to fall. Thus, during Stage 2, population growth was intense because of natural increase.

The next stage (Stage 3) was characterized by decreasing population growth due to lower birth and death rates. During this period fertility began to decline. In the final stage (Stage 4), called incipient decline, both fertility and mortality are very low. In Stage 4, populations grow only when there are increases in fertility, such as in the baby boom in the United States after World War II. During this stage, however, there are slight

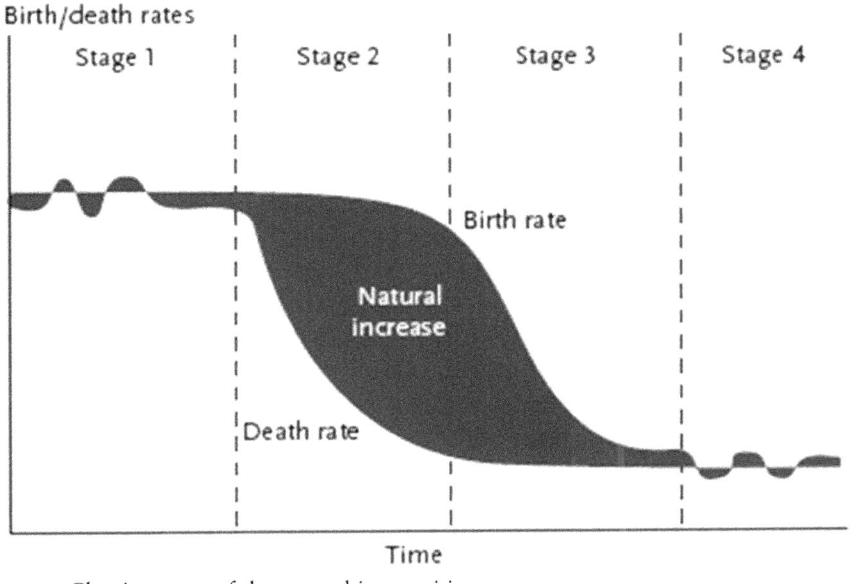

FIGURE 2.1 Classic stages of demographic transitions
Source: Joseph A. McFalls Jr., "Population: A Lively Introduction." *Population Bulletin* 62 (1) (2007): 1–31 (reprinted with permission).

fluctuations in fertility and there can be fluctuations in mortality due to pandemics. Thus, both natural increase and natural decrease will occur owing to these fluctuations. The term incipient is used because it is not really possible to determine how low fertility will go.

In recent years, fertility has fallen so low in many European countries and in Japan that the number of deaths exceeds the number of births (Poston, Johnson, and Field, 2015). Today about half of the world's population lives in countries that are experiencing – at least for now – natural decrease (Frejka, 2017). This finding has led to a hypothetical Stage 5 of the demographic transition, in which population numbers actually decline through natural decrease, at least for a while.

The theory of demographic transition is the most popular of the demographic theories of population change (Browning and Poston, 1980). There are numerous applications of the theory in European and other populations (Coale and Watkins, 1986). These studies show that the transition does not work the same way in every population (Hirschman, 1994; Knodel and van de Walle, 1979; K. Mason, 1997; Poston, 2000). Its major contribution is its utility less as a predictor than as a general description of population change (Poston, Zhang and Terrell, 2008).

The demographic transition in most less developed countries is not yet complete. Many African countries are early in Stage 3 of the transition, with falling death rates and high, though falling, birth rates, and others are late in Stage 2. This is also the case in much of the Middle East. Some countries in Latin America are moving toward the stage of incipient decline but are not there yet. This is also true of the United States.

These variations in demographic transition between the more developed and the less developed countries are resulting in some interesting changes in population distribution.

One in particular is that most of the population increase in the world between now and the year 2050 will mainly be among the developing countries and not among the developed countries. In 2022, over 83 percent of the world's population (6.6 billion people) lived in the less developed countries and just under 17 percent (just over 1.4 billion) in the more developed countries (UNCTAD, 2022). Just one century ago, the pattern was reversed, with a majority of the Earth's population residing in the more developed countries. "The conclusion is obvious: not only has population growth been enormous in the 20th century, it has also led to a complete reversal of population distribution with the poorer regions gaining and surpassing the richer sections in the process" (Bouvier and Bertrand, 1999: 10). The share of population living in the less developed countries will increase even further during the twenty-first century given the very low fertility rates in the developed nations.

We mentioned above that the fourth stage of the demographic transition is referred to as that of incipient decline because fertility and mortality are both low. However, there have occurred major changes throughout the society along with the very low fertility and mortality. Dirk van de Kaa (1987) and Ron Lesthaeghe (1995, 2010; Lesthaeghe and Neidert, 2006, 2009) have discussed these further fertility declines, along with accompanying demographic behaviors such as increasing age at first marriage, increases in cohabitation, increases in divorce, the emergence of same-sex partnerships and marriages, increasing rates of nonmarital childbearing, and voluntary childlessness. These have been subsumed under the heading of an extension of demographic transition theory that is popularly known as the **second demographic transition (SDT)**. In Chapters 4 and 8 we show that all the above changes are now occurring in the United States and in most of the European countries.

Demographic transition theory has been further revised with the recognition by Coleman (2006) of the increasing tendency, if not requirement, of low fertility countries to rely on immigration to maintain their population. This means that "the ancestry of some national populations is being radically and permanently altered by high levels of immigration of persons from remote geographic origins" and in some countries is accompanied by "accelerated levels of emigration of the domestic population" (Coleman, 2006: 401). These further changes are popularly referred to as the **third demographic transition (TDT)**.

A particularly instructive application of this perspective is Lichter's (2013: 364) observation that the "new immigration has altered America's fundamental character. Immigration has become a national political issue and not just a state or local one." Changes in the racial mix of the United States are first seen among the children and young people of the society (Johnson and Lichter, 2008, 2010), and many of these children are the children of immigrants. Lichter makes the point that these children are in "the vanguard of the Third Demographic Transition that will remake America" (Lichter, 2013: 364).

In summary the classic demographic transition, now referred to as the first demographic transition, involved the transition or movement of societies from high levels of fertility and mortality to low levels of fertility and mortality. This transition began in 1700 and later in Europe and is still ongoing in many Latin American and Asian countries and in virtually all of sub-Saharan Africa. We mentioned above the major changes that have occurred in demographic behavior in most European countries and other countries experiencing very low levels of fertility. These changes have led to what is now popularly known as the second demographic transition, which is an attempt by demographers to explain "the revolution in living arrangements and sexual behavior, and in the setting for childbearing, now transforming the lives of many inhabitants of Western societies and, it is argued, eventually in developed societies elsewhere" (Coleman, 2006: 402).

But given the very low levels of fertility, so low that in some societies there are more deaths occurring than births, there has been a tendency, if not a requirement, to rely on international migration to maintain their populations. Neither the first nor the second demographic transitions explicitly took into account the role of international migration. This lack of attention to the crucial role assumed by international migration has resulted in what has become known as the third demographic transition. This involves bringing increasing numbers of immigrants into the low-fertility countries, and in so doing, resulting in significant changes in the "composition of national populations and thereby [their] culture, physical appearance, social experiences, and self-perceived identity" (Coleman, 2006: 402). We discuss immigration further in Chapter 7. Next, we will discuss various theories that refer specifically to each of the three demographic processes of fertility, mortality, and migration.

FERTILITY THEORIES

Demographers have developed several theories of fertility. Prominent explanations are **wealth flows theory**, **human ecological theory**, and **political economic theory**. We now give each of these some attention.

Caldwell (1976) revised certain features of the classic demographic transition theory (just reviewed) with his fertility theory of wealth flows. It is based on the notion that the "emotional" nucleation of the family is crucial for lower fertility. This occurs when parents become less concerned with ancestors and extended family relatives than they are with their children, their children's future, and even the future of their children's children (Caldwell, 1976: 322). He noted that this depends largely on the direction of the intergenerational flows of wealth and services. If the flows run from children to their parents, parents will want to have large families. In modern societies where the flows are from parents to children, parents will want small families or maybe even no children (Poston and Terrell, 2006; Poston, Zhang, and Terrell, 2008).

Two other prominent theories of fertility change are based on human ecology and political economy. Both are extensions of demographic transition theory but in different ways. Human ecological theory is a macro-level explanation, that is, it focuses on societies and not on individuals. It argues that the level of sustenance-organization complexity of a society is negatively related to fertility growth and decline (Poston and Frisbie, 2019). In the first place, high-fertility patterns are dysfunctional for an increasingly complex sustenance organization because so much of the sustenance produced must be consumed directly by the population. High fertility will reduce the absolute amount of uncommitted sustenance resources, thereby limiting the population's flexibility for adapting to environmental, technological, and other kinds of societal changes and fluctuations. Low fertility is more consonant with the needs and requirements of an expansive sustenance organization. More sustenance would be available for investment back into the system in a low-growth and low-fertility population than in a population with high fertility. Hence, large quantities of sustenance normally consumed by the familial and educational institutions in a high-fertility population would be available as mobile or fluid resources in a low-fertility population. Sustenance organization in this latter instance would thus have the *investment resources* available for increasing complexity, given requisite changes in the environment and the technology. This leads to the hypothesis of a negative relation between organizational complexity and fertility and population change (Kasarda, 1971; London, 1987; London and Hadden, 1989; Poston and Frisbie, 2019).

The political economic approach is another way to analyze fertility. Diverse fields of knowledge are integrated into the political economy approach so that research reflecting this perspective is "multileveled," combining both macro- and micro-level explanations. Its complexity requires a methodology that embraces both quantitative and qualitative approaches (Greenhalgh, 1990b; 2008; Poston and Terrell, 2006).

The political economy of fertility is not really a theory of fertility per se but an investigative framework, or "analytic perspective," for the study of fertility (Greenhalgh, 1990b: 87). A good example of a political economy approach to fertility is Kertzer and Hogan's study of Casalecchio, Italy. The authors tracked one small, rural Italian community during a few change-laden decades of the nineteenth and twentieth centuries, using individual-level data and directed by a life-course perspective. They touched on historical events, such as labor and marriage patterns, often ignored by other studies of demographic change. They showed that fertility rates and fertility reduction vary depending on the class or occupation of the family, thus demonstrating that macro-level socioeconomic factors have idiosyncratic effects on different classes of people (Kertzer and Hogan, 1989).

A DEMOGRAPHIC THEORY OF MORTALITY

An important theory that demographers use to help them better understand societal changes in mortality and the changing structure of causes of death is **epidemiological transition theory (ETT)**. Epidemiological transition theory focuses on the society-wide decline of infectious disease to be replaced by chronic degenerative causes of death. According to ETT, as postulated by Omran (1971), there are three stages. The first stage is the age of pestilence and famine, in which the primary causes of mortality are influenza, pneumonia, smallpox, tuberculosis, and other related diseases, with high infant and childhood mortality and a life expectancy averaging between 20 and 40 years. In developed countries, this first stage lasted until around 1875. The second ETT stage is the age of receding pandemics, in which there is a decline in mortality due to improved sanitation and increases in standards of living and public health, resulting in a steady increase in life expectancy to between 30 and 50 years. According to Rogers and Hackenberg (1987), the stage of receding pandemics occurred around the period between 1875 and 1930. This stage should not be interpreted as meaning that infectious illnesses and pandemics disappear. New pathogens can arise for which the population has no immunity. The worldwide COVID-19 pandemic is one recent example, but other recent examples are AIDS and SARS/MERS. The point, however, is that even if these new diseases cause widespread death, the *proportion* of deaths from infectious disease continues to decline.

The third ETT stage is known as the era of degenerative and manmade diseases (heart disease, cancer, diabetes, and stroke), in which mortality declines are due primarily to medical advances in the prevention and treatment of infectious diseases. Life expectancy at birth rises rapidly so that fertility becomes the primary factor in population growth as life expectancy exceeds 70 years (Omran, 1971). About three-fourths of the deaths in this stage are the result of degenerative diseases in the advanced years (Olshansky and Ault, 1986).

Rogers and Hackenberg have noted a fourth ETT state that they have identified as an "hybristic stage" in which mortality is heavily influenced by individual behavior and lifestyle choices. Deaths in this stage are due to social pathologies such as accidents, alcoholism, suicide, and homicide, as well as to lifestyle issues such as smoking and diet (Fingerhut, 2003; Poston, Davis, and Lewinski, 2006; Robine, 2003; Rogers and Hackenberg, 1987).

These topics are discussed further in Chapters 5 and 12.

THEORIES OF INTERNAL MIGRATION

We now discuss some of the main theories developed by demographers to account for migration. In this section we focus on internal migration, or the changes in residence that occur within a country. In the next section we focus on international migration, or the changes in residence that occur between countries.

With respect to internal migration, why do people move or not move, and why do some geographic areas grow through internal migration and others do not? We note in later chapters that fertility and mortality occur in response to both biological/genetic and social factors. For example, the likelihood that a woman will have a child is due in part to her fecundity (biological) and in part to her education (social). The likelihood that a person will die or not die is also due in part to biological and social factors. Migration, however, has no such biological or genetic component. There is no genetic propensity in humans favoring or not favoring residential change. The likelihood that a person will or will not move is due entirely to factors in the physical and social environment at the areas of origin and destination, as well as to personal factors.

The eminent demographer Donald Bogue once wrote:

> [T]he human organism tends to remain at rest [that is, in the same residential location] until impelled to action by some unsatisfied need or by the threat of discomfort ... Migration [theories thus begin] with the premise that every departure for a new community, i.e., migratory movement, is either a response to some impelling need that the person believes cannot be satisfied in his/her present residence, or is a flight from a situation that for some reason has become undesirable, unpleasant, or intolerable. (Bogue, 1969: 753)

The question of who migrates depends in large part on what demographers refer to as the **push and pull factors of migration**. In every consideration of migration, there is usually some combination of factors pushing or not pushing the person from the area of origin and pulling or not pulling the person to the area of destination. Migration push factors include such considerations as loss of a job; discrimination; low availability of social and life partners; and community catastrophes such as floods, epidemics, or hurricanes. Migration pull factors include better chances for employment, education, or income; gentler environment in terms of climate and living conditions and in terms of race and sexual orientation; and the lure of new or different types of activities (Bogue, 1969; Lee, 1966).

Demographers have shown that people who migrate, i.e., change their residences, in response mainly to "pull" factors at the place of destination tend to be "positively" selected. They generally have more education than those who remain behind (Bouvier, Macisco, and Zarate, 1976). Hence, their departure lowers the overall level of educational attainment in the area of origin and often deprives the area of persons with skills that might be useful. These migrants tend to be more innovative and are often better planners. Indeed, that is one reason why they chose to move in the first place. To the extent that this selectivity is present, the area of origin will likely lose a valuable segment of its population (Macisco, Bouvier, and Weller, 1970).

In contrast, migrants responding mainly to "push" factors in the area of origin tend to be "negatively" selected. They are the people who cannot seem to succeed, either because of poor education, lack of needed talents, or losses through natural disasters. They are, in a sense, almost forced to leave to better their lot in life. They tend to have fewer positive characteristics that are valued in society. Other things equal, the area of origin is changed positively by the out-migration of such people (Bouvier, Macisco, and Zarate, 1976).

Lee (1966) noted, however, that there is more to migration than a person's calculating the advantages and disadvantages, the positives and the negatives, at both the areas of origin and destination. There are also intervening obstacles that must be considered. Between every two possible areas of origin and destination are various obstacles that may or may not intervene and have an impact on whether the migration will or will not occur. One is distance. Other things equal, the greater the distance between two areas, the less likely the migration. Physical barriers, the expense of transportation, and migration laws may also reduce the likelihood of migration.

Thus, at both the origin and the destination, there are positive and negative factors that the person typically considers when deciding whether to migrate. Between the origin and destination are obstacles that may or may not influence the migration decision. The pushes and pulls thus are evaluated in light of the costs of overcoming the intervening obstacles.

Many of the specific theories of internal migration developed by demographers to better understand the dynamics of migration begin with this framework. Each theory tends to focus more on certain pushes, pulls, or obstacles than on others. The main theoretical models seek to explain internal migration in terms of (1) the effects of distance, (2) income, (3) the physical costs of migration, (4) information, (5) personal characteristics, (6) individual expectations, and (7) community and kinship ties (Poston, Luo, and Zhang, 2006).

As already mentioned, the distance model states that long distance discourages migration (Lee, 1966) because the costs involved in migration are substantial and are closely related to distance. The income model argues that income and job opportunities provide a better explanation of in-migration than they do for out-migration (Perloff et al., 1960); destination characteristics also help determine the location to which the migrant will move (Poston and Frisbie, 2019). The physical costs model suggests that physical costs affect resource allocation and migration by influencing the private costs of migration (Greenwood, 1975). The information model emphasizes that "the availability of information concerning alternative localities plays a prominent role in the potential migrant's decision regarding a destination" (Greenwood, 1975: 405). The personal characteristics model argues that personal demographic characteristics (e.g., age, sex, education, number of dependents, networks, and race) exert important influences on the individual's decision or propensity to migrate (Grieco and Boyd, 1998; Nam, Serow, and Sly, 1990). The individual expectations model assumes that the dynamics of migration decision making are based on individual expectations about the advantages and disadvantages of the home community versus possible alternative destination communities (Fischer, Martin, and Straubhaar, 1997). And the community and kinship ties model points out that "the presence of relatives and friends is a valued aspect of life [that] ... encourages migration by increasing the individual's potential for adjustment through the availability of aid in location at an alternative area of residence" (Ritchey, 1976: 389).

The above theories of internal migration focus mainly on individuals and why they move or do not move. Demographers have developed other kinds of theories that are known as aggregate theories. They focus less on individuals per se and more on populations and their geographic areas. Rather than asking why individuals move, the aggregate theories ask why some areas increase in population size through migration, why others decrease through migration, and why still others are not influenced one way or the other via migration.

Sociological human ecology is an aggregate theory that provides a perspective for considering the effects of migration on populations and geographic areas. From the perspective of human ecology, migration is the major mechanism of social change and adaptability for human populations. Knowledge of migration patterns tells us about how "populations...maintain themselves in particular areas" (Hawley 1950: 149). The ecological approach asserts that human populations redistribute themselves via net migration in order to attain an equilibrium between their overall size and the life chances available to them (Poston and Frisbie 1998: 30; 2019; Poston, 2015).

The theoretical foundation of human ecology is based on the interdependence of the four conceptual rubrics of population, organization, environment, and technology. The interrelationships among and between these dimensions inform our understanding of migration patterns. All populations adapt to their environments. These adaptations vary among populations according to their social and sustenance organization, their technology, and the size, composition, and distribution of the population. The environment is comprised of both social and physical factors, and it sets constraints on the population and the form and characteristics of its organization. The technology at the population's disposal sets the boundaries for the form and kind of environmental adaptation that the population assumes. Human ecology posits that of the three demographic processes, migration is the most efficient agent for returning the human ecosystem to a state of equilibrium, or balance, between its size and organization (Poston and Frisbie, 1998, 2019; Poston, 2015).

An hypothesis typically investigated in ecological studies of internal migration (e.g., Poston and Frisbie, 1998; Saenz and Colberg, 1988) is that variability among human groups in their patterns of migration is a function of differences in their patterns of sustenance organization, technology, environment, and population. The ecological theory of migration thus focuses on characteristics of the population group to predict the level of migration. Individual attitudes and propensities do not play a role.

Finally, most theories of internal migration, both individual-level theories and aggregate theories, have been influenced in one way or another by the very early work of German geographer E. G. Ravenstein (1834–1913), who endeavored in two seminal articles written in 1885 and 1889 to identify the so-called laws of migration. Ravenstein set forth many laws or theorems of migration based largely on his research in England and a few other countries. Included are the following: (1) Migration is affected by distance; most migrants move only short distances. (2) Migrants often move in stages; as they leave one area, their places are filled by migrants from more distant areas. (3) Every migration stream has a compensating counterstream. (4) Migrants proceeding long distances often stop, temporarily, at major cities or centers of commerce that are located between the area of origin and the intended final area of destination. (5) Urban residents are less likely to migrate than rural residents.

Internal migration will be considered in more detail in Chapter 6.

THEORIES OF INTERNATIONAL MIGRATION

There are several theories of international migration, most of which focus on the determinants of voluntary migration. The **neoclassical economic theory of international migration** is perhaps the oldest and best-known theory of international migration. It focuses specifically on labor migration (Harris and Todaro, 1970; Massey et al., 1993, 1994). According to this model, migration occurs on account of individual cost–benefit decisions to maximize expected incomes through international movement. Workers are attracted from low-wage countries with adequate labor to high-wage countries with limited labor.

The **new economics theory of migration** is an international migration theory developed in recent years to challenge some of the hypotheses and assumptions of neoclassical economics. This theory argues that migration decisions are made not only by isolated individuals but also by larger units, such as families and households (Massey et al., 1993; Stark 1984, 1991). Migration occurs not only to increase individual earnings but also to minimize household risks and to protect the family from market failures.

An approach that differs from both of the preceding is **dual labor market theory**. This theory states that international migration stems from the demands of the economic structure of industrial societies (Massey et al., 1993, 1994; Piore, 1979). International migration is caused not only by the push factors of the origin countries but also by the pull factors of the destination countries. Inherent tendencies in modern capitalism lead labor markets to separate into two sectors: "the primary sector that produces jobs with secure tenure, high pay, generous benefits, and good working conditions; and the secondary sector typified by instability, low pay, limited benefits, and unpleasant or hazardous working conditions" (Massey et al., 1994: 715). Employers are inclined to turn to migrants to fill the jobs in the secondary sector.

The **world systems theory of migration** argues that international migration is the natural result of the globalization of the market economy (Massey et al., 1993; Portes and Walton, 1981; Sassen, 1988). In the process of global industrialization, a large number of people are released from traditional industries such as farming, state-owned industries, and handicrafts, and this creates a mobilized population to move both internally and internationally (Massey, 1988; Massey et al., 1993). The development of the global market economy attracts human capital to a relatively small number of global cities, among them, New York, Los Angeles, and Chicago (Castells, 1989).

Finally, **migration network theory** focuses on networks, that is, the interpersonal ties that connect migrants, former migrants, potential migrants, and nonmigrants in the origin and destination countries. The networks increase the likelihood of international movement by decreasing migrant risks and costs and increasing the net earnings to migration (Massey et al., 1993). Networks make it easier for new migrants to get information about the destination, to find jobs, and to gain access to required resources in their destination countries.

These theories and others endeavor to account for the causal process of international migration at different levels of analysis, namely, the individual, the household, the country, and the world. These different perspectives are not necessarily incompatible (Poston, Luo, and Zhang, 2006). Indeed, the key elements of each theory are sometimes all subsumed under the headings of "push" and "pull." There are push and pull conditions facilitating migration in most of the countries of the world. For an individual or group to decide to engage in international migration, there needs to be a push from the origin country and/or a pull to the destination country.

In addition to individual push and pull factors leading to international migration, there are also contextual factors operating. For example, after arriving in destination countries, migrants, particularly Asian migrants, sometimes gravitate into what are called ethnic enclaves. An **ethnic enclave** is a community that helps individuals transition into life as immigrants by providing support and environments much like those in their mother countries. The push and pull factors, individual and contextual, can be one or more of any of the characteristics defining the five theories outlined in this section (Cortes and Poston, 2008). We address international migration in more detail in Chapter 7.

SUMMARY

We began this chapter by exploring the meaning of "population." Next, we examined some of the early writings about population. We paid special attention to the work and contributions of Malthus, but also considered other population theorists, such as Marx. We next covered the major theory of demography, demographic transition theory, that was developed by demographers to help our understanding of overall population change that societies experienced as they transitioned from high fertility and mortality rates to low fertility and mortality rates. We discussed how demographers have revised the theory dealing with this classic, or first, demographic transition into extensions involving the second and third demographic transitions.

We then turned attention to theories focusing specifically on fertility and discussed some of the key perspectives. Next, we reviewed the major features of the main demographic theory of mortality, epidemiological transition theory. We followed this presentation with discussions of theories dealing with internal migration and with international migration. In later chapters we will have occasion to refer to many if not all of these theories in our reviews of the major substantive issues of demography.

Finally, it is clear from our discussions in this chapter that demography has an abundance of theories. Indeed, the theoretical perspectives of demography rival those of any of the other social sciences. Consider the many different theoretical perspectives reviewed in this chapter that focus on fertility and mortality and internal and international migration. Consider also the classic model of demographic transition and its elaborations. Charles Nam argued nearly fifty years ago that "the issues of demographic journals today are replete with theoretically based articles, in stark contrast to those of the past" (1979: 490; see also Riley and McCarthy, 2003). Occasionally, uninformed social scientists who do not know the demographic literature criticize demography as being atheoretical. They erroneously claim there is a paucity of theory in demography. The statement that demography is void of theory is incorrect (Burch, 2003).

A second point to note is that demographic theory has been shaped by many disciplines, including philosophy, sociology. history, economics, biology, and geography, among others. The interdisciplinary nature of demography adds to the usefulness of demographic knowledge and the appeal of demography to students from many majors.

DISCUSSION QUESTIONS

1. A prominent demographic theory of migration focuses on push and pull factors. Consider a recent migration of yours or of a relative or close friend. Tell us about the migration; where did it occur, when and where did it begin, when and where did it end? Were there any pull factors?; if yes, what were they? Were there any push factors?; if yes, what were they? Was this most recent migration more influenced by pull factors than by push factors? Why, or why not?
2. Discuss the views of Marx and Malthus about the importance of the population. How are their views similar? How are they different? They both stress the importance of the population. Do you personally prefer Malthus's views and arguments about the importance of the population, or those of Marx? Defend your preference.
3. What information would you need to decide which stage of the demographic transition characterizes a particular population?

3

The Sources of Demographic Information

INTRODUCTION

We noted toward the end of Chapter 1 that we demographers are more fortunate than many of our social science colleagues who must gather and develop their own data and databases. Generally speaking, most of the data we demographers use have already been gathered for us, although this is not always the situation. Indeed, some demographers do gather their own data, especially those using anthropological perspectives and who engage in ethnographic research (Greenhalgh, 1990b, 1994; Riley, 1998; Riley and McCarthy, 2003). However, most of us use data already gathered and developed by other organizations. In this chapter we discuss the three basic sources of demographic information.

The three basic sources of demographic data are national censuses, registers, and sample surveys. National censuses and registers differ in that the former are conducted on a periodic basis, such as every ten years (decennial) or five years (quincuennial), while the latter, theoretically at least, are gathered continuously. **Registration** data of population events are usually compiled and published annually or monthly, even though they are gathered continuously as they occur. A **census** may be likened to taking a snapshot of a population at one point in time, say, once every ten years or so, and in this snapshot getting a picture of the size of the population, its characteristics, and its spatial distribution. Conversely, a register may be thought of as a video that continuously compiles major population events, such as births, deaths, marriages, divorces, and sometimes migrations. When a birth or a death occurs, it is registered with the government; the registrations thus occur continuously.

Censuses and registers are intended to cover the entire population. In a national census, everyone in the population is supposed to be enumerated, and all the demographic events, that is, births, deaths, and so forth, that occur in the population are supposed to be registered. Sample surveys, on the other hand, are, by definition, administered only to a mathematically selected fraction, a sample, of the population. Surveys often contain data items that are also included in censuses and registers, plus additional items of interest that are not included in censuses and surveys. We will now cover in some detail each of these three sources of demographic data.

NATIONAL CENSUSES

A national census is "the total process of collecting, compiling, and publishing demographic, economic, and social data pertaining, at a specified time . . ., to all persons in a country or delimited territory" (United Nations, 1958: 3). The principal objective of a census is to obtain data about the size, composition, and distribution of the population. A typical census thus includes information about the size of the population and its geographic subpopulations, as well as data on their age and sex composition and other mainly demographic characteristics. Some censuses also include information about the population's educational composition, that is, levels of literacy and educational attainment and extent of school attendance, its economically active and inactive populations, the industrial and occupational composition of the working population, as well as economic, that is, salary and income, data. Other population data in a typical census might include information pertaining to country or area of birth, citizenship, language, recent migration experience, religion, and ethnic heritage, which refers to group distinctions based on shared cultural origins (Shryock, Siegel, and Associates, 1976).

The US decennial censuses, since 1940, included most of the above information, and this was the situation up through the census conducted in 2000. There were two census questionnaires known as the short-form or 100 percent questionnaire, and the long-form or sample questionnaire. Every household filled out the short-form instrument; it asked questions about one's sex, age, race, ethnicity, and household relationship. The long-form questionnaire was administered to all persons in about every one of six households, and it asked a host of additional questions dealing with socioeconomic status, place of birth, citizenship, migration, ancestry, and so forth. The US Census Bureau redesigned these questionnaires, so that the 2010 census included only the questions from the former short-form instrument. The more detailed long-form questionnaire is now the major component of a survey known as the American Community Survey; we discuss this survey later in the chapter.

The 2010 census questionnaire was one of the shortest questionnaires in US census history. It asked each person only to provide their name, sex, age, race, ethnicity, relationship, and whether they owned or rented their home. It took the average household about 10 minutes to fill it out. The 2020 census form was similar. In Figure 3.1 we have provided an information copy of the 2020 census questionnaire.

In the actual enumeration of the population, there are two ways to count people: by following a **de jure** method or by following a **de facto** method (Shryock, 1964). In the case of a de jure enumeration, the census covers the entire territory of the country and counts persons according to their "usual" or "normal" place of residence in the country. A de facto enumeration, on the other hand, also covers the entire territory of the country but counts each person according to his/her geographical location on the day of the census undertaking. For instance, a person who lives with her family in Dallas, Texas, but who is traveling on census day and is visiting a friend in College Station, Texas, and thus happens to be counted in College Station, would be counted as a resident of Dallas if the census was a de jure census, but would be assigned to College Station if it was a de facto census. Canada and the United States follow a de jure approach, as do European countries such as Austria, Belgium, Croatia, the Czech Republic, Denmark, Germany,

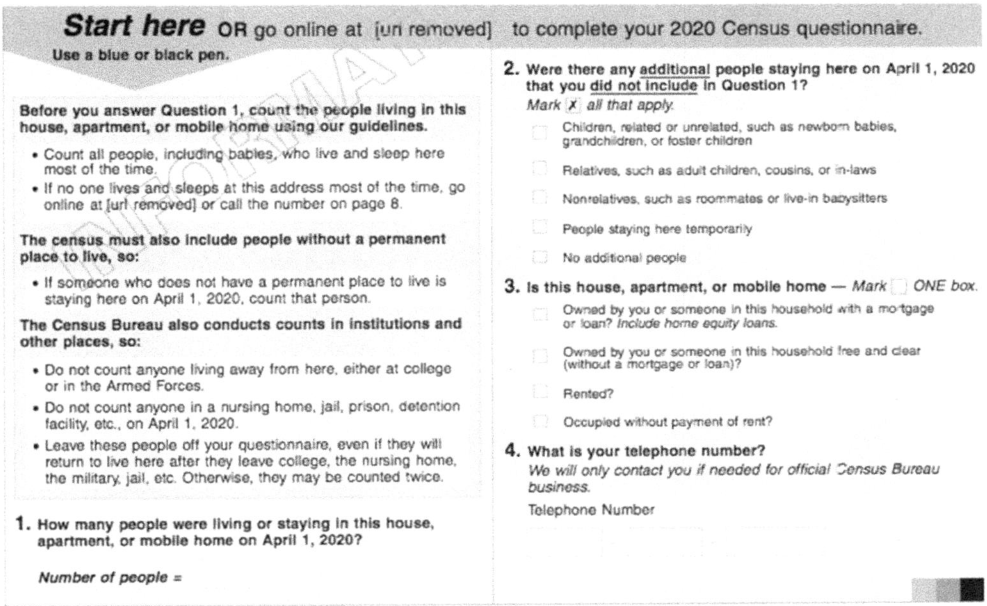

Start here OR go online at [url removed] to complete your 2020 Census questionnaire.

Use a blue or black pen.

Before you answer Question 1, count the people living in this house, apartment, or mobile home using our guidelines.

- Count all people, including babies, who live and sleep here most of the time.
- If no one lives and sleeps at this address most of the time, go online at [url removed] or call the number on page 8.

The census must also include people without a permanent place to live, so:

- If someone who does not have a permanent place to live is staying here on April 1, 2020, count that person.

The Census Bureau also conducts counts in institutions and other places, so:

- Do not count anyone living away from here, either at college or in the Armed Forces.
- Do not count anyone in a nursing home, jail, prison, detention facility, etc., on April 1, 2020.
- Leave these people off your questionnaire, even if they will return to live here after they leave college, the nursing home, the military, jail, etc. Otherwise, they may be counted twice.

1. **How many people were living or staying in this house, apartment, or mobile home on April 1, 2020?**

Number of people =

2. **Were there any additional people staying here on April 1, 2020 that you did not include in Question 1?**
Mark X all that apply.
- Children, related or unrelated, such as newborn babies, grandchildren, or foster children
- Relatives, such as adult children, cousins, or in-laws
- Nonrelatives, such as roommates or live-in babysitters
- People staying here temporarily
- No additional people

3. **Is this house, apartment, or mobile home** — *Mark ONE box.*
- Owned by you or someone in this household with a mortgage or loan? *Include home equity loans.*
- Owned by you or someone in this household free and clear (without a mortgage or loan)?
- Rented?
- Occupied without payment of rent?

4. **What is your telephone number?**
We will only contact you if needed for official Census Bureau business.
Telephone Number

FIGURE 3.1 Informational 2020 census questionnaire
Source: US Census Bureau. Note: Additional people in the same household answer as Person 2, Person 3, etc.

the Netherlands, Norway, Sweden, and Switzerland (United Nations, 1998). The censuses of Colombia have been both de facto (in 1963 and 1973) and de jure (since 1985). Of the more than 230 countries conducting national censuses, however, the de facto type is more common than the de jure (Wilmoth, 2004: 65).

We show in Figure 3.1 an information copy of a census questionnaire, the one that was administered in the United States in the 2020 census. The questions on this instrument were usually answered by one person in every **household** in the United States, and that person typically entered responses to each question for everyone residing in the household. As you can see, there were only a few questions on the 2020 questionnaire (Sullivan and Cork, 2023: 419–458). Census taking had its origins in ancient Egypt, China, and Rome, among other places, although only a few of these enumerations have survived. There may have been a census conducted in China as early as 3000 BC, but demographic records for China and other countries for the very early periods no longer exist. Several census counts are mentioned in the Bible. One was undertaken at the time of the Exodus in 1491 BC, and another was conducted during King David's era in 1017 BC. Roman censuses were conducted every five years for more than 800 years. The Romans extended the census enumeration to the entire Roman Empire in 5 BC, resulting in the popular biblical census story reported in St. Luke's Gospel (Bryan, 2004: 14).

It is difficult to determine with certainty when the first modern census was undertaken. Coverage was highly suspect in the very early censuses because censuses were seen as instruments of taxation and military conscription (Bryan, 2004). Indeed, the first

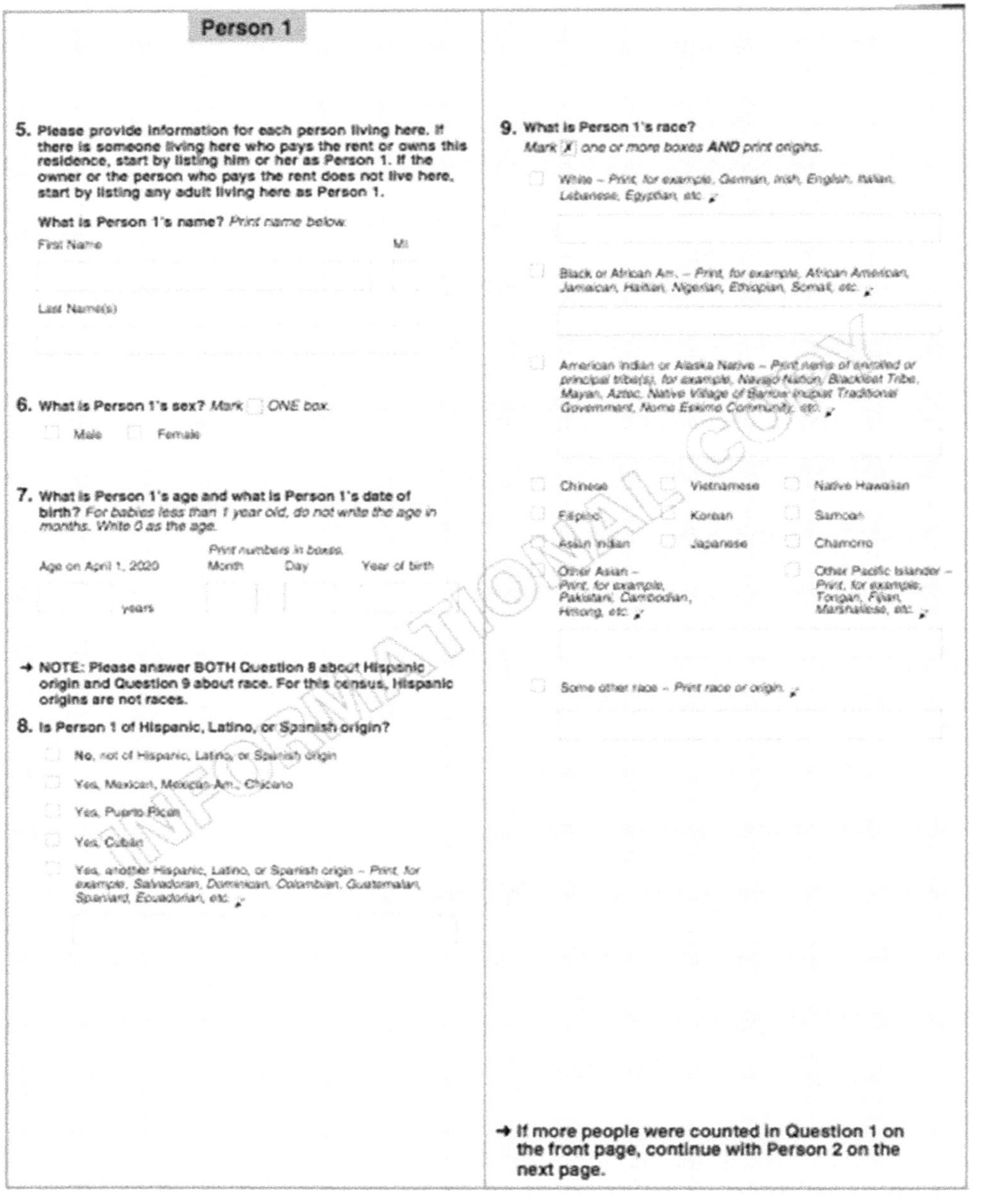

Person 1

5. Please provide information for each person living here. If there is someone living here who pays the rent or owns this residence, start by listing him or her as Person 1. If the owner or the person who pays the rent does not live here, start by listing any adult living here as Person 1.

What is Person 1's name? *Print name below.*

First Name MI

Last Name(s)

6. What is Person 1's sex? *Mark ☐ ONE box.*

☐ Male ☐ Female

7. What is Person 1's age and what is Person 1's date of birth? *For babies less than 1 year old, do not write the age in months. Write 0 as the age.*

Print numbers in boxes.

Age on April 1, 2020 Month Day Year of birth

years

→ NOTE: Please answer BOTH Question 8 about Hispanic origin and Question 9 about race. For this census, Hispanic origins are not races.

8. Is Person 1 of Hispanic, Latino, or Spanish origin?

☐ **No,** not of Hispanic, Latino, or Spanish origin

☐ Yes, Mexican, Mexican Am., Chicano

☐ Yes, Puerto Rican

☐ Yes, Cuban

☐ Yes, another Hispanic, Latino, or Spanish origin – *Print, for example, Salvadoran, Dominican, Colombian, Guatemalan, Spaniard, Ecuadorian, etc.*

9. What is Person 1's race?

*Mark ☒ one or more boxes **AND** print origins.*

☐ White – *Print, for example, German, Irish, English, Italian, Lebanese, Egyptian, etc.*

☐ Black or African Am. – *Print, for example, African American, Jamaican, Haitian, Nigerian, Ethiopian, Somali, etc.*

☐ American Indian or Alaska Native – *Print name of enrolled or principal tribe(s), for example, Navajo Nation, Blackfeet Tribe, Mayan, Aztec, Native Village of Barrow Inupiat Traditional Government, Nome Eskimo Community, etc.*

☐ Chinese ☐ Vietnamese ☐ Native Hawaiian

☐ Filipino ☐ Korean ☐ Samoan

☐ Asian Indian ☐ Japanese ☐ Chamorro

☐ Other Asian – *Print, for example, Pakistani, Cambodian, Hmong, etc.*

☐ Other Pacific Islander – *Print, for example, Tongan, Fijian, Marshallese, etc.*

☐ Some other race – *Print race or origin.*

→ If more people were counted in Question 1 on the front page, continue with Person 2 on the next page.

FIGURE 3.1 (*cont.*)

census conducted in the United States in 1790 was a rather crude undertaking; it included counts only of the number of "free white" males of age 16 and over and those under age 16, the number of "free white" females irrespective of their ages, the number of all other "free" persons irrespective of their sex or age, and the number of slaves irrespective of their sex or age. The US census of 1790 differentiated "free white" males by whether they were over or under age 16 as a rough measure of potential military capacity. Livi-Bacci (2012: 24) has stated that the 1790 US census that counted 3.9 million people, along with the 1787 census of the Kingdom of Spain that counted 10.4 million people, "are the first examples of modern censuses in large countries." Interestingly, Thomas Jefferson, then the Secretary of State, told President George Washington of his belief that the census represented a substantial undercount of inhabitants (Anderson, 2015: 15). That criticism has never disappeared (Sullivan, 2020a: 33–47).

Most countries of the world today conduct censuses. Some countries are late to census taking. For instance, the countries of Chad and Oman did not take their first censuses until 1993. The United Nations reports that of the more than 230 countries or areas in the world today, all but seven (Eritrea, Iraq, Lebanon, Pakistan, Somalia, Uzbekistan, and Western Sahara) completed a population census by the end of the 2010 "census round" which covers the time period between 2005 and 2014 (United Nations Statistics Division, 2013). This census round included around 96 percent of the world's population. This is a slight improvement from the 95 percent or so of the world's population covered in censuses in the 2000 round when as many as 26 countries did not participate (Johnson, 2000; United Nations, 2007).

Of the seven countries not conducting a census in the 2010 round, Lebanon stands out as the only country never to have conducted an official population census. Most likely owing to the way the country was formed by the French, Lebanon has used national population registries and household surveys for various enumeration estimates and has avoided, perhaps for political reasons, conducting an actual census (personal communication between Poston and Mary J. Chamie, July 10, 2007).

The United Nations recommended that all countries take a census during the two years 2020 and 2021. As it happened, however, these were the worst years of the COVID-19 pandemic. Almost surely, the pandemic resulted in conditions that will affect the quality of the data collected. Figure 3.2 shows the number of countries whose censuses were delayed or unscheduled. As a result, we cannot yet tell what this round of

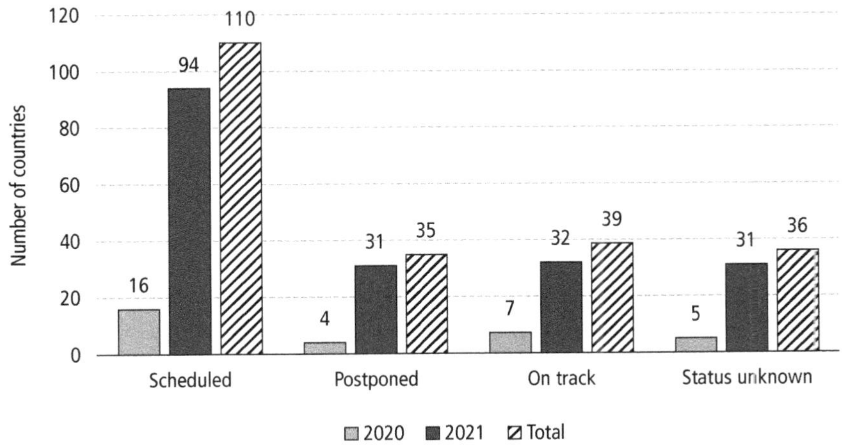

FIGURE 3.2 Number of countries delayed in the 2020 round of national censuses
Data source: United Nations Department of Economic and Social and Affairs (UNDESA), 2021.

censuses will tell us about world's population (United Nations Department of Economic and Social Affairs, 2021).

Population censuses were conducted relatively early in the United States, starting with Virginia in 1624–1625. Various colonial censuses were conducted through 1767. In the United States, the principal reason and justification for conducting a decennial national census is to provide population counts for the states of the country that are used by Congress to apportion the House of Representatives. The requirement for a decennial census was written in 1787 into Article 1, Section 2, of the US Constitution as follows:

> Representatives and direct taxes shall be apportioned among the several states which may be included within this Union according to their respective numbers .... The actual enumeration shall be made within three years after the first meeting of the Congress of the United States, and within every subsequent term of ten years in such manner as they shall by law direct.

It is useful to note that the language of the Constitution did not exclude nonvoters, which then included women as well as children, nor foreign-born persons. The one excluded group was "Indians not taxed." Enslaved people were counted, but the count was adjusted by 0.6 (three-fifths of a person) because of a political compromise between northern and southern states, but this provision was eliminated in the Fourteenth Amendment to the Constitution. Women were allowed to vote by the Nineteenth Amendment to the Constitution.

The first national census was conducted in 1790, and one has been conducted in the United States every ten years since. Today, censuses and census data are very important for the functioning of government bodies. As an illustration, we show in Box 3.1 exactly how the most recent apportionment of the US House of Representatives was conducted using data from the 2020 census.

Censuses are very expensive to conduct. The cost of the 2020 US census was around $13.7 billion, a figure that actually turned out to be 7 percent less than the $14.7 billion that had been appropriated for the 2010 count (Roberts, 2010; US GAO, 2023). Despite the disruptions caused by the COVID-19 pandemic, the 2020 census achieved cost-saving measures such as allowing people to respond over the internet using computers or cellphones (Sullivan 2020a: 37). Census data provide government officials with useful and necessary information about the people in their country. Governments use census data in virtually all features of public policy, for example, to determine how many children the public schools need to serve and where to place new roads. Census results also provide the denominator data for crime rates, death rates, per capita income figures, and other statistics that are needed to administer local and national governments. Most state legislatures rely on census data to draw boundaries for electoral districts, such as Congressional districts and legislative districts; this is a process known as redistricting, not to be confused with reapportionment. Private businesses require census data for their market analyses and for advertising activities (Anderson, 2003; Sullivan, 2020b). Many demographers and other social scientists use census data to test their theories and to conduct their analyses.

For instance, one of the questions in the 2020 census asked everyone living in a household with two or more persons about their relationship with the person who is

Box 3.1 Using Census Data to Apportion the US House of Representatives in 2020

The major objective when apportioning the US House of Representatives is to assign equitably the 435 seats to the fifty states. (The District of Columbia is not included in the apportionment; thus the residents of the District are not represented by a voting member of the House of Representatives). There are several constraints: (1) the total number of House seats must equal 435; (2) partial representatives cannot be assigned to states, nor can representatives be given fractional votes; (3) representatives may not be shared by two or more states; and (4) every state must be assigned at least one seat in the House.

The first fifty seats are automatically assigned, one per state. The purpose of the apportionment method is to divide up the remaining 385 seats. The apportionment method of Equal Proportions indicates which states should receive second seats, which states should receive third seats, and so forth. However, the US Constitution does not provide instructions on how apportionment should be carried out, only that the underlying assumption must be that no one person should have more of a voice than another person. As a result, representatives are assigned from states in proportion to their populations. The method of Equal Proportions was first used to apportion the House in 1940 and has been used ever since. It is a divisor method that first develops a target **ratio** of population to representatives that is based on data for the nation. In 2020, the apportionment population (the population counted by the Census Bureau residing in each state plus certain individuals living overseas who claim the state as their "state of residence," namely, military personnel and US government employees and their dependents) of the United States was 331,108,434. Hence, the target ratio in 2020 was 761,168.8 (or 331,108,434 divided by 435). This ratio, also called a divisor, is then divided into the apportionment populations of each of the states to obtain quotients. The method of Equal Proportions endeavors to ensure that "the difference between the representation of any two states is the smallest possible when measured both by the relative difference in the average population per district, and also by the relative difference in the individual share in a representative" (Schmeckebier, 1941: 22). The method gives to a state an additional representative "when its [apportionment] population, divided by the geometric mean of its present assignment of representatives and of its next higher assignment, is greater than the [apportionment] population of any other state divided by the geometric mean of the assignment to such other state and its next higher assignment" (Schmeckebier, 1941: 22).

The first step in using the method of Equal Proportions is to multiply the apportionment population of each state by the following fraction:

$$\frac{1}{\sqrt{N(N-1)}}$$

where N equals the particular seat being claimed, that is, the second seat or the third seat or the fourth seat, and so on. This provides numbers known as priority values. For instance, the proportion used in determining a state's claim to a second seat is:

$$\frac{1}{\sqrt{2(2-1)}} = \frac{1}{\sqrt{2}} = \frac{1}{1.41421356} = 0.70710678$$

The proportion used in determining a state's claim to a third seat is:

$$\frac{1}{\sqrt{3(3-1)}} = \frac{1}{\sqrt{6}} = \frac{1}{2.44948974} = 0.40824829$$

The rounding rule for this method is to round a state's quotient either up or down, "depending on whether or not the quotient exceeds the 'geometric mean' of these two choices" (Balinski and Young, 1982: 62). The geometric mean of two numbers is the square root of their product. Thus, according to the method of Equal Proportions, if a state had a quotient of 1.39, it would receive one representative because the geometric mean of 1 and 2 is 1.41; however, if a state had a quotient of 1.42, it would receive two representatives.

In the actual apportionment calculations, the rule per se need not be invoked. Instead, one may rely entirely on the proportions developed for the various seats. Thus, once the proportions are developed for determining the priorities for the various seats (we showed above the calculations of the proportions for seats 2 and 3), they are multiplied by the apportionment populations of each of the fifty states. That is, the proportion used for determining the states' priorities for a second seat (0.70710678) is successively multiplied by the apportionment populations of each of the fifty states; this procedure is then repeated using the proportion to determine the states' priorities for a third seat (0.40824829) and so forth. After all of these multiplications have been completed, the resulting priority values are then ranked in order, the largest first and the smallest last. The 385 House seats are assigned to the states with the 385 highest priority values.

In Table B3.1.1, we report the application of the Method of Equal Proportions in 2020 and identify the states receiving the first six seats and those receiving the last six seats. We also show the states that would have received the three seats beyond the 435th seat if more than 435 seats were available. In the 2020 apportionment, California received the 51st seat. Its priority value for a second seat, 27,984,993, was obtained by multiplying its 2020 apportionment population of 39,576,757 by the "second seat" proportion of 0.70710678. Texas received the 52nd seat with its priority value for a second seat of 20,635,702, which was determined by multiplying its 2020 apportionment population of

TABLE B3.1.1 *Application in 2020 of the method of Equal Proportions: allocating the first six and last few seats*

Numbered seat in House	State	Numbered seat in the State	Priority value
First six seats			
51	California	2	27,984,993
52	Texas	2	20,635,702
53	California	3	16,157,143
54	Florida	2	15,252,665
55	New York	2	14,294,694
56	Texas	3	11,914,028
Last six seats			
430	North Carolina	14	774,898
431	Oregon	6	774,388
432	Colorado	8	772,675
433	California	52	768,516
434	Montana	2	767,498
435	Minnesota	8	762,997
What states just missed? (beyond 435)			
436	New York	27	762,994
437	Ohio	16	762,257
438	Texas	39	758,071

Source: US Bureau of the Census, 2021.

29,183,290 by 0.70710678. The 51st and 52nd seats were thus assigned to the two largest states, California and Texas. Florida had the third largest population of all the states in 2020, but Florida did not receive the 53rd seat because its priority value for a second seat of 15,252,665 was smaller than California's priority value for a third seat of 16,157,143 (the priority value for California's third seat is obtained by multiplying California's apportionment population of 39,576,757 by the "third seat" proportion of 0.40824829). So, California received the 53rd seat and Florida the 54th seat. New York received the 55th seat as its second seat, and Texas received the 56th seat as its third seat.

Table B3.1.1 also shows the states receiving the last six seats in the House, the 430th through the 435th seats. Note, for instance, that North Carolina's priority value for a 14th seat was slightly larger than Oregon's claim for a 6th seat; therefore, the 430th seat was assigned to North Carolina and the 431st to Oregon. The last seat, the 435th, was allocated as Minnesota's 8th seat. The states of New York, Ohio, and Texas were next in line to receive the 436th, 437th, and 438th seats if there had been three more seats. Notice the very small difference in priority score between Minnesota, which received another representative, and New York, which did not (US Bureau of the Census, 2021).

For another discussion of apportionment, see Poston (2020b); for a discussion of its history and calculations see Burnett (2011) for the 2010 apportionment and Baumle and Poston (2004) for the 2000 apportionment.

On this topic of Congressional apportionment, we encourage you also to read Marta Tienda's (2002) very insightful article on "Demography and the Social Contract" that discusses issues involved in including and excluding immigrants from the apportionment populations of the states. There are some unexpected conclusions.

known as "Person 1." This person is often "the member of the household in whose name the home is owned, being bought or rented" (Barrett, 1994: 16). Operationally, it refers to the person taking the major responsibility for filling out the census form. Every person in the household, except Person 1, is also asked to respond to a question about his/her relationship to Person 1. (This question about the relationship to Person 1 is not actually shown in Figure 3.1 because the part of the questionnaire that we have included in Figure 3.1 only applies to Person 1.)

The numerous responses that Person 2 and Person 3 and the other persons in the household use to respond to the "relationship to Person 1" question include the so-called blood or family relationships of husband, wife, son, grandfather, and so forth, and the nonfamily relationships of roomer/boarder, housemate/roommate, unmarried partner, and so forth. The "unmarried partner" response permits researchers to identify a person in the household who is unrelated to Person 1 but who has a "marriage-like" relationship with Person 1. As of the end of June 2015 the Supreme Court of the United States ruled that the Constitution guarantees a right to same-sex marriage (Oyez, 2015). In the 2020 census, for the first time there were four "marriage-like" responses: opposite sex husband/wife/spouse; opposite-sex unmarried partner; same-sex husband/wife/spouse; same-sex unmarried partner.

More limited data were available after the 2010 census where the possible choices were "unmarried partner." When the sex of the unmarried partner matched the sex of Person 1, demographers made the assumption that these data on same-sex households (male–male or female–female) represented households inhabited by partnered gay men or partnered lesbians (Baumle, Compton, and Poston, 2009; Black et al., 2000).

Using such same-sex data from the 2010 census. Poston and Chang calculated gay male partnering rates and lesbian partnering rates for the 366 metropolitan areas of the United States (Poston and Chang, 2013, 2015). This research is covered in greater detail later in Chapter 9.

When analyzing the 2010 same-sex household data, Census Bureau researchers "discovered an inconsistency in the responses in the 2010 census summary file statistics that artificially inflated the number of same-sex couples." ("Census Bureau Releases Estimates of Same-Sex Married Couples," 2011). Poston and Chang adapted an adjustment method developed by Gates (2013) to address the above-mentioned problem (see Poston and Chang [2013] for the details).

The Poston and Chang research used a gay male/lesbian prevalence index that measures the over- or underrepresentation of "same-sex couples in a geographic area relative to the population" (Gates and Ost, 2004: 24). An index value of 1.0 for a metropolitan area means that "a same-sex couple is just as likely as a randomly picked household to locate" in the metro area (Gates and Ost, 2004: 24). An index value above 1.0 means that a same-sex couple is more likely to live in the metro area than a random household, and a value less than 1.0, less likely.

Their research showed that the mean index values across the 366 metropolitan areas for gay male households was 0.69 and was 0.86 for lesbian households. This means that in the "average" metropolitan area in the US in 2010, gay male couples were 31 percent less likely to settle there than would be a couple from a randomly selected metropolitan household (that is, [0.69 – 1.0] x 100); and that a lesbian couple would be 14 percent less likely to settle there than would be a couple from a randomly selected household. The research showed that the San Francisco-Oakland-Fremont, CA, metropolitan area (hereafter referred to as San Francisco) had the highest gay male couple ratio value, 2.78, and the Ithaca, NY, metropolitan area had the highest lesbian couple index ratio, 2.97. The value for the San Francisco area may be interpreted as indicating that a gay male couple is 2.8 times more likely than an "average" US couple to reside in the San Francisco area, or, in other words, 178 percent more likely (that is, [2.78 – 1.00] x 100). The Ithaca index value indicates that a lesbian couple is almost 200 percent more likely than an average US couple to live in Ithaca. San Francisco contains The Castro District, a neighborhood in San Francisco in the Eureka Valley, a well-known gay male enclave, making the high prevalence of partnered gay males in San Francisco not a surprise.

Have you ever wondered why San Francisco's gay communities are so world renowned? Why is San Francisco so welcoming to the gay male and lesbian populations? There are many answers to these questions, beginning with the emergence in the early 1900s of gay bars in San Francisco's tourist districts. See in particular Nan Alamilla Boyd's *Wide Open Town* (2003) for its vivid and fascinating chronicling of the history of queer San Francisco.

Regarding the lowest gay male and lesbian ratios of all the metropolitan areas, the Grand Forks, ND-MN, metro area has the lowest gay male couple ratio, 0.26, and Wausau, WI, had the lowest lesbian couple ratio, 0.32. Gay male couples were about one-quarter as likely (or 74 percent less likely) to live in Grand Forks as a randomly picked US metro household, and lesbian couples were about one-third as likely to live in Wausau as a randomly selected household.

For the most part, the gay male indexes tend to vary in the same way as the lesbian indexes. Metropolitan areas with high gay male partnering indexes have high lesbian partnering indexes, and areas with low gay male indexes have low lesbian indexes. But most of the metropolitan areas, 328 of the 366, have higher lesbian index values than gay male index values. From the data it seemed pretty clear that partnered gay men had a few favorite destinations in which to reside, including San Francisco, Miami, Seattle, San Diego, Washington, DC, Las Vegas, Los Angeles, Atlanta, Denver, New York, Tampa, Phoenix, Dallas, New Orleans, Honolulu, Chicago, and Houston, where their prevalence scores surpass those of partnered lesbians. Conversely, partnered lesbians-were concentrated more than were partnered gay men in metropolitan areas in general, tending not to prefer particular areas to the degree that gay men prefer them. We will return to some of these issues in more detail in Chapter 9.

Jones-Myer and Anderson (2024) did a similar analysis using 2020 data. In 2020 female same-sex couples made up 0.9 percent of US coupled households and male same-sex couples made up 0.8 percent of US coupled households. The geographic location of these couples showed a high correspondence with the patterns that Poston and Chang identified with the 2010 census data. San Francisco continued to have the largest concentration of male–male couples.

This is but one example of the many and different kinds of demographic research questions that may be answered with data from censuses. We turn next to a discussion of the second source of demographic data, **registration systems**.

REGISTRATION SYSTEMS

Whereas censuses provide a **cross-sectional** (one point in time) portrayal of the size, composition, and distribution of the population, a registration system pertains to the population's demographic events (births and deaths and, in some countries, migrations); it measures, that is, registers, them as they occur. While censuses are static, registers are dynamic and continuous. Registers apply principally to births and deaths, although many countries also maintain registrations of marriages, divorces, and abortions. Some countries maintain a migration registration system.

Strictly speaking, as Ostby (2003: 763) has noted, a **population register** is a list, that is, a register, of persons that includes the name, address, date of birth, and a personal identification number. Some registers have been maintained for centuries, such as those in church parishes that record the baptisms and the deaths of the parishioners. In Europe, the Nordic countries and the Netherlands maintain population registers, and many developing countries either have them in place or are planning to implement them. In Eastern Europe under the Communists, "population registers were used for control (of the people) as well as for administrative purposes, and the successor regimes for the most part have not maintained them" (Ostby, 2003: 763).

The United States does not maintain any kind of national population register. There are, however, partial registries in the United States. Some federal examples are Social Security, Medicare, Selective Service, and federal tax records. Access to these registries is tightly restricted to protect privacy and to prevent identity theft. States also have partial registries, such as voter rolls, driver's license registrations, and registries of convicted sex offenders. These state registries may be accessible to the general public, depending upon the laws of the state.

The earliest example on record of a population register of families and related household events was in China during the Han Dynasty (205 BC – AD 220). Indeed, as Taeuber (1959: 261) noted many years ago, a special demographic tradition of China and the East Asian region as a whole was population registration. Its major function, however, "was the control of the population at the local level" (Bryan, 2004: 25) and not necessarily the collection of continuous data on demographic events.

Population registers interest demographers because they contain birth and death records (certificates). But not all birth and death registrations occur in the context of population registers. In fact, since a large number of countries do not maintain them, the registration of many births and deaths occurs outside the population registers.

For most countries in the world, the recording of vital events – that is, births and deaths along with marriages, divorces, fetal deaths (stillbirths), and induced termination of pregnancies (abortions) – are part of their civil registration systems. But these registration systems need not necessarily be population registers. Indeed, many are not. Although civil registration data are not 100 percent accurate and complete in the countries of the developed world, their quality is far better than that in the poorer nations. Cleland (1996: 435) has observed that although civil registration systems in developing countries are "seriously defective, it would not be correct that the data are of little value to demographers." Demographers have developed special techniques for data adjustment and analysis, yielding a rough notion of trends and differentials in these demographic events (Popoff and Judson, 2004).

Freedman and Weed (2003: 960) have noted that "vital statistics form the basis of fundamental demographic and epidemiologic measures." **Vital statistics** are the data derived from civil registration systems, as well as from the actual records of vital events. The modern origin of vital statistics and their registration may be traced to the English ordinance in 1532 requiring that parish clerks in London maintain, on a weekly basis, the registration of deaths and christenings (Bryan, 2004: 25). These reports were begun in response to the plagues of the late sixteenth and early seventeenth centuries and were published in a nearly unbroken series for decades. Merchants used those data as a rough gauge of the likelihood of their clientele to flee to the countryside during epidemics (Kraeger, 1988: 129). John Graunt's ([1662] 1939) *Natural and Political Observations Made Upon the Bills of Mortality* is a well-known demographic analysis of these data (see Box 3.2).

With regard to the modern era, Szreter (2007) has written that the registrations of one's birth and death are fundamental human rights. The second clause of Article 24 of the International Covenant on Civil and Political Rights (ICCPR) of the United Nations states that "every child shall be registered immediately after birth and shall have a name" (Szreter, 2007: 67). The ICCPR also states that "for nation states to take appropriate measures to protect and enhance the life expectancy of their populations, they must have at their disposal accurate and detailed information about patterns and trends of mortality" (Szreter, 2007: 68), thus also requiring

Box 3.2 John Graunt

John Graunt is deemed by many demographers (Bogue, 1969: 9; Poston, 2006a: 254) to be the founder of demography. He was born in London in 1620, raised as a Puritan, and later in life became a Catholic. He died in London in poverty in 1674. Although lacking any higher education and untrained in the sciences or mathematics, he published in 1662 the first-known quantitative analysis of a human population, *Natural and Political Observations Made Upon the Bills of Mortality* (Graunt, [1662] 1939).

The "Bills of Mortality" were weekly accountings and reports of the London parish clerks of all the deaths and christenings. These reports were started in response to the plagues of the late sixteenth and early seventeenth centuries and were published in a nearly unbroken series for decades. Graunt studied this mass of data searching for regularities. He is credited for being the first to recognize that more males are born than females, and that females live longer than males. He also was one of the first to recognize the phenomenon of rural to urban migration. He developed a crude mortality table that eventually led to the modern life table. (In Chapter 5 we show that life tables are the basis for calculating life expectancy.) Graunt also set a precedent for one of demography's oldest traditions, namely, the evaluation of data "to learn the extent, types, and probable causes of errors" (Bogue, 1969: 9). He "carefully evaluated the bills for their numerical consistency and reliability of compilation, and presented his evidence at length so that his readers might judge it independently" (Kraeger, 1988: 129).

When Graunt died in 1674, he was presumably buried beneath the pews of St. Dunston's Church on Fleet Street in London (Aubrey, 1898). With his wife Patricia, Dudley Poston visited this church in London in 2012, but sadly they were not able to find any written record there of Graunt or of his burial. The church was rebuilt in 1930, so perhaps this explains why. Although Graunt died in obscurity, his lasting monument is his *Natural and Political Observations*, a very short book that to this day is a joy to read (Poston, 2006a).

death registration. (**Life expectancy** is the average number of years yet to be lived by people attaining a given age.)

How complete is the registration of births and deaths in the world today? The United Nations (UN) International Children's Emergency Fund (UNICEF) Research Center has estimated that worldwide in the year 2018 there were around 166 million children under the age of 5 who had not been registered, and 237 million children under the age of 5 who did not have a birth certificate, even though some of them might have been registered (UNICEF, 2019). Barriers for parents include not knowing how to register a child's birth, unaffordable fees for registering a birth or obtaining a birth certificate, further fees for late registration, and travel issues to reach the registration facility. Local customs, such as sequestering new mothers indoors, may impede registration (UNICEF, 2019). In some countries, gender discrimination and son preference also lead to female babies being excluded from birth registration (Hudson and den Boer, 2004).

Unregistered children most often live in countries where "there is little awareness of the value of birth registration, where there are no public campaigns, where the registration network is inadequate, or where the costs of registration of children are prohibitive" (UNICEF, 2002: 10). Most unregistered babies are born in low-income nations, largely because these countries are more likely to face political, administrative, and economic barriers to registration.

UNICEF has called for the registration of every child by 2030. Not being registered, and thus not possessing a birth certificate, has many serious consequences. For instance, the "lack of formal recognition by the State usually means that a child . . . may be denied health care or education. Later in life, the lack of an official identification document can mean that a child may enter into marriage or the labor market, or be conscripted into the armed forces, before the legal age. If accused of a crime, unregistered children may be prosecuted as adults, due to their inability to prove their age" (UNICEF, 2014: 6). Among the industrialized countries of the world, more than 90 percent of children under age 5 are registered. Many countries in the former Soviet Union have virtually universal coverage of births. This is likely due to their well-established birth registration systems, good medical facilities, and well-trained medical personnel. Between 2013 and 2020, the countries of South Asia made a determined effort to improve birth registration. In India, for example the birth registration proportions increased from 41 to 80 percent. In contrast, in sub-Saharan Africa the levels of registration remain low, with the lowest in Ethiopia (3 percent), Zambia (11 percent), and Chad (12 percent) (UNICEF, 2019).

Regarding deaths, we do not know as much about the completeness and coverage of registration around the world. Similar to the situation with birth registration, incomplete death registration occurs more frequently in low-income countries than in high-income nations. The World Health Organization (2024c) has estimated that nearly 40 percent of the world's deaths are not registered, and only 8 percent of reported deaths in low-income countries have documented causes. The estimated percentage of registered deaths ranged from 98 percent in Europe to 10 percent in Africa. Currently only around one-quarter of the population of the world lives in countries with 90 percent or more of their deaths registered, and these countries are almost always high-income countries.

We noted earlier that the US Constitution provides the requirement for a decennial census; but there is no such federal requirement for a national vital registration system. Legal authority for the registration of vital events in the United States lies entirely with the individual states. The first US census was conducted in 1790, but the complete coverage of births and deaths did not occur until 1933 (National Center for Health Statistics, 2009).

We already noted that in seventeenth-century England, the registration and maintenance of baptism, marriage, and burial records were the responsibilities of the clergy. This practice was also followed by the English colonies in North America. The registration of births, marriages, and deaths in the United States began with registration laws in Virginia in 1632 and later in other colonies. In 1639, courts in the Massachusetts Bay Colony declared that birth, death, and marriage reporting would be part of their administrative system. Bryan has written that the Massachusetts Bay Colony "may have been the first state in the Western world in which maintaining such records was a function of officers of the civil government" (2004: 26; see also Wolfenden, 1954: 22–23). But even here, registration was voluntary and therefore incomplete. By 1865 the reporting of deaths was fairly complete, but this was not the case for births (Bryan, 2004).

Little by little, other US states followed these practices. Since 1919, all of the states have had birth and death records on file for their entire areas, even though registration was not complete. Since 1903, Texas has had birth and death records on file for the entire state. For the state of California, the date is 1905.

The US federal government established a Death Registration Area in 1900 and recommended a standard death certificate form. A Birth Registration Area was established in 1915. Ten states and the District of Columbia were members, constituting just over 40 percent of the US population. States were added to the registration areas as they qualified. In theory, writes Bryan, "90 percent of deaths, or births, occurring in the state had to be registered for the state to qualify for admission into the Registration Areas; but ways of measuring performance were very crude" (2004: 27). In 1933, Texas was the last state (of the forty-eight states, at the time) to be admitted to the registration areas.

The US government required that the states in the registration areas transmit copies of their birth and death certificates to Washington every year. Although it is the responsibility of the states to register the births, deaths, and other demographic events, the federal government gathers the materials and publishes them for the country as a whole. Birth and death data are published annually by the National Center for Health Statistics (NCHS) in several series dealing with natality and mortality.

The registration of marriages and divorces in the United States has lagged behind the registration of births and deaths. The National Registration Areas for Marriages and Divorces were not established until 1957 (marriages) and 1958 (divorces). In the 1990s, the federal government stopped publishing yearly detailed marriage and divorce data from the states.

Birth certificates typically include the names and ages of the parents, their occupations, and, in some states, their levels of completed education. The mother normally provides the data, but according to Smith, "If she does not know or does not give the infant's father's attributes, they will not appear on the certificate" (1992: 4). Because birth certificate data about the father are sometimes missing or are incomplete, the study of male fertility is much more difficult than the study of female fertility. We discuss some of these issues in Chapter 4.

Birth certificates typically contain a lot of information about the mother and her baby. The birth certificate for Texas, for instance, has sections dealing with pregnancy history, birth weight, obstetric procedures, method of delivery, and congenital anomalies of the child. The states of the US do not all require exactly the same information on their certificates.

The Texas birth certificate also asks if the mother is married. However, this item and several others are reported as confidential information and are not included on the certified copies of the birth certificate. This practice is followed in most states.

A birth is registered in the following way: The physician, the midwife – or person acting as the midwife – the mother of the child, or the father, is required to file a certificate of birth with the local registrar of the district where the birth occurred within a certain number of days following the birth of the infant. In most states, the birth must be registered within five days.

Death certificates are usually filled out by funeral homes, with personal information about the decedent provided by one or more of the surviving family members, as well as by the physician in attendance at the death or by the coroner or medical examiner.

It is likely that sometime in your life, at the death of a parent or close relative, you will serve as the informant to provide personal information to a funeral home official. For one of us, Dudley Poston, this happened when his parents died in San Francisco in 1977 and 1979. On both occasions he and his sister Kathleen met with the funeral director and provided the personal information about their parents that was entered onto their death certificates.

In Texas, as an example, and most other states, death certificates contain basic personal information about the decedent (age, occupation, and so forth), and this is given by one of the surviving members of the decedent's family (the so-called informant) to a staff member of the funeral home, who fills in the certificate. Age "may be misreported by surviving family members, particularly for the elderly" (Smith, 1992: 4). The certificate also includes data on the facts of the death, usually including both the immediate and contributing causes of death, and these are filled in by the attending physician or by the medical examiner or justice of the peace. In most states, the person in charge of interment or of the removal of the body from the registration district (undertaker or funeral director) is responsible for filing a certificate of death with the local registrar. Generally, this registration must occur no later than ten days after the date of the death.

We noted previously that at the federal level, the NCHS gathers the birth and death data from each state and endeavors to make the various birth and death items comparable from state to state. **Nosologists**, that is, persons who study the classification and categorization of diseases and causes of death, then translate the descriptions of the cause of death into cause-of-death codes of the International Classification of Diseases. At the federal level, the United States also maintains a National Death Index (NDI), "which computerizes names and attributes of decedents as well as cause of death information. Among its ... uses, the NDI allows tracking of individuals lost to medical studies to confirm any deaths that have occurred" (Smith, 1992: 4–5).

One may think that demographic events such as births and deaths are so obvious that they need no definition. Actually, this is not true. We consider now the specific events of births, deaths, and fetal deaths. These are three mutually exclusive categories. A birth must occur before a death. If there is no birth, the **fetus** (the "product of conception") is then classified as a fetal death. We will define these terms very specifically.

First, consider a fetal death, which is defined statistically as follows:

Fetal death: the disappearance of life prior to **live birth**; that is, "the complete expulsion or extraction from its mother of a product of conception, irrespective of the duration of pregnancy. The death is indicated by the fact that after such separation, the fetus does not breathe or show any other evidence of life, such as the beating of the heart, pulsation of the umbilical cord, or definite movement of voluntary muscles" (Shryock, Siegel, and Associates, 1976: 221).

Fetal deaths include miscarriages, abortions, and stillbirths, defined as follows:

Miscarriage: the spontaneous or accidental termination of fetal life that occurs early in pregnancy.

Abortion: the premature expulsion of a fetus, spontaneous or induced, at a time before it is viable of sustaining life. An **induced abortion** is the termination of a pregnancy by human intervention that causes early fetal death.

Stillbirth: a late fetal death of 20 to 28 weeks or more of **gestation**. (Gestation is the carrying of a fetus in the uterus from conception to delivery.)

A death is different from a fetal death. A death must be preceded by a birth; a fetal death, conversely, is not preceded by a birth. A death is defined statistically as follows:

Death: "the permanent disappearance of all evidence of life at any time after a live birth has taken place (postnatal cessation of vital functions without the capability of resuscitation). A death can occur only after a live birth has occurred" (Shryock, Siegel, and Associates, 1976: 221). Deaths, therefore, do not include fetal deaths.

The third demographic event is birth. Here is its statistical definition:

Birth: "the complete expulsion or extraction from its mother of a product of conception, irrespective of the duration of pregnancy, which, after such separation, breathes or shows any other evidence of life, such as the beating of the heart, pulsation of the umbilical cord, or definite movement of voluntary muscles, whether or not the umbilical cord has been cut or the placenta is attached" (Shryock, Siegel, and Associates, 1976: 273). Strictly speaking, the period of gestation and the state of life or death at the time of registration are not relevant. After being separated from the mother, if the fetus shows any evidence of life (per the above definition), it is a live birth.

In the United States, births and deaths are tabulated on a de jure basis. That is, the births and deaths that occur in a state to residents of other states are excluded from the actual tabulations for that state. For example, deaths that occur to Texas residents, regardless of where they die, are included in the Texas death tabulations. A baby's parents might live in a rural area, even though the birth occurs in a large city hospital. In this case the birth would be tabulated for the rural area where the mother resides, not for the large city where the hospital is located. A small percentage of births and deaths to residents of a state occurs in other states and places. Knowledge of these events is obtained through an interstate transcript exchange, in cooperation with other states and the NCHS. However, if the death of, say, a Texan, were to occur in California, a California death certificate would be filled out for the decedent. The death information on the California certificate would then be provided to the Texas registration officials to be included in the Texas tabulations, and the death would not be included in the California tabulations.

SAMPLE SURVEYS

Many demographers rely on a third source of demographic data, sample surveys, because censuses and registration systems do not contain the extensive kinds of information needed to address many of the more critical demographic questions. This is particularly true with respect to the analysis of fertility, although it also applies to mortality and migration. Surveys are required for the collection of more detailed information. By administering surveys to carefully selected random samples of the larger populations, demographers are better able to uncover underlying patterns of demographic behavior than is possible with materials only from censuses and registration systems. For more general information on sample surveys, see Kalton (2021). We now discuss some of the major surveys that are used by demographers.

World Fertility Surveys

Beginning in the 1970s, coordinated cross-national fertility surveys were introduced into the statistical and demographic communities as an important source of fertility and related demographic information. Between 1974 and 1986, sample surveys to gather data on reproductive behavior and related social and psychological indicators were conducted in 62 countries, representing 40 percent of the world's population, under the auspices of the **World Fertility Survey** (WFS) (Cleland and Hobcroft, 1985; Cleland and Scott, 1987).

Demographic and Health Surveys

The WFS was followed by another coordinated international program of research, the **Demographic and Health Survey** (DHS), with more than 400 sample surveys carried out in 90 developing countries since 1984. DHSs are nationally representative household surveys with large sample sizes (usually between 5,000 and 30,000 households). These surveys provide data for many variables in the areas of fertility, population, health, and nutrition. Typically, the surveys are conducted every five years to enable comparisons over time. Interim surveys are conducted between DHS rounds and have shorter questionnaires and smaller samples than the DHS surveys (2,000 to 3,000 households). In 2024, DHSs were carried out in Nigeria, Malawi, Indonesia and Mali.

The DHS (as well as the WFS) provides demographic information previously unknown about the countries in which they are implemented. To illustrate, a DHS completed in 2013–2014 in Zambia, a small country of over 14 million people in eastern Africa, indicated that if current fertility levels were maintained, a Zambian woman would have, on average, 5.3 children by the time she completed her childbearing. The DHS data also showed that 45 percent of married women in Zambia used modern methods of contraception, a percentage lower than the 57 percent for married women worldwide, but higher than the 25 percent for married women in all of Africa. The 2013–2014 DHS data for Zambia also showed that 1 in every 13 children in the country did not survive to their fifth birthday. Although this figure is high compared to the much lower level of childhood mortality in high-income countries, it is a tremendous improvement compared to its value in 1997 in Zambia when 1 in every 5 children did not survive to their fifth birthday (Central Statistical Office, Zambia, and the DHS Program, ICF International, 2014). Important information such as the above would not be available were it not for the DHS.

Other Fertility Surveys

Less ambitious demographic surveys, typically focusing on a single country or community, have been part of the demographer's repertoire for decades. Early endeavors included the Indianapolis study (Kiser, 1953; Kiser and Whelpton, 1953), the

Princeton study (Westoff et al., 1961; Westoff, Potter, and Sagi, 1963), and surveys of family and reproductive behavior carried out in Puerto Rico (Hill, Stycos, and Back, 1959; Stycos, 1955).

The number of demographic surveys has grown steadily over the years. There are many surveys conducted in the United States, some of which are conducted by the federal government. Here now are several examples of federal surveys.

Current Population Survey

The **Current Population Survey (CPS)** is a monthly nationwide survey sponsored jointly by the US Bureau of the Census and the US Bureau of Labor Statistics. Its main purpose is to collect **labor force** data about the civilian noninstitutional population. Many of you have read newspaper stories or watched TV news reports every month or so about the levels of unemployment for the past month in the United States and in its major metropolitan areas. Have you ever wondered where these data come from? These are data that are gathered in the CPS.

CPS interviewers ask questions every month about the labor force participation of each member 14 years of age and older in every sample household. The survey covers around 60,000 occupied households each month and is a nationally representative sample of the US population. A household is in the CPS sample for eight rotations, and the samples are overlapping. Only 25 percent of the households differ between consecutive months. In addition to the basic CPS questions, interviewers also may ask supplementary questions. For instance, the March CPS includes a series of census-type questions (known as the Annual Demographic File) dealing with mobility, marital status, income, poverty, educational status, veteran status, and other census topics. Demographers' studies of the labor force are covered in more detail in Chapter 14.

National Survey of Family Growth

The **National Survey of Family Growth (NSFG)**, Cycle 1 was first conducted in 1973 and was followed by five more survey cycles in 1976, 1982, 1988, 1995, and 2002. After 2002, the NSFG has been administered on a continuous basis from 2006 to 2010, then from 2011 to 2015, and continuing beyond 2015.

The NSFG is a nationally representative multistage survey of male and female respondents between the ages of 15 and 44 that collects information on family life, marriage and divorce, pregnancy, infertility, use of contraception, and men's and women's health (National Center for Health Statistics, 2015). The 2002 NSFG was the first to include male respondents. In the first few years of the 2011–2015 period, the NSFG sample consisted of 10,416 men and women; approximately 5,000 more subjects were added in each of the following years of 2014 and 2015. The female questionnaire takes, on average, around 85 minutes to complete and the male questionnaire, 60 minutes. Respondent data addressing sensitive topics, such as sexuality, are collected using Audio Computer-Assisted Self-Interviewing (ACASI) "in which the respondent listens to the questions through headphones, reads them on the (laptop computer) screen, or both, and enters the response directly into the computer" (Mosher, Chandra, and Jones, 2005: 7). Such methods have been shown to "yield more complete reporting of sensitive behaviors, and they also avoid the large amounts of missing data often found on paper and pencil self-administered questionnaires" (Mosher, Chandra, and Jones, 2005: 8). Currently, the surveys have a response rate of 73 percent for women and 72 percent for men.

National Longitudinal Study of Adolescent to Adult Health

Another very important source of demographic information about young people is the National Longitudinal Study of Adolescent to Adult Health (Add Health), begun by Professor J. Richard Udry in the early 1990s at the Carolina Population Center at the University of North Carolina at Chapel Hill. It is a longitudinal study of a nationally representative sample of adolescents in grades 7–12 in the United States in 1994–1995. This adolescent cohort has been followed into adulthood with five in-home interviews, the last occurring in 2016–2018. Later in Chapter 4 of this book we discuss important research findings pertaining to adolescent pregnancy and fertility that used data from the Add Health survey.

American Community Survey

In the late 1990s, the US Bureau of the Census began redesigning its decennial long-form questionnaire (see our earlier discussion in this chapter) into an ongoing "continuous measurement" survey, known as the **American Community Survey (ACS)** (US Bureau of the Census, 2017). The ACS became fully operational in 2005. Beginning in 2010, it replaced the long-form questionnaire in the decennial census. The ACS is now conducted every year in all counties in the United States and Puerto Rico. It provides important economic, social, demographic, and housing data about all the communities in the United States every year, the same types of data that were previously provided only once every ten years. In this sense, the ACS may be thought of as "the decennial 'long form' spread out over 10 years; that is, the data collection occurs throughout the decade rather than just once in ten years" (Taeuber, 2006: 7).

US communities with 65,000 or more population receive ACS data estimates on all the long-form characteristics on an annual basis and have been receiving these data since 2006. Beginning in 2010 and every five years thereafter, national estimates are provided by combining the results of the previous five years' surveys. Hence, "the nation will have a five-year period estimate available as an alternative to the decennial census long-form sample, a community information resource that shows change over time, even for neighborhoods and rural areas" (US Bureau of the Census, 2006: 2–6). These five-year estimates are preferred over other ACS estimates because the error is smaller.

Beginning in 2005, a random sample of households in the United States started to receive the ACS questionnaire each month in the mail. Approximately 3.5 million households are contacted every year, or about 295 thousand households every month. Selected households receive a mailing, followed by a questionnaire that can be completed on the internet and is also available as a paper questionnaire. After the first mailing, there is a follow-up, and a face-to-face interview then follows for a subsample of the addresses that do not respond (US Bureau of the Census, 2017).

In closing, we emphasize that the ACS is a major change in census operations, indeed, a paradigm shift in census data collection. The ACS was developed so that the US Census Bureau would be able to address various problems encountered in recent censuses. These include, but are not limited to, difficulties in recruiting a sufficient number of qualified enumerators, a decline in the mail return of the census questionnaires, and an uncertainty about the completeness of the census address lists and counts, especially in so-called hard-to-enumerate areas. The ACS plan as summarized here (for more detail, see the ACS website, www.census.gov/acs/www/) simplifies the enumerators' job and makes response easier for many households who can self-respond to the questionnaire. The US Census Bureau expects that the ACS and its timely data will increase the confidence of users in its results, as well as reduce the number and types of problems encountered during the census operation (for more discussion, see Hillygus et al., 2006).

SUMMARY

In this chapter, we have discussed the three basic sources of demographic data: national censuses, registers, and surveys. Each is an important source of data for demographic study. Some demographers rely more on one or two of these than on the others. But demographic analysis generally requires data from all three sources. In later chapters, we will discuss the three demographic processes of fertility (Chapter 4), mortality (Chapter 5), and migration (Chapters 6 and 7). Our discussions in these and other chapters in this book are based on data from all three sources presented and elaborated on in this chapter.

DISCUSSION QUESTIONS

1. Look at Figure 3.1, It is an information copy of the 2020 census questionnaire. Assume that you have been identified as the person in the household where you are now living to fill out the form for your complete household. Your household would be the apartment where you are now living, or the home where you are now living, or the dormitory room where you are now living. Answer the census questions on the census form for your actual household for the current year, that is, this year, and not for the year 2020. (You may need to ask your roommates or suitemates or family members about answers to some of the questions.) Were there any questions you were not able to answer? Were any questions particularly difficult for you to answer?
2. The United States does not have a population register in the same way as the Scandinavian countries. But it does have partial registries dealing with Medicare, Social Security, Selective Service at the federal level, drivers' license records and voting registries at the state level, etc. But these do not cover the entire country. What do you believe would be the advantages and disadvantages of having the

US federal government develop a complete national population registry modeled on, for example, the registry of Denmark? For information on the Danish Civil Registry System, see https://ncrr.au.dk/danish-registers/the-population-statistics-register. Justify your arguments for and against the United States having a population registry.

4

Fertility

INTRODUCTION

Fertility refers to the production of children, which in the strictest sense is a biological process. A **zygote** is produced when the sperm of a male and the egg of a female are united, and around nine months later a baby is born. Most often in this process, although not always, a man and a woman have sexual intercourse, the woman conceives, and the **conception** results in a live birth. Even though the production of a child is a biological process, the various activities and events that lead to the act of sexual intercourse and, later, to giving birth are affected by the social, economic, cultural, and psychological characteristics of the woman and the man, as well as by the environment in which they live. The key to this paradox is that engaging in intercourse, conceiving, and giving birth are themselves behaviors that are influenced by other factors, most of them social and cultural. So, while we have no influence at all with regard to the family and parents we receive when we are born, we do have a significant influence on our own fertility. We will decide whether or not we produce children, and if so, the number and timing of the children produced. Whether we decide to engage in sexual intercourse, whether this intercourse results in a conception, and whether a live birth is the outcome are all driven largely by social and cultural considerations.

Fertility may be analyzed in different ways, one of which is cross-sectionally, that is, at one point in time; a cross-sectional perspective is also known as a **period perspective**. Were we to study the fertility behavior of women and men in the year 2025, we would develop cross-sectional fertility measures, also called period measures, that would show the number of births to women and men in the calendar year 2025. Most of the fertility measures we present in this chapter are period measures; they refer to a particular time period. A **period rate** is a rate based on behavior occurring at a particular point or period in time.

Fertility may also be studied over time to give us measures revealing the number and spacing of births to cohorts of women and men as they pass through the life cycle; this is known as **cohort analysis**. As an example, let us take the cohort of women who began their childbearing years at age 15 in, say, the year 1990. We would then follow them each year through the year 2025 when they were at the end of age 49 and had completed their 35 childbearing years, from age 15 to age 49; we could then tell how many babies they had produced. Fertility may be measured on a cohort basis, as well as on a period basis.

The demographic study of the fertility of individual women and men is known as a **micro-analysis** because it is an analysis of the fertility of persons. In contrast, if we were analyzing the fertility rates of the countries of the world we would be engaging in a **macro-analysis**.

There are several different ways to study fertility at the micro, that is, individual level: (1) examining the number of births a woman or man has produced by a given point in time, such as at the date of a census or survey; (2) examining the number of births a woman or man has had by the end of their childbearing years; and (3) focusing on the timing and spacing of births at various stages of the life cycle, say, between the ages of 25 and 29, or between the ages of 45 and 49.

As we noted above, another way to study fertility is to use a macro-level approach, that is, to determine the rate at which births occur in a population or subpopulation during a given period of time. Rather than studying the fertility of persons, macro-fertility analysis studies the fertility of populations (Poston and Frisbie, 2019). One reason demographers measure fertility at the macro-level is to then compare it with mortality, and to compute rates of overall population change. They also compare the fertility levels of different types of subpopulations over time.

In this chapter, we first consider the conceptualization and measurement of fertility. Second, we discuss the so-called **proximate determinants** of fertility. These are the mainly biological factors that lead directly to fertility and are themselves influenced heavily by social factors. We next consider world fertility patterns and how they have changed over time. We then focus on fertility trends and differences in the United States. We follow with a discussion of **adolescent fertility**, then **nonmarital fertility**, then **childlessness**, and then male fertility. We conclude the chapter with a discussion of popular and unpopular dates of birth.

CONCEPTUALIZATION AND MEASUREMENT OF FERTILITY

There are three main fertility concepts. **Fertility** is the actual production of male and female births and refers to real behavior. **Reproduction** is also the actual production of births, but refers to the production of only female births. (There is no demographic term to refer to the production of only male births.) **Fecundity** refers to the potential or the biological capability of producing live births.

The **crude birth rate (CBR)** is the first measure of fertility we will consider. It is a cross-sectional, that is, period, measure and refers to the number of births occurring in a population in a year per 1,000 persons. It is calculated as follows:

$$\text{CBR} = \frac{\text{number of births}}{\text{midyear population}} * 1{,}000 \qquad (4.1)$$

In 2024, the CBR for the world was 16/1,000. This means that in the world in 2024, there were 16 births for every 1,000 members of the world population. Among the continents, the CBR in 2024 ranged from a high of 31 in Africa to a low of 8 in Europe. In 2024 there were almost four times as many children per 1,000 population born in Africa as in Europe. Northern America had a CBR of 11 (and the CBR of the United States was also 11); Latin America and the Caribbean, 14; Asia, 14; and Oceania, 15. The major countries of the world had 2024 CBRs ranging from lows of 5 in South Korea; 6 in China, Japan, Taiwan and Italy; 7 in Thailand, Spain, Greece, Romania, Singapore, Lithuania, and Poland; to highs of 44 in the Central African Republic; 43 in Somalia; and 42 in Chad and Niger (Population Reference Bureau, 2024). Generally, CBRs above 30 are considered to be high, and those less than 15 to be low.

The CBR is referred to as "crude" because its **denominator**, the midyear population of the area, includes many people who are not at risk of childbearing, such as young women (under age 15) and postmenopausal women (older than age 49), and men. (An **at-risk population** is the population that is at risk of the event of interest occurring to them.) Strictly speaking, men do not bear children, so are thus not exposed to the risk of childbearing. However, some demographers do study male fertility, and we will consider this topic later in the chapter.

The **general fertility rate (GFR)** is another cross-sectional measure of fertility. It is superior conceptually and statistically to the CBR because it restricts the denominator to women of childbearing ages; its **numerator** is the same as that for the CBR. The GFR is calculated as follows:

$$\text{GFR} = \frac{\text{births}}{\text{midyear population}_{\text{f},15-49}} * 1{,}000 \tag{4.2}$$

where the numerator is the number of births in the population in the year, and the denominator is the number of females in the midyear population who are in the childbearing age range of 15 to 49.

In the United States in 2023, there were 75,905,647 women of ages 15 to 49; and 3,591,328 babies were born in 2023 (see Table 4.1). Dividing the latter figure by the former and multiplying the result by 1,000 gives us a GFR value for the United States of 47.31. This means that there were more than 47 babies born in the United States in 2023 for every 1,000 women between the ages of 15 and 49.

Sometimes the denominator of the GFR is restricted to women between the ages of 15 and 44. This occurs because, as we showed in Table 4.1, not many babies are born to women aged 45–49. For instance, of the 3,591,328 births in the United States in 2023, only 10,726, or 0.3 percent of them, were produced by women over the age of 44 (see Table 4.1).

In Figure 4.1, we show the number of live births and the GFRs for the United States for individual years between 2000 and 2023. The top line in the figure is the number of births and the bottom line is the GFR. Be aware that for the GFRs in Figure 4.1, the denominator is women in the age group 15–44, not 15–49.

In the years of the 2000s, there were around 4 million births each year; the number of births started to drop in around 2010, so that by 2023, there were just about 3.6 million babies born. The data in Figure 4.1 show that fertility as measured by the GFR (with a denominator of women aged 15–44) has been declining since 2007, and by 2023 rested right at about the mid-50s.

TABLE 4.1 *Fertility data and rates for the United States, 2023*

Age group	Women in age group (midyear population)	Live births to women in age group	Age-specific fertility rates (ASFR) (live births per 1,000 women)	ASFR × 5
15–19*	10,778,845	142,564	13.23	66.15
20–24	10,684,361	616,139	57.67	288.40
25–29	10,842,462	985,309	90.88	454.40
30–34	11,640,867	1,096,696	94.21	471.05
35–39	11,142,564	603,798	54.19	270.95
40–44	10,885,893	136,096	12.50	62.50
45–49**	9,930,655	10,726	1.08	5.40
TOTALS	75,905,647	3,591,328	47.31[a]	1618.85[b]

* Birth data are live births to mothers 19 years of age and less.
** Birth data are live births to mothers 45 years of age and older.
[a] GFR = (total births/female population$_{15-49}$) * 1,000 = (3,591,328 / 75,905,647) * 1,000 = 47.3
[b] TFR = $\sum$(ASFR * 5) = 1,618.9
Sources: Population data: US Bureau of the Census, "Annual Estimates of the Resident Population for Selected Age Groups by Sex for the United States: April 1, 2020 to July 1, 2023."
www.census.gov/data/datasets/time-series/demo/popest/2020s-national-detail.html
Birth data: Hamilton, Martin, and Osterman, 2024.
Calculations by DLP.

In the definition of the GFR, we referred to its denominator as females in the childbearing ages. We consider now what is meant by **childbearing ages**. In practice, as already noted, few women in a developed country such as the United States give birth before age 15 and after age 49, and so demographers usually use the age range 15–49 to mark the limits of the childbearing ages. But occasionally, births do occur to women before the age of 15 and after the age of 49. For example, in the United States in 2023, there were 1,763 births to women less than 15 years of age. But since so few births occur to women younger than 15 or older than 49, the ages 15–49 are used as the childbearing ages.

However, in developed countries, not only are there few births to women over age 49, there are not many births to women over age 44. Hence, as we have already noted, the denominator for the GFR is sometimes restricted to women aged 15–44, as is the case for the GFRs shown in Figure 4.1. So, a good rule of thumb when using the GFR is to use the 15–44 denominator if you are calculating the GFR for women in a developed and modernized country such as the United States.

Who is the oldest woman ever to give birth? The Guiness World Records reports that the oldest documented woman to ever give birth was a woman in Spain, Maria del Carmen Bousada Lara (1940–2009), who gave birth in Barcelona in 2006 by caesarean section to twin boys, Christian and Pau; she was then 66 years and 358 days of age (www.guinnessworldrecords.com/world-records/oldest-person-to-give-birth).

But we have found reports of two women, both in India, who gave birth at age 70. In July 2008, the British Broadcasting Corporation (BBC) News agency distributed a story about a woman, Omkari Panwar, giving birth to twins, at age 70. She and her

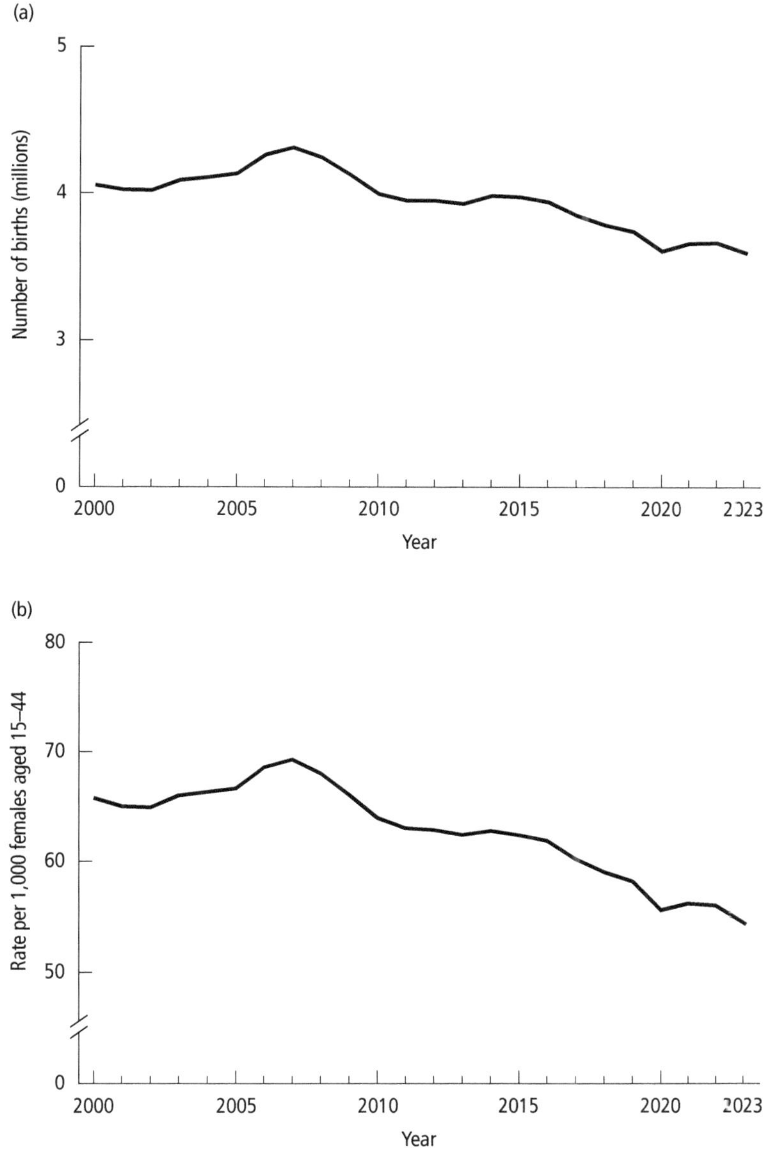

FIGURE 4.1 (a) Number of live births in millions in the United States from 2000 to 2023 and (b) General fertility rates per 1,000 women aged 15–44 in the United States from 2000 to 2023
Source: Modified from Hamilton, Martin, and Osterman, 2024.

husband, Charam Singh, a farmer in his mid-70s, already had two children, both girls. They badly wanted a son, so they took out a bank loan to pay the costs for **in vitro fertility** therapy, the result being a boy and a girl, both weighing around two pounds (BBC News, 2008).

The other elderly woman, also from India, reportedly gave birth to a baby when she also was 70 years old. Rajo Devi delivered a baby girl in 2008. Married for many years, she had always been trying to give birth, until she entered **menopause** when she was 50. She then used a donor's egg that was injected with her 72-year-old husband's sperm, and a baby was born (Belkin, 2008).

If you have data available only for the CBR but wish to approximate the value of the GFR, an estimated GFR value (for women in the age group 15–44) is given by the following formula:

$$GFR = CBR * 4.5 \tag{4.3}$$

To illustrate, CBR values in the United States in 1950 and in 2023 were 24.1 and 11.0, respectively. If we had no other data available and needed GFR values for these two years, we could multiply each CBR by 4.5 and arrive at estimated GFR values of 108.5 for 1950 and 49.5 for 2023. These estimated GFRs (for women aged 15–44) are not far from the actual GFRs of 106.2 for 1950 and 54.3 for 2023. The constant of 4.5 in this formula and those in other formulas that we show later are based on empirical and analytic relationships between the fertility measures (see Bogue and Palmore [1964]).

We noted earlier that the GFR addresses the major problem of the CBR by restricting the denominator to women in the childbearing ages. A problem still remains, however, with the GFR. It does not take into account the fact that within the childbearing years of 15 to 49, there are differences in the extent to which the women produce children. Fertility is low for women aged 15–19 and is then at its highest for women aged 20–29 and 30–34; the rates become lower in the late 30s and even lower in the 40s. To take into account the fact that fertility varies by age, demographers calculate fertility rates for specific age groups of women.

The **age-specific fertility rate (ASFR)** reflects exactly what its name indicates: It focuses on births to women according to their age. ASFRs are usually calculated for women in each of the seven five-year age groups of 15–19, 20–24, 25–29, 30–34, 35–39, 40–44, and 45–49. The general formula for the ASFR for women in age group x to x + n is as follows:

$$ASFR_{x\text{ to }x+n} = \frac{births_{x\text{ to }x+n}}{females_{x\text{ to }x+n}} * 1{,}000 \tag{4.4}$$

Although most demographic analyses using ASFRs calculate them for these five-year age groups, sometimes 35 single-year age groups are used, for example, age group 15, age group 16, age group 17, all the way up to age group 49.

Table 4.1 shows the numbers of women in the United States in 2023 in each of the seven age groups 15–19 to 45–49 (col. 2) and the numbers of babies born to the women in each of the age groups (col. 3). There were 10,684,361 women in 2023 in the age group 20–24. There were 616,139 babies born in 2023 to women in this age group. Dividing the latter figure by the former and multiplying the result by 1,000 produces an ASFR for women aged 20–24 of 57.67. This means that in the United States in 2023, for every 1,000 women aged 20–24, 58 babies were born to them. All seven ASFRs for US women in 2023 are shown in Table 4.1. The highest ASFR is for women aged 30–34, the next highest for women aged 25–29, and the third highest for women aged 20–24. ASFRs for women in the other four age groups are not quite as high.

When the seven ASFRs are plotted, they usually form an inverted U. Such a plot is referred to as the **age curve of fertility**. In Figure 4.2, we show age curve of fertility plots for 2023 for the United States and for the countries with very high and very low fertility rates in 2023, Chad and South Korea. The curves for South Korea and the United States are similar for the later ages, but they differ somewhat for women in the age groups 20–24 and 25–29. As we will see in the next section when we discuss the **total fertility rate,** in 2023 South Korea had a total fertility rate of 0.72 children per woman and the United States had a rate of 1.6 children per woman. The overall difference in TFRs for the two countries is mainly due to rate differences for the younger women.

In 2023 Chad had a total fertility rate of 6.1 children per woman, one of the highest in the world. Observe in Figure 4.2 how much higher Chad's rates are compared to the US rates. Women in the age group 20–24 in Chad in 2023 had 270 children per 1,000, compared to a rate for the United States of 58 per 1,000; that is, in 2023, for every 1,000 20–24-year-old women in Chad, more than one in four of them had a baby; for every 1,000 20–24-year-old women in the United States in 2023, around one in 20 of them had a baby. Chad women in the age group 25–29 had 274 babies per 1,000, compared to a rate for US women of 91. Chad's rate for women aged 40–44 in 2023 was 96 per 1,000; this rate for older women in Chad was higher than any of the age-specific fertility rates for US women in 2023. Clearly, fertility as measured by ASFRs is considerably higher in the African country of Chad than in the United States or in South Korea.

The **total fertility rate (TFR)** is the most popular of all fertility rates used by demographers. Like the ASFRs, the TFRs take into account the fact that fertility varies by age. Unlike the ASFRs, which are expressed quantitatively as a series of age-specific rates (usually seven, one for each age group), the TFR provides a single fertility value. The TFR is almost always calculated cross-sectionally, that is, for a specific period of time,

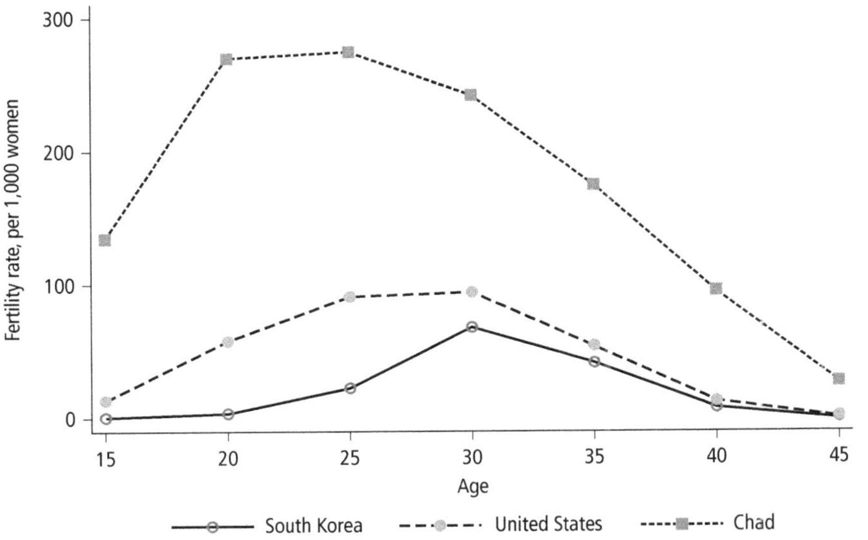

FIGURE 4.2 Age-specific fertility rates: South Korea, United States, and Chad, 2023
Data source: South Korea and Chad: United Nations, 2024b; United States: Table 4.1 above.

although as we will note later, it may also be calculated for cohorts. A cross-sectional TFR for a particular point in time is an estimate of the number of births that a hypothetical group of 1,000 women would produce during their reproductive lifetime, that is, between the ages of 15 and 49 (or, sometimes, 15 and 44), if their childbearing at each of their reproductive years followed the ASFRs for a given time period. This number of live births that the hypothetical group of 1,000 women would produce is calculated under the assumption that none of the women die during their reproductive years.

The TFR is calculated by summing the ASFRs after multiplying each by the width of the age interval of the ASFRs. If we use ASFRs based on five-year intervals, as is usually the case and as we have done in Table 4.1, we would multiply each ASFR by the value of 5. Here is the formula for calculating the TFR:

$$\text{TFR} = \sum(\text{ASFR}_{\text{x to x+n}} * \text{i}) \tag{4.5}$$

where i = the width in years of the age interval; in most cases, this will be 5.

In Table 4.1, we show the calculation of the TFR for the United States for the year 2023. The ASFRs shown in column 4 are multiplied by the constant of 5 and reported in column 5. These values are then summed, to yield a TFR of 1,619. This may be interpreted as follows: If 1,000 women went through their reproductive years from when they were age 15 to when they were age 49 and were subjected each year to the ASFRs of the United States for the year of 2023, by the time they reached age 49, they would have produced 1,619 babies, or an average of 1.6 babies each. The TFR refers to the average number of births to 1,000 women, as well as, when divided by 1,000, to the average number of births to a single woman. The TFR is a standardized rate; that is, it is not influenced by the differences in the numbers of women in each age. Its value is especially useful in interpreting the fertility that is implied by a given set of ASFRs for a particular point in time.

TFRs are shown in Figure 4.3 for the United States and South Korea for each year from 1950 to 2023. We noted earlier that South Korea in 2023 had the lowest fertility rate in the world, under 0.8 children per woman. But in 1950 Korea had a fertility rate of 6.0. In 1950 Korea's fertility rate was higher than the US fertility rate. But in 2023, Korea's fertility rate was lower than the US fertility rate. We will present here some of the reasons for the dramatic fertility decline in South Korea. Later in this chapter we will discuss the fertility changes in the United States starting in 1790, shortly after the country was established.

The Korean War began in late June of 1950 and ended in late July of 1953. Korea was destroyed economically and socially by the war. In the late 1950s, Korea was one of the poorest countries in the world. In 1961, the country's rate of recovery was slow, and annual per capita income was only about US $82. What happened in Korea since 1950? Why did its total fertility rate drop from 6.0 children per woman to 0.8 children per woman?

Korea's fertility decline began in the early 1960s when the government adopted an economic planning program, and then a year or so later a population and family planning program. The country's rapid fertility decline is due to both economic development and government family planning programs.

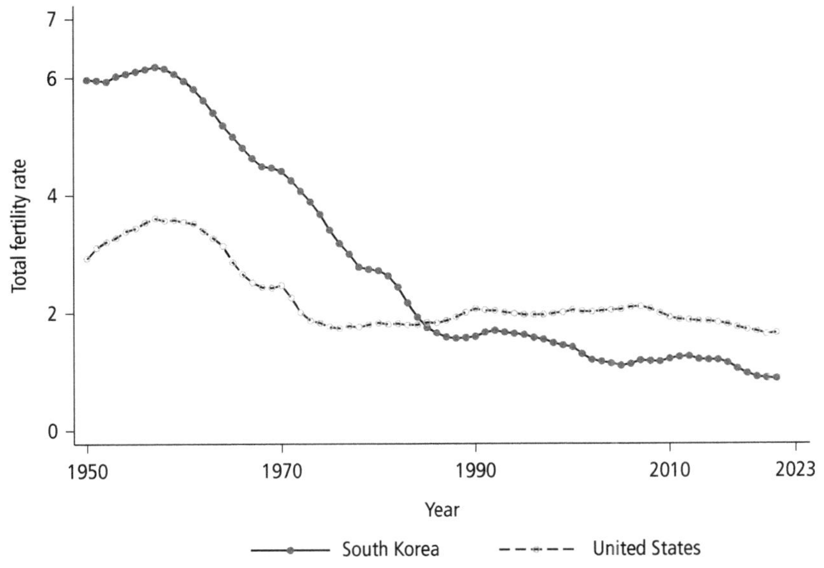

FIGURE 4.3 Total fertility rates: United States and South Korea, 1950–2023
Data source: United Nations, 2024b.

Dramatic increases in economic growth began after the Korean government introduced its five-year economic development plan in 1962; and the growth continued well into the mid-1990s and beyond. Increases in productivity, combined with an increasingly larger labor force and a gradual reduction of unemployment, produced average annual growth rates in GNP for many years of between 6 and 10 percent. Korea today is one of the richest countries in the world. According to 2021–2022 data from WorldData.info (www.worlddata.info/richest-countries.php), Korea was listed then as the 30th richest country in the world with an adjusted gross domestic product (GDP) per capita of US $46,889; the United States was ranked 11th.

Much of this transformation of Korea from a poor country to a rich country has been due to the **demographic dividend** that occurred during the country's fertility decline. This dividend refers to accelerated increases in a country's economy following a decline in its birth rates and subsequent change in its age composition. Economic growth occurs if the country introduces and implements social and economic policies.

Korea did both. With regard to population planning programs, Korea set a contraceptive use goal for married couples of around 45 percent. This further contributed to the fertility reduction when many couples realized that having fewer children often led to improvements in family living.

In the 1960s Korea was a very young country with a fertility rate of 6.0. Then from the 1960s to the mid-1990s, the country experienced high rates of annual growth in per capita GDP. These increases occurred because with many fewer births each year, Korea's young and dependent population grew smaller in relation to the working-age population. The country had proportionately fewer dependent mouths to feed. Korea's young dependent population became small, and its working-age population became large. This demographic dividend was mainly due to economic development and a successful family planning program.

What about the negative feature of the fertility decline? Now with an extremely low fertility rate of 0.8, Korea is on the way to becoming a country with a very large number of elderly people. Since the mid-1980s, Korean fertility has been below the replacement level of 2.1. (We later discuss the issue of replacement level fertility.) Birth cohorts are much smaller these days than they were several decades ago. The very low fertility rates, coupled with current and projected gains in longevity, will produce in the coming decades very large absolute numbers of elderly people (Poston, 2023b)

If one only has CBR data available for an area or country or, alternately, only GFR data, the TFR may be estimated with the following formulas:

$$TFR = CBR * 4.5 * 30 \tag{4.6}$$

$$TFR = GFR * 30 \tag{4.7}$$

In 2023, the world TFR was 2.2. It was 4.1 for the **least-developed countries**, and 2.4 for the **less-developed countries**. The **more-developed countries** had an average TFR in 2023 of 1.5. TFRs ranged around the world from highs of 6.7 in Niger, 6.4 in the Central African Republic, 6.2 in Somalia, and 6.1 in Chad, to lows of 0.8 in South Korea, 0.9 in Taiwan, and 1.1 in China, Spain, and Bosnia-Herzegovina (Population Reference Bureau, 2023). If during their childbearing years, 1,000 women followed the ASFRs for Niger in 2023, at the completion of their 49th year, they would have produced 6,400 babies, or an average of 6.4 each. In contrast, if during their reproductive lives, 1,000 women followed the ASFRs of South Korea for the year 2023, by the time they ended their childbearing years, they would have given birth to 800 babies, or about 0.8 each. These are tremendous differences in fertility. We will discuss TFR trends and differences among the countries of the world in a later section of this chapter.

We noted earlier that the TFR is most frequently calculated on a cross-sectional basis, that is, for a specific period or year, and is referred to as a period or cross-sectional TFR. Alternately, the TFR may be calculated for cohorts. Rather than subjecting a hypothetical group of 1,000 women to a schedule of ASFRs for a given point in time, that is, as with the cross-sectional TFR, the cohort TFR follows a real group of women through their childbearing years and tabulates their actual fertility as they pass through these years. Table 4.2 presents average annual ASFRs for the years 1970–1974, 1975–1979, and so forth, through 2010–2014. We will now show how to use these data to calculate both a period TFR and a cohort TFR.

The cross-sectional TFR may be calculated for any of the years 1970-1974, 1975-1979, up to 2010-2014 by summing the ASFRs across the respective row and multiplying the sum by 5. To illustrate, if we wanted the average annual cross-sectional TFR for the period 1970–1974, we would sum the seven ASFRs for that period, namely, 62.3, 137.1, 124.1, 62.0, 25.5, 6.3, and 0.4, and then multiply the total by 5 to produce an annual period TFR for 1970–1974 of 2,088.5 This value reflects the number of children that a hypothetical group of 1,000 women would produce if during their childbearing years they were subjected to the ASFRs of the United States for the 1970–1974 period. If we wanted the average annual cross-sectional TFR for the period 2010–2014, we

TABLE 4.2 *Age-specific fertility rates, United States, 1970–1974 to 2010–2014*

	15–19 years	20–24 years	25–29 years	30–34 years	35-39 years	40–44 years	45–49[a] years	Total fertility rate
1970–1974	**62.3**	137.1	124.1	62.0	25.5	6.3	0.4	2,088.5
1975–1979	53.0	**111.8**	109.1	56.1	19.2	4.2	0.2	1,768.0
1980–1984	51.9	110.7	**110.5**	63.9	21.2	3.9	0.2	1,811.5
1985–1989	52.4	109.5	112.9	**72.7**	26.5	4.5	0.2	1,893.5
1990–1994	59.8	113.2	115.5	80.0	**32.4**	5.9	0.3	2,035.5
1995–1999	52.0	107.8	109.4	83.7	35.9	**7.1**	0.4	1,981.5
2000–2004	43.4	104.4	115.0	93.5	42.2	8.4	**0.5**	2,037.0
2005–2009	40.1	102.1	115.8	98.6	46.9	9.6	0.6	2,068.5
2010–2014	29.1	83.6	106.6	97.8	48.3	10.4	0.7	1,882.5

Sources: Numerator data from the National Center for Health Statistics. Denominator data from the US Census Bureau.

[a] Before 1997, rates are for live births to women 45–49 per 1,000 women 45–49; beginning in 1997, rates are for live births to women 45–54 per 1,000 women 45–49.

Table produced by Rachel Traut Cortes and DLP.

would sum the seven ASFRs for that period – namely, 29.1, 83.6, 106.6, 97.8, 48.3, 10.4, and 0.7 – and then multiply the total by 5 to produce an annual period TFR for 2010–2014 of 1,882.5 This value would reflect the number of children that a hypothetical group of 1,000 women would produce were they to be subjected to the ASFRs of the United States for the 2010–2014 period.

In contrast, if we desired the cohort TFR for those women who started their childbearing years in 1970–1974 (we will refer to those women as the 1970–1974 fertility cohort because they initiated their childbearing in 1970–1974), we would take the ASFRs on the diagonal line in Table 4.2 for the 1970–1974 fertility cohort of women. (We have emboldened this diagonal line in the table.) When those women were aged 15–19 in 1970–1974, they had an ASFR of 62.3; when they were 20–24 in 1975–1979, they had an ASFR of 111.8; when they were 25–29 in 1980–1984, they had an ASFR of 110.5; and so forth until they were 45–49 in 2000–2004 and had an ASFR of 0.5. When we sum these ASFRs and multiply the total by 5, we have a cohort TFR of 1,986.5. This is the actual number of children that were produced on average by 1,000 members of the 1970–1974 fertility cohort.

But we would have had to wait until the women comprising the 1970–1974 fertility cohort completed their childbearing years to know what their cohort TFR would be. And by the time they completed their childbearing years, the TFR data for them would be dated and would apply only to an older group of women who had already completed their childbearing years. Hence period TFRs are often preferred over cohort TFRs; although period TFRs refer to a hypothetical (sometimes referred to as a synthetic) cohort, they are timelier and more current.

A period (i.e., cross-sectional) TFR refers to the fertility of a **hypothetical cohort** (an imaginary set) of 1,000 women. In contrast, a cohort TFR refers to the fertility of a real cohort of 1,000 women. A period TFR for a year, say, the year 2023, refers to the fertility produced by women of all ages in the year 2023, a particular period of time.

Alternately, a cohort TFR refers to the fertility of a group of women who have already completed their childbearing years and sometimes may be viewed as out of date. Both period and cohort TFRs are used by demographers, but, as we have already mentioned, period TFRs are preferred principally because of their currency.

There are two more fertility measures we will now discuss, although none is as popular as the TFR; these two are based on the concept of **population replacement**. Given a set of fertility rates, what does this mean with regard to replacing the population? Replacement refers to the production of female births, known among demographers as reproduction. In contrast, fertility refers to the production of babies of either sex.

The **gross reproduction rate (GRR)** is a standardized rate similar to the TFR, except that it is based on the sum of age-specific rates that include only female births in the numerators. Sometimes data are not readily available on the number of female live births reported by age of the mothers. Thus, the proportion of all births that are female is usually employed as a constant and is multiplied against the given TFR, as follows:

$$\text{GRR} = \text{TFR} * \left(\frac{\text{female births}}{\text{births}}\right) \tag{4.8}$$

The value of the constant multiplier, that is, the proportion of births that are female, varies only slightly from population to population. Most societies, but not all, have around 105–106 male babies born per 100 female babies. (See our earlier discussion in Chapter 1 of the sex ratio at birth.) Let us use the value of 105 male births; if we divide 100 (female births) by 205 (male births + female births) and multiply by 100, this results in a value of 48.8 percent being female births. Hence, we may use the following formula to calculate the GRR:

$$\text{GRR} = \text{TFR} * 0.488 \tag{4.9}$$

We reported previously in Table 4.1 that the TFR in the United States in 2023 was 1618.9. We can thus calculate the GRR for the United States in 2023 as follows:

$$\text{GRR} = \text{TFR} * 0.488 \tag{4.10}$$

$$\text{GRR} = 1618.9 * 0.488 = 790.0$$

This value of 790.0 may be interpreted as the number of daughters expected to be born alive to a hypothetical cohort of 1,000 women if none of the women died during their childbearing years and if the same schedule of age-specific rates applied throughout their childbearing years.

In Table 4.3, we show the calculation of the GRR for the United States in greater detail than we did above in formula 4.10. In this example, we calculate the GRR for the year of 2023. We begin with a listing of the seven age groups (col. 1) and the midpoint of the age interval for each age group (col. 2). For instance, the midpoint for the age group 15–19 is 17.5. Data on the number of women in each age group in the United States in 2023 appear in column 3. Data on the number of babies born to the women in each age group appear in column 4.

As noted earlier, we sometimes do not have easily accessible data on the sex composition of births by age of mother, so this is often approximated. In the United States, as in

TABLE 4.3 *Calculation of gross reproduction rate (GRR) and net reproduction rate (NRR), United States, 2023*

Age group (1)	Midpoint of interval (2)	Number of women in age group (3)	Number of births to women in age group (4)	Number of female births to women in age group (5)	Female births per woman (6)	Female birth rate during 5-year interval (7)	Proportion of female babies surviving to midpoint of age interval (8)	Surviving daughters per woman during 5-year interval (9)
15–19	17.5	10,778,845	142,564	69,571	0.00645	0.03225	0.9889	0.03189
20–24	22.5	10,684,361	616,139	300,676	0.02814	0.14070	0.9848	0.13856
25–29	27.5	10,842,462	985,309	480,831	0.04435	0.22175	0.9801	0.21734
30–34	32.5	11,640,867	1,096,696	535,188	0.04597	0.22985	0.9752	0.22415
35–39	37.5	11,142,564	603,798	294,653	0.02644	0.13220	0.9691	0.12812
40–44	42.5	10,885,893	136,096	66,415	0.00610	0.03050	0.9600	0.02928
45–49*	47.5	9,930,655	10,726	5,234	0.00053	0.00265	0.9462	0.00251
						0.78990 = GRR		0.77185 = NRR

* Rates are for live births to mothers aged 45–54 per 1,000 women aged 45–49.

Sources of data: Population data: US Bureau of the Census, “Annual Estimates of the Resident Population for Selected Age Groups by Sex for the United States: April 1, 2020 to July 1, 2023”: www.census.gov/data/datasets/time-series/demo/popest/2020s-national-detail.html

Birth data: Hamilton, Martin, and Osterman, 2024.

Calculations by DLP.

most other countries, the sex ratio at birth (SRB) is around 105 boys per 100 girls. This means that the proportion of US births that are female is 0.488. We thus multiply the birth data in column 4 by this constant proportion of 0.488, producing in column 5 the data on female births to women in each group. (If the SRB is not around 105, then another constant must be used. For instance, were we calculating the GRR for China in 2020, we would need to take into account the fact that China's SRB in 2020 was 108. Thus, the proportion of all births in China in 2020 that were female was 0.481. This constant of 0.481 would be the one we would use for calculating the GRR for China in 2020.)

Next, we divide the number of female births at each age (col. 5) by the number of women at each age (col. 3), to produce the age-specific rates of female births (col. 6); these age-specific rates have not yet been multiplied by 1,000.

The age-specific rates of female births in column 6 refer to only a single year, but we will assume that the hypothetical cohort of women will experience these rates during the entire five-year interval. So, we now multiply the rates in column 6 by 5 to obtain the female birth rates during the five-year interval; these are shown in column 7.

We then sum the values in column 7 to obtain the GRR. We multiply this sum by 1,000 to get the number of female births born to the hypothetical cohort of 1,000 women. The value of the GRR for the year is 0.7899 (see bottom of column 7 of Table 4.3). We multiply it by 1,000, yielding 789.9. This value of 789.9 may be interpreted as indicating that 790 daughters would be produced by a hypothetical cohort of 1,000 women if during their childbearing years they were subjected to the age-specific rates of the United States in 2023. Thus the 1,000 women would have produced 790 daughters, which would not have been enough daughters for the 1,000 women to replace themselves with 1,000 daughters. This value of 790, by the way, is exactly the same as the value we produced above with the GRR formula (formula 4.10).

We noted earlier that the GRR makes no allowance for the fact that some of the mothers will die before they complete their childbearing years. Thus, to obtain a more accurate measure of the replacement of daughters by their mothers, demographers have developed another rate, namely, the **net reproduction rate (NRR)**.

The NRR is a measure of the number of daughters who will be born to a hypothetical cohort of 1,000 mothers, taking into account the mortality of the mothers from the time of their birth. It may be thought of as the GRR net of mortality. Thus, the NRR subjects the 1,000 mothers not only to a schedule of age-specific reproduction rates but also to the risk of mortality up to the age of 49 (Rowland, 2003: 246). The formula for the NRR is the following:

$$\text{NRR} = \sum\left(\text{ASFR}_{x\ \text{to}\ x+n} * 0.488 * \frac{L_x}{5 l_o}\right) \tag{4.11}$$

The first two components of the NRR formula, namely, multiplying each ASFR by the constant of 0.488, are the major features of the GRR, as noted above. We have already mentioned that the GRR refers to the number of female births born to a hypothetical cohort of 1,000 women if none of the women in the hypothetical cohort die from the time they are babies until the end of their reproductive years. The NRR takes into account the probabilities that not all of the women will survive from age 0 to the end of their childbearing years.

So, returning to Table 4.3, column 8 presents **life table** values from a current life table for females of $\mathbf{L_x}$, multiplied by 500,000, for each of the age intervals. (We discuss the life table in the next chapter, Chapter 5.) The $\mathbf{L_x}$ values represent the total number of person years lived in the age interval. But since we need to have data on the proportion of women who survive to the midpoint of the age interval, we divide each of the $\mathbf{L_x}$ values by $5(l_o)$, or 500,000, giving us the proportion of women who survive from age 0 to the midpoint of each of the seven age intervals. (These values of $\mathbf{L_x}$ and l_o are discussed in detail in Chapter 5.)

To illustrate, for age interval 15–19, we take from the life table the value of $\mathbf{L_{15}}$ and divide it by $5(l_o)$, or 500,000, equaling 0.9889. This means that 98.89 percent of the women in the hypothetical cohort will survive from birth through the midpoint of the age interval 15–19. These proportions of surviving females appear in column 8.

We then multiply the five-year female birth rates (col. 7) by the proportions of surviving females (col. 8) to obtain in column 9 the number of daughters the women in each age group will bear, if they abide by a certain schedule of age-specific reproduction rates and a mortality schedule from the life table. We add up the values in column 9 to get a total of 0.7719, which is the average net number of female births per woman in the hypothetical cohort after taking into account the mortality of the mothers; the net number of female births is a value less than 1 per woman. We then multiply this figure by 1,000 for an estimate of the net number of female births for the entire cohort of 1,000 women, or 771.9 female births per 1,000 women (see the bottom of column 9 of Table 4.3).

The NRR is a "measure of how many daughters would replace 1,000 women if age-specific fertility and mortality rates remained constant indefinitely. Consequently, rates above 1,000 mean that eventually the population would increase, and rates below 1,000 mean that eventually the population would decrease, provided that the age-specific (birth and death) rates remained the same and no migration occurred" (Palmore and Gardner, 1994: 101–102).

PROXIMATE DETERMINANTS OF FERTILITY

Most demographers are primarily interested in ascertaining whether, how, and why various social, economic, cultural, and environmental factors influence both the likelihood of a woman having a baby and the number of babies she will have in her lifetime. It has been shown for instance that social class, economic status, religious beliefs, psychological disposition, attitudes about children, and other factors influence the decision to have a baby, as well as the number of babies, from zero to some positive number, a woman will have. Demographers have shown, for example, that the more years of education a woman has, the fewer children she will have. Why would this be? Why would more years of completed education result, on average, in a woman having fewer children? One reason is that women who are in school longer tend to marry later and postpone having children, compared to women who have attended school for a shorter period of time. So, the education variable has an influence on fertility through the so-called proximate or intermediate variables that lie between fertility and the social, economic, cultural, and environmental variables.

In 1956, two eminent demographers, Kingsley Davis and Judith Blake, wrote a very influential paper about the behavioral and biological variables that are "intermediate" and thus directly influence fertility. These particular variables were distinguished from all of the other kinds of variables because the latter variables, by necessity, influence fertility by operating through the few intermediate variables specified by Davis and Blake. Briefly, the authors stated that the three variables of intercourse, conception, and gestation/**parturition** (the act or process of giving birth) should be considered as intermediate to the many other social, economic, cultural, and environmental factors that influence fertility. These latter variables, they argued, can only be related to fertility if they work through, or pass through, one or more of the intermediate variables.

Davis and Blake expanded on the three intermediate variables in the following ways: (1) the amount of intercourse is affected by the proportion of persons who marry, the length of time these persons are married, and their frequency of sexual intercourse while married; (2) the probability of conception is affected by **contraception** and by voluntary or involuntary **infecundity**, that is, the inability to conceive; (3) the probability of a birth resulting from a given conception depends on the likelihood of miscarriage and abortion. They further emphasized that each intermediate variable can operate to increase as well as to decrease fertility. Not all of them need to operate in the same direction, however. The observed level of fertility in a population depends on the net balance of *all* the intermediate variables.

We will pause here for a moment and mention some of the fertility terms we will use. You already know the difference between fertility and fecundity. Fertility refers to actual reproduction and fecundity refers to the ability to reproduce. The opposite terms are **infertility**, also called childlessness, and infecundity, which is synonymous with **sterility**. Sterility implies the existence of infertility, but the reverse is not necessarily the case. A **fecund** woman may choose to remain infertile by not marrying or by practicing highly effective contraception. Infertility, then, is due to a voluntary decision not to have children or it is caused by (biological) infecundity.

With regard to fecundity, it is sometimes divided into five categories on the basis of the extent of fecundity impairment and the degree of certainty of the evidence (Poston, Zhang, and Terrell, 2008). That is, how able or unable are couples with regard to producing a birth?

First, all couples may be classified as either fecund or **subfecund**. Fecund couples are capable of giving birth. Second, subfecund couples have impairments of one sort or another and may be subdivided into the following groups: definitely sterile, probably sterile, **semifecund**, and **fecundity indeterminate** (Badenhorst and Higgins, 1962). Definitely sterile couples are those for whom conception is impossible because of certain physical or medical conditions, including an operation, some other impairment, or menopause. Probably sterile couples are those for whom a birth is improbable on the basis of specific medical evidence. Semifecund couples are those who have married or cohabited for a relatively long time without using contraception but have not conceived. Fecundity indeterminate couples are those who meet the criteria for semifecund couples, except that the woman sometimes reports douching "for cleanness only" soon after intercourse. These couples are defined as "fecundity indeterminate" (Badenhorst and Higgins, 1962: 281). Demographic research has shown that the majority of subfecund couples are impaired according to these definitions (Poston, Zhang, and Terrell, 2008).

Returning to our discussion of the proximate determinants, the distinguished demographer John Bongaarts, in two important papers written in 1978 and 1982, respecified the intermediate variables of Davis and Blake in a way that facilitated the quantitative specification of how they influence fertility. He referred to the intermediate variables as the "proximate determinants" of fertility, a term very commonly used these days by demographers. The proximate determinants perspective is one of the most elegant and useful frameworks in demography for understanding the process of fertility and how fertility is determined.

Bongaarts recognized that the "Davis and Blake framework for analyzing the determinants of fertility has found wide acceptance, [but] it has proven difficult to incorporate into quantitative reproductive models" (1982: 179). He thus set out the following seven proximate determinants: (1) marriage and marital disruption, (2) contraceptive use and effectiveness, (3) prevalence of induced abortion, (4) duration of **postpartum infecundability**, (5) waiting time to conception, (6) risk of intrauterine mortality, and (7) onset of permanent sterility. We now consider each of these in turn.

First, with regard to marriage and marital disruption, this variable was intended to reflect the proportion of women in the population who were of reproductive age and engaging in sexual activity on a regular basis; in traditional societies, sexual behavior occurred mainly within marriage. Second, the contraception variable reflects deliberate contraceptive behaviors, including abstinence and sterilization, that are undertaken to reduce the risk of conception. Third, induced abortion includes all practices and behaviors that deliberately interrupt pregnancies. Fourth, duration of postpartum infecundability, in Bongaarts's terms, may be considered this way: "Following a pregnancy a woman remains infecundable (i.e., unable to conceive) until the normal pattern of ovulation and menstruation is restored. The duration of the period of infecundity is a function of the duration and intensity of lactation" (Bongaarts, 1978: 107). Fifth, waiting time to conception refers to the fact that a woman who is not using contraception is able to conceive "for only a short period of approximately two days in the middle of the menstrual cycle when ovulation takes place. The duration of this fertile period is a function of the duration of the viability of the sperm and ovum" (Bongaarts, 1978: 107). Sixth, risk of intrauterine mortality reflects the fact that many conceptions do not eventually lead to live births because some of them end as miscarriages, spontaneous abortions, or stillbirths. Seventh, the onset of permanent sterility reflects the fact that "women are sterile before **menarche** . . . and after menopause, but a couple may become sterile before the woman reaches menopause for reasons other than contraceptive sterilization" (Bongaarts, 1978: 107–108). (Menarche is the beginning of the female reproductive period, signaled by the first menstrual flow, and menopause is the end of that period, signaled by the termination of menstruation.)

A considerable amount of demographic research focusing on fertility highlights three major kinds of variables that operate through the proximate determinants in predicting fertility. These are **family planning** variables, socioeconomic variables, and attitudinal variables. But for any of these variables to influence fertility behavior, they must work through the proximate determinants. As Knodel and his colleagues observed, "since many of the proximate determinants are influenced by volitional actions and choice, attitudes directly concerning fertility as well as attitudes about the proximate determinants themselves are an important feature of any exposition of reproductive change" (Knodel, Chamratrithirong, and Debavalya, 1987: 9).

Bongaarts (1982) has taken the first four of the proximate determinants and quantified them with indices ranging from 0 to 1, with the lowest value of 0 indicating the greatest possible inhibiting effect on fertility of the proximate determinant and the maximum score of 1 representing no inhibiting effect of the determinant. The marriage-pattern index, *Cm*, has a value of 1 when all women of reproductive ages are in a marital or consensual union and 0 when none of them is in such a union. The contraception index, *Cc*, equals 1 if no contraception is used in the population and equals 0 if all fecund women are using completely effective modern methods of contraception. The postpartum-infecundability measure, *Ci*, is an index that ranges from a value of 1 when no women are experiencing postpartum infecundability to a value of 0 when all women are. The index of abortion, *Ca*, ranges from a maximum value equaling 1 when there is no induced abortion practiced in the population to 0 if every pregnancy that occurs is aborted.

He then calculated the four indexes for 41 historical and contemporary, that is, developing and developed, countries and used them to predict the total fertility rates of these 41 populations. He showed that 96 percent of the variation in fertility could be explained solely by variation in the four proximate determinants of marriage, contraceptive use, postpartum infecundability, and abortion (see also Bongaarts and Potter [1983]). The other three proximate determinants were less important and did not vary significantly among the populations.

Bongaarts's demonstration is very important because it shows that virtually all of the variation in fertility is due to variation in only the four major proximate determinants. Thus, the effects of any and all of the socioeconomic and attitudinal and other kinds of variables that we mentioned above can only have an effect on fertility if they operate through the proximate determinants.

Stover (1998) has recommended several modifications and extensions to the Bongaarts model to include using sexual activity instead of marriage as the indicator of exposure to pregnancy, extending the sterility index to measure infecundity from all causes, revising the contraception index to take into account the fact that users of sterilization could become infecund before the age of 49, and changing the estimate of total fecundity. These revisions endeavor to take into account the demographic realities of modern societies. For instance, marriage no longer represents one's first exposure to sexual activity. In Chapter 11, we show data for the United States for the 2015–2019 period (Figure 11.4) indicating that among unmarried teenagers, 40 percent of both males and females have experienced their first sexual intercourse by age 17, and 60 percent of both males and females by age 19 (Abma and Martinez, 2023; see also Finer, 2007; Guttmacher Institute, 2014a).

The above are important revisions to the Bongaarts model, to be sure. But they should not be seen as reducing or minimizing in any way the contributions of Bongaarts.

His path-breaking conceptual and empirical studies, building on the earlier work of Davis and Blake, resulted in a paradigm shift among demographers and their analyses of fertility.

WORLD FERTILITY TRENDS AND PATTERNS

In the world in 2023 and in 2024, the total fertility rate (TFR) was 2.2, but this value hides the tremendous heterogeneity in fertility in the countries around the world. We first ask how many countries are there in the world? According to the United Nations, in 2023 there were 195 countries in the world, consisting of the 193 member countries of the United Nations, plus two recognized independent nations, the Holy See (Vatican City) and Palestine. (But only 145 of the 193 member countries recognize Palestine as a separate country.) Taiwan, Hong Kong, and Macao are not member countries of the United Nations because they are considered to be part of the People's Republic of China. And Kosovo is not included as a member UN country because it is considered to be part of Serbia.

The United States also recognizes 195 countries, but there are differences between the 195 UN countries and the 195 US countries. Kosovo is recognized as a country by the United States but is not a member country of the United Nations. And the United Nations includes Palestine as one of its 195 countries, but the United States does not officially recognize Palestine as a country. Taiwan is not recognized by both the United Nations and the United States as an independent country. But over the years the United States has provided Taiwan with considerable amounts of military aid and assistance to protect it from the People's Republic of China.

In demographic datasets produced by the United Nations in 2023, however, data were provided for 201 countries in the world. As defined by the United Nations (United Nations, 2014a), a country is included in the UN datasets if it is an internationally recognized country or a territory with a population of 150,000 or more; or, if it is smaller than 150,000, it is a member of the United Nations. Taiwan, Hong Kong, Macao, and Kosovo are not member countries of the United Nations, but they are included in many of the international datasets produced by the United Nations.

The Population Reference Bureau, a nonpartisan demographic research organization in Washington, DC, has been publishing annually since 1962 a *World Population Data Sheet*. The 2023 data sheet includes data for 210 countries; these include "all geopolitical entities with populations of 150,000 or more, and all members of the United Nations, including sovereign states, dependencies, overseas departments, and some territories whose status or boundaries may be undetermined or in dispute" (Population Reference Bureau, 2023: 22). Since the *World Population Data Sheet* is the most inclusive, we will use its data in our analysis here of current trends in world fertility.

The 210 countries included in the *World Population Data Sheet 2023* consist of 57 countries in Africa with an average total fertility rate of 4.3, 40 countries in the Americas with an average TFR of 1.8, 51 countries in Asia with an average TFR of 1.9, 45 countries in Europe with an average TFR of 1.4, and 17 countries in Oceania with an average TFR of 2.1. The average TFR of 4.3 in the African countries is the highest, and the average TFR of 1.4 in the European countries is the lowest.

There are major TFR differences among the African countries. Africa is divided into five regions: Northern, Western, Eastern, Middle, and Southern. The five countries of Southern Africa have an average TFR of 2.4, with the country of South Africa reporting a rate of 2.3. But the nine countries of Middle Africa have an average TFR of 5.6, with the countries of the Central African Republic, Chad, and the Democratic Republic of the Congo reporting TFRs of 6.4, 6.2, and 6.1, respectively.

Europe is divided into four regions: Northern, Western, Eastern and Southern. The countries of Europe are not as differentiated as the African countries regarding their fertility rates. The European average TFR is 1.4; the highest rate among the regions is 1.6 in Western Europe, and the lowest is 1.3 in Southern Europe. The small countries of Andorra and San Marino, in Southern Europe, have the lowest TFRs in all of Europe, rates of 0.9 and 1.0, respectively. Bosnia-Herzegovina and Spain, also in Southern Europe, report the next lowest TFRs of 1.1. The lowest TFRs reported by any of the 210 countries/territories on the 2023 *World Population Data Sheet* are 0.7 for Macao and Hong Kong and 0.8 for South Korea.

High-fertility countries are concentrated for the most part in sub-Saharan Africa (all of Africa but Northern Africa). In contrast, while the low-fertility countries used to be mainly in Europe, they are now becoming more diverse geographically, with many of them these days in Asia and a few in Latin America. Among the high-fertility countries, the United Nations expects fertility to decrease in some of them, particularly those in Asia. The fertility declines in other countries are expected to be much more gradual, especially those in Africa.

We now consider in more detail the low-fertility countries. We will refer to low-fertility countries as those with total fertility rates of 2.1 or less. A country needs a TFR of 2.1 to replace itself; that is, during their childbearing years women need to average 2.1 children each to replace themselves. In 2013, 79 countries had TFRs below 2.1. In 1970, there were only ten countries in the world with total fertility rates lower than 2.1; they were all in Europe and included Denmark, Finland, Sweden, Hungary, Russia, and Greece (Population Reference Bureau, 2014).

In 2023, there were 102 countries in the world reporting TFRs less than 2.1, and in 2024 there were 107 countries with TFRs below 2.1. In 2023, all but two of Europe's 45 countries reported fertility rates under 2.1; only Kosovo and Monaco had TFRs above 2.0. Of the eight countries in East Asia, only Mongolia had a rate above 2.1. Of the 17 countries in the Caribbean, only the Dominican Republic and Haiti reported rates higher than 2.1. Even Africa had four countries with TFRs under 2.1, Tunisia, Cabo Verde, Seychelles, and Mauritius.

No discussion of world fertility trends would be complete without mentioning **depopulation**, that is, the decline in the size of the population. This is so because depopulation is projected to occur in most countries of the world in the next 50 to 100 years. Despite the vast amount of attention paid since the late 1960s to the phenomenon of overpopulation (see esp. Ehrlich [1968]; B. Friedman [2005]; Meadows, Meadows, Randers, and Behrens [1974]; and Meadows, Randers, and Meadows [2004]), depopulation is expected to occur in around fifty or more countries by the year 2050 and in even more countries thereafter (Howden and Poston, 2008).

The United Nations in their *World Population Prospects 2024* stated that the total population of the world is projected to peak in the mid-2080s, growing from 8.2 billion in 2024 to 10.3 billion in the mid-2080s; the total size of the world population is then expected to drop back to 10.2 billion by the end of the century. Even though the population of the world is projected to continue to grow, reaching around 10.2 billion in 2100, a slowing of the rate of population growth is already underway, and the size of the world population will likely start to decline in size in around 2100. Europe is experiencing the greatest amount of depopulation, and most of Europe's countries are expected to have smaller populations by 2030.

In Europe as a whole in 2023, there was virtually no population growth. In 2023, Europe's crude birth rate was 9/1,000 and its crude death rate was 12/1,000, resulting in a percentage **rate of natural increase (RNI)** of -0.3. (The RNI is the difference between the crude birth rate and the crude death rate, expressed as a percentage.) Only five of Europe's forty-five countries reported RNIs of 0.3 or higher, Kosovo (0.7%), Ireland and Iceland (0.4%), Luxembourg and Lichtenstein (0.3%). Twenty-six European countries had negative rates of natural increase, that is, they had more deaths than births in 2023, the highest being Ukraine (-1.3%), Bulgaria (-1.0%), and Serbia (-0.7%). In 2023 four of Europe's six largest countries reported negative RNIs: Russia with a population of 146.9 million had an RNI of -0.5%; Germany at 84.9 million had an RNI of -0.4%; Italy at 58.8 million had an RNI or -0.5%; and Spain at 48.3 million had an RNI of -0.4%. Of Europe's six largest countries, only the United Kingdom and France reported positive RNIs (Population Reference Bureau, 2023; see also Johnson, Field, and Poston, 2015; and Poston, Johnson, and Field, 2016).

Indeed, Russia's population is expected to drop from 146.9 million in 2023 to around 133.1 million by 2050. In 2009, the demographer Nicholas Eberstadt (2009: 51) wrote about the severity of Russia's depopulation; his remarks still applied in 2024 when this chapter was being written:

> Russia's human numbers have been progressively dwindling. This slow-motion process now taking place in the country carries with it grim and potentially disastrous implications that threaten to recast the contours of life and society in Russia, to diminish the prospects for Russian economic development, and to affect Russia's potential influence on the world stage in the years ahead.

For the majority of countries, including Russia, the reason for depopulation is sustained low fertility. As we have noted, for a population to remain stable, TFRs need to be at or near replacement, that is, around 2.1 children per woman, and the cohorts in the childbearing ages cannot be larger than those in other age groups. If there are large numbers of the population in the parental ages, **replacement-level fertility** alone will not result in depopulation. This is due to what is referred to as negative **population momentum**, that is, the lag between the decline in TFRs and the decline in CBRs that is caused by large numbers of women still in their childbearing years owing to past high fertility. We have already noted that in 2023, there were 102 countries in the world with fertility rates lower than the replacement level of 2.1.

The depopulation of most of the countries in the developed world has significant economic impacts and implications. Major effects will likely be felt through the **aging of**

a population. As fertility declines, birth cohorts become progressively smaller. These smaller birth cohorts, coupled with increases in life expectancy, lead to an increasingly larger proportion of the population that is older than age 65 and a smaller proportion of the population in the working ages. For many countries, health care and pension programs are not well equipped to handle the large increases in the numbers of elderly, who themselves will live longer than their predecessors (Howden and Poston, 2008).

The case of China is particularly relevant. Up until a few years ago, China was the largest country in the world. But in 2021 India surpassed China and became the world's largest population. China in 2023 reported a total fertility rate of 1.1 children per woman, and the country is now having more deaths each year than births. China's future is one of declining population, with an enormous increase in the numbers of elderly.

In Figure 4.4, we show total population estimates for China for each year from 1950 to 2023, and population projection data for each year from 2024 to 2100. The data are from the United Nations *World Population Prospects 2024* (United Nations, 2024b), and the projections are based on the UN medium fertility scenario. In 1950, several months after the founding of the People's Republic of China, the country's population numbered 539 million people. For the next almost 70 years, it increased each year, reaching 1.427 billion in 2021, its highest ever population count. But in the past two years China has had more deaths than births and has lost population. And according to the UN population projections from 2024 to the end of the century, if current demographic trends continue, China's population will continue to decline, to below 1 billion in 2070, to below 800 million in 2086, to below 700 million in 2094, and to 633 million persons by 2100. This will be a loss of more than half its present population. Because China does not rely on international migration to provide young

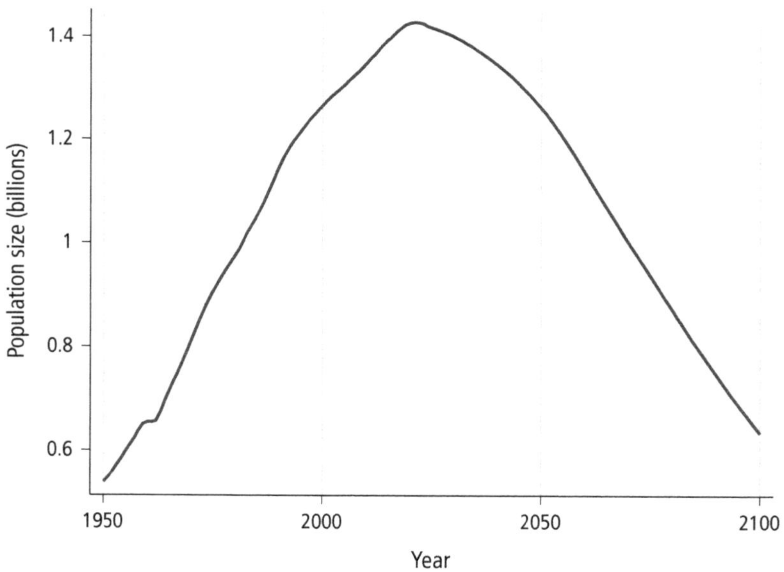

FIGURE 4.4 Total population size in billions: China 1950–2100
Data source: United Nations, 2024b.

workers and does not have an active immigration policy, the country is projected to lose more than half its population by 2100. It will end up less than half as large in 2100 as it is today, with a much older population and many fewer young workers and experienced workers. In the year 2023, just under 20 percent of China's population was at the retirement ages of 60 and over. But by 2100 this percentage is projected to be over 52 percent. Unless China addresses its serious demographic quagmire, in less than 80 years more than half its population will be elders. The population projection data for China do not bode well for the future of the country. The projections paint a picture of major population declines. If present trends continue, in 2100 China will be a country with 633 million people, more than half of them elders (Poston, 2024b).

FERTILITY CHANGE IN THE UNITED STATES

In less than 230 years, the United States has increased tremendously in size from fewer than 4 million people in 1790 to over 335 million in 2023 (see Chapter 17 for more discussion).

Earlier in this chapter we showed in Figure 4.3 the total fertility rates for the United States from 1950 to 2023. A high fertility rate was an important component of the rapid population increases in the United States in the early years between 1790 and 1860. Indeed, in 1800, the White population had a TFR of 7.0, which was likely the highest fertility rate of any country in the world at the time (Haines and Guest, 2008; Sanderson, 1979). The TFR in 1810 was still around 7.0 but by 1820 had dropped slightly to 6.7. It declined to 5.2 in 1860 and then to just under four births per woman by 1900 (Hamilton, Martin, and Ventura, 2007; C. Taeuber and I. Taeuber, 1958; US Bureau of the Census, 1975).

High fertility in the United States resulted from the fact that more than one-half of the population was fecund. The average age of the population was 15.9 in 1790, 17.0 in 1820, and 19.4 in 1860. Another reason for the high fertility was the high levels of rural and agricultural activity. When the first census of the United States was conducted in 1790, 95 percent of the population was rural. The rural portion comprised about 90 percent of the population through 1850 and had dropped to only 75 percent by 1900 (Kahn, 1974).

Between 1790 and 1860, when agriculture was dominant, income was directly related to the acreage of cultivated fields. Fields in the West were cheap and easy to obtain, and many people had more children in order to have more laborers. Big families were popular and normative and economically profitable.

Every modern, economically developed nation has undergone a demographic transition from high to low levels of fertility and mortality. The United States experienced a sustained fertility decline starting in the nineteenth century (Sternlieb and Hughes, 1978). The TFR (for Whites) dropped to 4.6 in 1870 and to 3.6 in 1900 (US Bureau of the Census, 1975). By 1920, just after World War I, the White TFR had dropped to 3.0.

In the several decades of the early twentieth century, the United States experienced a rapid transition in its economy, industrialization, and urbanization (C. Taeuber and I. Taeuber, 1958). In the late 1950s at the height of the baby boom era, the TFR reached a peak of 3.7. The high baby boom fertility following World War II was promoted in part by a need to take into account the population losses that occurred during the war.

In the 1960s, the fertility rate started to decline. Many factors influenced this reduction, such as higher living expenses, increases in educational opportunities and expectations, and more women employed in the labor force. Average US family size was reduced. Cheap, easily accessible, and more effective contraceptives, along with abortions (see our discussions in Chapter 11) gave couples greater control over births and hence were another factor in the fertility decline. In 1972, the US TFR dropped for the first time below the replacement level of 2.1 (Kahn, 1974; also see Figure 4.3); by 1975, it was 1.7. Even during the Great Depression years when fertility was low, it never dropped much below 2.2. Total population increase in 1972 was only 0.7 percent, almost one-half of the average annual increase during the 1960s (Kahn, 1974). US birth rates kept declining, although not as rapidly as in earlier years. Since 1990, the TFR continued to decline, sometimes ever so slightly, reaching a rate of around 1.7 in 2023 (see Figure 4.3).

The US population of 335 million people in 2023 has been growing slowly in recent years, with an RNI in 2023 of only 0.1 percent. The TFR in 2023 of 1.7 births in each woman's lifetime is below the replacement level of 2.1 but, nevertheless, is one of the highest of any of the developed countries in the world. If these trends continue, the American population is projected to be just over 383 million people in 2050 (see our discussions in Chapter 17). People are living longer, and the US population as a whole is aging.

ADOLESCENT FERTILITY

Adolescent fertility refers to the childbearing of young women. The **adolescent fertility rate** is measured with the ASFR for women aged 15–19. One reason why demographers study adolescent fertility is because

> [E]arly childbearing is likely to put a young mother on a lifelong path with different choices and opportunities than if she were to postpone her first birth to a later age. She is likely to have more births because of exposure to a longer period of childbearing. Early childbearing may also put a premature end to a young woman's schooling and threaten her economic prospects, earning capacity and overall wellbeing. [And] young mothers may pass on to their children a legacy of poor health, deficient education and meager means of living, creating a hard-to-break cycle of poverty. (United Nations, 2013a: 1)

The adolescent fertility rate for the world in 2023 was 41.3 per 1,000. That is, in the year of 2023, for every 1,000 young girls in the world of the ages 15–19, there were on average more than 41 babies born to them each year. In the European countries, the adolescent fertility rate was 13.1 per 1,000, but in the African countries excluding those in the Mediterranean region (Tunisia, Morocco, Egypt, Somalia, Sudan, Libya, and Djibouti), the rate was 97.1 per 1,000 (World Health Organization, 2024a).

The World Health Organization identifies several contextual factors contributing to the high levels of adolescent pregnancy in Africa and in many other developing countries. In many of these countries, young girls are heavily encouraged to marry and have children. Many go along with these pressures because they have little to no autonomy in influencing decisions to delay their childbearing. Moreover, outside of motherhood they have little if any opportunities for alternate life paths such as education and employment. Also, many medical and health workers are reluctant or unwilling to acknowledge the sexual health needs of the adolescent girls (World Health Organization, 2024a: 1).

UN data for the 2015–2020 period indicate that adolescent fertility rates were still relatively high, with rates exceeding 80 births per 1,000 young girls in 34 countries, many of them African. In several countries, the adolescent fertility rate exceeded 140 per 1,000, including the six African countries of Angola, Chad, Equatorial Guinea, Mali, Niger, and Mozambique, the four Latin America and Caribbean countries of the Dominican Republic, Nicaragua, Panama, and Venezuela, and one Asian country, Bangladesh (United Nations, 2020: 5).

We turn next to a discussion of adolescent fertility in the United States. The teen birth rate has fallen markedly in the United States in recent years, reaching a low of 15.4 in 2020; this is a decline of 75 percent from the 1991 teen birth rate of 61.8 (see Figure 4.5). Of the young women giving birth in 2020, over 91 percent of them were not married when their babies were born. Despite this marked decline in adolescent fertility to a record low of just over 15 per 1,000 in 2020, the teen birth rate in the United States is still one of the highest among the countries in the developed world. For instance, the teen birth rate in 2022 in all of Europe was 7 per 1,000, with lows of 5 per 1,000 in Austria and Iceland, 4 per 1,000 in Italy, 3 per 1,000 in the Netherlands, and 2 per 1,000 in Denmark (United Nations, 2024b).

We now discuss US trends in adolescent fertility since 1940 to provide some historical perspective. The US adolescent fertility rates show a long-term downward trend since 1940. The teen birth rate reached its peak in 1957, at 96.3/1,000. In that year, nearly one in ten teenagers gave birth. "The rate dropped almost one-third to 65.5 in 1969," increased slightly in the late 1960s, and then resumed "a decline that continued until 1979–1980 and again until 1986" when the teen rate equaled 50.2. But "from 1986 through 1991, the birth rate rose 23 percent. Since 1991, the rate has fallen ... and the decline has been (pretty much) continuous ... reaching 26.6 in 2013" (Ventura, Hamilton, and Mathews, 2014: 2–3) and reaching 24.2 in 2014. In 1957, nearly one in ten teenage women had a baby. In 2014, one in 41 teenage women in the United States had a baby.

One interesting change that has occurred among teenage mothers between 1940 and 2020 is the significant increase in the percentage of births to teenagers who are not married. In 1940 only 14 percent of the births to teenagers were to unmarried mothers. It increased slightly to 15 percent in 1960, and then had a very large increase to 48 percent in 1980, and another very large increase to 89 percent in 2013 (Ventura, Hamilton, and Mathews, 2014: 3). We noted above that in 2020 over 90 percent of teenage births were to unmarried mothers. These days very few teenagers are married.

Another way to examine the fertility of adolescents is to separate them into two groups: younger teenagers (aged 15–17) and older teenagers (aged 18–19). We show in Figure 4.6 the birth rates for these two groups, plus the larger group of all adolescents aged 15–19, for the years of 1991 through 2023. In 2023, the fertility rate for older teenage women in the United States was 24.9 per 1,000, and for younger teenagers it was 5.6 per 1,000. For every 1,000 older teenagers in 2023, one in around 40 had a

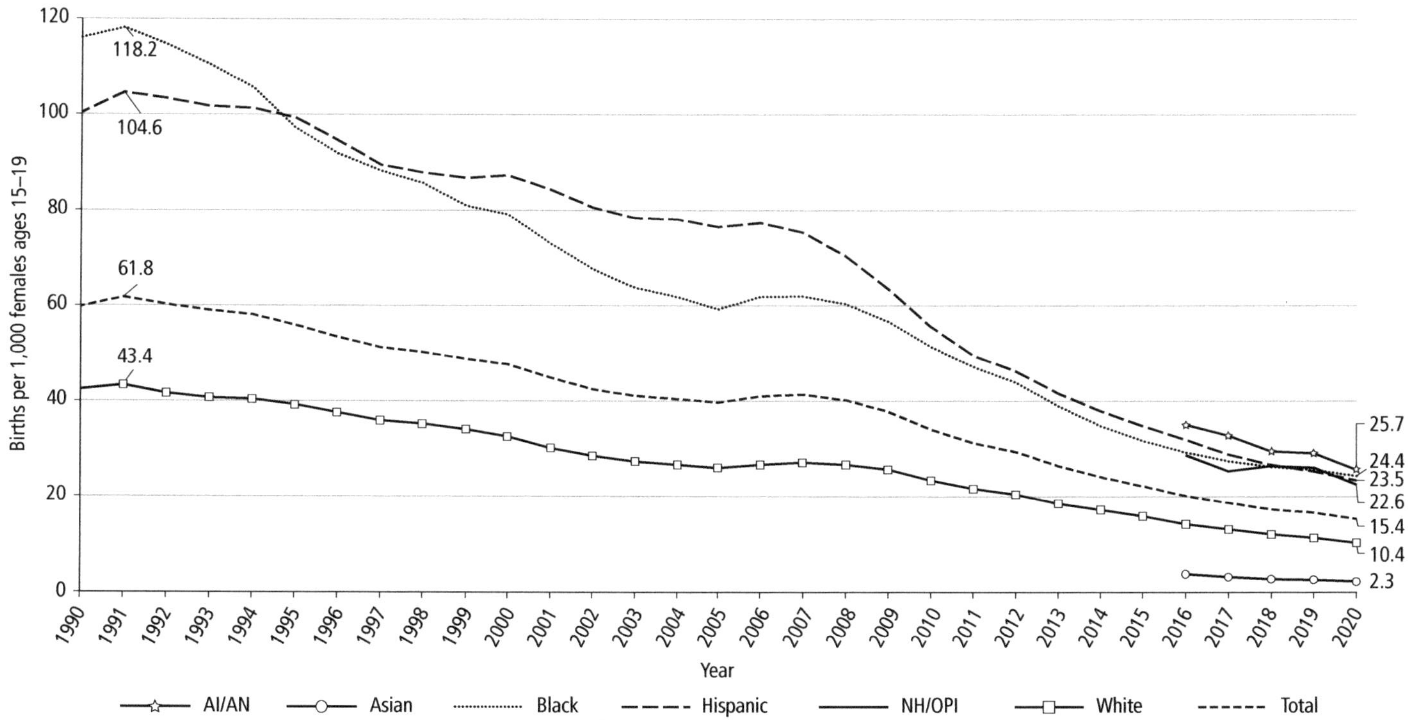

FIGURE 4.5 Adolescent birth rates among females aged 15–19, by race and Hispanic origin in the United States from 1990 to 2020.
Data source: US Department of Health and Human Services, 2022.

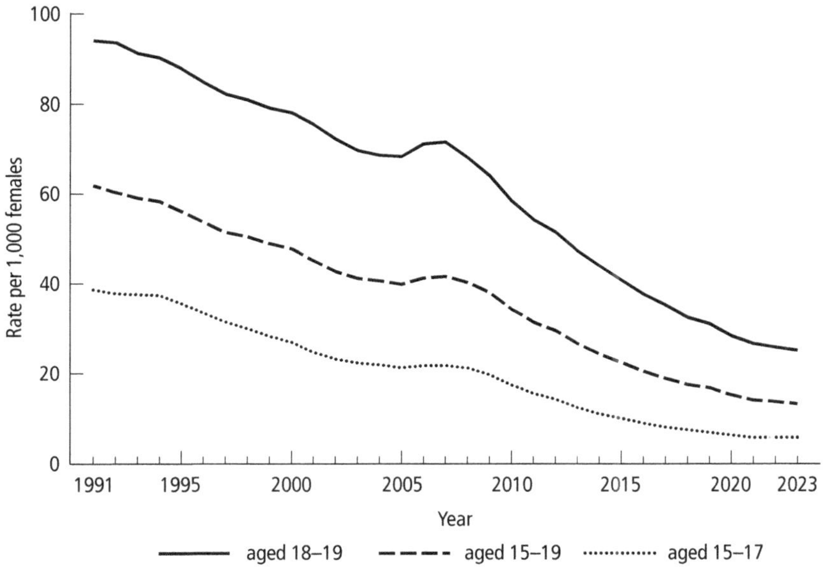

FIGURE 4.6 Birth rates per 1,000 female teenagers aged 15–17, 18–19, and 15–19 in the United States, 1991–2023
Source: Modified from Hamilton, Mathews, and Osterman, 2024.

baby; for every 1,000 younger female teenagers in 2013, one in almost 180 of them had a baby.

Figure 4.6 shows that the fertility rates of both the younger and the older teenagers have dropped markedly since 1991; data indicate declines in these rates for as far back as 1960. Between 1960 and 1975 the rates fell a little more rapidly for the older girls than for the younger girls, falling 50 percent for the former group compared to 18 percent for the latter group. Since the 1990s the rates have continued to fall a little bit more rapidly for the older teenagers, but the declines are very similar.

Adolescent fertility for US females varies considerably by race and ethnic group (see Figure 4.5). The lowest adolescent fertility rate for US women in 2020 was for Asian teenagers, 2.3/1,000. Following them with the next highest adolescent fertility rate were White teenagers at 10.4 per 1,000, and then Black teenagers and Hispanic teenagers. In 2020, AI/AN adolescents (American Indians and Alaskan Natives) reported the highest rate at 25.7 per 1,000. The rates for Black and Hispanic teenagers have declined the most since 1990. In 1990, 118 per 1,000 Black teenage girls gave birth, and 105 per 1,000 Hispanic teenagers gave birth. By 2020 the Black rate had dropped to 23.5 per 1,000, and the Hispanic rate to 22.6 per 1,000.

The adolescent fertility rates were much higher in 1990 than in 2020 for all the groups, especially Blacks and Hispanics. Indeed, the rates for 2020 are record lows. Every race/ethnic group has a lower adolescent fertility rate in 2020 than in 2010, and lower in 2010 than in 2000, and lower in 2000 than in 1990 (see Figure 4.5).

Why have these reductions occurred? In terms of the immediate causes, adolescents will have fewer births if they engage in sex less frequently, or if they become more effective users of contraception, or if there is some combination of the two.

There is evidence of a slight reduction in recent years in the percentages of teenagers engaging in sexual intercourse. In 2002, 45.5 percent of females aged 15–19, and 45.7 percent of males aged 15–19, reported that they had ever engaged in sexual intercourse; data for the 2015–2019 period indicate that these percentages had dropped to 40.5 percent for females and to 38.7 percent for males (Abma and Martinez, 2023). And there is evidence of a significant increase in the percentages of teenagers using contraception, especially for males. Data for the year 2002 showed that among those teenagers who have ever had sex, 74.5 percent of females and 82 percent of males stated they had used contraceptives the first time they engaged in sex; these percentages increased for the 2015–2019 time period to 77.3 for females and to 92.1 percent for males (Abma and Martinez, 2023: table 7).

NONMARITAL FERTILITY

In the preceding section, we noted that back in the 1940s very few babies were born to teenage women who were not married. In this section we focus on the **nonmarital fertility** of all women, not just teenage women. Nonmarital fertility refers to the fertility of women who are not married. An unmarried woman is one who is not married, widowed, or divorced.

When Poston, one of the authors of your textbook, was born in 1940, less than 4 percent of all births were to unmarried women. In those days, virtually all babies were born to married mothers. So prevalent was this association between the mother's marital status and her having a baby that the term "illegitimate fertility" was used, instead of "nonmarital fertility," to refer to births occurring outside marriage. Babies being born to unmarried mothers was so much against the norms of society that these babies were sometimes referred to as "illegitimate."

One reason why demographers study births to unmarried women is because the marital status of the mother is often an important "marker for the presence or absence of financial, social, and emotional resources. Infants of mothers who are not married have been shown to be at a higher risk for poor outcomes." For example, the mortality rate for infants of unmarried mothers is around 75 percent higher than "the rate for infants of married mothers" (Mathews and MacDorman, 2013: 8).

In 2022, almost 40 percent of all births were to unmarried women, a dramatic increase from the 4 percent in 1940. But there is considerable variability in the percentage of births to unmarried mothers among the race/ethnic groups: Asians have the lowest, 12 percent; they are followed by non-Hispanic whites at 27.1 percent, who are followed by Hispanics at 53.2 percent; following them are American Indians/Alaskan Natives at 68.1 percent; the group with the highest percentage in 2022 of births to unmarried mothers is Blacks at 69.3 percent (Osterman et al., 2024: table 9).

It is important to note that nonmarital births "include births to women in cohabiting unions and those to unmarried women not cohabiting" (Curtin, Ventura and Martinez, 2014: 4). Indeed, these days more than half of the births to unmarried women are to cohabiting women, and about one-half of the births to cohabiting women are intended births, that is, the women planned to have the births when they occurred. Whether or not the mother is cohabiting when she gives birth is sociologically very important because research has shown that cohabiting parents are more likely to eventually marry than are parents who are not cohabiting; thus, babies of cohabiting parents have a greater likelihood of growing up in a two-parent family (Carlson, McLanahan, and England, 2004). However, in the long-run, children of cohabiting parents are more socioeconomically disadvantaged and do not fare as well on a host of behavioral and emotional outcomes when compared to children who were born to a mother and father who are married (Child Trends, 2015).

CHILDLESSNESS

Childlessness refers to women having no children voluntarily or involuntarily. Recent years have seen dramatic increases in the percentages of ever-married childless women in the United States. In the 1970s almost half of White women were childless at age 25. Rindfuss and his colleagues (1988) expected that as many as 20 percent of these White women would still be childless at the end of their childbearing years (see also Morgan and Chen, 1992).

Childlessness is, and has been since the 1970s, much more prevalent than in the 1950s when childlessness was low and little of it, if any, was voluntary (Poston and Kramer, 1983). Indeed, demographers noted that in the 1950s, "voluntary childlessness ... [was] nearly extinct" (Whelpton, Campbell, and Patterson, 1966: 163). Until the early 1970s, the norms relating to marriage and procreation were pervasive and **pronatalist**, much more so than they are today. Research conducted more than fifty years ago indicated that childlessness was neither supported nor encouraged by the society's normative and value structure (Poston, 1974). The childed state was heavily valued in its own right (Griffith, 1973), and those remaining without children often experienced severe negative sanctions (Blake, 1974; Veevers, 1973).

We noted the very low prevalence of childlessness in the 1950s and 1960s in the United States. However, it would be a mistake to refer to the increases in childlessness since the 1970s as reflecting a so-called secular phenomenon and not as representing the more distant past. For instance, Morgan (1991) has shown that levels of childlessness in the nineteenth century were much higher than those reported for the 1950s and early 1960s. Nonetheless, little attention was given to childless women in the United States prior to the 1970s, and the research that was being conducted at that time focused mainly on involuntarily childless women. These early studies assumed that childlessness was caused primarily by sterility or subfecundity and not by voluntary decisions to stay childless (Poston and Cruz, 2016).

Interestingly, the percentages of married women aged 15–44 who were childless in the United States have fluctuated over time. In the 1970s when childlessness was increasing, researchers believed that most of the increase was due to women choosing to be childless. Recent studies have supported this idea of increased childlessness, especially at the older ages. For instance, Abma and Martinez (2006) focused on childlessness among older women (ages 35–44) and reported that voluntary childlessness rose from 5 percent in 1982 to 8 percent in 1988, and was maintained until 1995 at 9 percent before falling slightly to 7 percent in 2002. They also reported that women

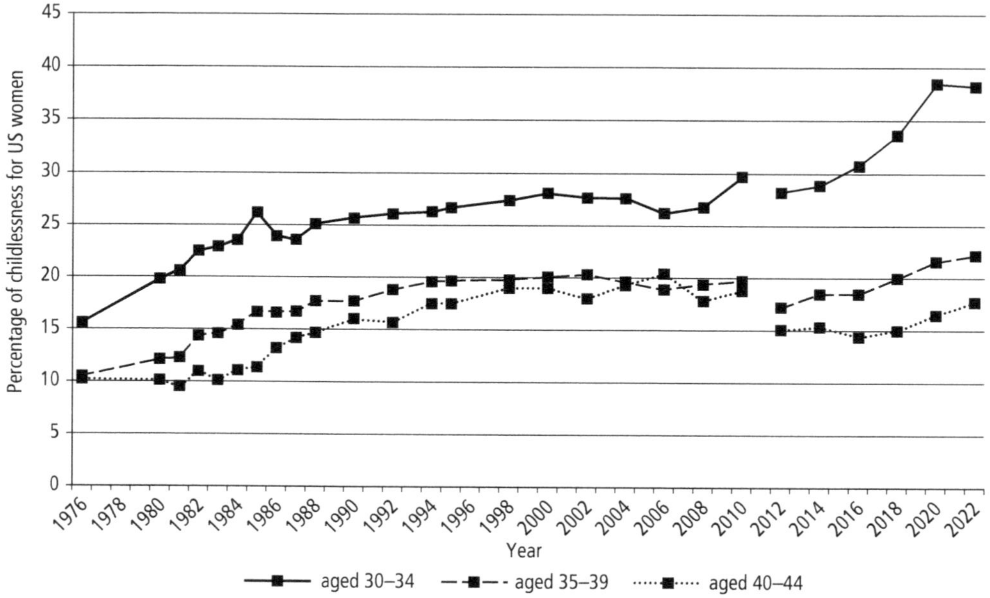

FIGURE 4.7 Percentage rates of childlessness, women aged 30–44 in the United States, 1976–2022
Data source: US Bureau of the Census, 2023b.

who were voluntarily childless tended to have the highest incomes, work experiences, and lowest religiosity (Poston and Cruz, 2016).

Figure 4.7 shows percentage rates of childlessness for US women aged 30–44 for the years 1976 to 2022. The increases in childlessness over the past several decades are clearly shown in the figure. Almost 39 percent of women aged 30–34 were childless in 2022, the highest ever for this group. The slight downturns for all three groups of women from 2010 to 2012 are mainly statistical and result from differential sampling weights applied in the surveys (Monte and Ellis, 2014: 7). The increases in childlessness since the 1970s are consistent and remarkable and are due mainly to increases in **voluntary childlessness**, resulting from changes in gender norms, as hypothesized by researchers in the 1960s. Cox and Pendell (2007) discovered that more than 80 percent of respondents in national surveys in the 1980s were neutral or agreed that childless individuals could have fulfilling lives. Their research showed that more positive attitudes towards childlessness were found among females who were college educated and/or childless; the less positive attitudes were found among older, less educated males who were religiously conservative. This suggests that attitudes and norms towards childlessness are becoming more positive overall, which explains in large part the increased levels of childlessness in the United States.

MALE FERTILITY

An important limitation of our discussions in this chapter is that the measures and concepts and research focusing on fertility are mainly derived from calculations and analyses of females. The fertility of males and the determinants of **male fertility** have rarely been examined and compared with those of females, but they need to be. Males are a neglected minority in fertility studies.

Several reasons have been proposed by demographers to justify the exclusion of males from fertility studies. The biological reasons are that the fecundity and the childbearing years of women occur in a more sharply defined and narrower range (15–49) than they do for men (15–79), and that "both the spacing and number of children are less subject to variation among women; a woman can have children only at intervals of 1 or 2 years, whereas a man can (theoretically at least) have hundreds" (Keyfitz, 1977a: 114). There are at least two methodological reasons: One, data on parental age at the birth of a child are more frequently collected on birth-registration certificates for the mothers than for the fathers; and two, when such data are obtained for mothers and fathers, there are more instances of unreported age data for fathers, especially for births occurring outside of marriage. A sociological reason is the belief that men are regarded principally as breadwinners and "uninvolved in fertility except to impregnate women and to stand in the way of their contraceptive use" (Greene and Biddlecom, 2000: 83; Poston, Zhang, and Terrell, 2008).

Biological and demographic studies provide us with evidence of the importance of men in fertility and related behaviors. Biologists have found that the male sex in most all species contributes an equivalent amount of genetic information to the next generation as does the female sex. But the variance contributed by the male sex to the next generation is often greater than that of the female sex, especially in species where **polygyny** (a union where a male is simultaneously married to two or more females) is practiced. That is, most females reproduce, some males do not reproduce, and other males have many offspring. This pattern has been found in most mammalian species (Coleman, 2000). In addition, it has been found in many species that there are more childless males than childless females.

Demographically, it has been shown that men have different patterns of fertility and fertility-related behavior. Males' age-specific fertility starts a little later, stops much later, and is typically higher than that of females (Paget and Timaeus, 1994). Also, the TFRs for males and females are not identical. Research has shown that in most industrialized countries, male TFRs are higher than female TFRs (Coleman, 2000). In the 1990s and later, in countries where the male and female TFRs were lower than 2.2, they tended to be more similar than dissimilar; and the opposite was found for countries with male and female TFRs higher than 2.2 (Zhang, 2013). This means that if men and women followed the sex- and age-specific fertility rates of an area at one point in time, and if they had more than 2.2 children during their childbearing years, they were more likely to have dissimilar than similar fertility rates, and vice versa (also see Myers, 1941; Smith, 1992).

The special importance of male fertility is also seen in the determinants of fertility and fertility-related behaviors, such as cohabitation and marriage. For example, in the United States, men's fertility is more likely to be influenced by their marital and employment status compared to women's. Being married and being employed significantly increase men's number of children ever born (CEB), while these factors do not have as strong an impact on women (Zhang, 2013). The relevance of labor-force participation for women's fertility has been emphasized repeatedly. Regarding education, the lower the level of education, the greater the difference between women and men with respect to the number of children ever born (Martinez, Daniels, and Chandra, 2012: 5). And with respect to income, research has shown that it has a positive effect on male fertility, but a negative effect on female fertility (Hopcroft, 2015; Hopcroft et al., 2024).

Men also have different cohabitation and marriage patterns compared to women. In the United States, for birth cohorts born during 1958 to 1987, living alone, being foreign-born, and living in fragmented families all tended to increase the likelihood of cohabitation for women but not for men. Foreign-born men have been shown to be more likely to marry than native-born men. But these factors do not seem to have as significant an impact on women's marriage behavior (Zhang, 2013). Researchers have conducted studies examining male and female transitions to adulthood in twenty-four European countries, using survey data for the 1980s and 1990s. They found that, in general, the negative effect on fertility of educational attainment is stronger for women than for men. Also, unemployment tends to lead to men's postponement of marriage, whereas it affects women in two distinct ways: It either accelerates or it slows down the timing of marriage. The effect of religion is stronger among women than among men. Furthermore, being Catholic and attending church services affect men's and women's parenthood timing in different ways in Catholic-prevalent countries. Other relevant factors such as parental influence seem to have a different impact for males than for females (Corijn and Klijzing, 2001).

Historically, women have been tied to motherhood, and this is deeply rooted in law and policy in the ways that jobs are structured and how family relations are navigated. Studies of fertility and parenthood have been undertaken by demographers in a similar way (Riley, 2019). These, together with the biological and methodological reasons noted previously, have resulted in the decreased attention given to males in fertility research. We noted earlier that biological and demographic analyses have shown that fertility and parenting are not simply female issues; they involve both men and women. The study of fertility should not focus only on females. Both Greenhalgh (1990b) and Riley (1998, 2019) have encouraged more discussion of gender issues among demographers, and critical demography has promoted bringing men into population studies (Coleman, 2000; Horton, 1999). It is necessary to incorporate gender studies into studies of demography in order to gain a more balanced picture of demographic issues. Indeed, male fertility is one of the emerging issues of demographic study. Demographers and sociologists need to give more attention to males in their analyses of fertility variation and change. It is essential to take men's roles and commitments into account when considering factors leading to decisions about the bearing and rearing of children.

DATES OF BIRTH

The last topic to be discussed in this chapter is dates of birth. The birthdates of babies are not distributed evenly across the 365 days of the year, or across the 366 days in a leap year. There are between 3.6 million and 3.8 million babies born in the United States each year. In 2023, there were 3,591,328 babies born. If we divide the total annual births by 365 days, the rough daily average for the past twenty years is about 10,000 births per day. But not every day has 10,000 births. Some dates are more popular than others.

The most popular birthdates are mainly in the middle weeks of September. The most popular birthdate is September 9th; the second most popular is September 19th, then the 12th, then the 17th, then the 10th, then July 7th, then back to the four September birthdates of the 20th, the 15th, the 16th, and the 18th. Of the 15 most popular of all 365 birthdates, 12 are in September. Of all the months in the year, most births occur in July, August, and September.

The 366th most popular date, that is, the least popular one, is February 29th. But this is because it occurs only once every four years. Considering only the dates that occur every year, the least popular birthdates occur mainly at the end, or at the beginning, of the year; the 365th most popular date is December 25th; the 364th is January 1st, then December 24th, then July 4th, then January 2nd, then December 26th, and then the three dates in late November, the 27th, the 23rd, and the 25th.

Why do the most popular birthdays mainly occur in mid-September? And why do more birthdays occur in the months of July, August, and September instead of in the other months?

Part of the answer to the first question is sociological, namely, that the mid-September babies were conceived around nine months earlier, which would be mid-December. For many people those are days when they are at home celebrating the holidays and having good times. Celebrations, lovemaking, and conceptions – they all work together.

Also, there are more births in July, August, and early September because among human and nonhuman mammals, intercourse resulting in conception tends to be more efficient when the climate is cooler, and the days are shorter. Remember that these July, August, and September births were conceived in October, November, and December. Also, it is believed that better sperms are produced in the winter months with respect to their motility and concentration.

As an aside, babies are not born exactly nine months after they were conceived. Yes, the average time from ovulation to birth is 268 days, but the lengths of the pregnancies vary by as much as 37 days.

What about the least popular dates? Why do they mainly occur on December 24th, 25th, or 26th, or January 1st or 2nd, or July 4th, or on days in late November? The unpopularity of these dates is also sociological, mainly due to decisions of obstetricians and parents with respect to the dates the babies will be delivered.

Cesarean section births in the United States in 2022 accounted for 32.1 percent of all births, versus only 5 percent in the 1970s. The low-risk Cesarean delivery rate in 2022 was 26.3 percent of all births (Osterman et al., 2024: 6). Yes, some of the Cesarean deliveries are medically necessary, but more than 80 percent of them are low-risk deliveries. These are often deliveries scheduled for nonmedical reasons, such as the obstetricians practicing defensive medicine, women giving birth at older ages, and women and doctors choosing C-sections for scheduling reasons. Parents and obstetricians often do not want to deliver babies on the days of Christmas and Thanksgiving and the days right before and after, and on other holidays like July 4th. Births more and more these days are much less likely to occur on holidays and on weekends.

If you wonder whether your birthday is a common one or an uncommon one, there is available online a complete list of all 366 birthdates from the most popular to the least popular in a piece published in late November 2022 by *USA Today*; see the list at: www.usatoday.com/story/news/2022/11/29/most-common-birthday/10765423002/

Find your birthdate and see how popular or unpopular it is. Find the birthdates of your relatives and friends and check out the popularity/unpopularity of their dates. How many of you and how many of them have really popular, or really unpopular, birthdates? You will have a lot to talk about the next time you are all together.

SUMMARY

In this chapter, we first considered various measures of fertility and next discussed the so-called proximate determinants of fertility. They are the mainly biological factors that lead directly to fertility and that are influenced heavily by social factors. Indeed, the various social, economic, cultural, environmental, and psychological factors that affect fertility do so only through the "proximate" variables. Both the societal birth rate and the fertility of individual women and men are produced by a combination of those factors. We then considered world fertility patterns and US fertility trends and differences. We next discussed adolescent fertility, nonmarital fertility, childlessness, and male fertility. We concluded the chapter with a discussion of dates of birth.

We close this chapter by summarizing some of the major fertility differentials. Fertility rates are much higher in many developing countries, especially those in sub-Saharan Africa, than they are in developed countries. Likewise, different types of people have different patterns of fertility. Generally, in developed societies, the higher a person's socioeconomic status, the fewer children that person is likely to have. In industrialized societies, women employed in the labor force tend to have fewer children than women who are not so employed. However, Hopcroft and her colleagues (2024) have noted that there is some evidence that in many developed societies, well-to-do men – especially those with higher incomes – may tend to have more, not fewer, children than men with lower status (also see Hopcroft, 2015).

Having a smaller family also tends to increase a woman's availability for employment, and her employment per se encourages a small family. Levels of childbearing also tend to be lower in urban than in rural areas. This is particularly true in more modernized countries, although in past decades, the difference between rural and urban childbearing rates has diminished. There are few if any differences in childbearing between Catholics and non-Catholics in the United States and other more developed countries. The differences are due mainly to differences in socioeconomic status. The fertility of Muslim women, however, is higher than that of Christian and Jewish women, in both developed and developing countries. These differentials notwithstanding, the most important point to remember about fertility is that fertility rates are heavily conditioned by social, economic, psychological, cultural, and environmental factors, all of which eventually affect fertility through the proximate determinants.

DISCUSSION QUESTIONS

1. List and briefly describe the main reasons why males are often excluded from the analysis of fertility. Then, list and briefly describe the main reasons why male fertility should not be excluded. What is your position? Should males be included or excluded from fertility analysis? Which reasons best support your decision?
2. Describe how the general fertility rate and the net reproduction rate are calculated; show and interpret their formulas. In your view, what is the main difference between the two rates? When do you believe one of the rates would be more useful than the other?
3. Your friend tells you that they believe that overpopulation is a growing problem for the world. Do you agree or disagree with your friend's claim? Provide data and examples from this chapter and from class lectures to support your answer.

5

Mortality

INTRODUCTION

As population actors, our last and final behavior on this earth is our death. When this demographic event occurs, people are likely to read about us either in the local newspaper or at a funeral home website in an **obituary** about our life. Our obituary might include when and where we were born, where we were educated, our surviving family members, and perhaps something about our main occupation while we were alive, our hobbies, and other items of interest.

The Oxford English Dictionary defines "obituary" as an "announcement of a death ...usually comprising a brief biographical sketch of the deceased" (2000: X: 640). What other time will a biographical sketch about you be written and published for everyone to read? Perhaps never. Our death is not only the last event in our life, but, indeed, one of the most important events in our life.

Every one of us has been born, and every one of us will die. This is a certainty. No one escapes death. In fact, the individuals in all species are born and the individuals in all species die. But we humans are the only species to actually think about and contemplate the act of dying.

Death will not occur at the same time for everyone. Some of us will die sooner than others. On average, death will come earlier to males than to females, and earlier to members of most racial minority groups than to members of the majority. However, if you are Latino, death will likely come later, not earlier. If you live in the United States and are a Latino female, you will have the longest average **longevity** (length of life). You will have the shortest longevity if you are an American Indian or Alaska Native male. According to 2021 life tables, Hispanic women in the United States may expect to live, on average, 81.1 years from the day they were born, compared with 62.2 years for American Indian and Alaskan Native males (Arias, Xu, and Kochanek, 2023). In this chapter we will explain, among other interesting facts, how life tables can yield such information.

We ourselves play an important role in deciding when we will die. In Chapter 1 in our discussion of our roles as population actors, we noted that our individual decision making is more obvious and apparent, say, with regard to fertility than with regard to mortality. We had absolutely no control over when or where we were born; our birth was the decision or at least the action of our biological parents. But we do have a lot of control and influence over whether, when, and where we ourselves produce children. Our dying is a similar kind of demographic act. We may exercise many options that result in extending or shortening our lives. While death is a certainty, the length of time we will live depends on many factors. Over some of them, such as our sex and race, we have no control, but over some other factors, such as smoking, diet, and exercise, we have a lot of control. Further, we ourselves have some influence not only on the timing and characteristics of our own death but also on the deaths of some others.

The impact of mortality varies significantly according to social and demographic characteristics. People in higher social classes live longer than those in the lower classes. Richer people live longer than poorer people. Married people live longer than single, separated, or divorced people. We discuss some of these issues later.

Mortality and its effects are best discussed from the vantage point of the society. Demographers often consider all individuals together as members of a single society, or state or country, and inquire about the factors that contribute to differences among them in their average length of life. For instance, in the year 2023, a baby girl born in Japan, South Korea, or San Marino had a life expectancy of 87 years; this means she could expect to live on average for about 87 years from the time she was born, assuming that the age-specific death rates did not change. This life expectancy of 87 is the highest in the world. By comparison, a baby girl born in 2023 in Nigeria could expect to live on average for about 54 years from the time when she was born, and a baby girl born in Chad about 55 years (Population Reference Bureau, 2023). Why do baby girls born in Nigeria or Chad have such a low average life expectancy compared with baby girls born in Japan, South Korea, or San Marino? Levels of development, medical conditions, and a host of other factors are involved, and we will discuss some of them later.

There have been major changes over the historical record in the main causes of death. People used to die mainly of infectious and parasitic diseases, but the major causes of death today in high-income countries such as the United States are chronic diseases such as heart disease, cancer, and stroke. Today the major causes of death are not always the same in countries with high and low levels of life expectancy. This topic, too, is covered in a later section.

This chapter has several sections. After addressing various issues of measurement, we will consider mortality and longevity from an international point of view. Then we will discuss the major causes of death in developed and developing countries and how these have changed over time. Another section is concerned specifically with changes in mortality in the United States, followed by a discussion of a special kind of mortality, that which occurs in infancy. We will also speculate about the future course of mortality and improvements in life expectancy. We now discuss the measurement of mortality.

MEASUREMENT OF MORTALITY

The quantification of mortality is central to demography. The measurement of mortality dates back to John Graunt (1620–1674) and his analyses of the "Bills of Mortality".

(See our discussion of Graunt in Chapter 3, Box 3.2.) **Mortality** refers to the relative frequency of death in a population.

Demographers use two different concepts when referring to mortality, namely, the **life span**, which is the numerical "age limit of human life" (Kintner, 2004: 307), and life expectancy, which is the average expected number of years of life to be lived by a particular population at a given time. An exact figure for the human life span or for the life span of any species is not known (Carey, 1997). However, demographers often use the "maximum recorded age at death" as an accepted operational definition of the human life span (Kintner, 2004: 307). As of the final writing and editing of this book in March of 2025, the longest known and verified life span is 122 years and 164 days, lived by the Frenchwoman Jeanne Louise Calment (see Box 5.1). The concept of life expectancy, which is used by demographers much more than the concept of the life span, is considered later.

Crude Death Rate

An easily understood and interpreted method for quantifying mortality, the **crude death rate (CDR)**, is the number of deaths in a population in a given year per 1,000 members of the population. It is expressed as:

$$CDR = \frac{\text{deaths in the year}}{\text{population at midyear}} * 1{,}000 \quad (5.1)$$

As an illustration, using data for the United States for 2022, equation (5.1) becomes

$$CDR = \frac{3{,}279{,}857}{333{,}287{,}557} * 1{,}000 = 9.8 \quad (5.2)$$

This means that in the United States in 2022, there were nearly ten deaths for every 1,000 persons in the population. This rate dropped in 2023 to 9.2.

Box 5.1 The Longest-Known Life Span (122+ Years)

As of the time Chapter 5 of this book was written in March 2025, the longest-known and verified life span is 122 years and 164 days, lived by the Frenchwoman Jeanne Louise Calment, who was born in Arles (a city in southern France) on February 21, 1875. She died in a retirement home there on August 4, 1997. In the later years of her life, Madame Calment reportedly made the following observations:

> "I've been forgotten by our good Lord."
> "I took pleasure when I could. I acted clearly and morally and without regret. I'm very lucky."
> "I've only got one wrinkle, and I'm sitting on it."
> "If you can't do anything about it, don't worry about it."

You may access the very interesting obituary of Ms. Calment that was written by Craig Whitney and published on August 5, 1997 in the *New York Times* at this link: www.nytimes.com/1997/08/05/world/jeanne-calment-world-s-elder-dies-at-122.html

CDRs for the countries of the world in 2023 ranged from a low of 1.5 in Qatar to a high of 15.6 in Bulgaria (World Population Review, 2024). The range of CDRs is narrower than that for the crude birth rates (CBRs) (discussed in Chapter 4).

However, CDRs must be interpreted with special caution. When CDRs are compared among countries, differences are sometimes due to differences in age composition. The fact that Qatar in 2023 had a CDR of 1.5 and the United States had a CDR of 9.2 means that there were more than six times more deaths per 1,000 people in the United States than there were in Qatar.

Why is the CDR of the United States so much higher than that of Qatar? Why were there so many more deaths per 1,000 people in the United States than in Qatar? The main reason is that Qatar is much younger in average age than the United States, and younger people have lower death rates than older people. In Qatar only 1.6 percent of the population is older than 65, but in the United States 17.3 percent of the population is older than 65. In other words, countries with large proportions of young people and small proportions of old people will usually have lower CDRs than countries with small proportions of young people and large proportions of old people.

CDRs also should not be used to compare the death experiences of the same population at different points in time, particularly if the population's age structure has changed over time. The crude death rate in the United States fell 27 percent from 10.9 in 1935 to 8.0 in 2010, but the population was much older in 2010. When the effect of the aging of the population is controlled by assuming that the age distribution for every year was the age distribution for the year 2000, then it turns out that the risk of dying actually decreased by 60 percent from 1935 to 2010 (Hoyert, 2012). This comparison using the **standardized death rate** (see our later discussion) is much larger than the decline in the CDR alone. It is misleading to use CDRs either to compare two populations or to compare the same population at two different points in time.

The CDR is referred to as crude because its denominator is comprised of the entire population, the members of which are not all equally at the risk of experiencing death. This is so because the risk of death varies by age, sex, race/ethnicity, socioeconomic status, and many other characteristics. Thus, although it is true that all persons in the denominator of the CDR will eventually experience death, they are not all equally exposed to the risk of death.

Death rates vary considerably by age. They are very high in the first year of life, but even then, the likelihood of death is not the same from month to month and from day to day. Indeed, in the first year of life, deaths are much higher in the first month of life than in the remaining eleven months, much higher in the first day than in the remaining days of the first month, much higher in the first hour than in the remaining twenty-three hours of the first day, and much higher in the first minute than in the remaining fifty-nine minutes of the first hour. This is the main reason why demographers who study mortality give such special attention to the study of **infant mortality** (Frisbie, 2005), a topic we cover later in this chapter.

Age-Specific Death Rate

Because death varies so considerably with age, demographers use **age-specific death rates (ASDRs)** as a more precise way to measure mortality. ASDRs are sometimes referred to as "M" rates. The ASDR (or $_nM_x$) is the number of deaths to persons in a specific age group per 1,000 persons in that age group. Its formula is

$$_nM_x = \frac{deaths\ to\ persons\ aged\ x\ to\ x+n}{persons\ in\ the\ population\ who\ are\ aged\ x\ to\ x+n} * 1{,}000 \quad (5.3)$$

where the subscripts n and x refer, respectively, to the width of the age group and to the initial year of the age group. For instance, the ASDR for age group 15–19 is referred to as $_5M_{15}$.

The ASDR is not crude because deaths to persons in the age group x to $x + n$ are examined in relation to the total number of persons who are at the risk of death in the age group x to $x + n$.

We noted already that death rates vary by age. Death rates are high in the initial year of life, then drop precipitously; they begin increasing again at around age 40 or so (although in societies highly affected by HIV/AIDS, they tend to increase even at the younger adult ages). ASDRs are very low for young persons after the first year or so of life. So, if we were to plot a schedule of $_nM_x$ values, we would produce what demographers refer to as the **age curve of mortality**. Remember in Chapter 4, the chapter on fertility, when we referred to the age curve of fertility as a chart of the age-specific fertility rates? You will recall that when we plotted the seven ASFRs, an inverted U curve was formed (see Figure 4.2).

Now were we to plot the age-specific death rates from the ASDR at the youngest age to the ASDR at the oldest age, a *U* curve would be formed. In Figure 5.1, we present an illustration of the age curve of mortality for the United States. The figure displays the

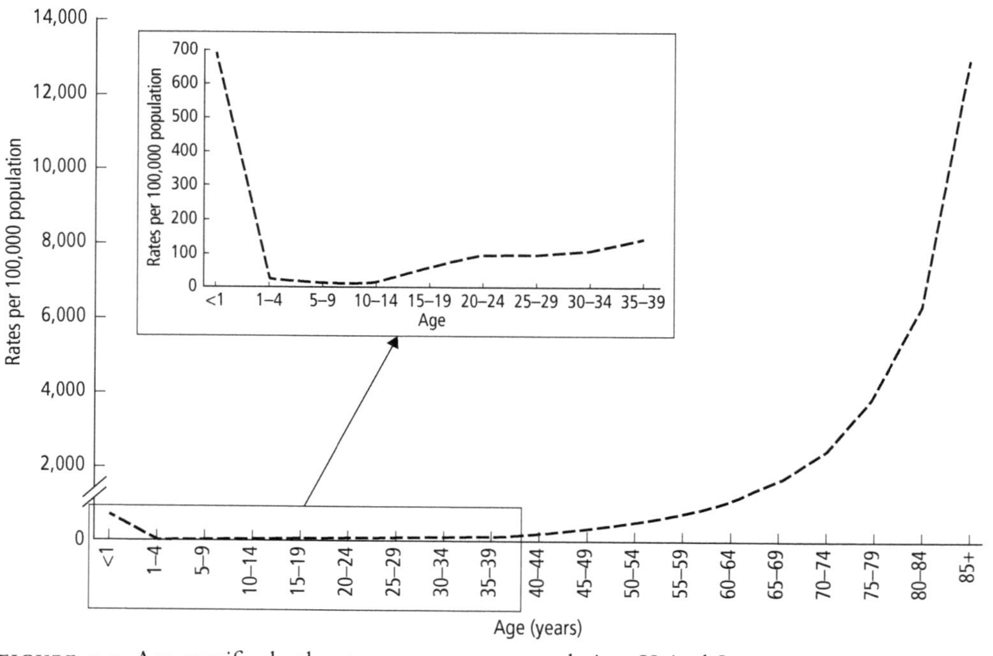

FIGURE 5.1 Age-specific death rates per 100,000 population, United States, 2007
Source: Minino et al., 2009.

ASDRs, that is, the $_nM_x$ values, starting at age <1 (less than 1 year of age), then 1–4, 5–9 and all the way to 85+. The death rate in the United States at age <1 is not reached again until age 55–59; from there the death rates increase rapidly, and even more rapidly after age 75–79. The ASDR for 5–9-year-olds is the lowest on the chart, and the ASDR for persons of age 85+ is the highest. Over 72 percent of all deaths in the United States in 2007 occurred to persons of age 65 and older, and almost 30 percent of all the deaths occurred to person of age 85 and older.

Standardization

ASDRs, and not CDRs, should be used to compare the mortality experiences of countries with known differences in age composition. We will elaborate this point with an example. The United States in 2006 had a CDR of 8, while Venezuela had a CDR of 4. This means that there were twice as many deaths per 1,000 people in the United States in 2006 than there were in Venezuela. But does this necessarily mean that young people and middle-age people and old people in the United States all die at higher rates than they do in Venezuela? To answer this question, we need to look at ASDR data and not CDR data.

In Table 5.1, we present ASDRs for the United States and for Venezuela for 2006. Observe the ASDR data in columns 2 and 4 of the table. At every age, except one, the United States had lower ASDRs than Venezuela. But we just mentioned in the preceding paragraph that the United States had a CDR twice as high as Venezuela's. How can this be? Why was Venezuela's CDR half that of the United States, while all but one of its ASDRs are higher than those of the United States?

The answer is shown in columns 3 and 5 of Table 5.1, namely, the proportions of people by age groups in the two countries. Venezuela had proportionately many more people in the younger age groups than the United States did. For instance, the population of age 10–14 comprised 10.2 percent of Venezuela's total population, versus 7.2 percent of the US population. The opposite held true with regard to people in the middle and older ages, with higher proportions in the United States than in Venezuela. Starting at age 35–39, the age-specific proportions became larger in the United States than in Venezuela. The population 65–69 was 3.4 percent of the United States versus 1.8 percent of Venezuela. The population in the age group 85–89 comprised 1.1 percent of the United States, compared with 0.2 percent of Venezuela. The United States is an "older" country than Venezuela, that is, the United States has more older people proportionately than Venezuela. In contrast, Venezuela is a much "younger" country than the United States. Because younger people die at lower rates than older people, many (but not all) "young" countries have lower CDRs than "old" countries.

Demographers have a method for taking into account a factor such as age composition when they compare death rates among different countries. It is known as **standardization.** We focus here on age standardization, the most popular form. Young populations tend to have low CDRs, and old populations have high CDRs. One way to consider this issue is to observe that the CDR can be viewed as the sum of the ASDRs weighted by the size of the population in each age group. In other words, the

TABLE 5.1 *Age-specific death rates (ASDRs) and age-specific proportions of the population, United States and Venezuela, 2006*

	United States		Venezuela	
Age group	ASDR	Proportion of population	ASDR	Proportion of population
<1	0.00654	0.0139	0.01623	0.0219
1–4	0.00029	0.0548	0.00064	0.0800
5–9	0.00014	0.0675	0.00032	0.1038
10–14	0.00018	0.0719	0.00041	0.1023
15–19	0.00064	0.0724	0.00146	0.1012
20–24	0.00091	0.0702	0.00238	0.0925
25–29	0.00090	0.0671	0.00221	0.0842
30–34	0.00106	0.0679	0.00203	0.0726
35–39	0.00153	0.0706	0.00215	0.0688
40–44	0.00231	0.0766	0.00289	0.0630
45–49	0.00341	0.0757	0.00411	0.0515
50–54	0.00493	0.0675	0.00568	0.0437
55–59	0.00742	0.0575	0.00775	0.0346
60–64	0.01150	0.0437	0.01173	0.0251
65–69	0.01780	0.0339	0.01877	0.0180
70–74	0.02771	0.0284	0.02838	0.0136
75–79	0.04350	0.0248	0.04270	0.0097
80–84	0.06958	0.0187	0.07531	0.0053
85–89	0.11056	0.0107	0.12769	0.0024
90–94	0.17477	0.0045	0.20820	0.0007
95–99	0.27656	0.0013	0.32576	0.0001
100+	0.43892	0.0003	0.48975	0.0001

Source: US Bureau of the Census, International Database. Calculations by DLP.

CDR may be thought of as the "weighted mean of the death rates at each age, the weights used being the numbers at each age in the population being studied" (Pollard, Yusuf, and Pollard, 1981: 71–72).

We presented earlier in formula (5.1) the formula for the CDR. The numerator of the formula, deaths in the year, or D, is nothing more than the sum of each of the ASDRs multiplied by the size of the population in the age group. Consider, therefore, the following formula for the CDR as an alternative to that shown in formula (5.1):

$$CDR = \sum ASDR_x\left(\frac{nPx}{P}\right) * 1{,}000 \tag{5.4}$$

where:

P = total population,
${}_nP_x$ = population in age group x, and
$ASDR_x$ = ASDR for age group x (Palmore and Gardner, 1994: 15)

Here is a very simple way to better understand formula (5.4). Imagine a hypothetical population with a CDR of 40. This population is divided into two broad age groups, 0–34 and 35+. Table 5.2 contains age data for this hypothetical population.

TABLE 5.2 *Age data for a hypothetical population*

Age	Midyear population	Deaths	ASDR
0–34	2,000	40	20/1,000
35+	1,000	80	80/1,000
Total	3,000	120	40/1,000

Source: Palmore and Gardner, 1994: 15–16.

The data in Table 5.2 may be arranged using formula (5.4) as follows:

$$\text{CDR} = \frac{\text{D}}{\text{P}} * 1,000 = \frac{120}{3,000} * 1,000 = 0.04 * 1,000 = 40 \tag{5.5}$$

Next, consider the CDR as a weighted sum of the ASDRs, and arrange the data in Table 5.2 using formula (5.4) as follows:

$$\text{CDR} = \left[\frac{2,000}{3,000} * 20\right] + \left[\frac{1,000}{3,000} * 80\right] = \left[\frac{2}{3} * 20\right] + \left[\frac{1}{3} * 80\right] \tag{5.6}$$

$$\text{CDR} = \frac{40}{3} + \frac{80}{3} = \frac{120}{3} = 40 \tag{5.7}$$

This example shows nicely and exactly how the CDR is a sum of the weighted (by population) ASDRs.

Now we will compare the mortality experiences of two or more populations. If a population such as the United States has more persons in the older age groups than in the younger age groups, then the death rates of the older groups (where there is more mortality) will be more heavily weighted than the death rates of the younger groups (where there is less mortality), and vice versa for a country such as Venezuela that has more persons in the younger age groups than in the older groups. This is seen clearly in the ASDRs in Table 5.1 for the United States and Venezuela. In other words, "if two populations of quite different age distributions are being compared, the weights used are quite different, and this method (i.e., the CDR) could give very misleading results" (Pollard, Yusuf, and Pollard, 1981: 72). Hence, demographers need to control for age composition.

Actually, there are other features of population composition that also need to be considered, that is, controlled, when comparing the death experiences of two populations. If one population has an excess of females and another an excess of males, and if the age compositions of the two are similar, the latter will have a higher CDR than the former because of the heavier representation of males. A similar statement may be made with regard to race composition, where the majority race usually has lower mortality rates than the minority group. Also, as we have already noted, it is not correct to compare the CDRs of the same population for different points in time, because the age structure of the population is likely to have changed over the time periods under consideration.

Although our discussion here is restricted to standardization for age composition, the basic techniques of standardization are easily extended to sex or race composition, marital status, educational attainment, or any other aspects of composition that the demographer believes could be influencing the death rates.

There are many statistical software programs available that demographers use to execute the statistical calculations for standardizing mortality rates for age composition. Poston prefers to use Stata Statistical Software, although many other statistical software packages also have standardization programs based on formula (5.4). (For a general introduction to Stata, see Acock, 2023.) We have used Stata's direct standardization program to standardize Venezuela's death rate by assigning to Venezuela the age composition of the United States. Recall that in 2006 Venezuela had a CDR of 4 and the United States had a CDR of 8. The result of the standardization exercise is that Venezuela has a directly standardized death rate (SDR) of 11.1. This means that if Venezuela had the age composition of the United States, while retaining its own ASDRs, it would have a CDR of 11.1, and not its actual CDR of 4. The fact that Venezuela had such a low CDR of 4 compared with the US CDR of 8 is due to its much younger age composition. Thus, if we assign to Venezuela the same age composition as the United States, Venezuela ends up having a directly SDR of 11.1, which is higher than that of 8 for the United States.

The Life Table

One of the most important and elegant measures of the mortality experiences of a population is the life table. It dates back to John Graunt (1620–1674) and his "Bills of Mortality" (see Chapter 3, Box 3.2). The life table starts with a hypothetical population (a radix) of 100,000 at age 0. Setting the radix at 100,000 is arbitrary but conventional. From each age to the next, the hypothetical population is decremented according to the actual age-specific mortality probabilities of a specific population until all members have died. The mortality schedule is assumed to be fixed so that it does not change over the life of the population. The basic life table consists of seven columns, including the probability of dying between age x and age $x + n$ ($_nq_x$), the number of survivors at each age x (l_x), and life expectancy at each age (e_x). In Box 5.2, we discuss and develop in more detail a life table for the US population for the year 2010.

Life expectancy, a statistic gleaned directly from the last column of the life table (see table in Box 5.2), is a primary indicator of quality of life. In 2024, life expectancy at birth in the world was 70.7 for males and 76 for females. Hong Kong had the highest life expectancy at birth, 83.0 for males, 88.2 for females. The lowest life expectancies were in Nigeria (54.3 for males, 55.0 for females), and Chad (53.4 for males, 57.2 for females) (Worldometer, 2024).

We need to be aware of the fact, however, that when considering life expectancy at birth, e_0, infant mortality plays a very important role. When e_0 is low, as in Nigeria, Lesotho, or Chad, for example, a major reason is their very high infant mortality rate. When comparing values of life expectancy at birth across countries, especially lower-income countries, therefore, we should not think of e_0 as, strictly speaking, a modal age at death.

Whereas John Graunt is referred to by most demographers as the founder of demography, many refer to Alfred Lotka (1880–1949) as the person most responsible for the

Box 5.2 The Life Table

Demographers use the life table to determine life expectancy, not only at birth but at any age. Like the total fertility rate (see our discussion of the TFR in Chapter 4), the life table is a synthetic or hypothetical measure. It tells us many things about a population. One of the most important questions it answers is the following: How many years of life, on average, may a person expect to live if the person during his or her lifetime is subjected to the age-specific probabilities of dying of a particular country or population at a given time? Thus, when we say that the population of the United States in 2010 had a life expectancy at birth of 78.7 years, we mean that if a cohort of 100,000 persons, throughout the years of their life, were subjected to the ASDRs, that is, the $_nM_x$ rates, of the total population in the United States in 2010, they would live, on average, 78.7 years.

In Table B5.2.1, we show an abridged life table for the US population for the year 2010. It is referred to as an *abridged* life table because it is calculated, for the most part, for five-year age groups, rather than for single-year age groups.

A life table starts with the radix, a population of 100,000 persons born alive at age 0. (See the figure of 100,000 at l_0 in column 3.) This initial group of 100,000 persons is then subjected to the probabilities of dying at each age, until all 100,000 are dead. We will now examine each of the seven columns of the life table for the total US population in the year 2010.

Column 1 refers to the age intervals of each group. The age groups shown here refer to the range of years between two birthdays. To illustrate, the age group 5–9 refers to the five-year interval between the fifth and the tenth birthdays.

TABLE B5.2.1 *Life table for the total population, United States, 2010*

(1) Age range	(2) $_nq_x$	(3) l_x	(4) $_nd_x$	(5) $_nL_x$	(6) T_x	(7) e_x
<1	0.006123	100,000	612	99,465	7,866,027	78.7
1–4	0.001071	99,388	106	397,294	7,766,561	78.1
5–9	0.000573	99,281	57	496,250	7,369,267	74.2
10–14	0.000708	99,224	70	495,989	6,873,017	69.3
15–19	0.002463	99,154	244	495,240	6,377,028	64.3
20–24	0.004317	98,910	427	493,529	5,881,789	59.5
25–29	0.004791	98,483	472	491,249	5,388,260	54.7
30–34	0.005497	98,011	539	488,744	4,897,011	50.0
35–39	0.006913	97,472	674	485,753	4,408,267	45.2
40–44	0.009979	96,798	966	481,758	3,922,514	40.5
45–49	0.016044	95,833	1,538	475,584	3,440,756	35.9
50–54	0.024343	94,295	2,295	466,066	2,965,173	31.4
55–59	0.035106	92,000	3,230	452,347	2,499,106	27.2
60–64	0.049847	88,770	4,425	433,348	2,046,759	23.1
65–69	0.074406	84,345	6,276	406,912	1,613,411	19.1
70–74	0.112315	78,069	8,768	369,612	1,206,499	15.5
75–79	0.174782	69,301	12,113	317,694	836,886	12.1
80–84	0.274384	57,188	15,692	248,038	519,193	9.1
85–89	0.430820	41,497	17,878	162,723	271,155	6.5
90–94	0.615282	23,619	14,532	79,720	108,432	4.6
95–99	0.783397	9,087	7,119	24,670	29,212	3.2
100+	1.00000	1,968	1,968	4,542	4,542	2.3

Source: Arias, 2014: 62.

Column 2 reports for each age group the probabilities of dying; these probabilities are designated as ${}_nq_x$. This is the most basic column of the life table. The ${}_nq_x$ values represent the probabilities that persons who are alive at the beginning of an age interval will die during that age interval, before they reach the start of the next age interval. While it is the case that the ${}_nq_x$ rates resemble the ${}_nM_x$ rates, there is an important difference between them. The difference has to do with their denominators; the denominator of the ${}_nM_x$ rates is the midyear population, whereas the denominator of the ${}_nq_x$ rates is the population alive at the beginning of the age interval. In most cases, the ${}_nq_x$ rates may be estimated from the ${}_nM_x$ rates with a straightforward transforming equation (Kintner, 2004). Given the radix of 100,000 babies born alive, the ${}_nq_x$ rates are expressed per 100,000.

Because of the curvilinear nature of death rates at the youngest and oldest ages, for a few age groups, namely, those less than 1, 1–4, and 100+, different formulas are used (see Kintner, 2004: 312). At the oldest age category (100+ in the life table shown here), the value of ${}_nq_x$ must equal 1.0 because all people alive at the start of that age interval must die at some point in that open-ended interval.

Column 3 shows values for the number of people alive at the beginning of the age interval; this column is designated as the l_x column of data and is sometimes known as "the little *l* column." It is calculated by subtracting the ${}_nd_x$ value (column 5) from the l_x value in the age interval immediately preceding the one being calculated. For example, of the 99,224 people alive at the beginning of the age interval 10–14 (i.e., l_{10}), 70 of them die during the age interval between their 10th and 15th birthdays (i.e., ${}_5d_{10}$). Thus, for the next age group, those aged 15–19, there are 70 fewer people; therefore, the value of l_{15} is 99,154 (i.e., 99,224 minus 70).

Column 4 shows the number of people who die during a particular age interval and is designated as ${}_nd_x$. It is arrived at by multiplying l_x by ${}_nq_x$. Thus, for the number of people who die during the age interval of 40–44, the ${}_5d_{40}$ value is 966; this equals the ${}_5q_{40}$ value of 0.009979 times the l_{40} value of 96,798.

Column 5 reports for each age interval the total number of years lived by all persons who enter that age interval while in the age interval. It is designated as ${}_nL_x$ and is sometimes referred to as "the big *L* column" of data. For instance, the life table shows that 98,011 persons are alive at the beginning of age interval 30–34 (i.e., the l_{30} value). If none of those persons died during that age interval, they would have lived 490,055 years during the period of time between their 30th and 35th birthdays, or 98,011 times 5. But we know that some of them died during the age interval of 30–34, namely, 539 died. (See the ${}_5d_{30}$ value of 539.) Demographers assume that these 539 deaths are evenly distributed during the five-year period for many age intervals. But this assumption does not apply to the first few age intervals. With regard to the first year of life, we noted in this chapter that it is erroneous to assume that deaths are evenly distributed throughout the first year. Different formulas are used to produce the ${}_nL_x$ value for the first few age groups (see Kintner, 2004: 313–315). At the other age extreme, 100+ in the life table, another formula is used (see Kintner, 2004: 314).

Column 6 reports the total number of years lived by the population in that age interval and in all subsequent age intervals; this column of data is designated as T_x. To determine the values of T_x for each age interval, one sums the ${}_nL_x$ from the oldest age backwards, using this formula:

$$T_x = \sum_{i=x}^{\omega} L_i$$

where:

L_i = entry i in the $_nL_x$ column, and

$\sum_{i=x}^{w}$ = the sum of the $_nL_x$ column starting at entry x through the last $_nL_x$ entry, namely, w.

We will calculate T_{95} from the life table for the US population in 2010, as follows:

$$T_{95} = {}_5L_{95} + {}_5L_{100+}$$

$$T_{95} = 24,670 + 4,542 = 29,212$$

Column 7 presents the average number of years of life remaining at the beginning of the age interval. This column of data, known as e_x, provides life expectancy at any age; it is calculated by dividing column 7 by column 4. We noted earlier that the total US population in 2010 has an average life expectancy at birth of 78.7 years. This refers to the e_0 value of 78.7 in the life table and is calculated as T_0 (7,866,027) divided by l_0 (100,000) = 78.7. If I wanted to know the average number of years of life remaining for the US population in 2010 who had reached their 25th birthday, I would use the e_{25} value of 54.7 in the life table; it is calculated as T_{25}(5,388,260) divided by l_{25} (98,483) = 54.71. This means that persons aged 25–29 could expect to live an additional 54.7 years on average if they were subjected to the age-specific probabilities of dying of the total US population in 2010.

Life tables are used for many purposes other than studying human mortality. Examples include estimating the failure rates of contraceptives, tracing the progress of a population of first-year students through college, and measuring marital formation and dissolution. Regarding the second example, one would take the number of first-year students entering college as the radix of the life table and then subject them to the multiple age-specific probabilities of dying, of dropping out of college, and of graduating from college. One could then determine, for example, the average number of years of college life for, say, male first-year students who entered four-year public colleges in the state of Texas in the fall semester of 2010, and compare this value of e_x with that for male first-year students who entered four-year private colleges in the state of Texas in the fall semester of 2010. Is the average number of years of college life larger or smaller for male first-year students in public versus private colleges? An educational life table would give us the answer.

development of modern demography. Lotka used life tables in the development of his **stable population theory**. The concept of a stable population was actually first set forth by Leonhard Euler ([1760] 1970), but its current development stems from the work of Lotka, who first introduced the concept in a brief note in 1907. Later, Sharpe and Lotka (1911) proved mathematically that if a population that is closed to migration experiences constant schedules of age-specific fertility and mortality rates, it will develop a constant age distribution and will grow at a constant rate, irrespective of its initial age distribution. We discuss this important demographic concept in more detail in Chapter 13.

Having covered some of the methodological issues involved in the study of mortality, we turn now to substantive issues. In the next section, we review briefly the history of mortality in the world and also cover the three positive checks of Malthus. Next, we discuss the major causes of death in developed and developing countries and how they have changed over time.

A SHORT HISTORY OF MORTALITY IN THE WORLD AND THE MALTHUSIAN CHECKS OF FAMINES, EPIDEMICS, AND WARS

Our knowledge of mortality levels and conditions prior to the Industrial Revolution is limited. We know that mortality then was high, but the availability and completeness of death data leave many questions unanswered. A life table for ancient Greece prepared from burial records shows a life expectancy at birth, e_o, of about 30 years (Dublin, Lotka, and Spiegelman, 1949). Age data from census records of Roman Egypt indicate an average life expectancy at birth in the first to third centuries AD of between 22 and 25 years, a finding that has been corroborated by data on tombstones in Roman North Africa (Scheidel, 2003: 45). A life table developed by John Graunt (see Chapter 3) reported that more than 35 percent of babies born in seventeenth-century London were dead by age 6. By comparison, according to a US life table for 2010, less than 1 percent of the US population born alive has died by age 6. (See the table in Box 5.2 above.) Graunt's life table showed that by age 56, 94 percent of those born were dead, while the respective figure for the US population in 2010 was around 8 percent. We are living quite a bit longer these days compared with Londoners four centuries ago. Thank goodness.

As late as the eighteenth century, life expectancy at birth ranged from only 30 to 40 years in much of Europe and the United States (Dublin, Lotka, and Spiegelman, 1949). As recently as 1901, the year Poston's father was born, US males had a life expectancy at birth of only 47.9 years and females, only 50.7 years (US Department of Commerce, 1921). (Dudley L. Poston, Sr. died in 1977 at age 75, so he exceeded by 27 years the e_o value when he was born.)

Mortality levels in past centuries were not constant from year to year. There were short-term fluctuations caused principally by changes in the major causes of high mortality, namely, famines, epidemics, and wars. These are the "positive checks" noted by Malthus that kept the death rate high (Malthus, [1803] 1989). (See our earlier discussion of Malthus in Chapter 2.) Poor living conditions in urban areas also contributed to high levels of mortality (Johnson, 2006).

Famines

We now consider famines as a cause of death. Populations in preindustrial times had much less control over their food supply than we do today. Agricultural output was severely limited by the vagaries of the weather, by the inefficiency of manual labor, by plagues of rodents and insects, and by plant diseases. Abundant harvests usually could not be exploited owing to inadequate food-storage facilities. Transportation technology and roadways were underdeveloped. Hence, isolated areas with food shortages were unable to import surplus food from other areas. Thus, famine was a major problem.

The demographic consequences of famines were often disastrous. Because famines have almost always taken place in rural and in poor populations, the precise nature of their toll is not easy to measure (O'Grada, 1999, 2001, 2003a). There were serious declines in population in much of Europe during the famine years of 1315–1317. In the 1690s, one-sixth of the population in some Swedish provinces died after severe crop failures.

The Irish potato famine of 1846–1851, known in Ireland as the Great Famine, killed around a million people, although some estimates place the number as high as 1.5 million (Foster, 1988: 324; Miller, 1985: 284). This is a huge number of deaths, amounting to between 12 and 18 percent of the population, when one recalls that the total population of Ireland in the early 1840s was just over 8 million. Besides the deaths, many Irish emigrated as refugees, especially to the United States, Canada, and Australia. As an Irish priest at the time observed, "Truly, the Angel of death and desolation reigns triumphant in Ireland" (Miller, 1985: 285). We also must not forget that these deaths do not include "averted births or allow for famine-related deaths in Britain and farther afield" (O'Grada, 2003b: 391; 1999). This famine illustrated the intersecting effects of public policy with the biological fact of the potato blight. Rather than feeding the Irish people, Ireland was exporting vast quantities of food because of the policies of the British government (Woodham-Smith, 1992).

One of the most destructive famines in the demographic record occurred in China between 1958 and 1961, and it illustrates the interaction of human and biological factors in producing famine. As industrial and grain production dropped to low levels, the standard of living declined, and the birth rate dropped to near replacement levels (Peng, 1987). First there were food shortages, followed by famine, and as happened in Ireland, food was exported, often from areas in China with food shortages. It is estimated that between 30 and 40 million Chinese died as a direct result of the famine, with 12 million of the deaths to children under the age of 10 (Ashton et al., 1984; MacDonald, 2003). The main cause of the famine stemmed from the ill-conceived and overly ambitious Great Leap Forward program, initiated in 1958 by Mao Zedong and designed to "involve a revolutionary struggle against nature to realize the great potential of agriculture by maximizing the advantages of the collective economy" (Aird, 1972: 278). The economic crisis and famine that followed were due to natural disasters, such as floods, plant diseases, and drought, as well as to bureaucratic inefficiency and improper management (Ashton et al., 1984; Dikotter, 2010; Yang, 2012). As disastrous as was China's famine, it killed "at most 2 to 3 percent of the total population" of the country (O'Grada, 2003a: 383).

Box 5.3 discusses the "Hunger Winter" in the Netherlands during World War II. This famine was engineered by an occupying army as a punishment of the population. Because of high-quality data in the Netherlands, it has been possible for researchers to study the long-term effects of famine on a population.

Throughout human history, unless famines occur in very small populations, famines seldom result in the deaths of a high percentage of people. More deadly in terms of widespread mortality are **epidemics** and **pandemics**. We discuss epidemics as a source of mass mortality in Chapter 12, with special attention to COVID-19. Putting aside for now the mortality due to epidemic disease, we now discuss war, the last of the Malthusian positive checks.

Wars

The demographic consequences of war with respect to mortality are not easy to determine. For one thing, there is the issue of definition. What is a war? Some military

Box 5.3 The Hunger Winter, 1944–1945

The Dutch Famine in western Netherlands during World War II is a case of the interaction of public policy, weather, war, and famine in producing mortality. What is unusual about this case is that historians and demographers were able to collect data from the survivors that have been used to understand the long-term effects of famine on a population.

The so-called "Hunger Winter" of 1944–1945 began while Nazi Germany was occupying the Netherlands. The Dutch government in exile supported the Allies, who had penetrated into the eastern Netherlands. In retaliation, Nazi officials ordered a blockade of food and fuel shipments from the farm towns to the western parts of the country. This was an unusually bitter winter in Europe, and so the shortage of fuel as well as food intensified the misery (van der Zee, 1998).

People from Amsterdam hiked into the countryside to find food on farms, but the farmers themselves soon had no food. Actress Audrey Hepburn, at that time a child living with her mother in several Dutch cities, recalled surviving by eating nettles and tulip bulbs (Garner, 1991). The famine ended in May 1945 when the Allies liberated the Netherlands.

The daily calorie consumption dropped as low as 580 calories per person (Dols and Arken, 1946; Stein et al., 1975). (For comparison, McDonald's Big Mac has 590 calories.) As the famine persisted, protein sources declined rapidly, leaving mostly carbohydrate-heavy foods such as bread and potatoes for consumption. The mortality increase was greatest among elderly men, and an estimated 45,000 excess deaths were attributed to the famine from among an affected population of about 4.5 million (Ramirez and Haas, 2022). Even the survivors, however, suffered malnutrition and showed later effects from it.

After food supplies returned to normal, men consistently showed worse outcomes from starvation than women, but the effects on women also showed up in later generations. Women who were pregnant during the famine gave birth to children with health issues such as obesity, diabetes, cardiovascular disease, and cognitive impairment. In the next generation, their grandchildren were smaller at birth and suffered increased health issues later in life compared with Dutch children born at the same time but whose families had not been exposed to the famine (De Zwarte, Ekamper, and Lumey, 2024; Hart, 1993; Lumey and van Poppel, 1994).

These conclusions were reached through the use of large-scale sample surveys and the Dutch population registry.

historians and archeologists define war as all kinds of conflicts involving more than two combatants. But this is an unrealistic approach. Scholars now tend to define war in terms of the number of deaths that have occurred. Wilkinson (1980) developed a register of wars since 1820 that includes 315 engagements where the number of deaths exceeded 300 (see also Etherington, 2003). In addition to the number of recorded military deaths, there is also the issue of civilian losses that occur as a consequence of war, including infection by diseases carried by the soldiers, killings associated with plunder, famine following the destruction of farmland, and hardships occurring as a result of economic and social disorganization.

Mortality data from war are best documented for activities in the twentieth century compared with previous eras. The greatest number of deaths, unquestionably, occurred during the first part of the last century. The range of estimates is considerable, but "plausible sizes of the military and civilian death toll would be around 8.5 million in

World War I and 40 million in World War II" (Etherington, 2003: 964). Often, the number of civilian deaths exceeds the number of military deaths. To illustrate, it is likely that during World War II in Russia, 60 percent of the deaths were civilian (Petersen, 1975: 269). And within the armies, the death toll from disease, accidents, and mishap often exceeded the deaths from actual combat.

In the United States, the Civil War resulted in the largest number of deaths to Americans of any war ever experienced by the country, before or after. An estimated 620,000 men, roughly half from the North and half from the South, died during the four years of fighting between 1861 and 1865. This is about the same number of Americans lost in the country's other wars from the Revolutionary War through the Korean War (Faust, 2008). The number of 620,000 Civil War deaths needs to be considered relative to the US population of around 31 million people at the time; approximately 2 percent of the country's total population died. This would be the equivalent of around 6.9 million people in terms of the US population in 2024.

MORTALITY TRENDS AND CAUSES OF DEATH IN DEVELOPED AND DEVELOPING COUNTRIES

The eminent demographer Donald Bogue noted that in many ways "it is superficial to treat death as a single unitary force.... In reality death is an event brought about by one or a combination of a great variety of causes, or diseases, and a full understanding of mortality requires an understanding of the trends in each of the major causes of death" (1969: 578).

Even today, data on causes of death are far from complete. Some deaths around the world are never registered. In many countries, a large proportion of deaths occurs outside the presence of physicians, and the causes are either unknown or incorrectly diagnosed. Sometimes, socially unpopular causes of death, such as suicide, syphilis, and HIV/AIDS, are misrepresented or camouflaged.

Moreover, international comparisons of cause-of-death data are difficult because countries often differ in terminology, method of certification, diagnostic techniques, and the quality of the coding and data-collection system. Nevertheless, some generalizations are possible about the general structure of the causes of death.

In the world today, most national governments classify causes of deaths according to the **International Classification of Diseases (ICD)** as developed by the World Health Organization (WHO) (World Health Organization, 2024e; 2024f). This classification undergoes periodic revision. ICD-11, the eleventh revision of the classification, was introduced in 2022 and is available in ten languages, with translations underway in another twenty-five languages. Causes of death in the United States have been classified according to ICD-10 since 1999, and the transition to ICD-11 is scheduled to take place between 2025 and 2026 (Feinstein, Gill, and Anderson, 2023).

According to the WHO, the ICD allows the systematic recording, analysis, interpretation, and comparison of mortality and morbidity data collected in different countries or regions and at different times. It also ensures that the recorded data are interoperable for uses such as statistics, decision support, resource allocation, third-party reimbursement, guidelines, and more. (World Health Organization, 2024e)

In the eleventh revision of the ICD, the causes of death are classified in twenty-four chapters. Here are these chapter headings, along with a few examples of specific causes for some of them (see World Health Organization 2024e, for more details), as follows:

- 01 Certain infectious or parasitic diseases (such as tuberculosis; HIV/AID)
- 02 Neoplasms (cancers)
- 03 Diseases of the blood or blood-forming organs
- 04 Diseases of the immune system
- 05 Endocrine, nutritional, or metabolic diseases (malnutrition; diabetes)
- 06 Mental, behavioral, or neurodevelopmental disorders (schizophrenia)
- 07 Sleep-wake disorders
- 08 Diseases of the nervous system (meningitis)
- 09 Diseases of the visual system
- 10 Diseases of the ear or mastoid process
- 11 Diseases of the circulatory system (ischemic heart disease; cerebrovascular disease)
- 12 Diseases of the respiratory system (influenza; pneumonia)
- 13 Diseases of the digestive system
- 14 Diseases of the skin
- 15 Diseases of the musculoskeletal system or connective tissue
- 16 Diseases of the genitourinary system
- 17 Conditions related to sexual health
- 18 Pregnancy, childbirth, or the puerperium
- 19 Certain conditions originating in the perinatal period (birth trauma)
- 20 Developmental anomalies (spina bifida)
- 21 Symptoms, signs, or clinical findings, not elsewhere classified
- 22 Injury, poisoning, or certain other consequences of external causes
- 23 External causes of morbidity or mortality (motor vehicle accidents)
- 24 Factors influencing health status or contact with health services

There is also another chapter providing codes for special purposes, such as new diseases.

This listing provides extensive detail about the structure of causes of death. Its presentation makes the general point that death is a complex behavior, and that there are literally many thousand different ways to die. But some causes of death occur more frequently than others.

To illustrate, in 2023, there were approximately 61 million deaths in the world (Ritchie and Mathieu, 2023). Worldwide, the top cause was ischemic heart disease at 7.4 million deaths, which accounts for 13 percent of all deaths; stroke caused 10 percent of all deaths; chronic obstructive pulmonary disease (COPD), a lung disease that interferes with normal breathing, accounted for 5 percent of deaths (World Health Organization, 2024i). The top ten causes account for over half of the world's deaths. The ordering of causes of death was seriously affected, however, by the surge of COVID-19 deaths in 2020–2022. This issue is discussed in greater detail in Chapter 12.

People do not all die of the same major causes, however. There are differences in causes of death, and these are largely due to the socioeconomic levels of the countries. People living in a low-income country are far more likely to die of a communicable disease than a noncommunicable disease. Despite the global decline, 8 of the top

10 causes of death in 2021 in low-income countries were communicable diseases. (World Health Organization, 2024i). Diarrheal diseases were also more common in these countries, although they have been declining.

In high-income countries, infectious diseases are less likely than chronic diseases to be the causes of death. Because average life expectancy is longer in these countries, diseases that are more common among elderly people are also more likely to be leading causes of death. Ischemic heart disease, stroke, and stomach cancer are among the causes of death in the top ten, and deaths from hypertensive heart disease are rising. Deaths due to Alzheimer's disease and other dementias have increased dramatically. This became the fourth leading cause of death in high-income countries in 2021 and is on track to overtake stroke as one of the top three (Davis, 2008; World Health Organization, 2024b, 2024i).

We have already mentioned that mortality was much higher in the past. The United Nations (2013d) has noted that the twentieth century was the era characterized by the most rapid decline in mortality in human history. In the early 1950s, life expectancy in the world was only 46 years, but reached 69 years by 2010. Figure 5.2 shows the estimated levels of life expectancy for the world and the three major development regions for the period 1950 through 2100.

Barring more unexpected mortality events such as COVID-19, the UN has projected that in 2050 life expectancy for the world will reach 76 years, and by 2100 it will reach 82 years. Life expectancy in the high-income countries in 1950 was already high, at 65 years; by 2010 it was 77, and is projected to be 83 years in 2050, and 89 years in 2100. In contrast, the 49 lowest-income countries, 20 of which have been severely impacted by HIV/AIDS, had a life expectancy of only 35 years in 1950; it reached 58 years in 2005–2010 and is projected to be 70 in 2050, and 77 by 2100.

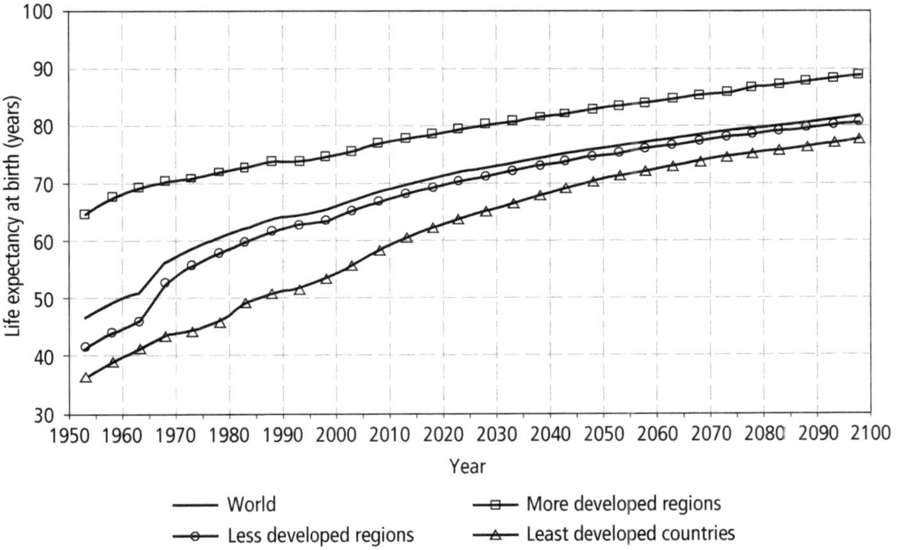

FIGURE 5.2 Actual and projected life expectancy at birth from 1950 to 2100 in the world, more developed regions, less developed regions, and least developed countries
Data source: United Nations, 2013d, 2024a.

The increases in life expectancy just noted for the high-income and low-income countries tend to hide the variation in these changes among the world's major areas. The countries of Asia, Latin America and the Caribbean, Northern America, and Oceania have been experiencing increases in life expectancy at a steady pace, but the countries of Europe for the most part have experienced a slowdown beginning in the late 1960s through the late 1980s. This is due to "severe reductions in life expectancy in countries of Eastern Europe, particularly in the Russian Federation and the Ukraine. The remaining regions of Europe have had increasing life expectancies which are currently equal to or higher than that of Northern America" (United Nations, 2013d: 15).

Unlike the situation in the other regions of the world, increases in life expectancy since the late 1980s in Africa have been slowing down.

> While this trend is due in large part to the HIV/AIDS epidemic, other factors have also played a role, including armed conflict, economic stagnation, and resurgent infectious diseases such as tuberculosis and malaria. The recent negative developments in many countries of Africa represent major setbacks in reducing mortality. [But life expectancy is expected to begin rising again] ... provided that efforts to reduce the expansion of the HIV/AIDS epidemic and to treat those affected by it succeed. (United Nations, 2013d: 17)

We turn next to a consideration of trends in mortality and longevity in the United States.

MORTALITY AND LONGEVITY IN THE UNITED STATES

The mortality declines that have taken place in the United States are consistent with demographic transition theory (as we have already described in Chapter 2). Mortality started dropping gradually in response to changes in the social and economic conditions and the environment that were part of societal modernization. Much of the mortality reduction started to occur before the initiation of any appreciable public health measures.

The Decline in Mortality

Mortality data for the United States are limited until about the middle of the 1800s. In fact, systematic information on US mortality has only been available since 1933 (see Chapter 3). It is believed that crude death rates (CDRs) during the colonial period were moderate, ranging from 20 deaths per 1,000 per population to just under 40 (recall, however, our earlier discussion about problems in using CDRs comparatively). Life expectancy certainly did not exceed age 40 and was much lower in many places. In New Hampshire and Massachusetts, life expectancy was about 35 and had increased to around 40 by 1850 (Kitagawa and Hauser, 1973). Indeed, for the states of the United States reporting data as of 1850, life expectancy at birth for Whites averaged just over 39 years and for Blacks only 23 years. Infant mortality was very high.

Since around 1850, some of the mortality decline has resulted in part from "improvements in public health and sanitation, especially better water supplies and sewage disposal. The improving diet, clothing, and shelter of the American population over the period since about 1870 also played a role. Specific medical interventions beyond more general environmental public health measures were not statistically important until well into the twentieth century" (Haines, 2007). We noted earlier that death rates were often high in the urban areas of Europe. The same was true in the United States. However, in the 1890s, many of the larger US cities initiated "public works sanitation projects (such as piped water, sewer systems, filtration and chlorination of water) and public health administration" (Haines, 2007). As a result of these efforts, the death rates dropped and rural–urban differences in mortality disappeared. Still, White–Black differences remained, as they do to this day, and this important issue is discussed in detail in Chapter 15.

Life expectancy in the United States increased dramatically from 46 for males and 48 for females in 1900 to 75 for males and 80 for females in 2024. Most of the improvements occurred from 1900 to 1950. The advances were due to the increased recognition of the **germ theory** of disease, resulting in the identification and control of many infectious and parasitic diseases, particularly among infants and children (Preston and Haines, 1991; Shrestha, 2006). The germ theory led to such interventions for the control of infectious disease as "boiling bottles and milk, washing hands, protecting food from flies, isolating sick children, ventilating rooms, and improving water supply and sewage disposal" (Shrestha, 2006: 3). Today, these preventive behaviors are taken for granted and practiced by nearly everyone.

Improvements in life expectancy since 1950 have been mostly due to the increased prevention and control of chronic diseases that affect adults, particularly heart disease and stroke. A major contribution to this improvement has been the decrease in tobacco use among Americans. Cigarette smoking declined to 11.5 percent of the population in 2021, the lowest rate recorded since 1965 (Centers for Disease Control, 2024e). About 450,000 deaths annually are still attributed to smoking, but because of smoking cessation, this number is expected to begin declining in 2030 (Thuy, Mendez, and Warner, 2024).

Nevertheless, life expectancy for the United States has not reached the high levels seen in Hong Kong, Japan, South Korea, and some other countries Recall in an earlier paragraph that we noted that in 2024 in the United States, life expectancy at birth was 75 for males and 80 for females. By comparison, in Canada in 2024, life expectancy at birth was 79 for males and 84 for females. In Japan in 2024, life expectancy at birth was 81 for males and 87 for females. In Hong Kong in 2024, life expectancy at birth was 83 for males and 88 for females (Population Reference Bureau, 2024). This is clearly a very important research issue that warrants more attention (Rogers, Lawrence, and Hummer, 2018).

Life expectancy has not increased uniformly at all ages. Most of the gains have occurred in the younger age groups. To illustrate, a boy born in the United States in 1900 could expect to live to the age of around 48 and a girl to around 51. As we just noted, by 2024, a boy infant in the United States could anticipate living for 75 years and a girl infant for 80 years. These are gains of 27 years for baby boys and 29 years for baby girls. For people in the older ages, the increases in the past century have not been as striking. A 60-year-old male in 1901 could expect to live for 14 more years and a female of the same age for 15 more years (Glover, 1921: 57, 61). In contrast, by 2010, a 60-year-old male could anticipate 22 more years of life and a 60-year-old female 24 more years (Arias, 2014: 3). These are gains during the 110-year period of 7 years for 60-year-old males and 9 years for 60-year-old females. As noted, the greater gains at the younger ages occurred because we can now pretty much control the various infectious diseases that in the past resulted in deaths of infants and young children. But we do not yet have control of the chronic diseases that cause death among older persons.

It should be noted, however, that life expectancy does not always increase. Remember that life expectancy is calculated in the life table by applying the current age-specific mortality rates, and those rates can change over time. During the COVID-19 years 2018–2021, for example, life expectancy for males declined from 76.3 to 73.5 years and for females from 81.4 to 79.3 years (Centers for Disease Control, 2023).

The improvement in life expectancy for women has slowed down, and it has slowed down more in the United States than elsewhere; the United States ranks thirtieth among the thirty-six most developed countries. The principal reasons appear to be higher death rates among women at younger ages with smoking, obesity, addictive behaviors, and suicide apparently among the responsible factors (Short and Zacher, 2022). In addition, the United States has a relatively high maternal mortality rate, and the majority of these deaths are regarded as preventable (Centers for Disease Control, 2024c; see the discussion of maternal mortality later in the chapter). As a result, the difference in longevity between men and women in the United States has been narrowing.

Prevailing Causes of Death

Recall Omran's (1971) theory of the epidemiologic transition, which we discussed in Chapter 2. According to this theory, as populations lived longer, on average, the prevailing causes of death would shift from infectious diseases to chronic and degenerative diseases that we associate with aging, such as heart disease, stroke, and cancer. Changes in causes of death in the United States, with some exceptions discussed in Chapter 12, follow Omran's general outline. Many decades ago, mortality from infectious and parasitic diseases decreased as major causes of death in the United States, and mortality from degenerative diseases increased. The main causes of death in the United States these days are associated with degenerative and chronic diseases.

However, this "general profile of leading causes varies substantially based on a decedent's age" (Minino, 2013: 4). Table 5.3 shows the five leading causes of death in the United States in 2021, for five broad age groups.

For children under 5, the two leading causes of death occur around the time of birth, namely, perinatal events and congenital abnormality (WHO, 2006). For persons aged 5–24, the three leading causes of death are all external causes, namely, unintentional injury (such as a motor vehicle accident), homicide, and suicide. Two external causes of death, unintentional injury and suicide, are among the top five for decedents aged 25–44, but heart disease and cancer also appear. And because these data are from 2021, COVID-19 is also a prominent cause of death. Among 45–64-year-old persons, only one external cause, unintentional injury, is among the five main causes for middle-aged decedents; most of the deaths in this age group are due to chronic conditions,

TABLE 5.3 *Five leading causes of death, by age group, based on age-adjusted deaths per 100,000 population, 2021*

Age	#1	#2	#3	#4	#5
<5 years	Perinatal event (53.2)	Congenital abnormality (24.4)	Unintentional injury (14.1)	Homicide (3.1)	Heart disease (2.1)
5–24 years	Unintentional injury (20.1)	Suicide (8.2)	Homicide (8.1)	Cancer (2.5)	COVID-19 (1.8)
25–44 years	Unintentional injury (80.2)	COVID-19 (26.3)	Heart disease (20.2)	Suicide (18.7)	Cancer (17.1)
45–64 years	Cancer (149.2)	Heart disease (133.5)	COVID-19 (122.7)	Unintentional injury (77.6)	Liver disease (31.9)
≥65 years	Heart disease (1,088.6)	Cancer (849.1)	COVID-19 (541.9)	Stroke (277.8)	Chronic lung disease (234.0)

Source: Centers for Disease Control and Prevention, National Center for Health Statistics, National Vital Statistics System – Mortality, 2018–2021, Single Race. Accessed on CDC WONDER Online Database, released in 2023.

namely, cancer, heart disease, and chronic liver disease, with COVID-19 also a leading cause of death. Among the oldest group of decedents, those aged 65 and over, the five main causes of their deaths do not include any external causes; their five main causes are heart disease, cancer, COVID-19, stroke, and chronic liver disease. So not only does the risk of mortality vary by age (remember the "age curve of mortality") but causes of death also vary by age.

Alzheimer disease (AD) is growing in its significance within the United States and worldwide. In 2022 there were more than 120,000 deaths from this disease. About 45 percent of nursing home residents and about 45 percent of hospice patients have a diagnosis of Alzheimer Disease (National Center for Health Statistics, 2024). AD ranks now as the seventh leading cause of death. There is currently no cure.

Socioeconomic Differentials in Mortality

Generally, the higher the socioeconomic status (SES), the lower the mortality. This relationship is found whether or not SES is measured in terms of income, occupation, or education (Stockwell, Wicks, and Adamchak, 1978). This inverse association is found in US data from the earliest times to the present, as well as in most other countries (Krieger et al., 1993; Rogers, Hummer, and Nam, 2000; Williams and Collins, 1995).

Two extensive and well-known studies of socioeconomic differentials deserve special mention. The first, *Differential Mortality in the United States* is the analysis by two of Sullivan's former demography teachers, Evelyn Kitagawa and Philip Hauser (1973). In this very important and path-breaking book, the authors examined a sample of US 1960 death certificates matched with 1960 census data. They showed that income and education have strong negative relationships with mortality, particularly for persons in the 25–64 age group. In other words, higher income and higher educational attainment are associated with lower rates of death. This was one of the very first analyses reporting the relationship between socioeconomic status and mortality.

A more recent and very noteworthy analysis is by Richard Rogers, Robert Hummer, and Charles Nam (2000), *Living and Dying in the USA*. In this invaluable study of adult mortality, the authors used two matched data sets to analyze the effects of social factors on mortality. One data set, the National Health Interview Survey (NHIS), was based on annual interviews of US residents about their health and sociodemographic characteristics. Data from the NHIS for persons aged 18 and older for several years in the late 1980s and early 1990s were then matched with death-certificate data for persons who were included in the NHIS but who subsequently died between 1986 and 1995. Rogers and his colleagues were able to relate a host of socioeconomic characteristics of persons interviewed in the NHIS with whether or not they died in the period through the mid-1990s. They showed statistically and concretely that mortality rates are not the same for all adults. The force of mortality is

> stronger for the poor, the less educated, the unemployed and the uninsured rather than for the rich, the highly educated, and the insured.... [Mortality is higher] for those who rarely attend religious services ... than for those who frequently attend.... [And mortality is higher] for those who smoke, drink heavily, and are inactive [compared to those] who have never smoked, who drink moderately, and exercise regularly. (Rogers, Hummer, and Nam, 2000: 321)

The data and results reported in their book provide solid evidence that we are indeed population actors and that our personal choices and decisions throughout our lifetime on a number of socioeconomic and behavioral dimensions can have dramatic effects on our longevity.

INFANT MORTALITY

An aspect of mortality that receives special consideration from demographers is infant mortality. This is due to at least two considerations. First, as Frisbie has written, "few, if any, human experiences are more tragic or emotionally devastating as the death of an infant or child" (2005: 251). Second, as we observed earlier, the death rate in the first year of life is much higher than in the succeeding several decades. Indeed, in high-mortality populations, the death rate in the first year of life is not reached again in the society until age 70 or later. And in some high-mortality populations, the highest death rate is in the first year of life. From the point of view of measurement, infant mortality has a disproportionate effect in lowering the expectation of life at birth. In societies with high mortality, the expectation of life at age 1 may exceed the expectation of life at birth. A baby who survives the first year of life in these societies has an improved life expectancy.

Infant Mortality Rate

The **infant mortality rate (IMR)**, the most common measure of infant death, is the number of deaths in a year to persons under age 1 per 1,000 babies born in the year. It is expressed as

$$\text{IMR} = \frac{\text{deaths in the year to persons under age 1}}{\text{live births in the year}} * 1{,}000 \tag{5.8}$$

Infant mortality rates of 200 or more per 1,000 births were the rule as late as 1800, even in countries of the higher-income world. This means that around one of every five babies born died before reaching their first birthday. IMRs were even higher in countries prior to their completing the demographic transition. During those early periods, "IMRs were probably on the order of 260 to 370 per 1,000 live births" (Frisbie, 2005: 260). As late as the 1870s, the IMR in European countries varied from 100 in Norway to nearly 300 in southern Germany (United Nations, 1973: 124). Infant mortality in China in the early 1900s was likely around 300. Indeed, China probably did not reduce its IMR countrywide to around 200 until the founding of the People's Republic in 1949 (Banister, 1992: 167).

High IMRs led to the cultural practice in China and Korea and in many other Asian societies of not giving a newborn baby a name until it had lived for several months and showed signs of continued viability. In Korea, for instance, even to this day, a small feast is prepared on the 100th day after a baby is born. Rice, red bean cakes, and wine are served. This day was originally celebrated as a feast in honor of the child's surviving the first few months of life, the most difficult period of time for survival. In ancient times, the child was not given a name until the 100th day celebration. It made little sense to invest emotionally in a newborn by assigning a name if the chances were only around four of ten that the baby would survive for a year.

During the latter part of the nineteenth century and into the twentieth century, most countries in the developed world experienced decreases in their IMRs. The transition to lower levels of infant mortality in the Western countries, as well as to lower child and adult mortality, was due in large part to reductions in infectious and parasitic diseases. Indeed, prior to the third and fourth decades of the twentieth century, "the role played by physicians and drug therapy in the reduction of mortality was relatively slight" (Frisbie, 2005: 260; McKeown, 1976).

The US IMR dropped from 11 deaths per 1,000 births in the 1980s to 9 in the 1990s to 7 in 2000 to 5.6 in 2022. Geographically, infant mortality rates in 2022 were highest among states in the South and in the Midwest, with ten states having IMRs in excess of 6.7 (Centers for Disease Control, 2024b). There is also a persistent racial difference in infant mortality. Black infant mortality is the highest of the major race/ethnic groups; non-Hispanic Black infant mortality has declined from under 14 infant deaths per 1,000 live births in 2000 to just over 10.9 in 2022. But Black infant mortality is still more than three times higher than the infant mortality rate of non-Hispanic Asians, which is 3.5 (Centers for Disease Control, 2024b).

Infant mortality in the contemporary world varies considerably from country to country. In general, the higher the income of the country, the lower its IMR. The estimated IMR of the world in 2023 was 29 infant deaths per 1,000 live births. The IMR was 4 in the high-income countries and 45 in the low-income countries (Population Reference Bureau, 2023).

We list in Table 5.4 the six countries with the highest estimated IMRs in 2024 and the six with the lowest.

TABLE 5.4 *Countries with the highest and the lowest infant mortality rates in the world, 2024 estimates*

Highest infant mortality rates		**Lowest infant mortality rates**	
Afghanistan	101.3	Slovenia	1.5
Somalia	83.6	Singapore	1.5
Central African Republic	80.5	Iceland	1.6
Equatorial Guinea	77.4	Monaco	1.7
Sierra Leone	71.2	Norway	1.8
Niger	64.3	Japan	1.9

Source: Central Intelligence Agency, *World Factbook*, 2024.

Afghanistan had the highest IMR in the world in 2024: 101.3 infant deaths per 1,000 live births. Somalia was second with an IMR of 83.6; the next highest IMRs are in the Central African Republic, Equatorial Guinea, Sierra Leone, and Niger. These are astoundingly high levels of infant mortality. Although great success in lowering infant mortality has been achieved in the last century, including in sub-Saharan Africa, these benefits have not been fully realized by the countries just mentioned.

The countries with the lowest IMRs in the world in 2024 were Slovenia and Singapore, both with 1.5 infant deaths per 1,000 live births; Iceland (1.6 infant deaths per 1,000 live births; Monaco (1.7 infant deaths per 1,000 live births); Norway (1.8 infant deaths per 1,000 live births); and Japan (1.9 infant deaths per 1,000 births). It seems likely that IMRs between 1 and 2 are about as low as will ever be attained.

The estimated IMR in the United States in 2024 was 5.1. Although this is certainly low compared with the IMRs in many other countries, it is higher than the IMR both in nearly all high-income and in some lower-income countries. Indeed, according to data from *The World Factbook* produced by the US Central Intelligence Agency (2024), fifty-three countries and territories had estimated IMRs for 2024 lower than that of the United States.

Why was the US IMR higher than the IMRs of these fifty-three other countries? Part of the reason is statistical. The United States counts as a live birth an infant showing any sign of life (see our discussion and definition of a live birth in Chapter 3), whereas many other countries are not as stringent. Dr. Bernadine Healy, the former director of the US National Institutes of Health, argued that it is incorrect to

> compare US infant mortality with reports from other countries. The United States counts all births as live if they show any sign of life, regardless of prematurity or size. This includes what many other countries report as **stillbirth.** In Austria and Germany, fetal weight must be at least 500 grams (1 pound) to count as a live birth; in other parts of Europe, such as Switzerland, the fetus must be at least 30 centimeters (12 inches) long. In Belgium and France, births at less than 26 weeks of pregnancy are registered as lifeless. And some countries do not reliably register babies who die within the first 24 hours of birth. Thus, the United States is sure to report higher infant mortality rates. (Healy, 2006)

However, statistical adjustments that attempt to take into account these differences in definitions still do not move the US IMR to the low levels of Japan and Sweden (Haub and Yanagishita, 1991). Also, if one used only the IMR for the US Anglo (non-Hispanic-White) population, the Anglo IMR would still be twice as high as that of the low IMR countries.

One reason for the United States faring so poorly is the powerful influence of the mother's socioeconomic status on the likelihood of the infant surviving death. The leading cause of infant mortality in high-income countries such as the United States is birth defects, a cause of infant death that can be reduced with good nutritional intake and prenatal vitamins. The next leading cause of infant death, preterm birth, can also be prevented in some cases with adequate health care. Mothers in poverty, however, often lack the socioeconomic resources needed to get adequate care. They also may be forced to forego full prenatal care, which could result in maternal complications at birth, another prime cause of infant mortality. Many countries provide universal health care to the entire population, and many of these countries have lower IMRs than the United States.

In the United States and in most high-income countries, around two-thirds of infant deaths occur in the first month after birth and are due in large part to "health problems of the infant or the pregnancy, such as preterm delivery or birth defects" (Federal Interagency Forum on Child and Family Statistics, 2007: 61). Deaths to infants during the first month of life are frequently analyzed separately from those that occur after the first month but during the first year of life.

Neonatal Mortality Rate and Postneonatal Mortality Rate

The IMR may be thought of as the sum of two rates, namely, the **neonatal mortality rate (NMR)**, that is, deaths to babies of 28 days of age or less per 1,000 live births, and the **postneonatal mortality rate (PMR)**, that is, deaths to babies of 29 days to 1 year of age per 1,000 live births. These two rates are expressed as follows:

$$NMR = \frac{\text{deaths of babies 0 to 28 days old}}{\text{live births in the year}} * 1{,}000 \qquad (5.9)$$

$$PMR = \frac{\text{deaths of babies 29 days to 365 days old}}{\text{live births in the year}} * 1{,}000 \qquad (5.10)$$

According to the WHO (World Health Organization, 2024h), there were 2.3 million neonatal deaths in 2022, which accounted for nearly half of all infant deaths. About 1 million newborns die in the first 24 hours after birth, and most neonatal deaths (75 percent) occur during the first week of life.

The great majority of newborn deaths take place in low- and middle-income countries. According to the WHO (World Health Organization, 2024h):

> In sub-Saharan Africa the risk of death in the first month of life is 11 times higher than that in the lowest-mortality region, Australia and New Zealand. At the country level, NMRs in 2022 ranged from 0.7 death per 1,000 live births to 39.4 deaths per 1,000 live births, and the risk of dying before the 28th day of life for a child born in the highest-mortality country was about 60 times greater than in the lowest-mortality country.

The main but not only causes of neonatal deaths are **endogenous conditions**, "such as congenital malformations, chromosomal abnormalities, and complications of delivery, as well as ... low birthweight" (Pebley, 2003: 534). These are usually related to genetic disorders or the birth process itself, but inadequate prenatal care of the mother and lack of quality health care at the birth also lead to the loss of babies whose lives could have been saved (World Health Organization, 2024h). Research has shown that the endogenous causes dominate infant mortality principally in the early days of life, and not for the entire first month of life (Bouvier and van der Tak, 1976; Poston and Rogers, 1985).

The post neonatal mortality rate (PMR) for the world in 2023 was 11 (UNICEF, 2024). Deaths in the postneonatal period, as well as in the first few years of life, are often due mainly to **exogenous causes**, such as infectious disease, accidents, and injury. In countries experiencing declining death rates, their PMRs tend to decline much more rapidly than their NMRs. The main reason is that "improved living standards, better health care, and public health programs have greater effects on exogenous causes of death than on endogenous causes" (Pebley, 2003: 534). An **exogenous cause of death** is one due mainly to environmental or external factors, such as infections or accidents. By contrast, an **endogenous cause of death** in an infant can occur because of genetic issues or conditions associated with fetal development or the birth process.

Stillbirth Rate

Demographers are also interested in the rate at which **stillbirths** occur. A stillbirth is a fetus not born alive after twenty-eight weeks of pregnancy. It is thus not registered as a death because it was not born. However, stillbirths are often identified in hospital reports dealing with obstetric procedures. A fetus may die prior to the onset of labor, that is, in utero, because of pregnancy complications or various maternal diseases. Or a fetus may be alive at the onset of labor but die during the process and, thus, emerge from its mother in a dead state. The WHO has reported that it "is therefore important to know at what point before birth the [fetus] died, so that appropriate interventions can be planned accordingly.... Where women receive good care during childbirth, [these] deaths represent less than 10 percent of stillbirths due to unexpected severe complications" (2006: 3). The formula for the **stillbirth rate (SBR)**, sometimes referred to as the **fetal death rate**, is the following:

$$\text{SBR} = \frac{\text{stillbirths}}{\text{live births plus stillbirths in the year}} * 1{,}000 \tag{5.11}$$

Not all countries report data on stillbirths, so demographers rely on estimates produced by UNICEF (2023). According to UNICEF, there were an estimated 1.9 million stillbirths in the world in 2021. Worldwide the SBR in 2022 was 13.9 stillbirths per 1,000 live births plus still births (remember that the denominator for the SBR is comprised of live births plus stillbirths). About one in every 72 pregnancies worldwide ended in stillbirth. In the United States there were 21,000 stillbirths in 2021, or about one in every 175 pregnancies (Centers for Disease Control, 2024d).

By far, most stillbirths occur in low-income countries. And almost half of all stillbirths occur when the woman is in labor. The major causes are complications during the birthing process, maternal infections, and maternal disorders, especially diabetes and hypertension. Most stillbirths are preventable, according to the WHO (2015).

Maternal Mortality Ratio

A final measure, the **maternal mortality ratio (MMR)**, gauges the extent to which mothers die immediately before, during, or after giving birth because of a problem or problems associated with the pregnancy or childbirth. The WHO has defined a **maternal death** as "the death of a woman while pregnant or within 42 days of termination of pregnancy, irrespective of the duration or site of pregnancy, from any cause related to or aggravated by the pregnancy or its management, but not from accidental or incidental causes" (Maine and Stamas, 2003: 628). The MMR is the number of deaths in a year to women dying as a result of complications of pregnancy, childbirth, and the puerperium (that is, the condition of the woman immediately following childbirth, usually ending when ovulation begins again), per 100,000 births occurring in the year. Sometimes the deaths (the numerator) are referred to as deaths due to puerperal causes. The formula for the MMR is the following:

$$MMR = \frac{\text{deaths in the year due to puerperal causes}}{\text{live births in the year}} * 100,000 \tag{5.12}$$

Observe that the MMR is multiplied by a constant of 100,000 because since 1940, maternal deaths have become increasingly rare in the high-income countries (Loudon, 1992, 2000). Almost 95 percent of all maternal deaths in 2020 occurred in low and lower middle-income countries, and most of them could have been prevented. (World Health Organization, 2024g). Since 2020, there has been a substantial decline in the MMR, so that even the highest levels are not as high as they were then.

Maternal deaths in earlier centuries were very common, even in Europe and the United States. Reliable data on maternal mortality were not collected in the Western world until the mid-nineteenth century. Loudon has noted that the levels were quite high until the 1930s: "The risk of women dying in childbirth in (England) in the 1920s and 1930s was still as high as it had been just after Queen Victoria came to the throne in the 1850s. Today, however, the risk of women in England and Wales dying is between 40 and 50 times lower than it was 60 years ago" (Loudon, 2000: 241S).

The two most important factors leading to maternal deaths are age and **parity** (the number of times a woman has given birth; it also refers to **birth order**; for example, a second-born child would be a second-parity child). Very young women and older women are more likely to die during pregnancy or childbirth than are women in their twenties and thirties. High-parity women and women with short birth intervals are also at high risk: "Underlying these [factors] are such conditions as chronic disease and malnutrition, poverty, unwanted pregnancies, inadequate prenatal and obstetric care, and lack of access to a hospital" (Lamb and Siegel, 2004: 352).

The WHO (World Health Organization, 2024g) reported that there were an estimated 287,000 maternal deaths in the entire world in 2020. Of these deaths, sub-Saharan Africa accounted for around 70 percent of maternal deaths (202,000), while Southern Asia accounted for around 16 percent (47,000). The MMR for the world for the year 2020 was estimated to be 223 per 100,000 live births (World Health Organization, 2024g). Sub-Saharan Africa was the only region in 2020 with a very high MMR of 545 per 100,000 live births, and the lifetime risk of maternal death there was estimated to be 1 in 40 (World Health Organization, 2023). The WHO has noted, however, that the number of maternal deaths reported for many countries is likely understated owing to the misclassification of maternal deaths, and should be inflated by a factor of around 1.5 (World Health Organization, 2004: 11).

In 2021 in the United States, 1,205 women died of maternal causes compared with 861 in 2020 and 754 in 2019. The maternal mortality ratio for 2021 was 32.9 deaths per 100,000 live births, compared with ratios of 23.8 in 2020 and 20.1 in 2019. What accounts for the US MMR increasing when decreases are noted in other parts of the world? In the United States, although large families have become less common, many more women are delaying childbirth to older ages. In 2021, the MMR for US women older than 40 was 136.5, which was about six times higher than the rate for women under the age of 25 (Hoyert, 2023). In addition, there is a significant racial gap in MMR, with non-Hispanic Black women having much higher ratios than non-Hispanic Whites. We will return to this topic in Chapter 15. Another factor to consider, although other countries also experienced medical disruption, was the effect of COVID-19 upon the provision of all medical care because of the overload of COVID-19 patients and the illness of some medical professionals.

THE FUTURE COURSE OF MORTALITY

Declining mortality has numerous social and economic implications. The efficiency and productivity of the labor force are increased because healthier adults are able to work better and longer. More surviving children translate into more potential and hopefully productive workers. Improved childhood survival often weakens and reduces the importance of some of the social, economic, and emotional rationales for high birth rates. At the same time, declining mortality has the direct effect of increasing rates of population growth, unless fertility rates fall as well; the mortality reductions will thus influence the population's age structure. Owing to these social, economic, and demographic implications, there is considerable speculation about the future levels of mortality (Bongaarts, 2006).

In 1950 the estimated life expectancy for the world was 46 years. In 2024 life expectancy for the world was 73.3 years. This is a dramatic increase in a relatively short period of time. In 2024 there were 17 countries in which life expectancy was 83 years or more, or ten years more than the world average. Will life expectancy continue to rise? There are two positions: One argues for a limit and the other argues against it.

A major advocate for an upper limit to human life expectancy is James Fries, who predicted in 1980 that humans have a maximum potential life expectancy averaging about 85 years (Fries, 1980; see also 1983). In a paper published in 2000, he commented on the increases in life expectancy that have occurred since 1980 when he made his stark prediction of 85 years, noting that life expectancy may increase a little beyond his earlier proclaimed average of 85 years, but not by much.

Jay Olshansky and Bruce Carnes (2001) support the contention of Fries and have noted that all living organisms are subjected to a "biological warranty" period. Arguing against an average life expectancy of, say, 100 years, they have written that "if most humans are capable of living to 100, there should be little evidence of significant functional decline and pathology" of older people today who reach ages older than 80. But they noted that there is no such evidence. Indeed, "there is substantial decline in functioning of all human biological systems by age 80" (Sonnega, 2006: 2). They have also contended that human life expectancy in the United States is not likely to exceed 90 years at any time in this century (Olshansky et al., 2005). Olshansky and his associates (2024) note that the rate of improvement in life expectancy has slowed since 1990, and they conclude that the survival rate to age 100 years is unlikely to exceed 15 percent for females and 5 percent for males.

The major proponent on the other side, proclaiming the real possibility of future and continued mortality declines, is the distinguished demographer James Vaupel. He has observed that every time a maximum life expectancy number is published, it is soon surpassed. He and his colleagues, particularly James Carey, have noted that death rates in human and many nonhuman populations do not continue to increase with increasing age, but that there is a slowing or deceleration of mortality at the oldest ages (Carey, 2003; Carey and Vaupel, 2019; Carey et al., 1992).

Vaupel and his colleague Jim Oeppen have examined what they refer to as "best practice life expectancy" data. They have gathered and graphed data for every year from 1840 to 2000 for the six countries of the world with the highest recorded life expectancy (i.e., Australia, Iceland, Japan, New Zealand, Norway, and Sweden). Their analysis led them to conclude that "the gap between the record [highest life expectancy] and the national level is a measure of how much better a country might do at current states of knowledge and demonstrated practice" (Oeppen and Vaupel, 2002: 1029). They showed that female life expectancy has increased linearly by about three months per year (or 2.5 years per decade) between 1840 and 2000. They have extrapolated from this linear trend and predict that if it continues, the average life expectancy at birth for females could well reach 100 years by the year 2060. Follow-up analyses have been undertaken by Shkolnikov, Jdanov, Andreev, and Vaupel (2011) with rather similar results.

Vaupel and Olshansky have debated for over 20 years whether life expectancies will continue to rise. As Couzin-Frankel (2011: 549) wrote several years ago, they have been "trying to answer a question that is essentially unanswerable: whether the future will resemble the past. Vaupel says it will, with life expectancies at birth rising unabated by about 3 months a year in countries where residents live the longest. Olshansky counters that sober realities, such as widespread obesity, will cut life spans short." Our review of the arguments and the data in an extensive body of literature leads us to conclude against a fixed biological maximum life expectancy. At the global level, life expectancy will probably continue to increase in the decades of this century. Whether life expectancy reaches 100 years is not as important as the expectation that it will not stagnate at just above 85.

In the lower-income countries, there will certainly be increases in life expectancy. Many of these countries still have high rates of infant mortality and general mortality, including maternal mortality. Infectious diseases remain a dominant cause of death in many of these countries. Modern medical and public health techniques can bring about further reductions in mortality from these causes. These countries also have a young age structure, and the young benefit and will continue to benefit from reductions in infectious and parasitic diseases. Consequently, further declines in mortality can surely be expected in many lower-income countries.

Progress in reducing the force of mortality in some countries of the world has stalled and has even reversed direction. This phenomenon of **mortality reversals** is a relatively new occurrence in demography. When Poston first began teaching demography to undergraduate students in 1970, any evidence of significant mortality reversals was for the most part unknown. Demographic transition theory proposed, and it was widely believed, that once death rates in a country began to fall, they would never change direction and start to increase (see our discussion of demographic transition theory in Chapter 2).

Since the early 1980s, however, we have seen more and more evidence of mortality reversals, first in some of the countries of Eastern Europe and later in sub-Saharan Africa. Russia and many of the countries of the former Soviet Union experienced mortality reversals in the 1980s and 1990s. Life expectancy for males in 2000 in Russia was 59 years, below its value of 60 in the mid-1950s. What is causing the mortality reversals in Eastern Europe? Possible factors include the "lack of preventative health programs and inadequate quality of medical services; smoking and alcohol abuse; [and] general neglect of individual health." These were caused by "a lack of life choices under the former Communist regimes, [as well as by] unemployment, relative deprivation, and inability to cope with the economic challenges of post-Communist times" (Shkolnikov, 2003: 677).

In many sub-Saharan African countries, there have been drastic increases in mortality and consequent declines in life expectancy since the mid-1980s. An analysis by Ashford (2006) examined mortality rates in the early years of the 2000–2010 decade for children under age 5 per 1,000 live births for the countries of Lesotho, Namibia, South Africa, Swaziland, and Zimbabwe, along with what the death rates would have been had there been no deaths to children via HIV/AIDS. The differences are striking. The mortality rates for young children are way above what they would have been without HIV. In Swaziland, the rate was 143 deaths to children under age 5, per 1,000 live births, but without the presence of HIV/AIDS, the rate would have been 73. In Lesotho, it was shown that 123 children under age 5 die for every 1,000 births, but without the presence of HIV/AIDS, this rate would have been 71. In sub-Saharan Africa, "one-third of children who are born infected with HIV (transmitted through their mothers) die before their first birthday, and about 60 percent die by age 5" (Ashford, 2006: 2).

The AIDS epidemic has halted or reversed gains in life expectancy in many sub-Saharan African countries: "For example, in Lesotho, where one-fourth of adults were estimated to be living with HIV/AIDS in 2005, life expectancy was nearly 60 years in 1990–1995" (Ashford, 2006: 2), but dropped to 44 for the year 2013 (Population Reference Bureau, 2014). Lesotho's life expectancy should have been approaching 69 years in this decade had the HIV/AIDS epidemic not hit the country. Instead, Lesotho's life expectancy will be considerably lower. The epidemic has taken a devastating toll on these countries.

In the United States, as well, there have been small reversals in life expectancy coming mostly from increased deaths among older teens and young adults. These deaths have been labeled "deaths of despair" because in these relatively healthy young people, death is coming from suicide, overdose, and alcoholic liver disease and violence (Case and

Deaton, 2020). This hypothesis, although controversial, is supported by analysis of ages at death and causes of death (Rogers et al., 2022).

The most notable reversal, which appears to be temporary if tragic, has resulted from the impact of the COVID-19 pandemic. An estimated 21 million persons worldwide died as a result of this disease, and most observers believe that estimate to be conservative.

Degenerative diseases rather than infectious diseases are the major causes of death in high-income countries. Because these diseases take years to develop, death is often postponed until ages after 60. Even the total elimination of a specific degenerative disease, say, heart disease or cancer, would not greatly increase life expectancy.

The increases in life expectancy resulting from the elimination of a specific degenerative disease are small mainly because these diseases occur principally in the older ages. The elimination of one degenerative disease will shift the cause of death from one degenerative disease to another, resulting in a gain in life expectancy of perhaps one or two years. We have already noted that the heart disease and cancer are two of the leading causes of death in high-income countries. If heart disease were eliminated as a cause of death in the United States, life expectancy at birth would increase only by a few years. If cancer were eliminated, life expectancy would increase by only three years (Arias, Heron, and Tejada-Vera, 2013: 5).

This finding illustrates a phenomenon known in demography as the **Taeuber paradox**, named after the demographer Conrad Taeuber, who pointed out many years ago that if a cure is found for one degenerative disease, this will provide the opportunity for death to occur from another. Or, in the words of Nathan Keyfitz, the demographer responsible for attributing the paradox to Taeuber:

> Everyone dies of something sooner or later, so that, when the effects of the eradication of cancer had shaken down, the same number of deaths would occur as before, and the only benefit would be the substitution of heart and other diseases for cancer. A cure for cancer would only have the effect of giving people the opportunity to die of heart disease. [Thus] all that this particular medical advance would do would be to increase the options: one could choose to die of heart disease rather than cancer. (Keyfitz, 1977b: 412; see also Rogers, Hummer, and Krueger, 2005; Rogers et al., 2019)

We close this chapter with a pithy and optimistic observation advanced by Rogers, Hummer, and Krueger (2005: 305):

> The question seems to be not whether mortality will improve in the future, but by how much it will improve, and what age, sex, race/ethnic, socioeconomic and geographical groups will reap the greatest benefits. Overall, continued improvements in health behavior, medical technology, and overall quality of life bode for a generally bright future, most likely with steady but deliberate increases in average length of life accompanied by an increasingly healthy population.

SUMMARY

Mortality is one of the three basic demographic processes and has great impact on families and entire societies. Mortality has systematic regularities by sex, socioeconomic status, race, and education, but by far the most important regularity is by age. Although the crude death rate appears in the demographic equation, it is an unreliable measure for comparisons across time and across geographic areas. The reason is that the age structure of populations has such a major impact on the number of deaths. For this reason, it is important to learn age-specific measures of death and to standardize death rates for purposes of comparison.

The life table is a mathematical model of the effect of a schedule of age-specific mortality rates on a hypothetical population, assuming that those rates persisted indefinitely. Life tables generate life expectancies, which measure how long a person could be expected to live given the assumption of constant age-specific mortality rates. The expectation of life at birth is an especially important indicator of the health of a population.

Infant mortality, or death to infants under the age of one year, has a major effect on life expectancies. Historically, infant mortality was very high. In some countries, infant mortality remains relatively high, with the result that life expectancies in those countries are lower than in countries with lower infant mortality.

In most high-income countries, life expectancy is high and deaths are concentrated among the older population. The causes of death to these older populations – except in the case of epidemics and pandemics – has shifted to chronic and degenerative causes of death.

Demographers have been interested in mortality reversals, which are changes in mortality rates that run counter to the generalizations above. Epidemic causes of death, such as AIDS in Africa or COVID-19, can cause a rise in mortality. Another example is the recent increase in mortality rates among apparently healthy young adults in the United States.

The long-term improvement in mortality rates and therefore in life expectancy is critical to understanding the demographic transition and to describing the health of populations.

DISCUSSION QUESTIONS

1. Death certificates in the United States are usually completed by the funeral director with the assistance of the doctor certifying the death, and sometimes also with the help of a principal member of the decedent's family. In your view, if you had to exclude one of these three persons when filling out the death certificate, the exclusion of which person, in your view, would result in the most amount of possible error in the death certificate; and the exclusion of which person, in your view, would result in the least amount of possible error? Defend your selections.
2. List some of the main reason why the HIV/AIDS virus has spread so rapidly throughout much of sub-Saharan Africa. For each reason, tell why it is important and how it works. Which of the reasons do you hold is the most important? Also, in your view, what measures might be put into place in sub-Saharan Africa to stem the spread of HIV/AIDS?
3. Infant mortality is sometimes analyzed in terms of endogenous and exogenous causes. Explain what is meant by those two terms and give examples. In your opinion, which category of causes is more susceptible to preventive efforts?

6

Internal Migration

INTRODUCTION

In earlier chapters, we discussed two of the three ways that populations change their size. People are added to a population through fertility (Chapter 4) and are subtracted from the population through mortality (Chapter 5). We now turn to the third and last way that populations change their size, namely, **migration**. People may be added to a population by moving into it or subtracted from it by moving away from it. Unlike a birth and a death, which occur to each of us once and only once during our lifetime, migration may occur to us on multiple occasions, or not at all.

There are two main types of migration, namely, within a country and between countries. The former is **internal migration**, and the latter, **international migration**. The dynamics of the two kinds of migration differ significantly, and many of their concepts and theories also differ. Although their theories are more or less governed by "push" and "pull" factors, they differ in their emphasis and focus. In this chapter, we cover internal migration. In Chapter 7, we cover international migration.

Internal migration is the change of permanent **residence** within a country, involving a geographical move that crosses a political boundary, usually a county or county-type geographical unit. Not all changes in residence are migrations. Indeed, demographers distinguish between **movers** and **migrants**. Any person who changes residence, whether the change involves moving across the street or moving from California to Texas, is a mover. A migrant is a person whose residential move involves the crossing of a political boundary. The US Census Bureau defines migration occurring within the United States as residential "moves that cross jurisdictional boundary (counties in particular)" (Mateyka, 2015: 3); if the residential move that crosses a jurisdictional boundary occurs within a country, it is internal migration; if it is a residential move between countries, it is international migration. These definitions of internal and international migration are pretty much the definitions used worldwide. Bear in mind that all migrants are movers, but not all movers are migrants. To be classified as an internal migrant, the mover must cross a jurisdictional boundary, usually a county, when changing residences; if the person moves to a new residence in the same county, they are referred to as a mover, but not as a migrant.

At least once in our lives almost all of us will be migrants. Usually this happens early in our lives, not later. In modern industrialized countries such as the United States, nearly everyone experiences migration. Our dear friend and (now deceased) colleague Leon Bouvier wrote the first edition of this book with Poston. As of 2010, when the first edition was published, Poston and Bouvier had taught demography courses to over eight thousand undergraduate and graduate students in a half-dozen different universities. They found that fewer than a dozen of these students had not yet migrated by the time they took their courses. And, if we broaden the concern from migration to **residential mobility**, Poston and Bouvier remembered teaching only a couple of students who had never ever moved; that is, they had never moved from the homes in which they lived as infants. Residential mobility and migration affect and will continue to affect nearly all of us.

Migration is a significant event not only for people but also for communities. Migration from one area to another has the effect of decreasing the size of the population in the **area of origin** and increasing it in the **area of destination**. Concerning the dynamics of population growth for communities, internal migration is the single most important of the three demographic processes of fertility, mortality, and migration. Differences in birth rates and death rates between communities of the same country are usually small compared with differences between the communities in migration. Migration is the major method for redistributing the population within a country (Bogue, 1969; Poston and Frisbie, 2019).

Let us start with a few facts about movers and migrants in the United States. The US Census Bureau asks questions in the Current Population Surveys and in the American Community Surveys about each household member's current place of residence and whether it has changed in the past year. In the 1950s, around 20 percent of the US population of one year of age or older changed residences each year (Ihrke, 2014). By 2006, the mover rate had fallen to 16.8 percent; it declined a bit more each year, to 13.7 percent in 2019 (Kerns-D'Amore et al., 2023), and to 12.6 percent in 2022 (Ismail, 2023). Of those persons in the United Sates who changed their residences in the one-year period, a little more than half move within their county and a little less than a half move between counties. In the 2021–2022 period, for example, 53.5 percent of the movers changed residences within the same county; these people are movers but are not migrants. Migrants must not only change their residence, but must cross a political boundary, that is, move from one county to another one. And 41.7 percent of people who changed residences between 2021 and 2022 moved to a different county (24.3 percent to a different county in the same state, and 17.3 percent to a different state); the remaining 4.9 percent changed residences between 2021 and 2022 from a different country (Kerns-D'Amore, 2023).

The cumulative effect of this mobility is striking. Census Bureau demographers have estimated that people in the United States can expect to move around eleven or twelve times in their lifetimes. At age 18, a person can expect to move another 8 or 9 times, and by age 45, still another 3 times (US Bureau of the Census, 2015b). The internal migration rates in the United States are comparable to those in Canada and Australia, but they are much higher than those in many other developed countries such as Sweden, Ireland, and Japan. Of course, these latter countries are smaller in size geographically than the United States, Canada, and Australia.

The next sections of this chapter cover the basic concepts and definitions used in analyses of internal migration. We will conclude the chapter with detailed discussions of domestic migration in the United States and of temporary, that is, "floating" migration in China.

CONCEPTS AND DEFINITIONS

Over the years, demographers have developed a standard set of concepts and definitions for studying internal migration. The most basic distinction, as we have already mentioned, is between migration and **local movement**. Local movement refers to the movers who make short-distance changes of residence within the same community, that is, county. Migration is the geographical movement resulting in the permanent change of residence that involves crossing a county boundary, and it typically involves additional changes: in one's school, job, church, doctor, dentist, library, pub, shopping center, nightclub, automobile mechanic, and the other institutional aspects of daily life. By contrast, a local change in residence does not usually involve changing the main institutions in the mover's daily life. "It is customary to define migration as intercounty mobility" because county units, most of the time, "correspond most nearly to the average size of a community" (Bogue, 1969: 756). A person's residential move from one county to another most likely will also involve changes in their institutions of daily life. A migration, but not necessarily a local move, is a sociological event of major magnitude.

A residential move, be it a local move or a migration, is necessarily defined as a "change in permanent residence, typically of a year or more in duration" (Frey, 2003: 545). Most countries have few or no restrictions on the internal movement of their peoples. In the United States, for example, there is a constitutional right to move to wherever we wish and whenever we wish, providing there is no intent to break certain laws, such as trafficking people. However, in China and in a few other countries such as North Korea, internal migration is tightly controlled. In these few countries, therefore, internal migrants are classified as either permanent migrants or as temporary migrants.

A permanent migrant in China is the same as a permanent migrant elsewhere; the migration involves a permanent change in residence and the crossing of a county boundary. The difference in China is that the permanent migration must first be approved by the government. A temporary migrant in China, and in the few other countries where internal migration is heavily controlled, is one whose residential move does not have governmental approval. In other words, the temporary migrant moves without permission. However, although termed temporary the migration is in fact permanent, or relatively permanent. The critical distinction is that this migration has not been officially sanctioned. Later in this chapter, we will discuss in more detail this phenomenon of temporary migration in China, referred to by the Chinese as "floating" migration. It is particularly important in China because its volume is so large.

Other concepts used by demographers in their studies of internal migration are the following: **In-migration** refers to the residential migration of persons to an area of destination; **out-migration** refers to the migration of persons from an area of origin. The **area of origin** is the area or community where the migration began, and the **area of**

destination is the area or community where the migration ended. **Return migration** is the migration of people back to their area of origin at some time after their initial out-migration.

Net migration refers to the migration balance of an area, consisting of the number of in-migrants minus the number of out-migrants; the net balance may be positive (representing a net population gain to the area) or negative (representing a net loss) or, conceivably, zero (Poston, Luo, and Zhang, 2006). Every time we migrate, we are simultaneously an in-migrant and an out-migrant. But we are never net migrants. The concept of net migration applies only to populations and geographic areas, not to individuals. In contrast, the concepts of in-migration, out-migration, and return migration apply to both people and geographic areas.

Like the concept of net migration, several other migration concepts apply only to geographic areas. **Gross migration** is the sum of migration for an area and is comprised of the in-migration into the area plus the out-migration from the area. **Migration efficiency** is an area's net migration divided by its gross migration. Migration in an area may be efficient or inefficient. For example, if there has been a lot of in-migration and little out-migration, that is, most of the migrants have moved in and very few have moved out, then the migration is positively efficient. This is a case with little turnover of people, that is, not much milling around. In contrast, the migration could be negatively efficient if there has been very little in-migration and a lot of out-migration. Migration is inefficient for an area when there are about the same numbers of persons migrating into the area as there are persons migrating out of the area (Shryock, 1964; Thomas, 1941). Consider, for example, a small town that houses a college or a military base. Every year there are likely to be relatively equal numbers of new residents and of former residents who are leaving. This migration is termed inefficient. High negative migration efficiency often characterizes areas of economic hardship, whereas high positive migration efficiency is usually found in areas experiencing economic expansion (Bogue, 1969: 784).

A **migration stream** is a body of migrants departing from a common area of origin and arriving at a common area of destination during a specified time interval. A **migration counterstream** is the migration stream, usually smaller in size, going in the opposite direction during the same time interval.

A **migration interval** refers to the time period during which the migration occurs. Because migration is a process that occurs over time, its analysis requires that time be broken into intervals, so that migration data may be assembled separately for each interval. Time intervals of one year, five years, or ten years are commonly used in demographic studies of internal migration. Irrespective of the length of the intervals chosen by the researcher, they need to be consistent in the analysis: "Two or more sets of migration statistics that have been collected for unequal intervals of time are therefore not fully comparable" (Bogue, 1969: 757).

Differential migration refers to the study of differences in migration according to the demographic, social, and economic characteristics of the population. This is also known as **migration selectivity** and points to the fact that some people are more likely to migrate than others. The strongest selectivity factor associated with both migration and local movement is age: "The incidence of making each kind of move is highest for persons in their early to middle twenties and then declines precipitously during the thirties and forties, with a sometimes small upturn in the early retirement years" (Frey, 2003: 546).

Residential change varies considerably by age. Indeed, the overwhelming importance for residential change of people in the young adult years is striking. Americans aged 18–24 have the highest annual rates of residential change, followed by those aged 25–29. "These ages cover busy points in the life course because several major events (college, employment and marriage) typically occur during these years" (Ihrke, Faber, and Koerber, 2011: 4; Ihrke and Faber, 2012). The percentage rates are the lowest for older people.

Another influential factor in the decision to migrate is education. Among migrants, there is "strong educational selectivity in movement. College graduates, who are likely to be in a national labor market, show higher [migration] rates ... than do those with lesser educational attainment" (Frey, 2003: 546). Homeownership is also important. Homeowners are much less likely to engage in local moves than renters. We will discuss migration selectivity in more detail later in this chapter in the context of domestic migration in the United States.

Many of these concepts are used by demographers in the different ways they measure migration. In the next section, we consider some issues involved in measuring migration.

MEASURES OF MIGRATION

There are inherent difficulties in measuring migration that are not generally encountered when analyzing fertility or mortality. Births and deaths are registered at the time of occurrence, but in most countries the residential move of a person is not. A few countries, for example, China and the Scandinavian countries, require people to register with government officials when they move from one place to another. However, in most countries, including the United States, there are no such requirements. Hence, it is necessary to rely on other types of data for measuring migration.

The US Census Bureau has used two items in its decennial censuses prior to the 2010 census that are now included in the American Community Survey. These are of particular benefit to demographers who use them to measure migration, namely, one's state of birth and one's place of residence five years, or one year, prior to the date of the census or survey. The Census Bureau also uses administrative data, namely, IRS tax return data, for this same purpose. By comparing one's state of birth with one's place of residence at the time of enumeration, it is possible to divide people into the following categories: 1. those living in a given state and born there; 2. those living in a given state but born somewhere else; and 3. those born in a given state but living in some other state.

People in the first category are referred to as nonmigrants, or natives. People in the second and third categories are classified as lifetime migrants. A caveat is needed here. Just because a person was born in Texas and was living there in 2020 does not necessarily mean that the person did not leave Texas between the time they were born and the enumeration date of 2020; the person could have moved from and back to Texas several times between birth and the year 2020. The same caution applies to measuring migration five years prior to the enumeration date.

Data concerning people in these categories can be used to estimate the presence (and size) of migration streams. It is also possible to estimate the proportion of a state's population that was born elsewhere. The "holding power" of a state (or region) can be estimated by calculating the percentage of the people born there who still live there when the survey or census is taken.

Having information about one's residence five years, or one year, before the enumeration date makes possible the determination of the proportion of a state's population that moved into the state within the past five years. People in this category are known as recent migrants.

Measures of migration are usually developed as rates that show empirically the relative frequency of a certain kind of migration. Four of the migration concepts presented above lead directly to rates, and one leads to a ratio, as follows:

$$\textbf{in} - \textbf{migration rate}(\textbf{IMR}) = (I/P) * 1,000$$

$$\textbf{out} - \textbf{migration rate}(\textbf{OMR}) = (O/P) * 1,000$$

$$\textbf{net migration rate}(\textbf{NMR}) = [(I - O)/P] * 1,000$$

$$\textbf{gross migration rate}(\textbf{GMR}) = [(I + O)/P] * 1,000$$

$$\textbf{migration efficiency ratio}(\textbf{MER}) = [(I - O)/(I + O)] * 100$$

where: "I" refers to the number of in-migrants moving into an area during a certain time interval (usually one, or five, or ten years);

"O" refers to the number of out-migrants moving out of an area during a certain time interval; and

"P" is the denominator and refers to the midyear or average size of the population of the area.

Determining the statistically correct denominator in calculating migration rates can be troublesome. Ideally, every individual in the denominator of a rate should have an equal chance to perform the event in the numerator. Obviously, this is not the case with respect to domestic in-migration rates, where, strictly speaking, the denominator should be the entire US population, excluding the resident population in the area of destination. To compare the migration rates more straightforwardly, demographers use as the denominator for all migration rates the resident population of the area for which the rate is being calculated. As indicated, the four rates are usually multiplied by a constant of 1,000, and the migration efficiency ratio by a constant of 100.

Bogue (1969: 758) noted many years ago that the OMR, the out-migration rate, is analogous to the crude death rate, and the IMR, the in-migration rate, is analogous to the crude birth rate. The parallel to the NMR is the rate of natural increase/decrease. These rates may be computed not only for the total population but also for specific subgroups of the population, such as sex groups, age groups, race/ethnic groups, and so forth. They may also be calculated for specific education groups and occupational groups.

We now present examples of these migration measures for a few selected states of the United States.

Table 6.1 presents domestic migration data for California, Nevada, New York, and Texas for the period of 2021 to 2022. The upper panel of the table shows the migration-flow data for each of the four states, and the lower panel, the values of the five migration measures. Between 2021 and 2022, California received 475,803 migrants from other states; for every 1,000 persons in California's population in 2022, over 12 were in-migrants. By comparison, during the same time period, 817,669 persons departed from California for other states, or over 21 persons per 1,000 population. The total number of migrants entering and leaving California during this period, that is, gross migration, was almost 1.3 million. Finally, California lost through migration 341,866 more persons than it gained; that is, between 2021 and 2022, almost 342,000 more persons departed from California for other states of the United States than entered California from other states. California's net migration rate (NMR) was −8.8, indicating that for every 1,000 persons in the population of California in 2022, there was a loss of almost 9 persons through net migration. California's MER was −26.4. For every 100 migrants to and from California during the period, there was a loss of over 26 migrants.

Of the four states shown in Table 6.1, Texas had the highest positive NMR; it gained almost 6 persons through net migration for every 1,000 members of its population in 2022. Of the states shown in the table, New York had the largest negative NMR, losing 12.5 persons during the 2021–2022 period for every 1,000 members of its population.

Regarding migration efficiency, of the four states shown in Table 6.1, Texas reported the highest positive efficiency ratio of 15.1, and New York reported the highest negative efficiency ratio of −28.7. Migration was considerably more efficient in New York than it

TABLE 6.1 *State-to-state domestic migration between 2021 and 2022: California, Nevada, New York, and Texas*

	Migration flows			
State	In-migrants	Out-migrants	Gross migrants	Net migrants
California	475,803	817,669	1,293,472	−341,866
Nevada	127,406	114,131	241,537	13,275
New York	301,461	545,598	847,059	−244,137
Texas	668,338	494,077	1,162,415	174,261
	Migration measures				
State	**IMR**	**OMR**	**GMR**	**NMR**	**MER**
California	12.3	21.2	33.5	−8.8	−26.4
Nevada	40.5	36.3	76.8	4.2	5.5
New York	15.5	28.0	43.5	−12.5	−28.7
Texas	22.5	16.7	39.2	5.9	15.1

IMR = In-migration rate
OMR = Out-migration rate
GMR = Gross migration rate
NMR = Net migration rate
MER = Migration efficiency ratio
Data source: US Bureau of the Census, 2024d. Calculations by DLP.

was in Texas, but in New York the efficiency was negative, and in Texas it was positive. The MER for Nevada was the lowest for the states shown in the table, a ratio of 5.5. In other words, for Nevada there was a lot of coming into and leaving the state, which produced a net gain of only 5.5 persons for every 100 migrants. Migration was considerably more efficient in Texas.

Having discussed the major concepts, definitions, and measures used in the analysis of internal migration, we next focus on internal migration trends and patterns in the United States.

DOMESTIC MIGRATION IN THE UNITED STATES

In Chapter 18 on population distribution, we will note that the major inter-regional flows of internal migrants in the United States have been from east to west and from north to south. During the nineteenth and early twentieth centuries, there was a steady movement urwestward as new areas beyond the Mississippi River were settled. Except for California, migration into the western states diminished during the first half of the twentieth century. Since then, it has accelerated considerably. Between 1970 and 1978, the western region of the United States had a net in-migration of 1.4 million people; that is, 1.4 million more people entered the region than left it. This was sufficient to account for almost half of the population increase in that area during that period.

The southern region of the country has long been an exporter of people, from late in the nineteenth century until well into the 1960s. Long the most underdeveloped and rural area of the nation, the South lagged behind as industrialization surged in the North (Biggar, 1979). The movement from south to north is an excellent example of rural to urban migration. Blacks often left behind limited economic opportunities in rural areas of the South when they moved to the big cities of the North to find jobs (Hamilton, 1964). The adjustment problems facing those migrants were enormous as they tried to adapt to the big-city norms of living. The move also contributed to the development of the urban ghetto and its attendant problems.

We show in Figure 6.1 one-year percentage mover rates from 2006 to 2019 for the total United States and for its four regions. (The states comprising the four regions are shown in Map 6.1.) Viewing the rates from the middle of the figure, the mover rates for the West region are shown in the very top row, followed by the rates for the South. The rates for the United States are next; these are followed by the Midwest rates and by those of the Northeast.

We already noted above that US mover rates have declined in recent years. The national mover rate in 2019 was 13.7 percent; its decline since 2006 is evident in Figure 6.1. Moreover, as we noted above, the rate has declined further to 12.6 percent in 2022 (Ismail, 2023). Another change, although not shown in the figure, is that from 2006 to 2022, the absolute number of movers declined, even though the total population of the United States increased in size; the number of movers dropped from 49.7 million in 2006 to 44.3 million in 2019. The changes from 2006 to 2019 in the regional rates follow the national mover rate. The region with the lowest rates of all the years is the

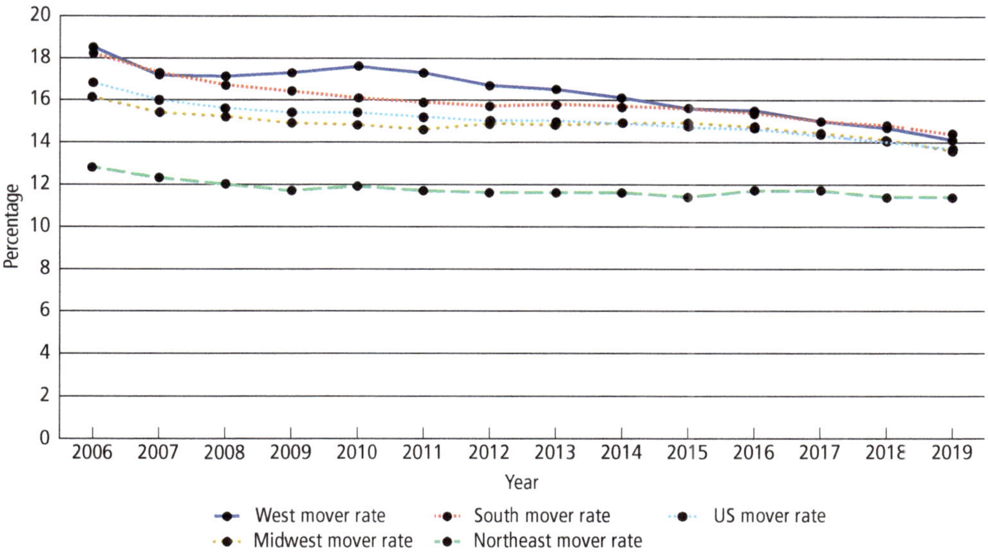

FIGURE 6.1 One-year percentage national and regional US mover rates, 2006–2019
Source: Modified from Kerns-D'Amore et al., 2023.

Northeast. And for most of the years the highest mover rate is found in the West region (Kerns-D'Amore, 2023: 2).

Migration Selectivity

We noted earlier the concept of **migration selectivity**. This refers to the fact that migrants are not all alike. For example, migration is selective based on age, race, sex, and socioeconomic status. We noted earlier that young adults between the ages of 20 and 29 are more likely to move than anyone else. Those between 20 and 29 leave their family homes to seek employment, to join the military, or to attend college. This is also a time when couples marry, which often involves at least one residential move, if not two. The somewhat higher levels of residential movement beyond age 29 differ a bit from previous decades. These days, people are getting married at later ages and frequently relationships break up. Also, more people are switching jobs. The level of residential movement is also high among the very young because children are moving with their parents, who themselves are relatively young. Beginning at around age 40, levels of residential mobility and migration drop considerably. The older the people, the less likely they are to move. There used to be a slight surge around the retirement age of 65, but this trend has not continued in recent years. The lack of an increase in residential mobility at the age of retirement owes in part to the fact that more people these days continue working beyond the age of 65.

Look at, for instance, the experiences of Poston and Sullivan, the two authors of your textbook. Poston did not retire from teaching classes at Texas A&M University until he was 79 years old. And Sullivan did not retire from teaching classes at the University of Virginia until she was 74 years old. Poston and Sullivan were both post-retirement

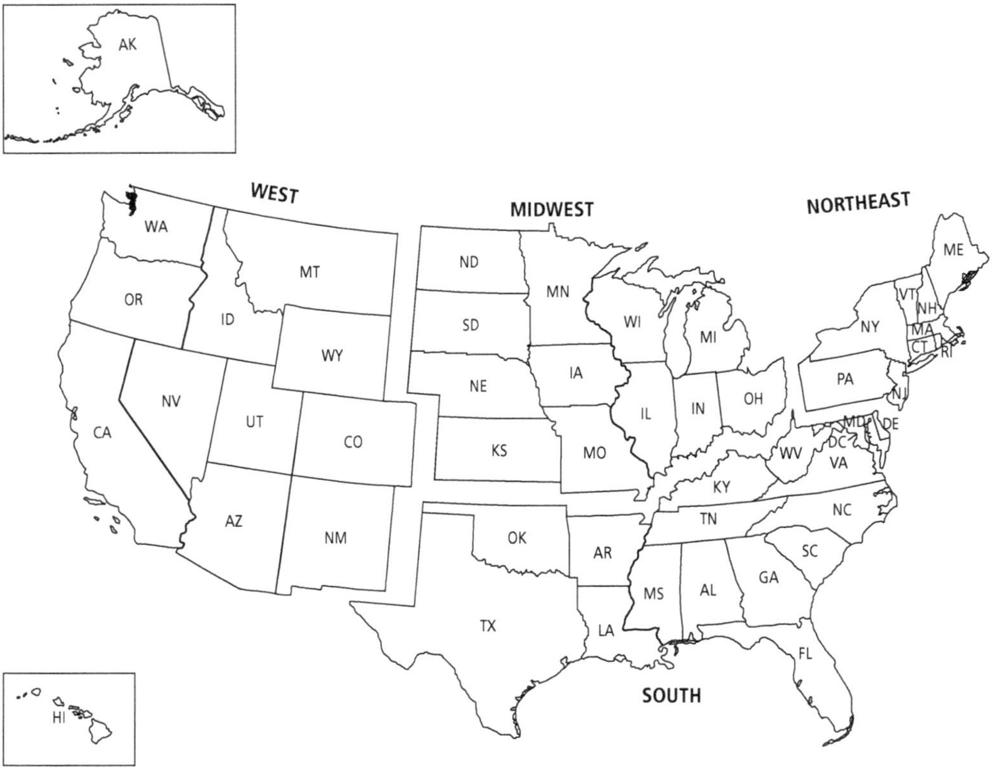

MAP 6.1 US census regions, divisions, and states
Source: US Census Bureau.

migrants, with Poston changing counties within Texas and Sullivan changing states from Virginia to Texas. And our deceased colleague and friend, Leon Bouvier, who coauthored with Poston the first edition of this book, was still teaching his classes at Old Dominion University at the time of his death at the ripe old age of 88. At the time of his death, Bouvier thus was neither a retiree nor a migrant.

Generally speaking, the higher a person's education, the more likely they will be to migrate. Indeed, the farther the move, the stronger the role that education plays in the decision to move. White-collar workers are the most migratory occupational group. Manual workers tend to be as mobile, but their moves are more likely to be local. Farm and service workers are the least mobile occupational group. People not in the labor force have high mobility. This, of course, is attributed in part to the fact that many of them are looking for more economic opportunities for themselves and their families.

A clear example of moving for economic opportunity was the **Great Migration** of African Americans away from the South. A few decades after the end of the Civil War, Black people started to migrate from the South to the Midwest and Northeast and the Pacific Coast. Between 1910 and 1970, over six million Black people moved out of the South. In 1900, almost nine of ten African Americans lived in the South. By 1970, the states of New York, Illinois and California had the most African Americans in the country. As recently as 1965–1970, the number of Black people leaving the South was 2.3 times greater than the number coming into the South.

This migration, however, started to reverse in the early 1970s and turned into a dramatic turnaround. The reversal "began as a trickle in the 1970s, increased in the 1990s, and turned into a virtual evacuation from many northern areas in the first decade of the 2000s. The movement is driven largely by younger, college-educated, and soon to be retiring baby boomer Black people, from both northern and western places of origin" (Frey, 2015: 107). The cities and metropolitan areas of Atlanta, Dallas, and Houston are among the destinations benefitting the most from the reversal. These places "are in the midst of new immigrant growth and white in-migration, which are shaping a region that is welcoming to blacks as well as new immigrant minorities" (Frey, 2015: 107). Of particular interest is the fact that the states that were the destinations of most of the Great Migration migrants, namely, New York, Illinois, Michigan, and California, are now among the several states sending the most Blacks to the South. However, there is one big difference between the migration patterns of those Blacks who participated in the Great Migration and those now participating in its reversal. The Black people who left the South were largely from rural areas, whereas those now migrating to the South are "younger and privileged migrants [who] are moving to a more prosperous and post-civil rights South that was unknown to their forebears" (Frey, 2015: 125).

In summary, migration is not a random event. Certain kinds of people are more likely to move than others; some move short distances and others move long distances. Whatever the nature of the moves, there are certain consequences for the areas involved. We now consider some of them.

Consequences of Domestic Migration

Contrary to fertility and mortality, migration affects two areas: the place of origin and the place of destination. In addition, moving affects the individual lives of movers and non-movers alike. Often, the consequences for the individual migrant differ from those of the aggregate population. For example, with increased immigration to the United States from Latin America into cities not generally prepared for such newcomers, the experience can be difficult for both the newcomers and the longtime residents of the cities. Allow us now to consider some of these influences at both the origin and the destination.

One way that migration affects the area of origin is by reducing its potential for population growth. This usually happens in two ways. People who move out of an area represent negative entries in the demographic equation that we discussed earlier in Chapter 1. (We show in Box 6.1 how to use the demographic equation that was discussed earlier in Chapter 1 to estimate net migration.) This loss may at least partially compensate for any reproductive increase that occurs. However, as we have already mentioned, those who move out of an area tend to be in the young childbearing ages, which thus tends to reduce the reproductive potential of the population at origin.

Until very recently, most large cities and states in the United States owed their population declines to out-migration, and not to an excess of deaths over births.

Box 6.1 Estimating Net Migration

In Chapter 1 in formula (1.1), we presented the demographic equation:

$$P_2 - P_1 = (B - D) + (I - O)$$

Suppose for the area you are studying you only have information about the size of its population at two points in time and the number of births and deaths that occurred in the area in the interval between the two points in time. Using the above equation, here is how you would use the population size and vital statistics data to estimate the amount of net migration for the area:

$$(I-O) = P_2 - P_1 - (B-D)$$

P_1 is the population size at an earlier date (T_1)
P_2 is the population size at a later date (T_2)
B is the number of births that occurred during the interval between T_1 and T_2
D is the number of deaths that occurred during the interval between T_1 and T_2
I is the number of in-migrants that entered the area between T_1 and T_2
O is the number of out-migrants that left the area between T_1 and T_2
B - D = natural increase/decrease; I - O = net migration; thus,
Net migration = population growth minus natural increase/decrease

However, as noted earlier this dynamic is changing as more areas in the United States are beginning to be characterized by more deaths than births. For instance, in each of the three years of 2020 to 2022, deaths exceeded births in 22 of the US states. It is the case that part of this increase in deaths was due to the COVID-19 epidemic. But "many of the demographic factors contributing to rising mortality and declining fertility predate the pandemic, so deaths will continue to exceed births in some states in the near term and in more states in the future" (Johnson, 2023: 1; Johnson, Field, and Poston, 2015).

The area of origin is affected as well by the type of people who migrate. The question of who migrates depends in part on whether migration is a response to push or pull factors. Migrants responding to pull factors at the place of destination tend to be positively selected, and migrants responding to push factors in the place of origin tend to be negatively selected. That is, for instance, migrants responding to pull factors tend to be of higher socioeconomic status than those responding to push factors.

Regarding the area of destination, migration tends to increase the population in two ways, directly and indirectly. The net number of in-migrants constitutes the direct effect. The number of children born to the in-migrants after their arrival is the indirect effect. The magnitude of the direct effect depends on the relative size of the migrant and the receiving populations. For instance, adding ten people via in-migration to Harris County, Texas (the third largest county in the United States with a 2020 census population of over 4.7 million), has far less of an impact on the area of destination than adding ten people to Loving County (a county in West Texas with a 2020 census population of 64, the least populous county in the United States).

The magnitude of the indirect effect depends on the relative levels of reproductive behavior of the migrants and the receiving population. If the in-migrants have more children than those already living in the area of destination, then there will be a larger impact on that area.

Each person added to the population means an additional individual who must be fed, clothed, housed, educated, transported, and given at least occasional medical care. Massive in-migration can put a severe strain on the receiving area to deliver these services. This is particularly true if the original population size of the area is relatively small. The extent to which the strains become real problems depends on the socioeconomic characteristics of the in-migrants and the extent to which the labor force can absorb them.

In-migration affects the size of the labor force in two ways. First, because of the (usually) younger age composition of the migrants, in-migration may increase the ratio of the economically active persons to the total number of persons. To be sure, there are exceptions, especially in retirement areas where the rapid growth of the elderly population presents special issues. Second, within the same age categories, the in-migrants may have higher rates of labor-force participation than the receiving population. Both these effects depend on the socioeconomic characteristics and the occupational skills of the in-migrants.

When people with different cultural and linguistic backgrounds migrate to a particular site, some cultural heterogeneity may develop. Cultural factors certainly have an impact on the tolerable levels of in-migration. Only a certain number of newcomers can be absorbed without the risk that the receiving population feels their social institutions and value systems to be threatened. We turn now to the impact of migration on the individual migrant.

Impact on the Individual Migrant

One important consequence for the migrant is the opportunity to live in an environment with the social, economic, political, or physical characteristics that they believe to be preferable to those of the old environment. Whether or not this is the case depends on the accuracy of the migrant's perceptions of the circumstances in both the old and the new environments, as well as the migrant's ability to use the advantageous features of the new environment. The latter, in turn, depends on whether the migrant possesses useful skills, and how rapidly they are assimilated into the prevailing culture.

In general, the difficulty that migrants experience in being acculturated depends on how different they are from the receiving population. Nonwhite groups (and here we are referring to Black people, Hispanic people, and Asian people) have found it more difficult to be "accepted" into mainstream American life than their White counterparts. Some are now beginning to be accepted by the whole of society, but this is not yet the case in some isolated heavily White areas.

While immigrants to America perhaps face more daunting problems, the native-born individuals moving within the country must also adapt to new situations as they join the residents of a new urban or rural area or leave the Northeast for the South or the West. Customs vary from region to region, and some "assimilating" is usually necessary if a newcomer needs to adjust to the unfamiliar surroundings. Despite the "nationalization" emanating from television and the Internet, many Americans still "speak funny" to other Americans.

In the preceding pages, we have discussed various aspects of domestic migration in the United States. We turn now to a consideration of domestic migration in China, particularly the so-called temporary internal migration.

TEMPORARY ("FLOATING") MIGRATION IN CHINA

Unlike the process of internal migration in most countries, "migration" in China is not defined merely as changing a residence from one location to another while crossing a geographical (county-level) boundary. To be allowed to migrate in China, one must first obtain permission to officially transfer their household registration (known in Chinese as the *hukou*) from the origin location to the destination location. People in China who move without permission are known as "floaters." These are people "who have crossed over some territorial ... boundary, [who] have not altered their permanent registration (*hukou*), and, [who] at least in theory, 'flow in and out'" (Solinger, 1999: 15; see also Zhou and Zhong, 2022; Poston and Zhang, 2008; Liang and Ma, 2004; and Poston and Mao, 1998). In China, thus, there are two types of internal migration: a move that is an officially permitted permanent change in the person's place-of-household registration; and a move with no such official sanction.

In 1948, China enacted the *hukou*, or household registration system. Urban residents were entitled to subsidized housing, social insurance, medical care, and, for the most part, employment. These rights and entitlements were denied to those holding rural *hukous*. In the late 1970s, Deng Xiaoping, the Chinese leader who succeeded Mao Zedong, established the economic reforms that changed the *hukou* controls. At about the same time, the state relaxed the rules; for instance, these days, one no longer needs coupons to buy grain in stores in China's cities. The economic reforms also resulted in a tremendous requirement for workforce in the cities in low-level construction and manufacturing jobs and, more recently, in many kinds of household service and related jobs. Concurrently, the incentives of Deng's so-called Household Responsibility System, whereby a household can keep much of what it produces, resulted in the release of many millions of farmers who in the past, during the communal regime, were inefficiently employed in agriculture (see Nolan, 1991; and Oi, 1999). There has existed in China for the past several decades a huge agricultural labor surplus that continues to grow because of the implementation of technology that increases even further the efficiency of agriculture.

So, what happens to this agricultural labor surplus? Much of it ends up migrating to the cities to the newly available low-level construction, manufacturing, and household service jobs; these migrants are the so-called **floating migrants**. The bulk of them are absorbed in the construction sector; others find jobs in manufacturing, services, and light manufacturing: "The predominance of construction jobs is one reason men migrate more often than women. In areas where light assembly jobs dominate, however, female workers ... outnumber males ..." (World Bank, 1997: 55; Chan, 2021).

The size of the floating population in China is enormous. Around 221 million floaters were counted in the 2010 census, there were an estimated 250 million floaters in 2012, and the 2020 census enumerated 376 million floaters. Of these 376 million floating migrants, over 88 percent of them migrated to big cities and towns. Guangdong

Province in southern China contains more than one-quarter of all the floaters, even though the province only contains around 7 percent of the country's population. Beijing and Shanghai, China's two principal cities, each has many million floaters in their populations (Zhou and Zhong, 2022). The growth of the floating population in Beijing has pretty much paralleled the growth of the floating population in the entire country (Poston and Duan, 2000). In Beijing in the early 1950s, the floating population was very "efficiently controlled" and, hence, small. But by the late 1980s, the number of floaters had reached more than 1.3 million, and by 1994 almost 3.3 million, or almost one-third of its population then of about 11 million. By 2000 the official number was 2.6 million, and it reached over 7 million by 2010 (Liang, Li, and Ma, 2014). And as noted above, Guangdong Province, in southern China, had over a quarter of all the floaters in 2020.

Who are the floating migrants? They are mainly young and unmarried males and females seeking employment in blue-collar, service, and household jobs. According to the World Bank (1997: 55), the "average [floating] migrant is less educated than the general population but more educated than the rural population. Few [floating] migrants come from the ranks of the absolute poor, who lack even the few years of schooling and basic Mandarin [Chinese language] required for most migrant jobs" (see Yang, 1994, 1996). The internal migration of floaters to China's cities constitutes the largest stream of peacetime mobility in recorded human history (Roberts, 1997). This is the main reason why this particular migration is so important.

But there is another reason. Many floaters could become international migrants and leave China, mainly as undocumented migrants. Here is how and why this might happen. The floating migrants in China's big cities earn wages that are several times greater than the wages earned by persons in their home villages in the rural areas, and they send as much as half of their salaries back to their home villages. This occurs even though the floaters' wages are quite a bit less than those of the permanent urban workers, as much as 20 to 40 percent less. In the rural counties of some provinces (e.g., Sichuan and Anhui Provinces), urban remittances from floaters account for almost half of household cash income (World Bank, 1997: 56–57).

If and when the floaters are unable to find jobs, or lose their jobs, in the cities of China, some may well look elsewhere, likely outside China, where there are jobs and where there are already established Chinese networks. In future years, there likely will be more rural surplus workers in China, as well as more floaters. Moreover, indications point to increases in unemployment in China's cities in the future. Many years ago Liang (2001: 693) wrote that the "likelihood of competition for jobs between internal migrants [i.e., the floaters] and unemployed workers [among the permanent residents of the cities] is clear ... Some members of the floating population and unemployed workers [may be pushed] onto the market for illegal transnational migration." His observations are still relevant today.

When floaters lose their jobs in the Chinese cities, some will not wish to return home to their rural villages, to which they have been sending remittances. Returning home unemployed would result in tremendous embarrassment and loss of "face." Many floaters may well look elsewhere, most likely outside China, to countries such as the United States, and many European countries. It is not inconceivable that there could well be many millions of floaters looking for jobs outside China in the next decade. The prominent demographer Douglas Massey has written that "China's movement towards markets and rapid economic growth may contain the seeds of an enormous migration . . . that would produce a flow of immigrants [to the United States] that would dwarf levels of migration now observed from Mexico" (1995: 649).

It is our belief that the United States, in particular, could be a popular destination for the floaters. In 2019 an estimated 4.4 million Chinese lived in the United States (Budiman and Ruiz, 2021). The Chinese in the United States form a potent interest group to China. Their ties could well draw several million floaters to Chinese American enclaves in Texas, California, and elsewhere in the United States. What might such a shift of human resources mean for Americans? "Opponents of immigration – including, understandably, jobless American workers – may not welcome more foreign newcomers. Nevertheless, established immigration networks anchored by longstanding family ties to particular destinations in Texas, California, New York, and other states will facilitate their arrival, surreptitiously or otherwise" (Poston and Morrison, 2011).

SUMMARY

Migration is a permanent shift of residence of such duration and distance that it results in changes in the physical and social environment. It is usually measured as a change of residence across political boundaries, generally between counties. We showed in this chapter that there is a great deal of geographic mobility in the United States, much of it created by people who move repeatedly. On average, every year one person in seven or eight changes residence. One person in twenty-five migrates by moving from one county to another. Until about 1950, a large part of the interregional migration was from east to west and south to north. Since then, the latter flow has reversed. Both White people and Black people are now moving into the South.

There are marked differences among those who migrate in terms of age, race, and socioeconomic status. Young adults are the most likely to move, as are young children, who move with their parents. Whites are more likely to migrate than Blacks, although the latter move locally more often. There is a positive relation between education and the possibility of moving: The better educated tend to migrate more often than the less educated.

In this chapter, we also considered the case of internal migration in China, where population movement is tightly controlled by the government. This is referred to as temporary, or floating, migration. Floating migrants are not expected to remain permanently in their areas of destination even though, in fact, most do. In 2020, there were around 376 million floating migrants in China. There are more floating migrants living in China than there are people living in the United States.

Migration is seldom explained in terms of the characteristics of only one place or factor. In any move, a decision has been reached that the area of destination offers advantages that outweigh the disadvantages of moving. Generally, it may be stated that people move "to better their lot" in life. This is happening today and will continue to happen if people believe that opportunities and living conditions are better elsewhere. Humankind is indeed peripatetic and will most likely always be so.

DISCUSSION QUESTIONS

1. Look at the discussions in this chapter and elsewhere of current patterns of internal migration in US cities; you will see that some are increasing in size, others are decreasing in size, and still others are neither growing nor declining. Then gather from the webpage of the US Census Bureau or some other organization some current data on three US cities and their migration patterns; one should be characterized by positive net migration, another by negative net migration, and a third by neither positive nor negative net migration. How do these three cities differ occupationally and economically? What might be the long-term and short-term consequences for these three cities? What would you as a demographer recommend to the leaders of these cities that they might do in the next few decades to maintain or change these demographic trends?
2. In this chapter we have noted that internal migration in a country is the geographical movement resulting in the permanent change of residence that involves crossing a political, often a county, boundary; it typically involves additional changes, in the migrant's school, job, church, doctor, dentist, library, pub, shopping center, nightclub, automobile mechanic, and other institutional aspects of daily life. Write a long paragraph about a recent internal migration of yours or of a friend. Where did the migration start and where did it end? In addition to this residential change, list a half dozen or more of the additional changes that occurred, as a consequence of the migration, in your daily life or in that of your migrant friend. Which one of these changes was the most important for you/your friend? Which one was the least important?

7

International Migration

INTRODUCTION

The first "international" migration of humans began around 60,000 years ago, and the migrations continue to this day (Busby, 2016; Gugliotta, 2008). Of all the demographic topics presented in this book, none is discussed these days by both laypeople and social scientists as frequently and as forcefully as international migration. **International migration** is migration that occurs between countries. Its dynamics differ from those of internal migration, that is, migration within the geographical boundaries of a single country (see Chapter 6). Thus, a separate chapter is devoted here to international migration.

We begin this chapter by considering some of the definitions and concepts used in the study of international migration. We next cover world immigration patterns over time. This is followed by a discussion of immigration to the US. We then consider some of the positive and negative economic issues pertaining to international migration. Considerations of legal and unauthorized immigration are next reviewed. We conclude the chapter with a discussion of the meaning of the concept of zero net international migration.

DEFINITIONS AND CONCEPTS

Similar to their study of internal migration, demographers have developed a fairly standard set of concepts and definitions for studying international migration. The first distinction is between **immigration** and **emigration. Immigration** refers to the movement of people *to* a new country for the purpose of establishing permanent residence; an **immigrant** is a person who moves to a new country to reside there and crosses an international boundary in doing so. These concepts are analogous in the study of internal migration to in-migration and in-migrant. Conversely, **emigration** refers to the permanent departure of people *from* a country; an **emigrant** is one who migrates away from a country with the intention of establishing a permanent residence elsewhere. The analogous internal migration concepts are out-migration and out-migrant.

In every international migration, a migrant is simultaneously an immigrant and an emigrant. The key element in the definition of an immigrant is the establishment of a permanent residence in the new country. This usually means residence in the destination country for at least one year and is referred to as **long-term immigration**. The number of long-term immigrants in the world has increased considerably in recent decades, from 75 million in 1965, to 120 million in 1990 (Martin, 2001), to 232 million in 2013 (United Nations, 2013b; 2013c), to 281 million in 2020 (International Organization for Migration, 2024). Approximately 3.6 percent of the world's population in 2020 was comprised of long-term immigrants. Although this is a relatively small percentage, it is a very large number, namely, 281 million persons. To provide some context, this number rivals the combined populations of Russia (144.8 million), the United Kingdom (69.1 million), and Italy (59.3 million) in 2024.

Remigration refers to the migration of international migrants back to their original countries of origin. A **remigrant** is an international migrant who moves back to and re-establishes permanent residence in their original country of residence. Sometimes international migrants return to their countries of origin in the later years of their lives; see the last section of this chapter. Say, for example a person leaves China and moves to the United States. This person is an emigrant from China and an immigrant to the United States. If at some later point in time the person decides to leave the United States and move back to China, we would refer to them as a remigrant. The analogous concept with respect to internal migration is return migrant.

We have already noted that international migration is the permanent movement of people from one country to another. International migrants are distinguished from **tourists** and visitors because tourists and visitors return home without establishing permanent residence in the destination country. People who travel to a foreign country as tourists, or to work for a short period, say as diplomats, are not regarded as international migrants (Münz, 2003). This demarcation, however, is not always an easy one to make in practice.

Immigrants in past decades to the major destination countries of the world (e.g., the United States, Russia, Germany, Saudi Arabia, the United Arab Emirates, and the United Kingdom, among other countries) may be grouped into four broad categories: refugees/asylees; migrants from former colonies; economic migrants; and "ethnic privileged" migrants (Münz, 2003).

A **refugee** or an **asylee** is one who involuntarily emigrates from his or her native country because of persecution, threat of violence, or extreme deprivation, often going to a neighboring country. **Postcolonial migration** began in the 1950s owing to the decolonization of mainly southern nations. Indigenous peoples moved from former colonial countries to the European countries that had colonized them to pursue better living conditions or to escape political persecution.

Economic migrants are voluntary migrants motivated by economic aspirations; this flow is more likely to occur from lower-income to the higher-income countries; the latter group of countries typically includes the United States and Canada, all the countries of Europe, plus the countries of Australia, New Zealand, and Saudi Arabia. Most international migration is economically motivated. Of the 281 million long-term immigrants in the world in 2020, around two-thirds of them resided in high-income countries (United Nations, 2013b).

Ethnic privileged immigrants are entitled to immigrate because they are ethnically similar to the people of the destination country.

Massey presents a slightly different set of international migrant categories, on the basis of whether the migration is voluntary or involuntary, and whether the migrants "are well or poorly endowed with human capital" (2003: 549).

Most people of the world never engage in international migration; "most live and die near their place of birth" (Martin and Zurcher, 2008: 3). Of the 3.6 percent of the world's population who are immigrants, about 12 percent are considered to be refugees (United Nations Department of Economic and Social Affairs [UNDESA], 2020). Those people who do engage in international migration often move between countries that are geographically close together. For the United States, this means that most immigrants come from Mexico and Central America. Some countries, however, attract migrants from longer distances. For instance, many international migrants to Germany hail from Turkey, a country around 1,500 miles away from Germany.

More recently, a large number of migrants have entered the United States from Asia. In 2021, Mexico was the birth country of the largest number of immigrants (150,000 people), followed by India (145,000 people) and China (90,000 people) (Moslimani and Passel, 2024). Even though China is geographically distant from the United States (over 7,000 miles away), making migration difficult and expensive, the push and pull factors of China and the United States are strong (Cortes and Poston, 2008; Poston and Luo, 2007).

According to the United Nations Department of Economic and Social Affairs (UNDESA, 2020) in 2019, roughly half of the international migrants in the world resided in just ten countries (see Table 7.1). Fully two-thirds of them resided in the largest twenty receiving countries. The largest number, about one-fifth of all the international migrants in the world by 2023, resided in the United States (Moslimani and Passel, 2024). The data shown in Table 7.1 indicate that the United States has received more immigrants than any other country in the world.

TABLE 7.1 *Top ten countries in 2019 with the largest number of foreign-born residents (immigrants)*

Country	# Immigrants
United States	50.6M
Germany	15.8M
Saudi Arabia	13.5M
Russia	11.6M
United Kingdom	9.4M
United Arab Emirates	8.7M
France	8.5M
Canada	8M
Australia	7.7M
Spain	6.8M

Source: UNDESA, 2020.

Table 7.1 refers to the **stock** of immigrants, meaning all those residing in the country regardless of the time at which they immigrated. In the case of the United States, this stock of immigrants represents decades of immigration. The **flow** of immigration refers to the immigration occurring within a specific time frame. In the period 2023–2024, for example, immigration was the driving change in population growth in the United States. The 2.8 million people entering the country in this time period accounted for 84 percent of the country's population increase in this time frame (US Bureau of the Census, 2024c). In 2022, about 1.6 million new immigrants entered the United States (Moslimani and Passel, 2024).

The COVID-19 epidemic caused a downturn in the flow of immigrants to most countries. Nevertheless, in 2020 some other countries with large numbers of international migrants were Germany with 15.8 million, Saudi Arabia with 13.5 million, and Russia with 11.6 million (UNDESA, 2020).

PATTERNS OF WORLD IMMIGRATION OVER TIME

The residential movement of large numbers of people spanning great distances goes far back into human history, way before the beginning of the establishment of nations and the creation of national boundaries. The first "modern" humans emerged in sub-Saharan Africa, as many as 195,000 years ago, and lived in Africa for the first two-thirds of their history. By 35,000 years ago, humans "thrived at opposite ends of Eurasia, from France to Southeast Asia and even Australia" (Goebel, 2007: 194). One of the greatest "untold stories in the history of humankind" is how humans went about colonizing "these and other drastically different environments during the intervening 160,000 years" (Goebel, 2007: 194). Humans began to migrate out of Africa around 50,000 to 60,000 years ago, first to southern Asia, China, and Java, and later to Europe. Evidence suggests that humans began migrating to the Americas around 14,000 years ago ("Before the Exodus," 2008: 101; Goebel, Waters, and O'Rourke, 2008; Meltzer, 2009). These "first Americans used boats, and the [west] coastal corridor would have been the likely route of passage ... Once humans reached the Pacific Northwest, they ... continued their spread southward along the coast to Chile, as well as eastward, ... possibly ... to Wisconsin" (Goebel, Waters, and O'Rourke, 2008: 1501).

Years later, movements were often across land areas and over short sea routes. The migration of a population was often preceded by an invasion of its armies. Sometimes the invaders would occupy the new lands permanently, perhaps intermarrying with the subdued population. The Norse peoples from Scandinavia illustrate this principle. They carried out numerous raids in Europe until the ninth century and then settled in England, Ireland, and France, where they were known as Normans. Occasionally the invaders would occupy the new lands only briefly, and later return to their original territory, leaving some of their members in the occupied region. Prior to the 1400s, many of the international migrations leading to the invasion and conquering of new territory did not involve oceanic crossings. The invasions of the Mongols in the fourteenth century, led by Tamerlane, seeking to conquer all of Eurasia, were the last time in human history when massive international migrations and invasions did not cross oceans. Thereafter, international migrations/invasions were transoceanic (Darwin, 2008).

Sometimes the international migrations/invasions were accompanied by the enslavement of the defeated peoples and their **forced migration** to the land of the conquerors.

For example, a single Roman military campaign could bring in as many as 50,000 prisoners. During the height of the Roman Empire, the population of Rome likely reached 1 million people, many of whom were slaves who had immigrated involuntarily. Earlier, during the fifth century BC, the population of Athens included between 75,000 and 150,000 slaves, from both Africa and Asia, representing around 25 to 35 percent of the population (Davis, 1974: 95).

Exploration also played a role in the dynamics of human migration in the thirteenth century from China, and in the fifteenth and sixteenth centuries from Europe. Zheng He, Marco Polo, Columbus, Magellan, and others led large naval expeditions to other parts of the world both to satisfy the curiosity of their governments, and to explore parts of the world unknown to them. They brought back treasures and stories about the new lands. Some settled in the new parts of the world then and later. For example, the Portuguese started colonies in Africa; the Spaniards, English, Dutch, French, and Swedish in the Americas; the Chinese in Southeast Asia; and the English in Australia and New Zealand (Davis, 1974; Dreyer, 2007; Menzies, 2003).

The greatest period of European migration overseas occurred between 1840 and 1930 when around 52 million people emigrated from European countries, primarily to North America. This number equaled around one-fifth of the population of Europe in 1840 and exceeded the number of Europeans already abroad after more than 300 years of settlement (Davis, 1974: 98). Haines (2003) has estimated that the transatlantic migration stream from Europe to the Western Hemisphere, from the beginning of colonization around 1500 until 1940, numbered 60 million and was "the greatest and probably the most consequential population movement in modern human history" (2003: 942).

Compared with the massive movements out of Europe, intercontinental migration from Asia before World War II was not quite as large. Asian Indians went to such places as Guyana, East Africa, Fiji, Mauritius, and Trinidad. Japanese and Filipino migrants went to Hawaii, and some Japanese settled in Brazil. Many Chinese migrated to the United States (Poston, Mao, and Yu, 1994).

Intercontinental migration from Africa differed from the preceding movements. The mass outpouring of Africans to other continents was mostly involuntary. Around 9.6 million enslaved Africans were taken to North and South America and the Caribbean islands between 1650 and the nineteenth century, when slavery was abolished. During these sea voyages, mortality was high, with as many as 25 percent who began the voyage dying before reaching the Americas. Thus, the total number of Africans taken from Africa was likely well over 11 million. This was the largest slave migration in recorded human history in terms of distance and numbers moved (Curtin, 1969).

These massive migrations have had a number of consequences for the world. World population increased after 1750 partly because emigration relieved the pressures of the population on land and resources in the origin countries, postponing a change in birth and death rates. In general, the greater the rate of emigration from a European country, the later the decline of its birth rate. In France, a country with low levels of emigration during this period, the birth rate began to fall as early as the mid-eighteenth century. Conversely, in Italy, a country with sizable levels of emigration, a significant fertility decline did not occur until early in the twentieth century. In the countries of destination, the immigrants often exhibited high birth rates. Indeed, some of the highest birth rates ever recorded were in French Canada in the latter part of the seventeenth century. Crude birth rates were as high as 65 per 1,000 among some of the immigrant groups to the New World (Bouvier, 1965; Sabagh, 1942).

Another consequence of these international migrations was the geographic redistribution of the global population. Between 1750 and 1930, the population of the main destination areas of European emigrants increased in size by fourteen times, while the population of all the other areas of the world was a little more than doubled. In 1750, these areas of destination of European emigrants comprised less than 3 percent of the population of the world; by 1930 they comprised 16 percent. The geographic distribution of the races also changed dramatically. By 1930 about one-third of all Whites no longer lived in Europe, and more than one-fifth of all Black people no longer lived in Africa (Davis, 1974: 99).

There have been several major international migration movements since the 1930s and the period of unrest preceding World War II to the present. Most of these migrants were refugees and asylum seekers. First, during Adolf Hitler's rise to power in the 1930s, large numbers of Jews and political refugees fled Germany. At the end of World War II, there were compulsory large-scale transfers of the European population as a result of repatriation. The uprooting of more than 20 million Eastern and Central Europeans via flight, expulsion, transfer, or population exchange represented a drastic solution to the presence of ethnic minorities in these regions (Bouvier, Shryock, and Henderson, 1977).

Second, after the end of World War II, about 3 million Japanese were returned by decree to Japan from other Asian nations. Third, in 1947 after the partition of India and Pakistan, more than 7 million Muslims fled from India to Pakistan, and a comparable number of Hindus, from Pakistan to India. In the Punjab area of Pakistan alone, the refugees who fled made up more than two-thirds of the population.

Fourth, in 1948, thousands of Palestinians were displaced from the territory that is now Israel. Israel is the classic example of an immigrant country drawing a population from dozens of other countries. The United States is another such example; indeed the US is the *ne plus ultra* of immigrant nations.

Fifth, in the 1970s, millions of South and Southeast Asians were uprooted owing to political and economic upheavals, resulting in one of the largest and most tragic refugee migrations in history. In 1971, 10 million refugees migrated from what had been East Pakistan (now Bangladesh) to northern India. Subsequently, millions of Asians escaped from Cambodia, Vietnam, and Laos into Thailand and elsewhere (Patrick, 2003).

Sixth, an often-overlooked international migration is that involving refugees fleeing Afghanistan following the Soviet invasion in 1979. More than forty years of conflict have generated both internal and international migration. There were as many as 6.5 million Afghan refugees between 1988 and 1991, and another 5 million from the early 1990s to 2000. By the early part of the twenty-first century, it is estimated that one in four Afghans were refugees (Patrick, 2003: 827). In 2023, the United Nations estimated that there were 2.2 million Afghan refugees registered in Iran and Pakistan alone. Another 3.22 million people were internally displaced by the end of 2023, having fled their homes in search of refuge within Afghanistan (UNHCR, 2024).

The modern refugee era began at the end of the Cold War in around 1991, when "many, mostly developing countries found themselves embroiled in often violent conflicts after they lost support of their superpower backer" (Patrick, 2003: 827). Several million additional refugees resulted from the US invasion of Iraq in 2003. The numbers of refugees and asylum seekers are astoundingly high.

The United Nations High Commissioner for Refugees (UNHCR) estimated that the number of displaced persons in 2023 was 11.7 million persons, an 8 percent increase from 2022. New refugee streams contained Sudanese, Venezuelans, and Palestinians. Not all displaced persons are refugees as the United Nations reports them. Another growing source of displacement is natural disasters and climate change. Displaced persons may become refugees, but some also leave their homes to seek a place of refuge within their country (UNHCR, 2023).

IMMIGRATION TO THE UNITED STATES

Nearly all the current residents of the United States, more than 97 percent, are immigrants to the US or are the descendants of immigrants to the US. In 2020, only 8 million people, or just about 2.4 percent of the population, identified themselves only as American Indians, Alaska Natives, or Native Hawaiians or as one of these identities in combination with other identities (Sánchez-Rivera, Jacobs and Spence, 2023). These groups are not considered to be immigrants. The American Indians are by far the largest of these three groups; they lived in North America for thousands of years before the arrival of the first European immigrants. Later, many of them coexisted with European settlers until the eighteenth century, when most were eliminated through either disease or war. These conflicts continued through the late nineteenth century, when only a fraction of the earlier Native American population remained (Snipp, 1989; Purcell, 1995; Cortes and Poston, 2008).

The United States receives the most immigrants of all the countries in the world. We reported above that according to the United Nations Department of Economic and Social Affairs, in 2019, over 50 million US residents, or over 14 percent of the total population, were born in foreign countries (Table 7.1). This is the largest number of immigrants residing in any country of the world. The US total immigrant number for 2019 provided by the United Nations is several million larger than that provided by the US Bureau of the Census, namely, 47.8 million in 2023, representing 14.3 percent of the US population (US Bureau of the Census, 2024c).

Some countries have larger percentages of foreign-born than the United States, but they have many fewer people; their foreign-born residents are mainly migrant workers and are seldom citizens of the host countries. For example, in 2022, 88 percent of the United Arab Emirates' total population of 9.5 million residents was foreign-born; this is the largest percentage of foreign-born residents in any one country. Three more countries with very large percentages of foreign-born persons in 2022 were Qatar at 77 percent, Kuwait at 73 percent, and Bahrain at 55 percent (IOM, 2024). These Gulf countries "tend to extend few rights to migrants; it is very hard for a guest worker to win immigrant status and naturalize" (Martin and Zurcher, 2008: 8).

One country, the Vatican City State (known officially as the Holy See, a term from the Latin *sancta sedes*, meaning "holy chair"), has a total population of just over 800 people, and nearly all are foreign-born. Its population consists of the Pope, priests and other members of religious orders, and laypeople (and their families) who work at the Vatican. Citizenship is given to people (and their families) who work there and is revoked when they are no longer employed there. Thus, not only are almost all the residents foreign-born, but there are also no permanent residents. The Vatican City State is the smallest country in the world with respect to both population size and land mass; it comprises less than one-fifth of a square mile (less than one-half of a square kilometer) and is completely surrounded by the city of Rome. The country is so small that it does not have street addresses (Central Intelligence Agency, 2015).

Now we review the history of immigration to the United States. Immigration has played a crucially important role in the American narrative. The sociologist and political scientist Seymour Martin Lipset (1997) once wrote about the "exceptional" character of the United States. He noted that when the thirteen colonies emerged from the American Revolution as a new nation, they relied on a broadly shared ideology based on human liberty, egalitarianism, populism, individualism, and republicanism. This made America exceptional, and Lipset referred to this as "American exceptionalism."

The demographic aspect of American exceptionalism needs to be mentioned. This feature results from America's populating the country with peoples from everywhere. Prior to, and after, the founding of America, virtually everyone and anyone was permitted to immigrate to the country (Cafferty et al., 1983: 35–64). As we noted previously, roughly 97 percent of the population of the United States today is comprised of either immigrants or the descendants of immigrants. This reliance on international migration has been crucial for the development of an "exceptional" America.

Why is this so? Because most international migration is selective of the very best people from other countries. Persons without motivation and without a striving for advancement and improvement, persons with few socioeconomic skills and talents, persons not willing to take risks and chances – these persons will more often remain at home where they were born and not emigrate abroad.

International migrants to the United States, both legal and undocumented, are less likely to commit serious crimes and are less likely to be imprisoned, compared with the native US-born population. Moreover, periods in the US of high levels of immigration are associated with low levels of criminal behavior. Extensive demographic and sociological research has shown the lack of any relationship between immigration and crime. This holds "true for both legal immigrants and the unauthorized, regardless of their country of origin or level of education. In other words, the overwhelming majority of immigrants are not 'criminals' by any commonly accepted definition of the term" (Ewing, Martinez, and Rumbaut, 2015: 1).

It is most unfortunate that US immigration policy is too often written more on the basis of fear and stereotype than on the empirical evidence provided by demographers and other social scientists. Consequently, "immigrants have the stigma of 'criminality' ascribed to them by an ever-evolving assortment of laws and immigration-enforcement mechanisms. Put differently, immigrants are being defined more and more as "threats" when there is little if any evidence for such a designation. Despite the overwhelming evidence that "immigration is not linked to higher crime rates, and that immigrants are less likely to be criminals than the native-born, many US policymakers succumb to their fears and prejudices about what they imagine immigrants to be" (Ewing, Martinez, and Rumbaut, 2015: 2).

The numbers of immigrants residing in the United States have varied greatly over time. Figure 7.1 shows the relative numbers of foreign-born and native-born residents in the United States over a long period of time. The foreign-born population in 2023 constituted about 14 percent of the population, which is the largest share of foreign-born persons in the United States since 1920. Immigration policies played a major role in these trends, and we will discuss the role of policy in more detail in Chapter 19.

In the following overview of US immigration history, you will note that the national origins of the immigrant stream changed over time. We will pay special attention to the most recent immigrant groups, especially the Chinese and Mexicans.

In 1598, Spaniards first came to what would later become the United States. They exploited the land and persecuted the indigenous peoples, but they differed from earlier explorers in that many remained permanently in the areas known today as the Southwest and Florida (Purcell, 1995).

The first really large stream of European immigrants to what is now the United States hailed from England, and they settled mainly in the present state of Virginia (Purcell, 1995). The first permanent settlement was Jamestown, established in 1607. These immigrants largely lived by selling their tobacco crops, which proved to be a profitable but labor-intensive product. This sustenance activity eventually led to the immigration of British indentured servants and African slaves. The arrival of the pilgrims on Plymouth Rock in 1620 marked the beginning of a large migration stream of English

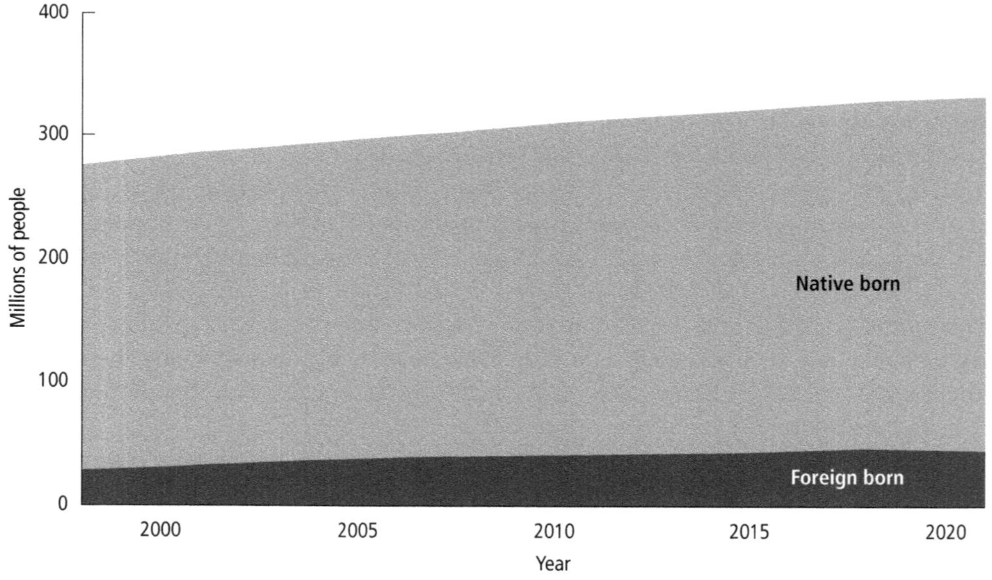

FIGURE 7.1 The US population by birthplace
Source: Congressional Budget Office, 2023.

people moving to North America for religious freedom. These early immigrant groups "of the 1600s and 1700s established the basic context of American society. English was the dominant language in America; English legal and government documents were the norm; and culture was for two centuries copied after English literature, drama, and art" (Purcell, 1995: 5). This model of American society set the standard and foundation during the next two centuries for the future discrimination and exclusion of certain immigrants and for the acceptance of others (Cortes and Poston, 2008).

In a previous section, we noted the sizable involuntary migrations of Africans that also occurred during this period. The first enslaved Africans were purchased in exchange for food provisions from a Dutch-flagged ship in Jamestown in 1619. The White-imposed slavery of Africans was relatively slow to develop in the colonies because Native Americans and White indentured servants were being used as cheap labor. However, by 1690 there were more African slaves than White indentured servants (Purcell, 1995). The Act Prohibiting the Importation of Slaves was a federal law passed on March 2, 1807, that took effect in 1808; it officially ended the transatlantic slave trade. Slavery persisted until the end of the Civil War, including the buying and selling of enslaved persons who had been born in the United States. The system of racism upon which slavery was founded remains a major hurdle for African Americans and other racial and ethnic minorities seeking socioeconomic success in America (Bonilla-Silva, 2013; Feagin, 2006, 2014).

The Dutch came to America in the 1600s and claimed much of present-day New York (Purcell, 1995). Swedish immigrants came to Delaware but were less successful than the British and the Dutch. Scotch-Irish immigrants came for economic reasons and settled mainly in Pennsylvania. As early as the seventeenth century, a considerable migration of German peoples began and it continued through the nineteenth century. They were the largest non-British and non-English-speaking immigrant group to come voluntarily to America. The cultural and linguistic differences of the Germans led to their being one of the first European immigrant groups to experience discrimination by earlier settlers in the country (Cortes and Poston, 2008). According to data from the American Community Survey, over 40 million people residing in the US claim German ancestry, making Germans the largest ancestry group in the country (US Bureau of the Census, 2023a).

Before 1830, the contribution of immigration to US population growth was minimal. Between 1821 and 1825, for example, the average number of immigrants every year was only about 8,000; this increased to almost 21,000 between 1826 and 1830. From 1841 to 1845, immigrants each year numbered more than 86,000. In the eight years between 1850 and 1857, the total number of immigrants to the United States was 2.2 million. In sum, between 1790 and 1860, the number of immigrants to the United States was almost 5 million, and most of them were from Europe (Cortes and Poston, 2008; Taeuber and Taeuber, 1958).

Starting on January 1, 1892, many immigrants, mainly from Europe, were processed through the portal of Ellis Island, a small island in New York Harbor. There were other ports of immigrant entry into the United States that were located in Boston, Philadelphia, Baltimore, San Francisco, Savannah, Miami, Galveston, and New Orleans, but Ellis Island was the major one. The Immigration Act of 1924 resulted in far fewer immigrants coming to the United States and also permitted the processing of immigrants at overseas embassies. By the time Ellis Island finally closed in 1954, more than 12 million immigrant steamship passengers had been processed into the United States through this port of entry (Coan, 2004: xiii). The National Park Service (2015) has estimated that around 40 percent of America's population today traces its ancestry to immigrants who entered the United States through Ellis Island. The immigrants had left behind their history, homeland, and people to come to the United States in search of a new and better life.

The first immigrant to enter the United States through Ellis Island when it opened on January 1, 1892, was Annie Moore (1874–1924), a young woman from County Cork, Ireland. She and her two brothers had traveled alone across the Atlantic Ocean to be reunited with their parents, who had emigrated from Ireland two years earlier (Coan, 2004: xxiv). Annie Moore has been immortalized in the popular song "Isle of Hope, Isle of Tears," written and composed by Brendan Graham and performed by, among others, the Celtic Woman and the Irish Tenors. Here is a link to a performance by the Celtic Woman: www.youtube.com/watch?v=yluUCjH6ONs

Listen to the song (it is preceded by a brief instrumental). The first two verses, and the chorus, illustrate well the hopes, fears, dreams, and courage of so many of the immigrants to the United States, feelings and attributes that continue to characterize immigrants to this day. To illustrate, one verse speaks of "her dreams for the future in the land of liberty." Keep in mind, however, that for most of the transatlantic and transpacific immigrants who came to the Americas a century or more ago, once they departed from their home countries they would likely never return home again. The song makes this point with the verse "the Isle [of home] you'll never see again ... is always on your mind."

When you listen to the song, you will learn that on January 1, 1892, when Annie Moore entered Ellis Island, she was 15 years old. As an aside, Brendan Graham, the author of "Isle of Hope, Isle of Tears," informed Poston in a personal communication (October 8, 2009) that Annie Moore was actually 17 years old when she moved from Ireland to the United States, not 15 as stated in his song. Years after writing and publishing the song, Graham obtained a copy of her birth certificate reporting her year of birth as 1874. It was then that he learned she apparently lied about her age and claimed to be 15. If she was 15, she could remain with her two younger brothers in the "family section" of the ship, but if she was 17, she would have to travel in the "adult section" of the ship and be separated from her brothers.

The last person to pass through Ellis Island was a Norwegian merchant seaman, Arne Petersson, who was processed on November 12, 1954 (Coan, 2004: xxiv).

In the nineteenth century, the combination of pro-immigration campaigns and the reduced cost of transcontinental transportation increased considerably the numbers of immigrants to the United States. There was a second influx of German and Irish immigrants. Germans found work in several established industries, aiding in the overall development of US commerce.

The Irish immigrants, mostly Catholics, suffered severe discrimination in the United States that reached a peak in the mid-1850s with the emergence of the Know-Nothings, an anti-Catholic organization dedicated to maintaining the dominance of Anglo-Saxon Protestants. Between the early seventeenth century and the 1920s, an estimated 7 million people left Ireland for North America (Miller, 1985: 3). Data from the 2021 American Community Survey indicate that in 2021 there were 31.5 million people in the United States claiming Irish ancestry; this is the second largest ancestry group in the US, after the Germans. US residents claiming Irish ancestry are more than four times larger in size than the total of the two large Irish populations in Europe, namely, Ireland (5.3 million) and Northern Ireland (1.9 million).

The end of the nineteenth century also saw immigration from some Scandinavian countries. These immigrants sought land for farming and developed the mostly unsettled Midwest (Cortes and Poston, 2008).

The Chinese have a long history of immigration to the United States. They first came to the US after the beginning of the California Gold Rush in 1849. An estimated 288,000 Chinese came during this period, although many returned to China before 1882 (Black, 1963; Poston and Luo, 2007). Like most immigrants, the Chinese came as laborers in search of work and wages. Their port of entry was San Francisco, which is where they hoped to become rich and realize their dreams. To this day, the Mandarin Chinese name for San Francisco is 旧金山 (*Jiù jīn shān*), or "Old Gold Mountain."

The Chinese were subjected to hostile discrimination because many American workers were threatened by the low wages the Chinese were willing to take. The passing of the Chinese Exclusion Act of 1882 ended the first period of Chinese immigration; it tapered off, eventually stopping by the end of the nineteenth century (Pedraza and Rumbaut, 1996; Poston and Luo, 2007).

The Act to Prohibit the Coming of Chinese Persons into the United States of May 1892, better known as the Geary Act, allowed Chinese laborers to travel to China and reenter the United States, but its provisions were more restrictive than the preceding immigration laws. The Geary Act required Chinese to register and secure a certificate as proof of their right to be in the United States. Those failing to do so could be put into prison or deported.

The Chinese Exclusion Act resulted from a concern about the large numbers of Chinese who had come earlier in response to the need for inexpensive labor, particularly to help with the construction of the western part of the transcontinental railroad. Competition with American workers and a growing nativism brought pressure for restrictive action, beginning with the Chinese Exclusion Act. This law suspended the immigration of Chinese laborers for ten years. However, it permitted Chinese who were in the United States in 1880 to stay, travel abroad, and return, but it prohibited their naturalization.

The next period of Chinese immigration began in 1882 and extended to 1965. For all practical purposes, Chinese immigration to the United States during this period was banned. The only exceptions were diplomats, merchants, and some students, as well as their dependents, but these were very small in number. The Chinese Exclusion Act was renewed in 1892, was made permanent in 1902, and was not repealed until 1943. The ban continued in force until 1943, at which time an annual quota of 100 immigrants was assigned to Chinese who wished to enter the United States (King and Locke, 1980; Poston and Luo, 2007).

In 1943, President Franklin D. Roosevelt signed the Act to Repeal the Chinese Exclusion Acts, mainly because China and the United States were allies during World

War II. The Act of 1943 also lifted restrictions on naturalization. However, until the Immigration and Nationality Act of 1965, various laws continued to restrict Chinese immigration. Chinese already in the United States were confined to highly segregated Chinatowns in major cities, such as San Francisco and New York, and in isolated regions in rural areas. Because the Chinese were deprived of their democratic rights, they sometimes made extensive use of the courts and diplomatic channels to defend themselves.

The US Civil Rights movement of the 1960s, particularly the enactment of the Civil Rights Act of 1964 and the Immigration and Nationality Act of 1965, began a new period of Chinese immigration, covering the years from 1965 to the present. The new laws restored many of the basic rights denied earlier to Chinese Americans. Since the 1980s, thousands of Chinese people have come to the United States each year. For instance, during the twenty-three years between 1980 and 2002, the volume of permanent Chinese immigration to the United States numbered more than 911,000, almost seven times the number between 1891 and 1979. It is during this latest period that the numbers of Chinese student immigrants increased substantially; in many cases, however, students are not included in the count of permanent immigrants (Poston and Luo, 2007). In the US in 2022 there were 4.7 million people who identify as Chinese, over 60 percent of whom are immigrants (Pew Research Center, 2024). We discuss immigration laws and regulations in more detail in Chapter 19.

Overlapping with early Chinese immigration to the United States, which was principally to the West Coast, were population movements from Eastern and Southern Europe, which were principally to the East Coast. These immigrants were not as welcome as the previous European immigrants because the "old" immigrants thought that these "new" immigrants would take their jobs (Purcell, 1995). The new immigrants were mainly Italians, Greeks, Poles, and Slavs who spoke different languages, had different religious beliefs in many cases, and had slightly different physical features than the Western Europeans. They were subjected to discrimination but were able to assimilate into White American culture with passing generations (Cortes and Poston, 2008).

Currently, the largest numbers of immigrants to the United States are from certain Asian and Latin American countries, particularly Mexico. (See Figure 7.2). These immigrants come for many of the same reasons that the European immigrants came in earlier decades. Population booms and increased industrialization, combined with the economic opportunities of the United States, created the push and pull factors that increased emigration from Asia. Many Asians move directly into ethnic enclaves where they find jobs and homes with people from their countries of origin. However, they are often criticized for not assimilating into "mainstream" White American culture (Portes and Rumbaut, 1990).

The end of the twentieth century through the first quarter of the twenty-first century has seen the immigration of millions of Mexicans to the United States. There is a long-standing social, economic, and geographical relationship between the two countries. As Massey and his colleagues have written, "the USA has invaded Mexico three times; it annexed one-third of its territory; it is the primary source of capital for Mexican investment; it is Mexico's largest trading partner; and Mexico is the second most important trading partner for the USA" (Massey et al., 2005: 67). Like most other

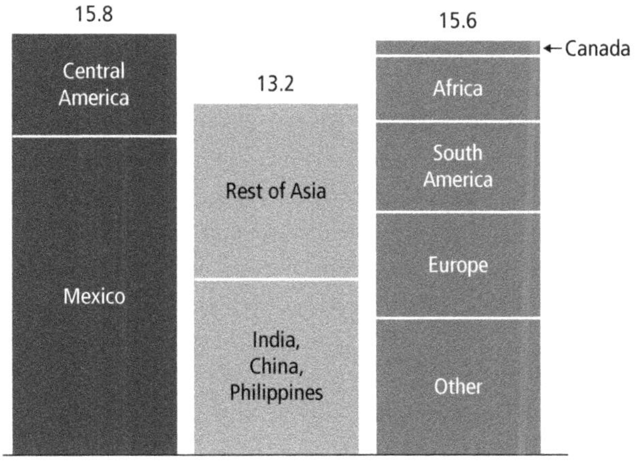

FIGURE 7.2 Number (millions) and country of foreign-born people residing in the United States, 2021
Source: Congressional Budget Office, 2023.

newcomers to the United States, Mexicans are seeking better working conditions and higher wages than are available in their home country. They are subjected to the same discrimination as earlier immigrant groups. Americans of Mexican descent vary in their levels of assimilation, based mostly on how long they or their ancestors have been in the United States (Cortes and Poston, 2008).

The first major migration of Mexicans took place after the Mexican Revolution (1910) and was motivated in large part by labor requirements in the southwestern United States (Donato, 1994). This migration was maintained until the immigrants became subjected to unfair treatment and were deported in large numbers during the 1930s. At about this time, the Immigration Act of 1924 was passed, which gave preference to Northern and Western Europeans. However, there was again a need for agricultural labor, so large-scale Mexican migration was resumed (Donato, 1994; Garcia, 2011).

Mexican migration to the United States may be categorized into three major periods: the *bracero* (i.e., guest worker) period (1942 to 1964), the post-bracero period (1965 through 1986), and the post-IRCA (Immigration Reform and Control Act) period (1987 to the present) (Donato, 1994; Durand, Massey, and Parrado, 1999). The **bracero program** (1942–1964) began as a response to the requirement for temporary agricultural labor. Attitudes toward immigration were tolerant during this twenty-two-year period. Mexicans were brought in on a temporary basis, and they maintained ties with their home country. Very little legal or unauthorized migration occurred during this period (Reichert and Massey, 1980). The bracero period is important because it established a precedent for Mexican migration to the United States as an opportunity to obtain earnings in the form of remittances. It also established the dynamic of a seasonal migration pattern (Garcia, 2011).

When the bracero program was terminated in 1964, around 200,000 of these guest workers lost their jobs, "leading to a buildup of social unrest" (Plankey Videla, 2008: 592). Several immigration regulations were then placed into effect. Only a person with family ties to a **green card** holder was allowed to work in the United States (Reichert and Massey, 1980). Thus, persons without such associations would need to use undocumented migration as a means to gain US employment, and more and more Mexican immigrants were women and children (Reichert and Massey, 1980). Unauthorized migration also increased because of the caps placed on migration from Europe. In fact, Mexican migrants could enter and leave the United States without much difficulty, and employer sanctions for hiring undocumented workers were minimal.

In the latter part of this period, however, the American public began discussing and debating the issue of unauthorized migration (Bean and Sullivan, 1987; Bean, Telles, and Lowell, 1987). Durand and his colleagues have written that "after 1973, wages stagnated, unemployment rates rose, income inequality grew, and the distribution of wealth became progressively more skewed" (Durand, Massey, and Parrado, 1999: 520). Some felt that the United States was losing control of its borders. These concerns and others resulted in the passage of the 1986 Immigration Reform and Control Act (IRCA) (Garcia, 2011; Warren and Passel, 1987).

The IRCA was designed to drastically reduce unauthorized migration from Mexico (Durand, Massey, and Parrado, 1999; White, Bean, and Espenshade, 1990) mainly by imposing strict employer sanctions, providing amnesty to long-term residents of the United States, and instituting stricter border control. The Act was successful in reducing undocumented migration. But as Passel (2006) has noted, rates began to increase in the early 1990s and have continued to increase until around 2010 (see also Garcia, 2011). Since 2010 or so the numbers of immigrants from Mexico have decreased, and net international migration from Mexico has even been negative in some years.

The period following the IRCA is known as the new era of migration (Durand, Massey, and Parrado, 1999). The immigrant population is no longer temporary, seasonal, geographically concentrated, and predominantly male but is now rather long-term, urbanized, and geographically dispersed. In the past three decades, there has been an increase in nativist sentiment (Espenshade and Hempstead, 1996) due in large part to a stagnating economy, a perceived threat to national security, particularly since the tragedy of 9/11, and the mistaken belief that immigrants, especially Mexicans, are taking away jobs from the permanent residents, even though extensive research indicates this is not true (Garcia, 2011).

An additional change has been a growing influx of immigrants, some of them seeking asylum, who come from the countries of Central America. Figure 7.2 shows the sizeable fraction of Central American immigrants, but also makes clear that Mexico remains the primary origin site of immigrants. Mexico and Central America together accounted for 15.8 million immigrants. Note that the rest of the world (including Canada, Africa, South America, and Europe) accounted for 15.6 million immigrants.

We noted earlier that the first immigrants were mainly from Northern and Western Europe. Indeed in 1850 and 1860 over 90 percent of the foreign-born persons in the United States were born in Northern and Western Europe. The share of the foreign-born from Northern and Western Europe was 87 percent in 1870 and 79 percent in 1890 (Gibson and Jung, 2006). Immigration to the United States began with immigrants from Northern and Western Europe and lasted among this group up to through the 1870s. In those times Northern and Western Europeans defined US immigration.

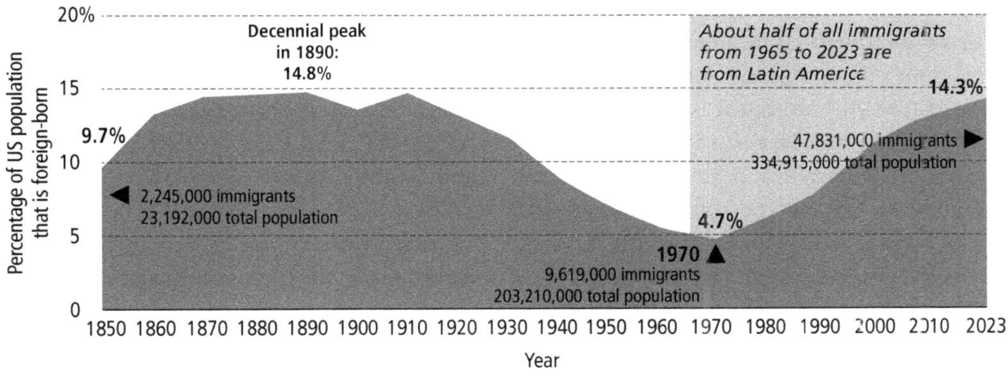

FIGURE 7.3 Immigrant share of the US population, 1850–2023
Source: Moslimani and Passel, 2024.

This pattern, however, began to change in the 1880s. Figure 7.3 shows that the foreign-born share of the US population peaked once in 1890 and again in 1910. After the depression in the US in the 1880s, the number of immigrants increased from 3.5 million in the 1890s to over 9 million in the first decade of the new century. By 1910 immigrants from Southern and Eastern Europe comprised over 70 percent of persons entering the United States. And the foreign-born population of the United States in 1910 was now one-third Southern and Eastern European (Gibson and Jung, 2006). During this period from the 1880s through the 1910s, Southern and Eastern Europeans defined US immigration. The character of US immigration had changed.

Immigration numbers declined considerably in the latter years of the 1910s because of World War I and the influenza pandemic (see Chapter 12). Population policies passed in the 1920s set a quota system for sending countries. These laws seriously restricted immigration to the United States, especially immigration from Southern and Eastern Europe. The share of foreign-born persons in the United States began declining after 1920 (Figure 7.3), reaching a low of fewer than 5 percent in 1970 (Figure 7.3). Then, in the 1970s and 1980s, the character of immigration changed again. The passage of the Immigration and Nationality Act in 1965, which took effect in 1968, opened up US immigration to peoples from all countries, including Latin America and Asia, so that by 2010 US immigration was no longer defined by Europeans but by Latin Americans and Asians. Figure 7.3 shows about half of all immigrants after 1965 were from Latin America, and Mexicans formed the greatest number of them.

So, the character of US immigration was first based on Northern and Western Europeans, then changed in the 1880s to one based on Southern and Eastern Europeans, and then changed in the late 1960s to one based on Latin Americans and Asians.

UNAUTHORIZED INTERNATIONAL MIGRATION

International migrants are often categorized as either legal or illegal. The main adjectives we use in this book to refer to international migrants who are not legally residing in a country are unauthorized and undocumented. What does this mean? An **unauthorized (or undocumented) immigrant** is a person who immigrates into a host country "through irregular or extralegal channels" (Armbrister, 2003: 512). More specifically, an unauthorized immigrant is an international migrant who resides in the host country of destination, but who is not a citizen of the host country, who has not been admitted by the host country for permanent residence, "and is not in a set of specific authorized temporary statuses permitting longer-term residence and work" (Passel, 2006: 1; see also Passel, Van Hook, and Bean, 2004). An international migrant is classified as unauthorized if (1) during the process of migrating to the host country, the person "avoided inspection by crossing borders clandestinely or ... traveled with fraudulent documents, e.g., a falsified visa or counterfeit passport"; such persons are referred to as **entries without inspection (EWIs)**; or (2) the migrant "overstayed the time limit of a legally obtained non-immigrant temporary visa"; such persons are referred to as **visa overstayers** or **visa overstays**" (Armbrister, 2003: 512).

The most frequent type of unauthorized immigrant in almost every country of the world is one who arrives legally in the host country often "as a non-immigrant (e.g., tourist, student, or temporary laborer), and [stays] beyond the legally sanctioned period" (Armbrister, 2003: 512), that is, a visa overstayer. In the United States, however, the majority of unauthorized immigrants "entered without inspection over land borders with Mexico and Canada" (Armbrister, 2003: 512); they were EWIs, and most were from Mexico. It is estimated that in 2005, among the unauthorized immigrant population in the United States, 25 to 40 percent were visa overstayers and the balance, the majority, were the so-called EWIs (Passel, 2006: 16). In 2022, more than two-fifths (40 percent) of the undocumented immigrants in the United States, or almost 4.7 million of them, were visa overstayers (Poston, 2025).

While the EWI immigration stream is primarily of Latin American origin, some undocumented immigrants from other parts of the world have also sought entry through the long southern border. Visa overstayers, by contrast, can come from any country. Demographers have noted that "visa-overstays do not come predominantly from any one country" (Brown, Bean, and Nasir, 2019: 441). Also, they differ markedly from EWIs. They most frequently enter the United States by air and are usually more socioeconomically advantaged than EWIs. At a minimum they need to possess resources to obtain a valid passport, a US visa, and transportation.

The exact number of unauthorized immigrants in the United States is difficult for government sources to measure with precision. Demographers can use existing data to make estimates about how many unauthorized immigrants there are, but without much detail as to who they are or where they live. Figure 7.4 shows the estimated share of unauthorized immigrants in 2022 to be 23 percent, or about one-quarter of all the foreign-born population. Figure 7.4 divides lawful immigrants into two segments: the naturalized citizens, who immigrated to the United States and have become citizens, and the temporary lawful residents. This latter category includes green card holders, international students, and other residents who hold visas. Some of them may leave the country, others may become naturalized citizens, and some of them may become visa overstayers and thus become unauthorized immigrants.

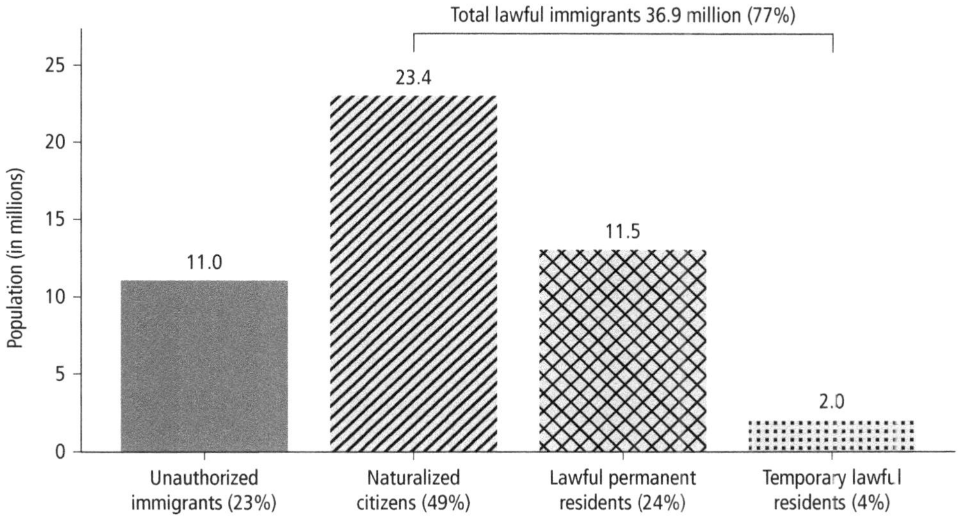

FIGURE 7.4 Groups of foreign-born population in the United States, 2022
Data source: Moslimani and Passel, 2024.

Regarding the volume of unauthorized immigrants worldwide, the International Organization for Migration (IOM, 2010: 29) estimated the number to be between 30 and 35 million persons, constituting around 15 percent or so of the estimated total number of 232 million international migrants. Most unauthorized immigrants go mainly to a few high-income countries, and they mainly hail from low-income countries. Visa overstayers in countries of the developed world are now believed to constitute a significant proportion of unauthorized immigrants. Some examples of countries that report substantial numbers of unauthorized immigrants include Russia, Germany, and Saudi Arabia. India has reported a large number of unauthorized immigrants from Bangladesh, and Mexico has reported an unauthorized immigration stream from Guatemala and other Central American countries over its southern border.

In the Western Hemisphere, the United States is the magnet country for unauthorized migrants. The numbers have increased considerably in past decades. In the United States, the estimated number of unauthorized immigrants grew from roughly 3.5 million in 1990 to around 8.6 million in 2000 and to about 12.2 million in 2007; the number declined to 11.2 million in 2012, and to around 11 million in 2022. Mexico has maintained its position as the prime source of unauthorized immigrants to the United States. The estimated number of unauthorized migrants from Mexico to the United States grew from 4.5 million in 2000 to 6.9 million in 2007 and then declined remarkably to 5.9 million in 2012, and to 5.5 million in 2023. "The sudden reversal of a long trend of growth in the number of Mexican unauthorized immigrants probably results from both a marked decline in new arrivals and an increase in departures [from the United States back] to Mexico" (Passel and Cohn, 2014: 19).

In the United States, under the Constitution anyone born in the United States is by definition a citizen and a legal resident (**birthright citizenship**). As a result, most of the children of unauthorized immigrants are themselves legal residents. Nearly 4.5 million of the 5.5 million children of unauthorized immigrants in 2010 were born in the United States and thus are themselves legal residents of the United States. Another group of interest is the so-called Dreamers. These are persons who were born in another country but whose parents brought them to the United States. Both they and their parents are unauthorized, but there have been temporary provisions to allow the Dreamers to remain legally, to work in the United States, and to get schooling in the United States, so long as they have no criminal record. The future policy for the Dreamers is as yet unknown. But over 80 percent of Americans report a willingness to find a way for them to remain in the United States (Jones, 2024).

ECONOMIC EFFECTS OF INTERNATIONAL MIGRATION

We noted at the start of this chapter that no demographic topic is discussed these days by laypeople and social scientists alike as frequently, as emotionally, and as forcefully as international migration. In 2024, a near-record 55 percent of Americans wanted immigration levels to decrease. By comparison, the highest number opposing immigration was 65 percent during the Great Depression in 1933. Immigration consistently ranks as one of the top problems facing the United States (Jones, 2024). It may perhaps seem paradoxical, but 65 percent of Americans in 2024 also said that they thought immigration was generally good for the country. These results indicate ambivalence about immigration, but the issue appears to be the number of immigrants and not the fact of continuing immigration.

There is a wealth of published literature by demographers and other social scientists dealing with the positive and negative aspects of international migration, considered from many different vantage points. These include economic effects, cultural effects, environmental effects, health effects, and security effects, to list several dimensions that have been examined. In this section, we draw on this literature and undertake a review of some of the positive and negative characteristics of international migration. We focus on the economic effects: What is good and what is not good economically about international migration?

In general terms, there are two basic perspectives on international migration: one permitting it, and one denying it. Organizations and bodies such as the Catholic Church and the World Bank argue for more and freer international migration because "people should not be confined to their countries of birth by national borders, and ... more migration would speed economic growth and development in both sending and receiving countries" (Martin and Zurcher, 2008: 4). An opposite approach is espoused by organizations in almost every high-income country of the world, arguing for reductions in the numbers of international immigrants. In the United States, two such bodies are Negative Population Growth (NPG) and the Federation for American Immigration Reform (FAIR). FAIR argues that "unskilled newcomers hurt low-skilled US workers, have negative environmental effects, and threaten established US cultural values" (Martin and Zurcher, 2008: 4).

The economic arguments about the costs and benefits of international migration, on which we concentrate here, are usually the main ones cited when scholars and laypeople argue for or against immigration. There is an impressive and extensive literature, and it is complex and diverse. We summarize some of this literature in the paragraphs below.

From the vantage point of the receiving (host) countries, there are several related concerns: Are immigrants taking away jobs from the local population, are immigrants driving down wages, and are immigrants a burden on the welfare system of the host country? Most analyses in Western Europe and the United States indicate that the impact of immigration on jobs and wages is weak or nonexistent. Immigrants often wind up in the "three D's jobs"; these are the "dirty, difficult and dangerous (or demeaning) jobs ... shunned by local workers" (Ghosh, 2005: 168).

Evidence shows little if any competition in these and in many other types of jobs between immigrants to a country and the local residents. Immigrants are often the first ones to be fired, and they are also "found to earn less than local workers in comparable jobs" (Ghosh, 2005: 169–170). Research on immigration's labor-market effects finds very little if any evidence that immigrants harm the employment or wages of similar natives (also see, Holzer, 2011). Some literature, however, shows how immigration can have a negative impact on industries or geographic areas with large concentrations of foreign workers; sometimes this results in "pressure on jobs and working conditions of the local labor force" (Ghosh, 2005: 169; see also Borjas, 2003; Borjas, Freeman, and Katz, 1997).

Regarding wages, some believe that even if immigrants do not take jobs from local workers, they will depress wages. Research from numerous studies in Europe and the United States is mixed, with most indicating little, if any depressing impact on local wages. Those studies showing negative effects of immigration on wages report a very small effect, on the order of –0.3 to –0.8 percent. In a study of US workers, Brucker (2002) found that a 10 percent increment in the number of immigrants has essentially a zero effect on nonimmigrant wages. Other analyses actually show that the presence of immigrants tends to increase local wages, especially those of the highly skilled.

What about the effect of immigration on social welfare costs? Studies in the United Kingdom show that immigrants contributed the equivalent of US $4 billion more in personal and employment taxes than they received in welfare benefits. Recent analyses conducted in the United States reach similar conclusions. Much depends on the degree to which immigrants access welfare. This varies from high levels in many Western European countries, sometimes higher than those of the local people, to levels in other European countries and in Canada where the welfare dependence of immigrants is lower than that of citizens. Immigrants to the United States, particularly in their early years in the new country, do add to some health and education costs. But, eventually, the immigrants and their descendants end up paying taxes that result in a net positive contribution (Ghosh, 2005: 171).

There is a real economic gain for many countries in admitting skilled workers. European Union member states, particularly Germany and the United Kingdom, are experienced users "of highly skilled foreign nationals, [and] are leading the way in selecting qualified workers from abroad" (Papademetriou, 2003: 571). Of all the developed countries, the United States has gained the most with respect to attracting skilled immigrants. In 2000, the United States had admitted more than 10.5 million highly skilled immigrants, while losing just over 431,000 graduates to other countries, for a net gain of 10 million (Legrain, 2006: 95).

In 2021, over 7 million persons, or about one in every five US workers in science, technology, engineering, or medicine (STEM) were foreign born. Over a quarter (26%) of foreign-born workers employed in the United States worked in STEM occupations (Taylor and Arbeit, 2024). Immigrants to the United States from low-income countries have roughly twice as much education as their compatriots remaining at home: "An extreme case is that of Jamaica in 2000, when there were nearly four times more Jamaicans with tertiary education in the US than at home. [Also], more Ethiopian doctors are practicing in Chicago than in Ethiopia" (Ghosh, 2005: 173). Skilled immigrants from developing nations play a very important role in the economic activities of high-income nations, a point often overlooked by those less accepting of international migrants.

Skilled immigrants have another type of impact on the economies of the host countries. Research has shown, for example, a positive association between the presence of foreign-born workers in California and exports from California to the home country. Specifically, "a one percent increase in the number of first generation immigrants generated a 0.5 percent increase in exports from California to the respective country" (Iredale, 2005: 224).

The immigrants also have an economic effect on the sending countries. Does international migration help or hinder the economic development of the origin countries? On the one hand, emigration is a safety valve, temporarily, on job losses and labor restructuring in the process of industrial development. But since emigrants involve only a small share of the labor force of the sending countries, no more than 2 to 3 percent at best, their departure does not appear to have much of a real and long-term impact on unemployment. In many low-income countries, labor emigration does not result in a rise in wages because these countries "generally suffer from a large backlog of unemployed and underemployed; this is one reason why employers normally do not oppose labor emigration" (Ghosh, 2005: 173).

Another economic effect is the remittances contributed by immigrants to the economies of the origin countries. A **remittance** is a transfer of money by a foreign immigrant worker from the host country to an individual in his/her home country. The many millions of migrants living outside their countries of birth send billions of dollars home each year. Worldwide, international migrants send over $626 billion annually to lower-income countries. This sum is larger than official development assistance and more stable than private capital flows to these countries. The United States is the destination for the most international migrants and, according to the International Monetary Fund and World Bank, the largest global source of remittances, sending $72.7 billion in 2021 (Weiss and Scott, 2023). "The economic importance of remittances is larger in poorer countries than in richer ones" and accounts for 8 percent of the "gross domestic product in low-income nations" (Connor et al., 2013: 6).

Remittances are valuable to the origin countries because their recipients have been shown to have a high propensity to save the funds. The remittances also result in credit that may be used as investment capital. Small business ventures grow via remittances. The remittances aid local community development and businesses, and they are an important and sometimes sizable addition to the gross national product (GNP) (i.e., the total dollar value of all goods and services produced for consumption in the society during a particular time period). However, one needs to be careful and not overestimate the effect of remittances on business development. "Businesses established through remittances cannot necessarily rely on their continued flow for sustainability" (Skeldon, 2005: 263).

Studies have also shown a positive association between remittances and poverty reduction. "A 10 percent increase in the share of remittances in country Gross Domestic Product (GDP) [leads] to a 1.2 percent decrease in the percentage of persons living on less than US $1.00 per day, and also reduces the depth or severity of poverty" (Ghosh, 2005: 179). Remittances are indispensable for the economic survival of many low-income countries (Skeldon, 2005: 260).

What is the economic cost to the origin countries when they lose skilled personnel via emigration? Is emigration always a "brain drain" that "can act as a serious brake on development and poverty alleviation?" (Laczko, 2005: 287). Actually, in nursing and teaching jobs, the international departure of residents, followed by their return, enables the migrants to obtain new skills, "and in many cases plays a useful role in exposing migrants, as well as the host societies, to new ideas and ways of doing things" (Laczko, 2005: 289). Research on the net effects of return international migration, that is, remigration, shows that the origin countries derive the greatest benefit when the skilled immigrants return home in, say, ten to fifteen years after their departure (Laczko, 2005: 289).

The literature on the effects of international immigration is extensive. We have discussed here only a small amount of the relevant research and have focused only on economic effects. Although there are, indeed, some important economic costs to international migration, on balance there are many more benefits, and this generalization may be made with regard to both the host countries and the sending countries.

We conclude this chapter by introducing a demographic concept that is very important in discussions of international migration and migration policy, **zero net international migration**. This concept is not as easily understood as it should be and is often used incorrectly.

ZERO NET INTERNATIONAL MIGRATION

Net international migration and natural increase (the difference between births and deaths) are the demographic processes that determine the amount of growth or decline in a nation's population. In many European countries that are today characterized by low levels of fertility and mortality, the contribution of net international migration to overall population change overshadows the contribution of natural increase. Some hold that international migration to the United States is too large and thus argue for **zero net international migration**. They state that if the number of people who leave the country each year is the same as the number who enter each year, then the effect of net international migration will be zero. For example, proponents of NPG have stated that the United States should place a ceiling on annual immigration so that it is balanced by emigration, and thus will not contribute to overall population growth (Mann, [1992] 2015). In this last section of the chapter, we draw on Poston's earlier research with Leon Bouvier and Nanbin Zhai (Bouvier, Poston, and Zhai, 1997) that shows why this reasoning is incorrect.

Zero net international migration should not be confused with no (i.e., zero) international migration. The former is characterized by the same numbers of people immigrating into a country as emigrating from it. In the latter, there is no international migration. The two concepts are not the same.

Zero net international migration is at least theoretically possible. Indeed, such has always been the intent behind temporary worker programs – whether in Europe or in the Middle East or in the Persian Gulf. Workers are allowed to enter the country for a specified period of time and then later are expected to return to their homelands.

Suppose we assume that zero net international migration could become a reality even in a country like the United States. If this were to occur, and if each year a number, say, 200,000, were to immigrate to the United States, and 200,000 were to emigrate from the United States, does this mean that immigration will no longer be a main contributor to population growth, as the NPG proponents conclude?

The answer is no. Even with zero net international migration, the impact of the immigration and emigration movements that produce it would result in considerable population increases in receiving countries, such as the United States, and substantial population losses in sending countries, such as Mexico.

In considering the direct impact of zero net international migration, we first need to note that immigrants to a country are usually younger than remigrants from that country. Immigrants often arrive in their countries of destination when they are in their 20s and early 30s; conversely, remigrants usually depart the host countries either fairly soon after their arrival, or much later when they are in their 60s or older when they reach retirement.

To simplify our hypothetical illustration about patterns of immigration to and remigration from the United States, we will assume that all immigrants enter the country at age 15, and that all remigrants leave the country at age 65. Thus, the immigrants tend to spend most of their adult lives in the United States, their country of first destination, for an average of about fifty years.

In this illustration, net international migration each year would be zero because 200,000 people would immigrate in each year and 200,000 would leave each year. We will use the life table (already discussed in Chapter 5) as a way of keeping track of the immigrants and remigrants. For most people, the life table indicates how many additional years a person can expect to live, on average, after having attained a specific age. If 200,000 people enter the United States at, say, age 15, and leave at, say, age 65, the total number of person-years spent in the country for any one of these cohorts of 200,000 persons would be 10 million (200,000 immigrants times 50 years) minus the person-years that would have been lived in the United States by those who died there before reaching age 65. If 200,000 persons immigrate to the United States at age 15, stay for fifty years, and then depart at age 65, this one cohort of 200,000 persons will have lived there for more than 9.5 million person-years (see our discussion in Chapter 5 of the "big L" column in the life table). Even though 200,000 persons leave the United States each year (at age 65) and 200,000 enter each year (at age 15), there is nevertheless a sizable direct effect of zero net international immigration. In the hypothetical case that we have constructed here, the direct effect of the net international migration involving 200,000 emigrants and 200,000 immigrants each year is in excess of

9.5 million person-years lived in the United States for each cohort of 200,000 immigrants who enter at age 15. Therefore, one must not confuse the two concepts of zero net international migration and zero (or no) international migration; they are very different from one another. The direct impact of zero net international migration can be quite substantial.

SUMMARY

This chapter focused on the demographic dynamics of international migration. No demographic topic is discussed by laypeople and social scientists as frequently, as forcefully, and as emotionally as international migration. Having considered in Chapter 6 the topic of internal migration and now, in this chapter, international migration, it is certainly the case that the dynamics of the two differ significantly.

We began this chapter by reviewing the definitions and concepts used by demographers in their analyses of international migration. World immigration patterns over time were next addressed, followed by a discussion of immigration to the United States, including legal and unauthorized immigration. Then we turned to a discussion of the positive and negative economic issues pertaining to international migration. We concluded the chapter with a section on the concept of zero net international migration.

This chapter completes our presentation in this book of the three demographic processes of fertility (Chapter 4), mortality (Chapter 5), and migration (Chapters 6 and 7). In the next four chapters, we address issues that are closely entwined with the demographic processes: the family (Chapter 8), sexual orientation (Chapter 9), sex composition and gender identity (Chapter 10), and contraception and birth control (Chapter 11).

DISCUSSION QUESTIONS

1. It is suggested in this chapter that international migration is one of the main reasons why the United States is "exceptional." Do you agree with this argument? If you do, what feature or characteristic of international migration do you believe leads to the US being exceptional? If you do not believe that international migration has resulted in the US being exceptional, why do you hold this position? How would you counter the reasons discussed in this chapter about why international migration leads to the destination country tending to become exceptional?
2. Over time the countries of origin of immigrants to the United States have changed. Immigrants first came to the US from Europe, mainly Spain, England, and Ireland. After the Civil War, there was immigration to the West Coast of the US from China and Japan, and to the East Coast from Eastern and Southern Europe. Since 1965, there has been a very large migration stream from Mexico and from countries in Central America. In your view, which immigration stream was the most beneficial for the US, and which one was the least beneficial? What do you mean by "beneficial"? Defend your selections.

8

The Family

INTRODUCTION

In this chapter we discuss a topic of special interest to demography, namely, the family. This is an important topic for demographers because most of the time it is the family that is responsible for the production of the next generation (Waite, 2005: 88). The family, however conceptualized and whatever its structure, is almost always the environment in which fertility, that is, the production of children, occurs.

We first undertake a historical review of the family, its structure and form. The traditional family consists of the "male breadwinner working outside the home and the stay-at-home mother taking care of the kids" (Iceland, 2014: 39). This is the kind of idealized family that represented much of America in the 1950s and may be revisited in the reruns of such television programs as *The Adventures of Ozzie and Harriet* and *Leave it to Beaver*. These were programs that many folks, including the two authors of this book, watched almost every week when they were children. But this family form was not really the "traditional" family. As Iceland has reminded us, it differed tremendously from the "traditional families of the colonial era and much of the nineteenth century" (Iceland, 2014: 39). The historian Stephanie Coontz (2000) makes a similar point in her book *The Way We Never Were: American Families and the Nostalgia Trap*. Our historical review of the structure and form of the family will show its significant heterogeneity over time.

We follow our historical review with an empirical depiction of the family today. The contemporary family has changed tremendously in the past 75 or so years. To illustrate, we show in Figure 8.1 that in 1960, almost 88 percent of children in the United States lived in two-parent "Ozzie and Harriet" type families; by the year 2000 the number had dropped to 69 percent, and it has remained at about that level; in 2023 just over 71 percent of children lived with both parents. We show later that these days people marry later, fewer people marry, pre-marital cohabitation is normative, and over 40 percent of children are born to unmarried mothers.

THE FAMILY

One would think that defining a "family" should not be a difficult task. After all, the family is so significant to society that it is universal. "The family is one of the most

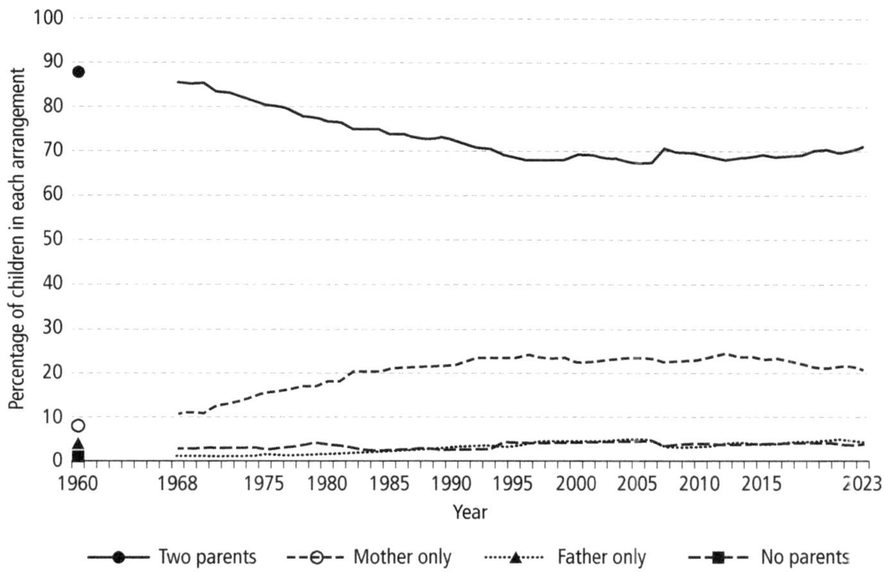

FIGURE 8.1 Parent/guardian living arrangements of children in the United States, 1960 to 2023
Source: US Bureau of the Census, 2024f.

important foundations and agents of socialization; the family is the first place we learn culture, norms, values, and gender roles" (Farris and Poston, 2014: vii). Families exist in all societies, but their constitution varies across cultures and over time. For example, the Western world has traditionally regarded a family as consisting of a husband, wife, and children. But we are seeing these days an increasing number "of one-parent families, gay and lesbian families, blended families and childless families." Moreover, in the United States and in many Western countries, "we use a bilineal system of descent in which we recognize that descent can be traced through both the mother's and the father's side of the family. However, in many parts of China, descent is patrilineal" (Farris and Poston, 2014: vii), that is, determined only through the father's side of the family.

Brief Historical Review

We start this review with Thornton and Fricke's very inclusive definition of the family: it is a "social network, not necessarily localized, that is based on culturally recognized biological and marital relationships" (1989: 130). One of the main functions of the family is to produce the next generation. Fertility almost always operates within the family setting. But as Waite (2005: 88) has observed, the "rise of alternative family structures, including gay and lesbian partnerships, and cohabiting couples, sometimes including children, raises the question of whether a family must have a culturally recognized biological or marital relationship." The answer depends on the extent to which the partners are recognized culturally as a family. Marriage clearly converts a cohabiting couple with one or more children into a family. But until recently, gay male and lesbian partners in the United States residing in states where same-sex marriage was illegal and often not recognized (Bryn and Holcomb, 2012) were denied the family-legitimizing function of marriage. This is, however, no longer the situation with the decision of the US Supreme Court on June 26, 2015, legalizing same-sex marriage everywhere in the United States (Poston, 2020a).

We mentioned earlier the historian Stephanie Coontz, one of the most prolific and articulate writers about marriage and the family. She has another interesting book *Marriage, A History: From Obedience to Intimacy or How Love Conquered Marriage* (2005). We draw on materials from this book in the next few paragraphs in our historical review of marriage and the family.

Coontz makes several points in her history of marriage that run counter to the idealized perception of the so-called traditional marriage. In the earliest times up to around the seventeenth century, marriages in most societies were not necessarily about love, sex, childrearing, and affection. Although these may have figured into the marriages, the principal objective of marriage was to gain in-laws who would bring legitimacy. The authority of rulers was justified on the basis of their ancestry. The best way to bolster one's ancestral legitimacy "was to marry someone who also had an august line of ancestors" (Coontz, 2005: 53). Moreover, marriage was used to establish military and commercial ties. Whereas today rulers and heads of states ratify treaties between countries with their signatures, in the past they would seal "their deals with a marriage ceremony" (Coontz, 2005: 54). And marriages worked in a similar way with similar benefits for the common people. The children who were married off had virtually no say regarding their new partners; for the most part their parents and grandparents and other male relatives made the decisions.

Marrying for the economic and political advantages accruing from such arrangements remained dominant until the eighteenth century. But several hundred years earlier, changes began to occur in Western Europe that led the way to the changes in the eighteenth century. One change was the prohibition, around the twelfth century, of **polygyny**. And "by the fifteenth century the children of mistresses had lost the inheritance rights they had had in the early medieval period" (Coontz, 2005: 124). Another change was that increasingly the newly married couple would establish their own household rather than move in with the parents of the husband. Despite these changes, however, women remained subordinate to men. But a wife in these new marital arrangements "could exert more pressure on her husband than in an extended family system, where the husband's authority was reinforced by all his kin" (Coontz, 2005: 130).

By the end of the eighteenth century in Western Europe, a new marriage system began to take hold. "For the first time in five thousand years, marriage came to be seen as a private relationship between two individuals rather than one link in a larger system of political and economic alliances" (Coontz, 2005: 145–146). And little by little, the roles of the husband and wife were transformed. The husband assumed the primary role of providing for the family. The wife focused herself morally and emotionally on family life. The "love match" became normative in England in the 1760s, in France in the 1800s, and in other parts of Europe at slightly different times. In America the norms were also starting to favor the "love match." A few decades after the American Revolution, "New Englanders began to change their description of an ideal mate, adding companionship and cooperation to the traditional expectations of thrift and industriousness" (Coontz, 2005: 147).

During the colonial era in the United States, the traditional family did not have the sharply divided roles and responsibilities we saw in the "Ozzie and Harriet" family where the husband was the provider, and the wife was the homemaker. The "husband was [still] considered [to be] the head of the family" (Gill, Glazer, and Thernstrom, 1992: 147). But the husband, wife, and children all worked together and contributed economically to the household and the household-related tasks. Think of the family farm one hundred or more years ago and the fact that everyone from the grandfather to the youngest child played a role in its maintenance.

Waite (2005: 88) has described how the societal and structural changes underway in Europe and America worked to influence the change in marriage form. Social changes – including industrialization, urbanization, productivity increases, rise of the market economy, and greater individualization – gradually shifted control and decision making away from the family and the extended family to the individuals. With increases in rural to urban migration, more and more adults were working in factories and other non-familial settings. With fewer people employed in family-based activities, such as the family farm, decision making became less based on familial issues and connections, resulting in the parents playing reduced roles in mate selection.

Pure demography also played a role in the changes in the importance and form of marriage. We reported in Chapter 4 that in the nineteenth century, US White women were having seven children each, on average. The total fertility rate (TFR) started to drop in 1820 but did not reach 4.0 children per woman until 1900. This means that for most of the nineteenth century most women were having their last baby when they were in their 40s. Consider an average woman having her last child (her fifth or sixth, or maybe her seventh) at age 45. She would be 60 years old when her last child was age 15. Female life expectancy at age 60 in 1901 was right at around fourteen years. So, the average White woman in the nineteenth century had fourteen years of life remaining after raising her last-born child to young adulthood. We do not have TFR and life expectancy data for Black women and Hispanic women for these periods, but the years of remaining life for Black women were surely less than those for Whites, and those for Hispanics and Whites would have been about the same.

Jump ahead to the second decade of the twenty-first century. As we will show below, the average non-Hispanic (NH) White woman today marries at around age 27 or 28. However, 40 percent of babies born today are to unmarried White mothers. (The percentages are higher for Hispanic and Black mothers.) So, marriage per se is no longer the precursor to fertility that it used to be. The average mother these days has her first baby at age 26. We will assume for the purpose of our illustration that she has her last birth at around age 35; 80 percent of the more than 3.6 million births in 2022 were to women of age 35 or younger (Osterman et al., 2024). By the time the last child of this average mother is age 15, Mom is age 50. Current life tables give this 50-year-old mother another thirty-three years of life. So, what does this mean?

The average woman in the nineteenth century had fourteen years of life remaining after she had raised her last child to age 15. In other words, by the time her last child was a young adult, the mother had already lived four-fifths of her life and had only one-fifth, or fourteen years left. In contrast, the average woman these days has thirty-three years of life remaining by the time she has raised her last child to age 15; she has used up

50 years of her life, but she has thirty-three more years left. The point we are making is that marriage and childbearing are no longer the defining events and activities of our lives. In earlier times they were our identity, and really our only identity. Now they are much less universal and exclusive than they once were. Or as Coontz (2000: 186) has remarked, "parenthood, like marriage, is a less salient, central, and long-lasting part of life than it used to be."

Marriage and the Family Today

We turn now to a discussion of marriage and the family today, focusing heavily on the situation in the United States. In 2024, Census Bureau data indicated that just about two-thirds, that is, 64 percent, of all households were classified as family households. This is a tremendous change from the mid-1970s when almost 80 percent of US households were so classified. Moreover, of all the family households in the United States in 2024, less than 40 percent included the householder's children under age 18.

A family household, by the way, is defined as a household with at least one adult heading the household, known as the householder or the household head, and with at least one other person living in the household who is related to the householder by birth, marriage, or adoption (US Bureau of the Census, 2024b). A nonfamily household is made up of unrelated individuals, such as college roommates living in an apartment. Who is living in the residence is the defining characteristic; not considered are how the finances are divided and how the meals are prepared.

There have been a lot of changes in recent decades. We now consider four main questions about the US family today to better assist us in understanding these changes:

1. How old are people today when they marry for the first time?
2. How many people get married?
3. How many people cohabit before marriage?
4. How many babies are born to unmarried women?

In the "traditional" Ozzie and Harriet type family of the 1950s, males married at around 22 or 23, and women at around age 20. Everyone, or nearly everyone, married. Very few people cohabited before marriage; the word "cohabitation" was not even in our vocabulary, even though the *Oxford English Dictionary* states that the word "cohabit" meaning "to live together as a husband and wife, often said distinctively of persons not legally married" appeared in the English language for the first time in as early as 1530 (2000: III: 448). And very few babies were born to unmarried women; if a woman did have a baby outside marriage, the baby was usually placed out for adoption. In the next several pages we will examine the above issues as they exist today and show how dramatically they have changed. Our discussions will allow us to paint a picture of marriage and the family in the contemporary United States and the changes that have occurred in recent decades.

1. How Old Are People Today When They Marry for the First Time?

We now consider the first question: How old are people today when they marry for the first time? Figure 8.2 presents data on the median age at first marriage for men and

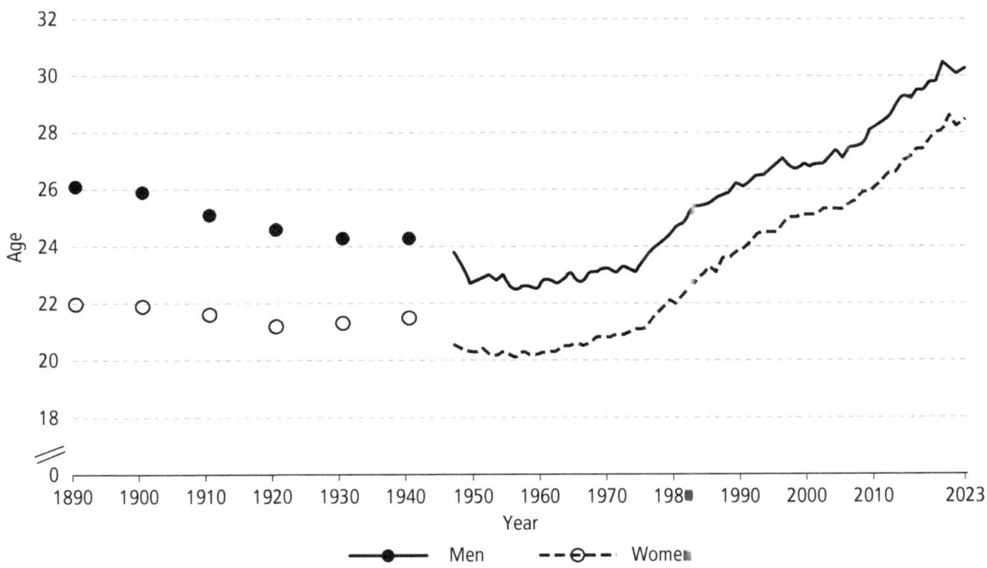

FIGURE 8.2 Median age at first marriage in the United States, 1890–2023
Source: US Census Bureau, 2024.

women, starting in 1890 and extending to 2023. Age at first marriage at the end of the nineteenth century was right at 26 for men and almost 22 for women. The trend lines show declines to about 1960 with median ages at first marriage then of 22.8 years for males and 20.3 years for females. These data almost perfectly represent the situations of the coauthors of this book. Poston and his wife Patricia married in 1963; he was just over 22, and Pat was four months shy of 21. The other coauthor, Sullivan, and her husband Doug married in 1971; she was 21 and he was 23. By the way, Poston and Sullivan and their spouses were not marrying early. They were marrying at about the same time as most of their similarly aged friends.

Iceland attributes the declines in median age at first marriage from 1890 to the early 1960s to "the growth of well-paid wage labor employment for men that accompanied industrialization ... [giving them] a sufficient income to support a family, even at a relatively young age" (Iceland, 2014: 40). And these were also the years of the baby boom, when men and women were marrying earlier and producing more children.

Since the 1960s the trend lines show progressively later ages at first marriage, rising to 26 years for men and 24 years for women in 1990, to 27 for men and 25 for women in 2000, to 29 for men and to 27 for women in 2015, and to 30 for men and 28 for women in 2023. These days, men and women in the United States are clearly marrying later than they did in earlier times. Indeed, there are no earlier periods in the United States, for which marriage data are available, that show later average ages at first marriage.

If women and men are marrying later, does this mean that some will never marry? If so, we should see increasing proportions never marrying and decreasing proportions marrying. This is our second question: How many people get married?

2. *How Many People Get Married?*

Figure 8.3 presents data on the marital status of US women 15 years of age and over from 1950 to 2023. In 1950, 66 percent of women of age 15+ were married, and 20 percent were never married. We do not show comparative data for men, but they are very similar to those for women. The percentage married trend line for women then goes down reaching 52 percent in 2010 and a low of 50 percent by 2023. (For males it is 52 percent.) And the never married trend line for women goes up, reaching 27 percent in 2010 and a high of 31 percent in 2023. (For males it is 37 percent.) We see a remarkably consistent reduction in the percentages of women and men marrying in the past almost seventy-five years, and a remarkably consistent increase in the percentages never marrying. In the 1950s more than two-thirds of women and men aged 15 and over were married; in 2023 half of women and just over half of men were married.

Another way to address the question is to consider data on the percentage of people 40 years old who have never married. Way back in 1910, 16 percent of 40-year-olds had never married; the figure reached a low in 1980 of only 6 percent of 40-year-olds who had never married; it then increased to 20 percent in 2010, and to 25 percent in 2021 (Fry, 2023). What of the years ahead? What about some of those 40-year-olds marrying when they are older? Consider the marrying patterns of 40-year-olds who had not married by the year 2001; "about one-in-four 40-year-olds who had not married in 2001 had done so by age 60" (Fry, 2023: 1). If that pattern holds, we would expect that some of the 40-year-olds not married in 2021 might marry later. But the numbers of late marriages will not make up for all the never marrieds in the earlier years.

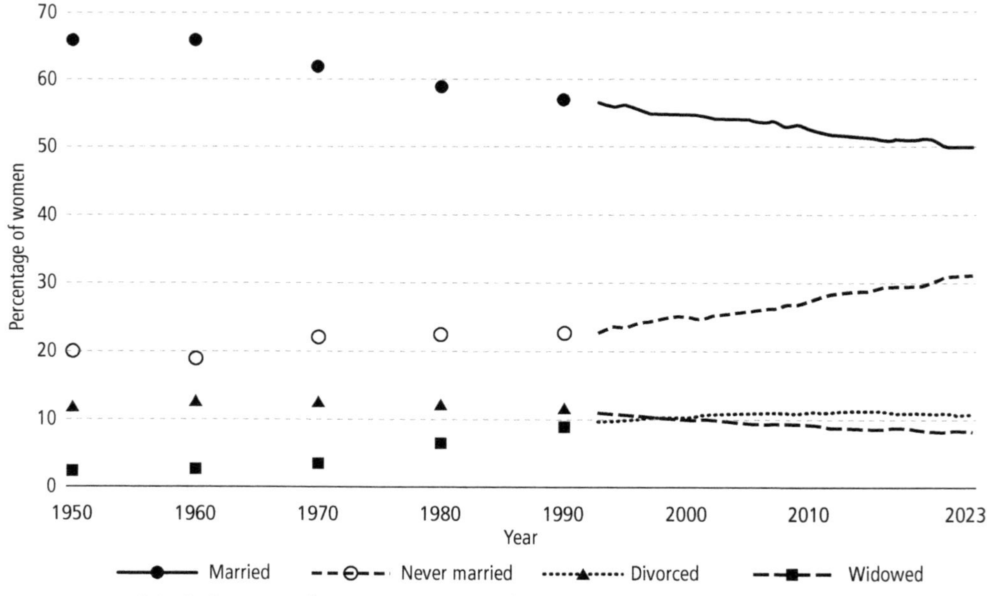

FIGURE 8.3 Marital status of women 15 years of age and older, United States, 1950–2023
Source: US Census Bureau, 2024.

Are women and men are opting out of marriage or are they marrying later? What are they doing? What are their living arrangements? This leads to our third question: How many people cohabit prior to marriage?

3. *How Many People Cohabit Before Marriage?*

We first examine data on cohabitation from the 2002 National Survey of Family Growth (NSFG) and from the 2013–2017 National Survey of Family Growth. (See our discussion of the NSFG in Chapter 3.) Let us look at the percentages of people who have ever cohabited in their lifetimes versus the percentages who have ever married. According to NSFG data for the 2013–2017 period, 59 percent of adults between the ages of 18 and 44 have lived with an unmarried partner at some time in their lives; that is, they have cohabited. Compare this ever-cohabited percentage of 59 percent with the percentage of adults who have ever been married, namely, 50 percent. "By contrast, in 2002, 54 percent of adults in this age group had ever cohabited and 60 percent had ever married" (Graf, 2019: 1). The NSFG data indicate that it is now more common for adults to have cohabited sometime in their lifetime than to have ever married.

Does cohabitation usually precede marriage? How many married couples these days cohabited prior to marrying? Manning and Carlson have examined NSFG data for several time periods; they have reported that among women between the ages of 19 and 44 marrying in the 1965–1974 period, 11 percent of them cohabited with their partners before marrying them. Among women in the same age group marrying between 1990 and 1994, 56 percent of them had cohabited prior to their marriages. Among the women marrying in the 2000–2004 period, 68 percent of them cohabited with their partners prior to marriage. Finally, the cohabitation data for women marrying in the most recent period of 2015–2019 show an even higher percentage. Among these women, 76 percent of them cohabited with their partners prior to marriage. Whereas 11 percent of women marrying in the late 1960s and early 1970s reported that they cohabited with their partners before marriage, 76 percent of women marrying between 2015 and 2019 lived with their partners before marrying them (Manning and Carlson, 2021). Regarding the levels of education of the women, the percentages who have cohabited prior to marriage have increased for all levels of education, with the largest increases for women with college degrees. Irrespective of one's level of education, the percentages who have ever cohabited have increased consistently.

4. *How Many Babies Are Born to Unmarried Women?*

We turn now to the last of our four questions: How many babies are born to unmarried women? We will first provide some perspective by drawing on the experiences and remembrances of coauthor Poston when he was the age of many of you readers of this textbook, back in his undergraduate student years in college in the late 1950s and early 1960s. Very few babies then were born to unmarried mothers, just over 5 percent of all births. In the 1950s and earlier, if an unmarried woman had a baby, she would most likely not raise the child. Keeping the baby if she was not married was seen as spoiling the reputation of her family. And abortion was illegal. So, what happened to the young pregnant unmarried woman? She was sent away, often to another city where no one knew her. She would go through her pregnancy there and give birth to the baby. And the baby would then be out-adopted at a very early age, often within the first few months of its birth. How was this done?

Poston grew up in the Parkside neighborhood in the southwestern part of San Francisco and lived there for most of the 22 years of his life before he married. In that neighborhood there was a private facility several blocks from his home that was referred to, in the vernacular of the day, as a "home for unwed mothers." Unwed pregnant women from outside San Francisco, and from outside California, lived there until their babies were born. Young pregnant women would often be seen walking about the neighborhood; most knew they were from the "home."

Poston's (now deceased) aunt and godmother, Dorothy Kara Zaro, worked for several decades in the 1960s to the 1980s as an office administrator at another of these "homes for unwed mothers" in San Francisco, known as St. Elizabeth's Infant Home for Unwed Mothers, run by the Daughters of Charity, an order of Catholic nuns. When a pregnant unmarried woman entered St. Elizabeth's, she was given a fictitious name which she used during her tenure there. Poston remembers his aunt telling him in as early as the 1980s that not as many pregnant unmarried women were now boarding any more at the facility. Fewer unwed pregnant women came to St. Elizabeth's in the 1990s, so the establishment changed its mission. Rather than caring for unmarried women as they progressed through their pregnancies, St. Elizabeth's started to care for married and unmarried mothers with young children. In 1993 St. Elizabeth's was renamed the Epiphany Center for Families in Recovery.

Pregnant unmarried women in the 1960s and earlier were stigmatized and shunned by society. If an unmarried daughter was found to be pregnant, her family would often send her away from her home to a home for unwed mothers in another city or state. She would enter the home – she would be perhaps in her late teen years or early 20s – in the fourth or so month of her pregnancy at about the time she was beginning "to show"; she would remain there until the baby was born. The baby would be taken from her soon after it was born, and it would be out-adopted; the mother would likely never see her baby again. From the start of the twentieth century until around 1970 or so, such establishments were pervasive. Most cities had several of them, and many were owned and operated by religious groups. Most of the young women in a home were from another city or town. The home offered them anonymity and safety. A movie and a recent book discuss these issues occurring in Ireland and in Italy. The 2013 film *Philomena*, starring Judi Dench and Steve Coogan, tells the true story of the experiences of an unwed mother (Philomena Lee, played by Judi Dench) in a home for unwed mothers in Ireland, and how she lost her son to a couple in the United States. Laurino's book, *The Price of Children* (2024), reveals how several thousand Italian children born to unmarried mothers in Italy between 1951 and 1969 were taken from their mothers and out-adopted to Catholic families in the United States, via a system maintained by the Italian government, the Vatican, and the National Catholic Welfare Conference, an arm of the American Catholic Church.

Figure 8.4 shows percentage data on babies born to unmarried women according to their race and Hispanic origin for the years 1980 through 2021. In 2021, 40 percent of all babies born that year were to unmarried mothers.

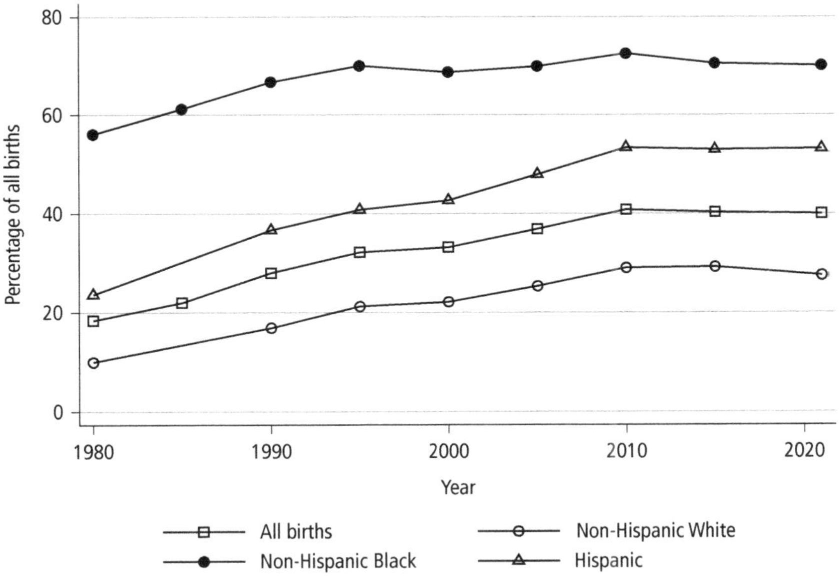

FIGURE 8.4 Percentage of births to unmarried women by race and Hispanic origin, United States, 1980 to 2021
Data sources: 1980–2015, National Center for Health Statistics; 2021: Osterman et al., 2023.

The trend data in Figure 8.4 show dramatic increases in the percentages of births to unmarried women, from a low of 18 percent in 1980, to 28 percent in 1990, to 33 percent in 2000, to 40 percent by 2021. The chart shown in Figure 8.4 starts in 1980. Data for the 1950s – not shown in the chart – report a value of 5 percent, indicating that for every 100 babies born in the 1950s, five were born to unwed mothers. By 2021, 40 of every 100 new births were to unwed mothers. The percentage of births to unmarried mothers increased eight-fold in seventy years.

Homes for unwed mothers still exist, but they are rare today. The reduction in the number of such establishments is due to several factors, such as the legalization of abortion, the widespread availability and enhanced effectiveness of contraception (see our discussions in Chapter 11), the increased percentages of unmarried mothers (see Figure 8.4), and the changing societal attitudes regarding single parenthood. The establishments that do exist are no longer called "homes for unwed mothers," but rather, "homes for expectant mothers" or "homes for babies and mothers" or "maternity homes." Often, the names of the establishments do not even contain the words "pregnant" and "unwed." The Edna Gladney Home in Fort Worth, Texas – renamed in 1991 as the Gladney Center for Adoption – was, and is, one of the most prominent institutions in Texas; it has provided services to pregnant single women since the 1930s up to this very day. "Maggie's Place" in Phoenix, Arizona, is another such establishment, as is "Good Counsel Homes" in Hoboken, New Jersey.

The percentage of births to unmarried mothers varies significantly by race and Hispanic origin (Figure 8.4). NH White women have the lowest percentage; it was 10 percent in 1980 and over 27 percent in 2021; since 1980 it has increased almost three-fold. These days, almost three of every ten births to NH White women are to unmarried NH White women.

NH Black women have the highest percentage of births. In 1980, over 56 percent of Black mothers were not married when their babies were born; the rate increased to over 70 percent by 2021. These days, more than seven of every ten births to Black mothers are to unmarried women. The Hispanic percentages are mid-way between those of the Whites and the Blacks. In 1980 almost one-quarter of all births to Hispanic mothers were to unmarried women; by 2021, the percentage had more than doubled to over 53 percent. Now, more than half of Hispanic women are unmarried when they have their babies.

Why are the NH Black percentages so much higher than the NH White percentages? In 2021, over 70 percent of Black births were to unmarried women, compared with over 27 percent of White births. The Black rate is 2.5 times higher than the White rate. First, the fact that a woman is not married when she has her baby does not mean that the unmarried mother is raising her baby alone. Of the 72 percent of births to unmarried Black women, one-third of the mothers are cohabiting (Martinez, Daniels, and Chandra, 2012), so there is a father in the household helping raise the child along with the mother. Another reason is purely demographic, namely, the availability of Black men; there are not enough of them. Of the 8 million Black men in the United States in the ages 25–54, 1.5 million are not available due to incarceration and higher mortality, the main factors responsible for taking these 1.5 million men out of the marriage pool. Mass incarceration accounts for 600,000 of them, and higher death rates for much of the balance. "Almost one in 12 Black men in this age group are behind bars, compared with one in 60 non-Black men" (Blow, 2015: A21).

Since there are many fewer Black men available in the marriage market, "some of the men have children by more than one woman, but they can only live in one home at a time" (Blow, 2015: A21). The fact that the father does not live with all his children at the same time, however, does not necessarily mean he is not relating to the children who are not living with him.

Recent research of demographer Joseph Chaime indicates that in the United States in 2023, across all the race and ethnic groups, around 25 percent of all children of age 17 years or less "were living in a household without their biological, step, or adoptive father," usually with their mother. He further notes that "living in a single-parent household with a father absent is [currently] the second most common US living arrangement [for children], and the proportion of these households has doubled since 1970" (Chamie, 2025: 1).

Sociologists Kathryn Edin and Maria Kefalas have written a very interesting and provocative ethnography, *Promises I Can Keep: Why Poor Women Put Motherhood before Marriage* (2007). Their book focused on 162 poor mothers living in Philadelphia who were Black, Hispanic, or White. Of their many interesting findings, one is of particular relevance for our discussions here: Among the poor young women they interviewed, many of them intentionally became pregnant because they wanted to have babies. Having a baby was a legitimation of their personhood. A baby was the woman's identity. Most could not imagine a life without a child, marriage or no marriage. Not having children was deemed a tragedy. (In our discussions of childlessness in Chapter 4,

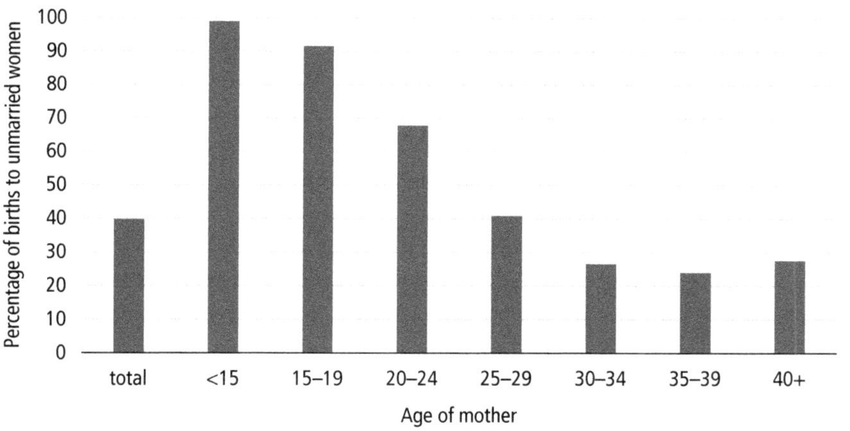

FIGURE 8.5 Percentage of all births to unmarried women by age of mother, United States, 2022
Data source: Osterman et al., 2024.

recall the much lower rates of childlessness among Black and Hispanic women than among Whites.)

Finally, we ask about the ages of the women who are unmarried when their children are born. How old are they? Figure 8.5 presents data for the year 2022 showing the ages of unmarried women giving birth.

Almost 40 percent of all births in 2022 were to unmarried women. The histogram data in Figure 8.5 indicate that in 2022 virtually all the births to women less than 15 years of age were to unmarried women; that is no surprise. In addition, there were very few births to women under age 15, only 1,816 in the United States in 2022. The next age group is 15–19; almost 92 percent of these women who had babies in 2022 were not married.

Most of the births in 2022 occurred to women in their 20s and early 30s. (Remember the "age curve of fertility" that we discussed in Chapter 4.) How many of them were unmarried? Almost 68 percent of 20–24-year-old women giving birth were unmarried, almost 41 percent of 25–29-year-olds, and over 26 percent of 30–34-year-olds. These data mirror very closely the increasing median age at first marriage (Figure 8.2). The older the woman, the more likely she has married, and the less likely she is not married when she gives birth.

SUMMARY

In this chapter we discussed several issues of marriage and the family in the contemporary US society. Men and women are marrying later these days than ever previously. Fewer people are marrying than in past decades. More men and women are cohabiting; indeed, cohabitation is now the norm. And, finally, 40 percent of all births are to unmarried women (69 percent for Blacks, 53 percent for Hispanics, 27 percent for Whites). These four issues we examined and discussed in this chapter are dramatically different quantitatively these days compared to in the 1950s. In the "Ozzie and Harriet" traditional family, men and women married early, most people married, very few cohabited, and hardly any babies were born to unwed mothers. The "Ozzie and Harriet" days are no longer with us.

DISCUSSION QUESTIONS

1. Think about the various characteristics of weddings, such as location, costs, timing, wedding participants, attendees, etc. Focus on four of the characteristics (you need not restrict yourself to the characteristics just mentioned) and speculate about how first-time weddings might be similar as well as different in these characteristics when the brides and grooms are in their late 20s or early 30s, compared to when the brides and grooms are in their late teens or early 20s. How do you think the weddings might be similar, and how do you think they might be different?
2. Trend data in Figure 8.4 show dramatic increases in the percentages of births in the United States to unmarried women, from a low of 18 percent in 1980, to 28 percent in 1990, to 33 percent in 2000, to 40 percent in 2021. The percentages of births to unmarried mothers vary significantly by race and Hispanic origin. NH White women have the lowest percentages, 10 percent in 1980 and over 27 percent in 2021. NH Black women have the highest percentages, over 56 percent in 1980 and over 70 percent in 2021. What do you believe are the two main reasons why the overall trends in percentages of births to unmarried women have increased from 1980 to 2021? And what do you think are the two main reasons why the percentages differ so much between White and Black women? Be sure to defend your answers.

9

Sexual Orientation

INTRODUCTION

The subject of this chapter is sexual orientation, and the subject of the next chapter is gender identity. Sexual orientation and gender identity are two distinctly different concepts. But populations engaging in these two behaviors are often combined in an acronym, expressed frequently as LGBTQ+, leading some to believe that the populations represented in the acronym are different versions of one common population. But they are not. The only common aspect is that the abbreviated populations in the acronym are all sexual minority populations.

In the first section of this chapter, we break down the acronym, consider each of the populations, and show that the acronym does not represent the same general population. Later sections discuss two basic strategies for conceptualizing sexual orientation, seven different dimensions of sexual orientation, and survey data for measuring the prevalence of sexual orientation. These sections are followed by sections reporting the results of empirical analyses of sexual orientation for females, for males, and for asexuals.

THE LGBTQIA ACRONYM

The LGBTQ abbreviations in the acronym represent sexual minority populations. The last category in the LGBTQ+ acronym shown in the preceding section is the "+" category; it is meant to indicate that there are additional sexual minority populations not captured with the first five LGBTQ. In our discussions here in this chapter, we will remove the plus sign and enter two more sexual minority populations, namely, the intersex population I, and the asexual population A. The acronym we will now use is LGBTQIA.

The LGBTQIA acronym lists seven different sexual and gender minority populations; these populations are grouped by sexual orientation, gender identity, or both. The groups are lesbians (L), gay males (G), bisexuals (B), transgender persons (T), queer/questioning persons (Q), intersex persons (I), and asexuals (A). Lesbians, gay males, bisexuals, and asexuals are sexual minorities grouped together owing to their sexual orientation; none of these populations interact sexually only and exclusively with members of the opposite sex. Lesbians (L) interact sexually with women, gay males (G) with men, and bisexuals (B) with both women and men; asexuals (A) do not interact sexually with others. Actually, as we note below, sexual orientation does not refer only to sexual behavior; there are several other dimensions of sexual orientation, and they are discussed in a later section.

Transgender persons (T) are grouped together not because of their sexual orientation, but because of their gender identity; they are a sexual minority group owing to their gender identity. Transgender persons identify their current gender as different from that assigned at birth; their current gender could be either male, or female, or neither, namely, gender nonbinary. As just noted, the classification of transgender persons is not one of sexual orientation, but one of gender identity.

Queer persons (Q) are grouped together either because their sexual orientation, or their gender identity, does not conform to societal norms or conventional labels. The Q label is also sometimes used to describe a person who is attracted to people of many genders. And the Q label is also sometimes used to represent questioning persons, that is, persons who are still exploring their sexual orientation or their gender identity.

Finally, intersex persons (I) are persons with a reproductive or sexual anatomy that does not fit the typical binary classification of male or female. Some persons are classified at birth as intersex; others are not classified as intersex until later, often during adolescence. Some intersex persons are chromosomally of one sex but hormonally of the other. The sexual orientation of an intersex person may be heterosexual, homosexual, bisexual, or asexual. The gender identity of an intersex person may be female, male, both, or neither.

The LGBTQIA acronym enables researchers to identify persons who are sexual or gender minorities (SGM); it also allows researchers to distinguish between SGM populations pertaining to sexual orientation and to gender identity.

CONCEPTUALIZING SEXUAL ORIENTATION

Most of the social science literature on sexual orientation conceptualizes the phenomenon using two basic perspectives or approaches, or a combination thereof. These two views are known as **essentialism** and **social constructionism.** Founded in biology, the essentialist view is one of dimorphism; it states that there is an "essential" biological or psychological characteristic or attribute that is common to all persons and that distinguishes them as either of one sexual orientation or not of that sexual orientation. This common characteristic, or essence, may be a fundamental drive or trait that establishes a person's inclusion, or not, in one of the sexual orientation categories of heterosexual or homosexual (Baumle et al., 2009: 19–21; Laumann et al., 1994: 285).

The social constructionist view, on the other hand, counters and critiques the essentialist perspective. Social constructionism argues against the notion of binary categories, that is, that one either is or is not in a specific sexual orientation category (Baumle et al., 2009: 20–2; Foucault, 1978). Instead, it argues for a continuum with varying degrees of the categories of sexual orientation. What in one culture may be defined as "homosexual" may not be so defined in another culture. Or as Blank (2012:

xviii) has written, "despite the fact that most of us use the term 'heterosexual' with enormous and cavalier certainty, there seems to be no aspect of 'heterosexual' for which a truly iron-clad definition has been established." And the same may be stated about "homosexual."

Up until the 1940s and 1950s when Alfred Kinsey and his colleagues (Kinsey, Pomeroy, and Martin, 1948; Kinsey, Pomeroy, Martin, and Gebhard, 1953) conducted their sexuality research, most researchers used an essentialist orientation. It was Kinsey who moved sexuality research away from a position of essentialism.

Perhaps the very best and certainly the most comprehensive analysis of sexuality in the United States is *The Social Organization of Sexuality: Sexual Practices in the United States* by Laumann, Gagnon, Michael, and Michaels that was published in 1994. In this book, and indeed in much of the literature on sexual orientation over the past few decades, a common finding is its *fluidity* over the life course. Most analyses show that the estimated prevalence rates of homosexuality and heterosexuality and bisexuality and asexuality vary, often considerably, according to the particular dimension of sexual orientation being used (Compton et al., 2015). We now turn attention to the dimensions of sexual orientation.

THE DIMENSIONS OF SEXUAL ORIENTATION

Seven different dimensions of sexual orientation have been discussed and delineated in the social science literature. Three of them, sexual self-identification, sexual attraction, and sexual behavior, the so-called trifecta, are especially prominent in the empirical literature, so we will give them special attention. In our discussions of the seven dimensions of sexual orientation, we draw especially on the writings of Edward Laumann and his associates (1994) and Anthony Bogaert (2012), and a few others.

We begin by asking what is meant when someone says they are lesbian or gay male or bisexual or heterosexual or asexual. Are the persons referring to their sexual behavior or to something more than their behavior? These days when demographers conduct research on sexual orientation, they tend to focus more on sexual behavior, with less attention to other dimensions. But when psychologists and sexologists study sexual orientation, they tend to focus more on sexual attraction. And sociologists tend to focus more on sexual self-identification. Often the dimension of sexual orientation used in the research depends on the social science background of the researcher.

Sexual behavior refers to overt sexual actions. There are lots of sexual actions, done by oneself or partnered, including masturbation, touching, oral sex, and intercourse. In the earliest analyses of sexuality – starting with the seven volumes by Havelock Ellis, *Studies in the Psychology of Sex* (1897–1928) up to the two volumes by Kinsey and his associates, *Sexual Behavior in the Human Male* (1948) and *Sexual Behavior in the Human Female* (1953) – the focus was almost always on sexual behavior.

But many social scientists and sexologists hold that sexual behavior is too limiting a dimension, and that the mind's key processes – namely, attractions, thoughts, and desires – also need to be considered. Bogaert has written that one reason why sex researchers these days consider other dimensions is because "we now have better ways of measuring them" (Bogaert, 2012: 17). In fact, some hold that "one's deep-seated sexual attractions always trump overt behavior when attempting to understand the essence of a human being's sexual orientation" (Bogaert, 2012: 18).

A second dimension is one's sexual self-identification, referring to how persons define themselves, namely, as heterosexual, lesbian, gay male, bisexual, or asexual. Using self-identity as the method for defining one's sexual orientation "respects the way someone chooses to label him or herself" (Bogaert, 2012: 23). But "because one's sexual identity is often formed by a variety of factors, such as knowledge of a label or labels, comfort level with coming out, and political and other factors," many sexologists, including Bogaert, "are often wary of using self-identification as the key dimension in defining sexual orientation" (Bogaert, 2012: 23).

A third dimension is sexual attraction, that is, the "sexual or lust lure for others" (Bogaert, 2012: 11). Whereas demographers seem to focus on sexual behavior, and sociologists on sexual self-identification, sexologists and psychologists focus on one's sexual attraction to others; they argue that sexual attraction "is the *sine qua non* of sexual orientation. So, for example, if you are a woman and primarily lust after – in other words are turned on by being with, looking at, thinking about, or fantasizing about – men, then you have a heterosexual orientation. Thus, you are sexually oriented to, or have sexual orientation toward, men" (Bogaert, 2012:12).

We have already noted that these three dimensions are the main ones. But there are several others. A fourth dimension is romantic attraction. This refers to a lure that draws us to someone or something. Romantic attraction is a "feeling of infatuation and emotional attachment" associated with pair bonding, often referred to as "love" (Bogaert, 2012; Diamond, 2003: 175). Romantic attraction is not necessarily the same as sexual attraction. Bogaert has noted that the two attractions are potentially independent and may well have evolved from different processes. "Reptilian brains are, after all, geared for sex, not for love" (Bogaert, 2012: 12). For some, sexual attraction may lead to romantic attraction; and for others romantic attraction may lead to sexual attraction. Diamond (2003) has written that romantic attraction followed by sexual attraction will tend to occur more often for women than for men.

A fifth dimension is sexual arousal; it refers to the "physical aspects of one's sexual response, or what happens in the genitals when sexual stimuli are encountered" (Bogaert, 2012: 15). In males, sexual arousal usually leads to erections and changing blood flows. In females, sexual arousal usually leads to engorged sexual tissues such as nipples, vulva, clitoris, vaginal walls, and lubrication (Bogaert, 2012: 15). The research by Masters and Johnson (1966, 1970) focused mainly on the sexual arousal dimension.

A sixth dimension is sexual scripts. This dimension deals with thoughts and how they are processed. Bogaert has observed that "our thoughts are often organized into 'knowledge structures' or 'schemas.' One form of knowledge structure is a script, ... [which is] a cognitive generalization about the 'appropriate sequence of events in a particular context'" (Bogaert, 2012: 20). Using scripts as a theoretical perspective for an analysis of sexuality is a major contribution of the research of Laumann and his associates (1994).

Bogaert has noted that humans engage in sexual scripts that are followed automatically by sexual behaviors. One needs to know the scripts for the various sexual behaviors. It will often take time to learn them, and it takes practice to make them "unfold in a relatively seamless way; sexual behavior is not without its complications, to say the least" (Bogaert, 2012: 20).

Finally, a seventh dimension is sexual desire, a dimension associated with the previous dimensions of sexual attraction, sexual arousal, sexual behavior, and sexual scripts, and also to some extent, with romantic attraction. Sexual desire may be defined as "a feeling that includes wanting to have a sexual experience, feeling receptive to a partners' sexual initiation, and thinking and fantasizing about sex" (Rosen et al, 2000: 191).

We have discussed seven different dimensions of sexual orientation. But three of these dimensions receive the most attention in the social science literature, namely, sexual behavior, sexual attraction, and sexual self-identification, the trifecta. One reason why these three receive more attention is that they are conceptually and methodologically preferred by social scientists over the other four; that is demographers tend to focus on sexual behavior, sociologists on sexual self-identification, and psychologists and sexologists on sexual attraction. Another reason why these three dimensions receive most of the attention in the empirical research literature is that data are more readily available in nationally representative surveys that capture these three dimensions than is the case for the other dimensions.

In the next section of this chapter, we look at data from the National Survey of Family Growth pertaining to the three sexual orientation dimensions of sexual behavior, sexual self-identification, and sexual attraction. For females and for males, we will compare and contrast the empirical prevalence in the United States of the sexual majority population, namely, heterosexuals, with the main sexual minority populations, namely, lesbians (L), gay males (G), bisexuals (B), and asexuals (A).

EMPIRICAL PREVALENCE OF SEXUAL ORIENTATION: DATA

There are several nationally representative social surveys of US adults that contain questions dealing with one or more of the three principal dimensions of sexual orientation. These are the General Social Survey (GSS), the National Health and Nutrition Examination Survey (NHANES), the National Health Interview Survey (NHIS), and two versions of the National Survey of Family Growth, one for females (NSFG-F) and one for males (NSFG-M). The GSS is conducted by the National Opinion Research Center (NORC) at the University of Chicago. The other four, NHANES, NHIS, NSFG-F, and NSFG-M are conducted by the National Center for Health Statistics (NCHS), a major division of the Center for Disease Control and Prevention (CDC). The CDC is a major operating component of the US Department of Health and Human Services.

The above five surveys do not all gather data on each of the three principal dimensions of sexual orientation, the so-called trifecta. The GSS and the NHANES both include questions on sexual behavior and sexual self-identification. The NHIS only includes questions of sexual self-identification. Only the NSFG, both the female and male versions, includes questions on all three of the trifecta. Since we wish in this chapter to appraise empirically the prevalence among US adults of sexual orientation according to all three dimensions, we opted to use only data from the NSFG. (See Baker-Hughes, 2019: chapter 3, for more discussion of these and other US surveys and their inclusion of questions dealing with the dimensions of sexual orientation.)

We noted in Chapter 3 that the National Survey of Family Growth is a nationally representative survey of female and male respondents between the ages of 15 and 44 that collects information on family life, marriage and divorce, pregnancy, infertility, use of contraception, and men's and women's health (National Center for Health Statistics, 2015). The NSFG is based on multistage and stratified probability sampling. We use data in this chapter from the 2015–2017 NSFG and from the 2017–2019 NSFG.

Here are the questions used in both NSFGs that tap the three dimensions of sexual behavior, sexual attraction, and sexual self-identification.

The following two questions dealing with the sexual behavior dimension were asked of female respondents:

At any time in your life, have you ever had sexual intercourse with a man, that is, made love, had sex, or gone all the way?
Yes or No.
Have you ever had any other sexual experience of any kind with another female?
Yes or No.

The following two sexual behavior questions were asked of male respondents:

At any time in your life, have you ever had sexual intercourse with a female; sometimes this is called making love, having sex, or going all the way?
Yes or No.
Have you ever had any other sexual experience of any kind with another male?
Yes or No.

Female respondents who stated that they have had sexual experiences with another female were classified on the sexual experience dimension as a sexual minority. And a similar classification was made of males who stated they have had sexual experiences with another male.

The following question dealing with the sexual attraction dimension was asked of both females and males:

People are different in their sexual attraction to other people. Which best describes your feelings?
Are you...
Only attracted to males 1
Mostly attracted to males 2
Equally attracted to males and females 3
Mostly attracted to females 4
Only attracted to females 5
Not sure 6

Respondents who reported that that they were only attracted to persons of the opposite sex were classified on the sexual attraction dimension as heterosexual. Respondents giving any of the other five answers were classified as sexual minority.

The following question dealing with the sexual self-identification dimension was asked of both females and males:

Which of the following best represents how you think of yourself?
Gay or lesbian. 1
Straight, that is, not gay or lesbian. 2
Bisexual 3
Something else 4

Respondents who answered the above question as "straight; that is, not gay or lesbian" were classified on the sexual self-identification dimension as heterosexual. Respondents giving any of the other three responses were classified as sexual minority.

We mentioned earlier that the NSFG is based on multistage and stratified probability sampling. Thus, in the empirical analyses reported below, we use the "svy" suite of statistical sample adjustment methods available in the Stata 17 statistical package (StataCorp, 2021) to adjust for the differential weighting and oversampling (Poston, Engin, and Cagatay, 2022).

EMPIRICAL ANALYSES OF SEXUAL ORIENTATION: FEMALES

We now examine female data from the 2015–2017 and 2017–2019 National Surveys of Family Growth capturing the three main dimensions of sexual orientation. Table 9.1

TABLE 9.1 *Adjusted percentage distributions of three dimensions of sexual orientation, females, National Surveys of Family Growth, 2015–2017 and 2017–2019*

Variable	NSFG 2015–2017	NSFG 2017–2019
Sexual Behavior		
Any same sex	19.2	20.2
No same sex	80.8	79.8
Sample size	5,493	6,069
Sexual Attraction		
Straight	76.3	72.8
Lesbian	1.5	1.6
Bisexual	19.8	23.5
Don't know/not sure	1.9	1.6
Refused	0.6	0.5
Sample Size	5,523	6,127
Sexual Self-Identification		
Straight	87.1	84.8
Lesbian	2.5	2.5
Bisexual	7.7	9.7
Something else	1.6	2.0
Don't know/not sure	0.3	0.3
Refused	0.7	0.7
Sample size	5,523	6,127

Data sources:
2015–2017: Baker-Hughes, 2019
2017–2019: National Survey of Family Growth, 2017–2019.

presents statistically adjusted percentage distributions using NSFG data from the 2015–2017 and the 2017–2019 surveys showing the responses of females to questions dealing with each of the three principal dimensions of sexual orientation. Regarding sexual behavior, the data from both surveys indicate that four-fifths of the females have engaged in sexual behavior only with males, and one-fifth have engaged in some form of sexual behavior with females.

The second dimension is sexual attraction. The sexual attraction question, as shown above, asks women to whom are they sexually attracted: only to males, mostly to males, equally to both males and females, mostly to females, and only to females. We have categorized women as straight if they report being only attracted to males, and as lesbian if they report being only attracted to females. If they report being mostly attracted to males, or mostly attracted to females, or equally attracted to males and females, we have categorized them as bisexual. The data on the sexual attraction dimension indicate that slightly less than four-fifths of females may be classified as straight, that is, they report that they are only attracted to males, with 76 percent in the 2015–2017 NSFG and 73 percent in the 2017–2019 NSFG. The rest of the women – minus a small portion who refuse to answer the question – are sexual minorities, namely, the lesbian, bisexual, and don't know/not sure categories ; they comprise almost 20 percent in the 2015–2017 NSFG and 25 percent in the 2017–2019 survey.

The third dimension is sexual self-identification. Among females in the 2015–2017 survey, 87 percent identify as straight, and in the 2017–2019 survey, 85 percent self-identify as straight. In both surveys, 2.5 percent identify as lesbian, 7.7 percent and 9.7 percent as bisexual, and 1.9 percent and 2.3 percent as something else or don't know/ not sure.

On each of the three dimensions of sexual orientation, the percentages of women in the two surveys in the various response categories are very similar. Most women by far may be classified as straight, that is, heterosexual, with considerably smaller percentages as sexual minority. The largest "straight" percentage is found in the sexual self-identification dimension, 85 percent of all women in the 2017–2019 survey, and the smallest "straight" percentage is found in the sexual behavior dimension, 80 percent of all women. *The percentage of women who are straight and the percentage of women who are sexual minority depends on which dimension of sexual orientation is being used by the investigator.*

Recall the earlier discussion in this chapter of essentialism and social constructionism as strategies for conceptualizing sexual orientation. We noted that essentialism is one of dimorphism, stipulating that there is an "essential" biological or psychological characteristic or attribute that is common to all persons and that distinguishes them as being either heterosexual or a sexual minority. We now use data from the 2017–2019 NSFG and apply an essentialist position to determine the percentage of females who may be classified as sexual minorities.

Recall from Table 9.1 that 20 percent of the female respondents identified as a sexual minority on the sexual behavior dimension, and that 27 percent of the respondents identified as a sexual minority on the sexual attraction dimension, and that 14.5 percent identified as a sexual minority on the sexual self-identification dimension. What percentage of respondents gave a sexual minority response to all three questions? If we use an essentialism argument to define and classify respondents as heterosexuals or as sexual minorities, a sexual minority would be expected to provide a sexual minority response to all three questions. It turns out that among the female respondents in the 2017–2019 NSFG, 10.4 percent of them gave the sexual minority response to all three questions. More than 10 percent of the female respondents in the 2017–2019 NSFG may be identified as sexual minorities if we use an essentialist strategy to decide who are sexual minorities.

Social constructionism is the alternative strategy for defining and classifying respondents as heterosexuals or as sexual minorities. This strategy would classify a female respondent as a sexual minority if she gives a sexual minority response to any one or more, or any combination thereof, of the three trifecta questions pertaining to sexual behavior, sexual identification, and sexual attraction. It turns out there are seven possible combinations of sexual minority responses on the three questions as follows: the respondent provides a sexual minority response (1) only to sexual self-identification, (2) only to sexual attraction, (3) only to sexual behavior, (4) to both sexual self-identification and sexual attraction, (5) to both sexual self-identification and sexual behavior, (6) to both sexual attraction and sexual behavior, and (7) to sexual self-identification, sexual attraction, and sexual behavior. Our calculations indicate that 33.7 percent of the female respondents in the 2017–2019 NSFG may be classified as sexual minorities using a social constructionist strategy, that is, they give sexual minority responses to any one or more, or any combination thereof, of the three trifecta questions of sexual self-identification, sexual attraction, and sexual behavior.

If we use an essentialist approach to classify female respondents as sexual minorities, more than 10 percent of adult females may be so classified. But if we use a social constructionist approach, almost 34 percent of the respondents may be classified as sexual minorities. The prevalence percentage of sexual minorities among adult women in the United States varies according to which of the two approaches is used for the classification.

EMPIRICAL ANALYSES OF SEXUAL ORIENTATION: MALES

We now examine male data from the 2015–2017 and 2017–2019 NSFG dealing with the trifecta of sexual self-identification, sexual attraction, and sexual behavior. Table 9.2 presents statistically adjusted percentage distributions using NSFG data from the 2015–2017 and the 2017–2019 surveys of the responses of males to questions dealing with each of the three principal dimensions of sexual orientation.

Paralleling the above analyses of females, Table 9.2 reports percentage distribution data from the two NSFGs showing the male responses on each of the three principal dimensions. Regarding the dimension of sexual behavior (top panel of the table), the data from both surveys indicate that 93 percent of male respondents report having engaged in sex only with females. This heterosexual response of 93 percent for males may be compared with a heterosexual response of 80 percent for females (Table 9.1).

Regarding sexual attraction, the second dimension, almost 90 percent of the male respondents in both surveys provide a “straight” response, that is, they are only attracted to females. In contrast, less than 80 percent of females may be classified as straight, that is, they are only attracted to males.

TABLE 9.2 *Adjusted percentage distributions of three dimensions of sexual orientation, males, National Surveys of Family Growth, 2015–2017 and 2017–2019*

Variable	NSFG 2015–2017	NSFG 2017–2019
Sexual Behavior		
Any same sex	7.0	7.0
No same sex	93.0	93.0
Sample size	4,501	5,150
Sexual Attraction		
Straight	89.4	88.4
Gay male	1.5	1.9
Something else	6.9	7.5
Don't know/not sure	1.1	1.3
Refused	0.5	0.8
Sample size	4,526	5,193
Sexual Self-Identification		
Straight	92.7	92.6
Gay male	2.8	2.8
Bisexual	2.6	2.4
Something else	1.0	1.3
Don't know/not sure	0.2	0.1
Refused	0.7	0.8
Sample size	4,526	5,193

Data sources:
2015–2017: Baker-Hughes, 2019
2017–2019: National Survey of Family Growth, 2017–2019.

The third dimension is sexual self-identification. Among male respondents in both surveys, 93 percent self-identify as straight. Lower percentages of females self-identified as straight. On all three dimensions, the percentages of males providing heterosexual responses are larger than those of females. And, correspondingly, the percentages of males providing sexual minority responses are smaller than those of females. Overall, on all three dimensions, many more males may be classified as straight than as sexual minorities. Moreover, a comparison of the percentage responses in Table 9.2 with those in Table 9.1 indicates that the straight percentages for males are higher than the straight percentages for females, and the sexual minority percentages for males are lower than those for females.

Finally, what percentage of males gives a sexual minority response to all three of the questions of sexual self-identification, sexual attraction, and sexual behavior? And what percentage of males gives a sexual minority response to any one or more, or any combination thereof, of the three trifecta questions? That is, does the prevalence of sexual minorities among males vary depending on whether one uses an essentialist strategy or a social constructionist strategy?

Only 4 percent (3.99%) of the male respondents in the 2017–2019 NSFG give a sexual minority response to all three of the questions of sexual self-identification, sexual attraction, and sexual behavior. In contrast, 14 percent of the males give a sexual minority response to any one or more, or any combination thereof, of the three questions pertaining to sexual orientation. The answer to a question about the percentage of adult males in the United States who are sexual minorities depends very much on which strategy is used for the classification, essentialism, or social constructionism.

By comparison, recall from our discussions of females in the previous section, that if we use an essentialist approach, 10.4 percent of them may be classified as sexual minorities. But if we use a social constructionist approach, 33.7 percent of them may be classified as sexual minorities. Our data indicate that the sexual minority percentages are clearly higher for females than for males, irrespective of which of the two classification strategies we use.

More generally, what then is the prevalence of sexual minorities in the United States for females and males in 2017–2019? *There is no one answer because it depends on how one defines a sexual minority*. Recall Blank's (2012: xviii) statement about heterosexuals that we quoted earlier, that "despite the fact that most of us use the term 'heterosexual' with enormous and cavalier certainty, there seems to be no aspect of 'heterosexual' for which a truly iron-clad definition has been established." The same observation may be made about sexual minorities. However, our above discussions do indicate that using a social constructionist strategy for classifying respondents as sexual minorities or as heterosexuals provides us with a much more encompassing understanding of sexual orientation than an essentialist strategy.

Also, the percentage calculations we have reported above assume the truthfulness of persons' responses when answering questions pertaining to sexual minority behavior, attraction, and self-identification. In an attempt to obtain complete and reliable data on these dimensions of sexuality, the NSFG used an expanded version of what is known as ACASI (audio computer-assisted self-interviewing). In ACASI "the respondent listens to the questions through headphones, reads them on the screen, or both, and enters the response directly into the computer. This method avoids asking the respondent to give his or her answers to the interviewer, and it has been found to yield more complete reporting of sensitive behaviors" (Chandra et al., 2011: 3).

EMPIRICAL ANALYSES OF SEXUAL ORIENTATION: ASEXUALS

We turn finally to a discussion of asexuality. Most human sexuality research has focused on sexuals, with comparatively little attention directed to asexuals (Baumle, Compton, and Poston, 2009; Baumle and Poston, 2011; Black et al., 2000; Laumann et al., 1994). But the literature does indicate that some individuals do not fall clearly into the heterosexual or sexual minority categories. Indeed, in recent years, asexuality has been gaining increasing attention in the popular media as a separate and distinct sexual orientation (Dahl, 2015; Decker, 2014).

What is asexuality? *The Oxford English Dictionary* (2000, vol. 1: 682) defines asexuality as "an asexual condition; the absence of sex; without sexuality." The *OED* gives the following three earliest known uses of the term "asexual":

(1) "The high estimation of virgin purity ... was advocated by the leaders of thought ... and ... the asexual existence ... was extolled as virtue in itself" (Eckenstein, 1896: 307).

(2) "All doctors will tell you that, athletic or not, women are more asexual than men" (*Daily Mail*, 1903: 2/7).
(3) "I feel I've shot it (i.e., the book) like a bomb against all their false sex and hypocrisy, as my Florentine doctor said, against all their asexual sexuality" (Lawrence, [1928], 1962: 1077).

The *OED* definition of asexuality and the three earliest uses of the term all represent a behavioral definition. Thus, an asexual is one who does not engage in sexual behavior. This definition is echoed in many studies of asexuality. Asexuals are often viewed as individuals who have "engaged in few or no sexual behaviors" (Brotto et al., 2010: 600; Rothblum and Brehomy, 1993). Researchers have quantified the prevalence of asexuality by ascertaining whether or not the respondents have engaged in sexual behavior.

Regarding the three dimensions of sexual orientation that we used earlier in this chapter, it turns out that few surveys have asexuality questions pertaining to asexual self-identification and asexual attraction. If an asexuality question is included in a survey, it almost always pertains to sexual behavior. In a survey conducted in Great Britain, Bogaert (2004) found that a small minority (1.05%) of the British population in 1990 claimed to have never felt sexual attraction to anyone. A follow-up study showed the asexual population to be even smaller (0.73%) in 2000 (Bogaert, 2013).

Regarding the sexual behavior dimension, Poston and Baumle (2010) analyzed data from the 2002 NSFG and found that 11 percent of women and 12 percent of men in the United States reported they had not engaged in sex in the previous twelve months. Laumann and his colleagues found that about 13 percent of their respondents reporting they had not had sex in the past year, and about two percent indicating that they had never had a sexual experience (Laumann et al., 1994). Sexual behavior, however, does not appear to be static across the life course. The literature indicates that the fact that people claiming to have no sexual activity at one point in time does not necessarily assure future sexual inactivity (Poston, Engin, and Cagatay, 2022).

We use data from the 2017–2019 NSFG to measure the prevalence of asexuality in the US adult population. Females were asked the following question with respect to sexual behavior: *At any time in your life, have you ever had sexual intercourse with a man, that is, made love, had sex, or gone all the way?* Males were asked a similar question about their sexual behavior with women. Our analysis is necessarily restricted to using data dealing only with sexual behavior, or the lack thereof, because the NSFG does not include questions dealing with asexual self-identification and asexual attraction.

But recall from our above discussions regarding NSFG questions on other dimensions of sexual orientation that the sexual self-identification question asked the following: *Which of the following best represents how you think of yourself?* The response of *asexual* was not one of the responses. But one of the responses was *something else*. One might suggest that a respondent who self-identifies as neither heterosexual or homosexual or bisexual, but as "something else" would likely self-identify as "asexual" if given the opportunity to do so. But it is also the case that the "something else" response would likely be the answer for persons self-identifying not as asexuals, but, say, as zoosexuals, masochists, exhibitionists, or as persons having a sexual fetish for such items as balloons, breasts, feet, panties, and so forth (Poston and Baumle, 2010). Even though the "something else" response would be the response for persons self-identifying as asexuals, there are too many other possible responses in addition to the asexual response. We opted therefore not to include data in our prevalence analysis pertaining to sexual self-identification because the self-identification question on the NSFG does not include an asexual response.

Similarly, recall that the sexual attraction question used in the NSFG first told respondents that *People are different in their sexual attraction to other people. Which best describes your feelings?* Respondents were not given as a possible response, *I am not sexually attracted to anyone*; but they were able to respond *Not sure* to the question. One might suggest that a respondent who is not sexually attracted to anyone, that is, a respondent who is asexual, would respond to the sexual attraction question as "not sure" because there were no other responses available. We opted against classifying as asexuals those respondents who answered they were not sure of their sexual attraction. There are too many reasons for answering "not sure" to the sexual attraction question other than the respondent being asexual.

What do we know about the prevalence of asexuality in the female and male populations in the United States? According to data from the 2017–2019 NSFG, 3.9 percent of females in the ages of 20–49 answered "no" to the question about sexual behavior; and 4.2 percent of males ages 20–49 answered "no" to the question about sexual behavior. These percentages of respondents classified as asexual are based only on their reported lack of sexual behavior in their lifetimes. Recall that Poston and Baumle (2010) analyzed NSFG data on sexual behavior for 2002 and found that 11 percent of women and 12 percent of men reported not having engaged in sex in the previous twelve months. And the analysis of Laumann and colleagues (1994) of data gathered in 1992 indicated that 13 percent of the respondents reported having no sex in the past year, and 2 percent in their lifetimes. These percentages, especially the lifetime percentages, are small. But they support a point we made earlier that asexuality has been gaining increasing attention, both in the social science literature and in the popular media as a separate and distinct sexual orientation. The sexual and gender minority (SGM) acronym, LGBTQIA, definitely needs to include the asexual population (A). Asexuals are not an insignificant population.

SUMMARY

This chapter focused on sexual orientation. We stated at the start that sexual orientation and gender identity are two distinctly different behaviors, and it is a mistake to treat them as similar. We noted there are two ways to conceptualize sexuality, essentialism and social constructionism. The latter is a much broader strategy than the former. We next indicated there are at least seven different ways or dimensions to consider sexual orientation. Of the seven dimensions, three receive the most attention from social scientists, sexual behavior, sexual self-identification, and sexual attraction. Persons may be classified as heterosexuals or as sexual minorities on the basis of their sexual behavior, their sexual self-identification, and their sexual attraction. We showed that an answer to the question how many heterosexuals and how many sexual minorities there are depends largely on which dimension one employs and whether one uses an essentialist or constructionist point of view.

When we used the three dimensions of sexual behavior, sexual self-identification, and sexual attraction and employed a social constructionist approach, we reported that 33.7 percent of adult females may be classified as sexual minorities, and 14 percent of adult males may be classified as sexual minorities. In contrast, using the same three dimensions and employing an essentialist approach indicated that 10.4 percent of adult females and 4 percent of adult males may be classified as sexual minorities. A social constructionist orientation clearly provides the more encompassing view of the prevalence of sexual minorities.

We concluded the chapter with an empirical analysis of the prevalence of asexuals, that is, persons who do not participate sexually with others. We were only able to undertake an analysis of asexuality using data on sexual behavior; there are no nationally representative data available permitting researchers to designate persons as asexual on the basis of their sexual self-identification and sexual attraction. We reported that almost 4 percent of females and just over 4 percent of males answered "no" to a question about sexual behavior in their lifetimes. These percentages are small, but they nonetheless support the point we made earlier that asexuality has been gaining increasing attention as a separate and distinct sexual orientation. Researchers studying sexual orientation should not overlook asexuality.

DISCUSSION QUESTIONS

1. In this chapter we discuss seven dimensions of sexual orientation. Select the three you believe are the most important and relevant for a true and thorough understanding of sexual orientation. Justify why you would select each of the three. Why do you believe the other four not to be as important and relevant? If you had to select only one dimension to use in an analysis of sexual orientation, which one would you select? Why do you deem it to be the most important and relevant?
2. Have another look at Table 9.1. How would an essentialist interpret this table with respect to the three listed dimensions of sexual orientation, and how would their interpretation differ from that of a social constructionist? Would the number or percentage of sexual minorities identified by the essentialist differ from those identified by the social constructionist? Why or why not?

10

Sex Structure and Gender Identity

Chapter 9 dealt with sexual orientation. One of the topics we will discuss in this chapter is gender identity. Keep in mind that sexual orientation and gender identity are two very different behaviors. But before dealing with gender identity, we first discuss several aspects of sex structure; sex is one of the most important and relevant concepts in demography and demographic analyses.

SEX STRUCTURE

In this section we first discuss sex as a demographic concept. Next, we consider the biological definitions of sex. Then we focus on demographic indexes of sex composition, particularly the sex ratio and the sex ratio at birth. We next discuss the importance of sex and the demographic processes. We conclude the section with discussions of the concept of intersex.

The Demographic Concept of Sex

Here are the definitions of sex, gender, transgender, cisgender, and nonbinary that we will use in this chapter. According to the National Academies of Sciences,

> *Sex* is a multidimensional construct based on anatomical and physiological traits that include external genitalia, secondary sex characteristics, gonads, chromosomes, and hormones .. *Gender* is a multidimensional construct that links gender identity, which is a core element of a person's individual identity; gender expression, which is how a person communicates their gender to others; and social and cultural expectations about status, characteristics, and behavior that are associated with sex traits ... *Transgender* refers to persons whose current gender identity is different from the sex they were assigned at birth ... *Cisgender* refers to people whose current gender identity corresponds to the sex they were assigned at birth ... [and] *[n]onbinary* is an umbrella term for gender identities that lie outside the gender binary. (National Academies of Sciences, Engineering and Medicine, 2022: 1; Davis, Compton, and Poston, 2025)

Sex and gender are of such significant importance in our daily lives that we usually do not realize that we are observing them. Whenever you walk across campus or on the streets where you live, one of the first characteristics you recognize about an approaching person is the person's sex and gender representation, and secondly the person's age.

We make these determinations mainly based on outward appearances, and we make them so automatically that they are done subconsciously.

The determination of a person's sex and gender representation is usually first. Often, the person's given name gives us important information. If you inform your mother that you just met someone with the name of Patricia, Nancy, Roberta, Kathleen, Kara, Haven, or Eva, she will certainly know that the person you met is female. If the person you just met has the given name of Douglas, Richard, David, Daniel, Christopher, Joseph, William, John, or Malcolm, your mother will recognize this person to be male right away. However, if you tell your mother that you just met someone with the given name of Taylor, Casey, Jordan, Quinn, or Kim, the first question your mother will almost certainly ask you is, "Is your new friend a male or female?" Try speaking to someone about another person who has an androgynous name like the ones just mentioned. Your conversation will not get very far until the other person wants to know the sex of the person being discussed.

To a certain extent, the classification, definition, and enumeration of persons by sex are more straightforward compared to the situation with most other demographic characteristics of human populations. For instance, the characteristics of race, marital status, and occupation "involve numerous categories and are subject to alternative formulation as a result of cultural differences, differences in the uses to which the data will be put, and differences in the interpretations of respondents and enumerators" (Shryock, Siegel, and Associates, 1976: 105). Still, the classification and definition of sex can be problematic.

Sex is an ascribed characteristic and, for most people, unchangeable. When a baby is born, its sex is determined on the basis of its genital tubercle. Or as the historian Helen King has written in her new book on the history of the female body, "From birth we are labeled on our external appearance. Because the body is supposed to tell us the truth, birth attendants definitively state sex simply by looking at the outside" (King, 2025: 9). On average, boys are born with penises ranging in length from 2.9 to 4.5 centimeters (1.2 to 1.8 inches) (Flatau et al., 1975). For girls, clitoral length at birth ranges from 0.2 to 0.9 centimeters (0.08 to 0.33 inches) (Fausto-Sterling, 2000: 60; Sane and Pescovitz, 1992). When the length of the tubercle is somewhere between the range for penis length and the range for clitoral length, sex determination is open for discussion and decision making by the parents and medical workers.

Sex is a biological concept, and we will note below how sex is determined. Once the person's sex is established biologically, the person then begins identifying their gender, usually male or female. One's gender self-representation mainly reflects how that person interacts with society and its social institutions.

When demographers identify the sex of a person or its distribution in a population, they are almost always referring to the person's self-identified gender. This is usually, but not necessarily always, based on the person's sex assigned at birth, and, subsequently, the person's self-identification of their gender. However, sex is determined biologically, in five ways, discussed next.

Biological Definitions of Sex

Figure 10.1 lists the five biological definitions of sex. The first is based on chromosomes, which are structures containing genetic material. Males have an X chromosome and a

- 1. Chromosomes:
    - Males: XY
    - Females: XX
- 2. Gonads:
    - Males: Testes
    - Females: Ovaries
- 3. Hormones:
    - Males: Androgens
    - Females: Estrogens
- 4. Internal Sexual Accessory Organs:
    - Males: Prostate, Vas deferens, Ejaculatory duct, Seminal vesicles
    - Females: Uterus, Fallopian tubes, Cervix
- 5. External Sexual Organs:
    - Males: Penis, Scrotal sac, Testicles
    - Females: Clitoris, Vagina

FIGURE 10.1 The five biological definitions of sex

Y chromosome, and females have two X chromosomes. The X chromosome is larger than the Y chromosome and carries more genetic material (Tavris and Wade, 1984: 135). Chromosome distribution is determined by one's biological parents. The ovum of the female and the sperm of the male each contain 23 chromosomes. When the sperm and the ovum come together in one of the female's Fallopian tubes, they produce a fertilized egg, known as an embryo. It contains 46 chromosomes aligned in 23 pairs. One of the pairs constitutes the sex of the embryo. An X chromosome is contributed by the mother and either an X or a Y chromosome is contributed by the father.

The second biological definition of sex is based on gonads, that is, testes in males and ovaries in females. If the embryo is chromosomally male, one theory asserts that a gene on the Y chromosome produces male gonads (testes) at about the sixth week after conception. If the embryo is chromosomally female, female gonads (ovaries) appear a few weeks later. Scholars are not entirely sure how this occurs.

The gonads produce the sex-specific hormones, which are the basis for the third biological definition of sex. Androgens are a class of hormones, found mainly in males, although also in females, of which testosterone is the most important. Testosterone is responsible for the differentiation of male and female primary sex characteristics at about the seventh week of fetal life. Men have roughly ten times more testosterone than women, but there is variation in the range; it is sometimes the case that some women will end up with higher levels of testosterone than some men (Kimmel, 2016). Without the release of testosterone and other androgens, the male fetus will not develop male external genital organs. Males also receive major surges of testosterone at puberty so that the task of sex differentiation can be completed. Estrogen surges also occur at puberty in females.

We noted above that androgens are considered as mainly male, and that estrogens are considered as mainly female. It is important to note, however, that all of us, regardless of our bodies, have both androgens and estrogens. Females and males need both hormones to function properly. In females, the ovaries, adrenal glands, fat cells, and skin cells produce the female body's supply of androgens. In males, the testes, adrenal glands, and fat tissues produce the male body's supply of estrogen. However, on average, there is a greater amount of androgen (testosterone) in biologically male bodies, and a greater amount of estrogen in biologically female bodies

Every embryo contains "two sets of ducts, one of which will become the internal reproductive structures appropriate to the embryo's sex" (Tavris and Wade, 1984: 137). These internal sexual properties constitute the fourth biological definition of sex. In males, these tissues are referred to as Wolffian ducts, and they result in the internal male accessories, namely, the vas deferens, the seminal vesicles, the ejaculatory duct, and the prostate. In females, they are known as Mullerian ducts, and they become the Fallopian tubes, the uterus, and the cervix. "In each sex, the ducts that do not develop eventually degenerate, except for traces" (Tavris and Wade, 1984: 137; see also Kimmel, 2016).

The sex-specific internal sex structures of the fetus lead finally to the development of sex-specific external genitals, namely, a penis, scrotal sac, and testicles for males, and a clitoris and vagina for females. The external sex structures are the basis for the fifth biological definition of sex. Moreover, it is this fifth definition that usually results in the assignment of sex at the birth of the baby.

Indexes of Sex Composition

Demographers use several methods to index sex composition: (1) the masculinity proportion, (2) the ratio of the excess or deficit of males to the total population, and (3) the sex ratio. The **masculinity proportion** is frequently used in nontechnical discussions of sex composition (Hobbs, 2004) and is calculated by dividing the number of males in the population by the number of males and females and multiplying the result by 100.

The **ratio of the excess, or deficit, of males** to the total population is obtained by subtracting the number of females from the number of males, dividing by the total number in the population and multiplying by 100.

The **sex ratio (SR)**, by far the most popular index of sex composition in demographic and other scholarly analyses, is defined as the number of males per 100 females, as follows:

$$SR = (\mathbf{P_m}/\mathbf{P_f}) * 100 \qquad (10.1)$$

An SR above 100 indicates an excess of males and an SR below 100 indicates an excess of females. In some Eastern European countries and in India, Iran, Pakistan, Saudi Arabia, and a few other countries, the SR is calculated as the number of females per 100 (or per 1,000) males. But the SR definition just shown in formula (10.1) is used by most demographers and by international bodies such as the United Nations (Poston, 2019).

In general, "national sex ratios tend to fall in the narrow range from about 95 to 102, barring special circumstances, such as a history of heavy war losses (less males), or heavy immigration (more males); national sex ratios outside the range of 90 to 105 should be viewed as extreme" (Shryock, Siegel, and Associates, 1976: 107).

Most societies have sex ratios at birth (SRBs) between 104 and 106; that is, 104–106 boys are born for every 100 girls. This so-called biologically normal SRB is likely an evolutionary adaptation to the fact that females have higher survival probabilities than males. (See Clarke, 2000, for another discussion). Since at every year of life males have higher age-specific death rates (ASDRs) than females, slightly more males than females are required at birth for there to be around equal numbers of males and females when the groups reach their marriageable ages.

If the biologically normal sex ratio at birth is between 104 and 106 in most human populations, what might be the average value of the sex ratio at conception (SRC)? Clearly, it is not possible to obtain a valid figure for the SRC, although much of the literature estimates the SRC to be between 110 and 120 (Carey and Lopreato, 1995; Hassold et al., 1983; Matthiessen and Matthiessen, 1977). Other research, however, suggests that the SRC may be even, that is, a value of 100, meaning that 100 males are conceived for every 100 females (Orzack et al., 2015). These authors suggest that the proportion of males increases relative to the proportion of females manly during the first trimester, and that female mortality exceeds male mortality throughout the pregnancy. Their arguments need additional theoretical justification and empirical support. We are inclined, for now, to set the SRC in the range of 110 to 120.

Biology dictates that the age-specific SR will be highest at the very young ages, starting around 104–106 at age 0, and should then decline with age, attaining a value of around 100 for persons in their late 20s and continuing to decline to levels around age 50 or 60 in the oldest ages.

Barring extreme forms of human intervention and disturbance, these types of SR patterns by age will occur in most populations. One such intervention would be a major war, such as the Korean War, which would reduce significantly the numbers of males in their 20s and 30s. Another would be high amounts of immigration and/or emigration. International migration is usually driven economically when, typically, males depart one country and enter another in search of employment. Such disturbances in some countries can be extreme, as we show later for some of the oil-producing countries in the Middle East. Another intervention would be female-specific abortion, resulting in an SRB well above 105.

One way to describe a population's sex structure is to examine sex ratios for each of its five-year age groups. Figure 10.2 is a graph of the age-specific SRs for South Korea in 1995. The figure shows SRs at the youngest ages that are much higher than would be expected biologically. These are the result of human interventions, namely, prenatal sex identification, followed by female-specific abortion (Poston, 2002, 2019). The SRs for age groups 0–4 and 5–9 are 113.4 and 110.6. Other than the higher-than-expected SRs at the very young ages, the declining trend in SRs in 1995 shown in Figure 10.2 for the remaining ages is pretty much as expected.

Some national populations have extreme imbalances by sex in certain age groups. The United Arab Emirates (UAE) is a good example. The UAE is one of several countries in the region of the world known as the Cooperation Council of the Arab States of the Gulf, originally and still colloquially, the Gulf Cooperation Council; the other member countries are Kuwait, Saudi Arabia, Qatar, Bahrain, and Oman. Most of these countries

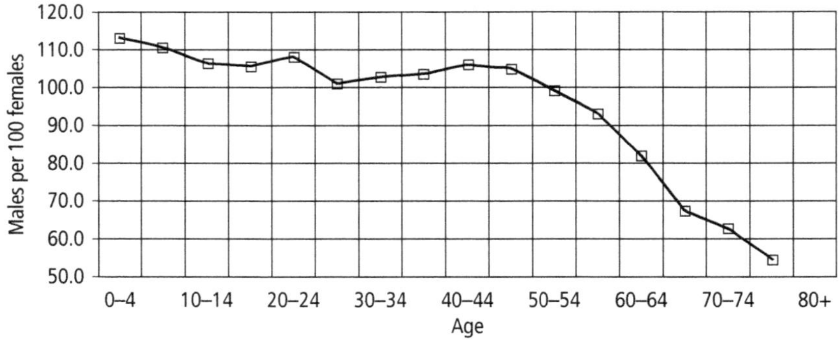

FIGURE 10.2 Sex ratios by age group in the Republic of Korea, 1995
Data source: US Census Bureau, International Database.

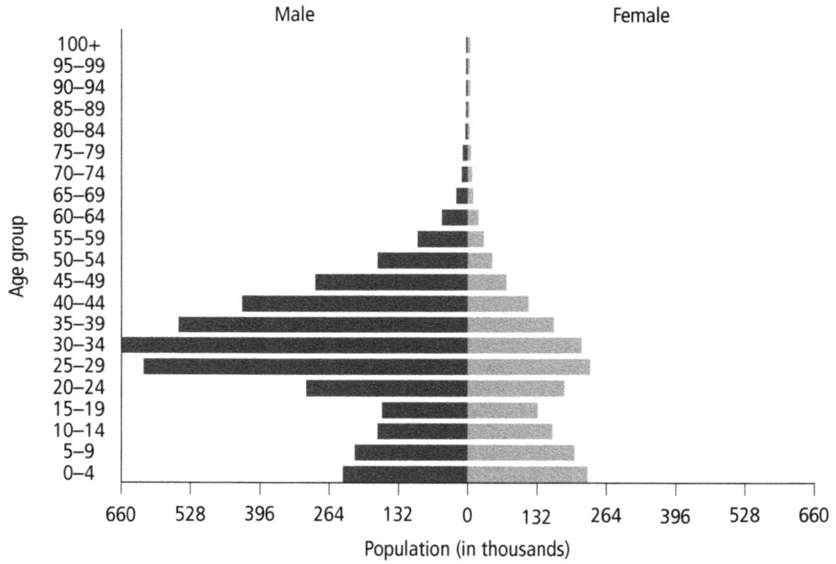

FIGURE 10.3 Population pyramid, age and sex composition, United Arab Emirates, 2015
Data source: US Census Bureau, International Database.

have very large percentages of foreign-born residents, often over 70 percent. Many of the foreigners are in the young working ages and are mainly male. They hail from Asia and other countries in the Middle East and are brought to the UAE and the other Gulf countries to work in the oil fields and in construction; these labor migrants are infrequently accompanied by family members (McFalls, 2007). These high concentrations of foreigners have a major impact on the demography of countries that are not large in population size. For instance, Qatar's 2024 population numbered 3.2 million residents and the UAE, just over 9.7 million. The immigration patterns that favor young working-age males result in extremely unbalanced distributions of SRs by age.

Figure 10.3 is a population pyramid for the UAE in 2015. We will discuss population pyramids in more detail in Chapter 13. All you need to know for now about a population pyramid (sometimes called an age–sex pyramid) is that it represents graphically the age and sex structure of a population at a given point in time; the sex groups are measured in one-year or five-year categories; the females are shown on the right side of the pyramid and the males on the left side. We see in Figure 10.3 that the males and females are near-balanced at the younger ages, but at age 25 the numbers of males begin to greatly exceed the numbers of females, and this continues up to the 65-year-olds and later ages. These tremendous sex imbalances are especially concentrated in around thirty years or so of the population's age structure. Not many national populations, other than the few Gulf countries just mentioned, have an age and sex population pyramid quite like that of the UAE in 2015.

Sex Ratio at Birth

We turn now to a specific example of the centrality of age and sex structure. We discuss the sex ratios at birth (SRBs) for China, South Korea, and the United States. The SRB in China has been and still is unbalanced; the SRB in South Korea was unbalanced but is back now to normal levels; the SRB in the United States is not now, and has not been, unbalanced.

We already noted that most societies have normal SRBs, of around 105; that is,105 boys are born for every 100 girls. Figure 10.4 shows time-series data for the SRB in China, South Korea, and the United States for the individual years from 1950 to 2021. The United States follows the normal SRB pattern. The SRB in the United States in 1950 was 105 and was still 105 in 2021; it has always been invariant in the US for as long as SRB data have been gathered. We should note, however, that the SRB in the US is slightly above 105 for some groups, and slightly below 105 for other groups. For instance, the older the mother, the lower the SRB. The higher the birth order, the lower the SRB. Also, SRBs vary slightly by race and ethnicity. Chinese and Filipinos have SRBs a little higher than 105, and Blacks and most Hispanics have SRBs a little lower. But

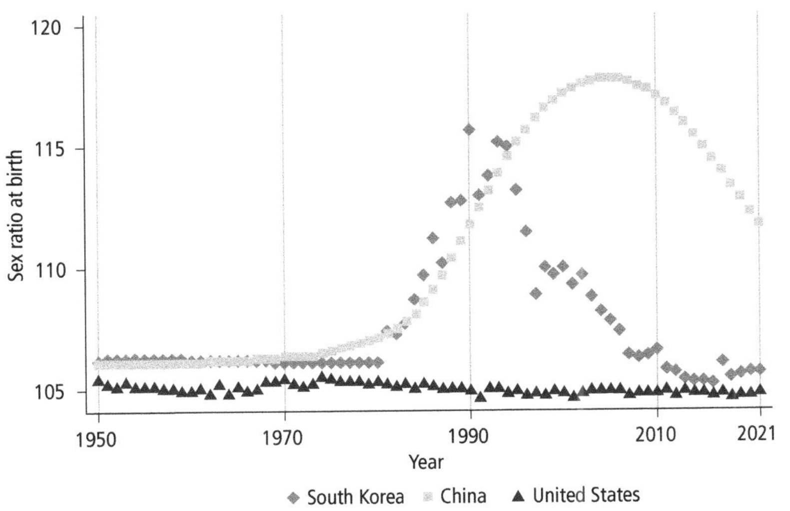

FIGURE 10.4 Sex ratios at birth, South Korea, China, and United States, 1950 to 2021
Data source: United Nations, World Population Prospects, 2022.

across the entire US population, the SRB averages out each year at around 105, as shown in Figure 10.4. This overall stability at 105–107 over time that we see in the US is observed in most populations if there are no human interventions operating to disturb the biological norm.

In contrast, between 1950 and 1980 China and South Korea had SRBs only slightly above 107, but they began to increase in the mid to late 1980s, reaching values in 1990 of 112 in China and 116 in South Korea. South Korea's SRB did not rise above its 1990 peak value of 116. It dropped to 110 in 1998 and back to the normal level of 106 in the late 2000s; its SRB value in 2021 was 106. But China's SRB continued to increase after 1990, rising to 117 in 1999, and to 118 a few years later. It began declining in the early 2010s and in 2020 reached a value of 112, which is still much above the normal value of 105 to 106.

As we already noted, if there are no human interferences with the biological processes, the SRBs will range from 104 to 107, with an average of around 105. What are the kinds of human interventions that might disturb the biological processes?

China, South Korea, Taiwan, India, and several other Asian countries have been reporting abnormally high SRBs since the 1980s (Arnold and Liu, 1986; Eberstadt, 2000; Goodkind, 1996, 2011; Gu and Roy, 1995; Hudson and den Boer, 2004; Jha et al., 2006; Kim, 1997; Poston, Conde, and DeSalvo, 2011; Poston, Gu, Liu, and McDaniel 1997; Poston and Zhang, 2009). These unbalanced SRBs occurred in these countries because of four events or phenomena: (1) a rapid fertility decline in a 20–30-year period from high to low levels; (2) the presence of a strong preference for sons; (3) the availability and relative ease of access to technologies allowing the determination of the sex of the fetus; and (4) the availability and relative ease of access to abortion, both physically and normatively. These four phenomena/events have all occurred or have been present in China, South Korea, Taiwan, and in several other countries in East Asia and South Asia.

The immediate and most influential cause of the unbalanced SRBs is the dramatic fertility declines that occurred in China and South Korea and the other countries noted earlier. Why would rapid fertility reductions lead to abnormally high SRBs? China and South Korea have Confucian patriarchal traditions where son preference is strong and pervasive (Poston, Gu, et al., 1997). A preference for sons is a part of Chinese and Korean history and culture. But when fertility was high, the chances that a boy would be born were good (Pison, 2004). When Chinese and Korean women were having six children on average, the probability was very low (less than 2 percent) that none of the six children would be male. By comparison, when women have only two children, the probability that neither will be a son is much higher (around 25 percent). When women have only one child, the probability that it will not be a son is just under 50 percent.

China and South Korea and the other countries noted earlier all showed or are still showing, in varying degrees, the same kinds of interventions leading to abnormally high SRBs. A main intervention is prenatal sex identification followed by gender-specific abortion.

Birth-planning policies as well as social, economic, and industrial transformations in China and South Korea have been responsible for the number of babies born per woman falling below replacement levels, and doing so quickly (Poston, 2000).

Couples now have fewer children than was the case just a couple of decades ago. However, the deeply rooted cultural influences of son preference still make it important for many families to have at least one son. Thus, many families implement strategies and interventions to ensure that they will have a son (Gu and Roy, 1995).

Since the late 1980s, ultrasound technology enabling the prenatal determination of sex has been widely available. Two decades ago China proposed a ban on the practice and launched a "pro-girl" campaign to help mediate the strong son preference (*China Daily*, 2004). This campaign, however, is not believed to have had much of an impact. Similar campaigns in Taiwan and South Korea had similar outcomes.

There is little evidence of female infanticide causing the high SRBs (Banister, 2004; Chu, 2001; Eberstadt, 2000; Zeng et al., 1993). The human interventions that disturb the SRB are mainly due to norms and traditions among Chinese and Korean families to have sons, within recent policies as well as a normative context to have fewer births.

How many excess boys will there be in China and South Korea who will be unable to find brides from their countries? In 2011, Poston and two of his former students, Conde and DeSalvo, examined population data for every year from 1978 to 2010 and calculated the numbers of males and females born every year, as well as the SRBs for each year. Using data from life tables (see Chapter 5), they next survived the males born each year to the ages of 29 and the females to the ages of 27, which are, or are near, the average marrying ages in China. They estimated that there have already been born in China more than 41 million Chinese males who, when they reach their mid-20s and are looking for brides, will not be able to find Chinese women to marry (Poston, Conde, and DeSalvo, 2011). Their number does not take into account the likelihood of some daughters at birth being underreported (Goodkind, 2011), so the figure of over 40 million may be a little too high.

We used a similar method to estimate the numbers of excess Korean males born during the thirty-year period of 1980 to 2010 when Korea's sex ratio at birth was so out of balance. We have estimated that in those 30 years, there were born in Korea between 700,000 and 800,000 or so extra boys who will not be able to find Korean girls to marry. Some of the extra boys started to reach marriage age as recently as 2015, and there will be lots more extra boys in Korea for another few decades (Poston, 2023c).

In Korea, starting about ten years ago and continuing for another two decades or so, there have not been and will not be enough young Korean women for young Korean men to marry. This is a particularly difficult situation because it is happening in a society where virtually everyone is expected to marry, and where marriage is nearly universal.

There will not be enough Chinese and Korean females in the marriage markets of these two countries for the excess Chinese and Korean males to marry. What will these young men do when they cannot find brides? Here are some speculations.

While it is true that throughout history, especially in Western Europe, "bachelorhood was an acceptable social role, and the incidence of never-marrying bachelors in the total population was high" (Eberstadt, 2000: 230; see also Hajnal, 1965), China and Korea, throughout their thousands of years of history, have never been so characterized. Unless in the next few decades China and Korea are "swept by a truly radical change in cultural and social attitudes toward marriage [the two countries are] poised to experience an increasingly intense, and perhaps desperate, competition among young men for [their] limited supply of brides" (Eberstadt, 2000: 230).

One solution to the demographic quagmires in the two countries is immigration, especially families with young workers and daughters. The United States and many European countries have relied for decades on international migration to increase their working-age populations. Currently, immigrants comprise nearly 14 percent of the US population, and around 18 percent of Germany's population. But China and South Korea throughout their histories have not relied much at all on immigration.

Currently, China has only 1 million residents who were born in another country, roughly 0.1 percent of its population; this is the lowest percentage of immigrants of any major country in the world. For immigration to have any reasonable impacts in China, the numbers of people coming into China will need to increase tremendously in the next decade or so – to around 50 million, perhaps higher. And it is not just the low numbers of immigrants that is a problem. China also faces the problem of growing numbers of its population moving to other countries, including the United States. In 2017, for example, around 10 million people moved from China to live and work in other countries (Poston, 2023a).

China must also change its immigration policies. Currently, foreign-born people cannot attain Chinese citizenship unless they are children of Chinese nationals. Also, foreigners are only allowed to purchase one piece of property in China, and it must be their residence. Changing immigration policies will likely require a change in mindset. China's current immigration policies are characterized by a deep-rooted belief in racial purity held by many leaders in the Chinese Communist Party. Many Chinese officials often refer to a single Chinese bloodline that stretches back for thousands of years. In 2017, Chinese President Xi Jinping told Donald Trump, who was then the US president, that almost all Chinese today are the original Chinese people, the descendants of the dragon. The best way to maintain this racial purity, many in China believe, is to limit or prohibit migration into China. Were the Chinese to relax their immigration policies, it would not only boost the numbers of people, but it would also bring in more younger people, many of them women. Immigrants are typically of prime working age and productive, and they also tend to have more younger children than native-born residents (Poston, 2023a).

South Korea is in a slightly better position than China with respect to international migration. Currently around 3 percent of Korea's population was born in another country (Poston, 2023c). South Korea could encourage the immigration to their country of Chinese-Korean women from the northeastern part of China, where more than 2 million Chinese of Korean ancestry reside, as well as women from other countries. This would enlarge the pool of wives. This new immigration flow to Korea has already begun. Financial assistance from the Korean government is already supporting the immigration to Korea of Korean women from northeastern China, and of foreign women from some less wealthy countries, such as Vietnam, the Philippines, and some Eastern European countries (Heo, Chang, and Abel, 2023).

Another possibility is that some of these Chinese and Korean bachelors will never marry and will have no other alternative but to develop their own lives and livelihoods. They could well settle with one another in "bachelor ghettos" in Beijing and Shanghai and in Seoul and Busan, and in other large cities in their countries, where commercial sex outlets will be more prevalent.

There is some historical precedent behind an expected growth of bachelor ghettos. In the nineteenth century, many thousands of young Chinese men immigrated to the United States to work in the gold mines and to help build the transcontinental railroad. When the work projects were completed, many stayed in the United States and resettled in Chinese bachelor ghetto areas in New York, San Francisco, and a few other large US cities (Kwong, 1988; Zhou, 1992). The sex ratios of the Chinese in these areas were extraordinarily high.

No one, of course, knows what this excess number of young Chinese and Korean males will do. We have entertained several possibilities. The only fact known for sure is that there have already been born in China and South Korea many, many more baby boys than there will be girls for them to marry. This issue needs the immediate attention of research scholars and policy- makers.

Sex and the Demographic Processes

The demographic processes themselves vary significantly by sex and, as we will show in Chapter 13, by age. Regarding fertility, we have already noted that more males are born than females, usually around 105–106 males for every 100 females. Regarding mortality, females have lower death rates than males at every age of life. Death rates are high in the first year of life and then drop to very low levels. In modern populations, they do not again attain the level reached in the first year of life for another five to six decades.

The sex difference in mortality deserves additional discussion. Females live longer than males. This differential has been observed through the centuries and may be attributed to both behavioral and genetic causes. Regarding behavioral factors, males are more prone than females to engage in risk-taking behaviors, and they also engage more than females in cigarette smoking. Regarding genetic factors, the sex chromosomes and hormones, such as testosterone and estrogen, increase longevity for females, but decrease it for males. Research by the actuary Barbara Blatt Kalben has shown that "the primarily female hormone, estrogen, is protective for females, while the primarily male hormone, testosterone, is detrimental. Estrogen protects the heart and blood vessels. Testosterone, in contrast, tends to promote higher blood pressure, suppress the effectiveness of the immune system, and increase thrombosis" (Kalben, 2003: 45). Kalben's research provides some evidence for both explanations, but the major determining component of the female advantage, she has argued, is the differences between the sexes in chromosomes and hormones.

That a genetic factor is the major reason for the physical superiority of women over men was also a conclusion of Madigan (1957) in his classic and very interesting study of the mortality patterns of Roman Catholic nuns (sisters) and brothers, all of whom were teachers in Catholic grammar schools and high schools. Madigan's subjects were similar in most behavioral characteristics, and none were married. The daily regimes of both the "brothers and sisters [were] extremely similar as regards time for sleep, work, study, and recreation, and with respect to diet, housing, and medical care" (Madigan, 1957: 204). The major difference was their sex.

Madigan found that the "sisters consistently exhibited greater expectations of life, and the brothers shorter expectations" (1957: 210). The title of his research paper was "Are Sex Mortality Differentials Biologically Caused?" He answered in the affirmative: "Biological factors played by far the chief part in differentiating the death rates" of the brothers and the sisters (Madigan, 1957: 221).

Intersex

We turn now to another issue of sex structure, the intersex population. We noted earlier that most embryos are consistent on the five biological definitions of sex (Figure 10.1). Usually, if an embryo is chromosomally a male, it will also be a male gonadally and hormonally, and it will possess male internal and male external sex genitalia, and similarly for females. But this is not always the case. Sometimes the embryos are inconsistent, resulting in intersexed births. **Intersex** refers to persons with atypical combinations of the biological attributes (e.g., chromosomes, gonads, hormones, genitalia) that are commonly used to distinguish males from females. The medical term for intersex traits is "variations in sex characteristics" (VSC). It has been estimated that over 1.7 percent of persons are born with VSC. Table 10.1 presents a list of intersex traits and their estimated percentages Also, note that the intersex trait "label is a biological category based on bodies and does not say anything about people's sexual orientation" or their gender identity (King, 2025: 11).

Far fewer than 1.7 percent of newborn babies are identified at birth with intersex traits. Indeed, the rate of newborn babies noticeably atypical in terms of genitalia has been estimated by some at around one in 2,000 births, that is, 0.05 percent of all births. We recently confirmed this approximate figure with data from the 2018 General Social Survey (GSS), a multistage probability sample survey of the US adult population that is conducted in even-numbered years by the National Opinion Research Center (NORC) at the University of Chicago. After adjusting these data for the complex survey design of the GSS, we found that only 0.067 percent of the 2018 GSS respondents noted that their sex at birth was reported as intersex. This 0.067 percent estimate is far too low an estimate of total intersex prevalence; compare this percentage with the 1.74 percentage

TABLE 10.1 *Estimated percentage rates of various intersex traits*

Intersex trait	Percentage of births
Turner syndrome (45, Xo)	0.0369
Klinefelter syndrome (47, XXY)	0.0922
Other non-XX or non-XY, e.g., XYY, XXX	0.0639
Androgen insensitivity syndrome (complete)	0.0076
Androgen insensitivity syndrome (partial)	0.0008
Classic CAH (congenital adrenal hyperplasia)	0.0078
Late-onset CAH (congenital adrenal hyperplasia)	1.5000
Other intersex traits	0.0332
TOTAL	1.7424

Data sources: Fausto-Sterling, 2000; Blackless et al., 2000; Nielsen and Wohlert, 1991; Merke and Kabbani, 2001; Hughes et al., 2012; Cui et al., 2018.

in Table 10.1. This owes to the fact that many persons with intersex traits are not so identified at birth. We note later that persons with the intersex trait with the highest percentage, late-onset congenital adrenal hyperplasia (CAH), a rate of 1.5 percent, are usually not so identified until their teenage or early adult years.

Many scholars of intersex studies agree that we do not have truly reliable estimates of the size of the intersex population. For one thing, as already noted, not everyone with an intersex trait knows they are intersex owing to the way this may have been addressed by medical providers when they were children, including intersex diagnoses which may have been withheld from them. Second, there is a lively debate among some researchers about what counts as intersex; for instance, some do not agree that late-onset congenital adrenal hyperplasia (CAH) and a few other intersex traits should be classified as intersex (Sax, 2002). Others question whether a chromosomal anomaly (we mention several of them below) should be classified as intersex when externally there is no observable ambiguity (Dreger, 1998). See also Stock's (2021) discussions and arguments, especially the second chapter of her book. These arguments are not as pervasive and, we hold, less persuasive now than they were several decades ago.

There are numerous intersex traits. We discuss below some of the major ones; the prevalence statistics we report in Table 10.1 are approximations.

In our view, one of the best definitions of intersex is that of the United Nations Office of the High Commissioner for Human Rights (UNOHCHR, 2019: 5): "Intersex people are born with physical sex characteristics that do not fit the normative definitions for male or female bodies. For some intersex people, these are apparent at birth, while for others they emerge later in life, often at puberty. Intersex persons may have any sexual orientation and gender identity." Intersex traits, as we discuss below, refer to variations in sexual and biological development that do not align with the binary categories of male or female.

One intersex trait is chromosomal (Nielsen and Wohlert, 1991). Occasionally, chromosomal inconsistencies occur, sometimes during sperm production, resulting in what Renzetti and her colleagues (2012) have referred to as a different complement of sex chromosomes. If the sperm fails to divide properly, that is, if what is called *nondisjunction* occurs, one kind of sperm produced will have neither an X nor a Y chromosome. If this sperm fertilizes a normal egg, the offspring will have only one chromosome, an X chromosome. This type of intersex is known as **Turner's syndrome** (Cui et al., 2018). The person appears to be a female because although they lack ovaries, they possess some external female characteristics. We report in Table 10.1 that this condition is estimated to occur in just under 0.04 percent of live births (Fausto-Sterling, 2000: 53).

Another case of nondisjunction is a sperm produced with two X chromosomes and one Y chromosome, or with one X chromosome and two Y chromosomes, resulting in the XXY and XYY chromosome abnormalities. The XXY configuration is referred to as **Klinefelter's syndrome** and occurs in roughly 0.09 percent of live births (Nielsen and Wohlert, 1991). A person born with this intersex trait has the height of a normal male, with long legs, an absent or weak sex drive, "feminized" hips, some breast development, and a small penis and testes (Money and Ehrhardt, 1972). The XYY chromosomal configuration is referred to as **Jacob's syndrome**. A person born with this intersex trait is an anatomical male with no physical abnormalities, except for unusual height. The extra Y chromosome does not appear to result in the person's having more androgens than an XY male. Such persons appear to be able to reproduce successfully and rarely come to the attention of investigators, except through large-scale screening of newborns.

Another chromosomal configuration is three X chromosomes, which is known as the XXX syndrome, or **Trisomy X.** People born with this chromosomal configuration are anatomically females and show few visible signs of abnormality, although they tend to be taller than XX females and have a slightly higher incidence of learning disorders (Nielsen and Wohlert, 1991; Renzetti et al., 2012).

These examples of intersex traits are chromosomal combinations other than the XY male or the XX female. The designation of the sex of these persons at birth is usually based on external sexual organs. Their combined prevalence is just about 0.2 percent of all births (Table 10.1).

There are other intersex traits in which the persons are chromosomally male (XY) or female (XX), but the sexual distinctions occur at the level of hormones. One hormonal example is when an XX fetus or XY fetus receives excessive amounts of androgens, mainly because the body is not able to properly produce cortisol, and thus excessive amounts of androgens are produced instead. This is known as the **adreno-genital syndrome (AGS)**, also referred to as **congenital adrenal hyperplasia (CAH)** (Berglund et al., 2023; Merke and Kabbani, 2001). Classic CAH is recognized at birth and is estimated to occur in 0.008 percent of all births. Late-onset CAH, as its label implies, is recognized later, at puberty or early adulthood. Untreated females with AGS have normally functioning ovaries and normal internal female sexual organs but a masculinized external appearance. This can vary from a slightly enlarged clitoris to a nearly normal-size penis with an empty scrotum. Untreated males with AGS may have partially or fully female external genitalia. Research shows classic CAH to be more prominent in females than males.

Classic CAH causes the children's bodies to produce an insufficient amount of cortisol. But if treated with cortisol from birth on, chromosomally females will have a later menarche than normal but will be able to conceive, lactate, and deliver babies (Merke and Kabbani, 2001; Money and Ehrhardt, 1972).

Regarding late-onset CAH, as we noted earlier, there is an extensive debate in the intersex literature about whether this intersex trait should be classified as intersex (Sax, 2002). This is mainly because persons with this trait are not recognized or diagnosed with CAH until puberty or later. But most intersex researchers include late-onset CAH as an intersex trait; we do also.

Sometimes there are no symptoms of CAH when the baby is born. It does not become evident until the teenage years or in early adulthood. In many instances, cortisol may be the only hormone that is deficient. Females with late-onset CAH may have normal appearing genitals at birth, but in their teenage and later years may experience irregular or absent menstrual periods. They also may have other masculine characteristics such as a deeper voice, facial hair, and premature development of pubic and underarm body hair. The percentage rate of late-onset CAH is the highest of all the intersex traits, estimated at 1.5 percent.

Another intersex trait at the hormonal level is a fetus that is chromosomally male with genitals that are ambiguous or that look more like a clitoris than a penis. This condition is known as **androgen insensitivity syndrome (AIS)** because of the inability to absorb androgens in utero. This trait cannot be treated by administering androgen after birth because the cells remain incapable of responding to androgen. At puberty, AIS persons develop breasts and a feminine body shape and often identify their gender as females. The incidence of AIS (partial and complete together) is estimated to be around 0.008 percent of live births.

We have discussed above a few of the several different intersex traits. Such persons are inconsistent on the five biological definitions of sex. Several well-known individuals are alleged to be/have been intersexed. These include the historical figure Joan of Arc (Gordon, 2000) and such Hollywood celebrities as Mae West, Greta Garbo, Marlene Dietrich, and Jamie Lee Curtis (Young, 2002). A search on the Internet of "intersex" will bring up these and many more names of historical and contemporary figures. In most of these instances, however, medical verification, for example, in the form of chromosomal data, is lacking.

The case of Joan of Arc is of particular interest. Joan may be "the one person born before 1800, with the exception of Jesus Christ, that the average Westerner can name" (Gordon, 2000: xix). In writings, movies, and plays about her, she is often referred to as a "girl/boy." She reportedly had "beautiful" breasts, yet she was not known to have ever menstruated (Gordon, 2000: 144, 145, 169). These observations are also made by Castor in her highly acclaimed *Joan of Arc: A History* (2015). Both characteristics are consistent with those of persons with AIS.

The sociologist Georgiann Davis has written a captivating book about intersex titled *Contesting Intersex: The Dubious Diagnosis* (2015). The book is part autobiographical; Professor Davis was diagnosed at age 13 with the androgen insensitivity syndrome (AIS), but she was not told she was AIS with undescended testes. Instead, the medical doctors informed her that she had underdeveloped ovaries that needed to be surgically removed. She had the surgery and did not learn until she was age 19 that she had an intersex trait. In her book she writes about how best to respond to these naturally occurring conditions of intersex. She describes in detail how intersex is defined, experienced, and contested in the United States today. It is a groundbreaking book, astute, and very readable. We recommend it highly.

GENDER IDENTITY

We turn now to gender identity. We noted earlier that once sex assignment is made at birth, it is usually permanent. However, there are instances of persons transitioning from the gender based on their sex assigned at birth to another gender or to no gender, namely, gender nonbinary. These persons are usually consistent on the five biological definitions but decide, often during adulthood, although not always, to change their gender; they are referred to as **transgender**. Keep in mind the definition we noted earlier that *transgender* refers to persons whose current gender identity is different from the sex they were assigned at birth.

Terminology

We note at the onset of this discussion on gender identity the

> vastness of identities and terms that are associated with the transgender, nonbinary, and gender minority populations ... We also recognize the dynamism of these populations, and how often or fast language and contemporary usage about them may change and be in flux ...We recognize that some individuals, e.g., nonbinary persons, may either reject or not identify with an umbrella term ... However, some of the data ... identify many groups, e.g., trans masculine, trans feminine, nonbinary, and genderqueer, under the umbrella term "transgender." (Davis, Compton, and Poston, 2025; Suárez et al., 2022: 74)

In our discussions we use the term "transgender" and "trans" as an umbrella term to represent the several identities associated with the transgender, gender nonbinary, and nonconforming, gender minority population. Also, our definition of transgender is based on self-identification. A transgender person is one whose gender identity is different from the sex assigned at birth. A cisgender person is one whose gender identity is the same as the sex assigned at birth. Many gender change strategies are taken in the transition from one gender to another. As part of their gender transition, some persons take one strategy, others take more than one. For instance, some persons undergo hormone therapy; some undergo surgery; some change their pronouns; some change their appearance. Some do many, others do a few. But please remember that the identification of a person as transgender does not depend on hormonal treatments or on gender-confirming surgery. The transgender population is diverse in many ways, especially with respect to gender identity, expression, and sexual orientation (Davis et al., 2025).

Some Early Transgender Persons

The term transgender has come into popular use only in the past few decades. But there have been people fitting the modern definition in almost every culture throughout recorded history. We know about some of them because they elected to undergo surgery. One of the first identifiable and recorded recipients of reassignment surgery was Lili Elbe (1882–1931), who had her surgery in Germany around 1930. She was born a male with the name of Einar Wegener. She wrote at length about her life as a trans woman. After her death, a friend, Niels Hoyer, collected her writings and edited them into Elbe's autobiography, *Man Into Woman: The First Sex Change* ([1933] 2004).

Christine Jorgensen (1927–1989), in her day, was one of the most well-known transgender persons in the United States. George Jorgensen was a former GI and professional photographer who had sex reassignment surgery in Denmark in 1952. Thereafter Christine Jorgensen "entered the public spotlight and became the catalyst for other would-be ... [transgender persons], many of whom went to Europe for surgery" (Haskell, 2013: 33; Jorgensen, 1967). She also was a patient of Harry Benjamin (see below) the endocrinologist and sex researcher.

Later, in 1965, sex-change surgery became possible for the first time in the United States with the establishment of the Johns Hopkins Gender Identity Clinic at the Johns

Hopkins Hospital in Baltimore, Maryland. The cofounder of the clinic was Howard W. Jones, Jr., who when learning that Christine Jorgensen had her surgery in Denmark, stated "that if the Europeans can do it, he could too" (Epstein, 2015). The clinic was closed in 1979.

In the mid-1970s the ophthalmologist and professional tennis star Richard Raskind underwent sex reassignment surgery and took the name Renée Richards. The New York Supreme Court later ruled that she was eligible to play in the US Open Tennis Tournament as a woman. She chose the name "Renée" because it is French for "reborn."

In June 2015, the magazine *Vanity Fair* published a lead cover story titled "Call Me Caitlyn" featuring the Olympic icon Bruce Jenner who had transitioned to Caitlyn Jenner. She had earlier announced formally her male-to-female transition in a television interview on April 24, 2015, with Diane Sawyer in which she discussed her life-long struggle with gender identity. In early February, 2016, the American Society of Magazine Editors named *Vanity Fair*'s "Call Me Caitlyn" cover story the Cover of the Year of 2015.

We mentioned Harry Benjamin (1885–1986) in an earlier paragraph. He was a medical doctor concentrating in hormonal research. He became acquainted with the sexuality researcher Alfred Kinsey (we discussed Kinsey in Chapter 9), who introduced him to his first transgendered patient. Benjamin's young patient was anatomically male, but claimed to be female (Rudacille, 2005: 81–82). Benjamin labeled the condition "transsexualism" and devoted much of his career to studying and treating such individuals. His book *The Transsexual Phenomenon* (1966) was for many years the definitive exposition of the subject (Poston, DeSalvo, and Kincannon, 2009).

A person who transitions from female to male, also referred to as a trans man, is a genetic female who thinks of himself and identifies as a male, and has "taken social, medical, or surgical steps to physically or socially masculinize his gender expression or body" (Shultz, 2015: 200). In a similar way, a person who transitions from male to female, also referred to as a trans woman, is a genetic male consistent on all five biological definitions who thinks of herself and identifies as a female, and has "taken social, medical, or surgical steps to physically or socially feminize her gender expression or body" (Shultz, 2015: 200–201). When a transgender person opts for sexual reassignment, this may be done with hormonal therapy, and sometimes also through surgery in which the external genitals are changed.

Empirical Analyses of the Transgender and Cisgender Populations

We turn now to empirical analyses of the transgender and cisgender populations. What are their rates of prevalence? Past studies conducted in the US have estimated transgender prevalence at between 0.4 percent and 0.7 percent of the adult population (Suarez et al., 2022: 74).

One of the best US surveys for addressing questions about the prevalence and characteristics of the transgender and nonbinary populations is the Behavioral Risk Factor Surveillance System (BRFSS). This survey is conducted by the Centers for Disease Control and Prevention (CDC) along with the health departments of the various states.

It started in 1984 with fifteen states participating; by 2024 all fifty states and the District of Columbia were included in the BRFSS. In our later analyses, we use data from the 2018 BRFSS.

Regarding measurement, two main types of questions have been used in empirical analyses of transgender persons. One type asks the respondent to self-identify as transgender or as cisgender. Most agree this is the best and most straightforward way for assessing transgender status. A second type is a two-step question that first asks the respondent about their assigned sex at birth, and next about their current gender identity. The BRFSS uses the self-identity method. Respondents were first asked "Do you consider yourself to be transgender?" If the respondent answered "Yes," the person was next asked, "Do you consider yourself to be 1. male-to-female, 2. female-to-male, or 3. gender nonconforming?" The respondent was allowed to answer with either the number or the text/word.

What is the rate of transgender prevalence according to data from the 2018 BRFSS? Our analysis of over 195,000 respondents with complete data in the BRFSS indicates that over 193,000 respondents answered "No" to the identity question asking if they considered themselves to be transgender, indicating that 98.9 percent of the respondents may be classified as cisgender. However, 0.67 percent of the respondents answered the question as "Don't know/not sure" or did not answer the question (see Table 10.2, top panel). We dropped the persons who responded, "Don't know/not sure," or refused to answer the question and then adjusted the data for its multistage survey design (see Table 10.2, bottom panel). The result is that 99.5 percent of the respondents identified as cisgender, and 0.51 percent as transgender. This one-half of 1 percent of the respondents identifying as transgender is well within the range of results of other empirical analyses.

Recall from our earlier discussion of the BRFSS transgender question that if the respondent answered "Yes," to the question "Do you consider yourself to be

TABLE 10.2 *Prevalence of the transgender and cisgender populations: data from the 2018 Behavioral Risk Factor Surveillance System*

Raw data from the BRFSS **Response**	**N**	**Percent**
1. Yes, transgender, male-to-female	324	0.17
2. Yes, transgender, female to male	330	0.17
3. Yes, transgender, gender nonconforming	206	0.11
4. No	193,725	98.89
7. Don't know/not sure	537	0.27
9. Refused	785	0.40
TOTAL	195,907	100.01

Survey adjusted data using BRFSS respondent sampling weights **Transgender/Cisgender status**	**Percent**
1. Transgender, male to female	0.18
2. Transgender, female to male	0.20
3. Transgender, gender nonconforming	0.13
4. Cisgender	99.50
Total	100.01

Source: Davis, Compton, and Poston, 2025.

transgender?" they were then asked, "Do you consider yourself to be 1. male-to-female, 2. female-to-male, or 3. gender nonconforming?" Our results indicate that the 0.51 percent identifying as transgender may be subcategorized as 0.18 percent male to female, 0.20 per cent female to male, and 0.13 percent gender nonconforming.

We now use demographic and socioeconomic characteristics data from the BRFSS 2018 and compare trans men with cis men, and trans women with cis women. We ask whether the trans groups differ from the cis groups on age, education, and marital status. In this analysis we do not include the transgender respondents who self-identified as gender nonconforming.

How different or how similar are the trans men and trans women to the cis men and cis women regarding (1) age, (2) education, and (3) marital status? In our analysis of single years of age (data not shown), we found that trans men are significantly younger than cis men; 30 percent of the trans men are between 18 and 27 years of age, compared to 18 percent of the cis men. And we also found that trans women are significantly younger than cis women; 30 percent of the trans women are in the young ages of 18 to 27, compared to 16 percent of the cis women.

How about levels of education? Are trans men more or less educated than cis men? We found that cis men are slightly more educated than trans men, and cis women are slightly more educated than trans women; these differences are statistically significant. For instance, we show in Table 10.3 (top panel) that 27.5 percent of cis men completed four or more years of college compared to 16.3 percent of trans men.

TABLE 10.3 *Characteristics of the transgender and the cisgender populations, frequency distributions, survey adjusted, Behavioral Risk Factor Surveillance System 2018*

	Trans men	Cis men	Trans women	Cis women
	percent	percent	percent	percent
Education				
none	0.2	0.2	0.0	0.3
grades 1–8	8.3	3.8	17.6	3.0
grades 9–11	14.2	8.7	17.0	7.5
grade 12 or GED	28.7	29.9	31.3	27.2
college 1–3 years	32.3	30.0	16.3	32.9
college 4 years +	16.3	27.5	17.7	29.2
Total	100.0	100.1	99.9	100.1
F-test	2.64***		10.49*	
Marital status				
Married	46.5	54.3	28.3	50.3
Divorced	10.7	10.5	12.2	12.3
Widowed	8.1	3.8	7.3	10.1
Separated	1.2	2.2	7.8	2.8
Never married	28.3	24.6	40.6	20.2
Cohabiting	5.1	4.6	3.8	4.4
Total	99.9	100.0	100.0	100.1
F-test	1.80+		7.31*	

Note: * = P<0.001, ** = P<0.01, ***P<0.05, + = P>0.05
Source: Davis, Compton, and Poston, 2025.

Similarly, 29.2 percent of cis women completed four or more years of college compared to 17.7 percent of trans women. The F-tests at the bottom of the panel are tests of statistical significance; if the F-test values have asterisks, the differences between the two groups are statistically significant; if the F-test values have pluses, the differences between the two groups are not statistically significant.

How about marriage? Do trans men differ significantly from cis men on marital status? How about trans women compared to cis women? Our marital status analysis indicates that trans men do not differ significantly from cis men, but trans women do differ significantly from cis women. Consider the percentage comparisons in the second panel of Table 10.4 Table 10.3; 10.7 percent of trans men compared to 10.5 percent of cis men are divorced; just over 28 percent of trans men have never been married compared to almost 25 percent of cis men. The largest difference for the two male groups is in the married category, 46.5 percent for trans men versus 54.3 percent for cis men. Overall, there are no statistically significant marital status differences when comparing trans men with cis men.

However, trans women do differ significantly on marital status from cis women. Over one-half (50.3 percent) of cis women are married compared to a little over one-quarter (28.3 percent) of trans women. The overall marital status difference is also seen in the never married category; over 20 percent of the cis women have never been married compared to almost 41 percent of the trans women.

TABLE 10.4 *Characteristics of transgender men and women and the transgender nonbinary populations, frequency distributions, survey adjusted, Behavioral Risk Factor Surveillance System 2018*

	Trans male	Trans NB	Trans female	Trans NB
	percent	percent	percent	percent
Education				
none	0.2	0.0	0.0	0.0
grades 1–8	8.3	17.7	17.6	17.7
grades 9–11	14.2	13.4	17.0	13.4
grade 12 or GED	28.7	18.3	31.3	18.3
college 1–3 years	32.3	28.3	16.3	28.3
college 4 years +	16.3	22.3	17.7	22.3
Total	100.0	100.0	99.9	100.0
F-test	0.86+		0.88+	
Marital status				
Married	46.5	26.3	28.3	26.3
Divorced	10.7	5.7	12.2	5.7
Widowed	8.1	15.3	7.3	15.3
Separated	1.2	1.3	7.8	1.3
Never married	28.3	42.4	40.6	42.4
Cohabiting	5.1	9.1	3.8	9.1
Total	99.9	100.1	100.0	100.1
F-test	1.96+		1.74+	

Note: * = P<0.001, ** = P<0.01, ***P<0.05, + = P>0.05
Source: Davis, Compton, and Poston, 2025.

We found that trans men and trans women differ significantly from cis men and from cis women on education and age. On marital status, trans women are significantly different from cis women, but trans men are not significantly different from cis men.

Finally, in other research we have shown that there is a clear income disadvantage for the trans population. We examined the incomes of trans men and trans women and compared them to the incomes of cis men and cis women. In our analyses we controlled for the effects on income of other variables known to influence income, such as employment, race, Hispanic ethnicity, age, and education. We found that the odds of trans men having higher incomes are 33 percent less than the odds of cis men; and the odds of trans women having higher incomes are 34 percent less than the odds of cis women (Davis, Compton, and Poston, 2025). Trans men and trans women are at significant economic disadvantages compared to cis men and cis women.

What about the characteristics of the gender nonbinary population? Do they differ from the trans male and the trans female populations on the characteristics of age, education, and marital status? We use the same BRFSS 2018 data and compare the trans male population with the transgender nonbinary population, and the trans female population with the transgender nonbinary population. In the previous analyses reported in Table 10.3, we did not include the transgender respondents identifying as gender nonbinary. We include them in this analysis.

How different or how similar are the trans male and trans female populations to the transgender nonbinary population regarding age? We compared five-year age data for the groups and found that neither trans men nor trans women differ significantly from gender nonbinary persons (data table not shown). The average age of the trans men is 43.4 years, and the average age of the trans women is 44.0 years; both are not significantly different from the average age of the transgender nonbinary respondents of 39.4 years.

How about education? In the top panel of Table 10.4 we show that trans male respondents do not differ significantly from transgender nonbinary respondents, and, also, that trans female respondents do not differ significantly from the transgender nonbinary respondents. The percentages of trans men in the various education categories are a little different from those of the gender nonbinary persons, but the differences are not large enough to be statistically significant. And the same conclusion holds for the comparisons of the trans women with the gender nonbinary respondents. The two percentage distributions by levels of education are remarkably similar for the two trans groups compared to the gender nonbinary group.

Finally, regarding marital status, trans men do not differ significantly from transgender nonbinary respondents, and trans women do not differ significantly from the transgender nonbinary group (see the bottom panel of Table 10.4). Once again, there are some minor differences in the marital status percentages, but the marital status distributions are far more similar than dissimilar. We conclude that trans men and trans women are not significantly different from transgender nonbinary respondents on all three characteristics of age, education, and marital status. The three groups of trans respondents are remarkably similar (Davis, Compton, and Poston, 2025).

In this last section of Chapter 10, we focused on gender identity. We specifically examined various issues dealing with trans men and trans women, transgender nonbinary persons, and cis men and cis women. Using data from the 2018 BRFSS social survey, we examined the overall prevalence of these groups in the US population. We next investigated socioeconomic patterns regarding age, education, and marital status by comparing these characteristics across gender identities. We also reported research comparing the incomes of transgender populations with cisgender populations.

We found that 99.5 percent of the respondents in the 2018 BRFSS data identified as cisgender, and 0.5 percent as transgender; these results are consistent with prior analyses that the trans population comprises between 0.4 and 0.7 percent of the general adult population. We then subcategorized the transgender respondents and found that 0.18 percent of them identified as transgender, male to female, 0.20 per cent as transgender, female to male, and 0.13 percent as transgender, gender nonconforming. In our analyses of age, education, and marital status, the data indicated that trans men and trans women are significantly younger than cis men and cis women. We found that cis men and cis women are more educated than trans men and trans women. Regarding marital status, over one-half of cis women are married compared to a little over one-quarter of trans women. Over 20 percent of the cis women have never been married compared to over 40.6 percent of the trans women. But trans men do not appear to differ much on marital status compared to cis men. Finally, we noted also that trans men and trans women are significantly disadvantaged economically compared to cis men and cis women.

SUMMARY

In the first part of this chapter, we discussed issues of sex structure. We considered sex as a demographic concept. Then we covered the five biological definitions of sex. We next focused on demographic indexes of sex composition, especially the sex ratio and the sex ratio at birth. We followed these discussions by noting the importance of sex and the demographic processes. We ended the section on sex structure with a discussion of intersex. In the next section of the chapter, we focused on gender identity; we discussed definitions and terminology dealing with gender identity, particularly transgender. We then examined various issues dealing with trans men and trans women, transgender nonbinary persons, and cis men and cis women. We discussed empirical research comparing trans persons with cis persons. We showed that there are significant differences between the trans male and trans female compared to the cis male and cis female populations.

Important points to take away from this chapter include the following: The definitions of sex and gender are not as straightforward as one might imagine; there are many complex issues involved in determining one's sex and gender identity; and empirically, comparing transgender persons with cisgender persons, there are many demographic and socioeconomic differences, and a few similarities.

DISCUSSION QUESTIONS

1. This chapter discusses several different sexual minority populations; two of the ones discussed are the transgender population and the intersex population. Distinguish each one from the other, and then tell us why both must be considered in demographic and sociological analyses of gender identity.

2. This chapter notes that biological sex is determined in five ways, on the basis of chromosomes, gonads, hormones, internal sexual organs, and external sexual organs (see Figure 10.1). Which one of the five do you hold to be the most important and relevant for the understanding of a person's biological sex, and which one is the least important. Be sure and justify your choices.

11

Contraception and Birth Control

INTRODUCTION

Discussions of the family and sexual orientation, the topics of Chapters 8 and 9, would not be complete without a consideration and review of **contraception** and **birth control**. Most married and unmarried sexually active women and men in the United States and in the countries of the developed world endeavor to limit their family size and/or to control the timing and spacing of their births. In the least-developed countries of the world, far fewer people use birth prevention methods. For example, family planning data for the past decade or so indicate that 74 percent of married (or in-union) women in the reproductive ages in the United States report using family planning methods, with 66 percent using modern methods; "modern methods include clinic and supply methods, including the pill, injectables, implants, IUDs, condoms, and sterilization" (Population Reference Bureau, 2024: 23). Compare these percentages with 40 percent of married women in the least-developed countries reporting using family planning methods, with 34 percent of them using modern methods (Population Reference Bureau, 2024). According to the United Nations classification, there are forty-five least-developed countries (LDCs); they are countries with agrarian economies and low levels of socioeconomic development, and they are mainly located in Africa (United Nations, 2024a).

There are many methods available to women and men to prevent births. The most popular ones worldwide are contraception, **sterilization**, and abortion. Some methods are more effective than others, and each has its advantages and disadvantages. In this chapter, we first present a brief review of the history of fertility control. Although fertility-control methods have been widely used and publicly accepted in the past seven or so decades, attempts to control fertility have characterized human populations for centuries. We follow this review with a description of the general situation worldwide and in the United States regarding the use of contraception, sterilization, and abortion. Then we present in the main part of the chapter a description of the major methods of birth prevention, including a discussion of their **effectiveness**.

BRIEF HISTORY OF FERTILITY CONTROL

The idea or notion of preventing births appeared early in human history. Of the many excellent and comprehensive accounts of contraception available, we call your attention to several. The classic is *Medical History of Contraception* by Norman Himes, first published in 1936, with a paperback edition in 1970. This is an exhaustive survey of contraception covering many cultures worldwide over three thousand years. It is a masterful collation of historical and anthropological evidence from preliterate societies to the early twentieth century.

In 1966, John T. Noonan wrote the superb *Contraception: A History of Its Treatment by the Catholic Theologians and Canonists*, with a paperback version published in 1986. As stated in the subtitle, it traces the very interesting history of contraception from the pre-Christian era to the 1960s, with the heaviest concentration on the interpretation and reception of contraception in the Catholic Church.

The third major treatment is the more recent (2008) book by Robert Jutte, *Contraception: A History*, published a few years earlier in German. Jutte's book extends and updates much of the earlier work of Himes and Noonan. All three books remind us that society's "attempts to control the increase in numbers reach so far back into the dim past that it is impossible to discern their real origins. Some forms of limitation on the rate of increase are undoubtedly as old as the life history of man" (Himes, [1936] 1970: 3).

Two other histories are also useful, namely McLaren's *History of Contraception: From Antiquity to the Present Day* (1992), and Riddle's *Eve's Herbs: A History of Contraception and Abortion in the West* (1999); the latter is particularly informative about the use of plant and herbal products to regulate fertility.

There are written records of contraceptive remedies and abortion techniques in Egyptian papyri (1900–1100 BC), in the Latin works of Pliny the Elder (AD 23–79) and Discorides (AD 40–90), in the Greek writings of Soranus (*c.* 100), and in works dealing with Arabic medicine in the tenth century. The oldest surviving documents describing contraceptive methods are the five Egyptian papyri dating from between 1900 BC and 1100 BC; each provided different recipes for contraceptive preparations. According to Noonan (1966: 9):

> The Kahun Papyrus [mentions] pulverized crocodile dung in fermented mucilage, and honey and sodium carbonate, to be sprinkled in the vulva. ... In the Ebers Papyrus it is said that pregnancy may be prevented for one, two, or three years by a recipe of acacia tips, coloquintida [a yellow lemon-sized bitter fruit sometimes used as a laxative], and dates, mixed with honey, to be placed in the uterus.

Until fairly recently, most fertility control methods were relatively ineffective, with the exception of induced abortion and **withdrawal**.

Virtually all of the contraceptive methods we review in this chapter, except for the hormonally based methods, were available and used by the end of the nineteenth century, some much earlier (Himes, [1936] 1970; Jutte, 2008). Condoms date back to the seventeenth century. Indeed, James Boswell, the famous diarist and author of *The Life of Samuel Johnson*, wrote about "using a condom with a prostitute in London in

1763" (Potts, 2003: 96). Intrauterine devices (IUDs) were first developed in Germany in the 1920s. However, owing to legal and other types of restrictions, it was not possible until much later to undertake IUD research in the United States. The manual vacuum-aspiration method of abortion was first described in the nineteenth century by Queen Victoria's gynecologist.

The physiological principles behind **oral contraceptives** were developed in the 1920s, "but the method made no progress, partly because of the lack of a cheap source of steroid and also because contraceptive research was not academically acceptable" (Potts, 2003: 96). Potts and Campbell (2002) have written about the vast historical disconnect between the acquisition of biological knowledge about birth control and its application.

In our presentations later about the specific types of contraceptives, we will have occasion to mention the historical precedents for some of them. We turn next to a discussion of fertility control in the world today.

CURRENT PATTERNS OF FERTILITY CONTROL WORLDWIDE

The Population Reference Bureau (2019) and the United Nations Department of Economic and Social Affairs (UNDESA) (2019, 2022) have published **family planning** and fertility control data from surveys conducted by a host of national governments and international agencies. Fertility control data for 2019 are presented for women between the ages of 15 and 49 who are married or in informal unions. These are the most comprehensive data currently available and portray a contemporary empirical picture of the reproductive revolution that has occurred in the world since the 1950s. We rely heavily on these data in our analyses of current fertility control patterns.

In 2019 in the world, 922 million women, or 48.5 percent, of the 1.9 billion women in the reproductive ages (15–49 years) were users of contraceptive methods; 842 million of them, 44.3 percent, used modern contraceptives; and 80 million, 4.2 percent, used traditional methods (UNDESA, 2019: 2). The main modern methods of family planning are the oral contraceptive (the pill), the **intrauterine device (IUD), contraception injection,** the **male condom,** and both **male and female sterilization.** Other modern methods include the **diaphragm, vaginal contraceptives** including various foams and jellies, several kinds of contraceptive implants, the **female condom,** and "natural" family planning methods – also known as **fertility awareness** methods, such as the **Standard Days Method®** and the **Billings ovulation method.** Traditional family planning methods include less effective "natural" methods, such as the calendar **rhythm method** (i.e., periodic abstinence), coitus interruptus (i.e., withdrawal), long-term abstinence, and prolonged breastfeeding. We discuss most of these and some other methods in a later section of this chapter.

We present in Figure 11.1 data on estimated numbers and percentages of contraceptive use worldwide for women of the reproductive ages (15–49). With 219 million users, the most common method used worldwide is female sterilization; almost 24 percent of all the contracepting women in the world use this method. The next three most popular methods worldwide are the male condom (189 million users, 21 percent of all contracepting women), the IUD (159 million users, 17 percent), and the pill (151 million users, 16 percent) (UNDESA, 2019: 3).

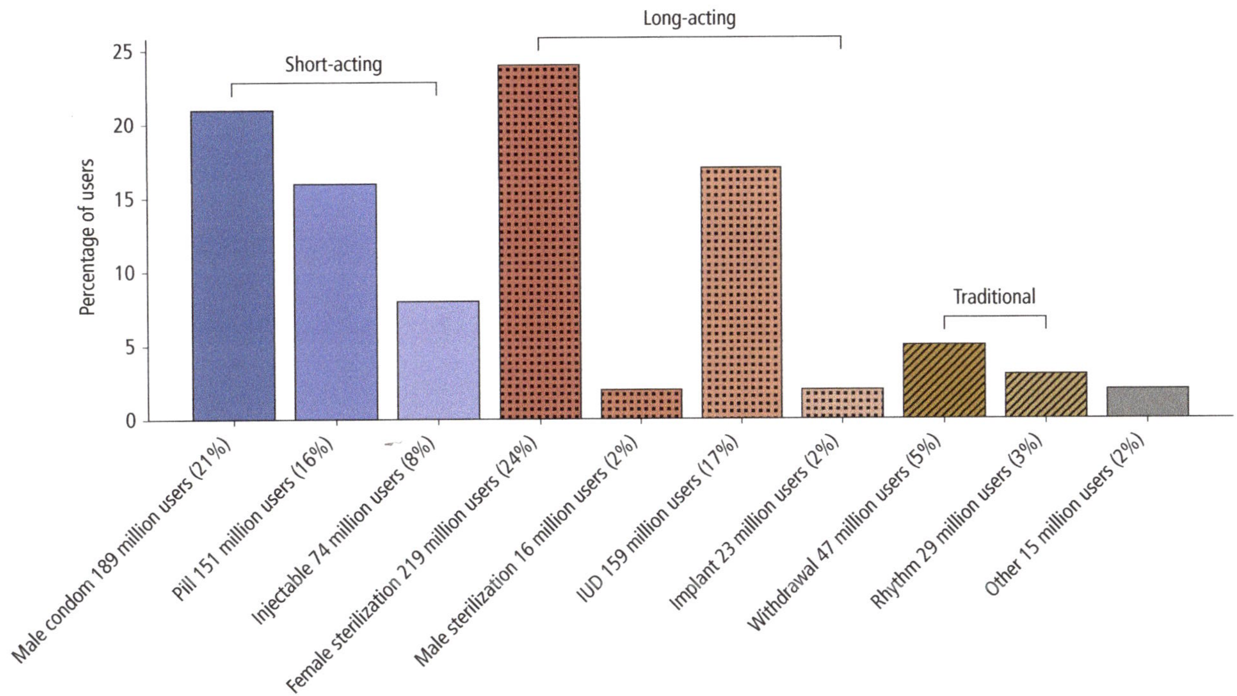

FIGURE 11.1 The estimated numbers and percentages of women of reproductive age (15–49) using various contraceptive methods worldwide, 2019 Contraceptive methods are grouped into short-acting, long-acting, traditional, and other.
Data source: United Nations Department of Economic and Social Affairs (UNDESA), 2019.

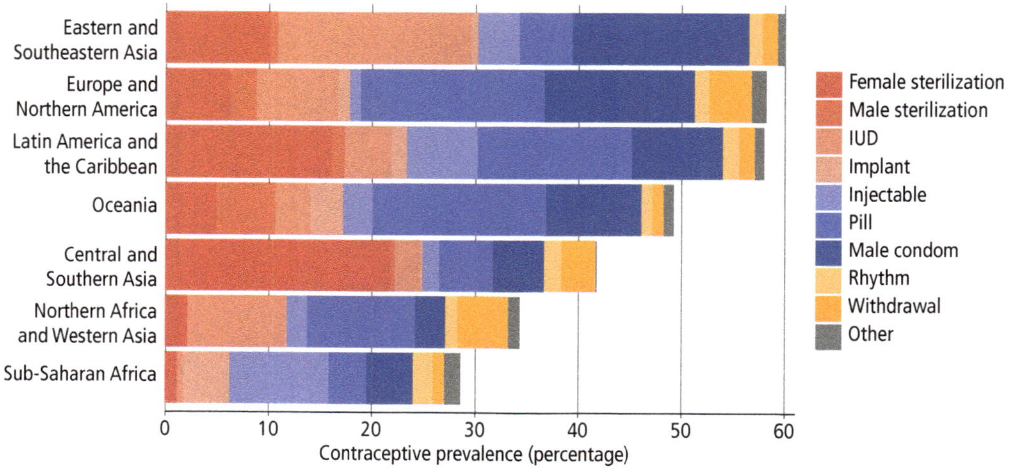

FIGURE 11.2. Contraceptive prevalence by method among women of reproductive age (15–49) by regions of the world, 2019
Data source: United Nations Department of Economic and Social Affairs (UNDESA), 2019.

Figure 11.2 presents data on percentages of overall contraceptive prevalence, and percentages using different methods, for women of the reproductive ages (15–49), for the different regions of the world. The three regions with the highest percentages of contraceptive prevalence are East and Southeast Asia (60 percent of all women in the reproductive ages using contraception), Europe and Northern America (58.2 percent), and Latin America and the Caribbean (58 percent). The two regions with the lowest rates of contraceptive prevalence are both in Africa: sub-Saharan Africa (28.5 percent) and Northern and Western Africa (34.3 percent).

In East and Southeast Asia, the most common of all the contraceptive methods is the IUD, with almost 19 percent of women in the reproductive ages using this method. The male condom (17 percent use rate) is the second most popular method. In Europe and Northern America, the pill (17.8 percent) is the most popular method followed by the male condom (14.6 percent). In Latin America and the Caribbean, the two most popular contraceptives are female sterilization (16 percent) and the pill (14.9 per cent). In sub-Saharan Africa, the region with the lowest overall contraceptive prevalence rate, the most popular method by far is injectables, at 9.6 percent; this is the only region in the world where injectables are the dominant contraceptive method (UNDESA, 2019: 4).

An injectable contraceptive is a shot administered every twelve weeks that contains hormones, usually progestin-only, but sometimes both a progestin and an estrogen; it prevents pregnancy by inhibiting the release of eggs from the ovaries and by thickening the mucus at the cervix, making it difficult for sperms to penetrate the cervix (Jacobstein and Polis, 2014). Depo-Provera® is a well-known injectable contraceptive used in many Western countries, including the United States.

Methods of contraceptive use vary significantly according to whether the woman is married or unmarried. "Married" women are those who are married according to the marriage laws and customs of their country, and also those who are in-union, that is, women living with their partners in the same households, namely, cohabiting.

"Unmarried" women are those who are not married and not in-union. We mentioned earlier that in the world in 2019 there were 922 million women in the reproductive ages who were users of contraceptives. Of these women, 779 million were married or in-union; almost 50 percent of them were users of permanent and long-lasting methods including female sterilization and the IUD. In contrast, 143 million of them were not married or in-union, and only 23 percent of them were users of permanent and long-lasting methods (UNDESA, 2019: 13).

Contraceptive use in the developing countries of the world has now almost reached the level attained in the developed countries, equaling in both regions around 60 percent of women in the reproductive ages (UNDESA, 2019: 4; Population Reference Bureau, 2024). This has occurred even though the use of family planning methods in the developing world is quite uneven across the various countries. The percentages of women in the reproductive ages using modern methods range from lows of 1 percent in Somalia, 4 percent in Albania, 5 percent in South Sudan, 7 percent in Chad, and 9 percent in Comoros, to highs of 82 percent in Finland, 81 percent in China, and 80 percent in Brazil. The countries with the highest percentages of women using any family planning method, not just modern methods, are Finland at 86 percent, China at 85 percent, and South Korea at 82 percent; the percentages of women in the reproductive ages in the United States using all methods and using modern methods are 74 percent and 66 percent, respectively (Population Reference Bureau, 2024). The reproductive revolution is surely one of the most remarkable demographic stories of the last seven or so decades.

So far, we have been presenting data on users of family planning methods. If we subtract the user percentage for a country from 100, we obtain the percentage of women who are not using contraceptive methods. In Finland, the percentage of nonusers is 14 percent, and it is 15 percent in China. However, in Somalia where only 7 percent of women in the reproductive ages are users of any contraceptive method, the percentage there of nonusers is 93 percent.

Who is a nonuser of contraception? There are roughly six categories of nonusers. Women in only one of the nonuser categories, the last category on the list we present below, are engaging in unprotected intercourse and are thus at risk of becoming pregnant. Here are the categories:

1. Women who are surgically sterile via a **hysterectomy**, that is, the surgical removal of the uterus and sometimes the additional removal of the Fallopian tubes and the ovaries, or by some other noncontraceptive operation; these women would not be expected to be using contraception because they are sterile.
2. Women who themselves or their male partners are nonsurgically sterile; these women would not be expected to be contraception users because they or their partners are sterile.
3. Women who are pregnant or postpartum, that is, those who have just given birth; pregnant women are not expected to be contracepting; and for postpartum women, there is very little risk of pregnancy for several months after giving birth; recall our discussion of postpartum infecundability in Chapter 4.
4. Women who are trying to become pregnant; they obviously would not be contracepting.

5. Women who have never had intercourse or have not had intercourse in the past three months; if the women have never had intercourse or have not had intercourse in the three months before they were questioned in the fertility survey interview, then they are not considered to be sexually active.
6. Women who have had intercourse in the last three months before the fertility survey interview; women in this last category are "sexually active" and hence are truly at risk of becoming pregnant. (Demographers define a "sexually active" woman as one who has had intercourse at least once in the past three months.)

Recent data indicate that around 63 percent of women in the reproductive ages worldwide, or almost two-thirds of them, are using family planning methods; therefore, 37 percent of them are nonusers. But we cannot tell from the international data how many of these nonusers are truly at risk of becoming pregnant involuntarily. That is, we do not know how many of the nonusers would fall into the sixth category of nonusers, as just described. However, these types of nonuser data are available for women in the United States, and we shall describe them in more detail later.

Having examined family planning methods worldwide, we turn now to a discussion of induced abortion. What are its current patterns worldwide? An induced abortion is termination of a pregnancy by human intervention with an "intent other than to produce a live birth" (Henshaw, 2003: 529). The most complete data on induced abortions are from countries where abortion is legal, but even here the quantity and quality of the data vary considerably. In Table 11.1, we show estimates of the rates of unintended pregnancy and of the rates of **induced abortions**, for the world and its major regions for 1990–1994, 2005–2009, and 2015–2019. By the 2015–2019 period in the world, the abortion rate (number of abortions per 1,000 women aged 15–49) had decreased very slightly from 40/1,000 in 1990–1994 to 39 per 1,000 in 2015–2019. The unintended pregnancy rate (number of unintended pregnancies per 1,000 women aged 15–49) experienced a much sharper decline, from 79/1,000 in 1990–1994 to 64 per 1,000 in 2015–2019. In 1990–1994, one-half of unintended pregnancies

TABLE 11.1 *Global and regional estimates of unintended pregnancy rates and induced abortion rates, 1990–1994, 2005–2009, and 2015–2019*

Region and subregion	Unintended pregnancy rate[a]			Abortion rate[b]		
	1990–1994	2005–2009	2015–2019	1990–1994	2005–2009	2015–2019
World	79	67	64	40	37	39
Region						
Africa	106	97	90	32	34	36
Asia	75	66	64	41	42	45
Europe	76	38	36	55	24	20
Latin America	94	78	69	35	35	32
Northern America	43	40	34	22	16	12

[a] Abortions per 1,000 women aged 15–49.
[b] Unintended pregnancy rate per 1,000 women aged 15-49.
Source: Guttmacher Institute, 2022.

worldwide ended in abortion; in 2015–2019, 61 percent of unintended pregnancies ended in abortion (Guttmacher Institute, 2014b, 2022).

Between 1990–1994 and 2015–2019, the abortion rates in some of the major regions of the world either declined a little or increased a little. The greatest decline in abortion rates occurred in Europe, from 55 in 1990–1994 to 20 in 2015–2019. Northern America also saw a decline in abortion rates from 22 in 1990–1994 to 12 in 2015–2019.

Abortions appear to occur less frequently in countries where they are legally performed versus in countries where they are not legally performed. To illustrate, the abortion data in Table 11.1 indicate that the rate in 2015–2019 was 36 in Africa where abortion is, for the most part, illegal, but it was 20 in Europe where it is mostly legal.

An unsafe abortion is defined by the World Health Organization "as a procedure for terminating a pregnancy that is performed by an individual lacking the necessary skills, or in an environment that does not conform to minimal medical standards, or both" (Guttmacher Institute, 2012: 2). Abortions are far safer in countries where they are legally performed than where they are illegally performed. There is a great disparity between the proportion of unsafe abortions in developed and developing countries. Almost all abortions in countries of the developed world are safe, but this is not at all the situation in the countries of the developing world. In East Asian countries abortions are very safe, but they are very unsafe in African countries.

CURRENT PATTERNS OF FERTILITY CONTROL IN THE UNITED STATES

We now turn attention to the contraceptive behavior of US women. Figure 11.3 presents data on the use and nonuse of contraception by US women aged 15–49, for the 2017–2019 period. These data were gathered via the National Survey of Family Growth (see our discussion of this survey in Chapter 3).

In Figure 11.3 we see that 65.3 percent of US women were using contraception in the 2017–2019 period, and, thus, 34.7 percent were not. The most popular method for US women is female sterilization (18.1%) with the oral contraceptive close behind (14.0%). Long-acting reversible contraception, namely, intrauterine devices and implants, are in third place at 10.4 percent. The male condom is the next most popular method (8.4%), with "all other contraceptive methods" (5.7%) in fifth place. Male sterilization (5.6%) is in sixth place. Unlike the situation worldwide, for US women, the IUD is not one of the most favored methods; but, as just noted, the category of long-acting reversible contraceptives is in third place, and the IUD is in this category.

What about the non-users of contraceptives? We noted in the previous paragraph that 34.7 percent of women were not contracepting. The data in the top part of Figure 11.3 refer to women who are nonusers of contraception. Of the almost 35 percent of all US women who are not currently using any form of contraception, almost one-half of them (16.8%) reported never having sexual intercourse or not having sex in the past three months. Almost 8 percent of them are pregnant, postpartum, or trying to become pregnant. Only 7 percent of the women who are nonusers of contraception are sexually active (defined by demographers as having had sexual intercourse at least once in the three months prior to being interviewed in the survey). Thus, most of the 35 percent who are not using contraceptives are women who are pregnant, seeking to become

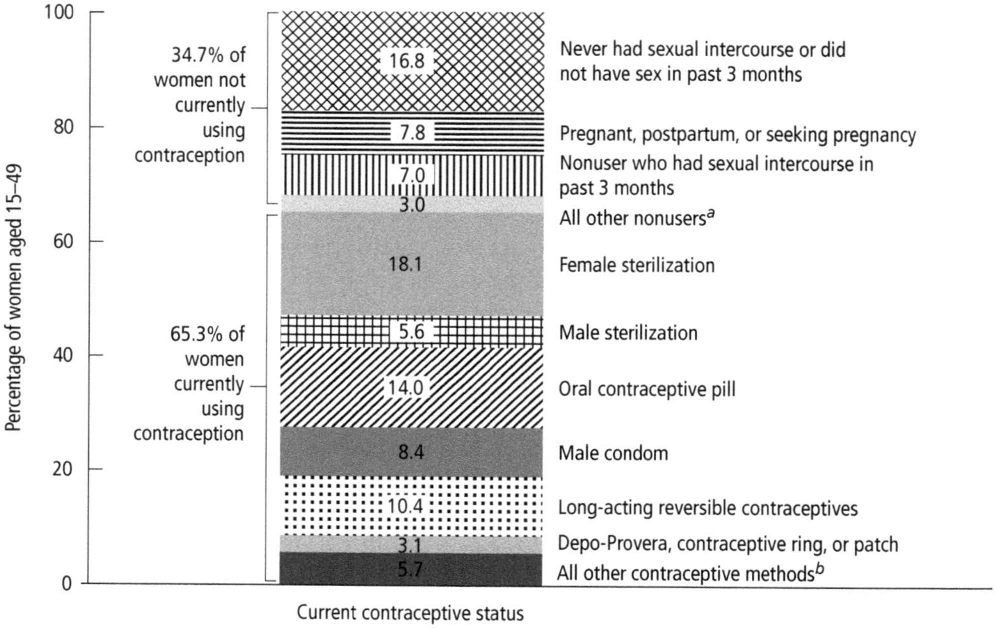

FIGURE 11.3 Percentages of women aged 15–49 by current contraceptive use in the United States, 2017–2019

[a] The nonusers include those who are nonsurgically sterile.

[b] "All other contraceptive methods" include diaphragm, periodic abstinence, and withdrawal.

Source: National Center for Health Statistics, 2021.

pregnant, postpartum, never had intercourse, or not sexually active. Only one in five of the nonusers of contraception are sexually active and do not fall into one of the other categories; it is only the sexually active group of women who are truly at risk of an unintended pregnancy.

What about contraceptive use by teenagers? Of the various methods we just discussed, which ones are the most popular and the least popular among teenagers in the United States? Before discussing contraceptive use among US teenagers, let us first examine recent data on sexual behavior of teenagers. Figure 11.4 presents data on the cumulative probability of male and female teenagers having first sexual intercourse by each age from 15 to 20. Sexual intercourse is defined "as vaginal intercourse between opposite-sex partners" (Abma and Martinez, 2023: 6). The age-specific probabilities of having had first sex are very similar for male and female teenagers. By age 17 the probabilities of having had sex were slightly above 40 percent for males and females, and they were above 60 percent by age 19.

Slightly different data for the year of 1971 show remarkably lower percentages for female teenagers. At age 17 among unmarried females living in metropolitan areas in the United States, 26 percent of them reported having had first sex. By age 19, 46 percent of them reported having experienced first sex (Zelnik and Kantner, 1980).

Race and ethnicity data are not reported in Figure 11.4. But it turns out that the probability "of having had sex by age 17 was highest for Black males (57%), followed

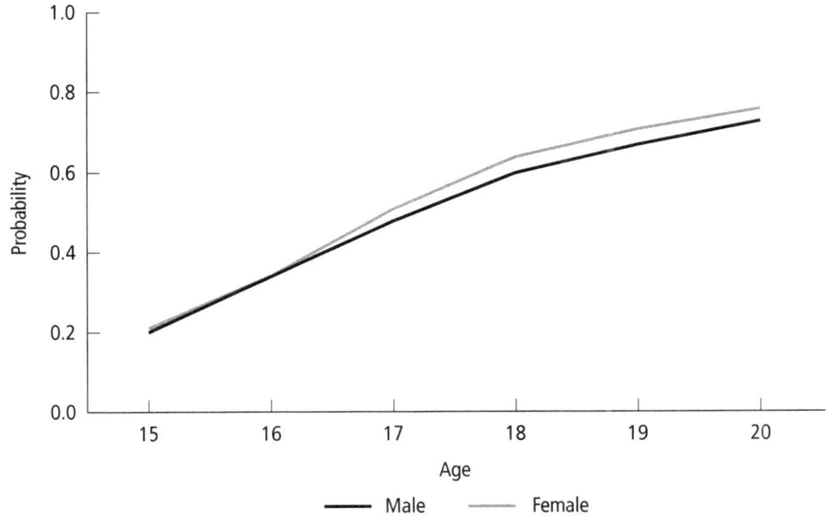

FIGURE 11.4 Probability of having had first sex by age 15, 16, 17, 18, 19, and 20 for females and males aged 15–24 in the United States, 2015–2019
Note: Sex is defined in this report as vaginal intercourse between opposite-sex partners.
Source: Abma and Martinez, 2023.

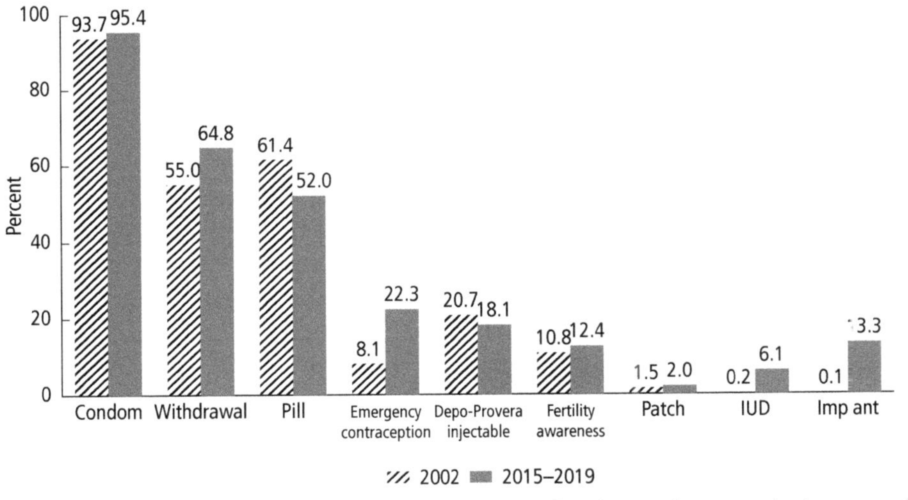

FIGURE 11.5 Methods of contraception ever used among females aged 15–19 who have ever had sex, United States, 2002 and 2015–2019
Source: Abma and Martinez, 2023.

by Hispanic (56%) and White males (44%). Among females, the probability of having had sex by age 17 was highest for Black females (58%), followed by White (51%) and Hispanic females (47%)" (Abma and Martinez, 2023: 6).

What methods are female teenagers using in their sexual activities? Figure 11.5 reports for the time periods of 2002 and 2015–2019 the percentages of sexually experienced female teenagers who had ever used each of several different contraceptives.

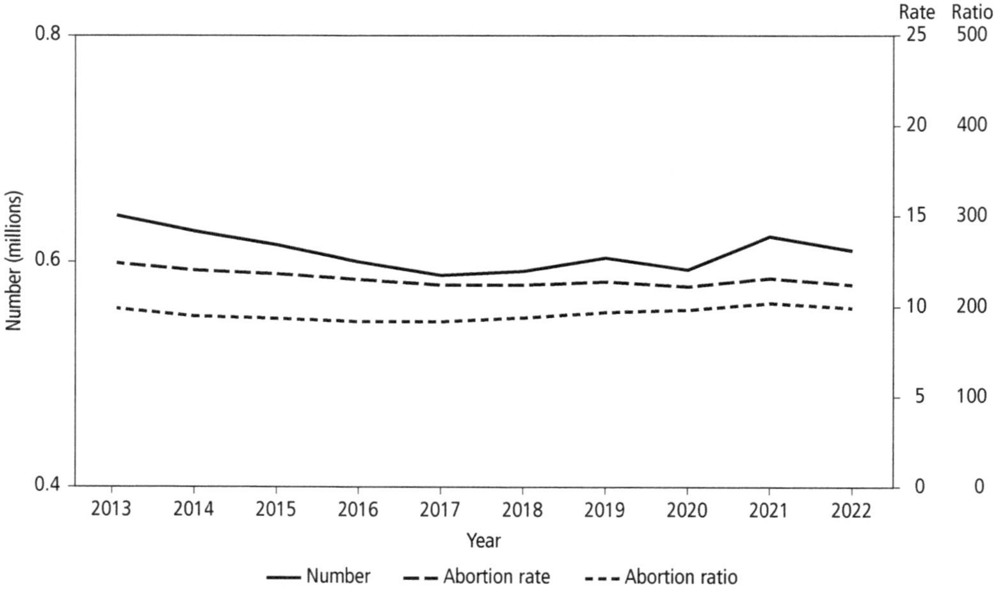

FIGURE 11.6. Number, rate,[a] and ratio[b] of abortions performed, by year – selected reporting areas,[c] United States, 2013–2022
[a] Number of abortions per 1,000 women aged 15–44 years.
[b] Number of abortions per 1,000 live births.
[c] Data are for 47 reporting areas; California, District of Columbia, Maryland, New Hampshire, and New Jersey are excluded.
Source: Ramer et al., 2024.

(A sexually experienced female is defined as one who has reported in the survey that she has had vaginal intercourse with an opposite-sex person.) In the 2015–2019 period the most-used contraceptive methods among experienced female teenagers were the condom (95.4%), withdrawal (64.8%), and the pill (52.0%). The data in Figure 11.5 also show that between 2002 and 2015–2019, the use by female teenagers of the oral contraceptive decreased from 61 percent to 52 percent, and the use of withdrawal increased from 55 percent to 65 percent.

What is known about abortion in the United States? Each year, the Centers for Disease Control and Prevention (CDC), a US federal agency under the Department of Health and Human Services, requests abortion data from the central health agencies of all fifty states, and the District of Columbia and New York City; 47 of these 52 areas provided data for each year from 2013 to 2022; New Jersey, New Hampshire, Maryland, California, and the District of Columbia did not provide consistent data. Figure 11.6 reports data from the 47 reporting areas for each year from 2013 to 2022 on the number of legal abortions, the abortion rate (number of abortions per 1,000 women aged 15–44), and the abortion ratio (number of abortions per 1,000 live births). "Among the 47 reporting areas with data each year . . ., in 2022, a total of 609,360 abortions were reported, the abortion rate was 11.2 abortions per 1,000 women aged 15–44 years, and the abortion ratio was 199 abortions per 1,000 live births. From 2021 to 2022, the total number of abortions decreased by 2% . . ., the abortion rate decreased by 3% . . ., and the abortion ratio decreased by 2%" (Ramer et al., 2024). We noted above that in the year 2022 there were over 613,000 reported abortions; this was a decrease of 5 percent from the over 640 thousand abortions reported in 2013, and a decrease of 10 percent in the abortion rate, from 12.4/1,000 to 11.2/1,000. Historically, the highest reported abortion rate for the United States was in 1981 when the rate was 29.3/1,000; since then, it has dropped fairly steadily to its rate in 2022 of 11.2/1,000.

Only 32 of the 48 reporting areas provided abortion data to the CDC that were broken down by race and ethnicity. The highest percentages of abortions in 2022 were among non-Hispanic White women and non-Hispanic Black women, 31.9 percent and 39.5 percent, respectively. Regarding marital status, over 12 percent of women receiving an abortion were married, and almost 88 percent were unmarried. And almost 41 percent of all the abortions performed in 2022 were to women who reported having had no live births previously, and over 24 percent of all the abortions in 2022 were to women who reported having had one live birth previously (Ramer et al., 2024).

Abortions became legal in the United States in 1973 when the Supreme Court in the *Roe v. Wade* decision declared that "women, in consultation with their physician, have a constitutionally protected right to have an abortion in the early stages of pregnancy, that is, before the fetus is viable, free from government interference" (Guttmacher Institute, 2008: 2). In June of 2022, the US Supreme Court in the *Dobbs v. Jackson Women's Health Organization* decision eliminated the federal constitutional right of women to have abortions. It was left to the states to regulate the practice of abortions or to ban them. As of March 2025, when this chapter was being written, abortions were banned in Alabama, Arkansas, Idaho, Indiana, Kentucky, Louisiana, Mississippi, Oklahoma, South Dakota, Tennessee, Texas, and West Virginia. In Florida, Georgia, Iowa, South Carolina, Nebraska, North Carolina, and Utah, there were gestational limits banning abortions running from 6 weeks to 12 weeks after the start of the pregnancy (McCann and Walter, 2025).

Having reviewed the patterns of family planning and abortion use and nonuse worldwide and in the United States, we turn in the next section to a discussion of each of the main methods of family planning.

METHODS OF FAMILY PLANNING

There are many kinds of family planning methods; some are controlled by females and others by males. This male–female categorization is "generally determined by which partner's body is most affected by the device's use" (Shepard, 1980: 72). There are several ways to categorize contraceptives. One way is whether or not the contraceptive serves as a barrier to keep the man's sperm from entering the woman. Another category is whether the contraceptive contains hormones. And another is whether the contraceptive requires continuous input (e.g., the pill or the condom) or whether it is long-lasting (e.g., IUDs and implants). Still another way is to categorize or rank them on the basis of their efficacy in preventing pregnancy. This is the approach we will follow. In this section, we first discuss the concept of contraceptive effectiveness and failure and show how failure rates are measured and determined and what they mean. We then review each of the major contraceptive methods.

Contraceptive Effectiveness and Failure

The effectiveness of family planning methods may be measured in two ways, in terms of **theoretical effectiveness** and in terms of **use effectiveness**. Theoretical effectiveness refers to the "efficaciousness" of the method when it is used "consistently according to a specified set of rules" and used all the time (Trussell, 2004: 91). In other words, it is the degree of effectiveness in preventing pregnancy that would occur with "perfect" use. Alternately, use effectiveness measures the effectiveness of the method taking into account the fact that some users do not follow the directions and the rules perfectly or carefully and/or may not use the method all the time; use effectiveness data tell us how effective the method is in **typical use**.

In Table 11.2, we report contraceptive failure percentage rates based on both use effectiveness and theoretical effectiveness data. Use effectiveness data are empirical data gathered in surveys conducted in past decades that covered the contraceptive and

TABLE 11.2 *Contraceptive failure rates (percentage of women experiencing an unintended pregnancy during the first year of use), by contraceptive method, according to use (i.e., typical) effectiveness and theoretical (i.e., perfect) effectiveness, United States, post-2000*

Method	Use effectiveness	Theoretical effectiveness
No method	85	85
Spermicides[a]	28	18
Fertility awareness methods	24	
Standard days method		5
Two-day method		4
Ovulation method		3
Symptothermal method		0.4
Withdrawal	22	4
Sponge		
Parous women	24	20
Nulliparous women	12	9
Female condom[b]	21	5
Male condom[b]	18	2
Diaphragm[c]	12	6
Combined pill & progestin-only pill	9	0.3
Ortho Evra patch	9	0.3
Vaginal ring, NuvaRing	9	0.3
Injectables, Depo-Provera	6	0.2
Intrauterine device (IUD)		
ParaGard	0.8	0.6
Mirena	0.2	0.2
Female sterilization	0.5	0.5
Male sterilization	0.15	0.10
Implant	0.05	0.05

[a] Foams, creams, gels, and vaginal suppositories.
[b] Without spermicides.
[c] With spermicidal cream or jelly.
Source: Centers for Disease Control and Prevention, 2014; Trussel, 2004; Trussel and Guthrie, 2011: Chapter 3, Table 3-2.

fertility behavior of women, mainly in the United States. Couples were surveyed about their use of specific family planning methods for specific periods of time, usually a year. The percentage of couples "typically" using a specific method and experiencing accidental pregnancies over the course of a year is the **failure rate** for that method according to use effectiveness data. One needs to keep in mind that typical use is broadly defined. In many of the surveys generating contraceptive use data, a woman is stated to be "using" a particular contraceptive method if "she considers herself to be using that method. So, typical use of the condom could include actually using a condom only occasionally" (Trussell, 2004: 91). Or "a woman could report that she is 'using' the pill even though her supplies ran out several months ago" (Trussell and Guthrie, 2011: 53). Thus, we need to keep in mind that "typical use is a very elastic concept" (Trussell, 2004: 91). It includes imperfect use and is not a measure of the "inherent efficacy of a contraceptive method when used perfectly, correctly and consistently" (Kost et al., 2008: 11).

The contraceptive failure rates based on theoretical effectiveness refer to pregnancies that would be experienced if a particular method was used under ideal, perfect conditions, that is, if the method was always used and used exactly according to the instructions and the rules.

We begin by first asking how many pregnancies will occur if no contraception is used. The failure rate for the nonuse of contraception is based on studies of "populations in which the use of contraception is rare, and on couples who report that they stopped using contraceptives because they want to conceive" (Trussel, 2011: 780). The failure rate for nonuse is 85 percent (see Table 11.2, top row of data). This means that if 100 sexually active couples were to use no contraception, that is, they were to engage in unprotected intercourse over the course of a year, 85 percent of the women on average would experience a pregnancy. The nonuse of contraception, obviously, has the highest pregnancy (or failure) rate.

Alternately, the contraceptive with the lowest failure rate, determined by both theoretical effectiveness data and use effectiveness data, is the implant; a popular implant brand is Nexplanon. Implants have an average failure rate of 0.05 percent (later we will discuss this method in more detail). This means that for every 10,000 women using an implant, about five or so would experience an unintended pregnancy in the course of one year of use.

Failure rates are shown in Table 11.2 for all the major types of contraceptives according to use effectiveness and theoretical effectiveness. We have ranked them from the highest failure rate to the lowest failure rate according to use effectiveness data.

Vaginal Spermicides

Vaginal spermicides are the least effective contraceptive method based on use effectiveness, but they are more effective than no contraception. Spermicides are contraceptive creams, jellies, and foams that are inserted into the vagina prior to the onset of genital contact and sexual intercourse. They are "commonly marketed for use with a diaphragm, but they can also be used alone for contraception" (Cates and Harwood, 2011: 395). They should be placed in the vagina several minutes before sexual activity commences. To be maximally effective, they should cover the vagina mucus and cervix. Some spermicides require the use of an applicator for correct insertion. The spermicide needs to be reapplied before each coitus. In addition to creating a physical barrier to the movement of sperm, many spermicides contain the sperm-killing chemical nonoxynol-9 (N-9), which further reduces the chance of conception (the beginning of pregnancy) by damaging and killing sperm in the vagina.

The idea of **vaginal contraceptives** is very old. Aristotle described the use of oil of cedar and frankincense in olive oil to block the cervical entrance. During the Middle Ages, rock salt and alum were frequently used as vaginal contraceptives (Himes, [1936] 1970: 80). Much later, a sponge moistened with diluted lemon juice and inserted into the vagina was described as an "effective" contraceptive. During the 1920s and 1930s, numerous vaginal suppositories and foam tablets were developed and sold widely.

There are many brands of vaginal spermicides available in pharmacies and supermarkets in the United States without a prescription, such as Encare, Endometrin, Gynol II, Prochieve, and VCF, among several others. Despite their large-scale accessibility and small expense, they are not very effective, from the vantage of either use effectiveness or theoretical effectiveness. Under typical use, the failure rate is 28 percent, and 18 percent under perfect use. Moreover, the effectiveness of a spermicide depends on the particular type. Aerosol foams and creams tend to be more effective than jellies and foam tablets. Foam compares favorably with the effectiveness of the calendar rhythm method (see our next discussion), but as indicated by the failure rate data just mentioned, produces more failures than most other methods.

Their relative ineffectiveness is the major disadvantage of vaginal spermicides. Also, as already noted, the preparations must be administered several minutes before intercourse, which will thus tend to interrupt foreplay and is often inconvenient. They must be inserted high into the vagina to be most effective, and some women may do this only reluctantly or not at all. On the other hand, their use does not require medical supervision. There are no known adverse side effects except for mild burning, which can be experienced by both the females and the males, and vaginal irritation, which can often be corrected by switching to some other type of preparation. A positive side effect is that spermicides provide some vaginal lubrication. A very small number of US women use spermicides as their regular contraceptive method, less than one-half of 1 percent.

Fertility Awareness Methods

Fertility awareness methods refer to several so-called natural family planning methods that employ an awareness of information about the woman's menstrual cycle to predict the time of the month when the probability is high that she will become pregnant. They "depend on identifying the 'fertile window,' or the days in each menstrual cycle when intercourse is most likely to result in a pregnancy" (Jennings and Burke, 2011: 417). In general, according to use effectiveness data, most of these methods are just slightly more effective than spermicides and a little less effective than withdrawal.

These methods require that a woman refrain from having intercourse during the time when the probability is high that she will become pregnant. Some of the fertility awareness methods are classified as "modern" and some as "traditional." The more effective ones use various kinds of symptomatic information about the woman and her menstrual cycle.

The traditional and least effective fertility awareness method is the **calendar rhythm method**, known also as periodic abstinence or continence. There are several calendar methods, the first of which was developed independently in 1920 by a Japanese scientist, Kyusaka Ogino, and by an Austrian scientist, Hermann Knaus. It was based on the idea that a women can avoid pregnancy if she refrains from intercourse around the time of ovulation, when the egg is produced. Generally, only one egg is produced per menstrual cycle, and it is potentially fertilizable for around twenty-four hours after ovulation. The sperm is believed to be viable in the female tract for as many as six or seven days (Ryder, 1993: 723; Segal, 2003: 171); it is thus capable of fertilizing an egg several days after intercourse occurs. Theoretically, couples who avoid intercourse during the period when the egg and sperm are viable should be able to avoid conception. The trick is finding out the exact time interval during which to avoid intercourse, which is not an easy task.

The notion that females cannot conceive during most of the menstrual cycle is very old (Himes, [1936] 1970), but some of the early ideas on which part of the cycle was not "safe" were incorrect. For instance, Knaus held that ovulation would always occur fourteen days prior to the start of the next menstrual cycle (Jutte, 2008: 204), a fact we now know not to be true. Others held that the woman was most likely to conceive immediately after her menstrual period ended; thus, the rest of the cycle was considered safe because she was thought to be sterile during that time. Frequently, women following these principles became pregnant, and the calendar rhythm method gained a poor reputation. In our classes we sometimes tell our demography students the joke that persons practicing the rhythm method are known as parents. Since the method was defined as "natural" and not "artificial," it was deemed to be acceptable by the Roman Catholic Church, and hence sometimes came to be called "Vatican roulette" or "calendar love."

The calendar rhythm method is usually applied as follows. The woman records the length of her menstrual cycles for a time period of a year or more. The presumed time of ovulation is then determined for the shortest and longest cycles. Nineteen is subtracted from the shortest and ten from the longest. These calculations inform the woman when it is safe and not safe to engage in intercourse. For example, if a woman determines that her menstrual cycles range in length from 31 to 35 days, it would be safe for her to have intercourse for the first through the twelfth days of the cycle (31–19 = 12), not safe on the thirteenth through the twenty-fourth days, and safe again starting on the twenty-fifth day (35–10 = 25) (Kipley and Kipley, 1996). Whereas few US women report using the calendar rhythm method (less than 1 percent), there are no acceptable failure rate data available because "no well-designed prospective studies have been conducted, and no data are available from national surveys" (Jennings and Burke, 2011: 419). Thus no data are shown for this method in Figure 11.3.

Another fertility awareness method, the Standard Days Method®, also involves "counting the days in the menstrual cycle to identify the fertile days" (Jennings and Burke, 2011: 418). It is easy to use for women with menstrual cycles that last between twenty-six and thirty-two days. It is a variant of the calendar rhythm method just described but, according to theoretical effectiveness data, it is more effective, and it is easier to learn and use. Developed by researchers at the Institute for Reproductive Health at Georgetown University, it is based on the principle that "women with regular menstrual cycles lasting 26–32 days can prevent pregnancy by avoiding unprotected intercourse on days eight through 19. This 12-day fertile window takes into account the variability in the timing of ovulation and the viability of sperm in the woman's reproductive tract" (Arevalo et al, 1999; Gribble, 2003: 188). Thus, for pregnancy prevention, it is safe to engage in intercourse for the first seven days of the cycle, not safe from the eighth through the nineteenth days, and safe again from the twentieth day until the end of the cycle.

CycleBeads®, a string of color-coded beads to indicate fertile and infertile days, may be used by a woman to keep track of the days in her menstrual cycle. The beads are colored either red, brown, or white; the white beads are designed to glow in the dark. There is one red bead on the necklace, and it is used to mark the first day in the woman's menstrual cycle, that is, the day she starts her menstrual period. Six brown beads follow the one red bead, and they signify the days when it is safe to have intercourse. Twelve white glow-in-the-dark beads follow the brown beads, and they signify days when it is not safe to have intercourse. They are then followed by brown beads signifying safe days until the menstrual period restarts, at which time the woman begins again by moving the ring to the red bead.

The woman is instructed to move a black marker ring each morning from one bead to the next. Prior to engaging in intercourse, she checks the color of the bead; if it is white and glowing in the dark, it is not a safe day, if she wants to prevent a pregnancy.

The Standard Days Method has been introduced in many developing countries to young women who are using contraceptives for the first time, and many find the method appealing. According to Gribble (2003: 188): "In trials conducted in El Salvador and India, up to one-half of women who adopted the method had never before practiced family planning, in large part because of concerns about side effects and a perceived threat to future fertility." There are no failure rate data available based on use effectiveness for the Standard Days Method. Its failure rate based on theoretical effectiveness data is around 5 percent.

The other fertility awareness methods involve the "actual observation of fertility signs such as presence or absence of secretions, changes in characteristics of cervical secretions, or changes in basal body temperature" (Jennings and Burke, 2011: 418). The estimated time of ovulation may be calculated by use of a **basal body temperature (BBT)** chart. It is based on the principle that ovulation produces a rise in the basic metabolic rate, causing a corresponding increase in body temperature of between 0.3 and 0.9 degrees Centigrade (between 0.5 and 1.6 degrees Fahrenheit). The time of one's ovulation may thus be determined by reading and recording one's temperature daily. This technique greatly reduces the length of abstinence as required in the calendar rhythm method, but there are drawbacks. For instance, changes in body temperature are slight and easily misinterpreted, and the principle of an increase in temperature at the time of ovulation may not necessarily apply to all women (Shepard, 1980).

Another way of determining the time of ovulation is based on the association between the presence of cervical mucus and ovulation. Vaginal mucus tends to become more moist and cervical secretions more watery, as the body prepares for ovulation. By slipping her finger into her vagina on a daily basis and checking on the moistness of the mucus and the consistency of the secretions, a woman, with appropriate training, can detect when ovulation is about to occur and when it has passed.

In Table 11.2, failure rate data based on theoretical effectiveness are presented for four different fertility awareness methods. We have already discussed the Standard Days Method and its failure rate of 5 percent. The **two-day method** and the ovulation method (sometimes known as the **Billings ovulation method**) are based on the presence or absence of cervical secretions, and follow the research undertaken by John Billings, Evelyn Billings, and others starting in the 1950s (Billings et al., 1972; Billings and Westmore, 2000; Billings, 1984).

The rules for using the two-day method are easier than the rules for the ovulation method (Jennings and Burke, 2011: 426–429), but the two-day method has a slightly higher failure rate (4%) than the ovulation method (3%); keep in mind that both of these failure rates are based on theoretical effectiveness.

The last fertility awareness method shown in Table 11.2 is the **symptothermal method.** It is a "combined, or symptothermal, approach (using) both cervical secretions and basal body temperature" to identify the times when pregnancy is likely. The rules for its use are more involved than those for the ovulation method (Jennings and Burke, 2011: 429–431), but its failure rate, based on theoretical effectiveness data, is the lowest of all the fertility awareness methods, 0.4 percent.

Except for the pregnancies that result from method failures, no known serious side effects are associated with any of the fertility awareness methods just reviewed. No special equipment is necessary, except, perhaps, for a calendar, or a thermometer, or a set of beads, or a chart. Their use does not require the interruption of sexual foreplay or the application of mechanical or chemical devices, and all of these methods are acceptable to the Roman Catholic Church. However, their effective use requires a high degree of motivation by both partners and the ability to estimate accurately the day of ovulation. There is also a mental disadvantage, that is, the extra worry some users may experience knowing in advance the probability of failure. The various fertility awareness methods have very low use rates among US women.

Withdrawal

The next method we discuss is withdrawal, also known as coitus interruptus and as the pull-out method. With coitus interruptus, "the couple may have penile-vaginal intercourse until ejaculation is impending, at which time the male partner withdraws his penis from the vagina and away from the external genitalia of the female partner. The man must rely on his own sensations to determine when he is about to ejaculate" (Kowal, 2011: 410). Coitus interruptus may be distinguished from a similar method with the same end result, namely, **coitus reservatus**, also known as **amplexus reservatus.** With the coitus reservatus method, the male enters his partner, does not ejaculate, and endeavors to remain at the plateau phase of sexual intercourse and excitement, thus prolonging and sometimes intensifying pleasure. It differs from coitus interruptus in that ejaculation does not occur or is delayed indefinitely.

Coitus interruptus is one of the oldest known contraceptive practices (Jutte, 2008). It is mentioned in the Old Testament (Genesis 38), and its use has been reported by field researchers in many parts of the world. In fact, demographers believe that withdrawal played a major role in the fertility decline that was part of the demographic transition in France during the nineteenth century (Ryder, 1959; Shepard, 1980: 74). As we will mention later in Chapter 16, the changes in the social and economic structure that accompanied industrialization rewarded smaller families and made large families much more costly. Modern contraceptives had not yet been developed, and withdrawal was a culturally acceptable method that was known and available. This illustrates nicely, we believe, how social, economic, and cultural factors affect the use of birth control methods.

To be used effectively, withdrawal requires a tremendous amount of self-control and trust. The male must have near-complete control of his sexual sensations and know exactly when he is about to reach the time of sexual excitement when ejaculation cannot be stopped or delayed; he must pull his penis out of the woman before this time occurs. But even if he withdraws his penis in time, the pre-ejaculate fluid often picks up enough sperm in the urethra from a previous ejaculation that an unintended pregnancy will still sometimes occur. Thus, the man should urinate between ejaculations to rid his urethra of leftover sperm. Even if the male withdraws his penis in time but deposits the ejaculate or pre-ejaculate on or near the woman's vagina, pregnancy will sometimes occur (Segal and Nordberg, 1977).

The Roman Catholic Church objects to the use of withdrawal on moral grounds, owing to the belief that every act of intercourse must have the possibility of resulting in conception (Jutte, 2008; Noonan, 1966). And some believe that withdrawal is a physically and psychologically damaging technique, although there is no solid evidence to support this view. However, the method does require the complete cooperation of the male partner, as well as practice and considerable motivation. Obviously, coitus interruptus is not a good method for males who tend to ejaculate prematurely. Also, it is not recommended for males with little or no sexual experience because a lot of experience is required before a male can predict with a reasonable amount of certainty that ejaculation is about to occur. On the positive side, there is no financial expense associated with the use of withdrawal, and it requires no special preparation or equipment.

Withdrawal has a high failure rate according to use effectiveness data, 22 percent (Table 11.2). Only a small percentage of all US women (3%) report this as their method of contraception.

Contraceptive Sponge

We next discuss the **contraceptive sponge**, a vaginal spermicide designed for a single use. It is a "small, pillow shaped polyurethane sponge" that contains one gram of spermicide. "The concave dimple on one side is designed to fit over the cervix and decrease the chance of dislodgement during intercourse ... The other side of the sponge incorporates a woven polyester loop to facilitate removal." The woman moistens it with water and inserts it deep into her vagina. It protects for 24 hours "no matter how many times intercourse occurs" (Cates and Harwood, 2011: 395–396). Its failure rates vary for different groups. For **parous women**, that is, women who have previously given birth, the failure rate based on use effectiveness is 24 percent. For **nulliparous women**, that is, women who have not previously given birth, the failure rate is half as high (Table 11.2).

Condom

Another barrier method is the condom, for both males and females. The male **condom** was not popularized until the late nineteenth century. However, it was first mentioned as far back as 1564 in the posthumous writings on syphilis of the Italian anatomist Gabriele Falloppio (who also described the Fallopian tubes, which were named after him). Falloppio recommended that condoms be used to prevent venereal disease (Jutte, 2008: 96). **Female condoms**, on the other hand, made a much later appearance; they were invented and popularized by the Danish medical doctor Lasse Hessel and launched worldwide in 1991. Under the brand name Reality®, female condoms were first marketed in the United States in 1992.

The male condom is a mechanical barrier that fits snugly over the penis and prevents the ejaculated sperm from entering the vagina. Condoms have many names, such as rubber, prophylactic, safe, raincoat, sheath, and jimmie. Himes has written that "the French call the condom 'la capot anglaise' or English cape; the English have returned the compliment; to them it is the 'French letter'" (Himes, [1936] 1970: 194).

The condom's first recorded appearance was in the sixteenth century when it was recommended as a prophylactic against venereal disease. Its contraceptive effects at that time were incidental. Condoms were made of linen and were not very effective. Those made from sheep intestines first appeared in the eighteenth century. Tietze, among others, has noted that this innovation "has been attributed to an Englishman named Cundum, sometimes identified, although erroneously, as a physician at the court of Charles II" (Tietze, 1965: 70; see also Bernstein, 1940; and Himes, [1936] 1970: 191–194). But it was not until the vulcanization of rubber in the mid-nineteenth century that condom use became possible on a large scale. The introduction of liquid latex in the mid-1930s greatly facilitated the production of condoms with greater tensile strength, allowing them to last longer before decaying.

Condoms are moderately effective. Almost all failures result from nonuse and/or incorrect use rather than from defects in the condoms themselves. The rules for perfect condom use are many (see Warner and Steiner, 2011: 382–384). The failure rate for male condoms based on use effectiveness is 18 percent (Table 11.2). Male condoms, especially when used with vaginal spermicides, are more effective than most of the other methods we have so far discussed. However, the male condom requires some interruption of sexual foreplay. An even larger drawback is decreased sensitivity for some males. Its major advantages are its effectiveness and the fact that it has no medical side effects. Condoms are easy to buy and store, and their use requires no special training. Medical examination, supervision, and follow-up are not necessary. Most importantly, in addition to providing visible postcoital evidence of effectiveness, condoms offer effective protection against venereal disease. More than 8 percent of all US women in the childbearing ages report that the male condom is their main method of contraception (Figure 11.3).

The female condom is a female-initiated barrier method, and its failure rate of 21 percent is only slightly higher than that of the male condom. It has many of the advantages of the male condom but fewer of its disadvantages. It is a soft and strong transparent polyurethane sheath about the same length as a male condom (around 6.5 inches), with a flexible ring at each end. It is inserted into the vagina prior to intercourse. The inner ring at the closed end of the condom is used to insert it into the vagina; the ring then moves into place behind the pubic bone. The outer ring at the open end of the condom is soft and remains outside the vagina. Since its use does not depend on the male having an erection, it usually does not interrupt the spontaneity of the sex act. Moreover, unlike the male condom, it does not need to be removed immediately after ejaculation. Because it lines the vagina loosely, not tightly, some persons, particularly males, find the female condom more satisfying sexually than the male condom. The distribution of the female condom has increased worldwide since first becoming available at a reduced cost in the mid-1990s. But it has nowhere near the impact on the world market as the male condom.

Diaphragm and Cervical Cap

Two more vaginal barrier methods are the diaphragm and the **cervical cap**. The vaginal diaphragm is a device that erects a barrier between the sperm and the ova. It is a soft rubber vaginal cup with a metal spring reinforcing the rim. It should be inserted into the vagina anytime from one to two hours before sexual activity and should be left in place for six to eight hours after the last ejaculation. It functions mainly to block the access of sperm to the cervix (the opening to the uterus) and is held in place by the spring tension rim, the woman's vaginal muscle tone, and the pubic bone. Although the diaphragm acts as a barrier to most of the sperm, it usually does not fit tightly enough to prevent passage of all of the sperm. Thus, the diaphragm should be used with a spermicidal cream or jelly.

A cervical cap is a small, thimble-shaped cup that also serves as a barrier contraceptive by fitting over the cervix. The first modern cervical caps were developed in 1838 by the German gynecologist Friedrich Wilde when he prepared custom-made rubber molds of the cervix for his patients (Himes, [1936] 1970: 211). Today, caps are made of latex or silicone. They provide a more effective mechanical block against sperm than diaphragms. Thus, spermicidal mixtures are not as necessary with cervical caps as they are with diaphragms, but they are still recommended. Cervical caps are much more effective when used by nulliparous women than by parous women.

Diaphragms and cervical caps were first developed for contraceptive use during the nineteenth century. The diaphragm was popularized in the early twentieth century by Margaret Sanger. (We will have more to say about her later when we discuss the oral contraceptive.) However, it lost favor "with the advent of non-event-related methods such as the IUD and oral contraceptive" (Shepard, 1980: 75). Combined with a contraceptive jelly or cream, the diaphragm and cap were the methods most often recommended by physicians in private practice and by birth control clinics throughout the United States and Europe during the 1930s and 1940s (Peel and Potts, 1969: 62–63). About one-third of American couples who tried to plan their families during the 1940s used diaphragms or cervical caps.

Even when properly used with a spermicide, the diaphragm has a relatively high failure rate, 12 percent, according to use effectiveness, although lower, 6 percent, according to theoretical effectiveness (Table 11.2). It is only somewhat more effective than spermicides and some other methods. In addition to nonuse because of insufficient motivation, diaphragm failures are due to lack of knowledge regarding proper insertion, improper fit, displacement during intercourse, and defects in the diaphragm itself. So few women report using the diaphragm or cervical cap that these two methods are included in the "all other contraceptive methods" category in Figure 11.3.

There are no known serious physiological side effects for either the diaphragm or the cervical cap. They do not require the cooperation of the male partner and are used only when needed. Hence, they are both convenient methods for women who engage in sexual intercourse infrequently and do not need continuous protection. Using a spermicidal cream or jelly also produces additional vaginal lubrication during intercourse. However, since the diaphragm or cervical cap should be inserted several hours before intercourse, as already mentioned, its use requires the user to know in advance when she will have intercourse; otherwise, she will have to interrupt sexual foreplay to insert the device. Regular use requires considerable motivation. Some women do not like the process of insertion, and other women view it as messy because of the spermicide.

Diaphragms and cervical caps must be fitted by trained personnel, who teach the user the proper insertion techniques. Both seem particularly ill-suited for use in many developing countries, where there is often a lack of privacy for insertion and removal, as well as a convenient source of clean water for washing the devices after use. Moreover, there tends to be a shortage of medical personnel available for fitting the devices, and the need for a constant supply of spermicidal creams or jellies makes this barrier method relatively expensive (Wortman, 1976).

Birth Control Pill

The next most effective and modern type of contraceptives is hormonal-based methods, of which the oral contraceptive – that is, the **birth control pill**, or "the pill" – is the most popular. We will first review how hormonal methods work. The first oral contraceptives marketed in the 1960s were known as "combined" pills because they contained the two hormones similar to the estrogen and progesterone produced by the ovary and governed by the pituitary gland. When a woman ingests the hormones contained in the pill, one might say that her pituitary is "fooled" into thinking that she is already pregnant. Thus, there is no need for the pituitary "to send out hormones to stimulate the ovaries [into egg production] if there are already [in the woman] high levels of ovarian-type hormones" (Guillebaud, 2005: 7). The combined birth control pill containing both estrogen and progestin (a type of progesterone) thus prevents conception primarily by preventing ovulation. There are two additional factors that contribute to its contraceptive effect. Because ovulation does not occur, the consistency of the cervical mucus is maintained in a state that the sperm cannot easily penetrate. Also, because the full secretory pattern is not reached, the inner lining of the uterus is usually not suitable for implantation of the fertilized egg.

Today, there are several different hormonal methods, and they differ according to the type of hormone(s) in the contraceptive, the amount of the hormone(s) in the contraceptive, the way the woman receives the hormone(s), and whether the exposure to the hormone(s) is continuous or periodic. As already noted, the hormones are estrogen and progestin, and they may be received by the woman orally or via a patch, injected under her skin, implanted into a tissue, or placed into her vagina.

The first hormonal-based method was the oral contraceptive. Margaret Sanger (1879–1966, of the Planned Parenthood Federation of America) with funds from Katherine McCormick (1875–1967, a suffragist and philanthropist from Massachusetts) supported a reproductive physiologist, Gregory Pincus (1903–1967, the Director of the Worcester Foundation for Experimental Biology in Shrewsbury, Massachusetts) and John Rock (1890–1984, a Professor of Gynecology and Obstetrics at the Harvard Medical School in Cambridge) to develop a simple and effective oral contraceptive. Their story and collaboration are recounted in a lively and extremely interesting book by Jonathan Eig, *The Birth of the Pill: How Four Crusaders Reinvented Sex and Launched a Revolution* (2014). We recommend it highly.

In 1953–1954, Pincus and his collaborators tested a steroid for ovulation inhibition. Pincus and Rock then began work formulating a birth control pill at the Worcester Foundation. Pincus headed the science side of the research, and Rock directed the clinical trials to show that this new pill was safe and effective. The pill was first tested on some of Rock's patients in Boston, but systematic trials could not be performed because it was a felony in Massachusetts at that time to dispense contraceptives. The tests were moved to Puerto Rico, and later to Haiti, Mexico, and Los Angeles. The work of Pincus and Rock led eventually to G. D. Searle and Company marketing the oral contraceptive in the United States in 1960 as Enovid-10®.

Also playing a part in these efforts was Carl Djerassi, a chemist, who in 1951 led a research team in the first synthesis of a steroid oral contraceptive. (See chapter 5 in his autobiography [Djerassi, 1992] for an interesting account of this discovery.) Pincus, Rock, and Djerassi are sometimes referred to as the "fathers" of the oral contraceptive, although Djerassi referred to himself as its "mother" (Marks, 2001:11). We would argue, however, that it is Margaret Sanger who is the "mother" of the pill.

John Rock was a devoted and devout Roman Catholic who believed that the newly invented birth control pill should and would be approved by the Roman Catholic Church. He compared the birth control pill to the calendar rhythm method, which had been approved earlier in 1951 by Pope Pius XII. Like the rhythm method, the pill did not kill sperm or obstruct the passage of sperm into the female tract. It suppressed ovulation with a combination of estrogen and progestin, much like a woman's body suppressed ovulation during pregnancy. Rock's landmark book published in 1963, *The Time Has Come: A Catholic Doctor's Proposals to End the Battle over Birth Control*, was a conscientious and honorable effort to justify the pill as a natural method of birth control. Although ghostwritten by professionals of the Planned Parenthood Federation of America, the book clearly represented Rock's views and opinions (Tentler, 2008). The book noted that "the pills, when properly taken, are not at all likely to disturb menstruation, nor do they mutilate any organ of the body, nor damage any natural process. They merely offer to the human intellect the means to regulate ovulation harmlessly, means which heretofore have come only from the ovary, and during pregnancy, from the placenta" (Rock, 1963: 169).

Rock was deeply disappointed in 1968 when Pope Paul VI published his encyclical *Humanae Vitae* (Latin for "Of Human Life") declaring that oral contraceptives and all other so-called artificial methods of birth control were immoral. The papal declarations in *Humanae Vitae* were exactly the opposite of the recommendations of the majority report of a papal committee, namely, the Papal Birth Control Commission, that was established by the Vatican to study and make recommendations regarding oral contraception. The Commission, by the way, had two demographers among its members; one was Thomas K. Burch (1934–2022), a friend of both of the authors of this textbook. Robert McClory's *Turning Point* (1995) is a dramatic story of the workings of the Commission. Margaret Marsh and Wanda Ronner's biography of John Rock, *The Fertility Doctor* (2008), is "a balanced portrait of a twentieth-century medical giant" (Tentler, 2008: 24) and describes in detail the kinds of conflicts that Dr. Rock had with his Catholic Church.

Once introduced in the United States and other countries in 1960, the oral contraceptive became extremely popular, and it remains so today. It is known simply as "the pill." If a woman informs her male friend that she forgot to take her "pill" for the past several days, he does not think to himself, "I wonder if she is referring to an aspirin or a sleeping pill or a vitamin pill or some other kind of pill." He knows exactly and immediately that she is referring to the birth control pill. We reported earlier (see Figure 11.3) that 14 percent of women in the United States are using the oral contraceptive.

When the oral contraceptive was first introduced in the early 1960s, its major disadvantage was adverse side effects. Some of them were nuisances, such as headaches, weight gain, and morning nausea, but many users found them so discomforting that they discontinued using the pill. Some of the side effects were life threatening. Thromboembolic (blood-clotting) disorders are but one example. Although the more common superficial leg thromboses (or phlebitis) are not very dangerous, cerebrovascular diseases (strokes that are also thrombic) are potentially fatal. The estrogen content of the pill was primarily responsible for the thromboembolic problems. Other negative side effects included increased blood pressure and vaginal dryness (Guillebaud, 2005). There is also a demonstrated interaction between cigarette smoking and pill use and the incidence of heart disease. However, the oral contraceptives produced these days "contain less than one-twentieth of the dose of the original pills, which results in a lower incidence of side effects" (Segal, 2003: 171).

Other side effects of the pill have been shown to be beneficial, such as those associated with the physical and emotional aspects of menstruation. These include decreased incidence of menorrhagia (heavy bleeding), dysmenorrhea (cramps), iron deficiency anemia, and premenstrual tension. Hence, for many women, oral contraceptives produce more regular menstrual cycles that are shorter in duration, produce less bleeding and abdominal discomfort, and are accompanied by less premenstrual tension than is normally the case (Potts, Diggory, and Peel, 1977: 38). There are several additional noncontraceptive health benefits, namely, "decreased risk of endometrial and ovarian cancer, decreased risk of colon cancer . . . and maintenance of bone density" (Segal, 2003: 171).

The modern oral contraceptive is either a combined pill containing estrogen and progestin, known as the **combined oral contraceptive**, or a pill containing only progestin, known as the **progestin-only pill**, or sometimes as the **mini-pill**. The combined pill is monophasic, biphasic, or triphasic, referring to the amounts of estrogen and progestin provided each day. A monophasic pill provides a constant amount of estrogen and progestin every day, while the other two types provide varying amounts (Nelson and Cwiak, 2011: 256–257). Depending on the manufacturer (there are around forty different combination pills produced), most combination pills come in either 21- or 28-day packages. With the former, the woman takes a pill each day for 21 days and no pill for seven days when menstruation occurs, and then the process is repeated. With the 28-day packet, the hormonal medication is present in the pills for the first 21 days, and the pills for the last seven days are placebos.

The progestin-only pill, or the mini-pill, the other type of oral contraceptive, was first marketed in the United States in 1973. It consists of a small dose of progestin, which is taken daily, even during menstruation. It reduces the side effects of the combined pill, and it also makes available an oral contraceptive for women who breast-feed their children or who should avoid estrogen for health reasons. The mini-pill does not include estrogen; therefore, it does not always result in the suppression of ovulation. Thus, many of the menstrual periods of progestin-only pill users are natural. The mini-pill functions as a contraceptive mainly "by interfering with the passage of sperm through the mucus at the entrance to the uterus" (Guillebaud, 2005: 176), whether or not an egg has been released. In this sense, the mini-pill acts more like a barrier method of contraceptive, albeit one that is taken orally. The mini-pill also prevents pregnancy; since the **endometrium** (the lining of the uterus) is altered, the result is that a fertilized egg is not being implanted, if indeed ovulation does occur (Raymond, 2011b: 237). The mini-pill is not as popular as the combined pill; there are a half dozen or so brands on the market.

Both the combined oral contraceptive pill and the mini-pill are very effective. The data in Table 11.2 indicate that according to use effectiveness data, the combined pill and the progestin-only pill have a failure rate of 9 percent and a much lower rate of 0.3 percent according to theoretical effectiveness. Most of the pregnancies that occur to pill users result from the failure to take it regularly. The major advantages are its high effectiveness and the fact that its use does not interfere with the sexual act in any way. It is not necessary to interrupt foreplay or to conclude sexual activity right after coition. Moreover, the pill allows the female to use contraception independently of any cooperation by the male (or even of his knowledge). Over 14 percent of all US women use either the combined pill or the mini-pill.

Other Hormonal Contraceptives

We noted previously that hormonal contraceptives need not only be administered orally. There are several other hormonal contraception delivery systems, one of which is the transdermal **contraceptive patch**. It was "approved by the US Federal Drug Administration (FDA) in 2002. It is a thin, flexible, 20cm^2 patch with three layers: a beige outer protective polyester layer; a middle medicated adhesive layer; and a clear liner" (Nanda, 2011: 343). The patch is about the size of a 50-cent piece that is placed on the buttocks, arm, or stomach. It works like the combination pill just discussed, except that instead of requiring the user to engage in a daily regimen, it is based on a weekly regimen. A new patch is placed on the skin once every seven days. The two hormones are released from the patch at a constant and continuous level each day. After three weeks, no patch is used for one week, to allow menstruation to occur. The birth control patch has the same effectiveness numbers as the combined pill and mini-pill. A small percentage of US women use the patch (Nanda, 2011).

A woman may also receive the contraceptive hormones by inserting into her vagina a **vaginal ring**, under the brand name NuvaRing®. It was approved by the FDA in 2001. It is a thin, transparent, flexible ring and is similar to the combined pill; it contains both estrogen and progestin, which are released on a continuous basis into the woman's body. It is inserted by the woman into her vagina usually during the first five days of her menstrual period and remains in place for three weeks. She then withdraws it, throws it away, and does not use a ring for a week, during which time menstruation occurs. A new ring is then inserted after seven days. Since the vaginal ring is not a barrier method like the diaphragm or cap or female condom, the exact and precise placement of the ring in the vagina is not a major issue. The vaginal ring has the same effectiveness numbers as the pill and the patch (Nanda, 2011).

Another way for women to receive hormonal contraception is through **contraception injection.** The most commonly used brand in the United States is Depo-Provera® and is similar to the progestin-only pill; it "prevents pregnancy primarily by inhibiting ovulation ... (it) also prevents pregnancy by thickening and decreasing cervical mucus ... (which) prevents sperm penetration" (Bartz and Goldberg, 2011: 210). Depo-Provera is administered via an injection by a health professional once every twelve weeks in the arm, buttocks, upper thigh, or abdomen. The economic cost is about the same as the birth control pill (Bartz and Goldberg, 2011).

Depo-Provera has a low use-effectiveness failure rate of 6 percent (Table 11.2). When failures (pregnancies) occur, they will mainly be due to the fact that the woman did not have her shots at the prescribed intervals. The failure rate based on theoretical effectiveness is a mere 0.2 percent. A woman typically stops having periods altogether after one year of use.

Still another way for the woman to receive hormonal contraception is via a **subdermal contraceptive implant.** The first implant was developed in the 1980s under the brand name of Norplant® (Sivin, Nash, and Waldman, 2002). It consisted of six small silicone capsule-type rods, each containing progestin, placed subdermally in the woman's upper arm, to remain in effect for five years. The implants were usually visible and resembled small veins. The Norplant implant has been phased out in favor of implants with fewer capsule rods. The main implant now available in the United States is Nexplanon®, containing one rod with protection for three years (Sivin, Nash, and Waldman, 2002; Raymond, 2011a).

An obvious advantage of the implant is that a single visit to a clinic once every three years for an implant is substituted for the daily consumption of birth control pills, or the weekly employment of a patch, or the triweekly insertion of a vaginal ring, or the monthly or trimonthly birth control shot. The major advantage of the implant, however, is its effectiveness. It is the most effective of all contraceptives, including male and female sterilization. According to both use and theoretical effectiveness data, the failure rate for the implant is a miniscule 0.05 percent (Table 11.2) (Raymond, 2011a: 195; Ramchandran and Upadhyay, 2007). This means that after a year of usage, five pregnancies will occur, on average, for every 10,000 users.

Actually, Raymond has noted that "to date [that is, as of 2011 when her research was published], no pregnancies have been observed in prospective or retrospective cohort studies of Implanon, which included a total of more than 4,500 women and more than 7,000 women-years of exposure" (2011a: 195). There have been a few failures reported to medical authorities of women not included in statistically representative surveys; but most of the few failures were due to the "non-insertion of the implant" or to the fact that the pregnancies had been conceived "before the women had Implanon inserted" (Raymond, 2011a: 195).

All of the family planning methods we have just reviewed are reversible; that is, a woman and her partner may use any of them and then decide later to stop using them if a pregnancy is desired.

Surgical Sterilization

The next method we discuss, **surgical sterilization** performed for contraceptive purposes, is rarely reversible. Surgical sterilization may be performed on both males and females. In the female, the sterilization is known as tubal ligation (tying of the tubes). It consists of cutting, tying, and removing a portion of the oviduct, that is, the Fallopian tubes. Female sterilization may be performed in one of several ways.

Laparoscopic sterilization is a sterilizing procedure using a laparoscope (from the Greek words *lapara*, meaning flank; and *skopein*, meaning to examine; the word thus means "look inside the abdomen"). It requires general anesthesia during which a small incision is introduced near the woman's belly button and a second incision may be made right above the pubic hairline. A laparoscope, that is, a telescope-like device, is then inserted through the first incision so that the physician or operator can view the Fallopian tubes. Rings or clips are then inserted through the second incision, or if there is no second incision, through the first, and used to close the Fallopian tubes.

Minilaparotomy is a surgical sterilization procedure performed on a woman a few days after she delivers a baby. A general anesthesia is required. The operator makes a small incision in the woman's abdomen and then cuts and removes a piece of each of the Fallopian tubes (Roncari and Hou, 2011: 450–451)

Hysteroscopic sterilization is performed using only a local anesthesia. A tiny coil insert is introduced into each of the Fallopian tubes through the vagina and uterus. Its introduction in each tube causes the development of scar tissues over a three-month period, resulting in both tubes becoming sealed (Conceptus, Inc., 2010).

Female sterilization is very effective. It has a failure rate of only 0.5 percent based on both use and theoretical effectiveness data. It frees the woman and her partner from ever again having to worry about an accidental pregnancy. But since it is a permanent form of contraception, it is not an appropriate method for persons who wish to delay a pregnancy to a later time, or who are not completely certain that they wish to have no more (or no) children. Over 18 percent of US contracepting women have been sterilized (Figure 11.3). Also, it is the most popular form of family planning worldwide.

Male sterilization is known as **vasectomy**. It involves cutting, tying, and removing a portion of the spermatic duct, that is, the vas deferens. There are several ways the surgery may be performed. We will discuss two approaches. The traditional vasectomy is a minor procedure that occurs under local anesthetic. The surgeon makes one incision in the skin on each of the two sides of the scrotum to expose the tubes of the vas deferens from each testicle. The vas deferens tube is lifted from the scrotum, cut, and tied, or sometimes cauterized. The separated tubes are then returned to the scrotum, and a few stitches are used to close the two incisions. After having a vasectomy, a man is still capable of ejaculating semen, but the semen no longer contains sperm.

A second approach to male sterilization is the **no-scalpel vasectomy**, also known as **keyhole vasectomy**. It was devised in 1974 by a surgeon in China, Li Shunqiang, and is now employed worldwide. It has been used in the United States since 1988. In this method, as its name indicates, no scalpel is employed, but there is still the need for a small opening to be made in the scrotum. The doctor applies a local anesthetic, which may be introduced without a needle, and then uses their hand to find the vas deferens under the scrotal skin. A very small set of pointed forceps then works to separate the scrotal tissue and to create a keyhole-type opening in the skin. Then, as with the traditional vasectomy procedure, the tubes of the vas deferens are lifted from the scrotal sac, cut, and tied, or sometimes cauterized, and then placed back into the scrotum. Because the scrotal skin opening is so small, it may not need to be closed with sutures (Roncari and Hou, 2011: 468–471).

Male sterilization is a very effective contraceptive method. Its failure rates of 0.15 percent and 0.10 percent based, respectively, on use effectiveness data and theoretical effectiveness data (Table 11.2) are even lower than those for female sterilization. Moreover, compared to female sterilization, male sterilization is faster to perform, requires only a local anesthetic, is less expensive, and presents less risk of complications. Finally, although sterilization reversal is a difficult operation and does not have high rates of success, it is sometimes a little easier to reverse a male sterilization than a female sterilization.

Overall, the effectiveness of sterilization varies according to the technique used by the physician and the gender of the patient. According to the rates just noted, there are very few failures. Most failures result from inadequate surgical procedures or because the tubes grow back together. Some men who obtain vasectomies have unprotected intercourse too soon after the operation. If this occurs before all the sperm containing semen already stored in the reproductive tract has been expelled, then pregnancy could result. However, this is a short-term problem that is easily avoided.

Because a sterilization is only performed once, this method does not require continuous motivation. It does not interfere with sexual enjoyment in any way. But it is difficult to reverse, so it is not suitable for persons who might change their minds about not wanting children or more children. Although the development and use of microsurgical techniques have greatly increased the chance of reversibility among vasectomy patients, most physicians still consider surgical sterilization a permanent form of contraception.

Surgical sterilization does not lower the sexual drive or capabilities of the male or female. Indeed, males with vasectomies often report increased enjoyment of sex, which is usually attributed to freedom from anxiety about their partners becoming pregnant. The male partners of almost 6 percent of contracepting women in the United States have been sterilized (Figure 11.3).

Intrauterine Device (IUD)

The intrauterine device (IUD), a device with or without hormones that is placed in the uterus, is the most widely used reversible contraceptive method in the world. The idea of placing devices in the uterus to prevent conception is fairly old. Giacomo Casanova, the eighteenth-century Italian adventurer and libertine, recommended the use of a gold ball for this purpose (Himes, [1936] 1970: 180). The antecedent of the modern intrauterine device was the **stem pessary**, developed in the late 1860s. This was a small button or cap that covered the opening of the cervix and was attached to stems extending into the cervical canal. In the 1920s, a German, Ernst Grafenberg, developed a silver ring that was placed in the uterus. In 1934, a Japanese scientist, Tenrei Ota, introduced a gold ring. Neither was accepted widely until the late 1950s (Peel and Potts, 1969: 128–129; Tietze, 1965: 79). The Lippes Loop was a popular type of IUD in the 1960s, as were several other types of plastic IUDs.

Research on modern IUDs was initiated at about the time oral-contraception research was in its final stages. But, as has been noted by Segal, "despite intensive research, scientists [still] do not fully understand why the presence of a foreign body in the uterus prevents pregnancy. The evidence clearly indicates that the IUD is a pre-fertilization method: the presence of fertilized eggs in IUD users cannot be demonstrated" (2003: 173).

The two main types of IUDs available in the United States today are both flexible polyethylene devices shaped like a "T." One has copper wire twisted about it and is known as the Copper T. Adding copper wire to the device increases its contraceptive effectiveness significantly, "although it is not known why the release of copper in the uterus is so effective in preventing pregnancy" (Segal, 2003: 173).

The other "T"-shaped IUD is formally known as Levonorgestrel IUD. It contains 52 mg of levonorgestrel, a second generation progestin hormone, "which is released directly into the endometrial cavity" (Dean and Schwarz, 2011: 149).

Either type of IUD is placed in the uterus by a health-care provider. Small strings extend from its end into the vagina, where they may be checked periodically by the woman to make sure that the IUD has not been ejected. If the IUD is going to slip out of the uterus, this will most likely occur during the first several months of use and/or during the days of the menstrual period.

Most earlier types of IUDs were nonhormonal; that is, they did not contain the female hormones used to suppress ovulation. The Mirena is hormonal. We referred earlier to the vaginal ring, which is also a foreign body placed in the uterus that contains hormones to be released into the woman's system. The vaginal ring contains both estrogen and progestin, unlike the Mirena IUD, which contains only progestin. Also, the vaginal ring needs to be replaced monthly, whereas the Mirena IUD remains effective for up to five years.

IUDs are very effective. The ParaGard has failure rates of 0.8 percent and 0.6 percent, based on use effectiveness data and theoretical effectiveness data, respectively. The Mirena has even lower failure rates, 0.2 percent according to both types of effectiveness. The undetected expulsion of these devices is the most common cause of pregnancy, a major disadvantage. The major advantages are that insertion is necessary only once every 10–12 years for the ParaGard and once every five years for the Mirena. Also, the IUD does not interfere with intercourse in any way.

IUDs that are expelled involuntarily may usually be reinserted successfully by medical-care professionals. Young women with no or few previous births may have higher rates of expulsion and pregnancy than older women with more births. In addition to the risk of involuntary expulsion, IUDs sometimes need to be removed for medical reasons, particularly, menstrual bleeding and pain. Another disadvantage is that unlike the case with vaginal rings, trained medical personnel are necessary for the insertion of IUDs. In the United States in 2018, around 14 percent of contracepting women reported using the IUD (Guttmacher Institute, 2021).

Emergency Contraceptive Pill (ECP)

We discuss now a special type of contraception, the **emergency contraceptive pill (ECP)**, also known as the **morning-after pill**. ECPs are contraceptive medications taken after unprotected intercourse and are designed to prevent pregnancy by interfering with the implantation of the fertilized ovum in the uterine lining. This is a different strategy from that of oral contraceptives and the other kinds of hormonal contraceptives that we discussed earlier; they prevent pregnancy primarily by preventing ovulation. The designation of "morning after" is actually a misnomer. ECPs are licensed for use for up to 72 hours after an unprotected intercourse.

There are several types of ECPs now available for use in the US. Three types are the following: **Plan B One-Step®**, a single 1,500 mcg levonorgestrel (a progestin hormone – see above) white pill, approved by the FDA in 2009; **ella®**, a single 30 mg uliprastal (an antiprogestin) white pill approved in 2010; and **Next Choice®**, a generic version of Plan B, taken as two peach pills, approved in 2009. Plan B One Step and Next Choice are available without prescription to persons aged 17 and over, but a prescription is required for ella (Trussell and Schwarz, 2011: 113–114).

Plan B One Step and Next Choice are progestin-only medications taken as either two doses twelve hours apart or as a single dose; the progestin acts to suppress ovulation and to thicken the cervical mucus so to immobilize the sperms. The ella ECP works in another way; it contains ulipristal which acts to suppress ovulation for up to five days. ECPs are not to be confused with abortifacients, that is, abortion pills. (We discuss them next.) ECPs are meant to function after fertilization has occurred but before the fertilized egg has settled into the uterine environment. Because ECPs have their effect prior to implantation, the International Federation of Gynecology and Obstetrics considers them legally and medically to be contraceptives. However, not all researchers and medical practitioners agree with this categorization.

These postcoital methods of birth prevention are particularly convenient for women who have sexual intercourse infrequently, and/or who did not have an opportunity to use contraceptives before intercourse, or who used a contraceptive that failed in the process, for example, a condom that broke open during use.

ECPs are regarded as a very effective means of preventing an accidental pregnancy. Those pregnancies that do occur result from (1) failure of an already established implantation, (2) an excessive lapse of time between unprotected intercourse and taking the ECP, (3) inadequate dosages, (4) regurgitation of the pill, or (5) failure of the drug itself. The major advantages of ECPs are effectiveness and suitability for use among women who had unexpected and unprotected sexual contact, particularly in situations of rape. The most common short-term side effects are nausea, headaches, menstrual irregularities, and breast tenderness (Trussell and Schwarz, 2011). Very low percentages of sexually active women and women using contraceptives, 0.2 percent and 0.2 per cent, respectively, report using ECPs (Guttmacher Institute, 2021).

Abortifacients

Finally, we consider **abortifacients**, which are pharmaceutical medications that cause the termination of an early pregnancy by interfering with the viability of an already implanted zygote (ferilized egg). A synthetic steroid compound with antiprogestational effects, known as RU-486, was discovered in 1982 by the French reproductive physiologist Etienne-Emile Baulieu and other researchers at the Roussel Uclaf Company in France, the eventual designer of the drug (hence, the designation "RU"). Since it contains antiprogestational agents, the medication works in a way opposite to that of progesterone, which functions to prepare and maintain the uterine environment for the fertilized egg. The generic name of the drug is mifepristone, and it is marketed in the United States under the trade name Mifeprex®. Mifepristone "blocks the action of progesterone, which is necessary to establish and maintain placental attachment" (Paul and Stein, 2011: 706). It is produced in China and has been approved by the US Federal Drug Administration as a drug to terminate an implanted zygote of up to forty-nine days' gestation. A 600 mg dose of mifepristone is administered by a physician, and is followed two days later by a large dose of a prostaglandin, misoprostol, to induce contractions (Paul and Stein, 2011; Spitz et al., 1998).

SUMMARY

A thorough understanding of a population's level of fertility requires knowledge of the extent to which people endeavor to limit family size. Whether or not a person uses a birth prevention method, and how effectively that method is used, depends on the person's motivation and the availability of the various methods. These, in turn, are influenced by social, economic, and religious factors.

The chief means by which people attempt to limit their family size are contraceptive techniques and devices, surgical sterilization, and induced abortion. Some methods are more effective than others. However, there is no perfect method of birth prevention. Each involves risks of failure or adverse effects.

Although the use of birth prevention methods is sometimes associated with medical risks, occasionally including mortality, these are usually much smaller than the mortality risks associated with pregnancy and giving birth. Generally, they are also smaller than the mortality risks associated with many widely accepted activities of daily life.

DISCUSSION QUESTIONS

1. One way of organizing the various contraceptive methods discussed in this chapter is in terms of barrier methods (e.g., diaphragm, condom); hormonal methods (e.g., contraceptive pills); and surgical methods (e.g., sterilization procedures). Which of these three methods do you yourself believe is the method most preferred, accepted, and understood by the adult female population? How about the adult male population? Make sure you define what you mean by "preferred," "accepted," and "understood."
2. One point made in this chapter is that different contraceptive methods are used more in some regions of the world, and less so in other regions (see Figure 11.2). Identify three or four factors that you believe may best explain the differences. Which one is the most inclusive? Why?

12

Epidemics and Pandemics

INTRODUCTION

In Chapter 5 we discussed the measurement of mortality and the significance of mortality as a demographic process. In this chapter we focus on the mass mortality and **morbidity** that result when an infectious disease affects many people at one time and one place, with a subsequent sharp increase in mortality. This situation is called an epidemic or a pandemic. After defining these terms, we will discuss the history of epidemics and pandemics and then the consequences of these mass mortality events for human populations.

DEFINING EPIDEMICS AND PANDEMICS

Infectious diseases are caused by pathogenic **agents**, such as bacteria, viruses, fungi, or parasites. These agents may infect a human directly from contaminated air, water, or food. The agents may also be spread from infected animals or infected humans, called **vectors**, to a healthy human. An **epidemic** is a major increase or upswing of an infectious disease in an area that results in a large number of cases, followed then by a decline. Many infections and contagious diseases have become epidemic, including scarlet fever, chicken pox, measles, influenza, and cholera, among others.

An infection in a human **host** results when the microorganism agent begins to reproduce within the host. The infected human is then able to spread the disease through coughing, sneezing, intimate contact, human waste products such as feces, or body fluids such as blood. When this happens, the infected human host becomes a vector of the disease.

When a large fraction of the human population has acquired immunity to the disease, either from previous exposure or from vaccination, then the disease may become **endemic**. This term means that the disease is still present in the population, but at much lower levels than in an epidemic.

Pandemics differ from epidemics in terms of the extent of affected geographic area. If an epidemic strikes several countries or continents, it is known as a **pandemic**. The term comes from the Greek words *pan*, meaning all, and *demos*, meaning people, and has been used since the mid-seventeenth century. With rapid air transportation, human vectors may travel to new countries and quickly introduce the infectious agent to a new population. COVID-19 is an example of a recent pandemic that was both deadly and disruptive. The existence of a pandemic is typically announced by the World Health Organization (WHO). Pandemics are much more disruptive demographically, economically, and socially than epidemics.

EPIDEMIC DISEASES

Epidemic diseases "break out, reach a peak, and subside; endemic diseases cause a relatively constant amount of illness and death over time" (Johansson, 2003: 303). If a disease is maintained at a fairly constant level, it is called **endemic** (Caldwell, 2006). Epidemics typically start out on a local level and are then diffused to nearby areas.

Caldwell (2006) has written that epidemics were important to the development of modern demography because it then became obvious that the tracking of deaths was necessary and important. For instance, the Spanish flu epidemic (see our later discussion) resulted in the establishment of the Growth Surveillance System by the League of Nations.

The Black Death

One of Europe's worst epidemics, the Black Death, was a virulent outbreak of a disease that likely originated in Central Asia, moved to the Mediterranean via the Silk Road, and then entered Europe from 1347 to 1352. The Black Death was caused by a disease called plague, an infectious disease caused by the bacterium *Yersinia pestis*. This bacterium infects small mammals and their fleas. It is transmitted between animals through fleas. Humans can be infected through flea bites, infected bodily fluids, or inhaling small droplets from the coughing or sneezing of a plague patient (WHO, 2022c).

The Black Death spread because of the growth of trade through shipping. Infected rats jumped to land from inbound ships, initially infecting port cities. Then infected humans, flea-infested goods, and even the rats themselves spread out to areas beyond the coast. The plague ultimately spread into northern Europe. It resulted in the death of around one-third of the continent's population (Caldwell, 2006; Herlihy, 1997; Martin, 2007). Subsequent epidemics of plague were so frequent and intense throughout Europe that the population was reduced by nearly 50 percent, and demographic recovery took more than two centuries (Johansson, 2003). The estimated number of deaths caused by the Black Death ranges from a low of 25 million up to as high of 60 to 75 million. A middle-range value is around 40 to 50 million deaths. This is an astounding value given that all of Europe in the fourteenth century likely numbered around 80 to 90 million inhabitants.

The Great Plague that hit London in the 1660s had continuing outbreaks for several decades thereafter, but its toll was lower than that of the Black Death. It was once believed to have been a bubonic plague, but many now hold that it was a disease similar to a viral fever (Caldwell, 2006). The "Bills of Mortality" analyzed by John Graunt (see Chapter 3) were produced during the era of the Great Plague.

Cholera

In the nineteenth century, Britain was subjected to four cholera epidemics. In 1854 when the epidemic was again sweeping through England and Wales, the mystery of the transmission of cholera was solved by "an ingenious physician named John Snow [whose discovery also] helped eliminate cholera from Britain and eventually from the Western world" (Epstein, 2007a: 41). In London, Snow showed that certain wells were yielding contaminated water, and that people drinking water from these sources were mainly the ones who were dying. He mapped the wells and the incidence of cholera for various areas of London, a map that some refer to today as "one of the most famous documents in the history of science" (Epstein, 2007a: 42). He convinced the local officials to remove the handle from the water well that was yielding much of the contaminated water; they did, and the incidence of cholera dropped precipitously. This was one of the first times that **geographic information systems (GIS)** were ever used to shape a policy (Swanson and Stephan, 2004). Steven Johnson's book *The Ghost Map* (2006) is a delightful, fascinating, and riveting account of Snow's pioneering work.

Today in London, there is a John Snow Pub located on Broadwick Street. It stands exactly where the bad well was located. Visit the pub the next time you are in London and salute and toast John Snow, who is recognized today as the Father of Epidemiology.

Influenza, 1918

A more recent epidemic was the Spanish flu epidemic, so named not because Spain was the first European country infected. Indeed, the epidemic appeared earlier in other countries, including the United States, Britain, and France. But most of the countries participating in World War I were maintaining media blackouts; thus few if any news stories about the epidemic appeared in their newspapers. However, Spain was neutral in the war, and their press was not censored, resulting in many stories being published in their newspapers about the problems the epidemic was causing in Spain. These stories were read widely throughout Europe and America. And since the stories about the flu originated in Spain, it became known as the Spanish flu (Spinney, 2017: chapter 5).

The flu spread throughout Europe in 1918 and then to the rest of the world. The death toll was especially high among troops living in close quarters. World War I was underway and there had been mass mobilization of young men in many countries, including the United States. Epidemiologists Niall Johnson and Juergen Mueller (2002) have estimated that the epidemic resulted in the deaths of around 50 million people; others place the toll even higher, perhaps as high as 100 million (Barry, 2004; Spinney, 2017). The Spanish flu may well have infected almost 1 billion people, or nearly half of the population of the world at that time. Some believe that large numbers of influenza deaths went unreported in less developed countries.

By the time the epidemic had run its course in North America, nearly 700,000 had died in the United States and around 50,000 in Canada. Some small villages in Quebec and Labrador were wiped out almost entirely. The most common victims of this epidemic were young adults, 20 to 40 years of age (Barry, 2004; Caldwell, 2006; Crosby, 2003; Kolata, 1999). If one examines month-specific death rates in the United

States for the years 1911–1917 and for 1918, the impact of the Spanish flu is particularly apparent in the last quarter of 1918, and especially in the month of October.

Few cities in the United States, or perhaps even worldwide, were as affected by this epidemic as severely as Dudley Poston's hometown of San Francisco, where "in only a few short months, the city recorded more than 50,000 cases and … 3,500 deaths" (Espey, 2014: 1). The situation was so serious that a law was passed in the city in 1918 requiring residents to wear masks when venturing outside the home to visit public places, and this slogan was promulgated by the city's Health Department: "Wear a Mask and Save Your Life! A Mask is 99% Proof Against Influenza" (available online at www.pbs.org/wgbh/americanexperience/features/general-article/influenza-san-francisco/). Some evidence suggests, however, that the wearing of masks was not that effective (Espey, 2014: 3, 24).

Among the victims living in San Francisco and nearby were three of Dudley Poston's grandparents and one aunt. We show in Figure 12.1 a copy of the actual death certificate of one of them, his maternal grandmother, Annie Kara. She died on December 20, 1918, at age 42, of "influenza" and was buried the next day in Holy

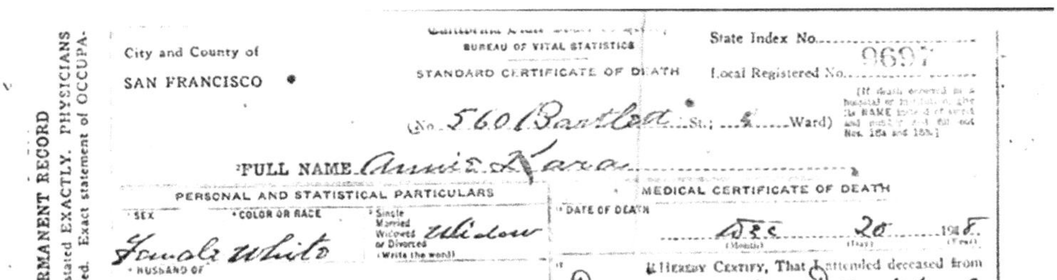

WRITE PLAINLY WITH UNFADING INK THIS IS A PERMANENT RECORD
N. B.—Every item of information should be carefully supplied. AGE should be stated EXACTLY. PHYSICIANS should state CAUSE OF DEATH in plain terms, that it may be properly classified. Exact statement of OCCUPATION is very important. See instructions on back of certificate.

City and County of SAN FRANCISCO

BUREAU OF VITAL STATISTICS
STANDARD CERTIFICATE OF DEATH

State Index No. 9697
Local Registered No.

(No. 560 Bartlett St.; ... Ward)

FULL NAME Annie Kara

PERSONAL AND STATISTICAL PARTICULARS

SEX Female; COLOR OR RACE White; Single, Married, Widowed or Divorced: Widow

DATE OF BIRTH 1876

AGE 42 years

OCCUPATION House Keeper

BIRTHPLACE (state or country) New Jersey

NAME OF FATHER Patrick Crosby

BIRTHPLACE OF FATHER Ireland

MAIDEN NAME OF MOTHER Catherine Gammon

BIRTHPLACE OF MOTHER Ireland

LENGTH OF RESIDENCE At Place of Death 38 years; In California 38 years

THE ABOVE IS TRUE TO THE BEST OF MY KNOWLEDGE
(Informant) Mrs. Byrne
(Address) 560 Bartlett St.

Filed DEC 21 1918

MEDICAL CERTIFICATE OF DEATH

DATE OF DEATH Dec. 20 1918

I HEREBY CERTIFY, That I attended deceased from Dec. 11 1918, to Dec. 21 1918, that I last saw her alive on Dec. 20 1918 and that death occurred on the date stated above at 4 a.m. The CAUSE OF DEATH was as follows:

Influenza

Contributory Pneumonia

John ... M.D. Dec 20 1918 (Address) 987 Valencia

PLACE OF BURIAL OR REMOVAL Holy Cross Cemetery; DATE OF BURIAL Dec. 21 1918

UNDERTAKER ... ADDRESS 435 Valencia St. 581

FIGURE 12.1 Death certificate of Annie Kara (Dudley Poston's grandmother): a victim of the flu epidemic, San Francisco, 1918

Cross Catholic Cemetery in Colma, a small town south of San Francisco. His mother, Kathryn Kara, who was then 9 years old, also contracted the Spanish flu in San Francisco in the fall of 1918, but, thankfully, she survived. In 1936 she married his father Dudley Poston, Sr., and gave birth to him in 1940, and to her daughter Kathleen in 1943. Kathryn Kara Poston, who died in San Francisco at age 69 in 1979, had a tremendous influence on the lives of her children and grandchildren during her lifetime. So powerful and long-lasting was her influence that Nancy, her granddaughter and Dudley's daughter, named her first daughter Kara after Kara's great-grandmother. Had the vagaries of mortality and the 1918 flu epidemic operated in another way, and had Kathryn Kara died in 1918 along with her parents and sister and 3,500 other residents of the San Francisco area, many persons named in this paragraph would not have been born, this demography textbook would not have been written, and the lives of countless others would be very different today.

Before leaving our discussion of the Spanish flu epidemic, let us mention two references deserving your attention. First, we have read several books about the 1918 flu epidemic. In our opinion the best and the most readable one is Crosby's (2003) *America's Forgotten Pandemic*. It is fascinating reading and may well be the most thorough exploration of the epidemic. Second, the novelist Katherine Anne Porter's 1939 book *Pale Horse, Pale Rider* consists of three novellas. The third is the eponymous "Pale Horse, Pale Rider" and is about a newspaper woman and a soldier and their relationship. She contracts the flu, and he does also, and he may have caught it from her. It is a gripping story, only 60 pages long, and well worth reading. Porter herself was stricken by the flu, so the story is somewhat autobiographical. Alfred Crosby (see above) considered this short piece of fiction to be such an exceptional work that he dedicated his *America's Forgotten Pandemic* "To Katherine Anne Porter, who survived" (Crosby, 2003: v).

HIV/AIDS

In the preceding paragraphs we noted that the Black Death resulted in around 50 million deaths, although this number might be too low; and the Spanish flu epidemic also resulted in around 50 million deaths, although this number also might be too low. The HIV/AIDS epidemic could eventually be responsible for more deaths that the combined 100 million toll of the Black Death and Spanish flu epidemics.

The first cases of HIV infection were noticed in the United States in 1981, initially among gay men (Shilts, 1987; hiv.gov, 2023). Hemophiliac cases of AIDS were first reported in 1982. The human immunodeficiency virus (HIV) causing AIDS was isolated in 1983 at the Pasteur Institute in Paris, and by the late 1980s and into the 1990s, HIV/AIDS had been identified in every region of the world. HIV is spread from person to person via contact with body fluids. As Zaba (2003: 37) has written, "this may occur during sexual intercourse, or as a result of mother-to-child transmission during pregnancy, delivery, or breastfeeding. The virus may also be transferred in blood used for transfusions ... [Also] it can be spread by unsterilized hypodermic needles and surgical instruments." The virus is most commonly spread by having sex with someone with HIV, and secondly by sharing needles and syringes with someone who has HIV.

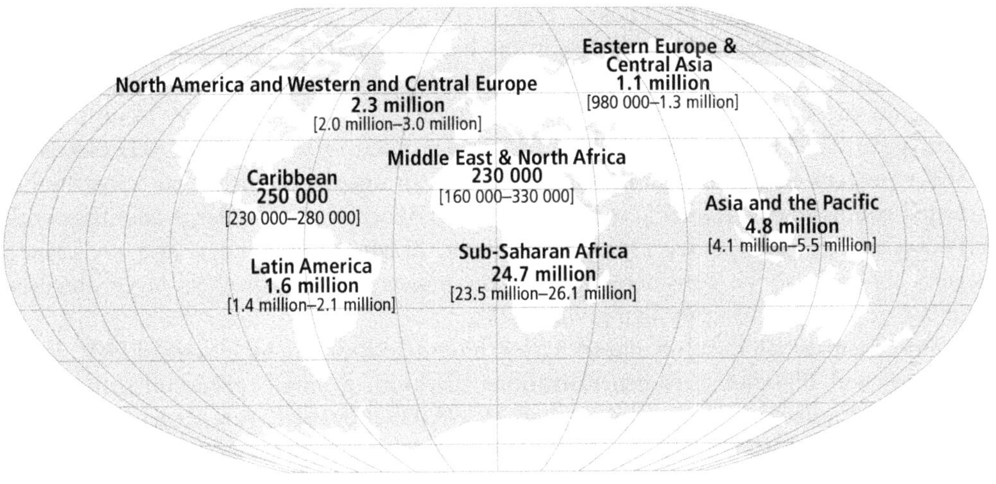

Total: 35.0 million [33.2 million–37.2 million]

FIGURE 12.2 Estimated numbers of people (millions) living with HIV, worldwide, 2013
Source: UNAIDS.

According to the WHO, "[S]ince the beginning of the epidemic, 88.4 million [range of 71.3–112.8 million] people have been infected with the HIV virus and about 42.3 million [range of 35.7–51.1 million] people have died of HIV" (WHO, 2024d). In 2023, 630,000 people died of HIV/AIDS.

In the world as a whole, 39.9 million (range of 36.1 million – 44.6 million) people were living with HIV at the end of 2023. The WHO estimated that 0.6 percent (range of 0.6–0.7%) of adults aged 15–49 years worldwide are living with HIV, although the burden of the epidemic continues to vary considerably between countries and regions (WHO, 2024d). The WHO African region remains most severely affected, with one in every 30 adults (3.4%) living with HIV and accounting for more than two-thirds of the people living with HIV worldwide. Moreover, 70 percent of the global total of new HIV infections occur in sub-Saharan Africa (WHO, 2014).

Figure 12.2 is a map of the world showing the numbers of children and adults in 2013 living with HIV in each major region of the world. The confidence intervals are shown in brackets. The map shows clearly that the region with the most cases in 2013 was sub-Saharan Africa with almost 25 million of the then-35 million cases.

One reason for the very high levels of HIV infection in sub-Saharan Africa is partner concurrency, the practice of men and women having more than one partner concurrently, that is, simultaneously. A man might have a wife and one or two steady girlfriends, all at the same time. A woman might simultaneously have a husband and a couple of boyfriends. This pattern adds significantly to the risk of contracting the virus (Epstein, 2007b).

Although sub-Saharan Africa is by far the most affected region in the world, epidemics are also underway in Central Asia and in Eastern Europe. Also, there is an enormous potential for a massive HIV/AIDS epidemic in China owing to the 30 to 40 million excess males already born in China who will not be able to find Chinese brides (Poston,

Conde, and DeSalvo, 2011; Tucker, Henderson, et al., 2005; Tucker, Poston, et al., 2009). These bachelors will likely live in the big cities and patronize sex workers.

It is clear that the HIV/AIDS epidemic has had, and continues to have, an enormous impact on the populations of many countries of the world (Lamptey, Johnson, and Khan, 2006). The United Nations (2013d) reported that HIV prevalence was estimated to be 2 percent or higher among the population of age 15–49 in the 39 most highly affected countries of the world, 36 of which are in Africa. Four very large countries with HIV prevalence rates under 1 percent, namely, Brazil, China, India, and the United States, should also be considered in this discussion because of their large absolute number of persons currently living with HIV.

Nine countries, all in sub-Saharan Africa, have astoundingly high rates of HIV. Some examples will illustrate this generalization. Eswatini, a small, predominantly rural, landlocked country has the world's highest HIV/AIDS prevalence rate, nearly 28 percent of adults. Lesotho had the second highest HIV/AIDS prevalence rate in 2021. Mozambique ranked among the worst in the world for HIV/AIDS prevalence and deaths as of 2022. Zimbabwe's HIV/AIDS prevalence rate has dropped from about 29 percent to 15 percent, still among the world's worst (CIA, 2024).

There is hope, though, as illustrated by the drop in prevalence in Zimbabwe. There is no cure for AIDS, but there are antiretroviral medications that can substantially reduce the viral load, sometimes to the point that there is no detectable virus. This medication remains in short supply in Africa, but public health campaigns have stressed educating people about AIDS and encouraging them to change their sexual practices. In Zimbabwe and some other countries, these campaigns appear to be having an effect in reducing new infections. The WHO reports that 230 million people in 103 countries were tested for HIV in 2023 (WHO, 2024d). There has been intensive research into possible vaccines that would be effective against HIV.

Until these measures have greater effects, however, HIV/AIDS continues to have severe consequences. The HIV/AIDS epidemic has resulted in several African countries recording increases in past years in their levels of mortality. Life expectancy in some of the most affected countries has declined. To illustrate, in Botswana, "life expectancy has fallen from 64 years in 1985–1990 to 47 years in 2005–2010 ... In Southern Africa as a whole, where most of the worst affected countries are, life expectancy has fallen from 61 to 52 years over the last 20 years" (United Nations, 2013d: 18).

Yellow Fever

Yellow fever is caused by the bite of an infected *Aedes aegypti* mosquito. This mosquito is an invasive species and has traveled with humans to many countries from its origin, believed to be in Africa. Yellow fever is endemic in Africa and has been for centuries. It appears that the mosquito came to the Americas through the North Atlantic slave trade. The mosquito is very adaptable, and it can also be the vector for other diseases such as Zika fever, dengue fever, and chikungunya (Kent, Schrider, and Matute, 2024).

Many of the enslaved persons already had an immunity to yellow fever, likely from having contracted a relatively mild case of it as a child. The European stock of North America, however, had no such immunity and during the mosquito season there were many new cases, some mild but some of them severe enough to produce liver damage and jaundice (the source of the name "yellow" fever). In severe cases, 20–50 percent of infected people died. When the mosquito bit an infected person, that same mosquito could then bite another person and infect that person too. It also appears that the virus could be transmitted by the female mosquito to her eggs, and thus to the next generation of mosquitoes.

The first North American cases reported in the historical record were in 1693 in Boston, Philadelphia, and Charleston, SC. The pattern of infections breaking out in Atlantic ports persisted through the 1700s, but soon Gulf of Mexico ports such as New Orleans, Mobile, and Galveston began having outbreaks. In the mid-1800s, the outbreaks came to be concentrated in the American South, an especially favorable climate for the mosquitoes. Steamboats carried the mosquito up the Mississippi River, with outbreaks resulting as far as Cairo, Illinois. The Mississippi River region experienced up to 20,000 deaths in the year 1878 alone (Patterson, 1992).

The devastation of Memphis was especially notable. There was very little immunity in the population, and the yellow fever spread rapidly throughout the city. Writer Molly Caldwell Crosby noted that in the single summer of 1878 in Memphis, yellow fever claimed more lives than the Chicago fire, the San Francisco earthquake, and the Johnstown flood combined (Crosby, 2007).

Frightened citizens tried enforcing quarantines, but of course the mosquitoes did not respect quarantines. It was noted that newcomers, especially new immigrants, often succumbed to the disease; it was sometimes called the "stranger's disease." The reason, of course, was that the newcomers to the area had not previously been exposed to the virus, but the observation reinforced suspicion of migrants.

The Spanish–American war, in which American troops went to Cuba, led to a high rate of infection among the soldiers. It was said that there were five yellow fever deaths for every combat death among the Americans. A group of American army doctors, led by Walter Reed, traveled to Cuba to learn the origin of the disease. There they ran controversial experiments on volunteer soldiers, exposing them to infected mosquitoes and eventually (although with resulting deaths among both doctors and volunteers) demonstrating that the mosquito was the vector.

Today there is a vaccine for yellow fever, and some countries require it for travelers to enter. Despite the existence of the vaccine, however, yellow fever is increasing in incidence in subtropical areas of Africa and South America. Contributing factors are population growth, urbanization, climate change, and globalization, along with inadequate public health facilities and the unaffordability of the vaccine (Gianchecchi et al., 2022).

COVID-19: A CONTEMPORARY PANDEMIC

In December 2019, some patients in Wuhan, China, reported the symptoms of an illness similar to pneumonia that did not respond to the usual treatments. The first death in China was reported in January 2020. By January 10, the WHO labeled the new disease the "2019 Novel Coronavirus" or "2019-nCoV" as the cause of the outbreak in Wuhan, China. Later that day, scientists in China and Australia uploaded the genetic sequence of the new coronavirus. In the following nine days, cases were reported in Thailand, Japan, and South Korea. By January 27, five cases had been identified in the United States in Washington, Illinois, California, and Arizona. By the end of January, the WHO declared a Public Health Emergency of International Concern (PHEIC), and the United States declared a public health emergency. By March, with at least 118,000 cases in 114 countries and 4,291 deaths, the WHO declared COVID-19 a pandemic (David J. Senser CDC Museum, 2024).

Scientists began immediately to develop clinical tests that would correctly identify the infection, and also to work on potential vaccines. Meanwhile there were dramatic responses in nearly all countries. Countries imposed travel restrictions on both air and ship traffic. Lockdowns began in many countries, allowing people to go outdoors only for walks and buying food or medicine. Many businesses offering personal services – such as gyms, beauty salons, bars, and restaurants – either closed or curtailed their services; restaurants, for example, switched from in-person service to carry-out only. Many workplaces shifted to at-home work, a change that worked for many technical and office workers, but not for blue-collar workers, many of whom were members of minority groups (Sullivan, 2020c). The NCAA canceled its annual basketball tournament, and by mid-March most US colleges and universities had closed, with courses offered only through distance learning. After the first case was confirmed in Michigan, Teresa Sullivan, who was the interim Provost at Michigan State University in 2019–2020, was charged with changing the entire University and its 50,000 students to online learning. Many K-12 school districts turned to online learning only.

Meanwhile, the death toll mounted, and many hospitals (and mortuaries) were overwhelmed. Doctors' offices closed and hospitals postponed elective procedures. Hospitals ran short of ventilators and the personal protective equipment needed for their doctors and nurses. By April there had been nearly 19,000 deaths and in New York City coffins were being buried in mass graves (CDC, 2024f). When the pandemic ended, the United States had recorded over 1.2 million COVID-19 deaths; another nearly 110 million people recovered after having the infection. Figure 12.3 shows the cumulative number of US deaths over a four-year period. Worldwide by 2022 there were 14.9 million "excess deaths," or deaths in excess of what would have been expected without the pandemic (WHO, 2022a).

There was a significant drop in US life expectancy between 2019 and 2021. Life expectancy at birth in the United States declined to 76.1 years, the lowest level since 1996. COVID-19 deaths explained 74 percent of the decline from 2019 to 2020 and 50 percent of the decline from 2020 to 2021. The two-year decline in life expectancy was the sharpest since 1921–1923 (NCHS, 2022).

COVID-19 did not affect all parts of the population equally. The elderly, especially those with a pre-existing condition such as heart disease; persons living on reservations; and members of minority groups were more affected (Dwyer-Lindgren et al., 2024). The initial deaths were concentrated in the largest urban areas, although eventually the disease spread to rural areas as well.

COVID-19 will apparently become endemic, at least in the United States, much as influenza is endemic. The endemic condition does not mean that there will be no more deaths, but it does mean that the sudden catastrophic rise in cases is unlikely to reoccur.

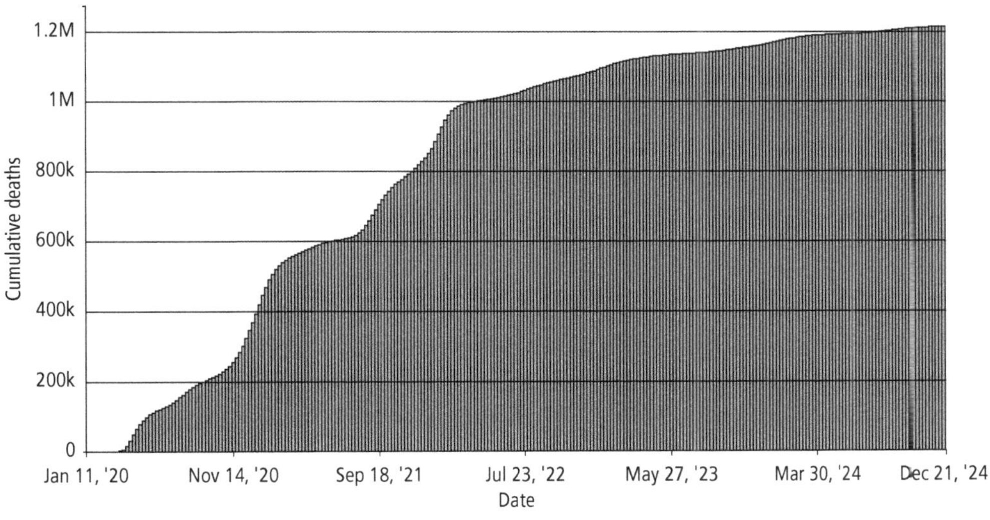

FIGURE 12.3 Cumulative number of COVID-19 deaths in the United States by week over a four-year period from January 2020 to December 2024
Source: Centers for Disease Control and Prevention, 2024f, COVID-19 Data Tracker.

CONDITIONS FOR EPIDEMICS AND PANDEMICS

What explains the sudden and catastrophic explosion of deaths in epidemics and pandemics? Briefly, we can identify several conditions.

- A novel agent. Humans did not have immunity to the COVID-19 virus when it first appeared. Over time, there can be immunity acquired through surviving the disease or through vaccination. Viruses, however, can mutate quickly; this is one of the reasons that influenza remains endemic, because new strains appear on a regular basis.
- A novel population. The European explorers brought a number of infectious diseases with them to the Americas, and the indigenous populations did not have resistance to these diseases. In both Mexico and Peru, for example, smallpox and then measles killed a large fraction of the population; the Spanish explorers, however, had immunity to these diseases, many of them having experienced them as children (McNeill, 1976). Eventually some colonizers deliberately introduced infectious disease to help clear away indigenous populations (Patterson and Runge, 2002).
- Lack of medical treatment. Without effective vaccinations, prevention of infection is difficult; sometimes, with especially virulent pathogens, the standard methods for treating infections are ineffective. This was the case early in the COVID-19 epidemic.
- Rapid transportation. The relatively inexpensive availability of rapid transportation, such as air travel, has made it possible for a single infected individual to travel to new populations that have no immunity to the disease. The rapid spread of COVID-19 was due in part to travel by infected people. The initial infection of port cities with plague and with yellow fever came about because of shipping that inadvertently carried the disease vectors (fleas, mosquitoes, and infected individuals).

There are also demographic conditions that foster epidemic conditions. Crowded conditions in urban areas facilitate the spread of diseases that are airborne, such as influenza or COVID-19. Inadequate sanitary conditions in crowded cities facilitate waterborne diseases, such as cholera in London in the nineteenth century. Pregnancy affects the immune system; it was noted during the plague that pregnant women were often the first to die, although women were also more likely to be nursing the sick and thus exposed to the fleas or airborne droplets that spread the plague.

WIDER CONSEQUENCES OF EPIDEMICS AND PANDEMICS

High mortality is an obvious and fearsome consequence of epidemics and pandemics. Demographically, human populations, unless quite isolated, replace the lost mortality fairly quickly. There may also be a decline in fertility, and some changes in age composition. These consequences may also be temporary. Migration, especially to infected areas, stops, and migration from infected areas may be prohibited.

But epidemics and pandemics have substantial social, economic, and political consequences that range well beyond the immediate demographic consequences. Both epidemics and pandemics cause widespread disruptions in the society and economy of countries, including funeral customs and religious ceremonies (Mikles, 2024), work arrangements (Sullivan, 2020c), and education (Annie E. Casey Foundation, 2024).

Socially, there is often widespread horror of the disease, and the sick may be shunned for fear of contagion. This is especially true if, as with yellow fever, the disease agent is unknown.

The economic consequences can be severe. During the COVID-19 pandemic, for example, many small businesses closed, and unemployment soared (Sullivan, 2020c). A pandemic such as this caused disruptions in international supply chains, which in turn caused factories to furlough workers. Even the move to at-home work has had interesting effects, with some workers unwilling to return to their former work schedules even after the disease threat had passed. COVID-19 led to an unexpected increase in retirements, job quits, and other unanticipated responses by workers. The US Congress enacted extraordinary subsidies for payroll support, tax relief, and living expenses; these had the effect of expanding the national debt and fueling more political controversies. These issues are still unfolding.

Epidemics and pandemics, especially when they are barely understood, also lead to political discontent and scapegoating (Markel, 2004). Immigrants are a frequent target of this scapegoating because they are blamed for carrying the disease, even if, as with yellow fever, they are more likely to contract the disease. The United States experienced an increase in anti-Chinese sentiment because COVID-19 had originated in China.

PREVENTING EPIDEMICS AND PANDEMICS

Public health authorities have a set of tactics that they use to slow down an epidemic or pandemic. During COVID-19, the authorities turned to the scientific literature on the 1918 influenza epidemic (e.g., Tomes, 2010). Some measures tried in 1918 and again in 2020 were banning large gatherings, such as in churches and schools; social distancing;

quarantines; isolation; masking; and limiting travel. These measures, however, were mixed in their effectiveness.

The best measures eliminate the causative agent. This is what John Snow (see our earlier discussion of him in this chapter) was able to do by eliminating the use of the contaminated well in London. Yellow fever was harder to eliminate without widespread mosquito control, something the *Aedes aegypti* has been good at evading. And airborne diseases, such as influenza and COVID-19, are especially hard to eliminate.

Vaccinations help to prevent epidemics and pandemics by expanding the immunity of individuals. Both coauthors of this book were vaccinated against smallpox, which was routine in their childhoods. Chances are that you have not been vaccinated for smallpox, because in 1980 the WHO declared smallpox to be extinct, thanks to vaccination (CDC, 2024a). Polio is another disease on the verge of extinction because of vaccines. On the other hand, both of the coauthors contracted measles, mumps, and chicken pox as children because effective vaccines were not yet available for these diseases. Again, chances are that you have not contracted these diseases in childhood, and you were protected because of widespread vaccination programs.

Ever since smallpox vaccination was first developed by English physician and scientist Edward Jenner in 1796, some people have been fearful about the motivations of vaccinators and the efficacy of the vaccines. During COVID-19, there was substantial pushback against the vaccine that was developed under the first Trump Administration, and there is now an anti-vaccination social movement among some Americans. The balance of public health history, however, supports vaccinations when available as an important barrier to infectious disease.

SUMMARY

In this chapter we reviewed the terms "epidemic" and "pandemic." We introduced the terms *agent*, *vector*, and *host* to clarify how an infectious disease can spread. We offered examples of the Black Death, cholera, influenza, HIV/AIDS, yellow fever, and COVID-19 as historically important epidemics. Some of these diseases are now endemic, and others we have learned to prevent. Vaccination remains the most effective means of preventing infectious disease.

COVID-19 was a challenge to the world because it spread so rapidly, it was initially so deadly, and there was a lack of good tools for dealing with it. The disease came on so quickly and in such numbers that medical facilities were overwhelmed. Responses such as lockdowns led to serious social, economic, and political consequences.

Will there be future epidemics? Infectious agents can mutate, jump from animal hosts to human hosts, and quickly travel internationally. These factors make it unlikely that the era of infectious diseases has ended, despite the hopeful theorizing of Omran (1971: chapter 5).

Demographic conditions such as rapid population growth and urbanization can affect the future severity of epidemics. Increased mortality, temporarily decreased fertility, and interrupted migration are also effects of epidemics, but the more problematic effects are social, economic, and political.

DISCUSSION QUESTIONS

1. Sometimes increases in mortality from a chronic disease will be described as an *epidemic*, such as "an epidemic of cancer" or "an epidemic of diabetes." Does this use of the word *epidemic* raise any questions or concerns for you?
2. Faced with a novel Coronavirus in the COVID-19 pandemic in 2020, public health authorities recommended measures that had been used in the 1918 Spanish flu epidemic, even though those measures had not been rigorously tested. Examples were closing schools and churches, introducing social distancing, and wearing masks. Later, when a vaccine was introduced, many workplaces made vaccination a necessary condition for employment. In your opinion, were these measures justified? Why or why not?

13

Age Composition and Aging Societies

INTRODUCTION

In this chapter we discuss age composition, that is, how a population is divided among children, young and middle-aged adults, and older adults. **Aging** is a biological process, but there are many social expectations associated with certain ages, referred to as **age grading**. There are minimum ages, for example, for starting school; for obtaining a driver's license; for voting; for drinking alcohol legally; and for qualifying for Social Security and Medicare. The US Constitution specifies minimum ages for members of Congress, and the presidency. People of the same age tend to have much in common because they have had similar experiences at similar ages.

The age composition of a population changes with the basic demographic processes of fertility, mortality, and migration (see Chapters 4 through 7). As a society grows older or younger, its social and economic life changes as well. As a result of the demographic transition, throughout the world there are now many aging societies, which is a novel experience for humanity. Age composition, in turn, also affects the demographic processes. You have already seen how fertility, mortality, and migration rates vary by age; this is the reason demographers use **age-specific rates**, such as the age-specific fertility rate (see Chapter 4).

In this chapter we will discuss the definition and measures of age and age distribution, the concepts of age heaping and age dependency, and population pyramids. Then we will examine in detail some of the issues posed by aging populations, including healthy aging. Finally, we will discuss the concepts of cohort and generation.

DEFINING AND MEASURING AGE

To a certain extent, the classification, definition, and enumeration of persons by age are more straightforward compared with other characteristics of human populations such as marital status, race, or occupation. These other characteristics "involve numerous categories and are subject to alternative formulation as a result of cultural differences, differences in the uses to which the data will be put, and differences in the interpretations of respondents and enumerators" (Shryock, Siegel, and Associates, 1976: 105). By contrast, age can be reported as a single number.

Age is an **ascribed** characteristic, meaning that individuals have no control over their chronological age. It is also a changeable characteristic because its value changes every year. Age is usually defined in population censuses in terms of the age of the person at their last birthday. The United Nations (1998: 69) defines age as "the estimated or calculated interval of time between the date of birth and the date of the census, expressed in complete solar years" (see also Hobbs, 2004). In most censuses, respondents are asked their current age, as well as their date of birth. Adjustments are then introduced by census-editing procedures if the respondent's current age does not correspond to the age denoted by the date of birth.

Age is considered an interval variable, which means that the distance between two values, such as 3 years of age and 4 years of age, is the same as the distance between any other two adjacent values, say 68 years and 69 years. The distribution of an interval variable can be summarized with measures of central tendency. The **mean** is the arithmetic average of ages, but not too useful for demographers because the older ages will tend to skew the value upward. The **mode** is the most commonly occurring value, which is again rarely of value to demographers. The measure used most often is the **median**, which is the value that divides the population in half. This measure is not affected by extreme values such as very young or very old ages. The median age in the United States in 2025 was 38.3 years, compared with 40.5 years for Canada and 29.3 years for Mexico (Worldostats, 2025). As you have seen in Chapters 4 and 5, demographers often report ages in five-year age groups, such as 10–14 and 60–64 years of age. Sometimes you will find ages reported in ten-year intervals.

Errors in age reporting are fairly common, and that is one reason that interviewers may request both actual age and date of birth. Now that date of birth is commonly used for identification purposes in the United States, especially by health providers, there is more sensitivity to providing the exact date of birth for fear of identity theft. The report of age only in years is also subject to errors. One such error is exaggeration, such as when 20-year-olds report their age as 21 to purchase alcohol, or when respondents near a landmark birthday date exaggerate their age to show their having already reached that date.

PROSPECTIVE AGE

The major definition of age is chronological age, as defined and discussed in the preceding paragraphs. However, one's chronological age may not always tell us much about how old the person really is. For many decades the United Nations has defined an "older" person as one who is 60 years old or older, and more recently, as one who is 65 years old or older (United Nations, 2025: 1–2). But a 60- or 65-year-old person in the year 2018 is not as old physically as was a 60- or 65-year-old person in the year 1918. Similarly, a 60- or 65-year-old person living today in Niger is older physically than a 60- or 65-year-old person living today in Japan. Demographers have thus introduced the concept of **prospective age**, referring to the average number of years a person has left to live (Sanderson and Scherbov 2010, 2019). Everyone thus has two ages, a chronological age and a prospective age; one refers to the number of years the person has lived, and the other refers to the average number of years the person has remaining to live.

Let us define an older person not as a person who is 65 years of age or older, that is, by chronological age, but as a person who has an average of fifteen years of life remaining, that is, prospective age. According to period life tables for the years 1900 and 2000 produced by the US Social Security Administration (Bell and Miller, 2005), males in the year 1900 needed to live to age 58, and females needed to live to age 60, before they reached the age at which they would on average have fifteen years of life remaining. In the year 2000, however, males needed to live to age 66, and females to age 70, before they reached the age at which there was an average of fifteen years of life remaining. And according to projected life tables for the year 2050, when males are age 70 and when females then are age 73, they are projected on average to have fifteen years of life remaining. So according to prospective age, men and women reached old age in 1900 when they were ages 58 and 60, they reached old age in 2000 when they were ages 66 and 70, and they are projected to reach old age in 2050 when they are ages 70 and 73.

Chronological age is a backward way of defining one's age. It is based on how many years of life the person has lived. Prospective age is a forward way of defining age. It is based on the number of years the person has left to live. Age thus is two-dimensional. As Sanderson and Scherbov (2005) have noted, persons sharing the same chronological age have been alive for the same number of years. Alternately, persons sharing the same prospective age have the same average number of years life left to live. Demographers almost always use chronological age when discussing age structure and age composition (Poston, 2019).

AGE HEAPING

Age exaggeration is related to the concept of **age heaping**, which is a preference for ages ending in certain digits. Age heaping tends to be more pronounced among populations or population subgroups with low levels of education: "The causes and patterns of [age heaping] vary from culture to culture, but preference for ages ending in '0' and in '5' is quite widespread" (Hobbs, 2004: 136), particularly in the Western world. In Korea, China, and some other countries in East Asia, there is sometimes a preference for ages ending in "3" because the number "3" sounds like the word or character for "life."

In some cultures, certain numbers and digits are avoided; for example, "13" is frequently avoided in the West because it is considered unlucky. The number "4" is avoided in Korea and in China because it has the same sound as the word or character for "death." For example, hotels in the United States and in some Western countries sometimes do not have floors designated as 13. Similarly, hotels in China, South Korea, and some other East Asian countries sometimes do not have floors designated as 4.

Age heaping is easily detected using graphs and indices. Figure 13.1 is a graph of single years of age for females in South Korea in 1995. Aside from some heaping on ages 43, 53, and 63 (note the preference for ages ending in the numeral 3), there is little evidence elsewhere of age heaping. Compare the situation of females in South Korea in 1995 with that of males in Pakistan in 1981 (Figure 13.2). In Pakistan in 1981, there was an astounding amount of age heaping on ages ending in 0 and 5.

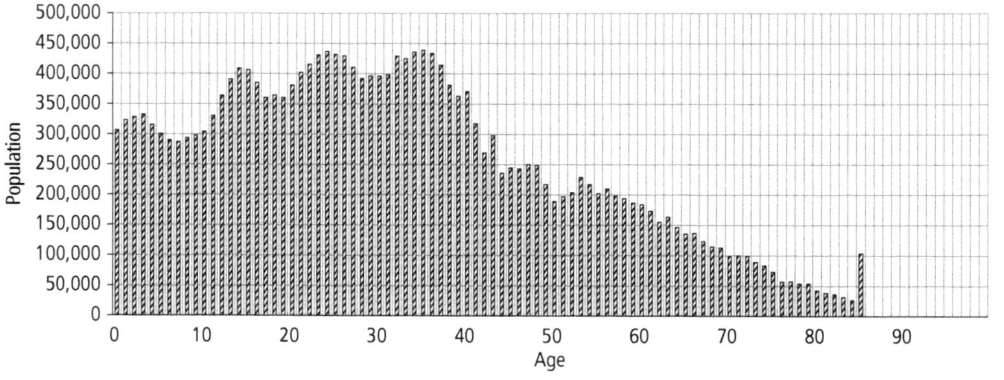

FIGURE 13.1 Single years of age, female population, Republic of Korea, 1995

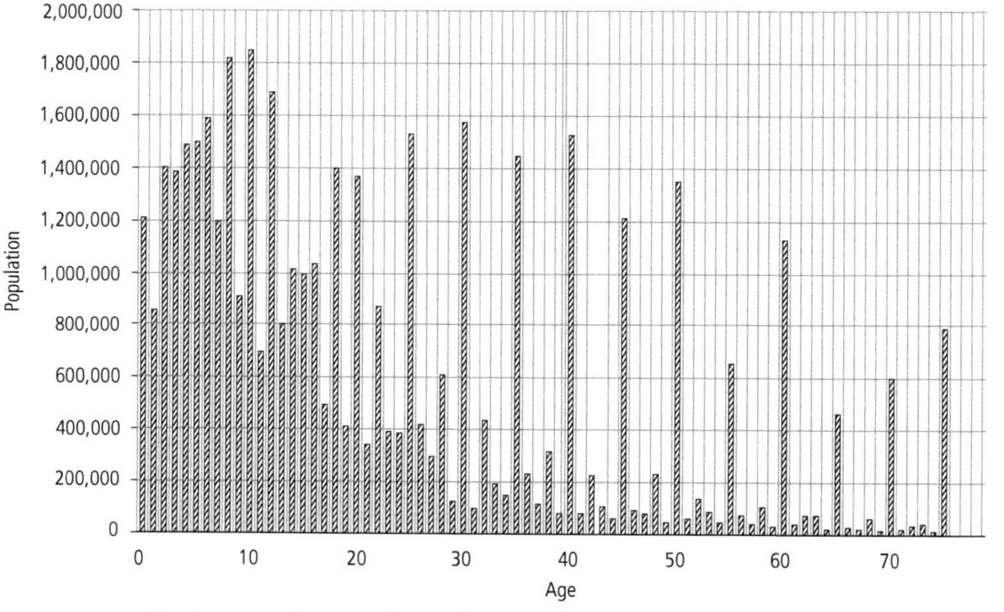

FIGURE 13.2 Single years of age, male population, Pakistan, 1981
Data source: US Census Bureau, International Database.

Figure 13.3 shows age heaping in the 2020 US census. The spikes indicate higher net overcount, or in other words, more age heaping at certain ages compared with what we would expect from vital statistics records.

This age heaping in 2020 was greater than was seen in the 2000 and 2010 censuses, and there is still some controversy over the reason. Because of the COVID-19 pandemic, the 2020 census was delayed, and many college students had left their campuses; the peak at age 20 may reflect the use of proxy respondents who did not know the actual ages of students. There was much more age heaping among individuals who did not live in a family household, such as college roommates (Jensen, Roberts, and Rogers, 2023).

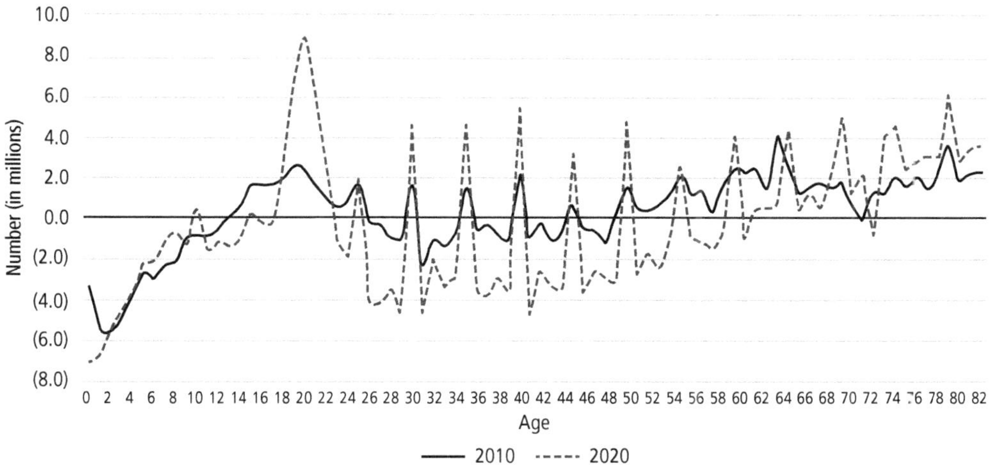

FIGURE 13.3 Age heaping estimates: percentage net under/overcount, single years of age, 2010 and 2020 US censuses
Source: Sullivan and Cork, 2023.

Similarly, apartment managers or other proxy reporters might have indicated that their renters were "forty or so" because they could not be sure of the actual ages (Sullivan and Cork, 2023: 61–63).

The extent of age heaping may be ascertained more precisely with indices. A popular one is **Whipple's method (WM)**, an index designed to reflect preference for the terminal digits of "0" and "5," usually in the age range of 23 to 62 (cf. Hobbs, 2004). WM varies from 0 (when the digits 0 and 5 are not reported in the census data) to 100 (when there is no preference for 0 or 5 in the census data) to a maximum of 500 (when only the digits 0 and 5 are reported in the census data). The United Nations (1990) has noted that if the values of Whipple's Index are less than 105, then the age distribution data are "highly accurate." If the WM values are between 105 and 109.9, the age data are "fairly accurate"; if between 110 and 124.9, "approximate"; if between 125 and 174.9, "rough"; and if 175 or more, "very rough" (United Nations, 1990: 18–19). WM is calculated as follows (Hobbs, 2004: 138):

$$WM = \frac{\sum(P_{25} + P_{30} + \cdots + P_{55} + P_{60})}{1/5\sum(P_{23} + P_{24} + P_{25} \cdots P_{60} + P_{61} + P_{62})} * 100 \tag{13.1}$$

The UN has reported that "although Whipple's Index measures only the effects of preferences for ages ending in 5 and 0, it can be assumed that such digit preference is usually connected with other sources of inaccuracy in age statements, and the indexes can be accepted as a fair measure of the general reliability of the age distribution" (1990: 20).

The decision in Whipple's Index to focus on the age range of 23 to 62 is partly an arbitrary one. The ages of early childhood and old age are excluded because, frequently, they are more influenced by other types of errors and issues than digit preference; also, "the assumption of equal decrements from age to age is less applicable" at the older ages (Hobbs, 2004: 138).

The WM value for South Korean females in 1995 (see Figure 13.1 above) is 100.1; the WM value for Pakistani males in 1981 (see Figure 13.2 above) is 330.8. Among Korean females in 1995, the WM Index indicates virtually no age heaping on digits ending in 0 and 5. This means that in South Korea, the numbers of females counted in 1995 at ages ending in 0 and 5 overstate an unbiased population, that is, one in which there is no age heaping on 0 or 5, by a mere 0.1 percent. Conversely, in Pakistan in 1981, males counted at ages ending in 0 and 5 overstate an unbiased population by almost 231 percent.

The Whipple's Index for the 2000 US census was 101.8; for 2010 it was 102.2, and for 2020 it was 105.9 (106.6 for males and 105.3 for females; Jensen, Roberts, and Rogers, 2023). This index shows some loss of accuracy in the successive censuses from "highly accurate" to "fairly accurate," to use the United Nations' terminology.

To illustrate the range of WM values, we calculated WM scores for three higher-income countries, namely, Japan in 1985, Denmark in 1988, and Hong Kong in 1995; and for two lower-income countries, namely, Iran and Mexico, both in 1988. Their WM scores are 98.4 for Japan, 101.5 for Denmark, and 101.7 for Hong Kong, versus 122.7 for Iran and 133.4 for Mexico. The WM values for the higher-income countries, as expected, are lower and closer to 100 than those for lower-income countries.

Several other summary indexes of age heaping and digit preference have been developed by Myers (1940), Bachi (1951), Carrier (1959), and Ramachandran (1967). These differ only slightly from one another and from the WM as general indicators of heaping.

THE POPULATION PYRAMID

The population pyramid (sometimes called the age/sex pyramid) is an important visual representation of the age and sex structure of a population at a given moment of time. Another way to think of it is the aggregation of cohorts born in different years; the pyramid shows for a specific point in time the different surviving cohorts of persons of each sex. A population pyramid is one of the most elegant ways of graphically presenting age and sex data (Poston, 2019).

A population pyramid is two ordinary **histograms** (bar graphs), representing the male and female populations in, usually, one- or five-year age categories, placed on their sides and back-to-back. By convention, women are on the right side of the pyramid and men on the left side. The base of the pyramid, representing the size of each of the age/sex population groups, is presented in either absolute numbers or in percentages. When using percentages as the metric, one must be sure to "calculate the percentages on the basis of the grand total for the population, including both sexes and all ages" (Hobbs, 2004: 162).

Figure 13.4 is a population pyramid for the United States in 2020, presented in absolute numbers. Compared with some pyramids we will view later, the two sexes are relatively balanced, although there are more women at the older ages. Look also at the larger numbers of males and females between the ages of 55 and 70. These persons were born during the "baby boom" years after World War II, when the total fertility rate in the United States reached its peak level of 3.7 children per woman in the late 1950s.

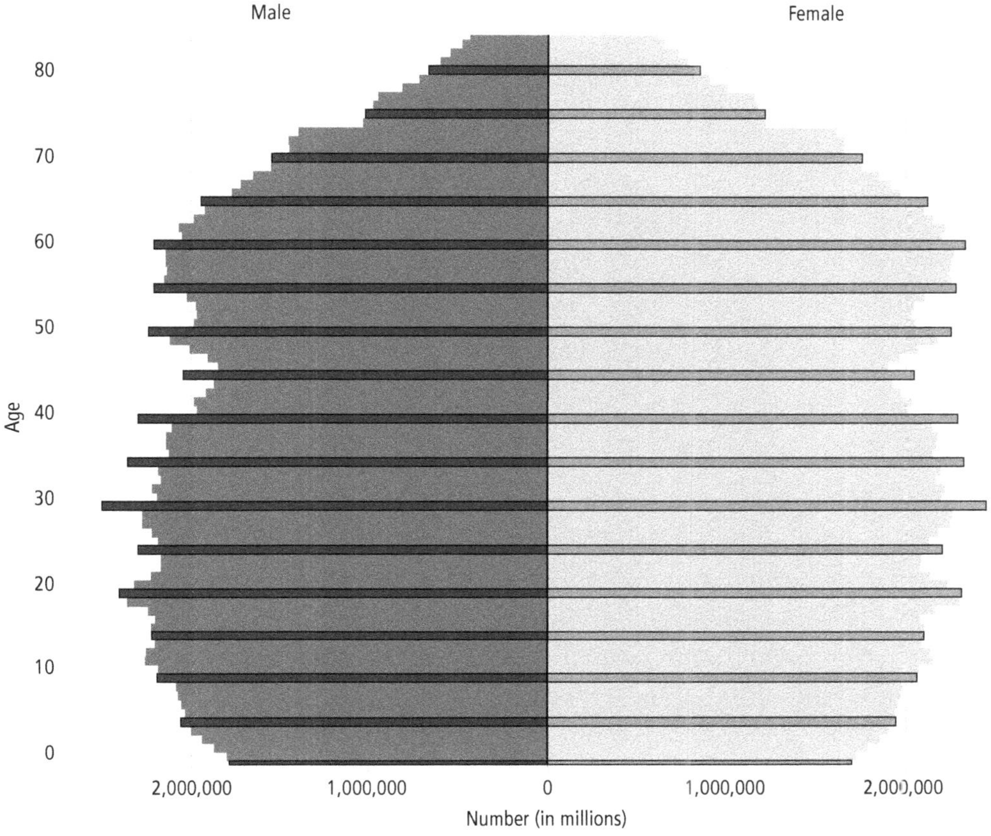

FIGURE 13.4 Population pyramid, age, and sex composition, United States, 2020
Outlined bars represent ages ending in "0" or "5."
Source: Jensen, Roberts, and Rogers, 2023.

Observe the slightly larger cohorts of ages 28 to 40 years as well. These are mainly the babies of parents born during the baby boom, that is, the babies of the baby boom babies. We see, thus, an echo of the baby boom one generation later, the so-called **echo effect.**

Figure 13.5 is a population pyramid for France in 2025 and "reflects various irregularities associated with that country's special history" (Hobbs, 2004: 164). This pyramid was constructed with data for individual years of age. There are five special aspects of this pyramid worth mentioning, and they are identified at the bottom of the pyramid. The first represents the very small birth cohorts born in France during World War I. One also sees at the older ages of the pyramid the larger number of females than males; this latter consideration characterizes most national populations, not only France, but also reflects male mortality during war. The second special feature of the pyramid points to the smaller number of persons born during World War I who reached the reproductive years in 1940. The third feature worthy of note refers to the larger numbers of babies born in France after World War II in their baby boom. The fourth special aspect of the

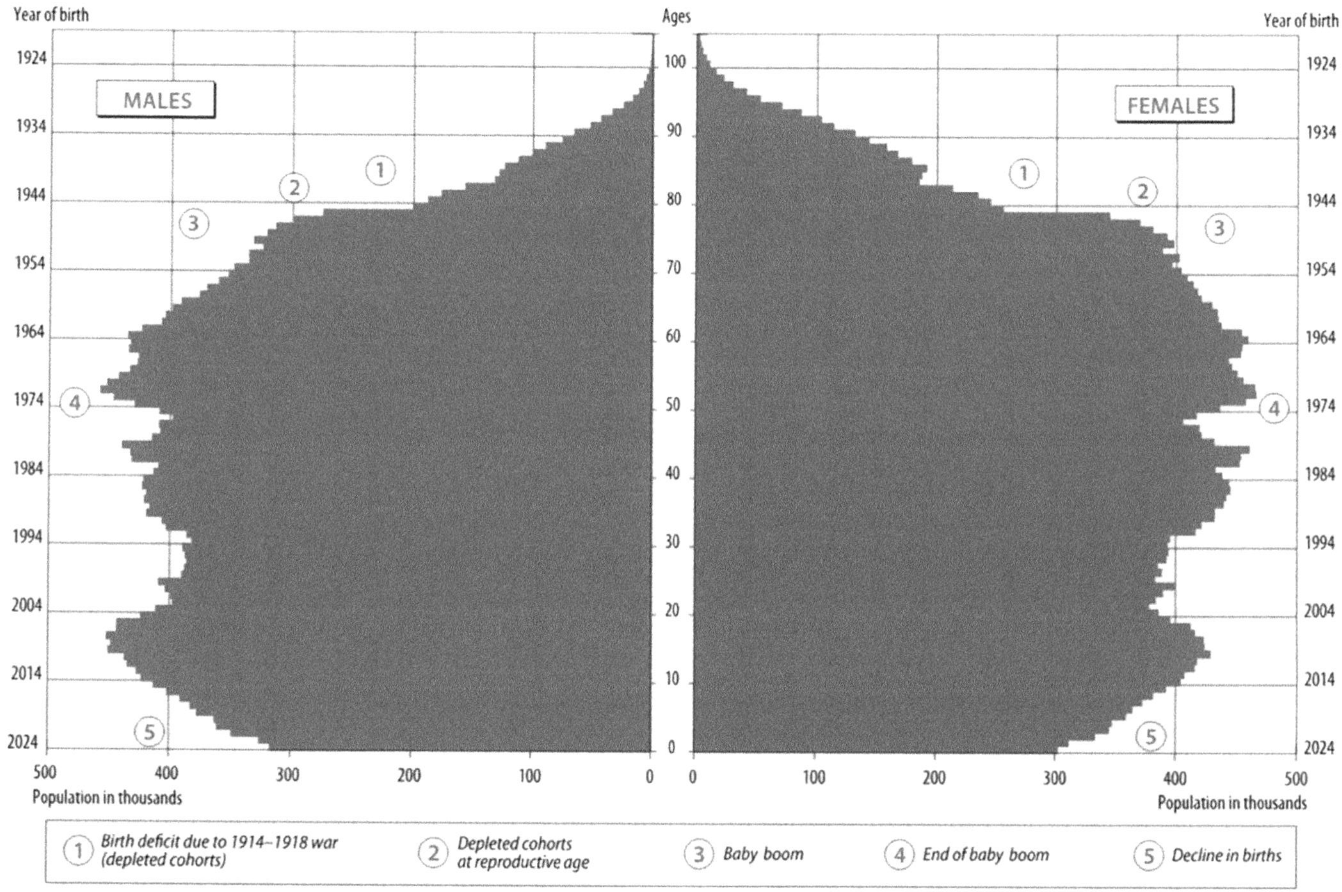

FIGURE 13.5 Population pyramid, age and sex composition, France, 2025
Source: Gilles Pison and Laurent Toulemon, "Is the French Population on a Path to Decline?" *Population and Societies* 631 (2025): 1–4. https://doi.org/10.3917/popsoc.631.0001 (reprinted with permission).

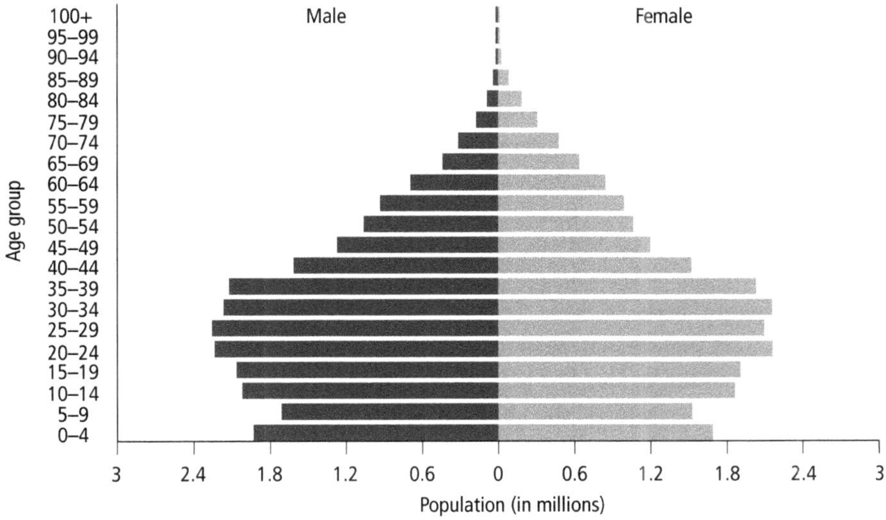

FIGURE 13.6 Population pyramid, age and sex composition, South Korea, 1995
Source: US Census Bureau, International Database.

French pyramid refers to the smaller numbers of babies born after the end of the baby boom. And the fifth special feature shows the recent declines in births in France. Knowing the age and sex structure of the population tells us a great deal about its history. This is certainly the case for France.

Figure 13.6 is a pyramid for the Republic of Korea in 1995. The bottom bars of the pyramid show the effects of the fertility reduction in South Korea since the 1970s. In 1995, less than 12 percent of Korea's population was male aged 0 to 14 (compared with more than 21 percent in 1970), and also less than 12 percent was female aged 0 to 14 (more than 20 percent in 1970). The lower bars also indicate the much larger numbers of males, compared to females, born in Korea since the mid-1980s. The lowest two bars of the pyramid indicate that the sex ratio for Koreans in 1995 in the age group 0–4 was 113.4; this suggests a much higher sex ratio at birth (SRB) than that regulated by biology and is evidence of son preference (see Chapter 10). Also shown in the South Korean pyramid is a relatively smaller number of men between the ages of 65 and 74. This is the special population that was heavily depleted through mortality during the Korean War.

Despite their descriptive utility, however, population pyramids are a graphic representation of age and sex structure only at a particular point in time. We will now discuss several indexes that may be used to examine patterns of age data.

AGE DEPENDENCY

One may analyze the **age distribution** of a population in many ways (Arriaga and Associates, 1994; Hobbs, 2004). A popular measure of age structure is the **dependency ratio (DR)**. The DR is the ratio of the dependent-age population (both young persons [0–14 years old] and old persons [65 years of age and older]) to the working-age population (persons 15–64 years old). The DR is usually multiplied by a constant of 100. The higher the ratio, the more people each worker needs to support; the lower the DR, the fewer the number of dependents. Demographers usually split the DR into the **youth-dependency ratio (YDR or Youth-DR)** and the **old-age dependency ratio (Old-Age-DR)**, also known as the **aged-dependency ratio (ADR or Aged-DR)**; both have the same denominator, namely, the population 15–64. The numerator of the Youth-DR is the population 0–14 and the numerator of the Old Age-DR is the population 65+. The Youth-DR plus the Old-Age-DR equals the DR.

An index analogous to the old-age dependency ratio is a measure of elderly support, known as the **parent support ratio (PSR)**. It takes the number of persons 80 years old and older, per 100 persons of ages 50–64 (Wu and Wang, 2004). It represents the relative burden that the oldest-old population, that is, the elderly parents, has on the population aged 50–64, that is, the children of the elderly parents.

In 2021 the **total dependency ratio (Total DR)** for the world was 54.1; the world youth dependency ratio was 39.3 and the world old age dependency ratio was 14.8 (CIA, 2024). Presented in Table 13.1 are values of the Youth-DR, the Old-Age-DR, and the total dependency ratio (Total DR) for fifteen countries of the world. We selected these countries to show a range of values for Total DR, and low or high values of the component DRs. The countries are ranked according to their Total DR values, from lowest to highest. The United Arab Emirates, South Korea, and China have Total DRs that are among the lowest in the world. For every 100 persons in the economically producing ages (15–64) in South Korea and China, for example, there are about 17 and 26 young people, respectively, in the dependent ages that the producers must support.

The United States and Spain have Total DRs of 52–53, indicating that for every 100 persons in the producing population, there are more than about 52 or 53 dependents. But in the US the old-age dependency ratio is 25.6 and in Spain it is 30.2. At the

TABLE 13.1 *Values of youth-dependency ratio, old-age-dependency ratio, and total dependency ratio, selected countries of the world, 2024 (ordered by total dependency ratio)*

Country	Youth-DR	Old-Age-DR	Total DR
United Arab Emirates	18.2	2.1	20.3
South Korea	16.6	23.3	39.9
China	25.5	19.0	44.5
Mexico	37.3	12.2	49.4
Russia	26.6	23.4	50.0
Canada	23.9	28.2	52.1
Spain	21.9	30.2	52.1
United States	28.0	25.6	53.7
Italy	19.9	37.2	57.1
Iraq	65.2	5.8	71.0
Japan	20.1	51.0	71.1
Afghanistan	80.2	4.8	84.6
Nigeria	80.6	5.5	86.0
Chad	94.7	4.0	98.7
Niger	100.4	5.0	105.4

Data source: CIA, 2024. Total DR may not sum to Youth-DR and Old-Age-DR because of rounding error.

other extreme are the three African countries of Nigeria, Chad, and Niger, with Total DRs that are among the highest in the world. For every 100 persons in the economically producing ages in Niger, there are 100 persons in the dependent ages that the producers must support. Nearly all of these dependents are young people. Compare the United Arab Emirates and Niger, the countries with the lowest and highest Total DRs in the table. The producers in Niger are supporting more than five times as many dependents as are the producers in the United Arab Emirates.

Knowing the values of Youth-DR and the Old-Age-DR is important because the needs of the young and the old are different. Both dependent populations need food, clothing, and shelter, but the youth population also needs education and preparation for work, and the old-age population needs pension support and much more medical care.

THEORETICAL AND SUBSTANTIVE ISSUES OF AGE

The population pyramid is an important piece of information because it maps the demographic history of the population for the past 85–100 years, depending on how high the age categories go. Persons of the same age constitute a group or cohort of people who were born during the same period, and therefore have been exposed to similar historical facts and conditions. For instance, military personnel who participate in wars are usually restricted to a narrow age range and are comprised of more males than females. For decades after the cessation of fighting, one will observe heavier attrition among the veterans owing to war casualties. Major events in a population's immediate history, say, those that occurred within the previous eight decades, are easily recognized when only the population's current data are examined.

Both policymakers and social scientists are interested in the age composition of populations because so many activities are age graded. It is important to know, for example, how many children will start school next year, or how many additional retirees will qualify for social security.

Age is also important theoretically. Bogue (1985: 42) has written that "almost any aspect of human behavior, from states of subjective feeling and attitudes to objective characteristics such as income, home ownership, occupation, or group membership, may be expected to vary with age." Populations with large proportions of young members differ in many ways from those with large proportions of elders.

AGE AND THE DEMOGRAPHIC PROCESSES

The demographic processes themselves vary significantly by age. The fecundity and, hence, the childbearing years of females and males occur within certain ages, for females between the ages 15 and 49 and for males usually a few years later in the teen years and up to age 79. Regarding mortality, death rates are high in the first year of life and then drop to very low levels. In modern populations, they do not again attain the level reached in the first year of life for another five to six decades. Also, as we noted earlier in Chapter 5, cause-specific mortality is often age-related. Chronic diseases, such as cardiovascular disease, are far more common among older adults. In fact, age by itself is often a risk factor for certain diseases.

Migration is also age-selective, with the largest numbers of migrants found among young adults (Stone, 1978; Tobler, 1995; Benetsky et al., 2015). Goldscheider has observed that "given different political, social, economic, cultural and demographic contexts, age remains as a critical differentiation of migration ... [These contexts] determine the specifics of age and mobility" (1971: 311).

DEMOGRAPHIC THEORIES OF AGE

Demographers are well known for their formal theories and have developed some of the most mathematically elegant theories in the social sciences. Age is the centerpiece of most formal theory in demography. Examples of formal age models include Ansley Coale's (1971) development of marriage patterns by age, Andrei Rogers's (1975) elaborate presentation of migration patterns by age, and Louis Henry's (1961) description of fertility patterns by age in the absence of voluntary fertility control. But the most powerful and elegant formal mathematical theory in demography that incorporates a population's age and sex structure, but particularly age, is **stable population theory**. Many claim this theory to be the most important aspect of the entirety of the mathematics of population (Pollard, Yusuf, and Pollard, 1990; Yusuf, Martins, and Swanson, 2014).

We have already mentioned stable population theory in Chapter 5. We noted that if a population closed to migration experiences constant schedules of age-specific fertility and mortality rates, it will develop a constant age distribution and will grow at a constant rate, irrespective of its initial age distribution. Its mathematical bases and foundation are laid out and discussed in many places, one of the best expositions being Coale's masterpiece, *The Growth and Structure of Human Populations* (1972). (See also Keyfitz, 1977a; Pollard, Yusuf, and Pollard, 1990; Preston, Heuveline, and Guillot, 2001; Schoen, 1988; and Yusuf, Martins, and Swanson, 2014.)

The age distribution of the stable population depends on two items, namely, the underlying age-specific mortality rates, and the rate of growth: "The higher the mortality, the more rapidly the age distribution falls with increasing age; and also, the higher the rate of growth, the more rapidly the age distribution falls with age" (Pollard, Yusuf, and Pollard, 1990: 106).

An important point to remember about a stable population is that it eventually converges to a constant age distribution, irrespective of the age distribution with which it began. Thus, demographers sometimes state that "stable populations forget their past." In other words, when fixed fertility and mortality rates have prevailed, a stable population eventually ends up with an unchanging age structure that will be completely independent of its form at any earlier time.

Actually, Coale (1957) demonstrated that all human populations, not just stable populations, forget their pasts: "The age distribution of France is no longer much affected by the excess mortality and reduced numbers of births experienced during the Napoleonic Wars, and the age distribution of Greece is no longer affected at all by the Peloponnesian Wars" (Coale, 1987: 466). Obviously, when fertility and mortality schedules constantly change, the age structure constantly changes. Thus, following Coale, one may state that all populations, whether stable or not, have forgotten the past. But the stable population, in addition, has a fixed form, and fixed birth and death rates.

This theorem is very nicely illustrated by van de Walle and Knodel (1970) in their demographic simulation known as "The Case of Women's Island," an exercise that reports quantitatively the hypothetical "story" of a thousand young women marooned with five men on an island that is forever closed to migration. After a hundred years have elapsed, "one cannot find any evidence that the initial population [of the island was so] ... distorted in both its [initial] age and sex composition" (van de Walle and Knodel, 1970: 436). This is an interesting demonstration of the statement that a population, stable or not, "forgets" its past and "stabilizes itself in due time with a structure that is entirely dependent on fertility and mortality levels" (van de Walle and Knodel, 1970: 436).

Stable population theory has many implications for age distribution. One is that changes and fluctuations in fertility cause far greater changes in a population's age distribution than do changes and fluctuations in mortality. Coale and Demeny (1983) have shown that populations closed to migration that have near stable fertility rates but differ only in their mortality schedules will have similar age and sex structures (see also Hinde, 1998; and Yusuf, Martins, and Swanson, 2014).

We have limited our discussion here of the stable model to the **closed population**, that is, a population in which migration does not occur. However, it has also been shown mathematically that even when migration is taken into consideration, a stable population (indeed, a **stationary population**, that is, one with the same birth and death rates) can eventually be reached. As long as fertility is below replacement levels, a constant number and age distribution of in-migrants (with fixed fertility and mortality rates) will lead to a stationary population. Neither the level of the net reproduction rate nor the size of the in-migration stream will affect this conclusion; a stationary population will eventually emerge (Espenshade, Bouvier, and Arthur, 1982).

We can link this discussion of age structure to our earlier discussion of demographic transition theory (see Chapter 2). Because fertility and mortality rates shape the age structure, and because the stages of the demographic transition vary by fertility and mortality rates, there are distinctive population pyramids associated with each stage. Figure 13.7 shows the characteristic pyramids associated with the stages of the demographic transition.

The top panel of Figure 13.7 shows the stages of the demographic transition, including stage 5, the most speculative of the changes. (Most of our earlier discussions of the demographic transition have not included stage 5.) The bottom panel of the figure shows the shapes of the pyramids. Notice that in stage 2 of the transition, the pyramid is a triangle shape. Because of high fertility, each cohort added at the bottom is slightly larger than the one preceding it. And because of high mortality, the pyramid tapers to a fairly small peak. By contrast, in stage 4 with relatively stable fertility, the base of the pyramid is roughly the same from year to year and the tapering at older ages is much less pronounced. The pyramid has begun to resemble a rectangle. By looking at the population pyramid of a country, a demographer can make a rough guess about where the country is in terms of the demographic transition.

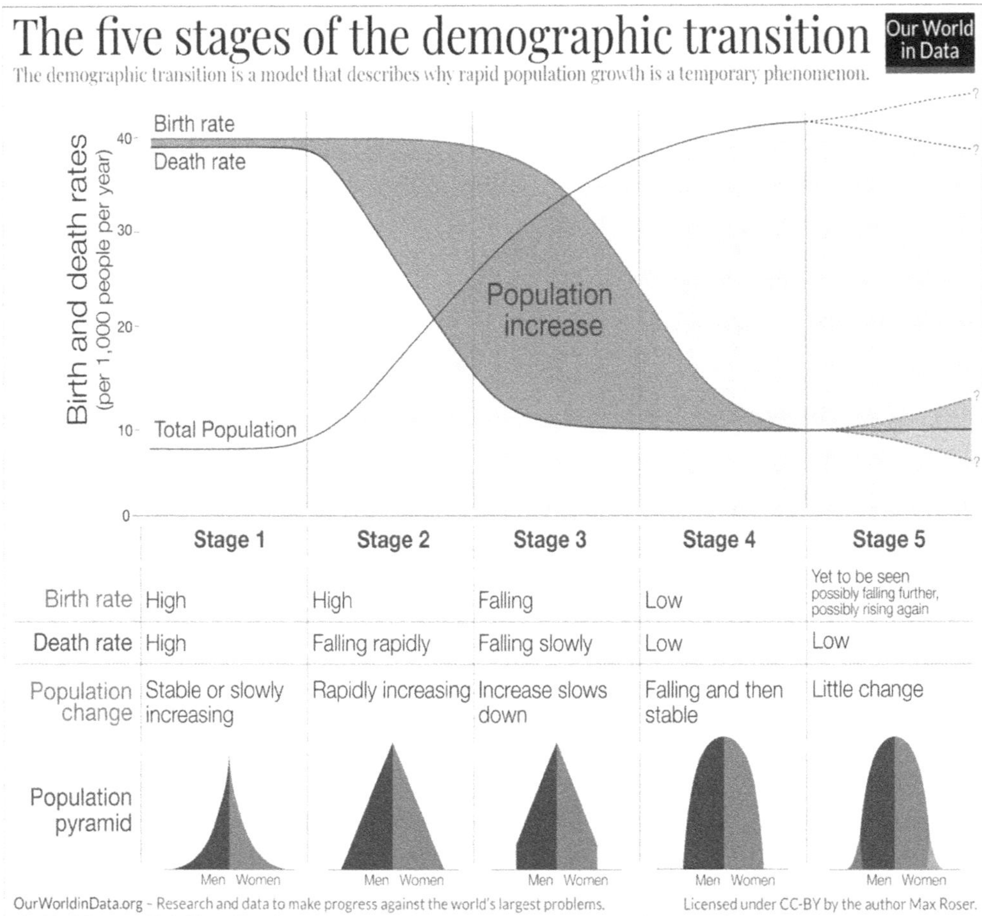

FIGURE 13.7 The five stages of the demographic transition (top) and corresponding population pyramids (bottom)
Source: Roser, 2023.

POPULATION AGING

As Figure 13.7 shows, as countries progress through the demographic transition, the size and proportion of their older populations increase. China is the second largest country in the world (after India), with a population size in 2025 of more than 1.4 billion. The United States is the third largest country in the world (after India and China), with a population of more than 341 million. China has a land mass just slightly less than that of the United States (China has 9.6 million square kilometers of surface area compared with the United States with 9.8 million square kilometers) but a population that is more than four times larger than that of the United States. An interesting issue we will now address is the size of the older and oldest-old populations in China and the United States and the issues they pose.

The World Health Organization (WHO) and the American Geriatric Society define the oldest-old as persons aged 80 and over, and they are a rapidly growing population worldwide (Escourrou, 2022). Two other categories of older people often used are the youngest-old (aged 60–69) and the middle-old (ages 70–79) (Lee et al., 2018). The size of the world population aged 60 years and over is projected to increase from 1 billion in 2020 to 1.4 billion in 2030. The number of persons aged 80 years or older is expected to triple between 2020 and 2050 to reach 426 million (WHO, 2024b).

According to the WHO (2024b), "China has one of the fastest growing ageing populations in the world. The population of people over 60 years old in China is projected to reach 28 percent by 2040, due to longer life expectancy and declining fertility rates." Roughly one in every five persons in China is aged 60 or older, or about 291 million people. If the older population of China in 2023 were a single country, it would be the fourth largest country in the world, outnumbered only by India, the nonelderly population of China, and the United States.

In the early 1970s, China came to grips with the burgeoning size of its population and established a nationwide fertility control program that stressed *later* marriages, *longer* intervals between children, and *fewer* children. However, the large numbers of children born during China's baby boom in the early 1960s caused China's leaders in the middle to late 1970s to become increasingly worried about demographic momentum and the concomitant growth potential of this extraordinarily large cohort. Thus, in 1979, they launched the One-Child Campaign, with a goal of eliminating all births above or equal to three per family and encouraging most families to have no more than one child, especially those living in urban areas. These two policies, along with increasing levels of socioeconomic development, resulted in a drastic decline in China's fertility rate, from levels greater than six children per woman in the early 1950s to less than two in the late 1990s, to around 1.5 in 2015. These policies are discussed in more detail later in Chapter 19.

In the United States, the 2020 census indicated that 55.8 million or 16.8 percent of the population was aged 65 or older. This population of older people grew five times faster than the total population growth between 1920 and 2020. One reason for this rapid growth is the aging of the Baby Boomers, who will all have reached age 65 by 2030. After that time, the growth of the US aging population is expected to slow down (Roser, 2023). The United States has also experienced a fertility reduction, although not as dramatic as China's (please review Chapter 4 for details).

It is important to remember that the relatively large numbers of the older and oldest-old populations of China and the United States were generated during demographic regimes in which fertility and mortality rates declined. A consequence of these transitions, and especially unanticipated in China, are the extremely large older and oldest-old populations projected for the decades of this new century.

A large number of elderly persons in a population is not problematic if there exists at the same time in the population a large number of producers. It is only when the ratio of elderly to producers becomes high that a host of economic, social, and related problems occur. We will compare China with the United States to describe the anticipated changes.

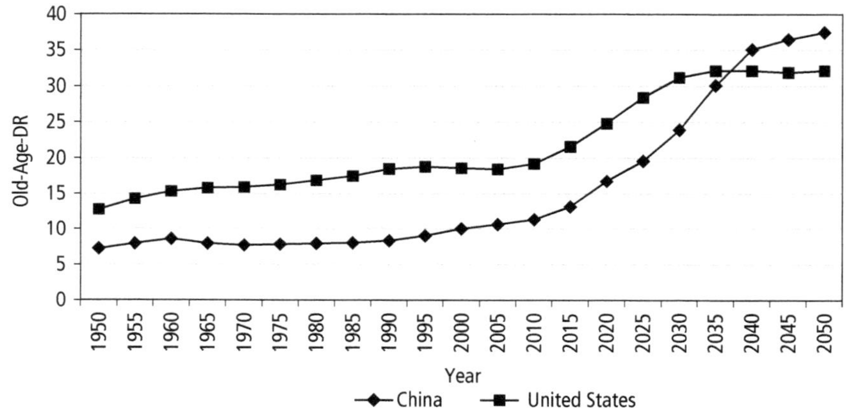

FIGURE 13.8 Old-age dependency ratios, China and the United States, 1950 to 2050
Data source: US Bureau of the Census, International Database.

China's Old-Age-DR increased from 11 aged dependents per 100 producers in 2010 to 19 in 2024 (see Table 13.1). As Figure 13.8 shows, the Old-Age-DR is projected to grow to 37 aged dependents per 100 producers in 2050. The United States also is projected to have grown older; its ADR increased from around 20 in 2010 to 25.6 in 2024, with an expected value of 32 in 2050.

Meanwhile, the YDRs in China and the United States are not projected to change significantly between 2010 and 2050.

The aged-dependency situation changes remarkably when we consider 2050. China is expected to have made the transition to a demographically very old country. The United States also will have become quite old, but not as old as China. The two countries will have become demographically top-heavy. Policymakers in both countries are watching Japan, today the world's oldest population with an Old-Age-DR of 51. The Japanese have had to make many adjustments to this older population. One example is that Japan's largest manufacturer of baby diapers now produces only adult diapers (Oi, 2024). What are the other implications of a very old population, particularly for China?

Traditionally in China, the support of one's elder parents has been the responsibility of the sons. Often the parents lived with the oldest son and either with or nearby the other sons. The eldest son and his brothers were responsible for providing the parents with economic support. The sons would rely on one of their sisters, or sometimes on their wives, to provide their parents with emotional support. These norms have been adjusted or modified in past decades, especially since the founding of the People's Republic in 1949, and particularly among urban residents. Nevertheless, the provision of economic and emotional support to one's parents has seldom been a major burden. As one might expect in a population with modestly high levels of fertility, there have usually been many more producers in the Chinese population than aged dependents. The parental support ratio in China is 5.3. Similar traditional norms have not governed the US family, where the parental support ratio is 3.9, to the same extent as in China.

However, given the very low levels of fertility in contemporary China, as well as a highly unbalanced SRB since the 1980s, the provision of elder care will be a major concern in the years of this new century. For one thing, as we have already noted, there are projected to be many more aged dependents per producer in China in the years ahead. The number of aged dependents per 100 producers in China in 2050 is projected to be 3.4 times larger than China's number in 2010.

When we couple this very high Old-Age-DR for the year 2050 for China with the abnormally high SRBs in China (Poston, Conde, and DeSalvo, 2011), the issue of elder-care provision in the years ahead becomes even more complex. We noted earlier that there have already been born in China 30 to 40 million boys who will be unable to find Chinese brides when they reach the marriageable ages. And if the higher SRBs continue to 2030 and to 2040, an enormously large number of Chinese males will find it difficult if not impossible to meet Chinese females to marry. Many of these single males will have the responsibility for providing both the economic and emotional support for their parents. Since they are not likely to marry, they will have no sons or daughters to take care of them. Since many of them will be only children, they will have no siblings with whom to grow old.

In the United States the Old-Age-DR will produce economic consequences because there will be fewer workers to support Social Security and Medicare, and more beneficiaries of both programs. The need to provide sufficient income support and medical care for an elderly population will be borne by a smaller number of workers, and smaller families mean that many of the elderly will have little or no family support.

Demographically, a high Old-Age-DR population is anomalous, and so most societies find themselves without a well-established portfolio of policy solutions. One solution that is being promoted is healthy aging, which would reduce some of the problems associated with the dependent elderly.

HEALTHY AGING

The cases of China and the United States are especially dramatic, but in fact there will be an increase in the Old-Age-DR in many countries as fertility and mortality rates decline. The United Nations, which has recognized the challenges of aging societies, has declared a Decade of Healthy Ageing (2021–2030). This is a campaign to reduce health inequities and improve the lives of older people. The campaign focuses on four areas: (1) changing how people think, feel and act towards age and ageism; (2) developing communities that foster the abilities of older people; (3) delivering integrated care and primary health services responsive to older people; and (4) providing older people who need it with access to quality long-term care (WHO, 2024b).

As we said at the beginning of this chapter, aging is a biological process. For the aging human, molecular and cellular changes accumulate, making the older person more susceptible to physical and mental decline and to disease. It has long been noted, however, that biological age and chronological age are not necessarily the same. Healthy habits of diet, regular exercise, intellectual stimulation, and socializing have been shown to improve the health and longevity of older persons (Scommegna et al., 2024). Avoiding unhealthy habits, such as smoking and excessive use of alcohol or other substances, also plays a role in healthy aging.

Box 13.1 Blue Zones: Proof of Healthy Aging?

The term Blue Zones was first used in a 2004 academic article to describe villages in Sardinia, Italy, with large numbers of centenarians (Poulain et al., 2004). The term came about because villages were marked on a map with a blue pen. The term was subsequently popularized by *National Geographic* writer Dan Buettner (Buettner, 2012). The consensus Blue Zones were identified in Okinawa Prefecture, Japan; The Nicoya Peninsula, Costa Rica; and Icaria, Greece. European demographers were involved in the early work to verify the ages of the centenarians.

The long lives of residents in these areas were attributed to certain healthy practices, including a diet made up of whole foods with lots of fruits and vegetables. They were also described as being physically active and leading low-stress lifestyles, with close integration into families and the community to provide frequent socializing.

No doubt these are healthy practices and indeed they are the foundation of efforts to foster healthy aging. But is there really something special about the Blue Zones that would not translate to your town or city?

Some research has begun to question the data that led to the identification of the Blue Zones, specifically the large number of persons aged 100 or older (Amigo, 2024). Newman (2024) argues that the large number of centenarians is hard to verify because of inadequate record-keeping that goes back a full century and because of age exaggeration and some age heaping among respondents. In addition, he argued that in some cases pension fraud led to age exaggeration or even to covering up the death of a family member so as to continue the pension payments. Demographers have long been suspicious that the ages of centenarians are exaggerated (Shryock and Siegel, 1980, vol. 1:228).

The healthy aging movement has led to improvements in elder care and support for adult children of elderly parents. And not surprisingly, there has been great interest in which practices most influence health at older ages. The so-called Blue Zones are discussed in Box 13.1. The Blue Zones are communities where a disproportionate number of people are centenarians. This concept has generated some interesting demographic research that addresses the quality of the underlying age data.

COHORTS AND GENERATIONS

The last topic we discuss in this chapter is the **cohort**, defined by demographers as a group of persons who "have in common the fact that they all experienced a given event during a given time interval" (van Imhoff, 2003: 155). Birth cohorts are of special interest to demographers; these are groups of persons born during the same time interval. Birth cohorts are sometimes referred to as generations. The birth cohort of 1983–2001, for example, has been given the name "New Boomers." But the cohort has other names, such as "Millennials," "Generation Y," and the "Boomerang Generation"; this latter name is due to the trend of many members of the 1983–2001 birth cohort living with their parents for longer periods of time than did members of previous cohorts (Farris, 2016).

As we mentioned earlier in Chapter 1, Poston is a member of the birth cohort born between 1929 and 1945 (he was born in 1940). His birth cohort is often referred to as the **Lucky Few** cohort, because there were many fewer of them born compared with the much larger number of persons in the cohort immediately following, those born between 1946 and 1964, the **Baby Boomer** cohort. There were around 44 million "Lucky Few" births versus 76 million Baby Boomer births (Carlson, 2008: 25). The smaller size of the Lucky Few has enabled them to enjoy higher employment rates and a greater variety of social opportunities than members in the preceding or following cohorts.

Sullivan is a Baby Boomer, born in 1949. She experienced the opposite effects because of the large size of her cohort. In Little Rock, Arkansas, where she grew up, some elementary schools had so many children to serve that the school day was divided into a morning session, attended by half the class, and an afternoon session, attended by the other half. Admission to colleges was very competitive, and unemployment was higher for them as young adults. Now the Baby Boomers are swelling the numbers of the elderly. The last Baby Boomers will reach age 65 by 2030.

One of the very best books written about birth cohorts is Elwood Carlson's *The Lucky Few: Between the Greatest Generation and the Baby Boom* (2008). This is one of Poston's favorite demography books, and both authors of this book highly recommend it to you. In Carlson's very engaging book he discusses the seven birth cohorts born between 1871 and 2001. They are: (1) the "New Worlders" (1871–1889); (2) the "Hard-Timers" (1890–1908): (3) the "Good Warriors" EmptyTargetElement (1909–1928); (4) the "Lucky Few" (1929–1945); (5) the "Baby Boomers" (1946–1964); (6) "Generation X" (1965–1982); and (7) the "New Boomers," known also as "Generation Y," and also as the "Millennials" (1983–2001).

Carlson's book stopped with the Millennials. There are three additional birth cohorts, not covered by Carlson; they are "Generation Z" (2002–2012), "Gen Alpha" (2013–2024), and "Gen Beta" (2025–2039).

The New Worlders is Carlson's first birth cohort; it is so named because a large number of its members immigrated to the US, the so-called new world, from other countries. The Hard-Timers, the second cohort, is so named because its members lived during the years that "included a world war, a disastrous economic depression, and then another world war, a string of calamities that all but smothered their adult lives" (Carlson, 2008: 18). The third birth cohort, the Good Warriors, received its name "because this one generation essentially did all the fighting for the United States in the Second World War" (Carlson, 2008: 20). It was also called "the Greatest Generation" for the same reason (Brokaw, 1998). We have already mentioned the fourth birth cohort, the Lucky Few. The fifth, the Baby Boomers, is so named because there was a "boom" in the number of births produced during the years after World War II when the birth rates skyrocketed, reaching a high of 3.7 births per woman. Almost 76 million Baby Boomers were born in the United States between 1946 and 1964, "nearly double the 44 million Lucky Few births" (Carlson, 2008: 25). The sixth cohort, "Generation X," has its name because, according to Carlson (2008: 27), "perplexed marketing specialists who couldn't think of any other name simply took to calling these people Generation X, and that label with all its implications of confusion and alienation has persisted." Finally, the seventh cohort, the New Boomers, more popularly known as the Millennials, began to be born in 1983. Its number of births was large because the parents of most of its members, namely, the Baby Boomers, were very large in number.

The New Boomers generation is also sometimes referred to as "the echo effect," because when the Baby Boomers began to have their babies, there were a lot of them having babies, thus producing the large number of New Boomers born between 1983 and 2001. Sullivan's first baby was born a few years before the echo effect, in 1980, but her second son was a New Boomer born in 1987. Conversely, Poston's first child, a daughter, was born in 1964, the last year of the baby boom. His second child, a son, was born in 1966, the early years of Generation X.

In Figure 13.9 the numbers of persons in each of the seven birth cohorts are graphed according to their size in each of the US decennial censuses of 1900 to 2010 in which they were enumerated. The oldest cohort, the New Worlders, appears first on the left side of the figure, followed by the next cohort, the Hard-Timers, and so forth up to the last and youngest cohort, the New Boomers. Each cohort "changes in size as successive censuses count its members over the course of their lives" (Carlson, 2008: 12). Obviously the New Worlders were enumerated in the 1900 census, but as you can see in Figure 13.9, most of the cohorts were not counted for the first time until later censuses. The number at the top of each cohort's figure is the largest number of persons in that cohort in any one of the census years. Thus, of all the members of the Lucky Few who were born, there were 41.3 million of them enumerated in the 1980 census.

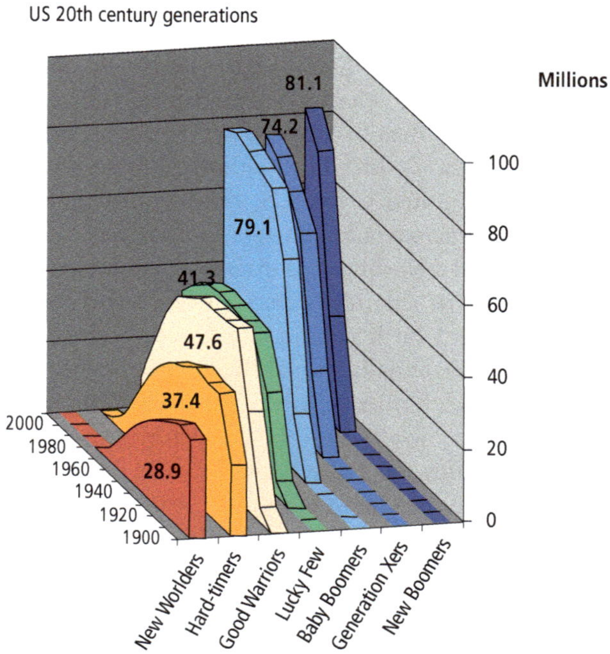

FIGURE 13.9 Seven US birth cohorts by size: census years of 1900 to 2010
Source: Figure prepared by Elwood Carlson.

Let us show you how to read all the information in Figure 13.9. It looks complicated, but it is really quite easy. We will use Poston's birth cohort, the Lucky Few (LF), as the example. For the first three decennial censuses (1900, 1910, and 1920) there were no members of the LF generation counted; the LF birth cohort did not start until 1929. The 1930 census is the first census to count some LF members; the chart shows that there were only around 4.5 million LF members in 1930. In 1940, the year Poston was born, the number in the LF cohort was around 26 million; by 1960 the count of the LF cohort was almost 40 million. The Lucky Few cohort reached its maximum size in the 1980 census, with a count of 41.3 million (the number shown at the top of the LF graph in the figure). The LF members have started to die in past decades, so that by the 2010 census, the number of LF members had dropped to 32 million.

Why do demographers study birth cohorts, that is, **generations**? More broadly, why do generations matter? For instance, what is so different about the Lucky Few generation compared with the New Boomers generation? If we are knowledgeable about the different birth cohorts (generations) and their similarities and differences and the different societal contexts characterizing the time periods when their members were born and grew to adulthood, this will help us better understand ourselves and our older parents and grandparents because we will be cognizant of the ways their lives and our lives unfolded and the differences and similarities in these processes.

Carlson noted in an interview that if "you understand what distinctive opportunities and problems you have faced, you can find common ground with others in your generation" and in other generations (Zuehlke, 2008). Generations have a clear impact on our lives, indeed a life-long impact. The lives of the members of the Lucky Few generation are different in many ways from the lives of the New Boomers generation, and these differences are due largely to the societal contexts that defined the years of our childhood and early adulthood. Certainly, our individual and personal efforts have an important influence on our destiny. But we must not overlook the societal contexts when we were born and during the years we grew to adulthood, such as political events or new technologies. These are forces beyond our control; they play a crucial role in determining our lives and our life chances (Easterlin, 2008: xvii; Pampel and Peters, 1995).

Finally, our discussion of cohorts stops with the New Boomers cohort, also known as the Millennials; the last members of this cohort were born in 2001. But what about the birth cohort following the New Boomers, that is, what about the generation born in 2002 and later? What might characterize them? What might be their name?

Poston asked Elwood Carlson precisely these questions. He said that since generations usually do not start to show their formative influences and distinctive character until they enter adulthood, it is premature to try to label at this time (in the winter of 2024 when we are writing this chapter) the birth cohort that began in 2002. The oldest of them now are likely to be finishing their education or embarking on their work careers. But one thing we can safely say about them is that they will probably be the most "global" generation that we have seen in the United States in more than a century. They will likely have more foreign-born members than was the situation in the early twentieth century in the peak immigration years. Also, Carlson said that they will not be small in size; they will not be a small generation following a larger one, as were the

Lucky Few and Generation X. Declining death rates, stable birth rates, and high immigration rates could well make this cohort as large as, if not larger than, the New Boomers, which is already the largest generation in US history.

Regarding the name of this birth cohort that began in 2002, it could well be based on the diversity of the cohort's backgrounds. Also, its members will likely be increasingly fragmented by more and more personally customized media that will have different content from one member to another. Carlson suggested that maybe the name of "Divergents" will be used for this generation born in 2002 and thereafter (personal communication between Poston and Elwood Carlson, June 2, 2015).

SUMMARY

In this chapter, we first discussed the definition of age and its measurement. We highlighted the issues of age heaping, and we presented the concepts of the age dependency ratio, the youth dependency ratio, and the old-age dependency ratio. We introduced the population pyramid as a useful tool and a shorthand guide to a country's place in the demographic transition. We then introduced the concept of prospective age, as another way to think about and measure age. We next discussed some of the key theoretical issues in demography dealing with age and sex structure, particularly stable population theory. We discussed population aging and how aging societies could encourage healthy aging. We concluded the chapter with a discussion of cohorts and generations.

DISCUSSION QUESTIONS

1. There are fears that artificial intelligence (AI) will eliminate many jobs. Given that American society is aging, could AI be a potential substitute for a shrinking number of middle-aged workers? Do you agree or disagree? Defend your decision. Also, what issues or concerns would this development raise?
2. Many age-graded activities in the United States have minimum ages, such as to vote, to buy alcohol, and to run for Congress. Maximum ages, however, are rare. Many jobs once had mandatory retirement ages, or maximum ages for working at the job, but legislation has made mandatory retirement ages illegal with few exceptions. Should there be maximum ages for some activities, and if so, which activities?

14

The Labor Force

INTRODUCTION

The **labor force** refers to all members of the population above a minimum age who are either working or looking for work. An equivalent term is the economically active population. In most societies, child labor is no longer considered legal; as a result, there is a lower age limit for inclusion in the labor force. There is no upper boundary, for some people continue to work well beyond what might be considered the normal retirement age. Good examples are the two coauthors of this book, both of whom are working well past the customary retirement age of 65.

In this chapter, we will discuss how the labor force is measured, how the labor force interacts with the basic demographic processes of fertility, mortality, and migration, and changes in the composition of the labor force, especially the dramatic increase over time in women workers. There are also important composition variables that are usually measured within the labor force, such as occupation, industry, and class of worker. We will also discuss how the size and composition of the labor force affect the economy (Sullivan, 2019). The study of the labor force is one specialty within demography that closely overlaps economics. Finally, we will discuss the future of work.

MEASURING ECONOMIC ACTIVITY

In preindustrial societies, many families lived and worked in the same place. They farmed for a living and lived on the farm. In a village, they might offer a service such as carpentry or blacksmithing, and their residence and shop were in the same place. With the development of factories, workers more commonly left home to go to work in a factory or other centralized location. The separation of workplace from home has been a strong trend for the past 150 years. The COVID-19 pandemic changed this trend and, aided by technology, many workers returned to the earlier practice of working from home. Even after the pandemic emergency ended, substantial numbers of workers were able to continue to work at home. In 2023, 35 percent of US workers worked at home for at least part of the week (US Bureau of Labor Statistics, 2024c).

Another important difference is that in pre-industrial society there was less need for money per se. Agricultural products could be consumed at home or bartered for other needed goods and services; artisans could similarly barter their work to meet their needs. Industrial society firmly cemented a cash economy, in which workers were paid cash wages, usually by the hour or sometimes by the piece. The cash could then be spent on any goods or services. The expansion of the cash economy accelerated the development of national economic accounts, which were used to measure the extent and volume of economic activity for a given place or time.

In terms of national economic accounts, especially GDP and GNP, the labor force is a measure of the labor supply, that is, the people who produce the goods and services whose value is counted in the Gross Domestic Product (GDP) and the Gross National Product (GNP). GDP refers to goods and services produced in the country, whereas GNP refers to goods and services produced by the residents of a country, regardless of their location in their home country or abroad. For instance, US GNP refers to goods and services produced by Americans working for American companies everywhere, whereas US GDP refers to goods and services produced in the United States. The difference can be described this way: "if a German-owned company has a factory in the United States, the output of this factory would be included in US GDP, but in German GNP" (Callen, 2022: 14).

The GDP and GNP measure the market (cash) value of goods and services produced by the workers. Jaffe (1959) explains that all members of a population consume goods and services, but only the members of the labor force produce those goods and services.

Because the labor force is so closely related to sustenance organization – production and consumption of goods and services – its size, composition, and changes are of significant interest to demographers, sociologists, economists, and policymakers. Particularly in modern economies, where work has become separated into times and places distinct from other life activities, the labor force is a useful subdivision of the adult population for further study (Sullivan, 2019).

There are still many goods and services that are produced but not counted in the GDP because they are not sold. Consider a chef who prepares a dish of chicken for her family; her service and the final product would not be part of the GDP because no money changed hands. If she cooked the same dish in her restaurant and served it to her paying customers, then it would be counted. Much of the childcare, nursing care, housekeeping, gardening, and cooking are services provided to members of a family or household. Although volunteers and homemakers provide valuable goods and services, their output is not counted in the GDP – and therefore they are not in the labor force – because they are not paid.

One measure sometimes used in demographic analyses of the labor force is the **total dependency rate**, which you learned about in Chapter 13. The dependency rate is useful because it requires only an age distribution to calculate, so it can be produced when more sophisticated data are unavailable. There are, however, limitations to this measure for economic activity. The calculation assumes that no one younger than 15 nor older than 65 is working, and that everyone in the working ages is at work. A more refined measure has been developed, but understanding it requires learning how the labor force is defined and measured.

Unemployment and the Labor Force Concept

Because unemployment rises and falls in business cycles, the numbers and characteristics of unemployed persons in the working ages are of great policy interest. The COVID-19 pandemic was associated with a sharp business downturn during the lockdowns. During this rise in unemployment, African American males suffered much higher unemployment rates than White males (Sullivan, 2020c; see also Couch and Fairlie, 2010). This result could not be determined based solely on the dependency ratio.

Administrative records are also insufficient for measuring unemployment, even though there is an unemployment compensation program in the United States and in many other countries. Unemployment compensation records undercount unemployed workers who have exhausted their benefits or who never qualified for benefits (US Bureau of Labor Statistics, 2015). In addition, potential workers looking for their first jobs are ineligible for unemployment compensation, and some firms and industries are not covered by the program.

Payroll data, which could provide counts of the employed, are also inadequate to measure unemployment because of the potential double-count of moonlighters (people who work more than one job), and the exclusion of people in casual employment. In addition, there are adults who attend school, retire early, are ill, or for other reasons are not counted either as employed or unemployed.

The development of the labor force concept was precipitated by the need of policymakers to measure unemployment (Hauser, 1949, 1964; Sullivan and Panuska, 2020). During the Great Depression of the 1930s, US demographers and statisticians began a series of studies attempting to quantify unemployment (Dunn et al., 2018; Hodson and Sullivan, 2012; National Commission, 1979). To minimize the politicization of the measure, it was important to develop a method that was objective and could be repeated in succeeding time periods. The method that emerged relies on answers to a series of nested questions, which are asked concerning every working-age member of a household; in the United States, the sample survey that is used is the Current Population Survey (CPS), which we discussed in Chapter 3. Because labor force data vary with the business cycle, it is best to have repeated labor force measures for a population, so a regular survey is preferable to a census.

The CPS questions identify behaviors that occurred within a specified time period, to reduce issues of faulty recall. Based on the survey responses, every adult over the minimum working age is assigned to one of three statuses: employed, unemployed, or not in the labor force (NILF), with the priority in that order. The minimum working age in the United States is 16, although in many other countries it is 15 or sometimes even 14. Unlike the dependency ratio, the labor force measure has no maximum age.

The first question asked in the CPS is whether the individual was at work for at least one hour for pay or profit during the week preceding the survey. If the answer is no, the next question asks whether the person worked at least fifteen hours unpaid in a family-owned enterprise, such as a farm or a retail store. If this answer is again no, the person is asked whether they had a job but were not at work; an example of a reason would be that the person was on vacation or was temporarily ill. A yes to any of these questions results in a classification of the person as employed (US Bureau of Labor Statistics, 2015, 2024a).

Box 14.1 Behaviors that Would Classify a Nonworking Adult as Unemployed: the Distinction between Active and Passive Job Search

Active job search methods are defined as those that have the potential to result in a job offer without any further action on the part of the job seeker. Examples of active job search methods include:

- contacting an employer directly about a job
- having a job interview
- submitting a resume or application to an employer or to a job website
- using a public or private employment agency, job service, placement firm, or university employment center
- contacting a job recruiter or headhunter
- seeking assistance from friends, relatives, or via social networks; for example, asking friends and family for job leads or indicating one's job seeking status on social media
- placing or answering a job advertisement
- checking union or professional registers

Passive job search methods are methods that do *not* constitute an active job search. Passive methods are those that could not result in a job offer unless additional steps were taken. Examples include simply looking at job postings without taking further action or taking a training course.

Only people reporting at least one active search method are counted as unemployed. Those who report only passive methods or no methods at all are classified as NILF.

Source: US Bureau of Labor Statistics, 2024a. "Concepts and Definitions – CPS." www.bls.gov/cps/definitions.htm

Those who are not employed are then asked if they were available for work and actively looking for work during the past four weeks, waiting for the result of a job search, or waiting to report to a job within the next month. Anyone answering yes to any of these questions is classified as unemployed. (See Box 14.1 to understand what is meant by "actively looking for work.") Anyone who is not classified as employed or unemployed is considered NILF. The principal reasons for not being in the labor force are retirement, disability, school attendance, and home responsibilities (Hipple 2015).

The employed and the unemployed together are termed the **labor force**. The **unemployment rate** is the ratio of the number of unemployed to the number in the labor force, that is, the employed plus the unemployed, times 100.

$$\textbf{Unemployment rate} = \frac{\textbf{Number Unemployed}}{\textbf{Number in Labor Force}} \times 100 \tag{14.1}$$

The unemployment rate is then interpreted as the percentage of the labor force that is actively seeking employment, and some analysts call this number the most significant statistic issued by the federal government. The United States unemployment rate for the previous month is released in the morning of the first Friday of every month, and it is carefully watched as an economic indicator (Öner, 2010).

The **labor force participation rate** (LFPR) is the ratio of the labor force, that is, the sum of the employed and the unemployed, divided by the noninstitutionalized civilian

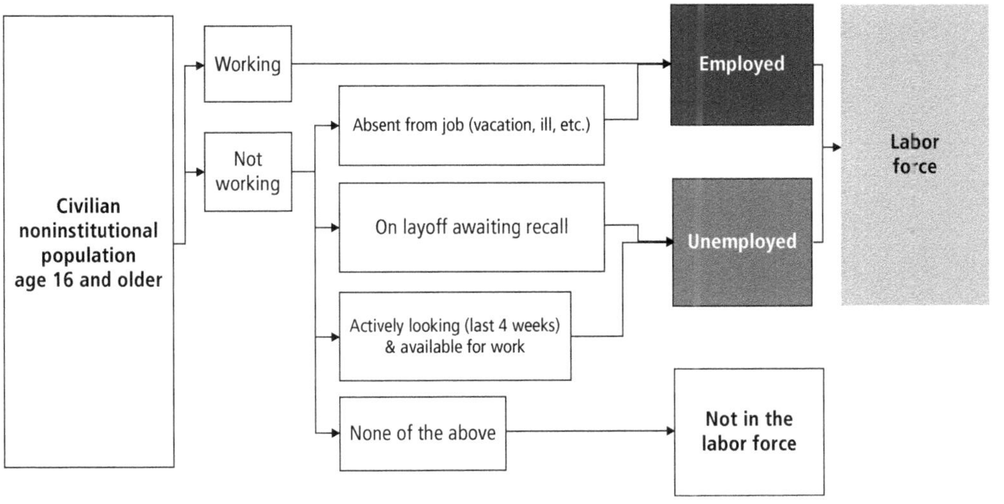

FIGURE 14.1 The relationship of the labor force to its constituent parts
Source: US Bureau of Labor Statistics, 2024a.

population older than the minimum working age, times 100. The denominator is calculated with whatever the legal minimum age is in the country, and with no upper age limit. The denominator omits anyone who is full-time in the military or who is institutionalized (such as in a prison).

$$\text{LFPR} = \frac{\textbf{Number of People in Labor Force}}{\textbf{Civilian Noninstitutionalized Population aged 16+}} \times 100 \qquad (14.2)$$

Figure 14.1 shows the relationships among the parts of the labor force.

The labor force participation rate can be calculated for specific population groups. The female labor force participation rate is particularly interesting because fertility and childcare compete with paid work for adult women's time. Labor force participation rates can also be calculated for specific age groups, for racial/ethnic groups, and for levels of educational attainment (Hipple, 2016). With a sufficient sample size, labor force participation rates and unemployment rates can be calculated for geographic areas such as states, counties, and cities. Table 14.1 shows labor force participation rates for a variety of countries as of 2022, when the COVID-19 pandemic had largely subsided.

Labor force participation rates vary for a variety of reasons. On the demand side, there may be relatively few jobs available. On the supply side, there may be cultural or social restrictions on paid work by women. Where higher education is common, students may be completing their education and not available to work. There may be strong preferences for retirement by a certain age, with the result that most older people leave the labor force.

It is common for unemployment rates to vary between urban and rural areas, and to vary among states and regions depending upon local economies. These rates also vary by demographic group. In the United States, men's unemployment rates are higher than women's rates, and African American unemployment rates are typically twice as high as

TABLE 14.1 *Labor force participation rates (% of total population aged 15–64), various countries, 2022*

Country	Value
Afghanistan	38.5
Australia	79.5
China	75.9
Egypt	46.5
Germany	79.9
India	55.4
Mexico	65.4
Nigeria	59.1
Peru	75.6
United States	72.7
High-income countries	74.7
Low-income countries	65.8

Source: World Bank Group. https://data.worldbank.org/indicator/SL.TLF.ACTI.ZS

those for Whites, with Asian and Hispanic unemployment rates intermediate between the African American and White unemployment rates (US Bureau of Labor Statistics, 2025b, 2025c). Teenagers have persistently high unemployment rates, usually at least double the rates for adults.

A measure that is sometimes used instead of the unemployment rate is the **employment–population ratio**, which is calculated as

$$\textbf{Employment–population ratio} = \frac{\textbf{Number of Employed People}}{\textbf{Civilian Noninstitutional Population aged 16+}} \times 100 \tag{14.3}$$

In December 2024, the employment–population ratio in the United States was 60.0, down from 60.1 one year earlier (US Bureau of Labor Statistics, 2025c). Both the employment–population ratio and the unemployment rate can rise at the same time, because it is possible for there to be both more employed people and more unemployed people when the labor force grows. The employment–population ratio is sometimes seen as a more positive measure because it emphasizes employment rather than unemployment.

Limitations of Labor Force Measures

Each of the above measures is subject to limitations. One limitation is sensitivity to age structure. Relatively young populations typically have lower labor force participation rates because of full-time school attendance and childbearing. Teenagers have higher unemployment rates than older workers because they are trying to establish themselves as workers. In a population that is aging because of declining fertility, measures such as the employment–population ratio will change because of age structure changes independently of the current economic conditions. Aaronson and colleagues (2014) found that the decline in US labor force participation rates after the Great Recession that began in 2008 reflected structural changes, such as age structure, and not merely cyclical changes in labor demand.

The definition of employment is criticized both for being too generous and for being too restrictive. The fact that a person can be counted as employed with as little as one hour of paid employment may seem overly generous, especially if that same person spends the rest of the week actively looking for work. The definition of employed covers a wide range of employment arrangements and contexts (Kalleberg, 2000, 2011).

On the other hand, the employment measure can be criticized as too restrictive for omitting the productive work of volunteers, homemakers, and caregivers whose work would be counted if they received a wage (Bener'ia, 1999). Inmates of institutions are excluded by definition from the labor force, even if they receive a wage. In the United States, the reported labor force data are nearly always for the civilian labor force. By definition the military are omitted from labor force statistics despite receiving pay.

Similarly, the unemployment rate is criticized for omitting people who are no longer actively seeking work because they believe that no work is available. These people are officially NILF, but they are classified as marginally attached to the labor force if they sought work in the last twelve months and are available for work. A subset of this group, called **discouraged workers**, report believing that no work is available for them (Buss and Redburn, 1988; Hipple, 2015). In December 2024, there were 480,000 discouraged workers in the United States (US Bureau of Labor Statistics, 2025c). They form a sort of labor reserve that could perhaps be re-engaged in the labor force if work became available.

THE LABOR FORCE AND THE DEMOGRAPHIC PROCESSES

In Chapters 4 through 7, you learned about the basic demographic processes of fertility, mortality, and migration. These processes affect the labor force; but in addition, the state of the economy – especially the demand for labor – affects which members of the population will seek employment. For example, when the demand for highly educated workers rises, then members of the population who have pursued more education will have an edge in becoming employed.

Fertility and Labor Force Participation

One obvious way that fertility affects the labor force is through the age structure. Fertility provides the newcomers to the labor force, with a time lag of 14–22 years depending upon the country's minimum working age and the child's length of education. When fertility rates are declining, the entering cohorts of new workers will be smaller and they might find expanded work opportunities; see our discussion of the Lucky Few in Chapter 13. On the other hand, high fertility rates lead to more new workers competing for jobs, as happened to the baby boomers when they reached working age.

The issue that has most preoccupied demographers, however, has been the effect that working has on a woman's fertility. Why some women, and not others, pursue paid work in the labor force is an important issue that is closely related to fertility (Brewster and Rindfuss, 2000). Women's family responsibilities as wives, mothers, and daughters may affect their labor force participation even if they are well prepared for work. The family–work relationship varies by generation, ethnicity, and immigrant status (Stier and Tienda, 1992), and by religion (Hayford and Morgan, 2008).

Some jobs facilitate or impede women's labor force participation. Teaching has been viewed as especially compatible with having children because the teacher and the child will have similar hours to be at home and to be at school. Women workers are particularly likely to engage in part-time work (Presser and Gornick, 2005). The availability of childcare, or the ability of husbands and wives to work different shifts so that they can care for their children themselves, are additional examples of job arrangements that help mothers participate in the labor force (Fallon et al., 2017; Ma, 2016; Matysiak and Vignoli, 2008; Morrissey, 2017; Presser and Gornick, 2005; Rindfuss et al., 2003). England and colleagues (2016) have argued that women with relatively high paying jobs pay a heavier price for fertility than other women in terms of their incomes because seniority and experience are rewarded in their careers.

Economic considerations play a key role when households decide who should work. If one member of a couple is unemployed, the other might go to work just to keep a paycheck and health insurance in place for the family. Both spouses may choose to be employed for a variety of reasons, including securing enough funds for the family's needs.

Mortality and the Labor Force

High levels of mortality may lead to changes in the labor force, but these changes may well be temporary. For mortality to have a significant effect, not only do mortality rates have to rise but deaths need to occur among the working-age adults. The Black Death in England killed so many people of working age that agricultural production dropped, and the workers' wages rose by one-third, at least temporarily, because of limited supply (Jedwab, Johnson, and Koyama, 2022). By contrast, COVID-19 tended to cause the greatest mortality among older, often retired, people.

If a labor shortage arises, employers may substitute technology to compensate for the missing labor. If this substitution is successful, then the jobs lost may never return. If the labor shortage is limited to a single area, however, then the labor supply may be increased through hiring more women, teenagers, or the elderly, or by increasing immigration (see the next section of this chapter).

In most societies today the working life of adults ends in retirement rather than death, and so the principal issues for them will be having earned enough during their working years, or having sufficient pension funds, to fund their retirement years. As an economy grows, there is often a more generous provision of disability payments and retirement income. These alternative income supports encourage older workers to retire from the labor force and affect the timing of retirement. Elsayed and colleagues (2018) show that workers would prefer to work one year longer if offered a gradual retirement program.

In an aging society, the solvency of retirement income programs, such as Social Security, may become an issue because there are few younger workers to maintain funding.

Migration and the Labor Force

Historically, migration has been the way that excess labor demand or supply has been remedied. Young adults often migrate in search of work. Where jobs are abundant, employers may advertise deliberately in areas with high unemployment to attract new workers. If there are insufficient native-born workers, then employers may seek to hire immigrants.

Most of the high-income countries have programs to hire highly skilled workers, for whom there may be an insufficient domestic supply. In the United States, skilled immigrants in high demand have included healthcare professionals, engineers, and technology specialists. In countries with aging populations, which describes most of the high-income countries, there is also a growing need for people to care for the elderly.

Another labor need in many countries is for jobs characterized by the "three D's" – dangerous, dirty, and demeaning. These jobs typically do not require specific skills, but the work may be hard and physical. Examples include crop harvesting, unskilled construction, and some factory work. These workers may be hired as guest workers under programs that provide them with temporary permission to stay in the host country. In other cases, they may be working illegally.

In the high-fertility countries, especially those that are also low-income countries, there is a ready supply of would-be immigrants who would accept even hard physical work for the ability to earn a higher wage and perhaps remit some of their pay to their families in the home countries.

Public immigration policies, which are in flux around the world, attempt to determine which workers, and in what numbers, may enter a country. These policies are discussed in more detail in Chapter 19.

CHANGES IN THE COMPOSITION OF THE LABOR FORCE

Age structure plays an important role in the composition of the labor force. As seen in previous chapters (see Figure 13.7, for example), there is a characteristic age structure of the population at different stages of the demographic transition. In stage 2, the population pyramid is a triangle, with the working-age population supporting many children and only a few elderly people.

In stage 3, the shape of the pyramid begins to change because fertility is dropping. One notable change is a bulge of young adults with fewer children and still not too many older adults. This stage provides what demographers call the "**demographic dividend**," which is the temporary increase in young workers whose employment would encourage economic growth and perhaps lead to greater societal savings (Madsen, 2018). The term demographic dividend refers to the potential for economic growth from the relative increase of workers in the labor force due to declining fertility (Kinugasa, 2018). The declining fertility also potentially increases the labor force because women with fewer children have more time for paid work. If productive work can be provided for the new workers, society could experience a boost in productivity and economic growth. The demographic dividend is time-limited because if fertility remains low, the number of potential new workers available every year will stabilize or decrease. The demographic dividend is temporary because the later stages of the demographic transition will have smaller birth cohorts reaching working age.

The demographic dividend offers a great opportunity to a society, but only if there are enough jobs available for young workers. With enough jobs, there can be improvement in the level of living for families and for society at large. Without enough jobs, young people may be unemployed, or they may turn to illegal or marginal activities, never establishing a strong work record and usually only scraping by in terms of finances.

The **economic dependency ratio** (EDR) links the age structure with the labor force measure. The economic dependency ratio is calculated as:

$$\text{EDR} = \frac{(\text{Persons aged } 0-16 + \text{Unemployed persons} + \text{NILF})}{\text{Employed Persons}} \times 100 \qquad (14.4)$$

The numerator is the number of children below the minimum age for working, plus people of working age looking for work, plus anyone of working age who is not in the labor force (such as students, homemakers, and the retired). The minimum working age varies in different countries. The denominator is the number of employed persons in the labor force. Then the result is multiplied by 100. In the United States the military and anyone institutionalized are omitted from the calculation.

In 2021, the economic dependency ratio for the United States was estimated to be 110.2 (Henesy, 2021). This can be interpreted to mean that every 100 workers supported 110 dependents, where dependent means the numbers of children under age 16, plus the unemployed, plus the NILF. By contrast, in the same year the total age dependency ratio (ADR) was 64 (note that ADR uses children aged 0–18 and not 0–16 as the labor force calculation uses) (Henesy, 2021). The ADR shows considerably fewer dependents, because the ADR implicitly assumes that everyone in the working ages is in fact working. This is an assumption that is corrected by using labor force data.

For 2024, the economic dependency ratio (EDR) for the United States was estimated to be 104.7 (calculated by the authors; data from US Bureau of Labor Statistics, 2025c and census age data). This EDR can be interpreted as meaning 100 workers are supporting fewer than 105 dependents. This is apparently an improvement from 2021, but the comparison with 2021 does not explain the reason without further investigation.

The EDR fluctuates both with age structure and the business cycle. To give some examples, the ratio can rise because of a recession that leaves more people unemployed; because of increased fertility rates; because of an aging population that leads to more retirements; or because of a lower labor force participation rate. This ratio can decrease because of an economic expansion that leads to lower unemployment, increased labor force participation, or a declining fertility rate. Between 2021 and 2024, for example, the civilian labor force grew by about 7.5 million persons, and the number employed grew by about 5.7 million persons (calculated by the authors from US Bureau of Labor Statistics data). This also marked a time period in which the US economy was recovering from COVID-19. During these four years, the change in age structure was minimal. Thus, labor force dynamics appear to have played a larger role than age structure in the lower EDR.

Both the calculation and interpretation of the EDR are more involved than the ADR, and thus the EDR is not used as frequently.

INTERNAL COMPOSITION OF THE LABOR FORCE

Occupation, industry, and class of worker are three variables that are often used to analyze the labor force by concentrating on the type of work that is being done.

Occupation refers to the type of work that a worker is doing. Some occupations, such as secretary or administrative assistant, can be found in many different types of workplaces. Other occupations, such as farmer, are found at one type of workplace, namely, farms.

The terms "white-collar" and "blue-collar" reflect an older effort to classify occupations. White-collar jobs were office and other "clean" jobs (hence white shirts), while blue-collar referred to jobs requiring more hands-on or physical labor. This distinction once implied a sharp distinction in income, because there was a limited supply of workers with sufficient education to work in offices, and because factories and farms hired workers with lower skill levels. This income differential is much less likely now, with some office and sales workers earning little more than minimum wage, and skilled trades workers (such as plumbers or electricians) earning much higher incomes. Moreover, technology has transformed many factory jobs and relocated some of them to "clean" rooms. Table 14.2 shows the median annual wage for full-time workers in a variety of occupations.

While the white-collar/blue-collar distinction is mostly obsolete, some classification system is necessary for analysts. In a complex economy such as that of the United States, there are thousands of occupations. The US Bureau of Labor Statistics uses a detailed occupational list that can be found here: www.bls.gov/oes/current/oes_stru.htm

Industry refers to the type of service or goods that the worker produces. New industries are born when new products, new services, or new technologies are developed. Within a single industry, there are usually a wide variety of occupations, from the top managers and production staff to the janitorial staff. Again, because the United States has a complex economy, it has a large number of industries. The US Census Bureau and the US Bureau of Labor Statistics use a classification system called the North American Industry Classification System (NAICS), which has 1,057 industries coded (Knoll et al., 2024).

So many codes are difficult to use for many purposes. As a more workable approach, industries can be loosely grouped into three general **industry sectors.** The first sector, agricultural and extractive, includes farming, fishing, mining, and lumbering. These industries produce goods taken from the earth and we believe that these were the dominant industries nearly everywhere in the earliest stages of the demographic transition. With urbanization (and generally lower fertility rates) the transformative sector became more important; this sector includes manufacturing and construction.

TABLE 14.2 *Mean annual wage for selected occupations, 2023*

Occupation	Mean annual wage (US$)
Cook, fast food	29,260
Childcare workers	32,070
Security guards	40,440
Bill and account collectors	46,020
Home appliance repairers	50,650
Firefighters	60,390
Chefs and head cooks	62,640
Dieticians and nutritionists	71,280
Editors	85,110
Power plant operators	91,880
Life scientists	100,630
Engineers	111,890
Nurse practitioners	128,490
Air traffic controllers	136,790
Dentists	200,870

Source: Adapted from US Bureau of Labor Statistics, 2024b. Mean annual wages have been adjusted to reflect full-time full-year work. This table shows only a few occupations as it is intended to show a range of wage levels. The source table lists 1,105 occupations.

The third sector, services, has become relatively more common in the later stages of the demographic transition. With increases in productivity in the first and second sectors, new workers have often been absorbed into the service sector. Examples of services include professional services (such as legal and medical services), distributional services (such as transportation and retail), and business services (such as accounting, advertising, and marketing). As these sectors have developed, the share of the labor force in each one has changed from predominantly agricultural, to predominantly transformative, to predominantly services. Most developed countries today are considered service societies, although they still produce agricultural and manufactured products (Singlemann, 1978).

Table 14.3 shows the estimated sector composition for a variety of countries. Notice the relative size of the extractive sector among these countries; in most countries this sector is composed principally of agricultural workers. Notice that in Nigeria, one of the low-income countries, 70 percent of the labor force works is in this sector, compared with less than 2 percent in Belgium.

The extractive sector refers to agriculture but may also include fishing, forestry, and mining. The transformative sector includes manufacturing and construction. The services sector includes professional services, business services, transportation, retail and wholesale, and personal services. Totals may not add to 100 percent because of rounding or exclusions.

Class of worker refers to the ownership of the workplace. Most workers are *wage and salary workers*. In the private sector, an individual or corporate owner has hired them and provides their compensation. In the public sector, some agency of government is the employer, but the employees are still considered wage and salary workers. Entrepreneurs are considered *self-employed* because they own the workplace, which

TABLE 14.3 *Sector composition of the labor force, various countries (estimates and data for dates between 2011 and 2017)*

Country	Extractive sector (%)	Transformative sector (%)	Services sector (%)
Afghanistan	44.3	18.1	37.6
Belgium	1.3	18.6	80.1
Brazil	9.4	32.1	58.5
China	27.7	28.8	43.5
India	47	22	31
Indonesia	32	21	47
Mexico	13.4	24.1	61.9
Nigeria	70	10	20[a]
Russia	9.4	27.6	63

[a] Estimate from 1999.
Source: Adapted from CIA, *The World Factbook*, 2025.

could be a farm, retail store, or online enterprise. Independent contractors are also self-employed, although there may be a faint line between being an independent contractor and being an employee. Uber and Lyft drivers, for example, usually own their automobiles, which are their workplace, but they rely for communication technology and fee collection on the company's software. The final, small class of worker is the *unpaid family worker*, who must work at least fifteen hours a week to qualify as employed. These workers are working in an enterprise owned by the family; instead of receiving wages, they share in the profits of the enterprise through the provision of food, clothing, and shelter to the family. Many farm families, for example, have unpaid family workers.

HOW THE LABOR FORCE AFFECTS THE ECONOMY

The labor force concept assumes a market-based economy because of the criterion of working at least one hour for pay or profit. There are certainly goods and services produced at home for home consumption, but increasingly services that were previously performed at home, such as cooking, childcare, cleaning, and eldercare have been purchased by households.

In this process, many women became labor force participants. The work of Charles (1992) suggests that the incorporation of more women into the labor force may intensify **occupational segregation** because many of the new women workers are still doing traditionally women's work, only now for pay. Occupational segregation refers to the implicit or explicit preference for workers with specific demographic characteristics for specific jobs.

Because the labor force assumes a cash economy, it might be less satisfactory as a measure in countries with lower levels of economic development. The self-employed, especially those in subsistence agriculture, have not always been adequately accounted for in labor force measurement. Self-employment has sometimes been seen as a face-saving alternative to what is referred to as disguised unemployment, for it could represent a stopgap effort at any sort of productive activity, however marginal or informal. For this reason, the labor force has not always adequately measured the productive population in low-income countries and may overcount workers.

On the other hand, the labor force concept may also undercount workers. In a setting where many people are employed by other members of their own household, or where they may receive their pay as shares of produce or other in-kind provisions, the identification of unpaid family workers may be inefficient, and actual labor force participants may thus be undercounted.

The assumption that economic development always leads to a formal separation of the workplace from the home is now undergoing substantial challenge. With internet technology, employment contracts have changed, with a reconvergence of home with work for at least some workers. Telecommuting and compressed work schedules have made market-based work possible even from workers' homes, with far less need for a formal office. In the so-called gig economy, workers may have sporadic contact with several employers and function as independent contractors. Because of the definition of employment, these workers are counted as employed and in the labor force, but their level of job security might be lower than those with long-term relationships with a single employer.

Size of the Labor Force

The size of the labor force, especially relative to the entire population, is an important indicator. For example, Bauer (1990) examined labor force growth and labor costs in Asian countries. A relatively large labor force indicates a large number of productive people to support the dependent population. A relatively small labor force may imply high levels of dependency, either because the age structure is relatively young or old, or because many people in the usual working ages are unable or unwilling to work.

The size of the labor force changes because of the entrance of new workers, the retirement of older workers, and the movement in and out of the labor force by students, seasonal workers, temporary workers, or parents reentering the labor force because their children have reached school age. Two labor forces may be of similar size, but if one is made up of full-time workers and the other has many part-time or seasonal workers, then the economic product of the two will be quite different.

The size of the labor force may also change over the seasons, depending upon the mix of industries in a locality. To take one example, in a seaside resort the size of the labor force may grow during the high tourist season, when local businesses hire additional lifeguards, food servers, hotel workers, and tour guides. Six months later, the local labor force of a city may grow because retail establishments, restaurants, and delivery services take on extra employees for the holiday rush period.

There are two ways to deal with this seasonal variation in measuring the labor force. One way is called seasonal adjustment, which is a statistical adjustment to account for seasonal changes. The seasonal adjustment to the unemployment rate at the beginning of summer, for example, accounts for students who are looking for summer jobs. The other way is to use annual averages.

The labor force participation rate is the most commonly used measure for comparative labor force studies. The labor force participation rate can be calculated in a time series, and because it can be calculated for geographic subregions, it is often used to evaluate local or regional labor markets (Besamusca et al., 2015; Hipple, 2016; Odland, 2001).

Composition of the Labor Force

Labor force participation varies by different demographic groups. We discussed above how age structure affects the labor force. Other important demographic variables are sex, race or ethnicity, level of education, marital status, and migration status. In the United States, for example, the labor force participation rate of Black women has historically exceeded that for White women, but the unemployment rate for Blacks has typically been twice that of Whites. Labor force participation has been shown to be relatively high for the well educated (Hill, 1995), and for married men. For migrants, especially men, labor force participation is usually high (Borjas and Tienda, 1993), but for women migrants higher participation appears to occur over a longer time frame (Rebhum, 2008).

Knowing that there is a difference in labor force participation is not by itself explanatory. Local labor market conditions help determine labor demand, and the demand in one locality may be very different from another locality in the same state or parish.

Lower participation by women, for example, may be a function of their family responsibilities, education levels, previous work experience, and social norms (Costagliola, 2021). Lower participation between two racial and ethnic groups could be explained by differences in health status, level of education, or labor market discrimination. A more sophisticated understanding of labor force behavior requires a statistical model that uses multiple variables such as sex, age, education, and migration status.

THE FUTURE OF WORK

Demographers use current labor force data to project the future labor supply, including the composition of potential workers. Understanding more about the labor force requires additional information concerning labor demand and how it affects employment numbers and the desired characteristics and skills of workers. We can expect that technology and improved productivity will affect the demand for labor. But there are a variety of institutional and policy issues, such as immigration and pension policies, that are difficult to forecast and that are likely to play a key role in shaping the future labor force.

SUMMARY

In this chapter we have introduced the labor force. We began by explaining how the labor force is related to the Gross Domestic Product (GDP) and the Gross National Product (GNP). Next, we introduced the concepts and measurements of the labor force and unemployment and examined the employment–population ratio. We also discussed the limitations of these measurements.

Then we showed how the labor force is related to the basic demographic processes of fertility, mortality, and migration. Fertility is of particular interest because of its effect on women's labor force participation. Migration and immigration policies also affect the numbers and skill levels of migrant workers available to take jobs in a host country or locality. Mortality has some effect, although the effect tends to be of brief duration.

Then we turned to demographic transition theory and how the age structure at different stages of the transition affects the labor force. We introduced the term demographic dividend, which refers to a temporary boost in the number of available workers when fertility declines. The economic dependency ratio was introduced and discussed. We also introduced the terms occupation, industry, and class of workers, which are terms used to describe the internal composition of the labor force. Finally, we addressed the effects of the labor force on the economy, including the future of work.

Most students reading this book are preparing for a life as workers. If that includes you, the information in the chapter can help you become an informed consumer of some demographic indicators that can influence how and when you launch your job search.

DISCUSSION QUESTIONS

1. We note that discouraged workers are not counted as unemployed workers and therefore are not counted in the labor force. In your opinion, should discouraged workers be considered members of the labor force? Why or why not?
2. What uses can you think of for the detailed classifications of industries, such as NAICS, that are available?

15

Race and Ethnic Relations

INTRODUCTION

This chapter deals with the demography of race and ethnicity. We are mainly concerned here with demographic issues pertaining to race and ethnicity, their implications and consequences. We first discuss why demographers are interested in race and ethnicity. We review briefly the history of categorizing people according to race and ethnicity and then show how in the United States the statistical concepts of race and ethnicity evolved over time, from the 1790 census to the 2020 census. We examine current patterns of race and ethnicity in the United States and show how these groups differ in terms of the basic demographic processes. In particular we discuss differential fertility and differential mortality. These topics are significant because the United States is approaching a time when there will no longer be any numerical majority racial or ethnic group.

WHY DO DEMOGRAPHERS STUDY RACE AND ETHNICITY?

Very early in Chapter 1 of this book, we noted that demography is concerned with "how populations are composed according to age, sex, race, marital status, and other characteristics." In earlier chapters we discussed marital status, age, sex, and labor force status. In this chapter we cover yet another feature of population composition, race and ethnicity. So why are demographers so interested in the race and ethnicity of human populations? What is it about race and ethnicity that is so important for demography?

Do you remember in Chapter 1 our discussion of the basic demographic equation? It will be worth our time to spend a few paragraphs here reviewing it. The basic demographic equation states that the change in the size of a population that occurs between two points in time, say, between times t and $t + 1$, is due to the changes in the levels of fertility, mortality and migration that occur in the interval between times t and $t + 1$. Take another look at Equation (1.1) in Chapter 1.

So, suppose we wish to analyze population change in the United States in the period between April 1, 2020, and July 1, 2024. The US population grew by 10.6 million, from 329.5 million residents in 2020 to 340.1 million residents in 2024. To figure out how this change came about, we need to examine the difference of 10.6 million and determine how it occurred via the three demographic processes of fertility, mortality, and migration. In doing so, we would find out that there were 18.9 million babies added to the population, 16.2 million decedents were subtracted from the population, and a net gain of a little less than 8 million international migrants added to the population, to equal the overall population change of 10.6 million.

Race and ethnicity enter into consideration because the different race and ethnic groups do not contribute in the same way to the three demographic processes. Hispanics have higher birth rates and lower death rates than non-Hispanic Whites, Blacks, and Native Americans. And Hispanics and Asians have higher international migration rates than either non-Hispanic Whites, Blacks, or Native Americans.

So, for instance, if we wanted to figure out how and why there were 18.9 million births in the United States between 2020 and 2024, we would need to account for the proportional representation of the race and ethnic groups in the population and for their different birth rates. As Saenz and Morales (2019: 164) have written, "race and ethnicity are important dimensions in understanding the demography of the United States, for racial and ethnic groups vary tremendously with respect to population composition [and] population processes." See their detailed and quite excellent discussion of the differential impacts of race and ethnic groups on the three demographic processes (Saenz and Morales, 2019: 172–178).

BRIEF HISTORY OF RACE AND ETHNIC CATEGORIES

The categories of race and ethnicity are often used interchangeably by demographers, but they are really two different terms. "Race is mainly associated with physical characteristics, and ethnicity is largely related to behavioral or cultural attributes" (Saenz and Morales, 2019: 165). The questionnaire instruments of the US Census and the American Community Survey (ACS) (see Chapter 3) contain two questions dealing with race and ethnicity (see Figure 3.1 in Chapter 3, questions 8 and 9). One question asks whether the person is of Hispanic, Latino, or Spanish origin. The second question asks about the person's race. Respondents are required to answer both questions on the census and ACS forms. In the 2020 census, demographers used the answers to these two questions to develop population counts for the five major race/ethnic groups.

The demographer Rogelio Saenz has recommended a procedure to classify people into the various race/ethnic categories using the answers to the above two questions, an approach which many demographers now follow (Saenz, 2010). According to Saenz,

> Because Latinos [i.e., Hispanics] can be of any race, in doing comparative analysis, one should first place all persons who identify as Latino into a specific group and subsequently place all others [non-Latinos] into specific categories based on their own race. This assures that the groups are mutually exclusive and that, for example, the White category does not include Latinos who identify themselves racially as White. (personal communication between Poston and Rogelio Saenz, July 8, 2015)

The large residual group, then, is composed of non-Hispanics; they are separated by their answers to the race question into the four non-Hispanic (NH) race groups of NH-Whites, NH-Blacks, NH-Asians, and NH-Native Americans (or American Indians).

Hispanics may be further subdivided into Cubans, Mexicans, Puerto Ricans, and Other Hispanics. Similarly, Asians may be further subdivided into several Asian groups, e.g., Chinese, Korean, Japanese, Filipino, Vietnamese, Asian Indians (to distinguish them from American Indians), and Native Hawaiians (see the listing in Figure 3.1 for all the groups).

In the 2030 census these two questions might be merged into a single question about identity, but that decision is not final, so we will continue to use the 2020 census procedures in our discussion.

But how did these race/ethnic categories come about?

Carl Linnaeus (1707–1778) (also known as Carl von Linne) was a Swedish scientist and is recognized as the father of **taxonomy** (the branch of science concerned with classification). He published the first edition of his *Systema Naturae* (*System of Nature*) in 1735; it was only twelve pages long. By the time it reached its tenth edition in 1758, it classified over 4,000 species of animals and over 7,000 species of plants. According to Prewitt (2013: 15), the book "offered the first authoritative, systematic classification of human variation ... it favored skin color as the distinguishing trait ... [the colors were] reddish, sallow, black and white," and they represented, according to Linnaeus, the categories of Americanus [i.e., American Indian], Asiaticus, Africanus, and Europeaeus. Although neither a psychologist nor an anthropologist, Linnaeus claimed that temperament and behavior and character varied significantly among these color groupings. Racial essentialism, i.e., "the idea that there are characteristics that any member of a given race must possess" became an accepted tenet with Linnaeus. Henceforth, "race, more or less as we know it today, entered the scientific canon as a fact of nature" (Prewitt, 2013: 15; Charmantier, 2020).

Other natural scientists followed Linnaeus in the eighteenth and nineteenth centuries proposing other "rudimentary human classification scheme(s) that conflated color and culture" (Prewitt, 2013: 16). Foremost among them was Johann Blumenbach (1752–1840), a German physician and naturalist, who published in 1775 his *De Generis Humani Varietate Nativa* (*On the Natural Varieties of Mankind*) in which he "offered the first explanation for the presumed superiority of the White race ... [attributing it] to the influence of climate, diet, and living habits" (Prewitt, 2013: 16). In the second edition of the book published in 1776, he added a fifth category to the four categories of Linnaeus, and he ranked the five in order of their superiority, namely, "Caucasian, Mongolian, Malay, American Indian and Negro (Ethiopian). This taxonomy bequeathed to Western science and culture the all-too-familiar color-denominated racial pentagon: white, yellow, brown, red and black" (Prewitt, 2013: 17). These are the same five race/ethnic group categories that have been used by the US federal government to cross-classify virtually all the micro-data produced by the government, from birth and death and marriage and divorce records, to educational and income data, and residence, and military records; moreover these categories have been part and parcel of federal and state laws, policies, and regulations.

(Blumenbach's five categories did not include, specifically, one for Latinos/Hispanics. His "brown" race referred to "Malays," namely, persons from Malaysia, Indonesia, the Philippines, Brunei, and certain other Southeast Asian areas, plus Polynesians and other Pacific Islanders. Hollinger [2006] and Hochschild and Powell [2008] use Blumenbach's "brown" category to refer to Latinos/Hispanics.)

THE CATEGORIES OF LINNAEUS AND BLUMENBACH ARE EMBEDDED IN US RACIAL CATEGORIES

The racial categories first set out in 1735 and in 1775/1776 by Linnaeus and by Blumenbach still existed in the US government's census enumeration procedures through the 2020 census. Race has been part of every census since the first census conducted in 1790. Recall in Chapter 3 that the 1790 census had items on its questionnaire differentiating the population according to whether they were free "white" males and free "white" females, other free persons who were not White, and persons who were neither free nor White, namely enslaved persons. "Various racial distinctions and taxonomies came and went over the next twenty-two censuses, but never was there a census without a racial classification" (Prewitt, 2013: 20). Waters has further stated that the racial and ethnic categories used by the US federal government are "subject to a great deal of flux and change, both intergenerationally, over the life course and situationally" (Waters, 2002: 25).

Here are some examples of race questions in the various censuses. In the 1830 census there was a new question about White persons who were foreign-born and not yet naturalized. In the 1850 census the enumerators were instructed to identify free persons with different designations depending on their color: The "color" column on the census questionnaire was left blank if the person was White, was scored "M" if the person was Mulatto, and "B" if the person was Black. In the 1870 census two more race codes were added to the above question, "C" if the person was Chinese, and "I" if the person was American Indian. In the 1890 census, some of the different East Asian groups were distinguished, for example, Japanese. The 1890 census was also the first census to actually use the term "race" on the questionnaire. Among the racial categories the census enumerators could write in were "White," "Black," "**Mulatto**," "**Quadroon**," "**Octoroon**," "Chinese," "Japanese," or "Indian" depending on the perceived race of the respondent. The term "Mulatto" was taken out of the 1900 census but reappeared in the 1910 census (US Bureau of the Census, 2014).

In the 1930 census, the term "Mulatto" was removed again. Enumerators were required to report the race of mixed-race persons as "Negro," no matter the fraction of the racial categories. This was an application of the so-called "one-drop rule," whereby a mixed-race person was to be recorded as "Black" irrespective of how small the Black lineage might be. Also, in this census for the first and only time, "Mexican" was added as a racial category. In the 1940 census, the race category of "Mexican" was removed and Mexican origin persons were assigned the race of "White." In the 1950 census the term "color" was removed from the race question, but it was added back in the 1960 census (US Bureau of the Census, 2014).

The 1960 Census was notable because many individuals being enumerated could self-identify their race. Prior to this time, a census enumerator had marked the person's race by visual inspection – a process that no doubt led to errors. By 1970, self-identification was the uniform process for racial identification.

For a sample of the respondents in the 1970 census, a question pertaining to Hispanic/Latino origin was added for the first time. Specifically, on the 5 percent sample questionnaire of the 1970 census, this question was added:

Is this person's origin or descent:

- *Mexican*
- *Puerto Rican*
- *Cuban*
- *Central or South American*
- *Other Spanish*
- *None of these*

Since then, a similar question has remained on all decennial censuses and American Community Surveys. The 1970 census was also the first census to be conducted as a mail-out, mail-back enumeration system. Census enumerators were used only to visit households that had not returned their questionnaires (US Bureau of the Census, 2014).

In the 1980 census more options were added to the race question, including Vietnamese, Guamanian, and Samoan. And the Hispanic/Latino origin question (above) was moved to the 100 percent census questionnaire (i.e., the questionnaire that everyone in the population answers), where it has remained to this day. The race question has always been included on the 100 percent questionnaire. In the 1990 census, persons who wrote in a multirace response to the "other" category on the race question were assigned the race of the first part of their response; thus, someone who wrote in White-Asian was coded as "White," whereas someone who wrote in Asian-White, was coded as "Asian."

Census 2000 was the first census to allow persons to check more than one category on the race question (see question #9 in Figure 3.1, in Chapter 3). The race question and the Hispanic/Latino ethnicity question on the 2010 census were pretty much the same as they were on the 1990 and 2000 censuses; the major difference was that in 2000 persons had the option of checking more than one response on the race question (US Bureau of the Census, 2014). In the 2010 census, 2.9 percent of the US population selected "two or more races," an increase from the 2.4 percent choosing two or more races in the 2000 census (Jones and Bullock, 2012). Figure 15.1 shows the percentages of racial groups as enumerated in the censuses of 2010 and 2020.

The Black percentage remained about the same. The Asian percentage increased slightly. The percentage of people checking two or more races increased substantially. While the reasons for the increase are not entirely understood, an increase in intergroup marriages and a decline in the stigma previously attached to biracial children may be part of the reason.

Another reason might be census tabulation procedures. In the 2020 census, respondents were asked for the first time not only to indicate their race but also to write in their national origins. Both Poston and Sullivan, for example, wrote in "Irish." Depending on the answers given, some respondents were reclassified as "two or more races." This change might have affected the rather drastic decline in the proportion of the population coded as White from 72.4 percent of the population in 2010 to 61.1 percent in 2020; meanwhile the two or more races category increased from 2.9 percent to 10.2 percent (Sullivan and Cork, 2023: 273).

The addition of the write-in options led to some additional people being classified as Hispanic. Suppose, for example, that someone failed to answer the Hispanic question and then checked "White" on the race question and wrote in "Puerto Rican." Then the

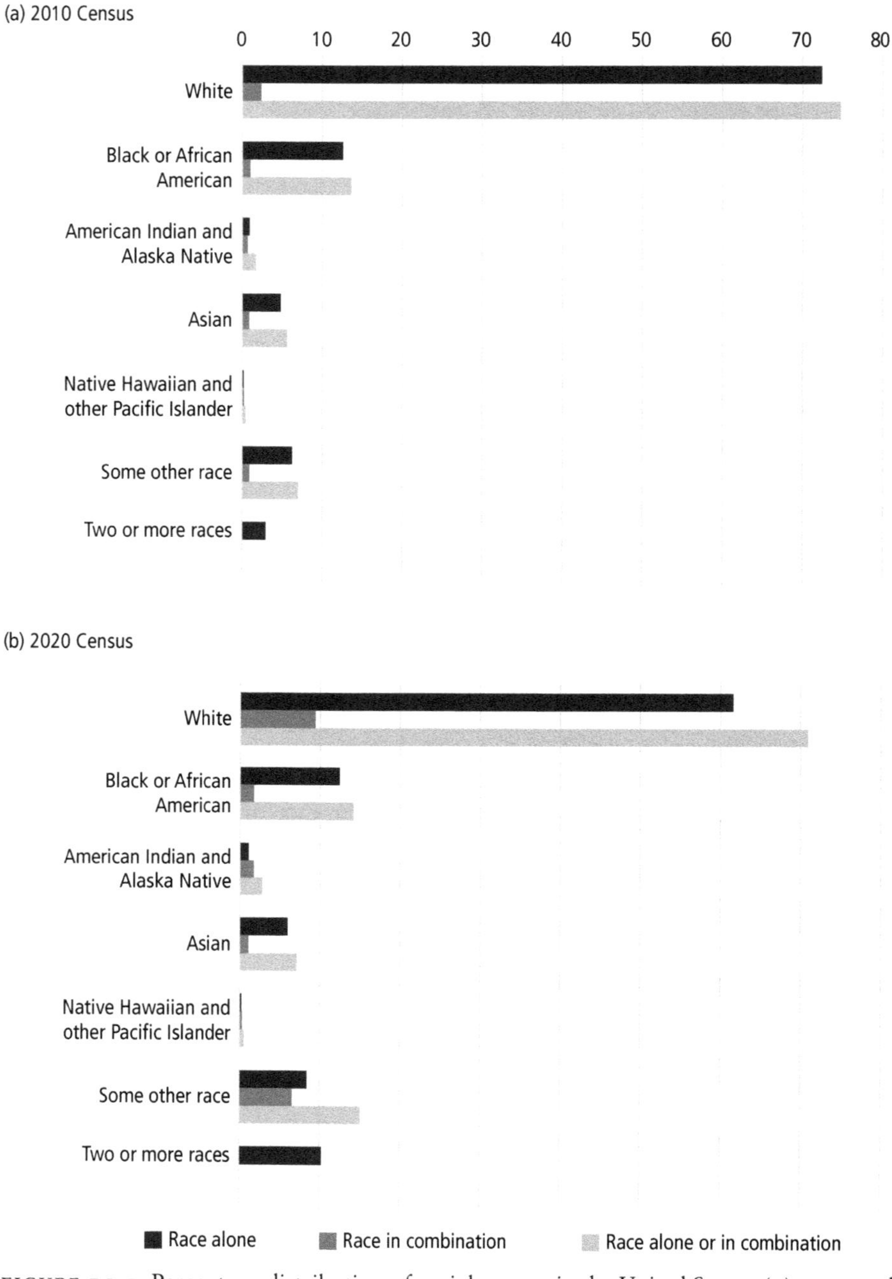

FIGURE 15.1 Percentage distribution of racial groups in the United States, (a) 2010 and (b) 2020
Source: US Census Data.

census procedure was to code that person as Hispanic. Figure 15.2 provides a flow-chart to explain this process.

A smaller but notable increase, from 6.2 percent in 2010 to 8.4 percent in 2020, was the population indicating they were "some other race." Some Hispanic people checked

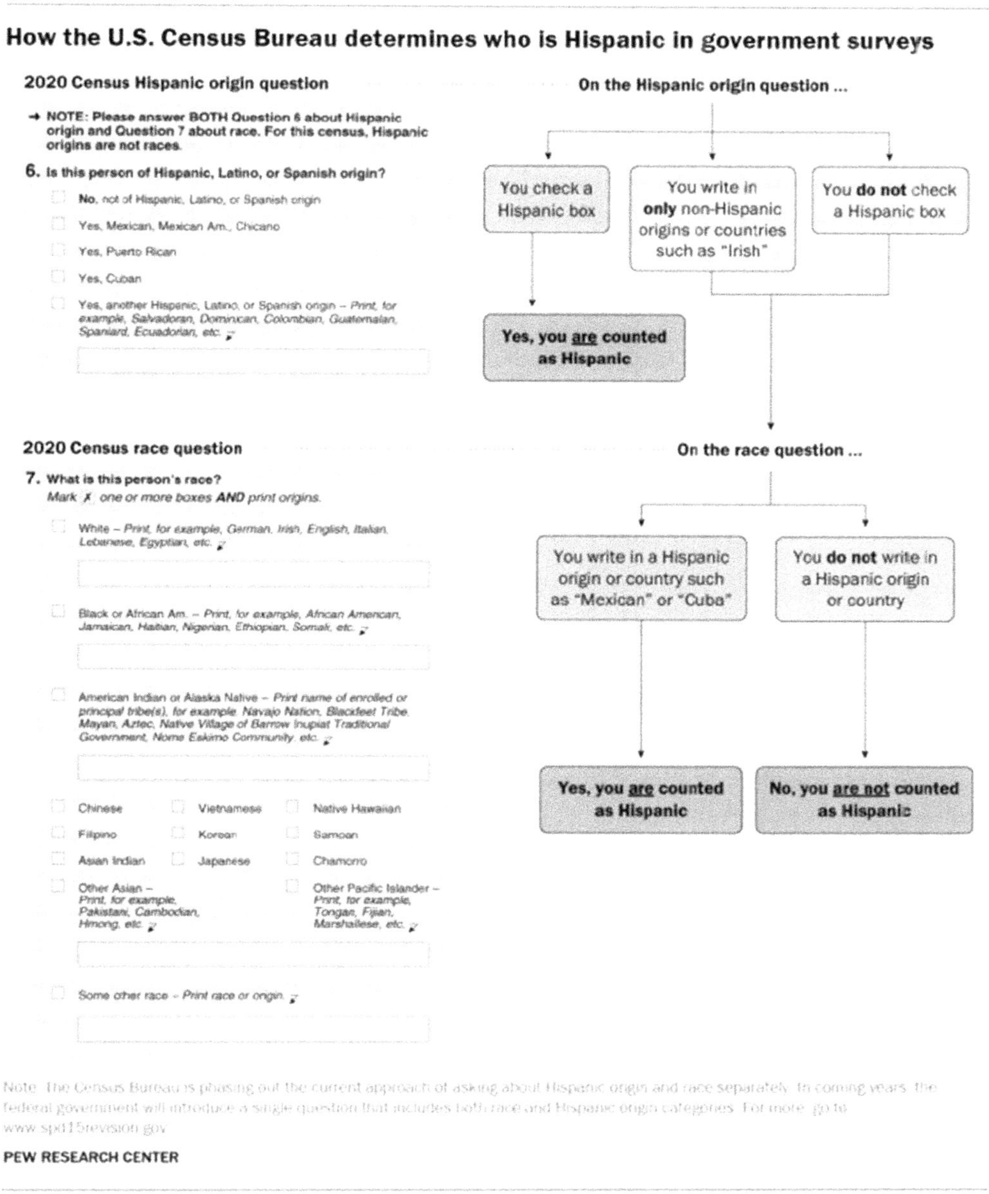

FIGURE 15.2 Who is Hispanic? How the US Government classifies persons of Hispanic origin
Source: Lopez, Krogstad, and Passel, 2024.

this race option. Others enumerated in the census did not see an identification that seemed to fit their identity. There were petitions to the government, for example, to add a "Middle Eastern and North African" racial category. The argument was that persons whose origins were, for example, in Jordan, Egypt, or Morocco might be counted as "White" but were treated in everyday life as if they were non-White. This change remains under discussion.

We have reviewed some of the key changes pertaining to the census classification of race and ethnicity starting in the 1790 census up to and including the 2020 census. The principal race/ethnicity categories used today by the Census Bureau (see Figure 15.1) are pretty much the same categories developed by Blumenbach in 1775 and 1776, namely, the five we specified above: Hispanics, and the four non-Hispanic (NH) race groups of NH-Whites, NH-Blacks, NH-Asians, and NH-Native Americans (or American Indians). These represent the same all-familiar color groupings of brown, white, black, yellow, and red.

In Kenneth Prewitt's (2013: 8) words,

> Today, nearly two and a half centuries [after a German doctor divided the human species into five races], these are the same five races into which the US Census divides the American population, making America the only country in the world firmly wedded to an eighteenth-century racial taxonomy ... [in which] there were not just different races but superior and inferior races.

There have been a lot of changes in the statistical categorization of race and ethnicity in the United States since 1790. But despite all the many changes, we are still using today pretty much the same racial categories that were first developed in 1776.

PATTERNS OF RACE AND ETHNICITY IN THE UNITED STATES

According to the 2020 census, 61.6 percent of the American population identified themselves as White alone. This is a sharp change from the first census in 1790 when Whites comprised 81 percent of the total. The White percentage reached 90 percent in 1920 and remained at or above 90 percent until 1950. By 2000 the White percentage had dropped to 75 percent, and to 72 percent by 2010.

But here we run into a classification issue with the statistical data. Up until 1970 when a question was added to the census pertaining to Hispanic/Latino origin (see our discussion above), persons of Hispanic origin were usually counted as White. Therefore, the White percentages almost always included persons of Hispanic origin who identified themselves as White. It was not until 1980, and certainly by 1990, that demographers began to distinguish among the various race groups (White, Black, Asian, and Indian) by whether they were Hispanic or non-Hispanic. This is especially important with regard to Whites because the White race group, by itself, includes the greatest number of Hispanics.

The percentages of the White race group in the US population for the years 1990, 2000, 2010, and 2020 are, respectively, 80 percent, 75 percent, 72 percent, and 61.6 percent. The percentages of the White race group who are not Hispanic, namely, the non-Hispanic White group, for 1990, 2000, and 2010 are, respectively, 76 percent, 69 percent, and 64 percent. Thus, irrespective of how Whites are counted, their representation in the US population has been declining since 1950.

Figure 15.3 shows the rapid growth of the Hispanic population over time. Recall that Hispanics may be of any race. In 1980 there were about 14.8 million Hispanics, and they were only 7 percent of the population. By 2021 there were over 62 million Hispanics, or approximately 19 percent of the total US population (Moslimani and Noe-Bustamente, 2023). Between 2010 and 2020, the increase in the numbers of

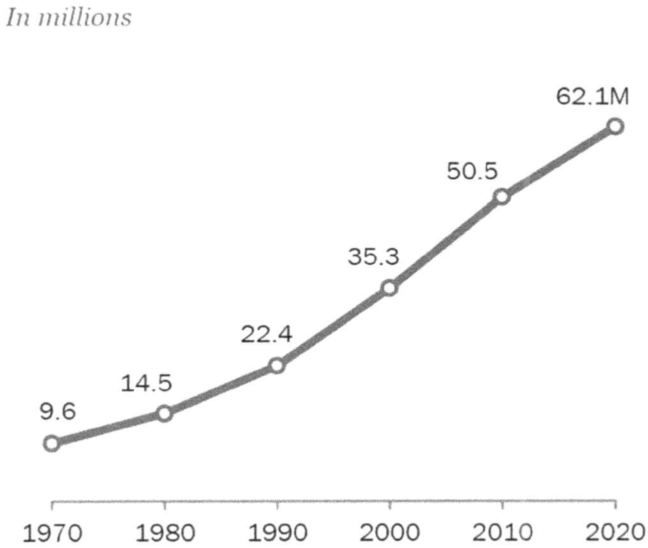

FIGURE 15.3 Growth of the Hispanic population between 1970 and 2020
Source: Funk and Lopez, 2022.

Hispanics accounted for about half of US population growth. People who self-report Hispanic origin are the largest minority group in the United States.

We can conclude from Figures 15.1 and 15.3 that two important population trends in the United States between 2010 and 2020 are a declining White-only population and an increasing Hispanic population.

If we speak of the minority population as a whole, then Blacks, Asians, Native Americans, and Alaska Natives are also part of the minority population. The various minority groups, however, have different residential patterns. Map 15.1 shows the most prevalent minority group in each part of the country. Notice that although the NH-White population has been declining, Whites are still the prevalent group in much of the land mass of the continental United States. Blacks are the most prevalent group in parts of the Mississippi River delta, the southern states, and the Washington, DC, area. Hispanics are most prevalent along the southwestern border states and Puerto Rico, and Native Americans or Alaska Natives are most prevalent in areas of the Great Plains, the Four Corners area, and most of Alaska. Asians, although residing in many parts of the United States, are the most prevalent group only in a bit of coastal California.

In 1980, only Hawaii and the District of Columbia had more than 50 percent of its population minority; they were the so-called **majority–minority populations**, that is, over 50 percent of their populations were comprised of minorities. By 2000, California and New Mexico had joined Hawaii as majority–minority states. In 2000, Texas was 48 percent minority but became a majority–minority state in 2004 (Humes, Jones, and Ramirez, 2011: 18–19). Figure 15.4 shows for the United States as a whole the projection of the relative proportions of minority populations to NH-Whites. This figure shows that a slim majority of children were members of minority groups by 2020, and by 2044 a slim majority of all Americans is projected to be minority group

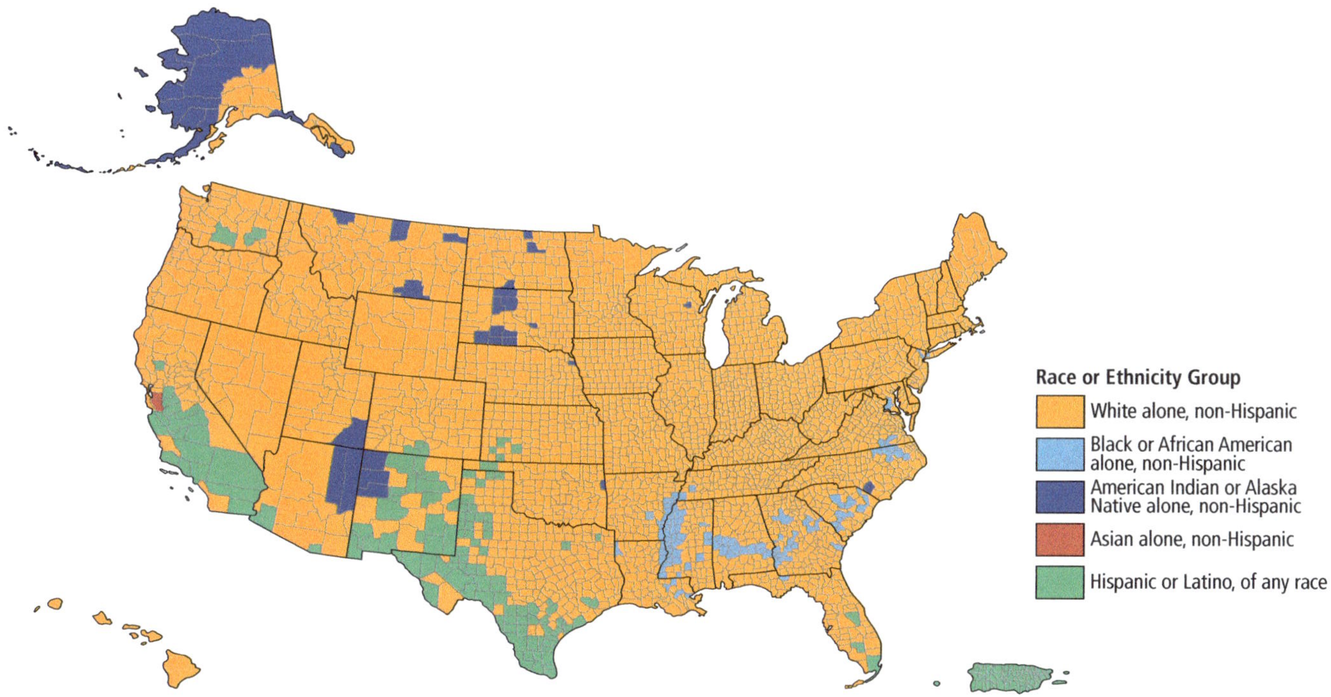

MAP 15.1 Classification of each US county in 2020 according to its most prevalent race or ethnicity group
Source: US Census Bureau, 2020 Redistricting Data.

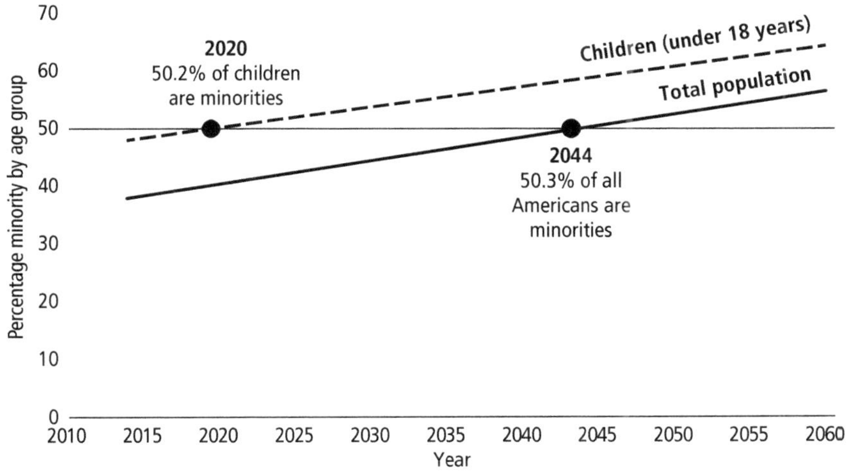

FIGURE 15.4 Projections of the non-Hispanic White population from 2014 to 2060, including both total population and population under 18 years of age
Source: Colby and Ortman, 2015.

members. Projections, of course, make strong assumptions about current demographic conditions continuing indefinitely.

We have discussed the Hispanic population in many places throughout this chapter. Some people prefer the terms Latino or Latinx. The term "Hispanic" is objectionable to some people as a government-invented blanket term that identifies many people by their former colonial power (i.e., Spain). This term obscures the fact that these people's origins arose in a variety of places – Mexico, Central America, South America, and Spain. Because we rely on government statistics, we continue to use the term "Hispanic," but we will specify in greater detail the ethnic composition of this population group. We will answer next the question: who are the Hispanics?

In 2020 there were 62.1 million Hispanics in the United States, or about 19 percent of the population. Based on 2019 ACS data, the largest group among them was Mexican origin, who accounted for 37.2 percent of Hispanics. Puerto Ricans were second, with about 6 million people counted. By the way, Puerto Ricans are not immigrants; even if they migrate to the US continent from the island, Puerto Ricans are born as US citizens. Then Cubans, Salvadorans, Dominicans, Guatemalans, Colombians, and Hondurans have at least one million people each. The fastest growing immigrant group among them were Venezuelans (Funk and Lopez, 2022).

The major changes in racial and ethnic composition in the United States and some other countries are the result directly and indirectly of immigration. Immigration has a direct effect because the immigrants are added to the population; it has an indirect effect because the immigrants have children in the host country, and the children are then added to the population (Lichter, 2013). This indirect effect occurs because of their children who are born after immigration. Although immigrant populations tend to converge toward the fertility rates of other Americans after a time in the country, they may initially have higher birth rates. The issues of **differential fertility** and **differential mortality** are therefore important in understanding the growth or decline of minority populations. These issues are addressed in the next section.

DIFFERENTIALS IN THE BASIC DEMOGRAPHIC PROCESSES

As we have already mentioned, aside from immigration rates, the relative numbers of the various racial and ethnic groups depend upon both their birth rates and their death rates. Differential fertility refers to differences among groups – in this case, racial and ethnic groups. (We note that there is also differential fertility based on age distribution, income, education, religion, and other characteristics, and racial groups differ in terms of these other characteristics.)

Differential Fertility

Recall from Chapter 3 that we defined the general fertility rate (GFR) as the number of births to women in the childbearing ages. We will use the GFR per 1,000 women to compare the fertility rates of various racial ethnic groups. Using the average of years 2021–2023, these rates were as follows (March of Dimes, 2024):

Total	55.6
Hispanics (may be any race)	64.4
Black	55.2
White	52.5
American Indian / Alaska Native	49.3
Asian /Pacific Islander	48.1

The highest GFR, 64.4, is for Hispanic women, but Hispanic fertility has been dropping over time. Alvira-Hammond (2019) has noted the following: "The general fertility rate of US women has declined substantially... [S]ome of the largest declines have been among Hispanic women, whose fertility rate fell by 31 percent from 2006 to 2017, compared to 5 percent for White women and 11 percent for Black women." In general, native-born Hispanic women have lower fertility than foreign-born Hispanic women (Parrado and Flippen, 2012).

Frejka (2011) noted that during the baby boom, fertility among Black women was higher (total fertility rate [TFR] greater than 4) than fertility among White women. Since the mid-1960s, however, Black fertility has rapidly declined to TFRs closer to 2 – in other words, very similar to the TFR of White women. During 2024, 5.8 percent of Black women gave birth (Martinez and Passel, 2025). There are remaining Black–White differentials in terms of fertility timing, and the Black population is generally younger than the White population, but in terms of contribution to population growth, the current differential is small.

The American Indian / Alaska Native population (AIAN) has lower fertility than the overall female population and also lower than the White population. It does appear, however, that AIAN women may begin their childbearing at younger ages than the other groups (Office of Child Support Services, 2023). Younger childbearing does not necessarily lead to higher fertility, however, if the childbearing also stops at an earlier age.

The lowest fertility level is among Asian and Pacific Islander women, although it is only a little lower than for the AIAN women. Espenshade and Ye (1994) have argued that one reason for Chinese American women's lower fertility is that they try hard to find a place in the American labor market, and because of the resulting delay in childbearing, they have lower fertility. A related argument is that delaying their first birth to older ages makes infertility issues more likely for Asian American women. Other possibilities being explored are genetic susceptibilities to infertility, cultural stigma in seeking treatment, and availability of treatment (Vu, Nguyen, and Alur-Gupta, 2021).

As this brief overview suggests, differential fertility persists despite a long-term convergence toward lower fertility in line with the American majority.

Differential Mortality

Despite the improvements in life expectancy since the nineteenth century, a sizable racial difference remains. The gap has narrowed, but there are still differences among the races. Whites had a much higher life expectancy at birth than Blacks at the start of the twentieth century. In 1900, a White female infant could expect to live 51 years, compared with 35 years for a Black female infant. A White male infant had a life expectancy in 1900 of 48 years, compared with 33 years for a newborn Black male. So, in 1900 the White advantage for female infants was 16 years, and for male infants it was 15 years.

By 2010, the life expectancy advantage for White females over Black females had fallen to 3 years, and the advantage for White males over Black males had dropped to almost 5 years. These gains are impressive, but the racial differences are still present. The racial differential in mortality in the United States has been studied and analyzed by medical and social scientists for many decades, but the differences have remained.

A major reason for the racial differential is the socioeconomic consequences of lower income. Possible factors in childhood are low birth weight and low levels of childhood nutrition. Factors operating in midlife include the lack of access to health insurance provided by one's employer, "the strain of physically demanding work, and exposure to a broad range of toxins, both behavioral (e.g., smoking) and environmental (e.g., workplace exposures)" (Shrestha, 2006: 17). In addition, one cannot discount the unfortunate experiences of racial discrimination, which not only have serious and adverse psychological and physiological effects but also limit the potential quantity and quality of healthcare available (Shrestha, 2006).

Of particular interest in any analysis of majority–minority group differences in mortality is the very consistent finding that Hispanics in the United States, particularly Mexican Americans, have a life expectancy similar to, and sometimes higher than, Anglos (i.e., non-Hispanic Whites) (Rogers, Hummer, Nam, and Peters, 1996; Rogers, Hummer, and Nam, 2000). This is a demographic situation exactly the opposite of that of Blacks. Mexican Americans and African Americans "are more likely to be unemployed, poor, and without a high school degree and...have [also] experienced a long history of discrimination" (Rogers, Hummer, and Nam, 2000: 55; see also Bean and Tienda, 1987). But Mexican Americans compared with Anglos are not at all disadvantaged with regard to life expectancy and other measures of longevity ; in fact, they are advantaged, but African Americans are disadvantaged.

Several hypotheses have been offered to account for this so-called Hispanic **epidemiological paradox** (Markides and Coreil, 1986), also referred to as the Latino mortality paradox (Abraido-Lanza et al., 1999) and the **Hispanic paradox** (Palloni and Morenoff, 2001), that is, the empirical finding that Hispanics, especially those of Mexican origin, have death rates of about the same magnitude as, and sometimes lower than, majority Whites (Markides and Eschbach, 2011; Riosmena et al., 2015). The hypotheses may be subsumed into three groups, namely, data artifacts, migration effects, and cultural effects. Under data artifacts are such reasons as the possible under-reporting of Hispanic origin identification on death certificates (Palloni and Arias, 2004; Rosenberg et al., 1999) and the misstatement of age, perhaps overstatement, at the older ages (Rosenwaike and Preston, 1983). There are two principal migration effects: First is the **healthy migrant effect**, which states that the longevity advantage is due to the facts that many Mexican Americans in the United States were born elsewhere (Rogers, Hummer, and Nam, 2000: 56), and that migration is known to be selective of persons in better physical and mental health (Palloni and Morenoff, 2001; Rosenwaike, 1991.) (See our discussion of migration selectivity in Chapter 7.) Second is the **return migrant effect**, also known as the **salmon bias**, which states that Mexican Americans in poor physical health often return to Mexico at old ages to live out the rest of their lives and, thus, their deaths are not counted in the US statistics (Abraido-Lanza et al., 1999; Palloni and Arias, 2004). Third are various cultural effects including the better dietary practices of Latinos compared with other US residents and the stronger family obligations and relationships among Latinos compared with non-Latinos (LeClere, Rogers, and Peters, 1997; Markides and Coreil, 1986; Scribner, 1996; Scribner and Dwyer, 1989).

Figure 15.5 shows age-adjusted death rates per 100,000 population by race, sex, and Hispanic origin, for 2020 and 2021. Recall that these were years of the COVID-19 pandemic, so we would expect these figures to be higher than normal. Even so, we can see the Hispanic paradox for both males and females. The death rate for Hispanic males is much lower than for Black males and for White males. Similarly, the death rate for Hispanic females is lower than the rate for either Black or White females.

Some research has found limited support for the salmon bias and the healthy migrant effects (e.g., Palloni and Arias, 2004). But other analyses (e.g., Turra and Ilo, 2008) find little support for these effects, particularly those involving the salmon bias.

The paradox has also been studied with cause of death data. Hispanics, especially those of Mexican origin, have lower death rates compared to NH- Whites for nine of the fifteen leading causes of death (Dominguez et al., 2015). For instance, the prevalence of smoking is lower among Hispanics compared with NH-Whites, which could contribute to lower Hispanic mortality.

And the paradox has also been analyzed by focusing on the presence of sexually transmitted infections (Obregon, 2015) and the prevalence of criminal behavior (Martinez, 2010, 2014; Martinez and Valenzuela, 2006 Romero, 2014). The presence of sexually transmitted infections (STIs) should be associated with socioeconomic status (SES); that is, the higher the SES, the less the presence of STIs. But Obregon's (2015) analysis demonstrated that Mexican-origin birth-giving women have lower odds of having STIs than NH-Blacks.

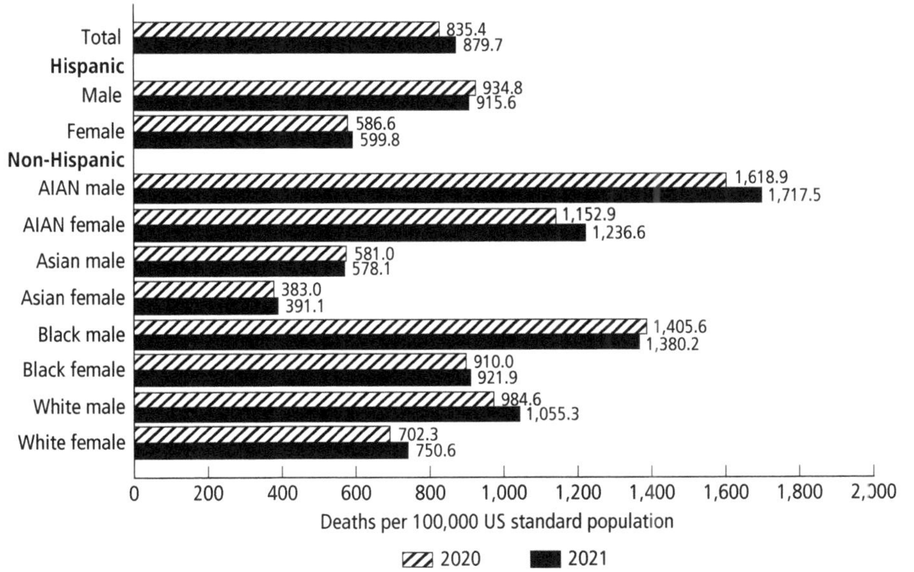

FIGURE 15.5 Age-adjusted death rate by race and Hispanic origin and sex: United States, 2020 and 2021

[a] Includes races and origins not shown separately.

[b] Statistically significant increase from 2020 to 2021 ($p < 0.05$).

[c] Statistically significant decrease from 2020 to 2021 ($p < 0.05$), AIAN is American Indian or Alaska Native, race groups are single race, data by race and Hispanic origin are adjusted for race and Hispanic-origin misclassification on death certificates.

Source: National Center for Health Statistics, National Vital Statistics System, Mortality.

Poston's student Fabian Romero conducted research showing that neighborhood crime rates, especially murder, were higher for Blacks living in segregated neighborhoods, but this relationship did not hold for Hispanics living in segregated neighborhoods. His analyses indicated that the return to crime for residentially segregated Blacks was much higher than it was for residentially segregated Hispanics, particularly for violent crimes (Romero, 2014: 107).

Thus, research shows that Latinos have an advantage over Blacks, and in some cases over Whites, with respect to higher life expectancy and lower death rates for most of the main causes of death. Mexican-origin women have a much lower likelihood of contracting sexually transmitted infections compared with Black women. And Hispanic men living in segregated neighborhoods have crime rates significantly lower than those of Black men living in segregated neighborhoods. This research points to a Hispanic advantage on several dimensions. This is an unexpected finding given the lower levels of socioeconomic status for Hispanics, their higher rates of poverty, and the decades of discrimination they experienced.

There is another racial difference in mortality that deserves our attention. We showed earlier that life expectancy at birth, e_0, is the lowest for Blacks compared to Hispanics and Whites. Indeed, for most of the years of their lives, Blacks have higher death rates than Hispanics and Whites. But the situation changes at the very oldest ages. By late life,

TABLE 15.1 *Expectation of life at ages 70, 80, 90, and 100, by sex and by race and Hispanic origin, United States, 2010*

	Hispanics		NH-Whites		NH-Blacks	
Age	Males	Females	Males	Females	Males	Females
70	15.4	18.0	14.2	16.4	12.8	15.7
80	9.0	10.8	8.1	9.6	7.8	9.6
90	4.5	5.4	4.0	4.8	4.4	5.2
100	2.3	2.6	2.0	2.3	2.5	2.8

Source: Arias, 2014.

death rates for Blacks become lower than those for Whites, and in some cases lower than those for Hispanics. This is what is known in demography as the **racial mortality crossover.**

Poston extracted life expectancy data from a 2010 US life table (Arias, 2014) to develop Table 15.1. The table shows values of life expectancy for ages 70, 80, 90, and 100 for Hispanic males and females, for non-Hispanic White males and females, and for non-Hispanic Black males and females. Looking first at males at age 70, Hispanics have an expectancy value of 15.4 years, NH-Whites, 14.2 years, and NH-Blacks, 12.8 years. And the same pattern holds for females at age 70. This is the pattern we see throughout most of the life table, that is, Hispanics live the longest, then NH-Whites, and last, NH-Blacks.

But observe what happens at age 80. Among females at age 80, NH-Blacks and NH-Whites have the same value, 9.6 years. At age 80, the racial crossover is beginning to occur for females. But it has not yet started for males. Among males at age 80, Hispanics still live the longest, then NH-Whites, and last, NH-Blacks, the same pattern observed in most of the life table.

At age 90, NH-Black males and NH-Black females show a life expectancy advantage over NH-White males and females. And at age 100, NH-Black males and NH-Black females have the highest life expectancy values compared with NH-White males and females and with Hispanic males and females.

The racial crossover has been studied extensively by demographers and other social scientists (Corti et al., 1999; Dupre, Franzese, and Parrado, 2006; Eberstein, Nam, and Heyman, 2008; Johnson, 2000; Manton, Poss, and Wing, 1979; Manton and Stallard, 1997; Nam, Weatherby, and Ockay, 1978; Sautter et al., 2012; Wing et al., 1985), and the findings have been rather consistent, showing results for the US much like those reported above in Table 15.1. Moreover, other analyses have found evidence of a racial mortality crossover in different time periods and in different parts of the world (Nam, 1995).

The issue, thus, is not whether the crossover exists. Clearly it does. The question is why. Specifically, why do Blacks at the oldest ages have higher life expectancies than Whites? Demographers have set forth two main explanations: age misreporting on death certificates, and "population heterogeneity in frailty" (Sautter et al., 2012).

With respect to the first reason, Sautter and her colleagues (2012) have noted that "age misreporting, i.e., the overstatement of age, on death certificates occurs and is more common among Blacks; this error can bias mortality estimates downward at the oldest ages. However, some analyses show that … crossovers are postponed to later ages rather than eliminated when data are adjusted for age misreporting" (Sautter et al., 2012: 1566).

The second reason, "population heterogeneity in frailty," refers to the fact that socioeconomically disadvantaged groups, such as Blacks in the United States, will suffer higher death rates throughout most of their lives, compared to the majority population, for the reasons we discussed earlier in this chapter. This ends up producing in the surviving elderly Black population "a more robust group of disadvantaged individuals." As their age increases, the likelihood of dying is now "weighted toward the robust members of the disadvantaged subgroup who now exhibit lower mortality than the advantaged subgroup (i.e., the Whites), who experience an acceleration of mortality at older ages" (Sautter et al., 2012: 1566). In a sense this is a "survival of the fittest" argument. The frailer Blacks die before they are aged 80 or 90, and this produces a more robust group of Blacks, who have survived the previous 70–80 or so years, and hence live longer than the majority. The racial mortality crossover is certainly a phenomenon of considerable interest to demographers. Like the Hispanic paradox reviewed earlier, it is an area that will continue to be debated and analyzed by demographers in the decades ahead.

To return now to Figure 15.5, we have not yet discussed the age-adjusted death rates for American Indian / Alaska Natives (AIAN) and for Asian Americans. Interestingly, these two groups represent the extreme ends of the differential mortality spectrum. AIAN males have the worst experience of any group of males, and AIAN females have the worst experience of any group of females. It is worth remembering that COVID-19 hit Indian reservations with particular ferocity. There is relatively little research to explain the poor mortality experience of the AIAN populations, but the adequacy of medical care and access to medical care would be important avenues of research.

The other group of note, Asian males and Asian females, have the best (that is, lowest) mortality rates of all the groups in Figure 15.5. Indeed, Asian male death rates are just slightly below the rates for Hispanic females. And Asian females have the lowest death rate in the figure, below 400 per 100,000 in both 2020 and 2021. Again, what explains this result? Along with Hispanics, the Asian group is most likely to have immigrants, and we have already explained that selective migration (see Chapter 7) means that immigrants tend to be healthier than the average person in their home country. In addition, the Asian population tends to be well educated and to have strong family ties, two factors that contribute to good health. Here again, however, we have had relatively little definitive research.

SUMMARY

In this chapter on the demography of race and ethnicity, we first discussed why demographers are interested in race and ethnicity. Next, we reviewed briefly the development of racial categories, as set forth principally by Linnaeus and Blumenbach. We next discussed how the statistical issues of race and ethnicity evolved in the United States, resulting in the basic categories used today by the US federal government. We then examined some of the current patterns of race and ethnicity in the United States. We concluded the chapter with a discussion of differential fertility and differential mortality among racial and ethnic groups.

DISCUSSION QUESTIONS

1. Carl Linnaeus used skin color in his classification of humanity. To what extent do you think skin color is important today in racial identification? Please be sure to justify your reasoning.
2. The Hispanic paradox refers to the mortality experience of Hispanics compared with other groups. We offer several possible hypotheses for why the Hispanic paradox exists. Which of these hypotheses seems to you to be most worth further investigation, and why? Which hypothesis is least important in your estimation?

16

World Population Change over Time

INTRODUCTION

We have already discussed the three demographic processes of fertility, mortality and migration in Chapters 4, 5, 6, and 7. We may now put them all together and analyze overall population change. This chapter deals with the dynamics of population change in the world, and the next chapter (Chapter 17) deals with population change in the United States.

To help us better understand the issues that we discuss in this chapter, we first ask how many people have ever lived on the earth. We next review, albeit briefly, the main theory of population change, namely, **demographic transition theory** (DTT). (Please look over our more detailed discussions of this theory, and other writings on population change, in Chapter 2.) Then we look specifically at the dynamics of world population change, taking both a long and a short view. We conclude this chapter with a discussion of the future of the world's population.

How Many People Have Ever Been Born?

How large is the population of the world right now, and how rapidly is it growing? We wrote the first draft of this chapter on February 11, 2025. On that date the population clock of the US Bureau of the Census (2024f) estimated that the population of the entire world numbered 8,100,146,420 people. The crude birth rate (CBR) of the world in 2024 was estimated to be 16/1,000, and the crude death rate (CDR) to be 8/1,000. Thus, the rate of annual population growth in the world was an estimated 0.8 percent. So, if these birth and death rates were to continue unchanged into the future, the size of the population of the world would double almost every eighty-seven years. (See our discussion of **doubling time** later in this chapter.) Of course, such astronomical numbers are unlikely to occur. Either the birth rate will fall or the death rate will rise, and it will most likely be the former, not the latter.

There were an estimated 8.1 billion people on the earth in mid-year 2024. We already mentioned in Chapter 7 that the first humans emerged in sub-Saharan Africa, as many as 195,000 years ago, and lived there for the first two-thirds of their history. But given that we humans first appeared on earth nearly 200,000 years ago, we might want to ask right now how many people have ever been born, namely, how many people have ever lived on the earth. Carl Haub (1945–2025) was a distinguished demographer at the Population Reference Bureau in Washington, DC; he first posed the above question back in the 1990s because at the time there was a factoid circulating that claimed that 75 percent of persons ever born in the world were now alive. This seemed to Haub to be a ridiculous statement, and we agree, it certainly was. Haub answered the question in 1995, updated it in 2002 and again in 2011 (Haub, 2011).

To obtain an estimate of the number of people ever born, Haub needed to estimate the birth rates at the various eras since humans first appeared on the earth. He began the human race with two people 50,000 years ago with a birth rate of 80/1,000, dropped the rate to 60 starting in AD 1200, and continued dropping the rate until the year 2011 when it was 23. He then did the calculations and determined that as of 2011 there had been 108 billion people ever born on this earth. Thus the 2011 population of the earth was but 6.5 percent of all people ever born, a much more realistic figure than the 75 percent factoid.

Since evidence indicates that the first "modern" humans emerged as many as 195,000 years ago (see Chapter 7), Poston (2024a) revised Haub's estimate by starting the first two humans on earth 195,000 years ago, and not 50,000 years ago. He also extended Haub's analysis from 2011 up to 2024. As an aside, we note that it is probably not the case that we humans have descended from a single pair of individuals (cf. "All About Adam," 2013; Fagundes et al., 2007). Nevertheless, we will begin the human population with two people to make our demographic model less complicated.

We set the birth rate at 80/1,000 for the period 195,000 years ago to 50,000 years ago, and this results in an estimated 8 billion births for that period. (Remember that Haub assumed humans began 50,000 years ago, so we first needed to estimate how many babies were born for those first almost 150,000 years of our existence.) We show later in this chapter that there was very little growth in the human population then and for most of its history. Yes, birth rates were high, around 80/1,000, but so were death rates.

Next, we needed to extend Haub's analysis by thirteen years from 2011 to 2024. Around 130 million babies are born in the world each year, so we added another 1.7 billion births to carry us up to the present.

Our answer to Haub's question of "How many people have ever lived on earth?" from their beginnings 195,000 years ago up to the year of 2024 is around 117.7 billion. We will round up to 118 billion. The present population of the earth of 8.1 billion is only 6.9 percent of all persons who have ever been born.

Livi-Bacci (2012: 26) also developed an answer to the question of how many people have ever lived on the earth, with slightly different assumptions about when the human population began and the levels of its birth and death rates over time. He comes up with a number of 82 billion, a little less than our above number of 118 billion that we developed with revisions and extensions of Haub's calculations. No one will ever know which number is the closest to the true number.

Figure 16.1 presents United Nations (2024b) annual population growth rate data for the world from 1700 to 2020 and then projected to 2100. There was very little growth in the population of the world up to around 1700. We noted earlier that birth rates were high, and so were death rates, so there was very little growth in the population. This was

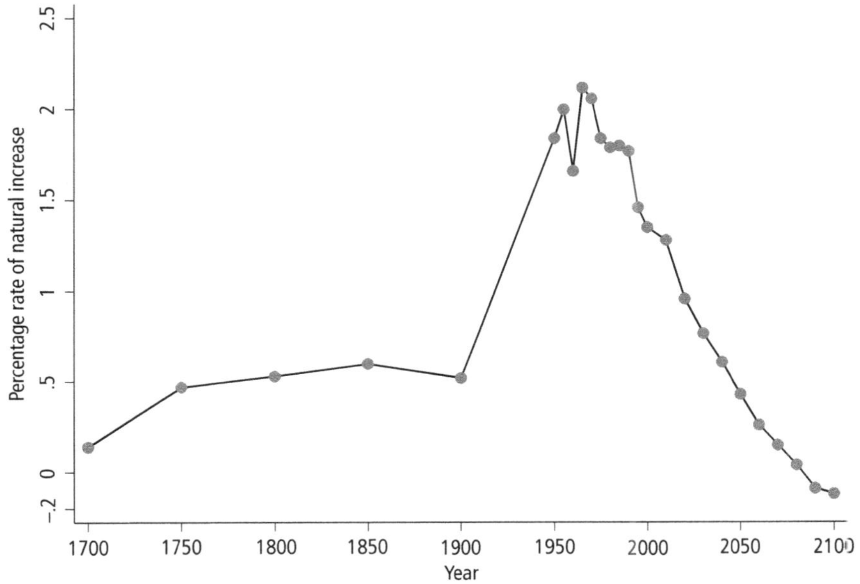

FIGURE 16.1 Population growth rates: world, 1970 to 2020 and projected to 2010
Data source: United Nations, 2024b.

the first stage of the demographic transition, as discussed earlier in Chapter 2. The current growth rate of the world's population in 2020 of just over 0.8 percent has not been constant in past years. The data in Figure 16.1 indicate that the annual rate of world population growth started going up from around 0.1 percent in around 1700, reached a rate of around 0.5 percent by 1800, continued increasing to 1.8 percent in 1950, and then to a high rate of just around 2.1 percent in the mid-1960s. The rate then started to decline around 1970, reaching 1.8 percent in 1980, 1.4 percent in 2000, and 0.96 percent in 2020. We then used population projection data from the medium variant of the United Nations (2024b) to show that by around 2060 the world population growth rate is projected to have dropped to 0.3 percent, and then to 0.04 percent by 2080. By 2090 it is projected to become negative at -.0.09 percent, and then to -0.12 by 2100. In 2100 the world is projected to have the same near zero rate of increase that characterized the world prior to 1700.

Some demographers, ourselves included, believe that the period in the late 1950s and 1960s when the world started to have a decreasing growth rate (dropping below 2 percent) may be one of the most important demographic dates in human history. It marks the start of the movement to eventual no population growth in the world, which is projected to occur around 2100.

The increases and decreases in the world's population growth rates have not always been steady. Indeed, the slowing down for a few years of the growth rate in the late 1950s and early 1960s was due almost entirely to events in China, namely, the natural disasters and decreased agricultural production there that resulted in a great famine following the calamitous years of the Great Leap Forward. (We discussed this famine earlier in Chapter 12.) This means that the notion of a "world population" may be misguided because there is not really a "world society." Changes and trends in world demographic behavior result from the differential demographic behaviors in the major world regions. This point is made more apparent later in this and in other chapters.

Demographic Transition Theory

As we have already discussed in Chapter 2, the most prominent explanation of population change is the theory of demographic transition. The current version of the theory has four stages of mortality and fertility change that occur in the process of societal modernization. We showed these four stages in Chapter 2 in Figure 2.1. Stage 1 is the pretransitional or preindustrialization stage. It lasted worldwide for thousands and thousands of years when the world was characterized by high birth and death rates and stable population growth. Because of the high birth rates that occurred during this stage, it is sometimes referred to as the stage of high growth potential because of the great potential for population growth if mortality were ever to fall. No countries today are located in Stage 1. This is truly remarkable when we realize that prior to the eighteenth century most of the countries of the world were located in Stage 1.

The pretransitional stage is followed by the first transitional stage, known as Stage 2. Stage 2 likely started worldwide around 1700 or so. The forces of modernization and industrialization were responsible for moving countries of the world from Stage 1 to Stage 2, and the first effect was a reduction in mortality. This intermediate stage resulted in rapid rates of population growth because fertility remained high after mortality had declined. During Stage 2, the rate of population growth is high. There are a few countries today still in Stage 2, mainly very poor developing countries such as Afghanistan, some African countries such as Niger, Somalia, Chad, and Uganda, and some Middle East countries such as Yemen.

The next stage (Stage 3) is characterized by decreasing population growth due to lower birth and death rates; it was during this stage that fertility began to decline. Some of the countries today in Stage 3 include Malaysia, Botswana, Colombia, Mexico, and South Africa.

In the final stage (Stage 4), called incipient decline, both fertility and mortality are very low. During this stage, however, there are often slight fluctuations in fertility; thus both natural increase and natural decrease will occur owing to these fluctuations. Included in Stage 4 are most of the countries of Europe, the United States, Canada, Brazil, Japan, South Korea, Taiwan, and several others. The world is projected to reach Stage 4 by around the year 2080 (Figure 16.1).

Demographic transition theory is the most popular of the demographic theories of population change. But be sure you keep in mind the revisions of the theory, discussed already in Chapter 2, particularly the revisions resulting in the "second" and the "third" demographic transitions.

DOUBLING TIME AND HALVING TIME

How fast or how slow is the world's current population growth rate of 0.8 percent? We noted in the first part of this chapter that in the 1960s, the world was growing at around 2 percent, and now it is growing at around 0.8 percent. Demographers sometimes use the **Rule of 69.3** to gain an idea about whether a population's growth rate is fast or slow. Where did the Rule of 69.3 come from? What does it mean?

One way to determine the significance or relevance of a population's rate of growth is through the concept of doubling time. That is, if a population maintains its present birth rates and death rates year after year after year, how long would it take to double its size? The answer may be presented using natural logarithms. The **natural log** of 2 is 0.693. We multiply 0.693 by 100 to equal 69.3.

To illustrate, if we divide 69.3 by the population's positive growth rate expressed as a percentage, the answer tells us how many years it will take for the population to double its size if it maintains its current birth and death rates. The world's CBR in 2024 was 16/1,000 and its death rate was 8/1,000, for a difference between the two of 8/1,000, or 0.8 percent, that is, 0.8/100. Dividing 69.3 by 0.8 equals 86.6, which is the number of years it would take the world to double its size from 8.1 billion to 16.2 billion if it kept its birth and death rates steady. If its present birth and death rates were maintained, the world would number 16.2 billion in 2111, that is, 2024 plus 87, and it would reach 32.4 billion in 2198, that is, 2111 plus 87. A population growth rate of 0.8 percent is a high rate of growth, leading to a doubling of the population every 87 years. This growth rate of the world today of 0.8 percent is not as high as it was in the 1960s when the world was growing at 2 percent (a doubling time of almost 35 years). Indeed, population growth rates greater than 1 percent have not been common in the world until just a few centuries ago (see Figure 16.1).

If you are wondering about how many years it would take a population to triple its size if its birth and death rates did not change, then use the natural log of 3 (which is 1.10), multiply it by 100, and divide into it the percent growth rate. How long will it take the world to triple its current size of 8.1 billion to 24.3 billion? Dividing 110 by 0.8, equals 137.5. This means that in around 138 years from now (the year 2024 when we are writing this chapter), that is, in around the year 2162, if the world maintained a growth rate every year of 0.8 percent, the population size of the world would be around 24.3 billion.

We will now compare the population growth rates of two countries of about the same size with very different rates of growth. The Middle African country of Chad had a mid-year 2024 population numbering around 18.7 million, with a crude birth rate of 42 and a crude death rate of 11, equaling an annual growth rate of 3.1 percent. The Western European country of the Netherlands had a mid-year 2024 population of around 18 million people, with a crude birth rate of over 9/1,000 and a crude death rate of under 9/1,000, resulting in a population growth rate of 0.1 percent (Population Reference Bureau, 2024).

Here are two countries with populations of nearly the same size, between 18 and 18.7 million. Their growth rates are 3.1 percent and 0.1 percent. How different are these rates? The difference between the two, one might say, is only 3.0 percent; this is not very much.

But it is a very large difference, a huge difference, if one answers the question in terms of doubling time. If Niger maintains its current birth and death rates, its population will double in size in just over 22 years, that is, 69.3 divided by 3.1 equals 22.4. If the Netherlands maintains its current birth and death rates, its population will double in size in around 693 years.

Keep in mind that the doubling time concept does not necessarily reflect what will actually happen in the future because a country's birth and death rates hardly ever remain the same from year to year. But the doubling time concept enables us to appraise the relevance or significance of a particular percentage rate of population change.

What happens if the difference between the population's crude birth and death rates is not positive but is negative? May we still use the Rule of 69.3 to tell us about the significance or relevance of a negative rate of growth? Yes, we may.

For example, Germany in mid-year 2024 had a population of 84.9 million people; its birth rate was 8/1,000 and its death rate 12/1,000, for a percentage rate of population change of –0.4 percent (Population Reference Bureau, 2024). If we divide this negative percentage rate into 69.3, the answer is -173. This means that if Germany were to maintain its current birth and death rates of 8/1,000 and 12/1,000, respectively, its population would become half as large in 173 years (i.e., a **halving time**). We noted earlier that many countries, including most of Europe, are experiencing population decline because of their low birth rates. Germany is certainly one of them.

We turn next to a discussion of population change in the world. We look first at population growth before 1650 and then since 1650.

World Population Growth

Population Growth Before 1650

Figure 16.2 shows estimated numbers of the size of the population of the world beginning around 65,000 BC. The world population then was estimated to number between 400,000 and 500,000 people. For thousands of years, the world grew very slowly. About 35,000 BC, the population of the world numbered around 4 million. By around 8000 BC, the world's population was about 6 million. That was about the time, give or take a thousand years, when the first Agricultural Revolution had its start. With settled agriculture and the domestication of animals, it was possible to support a denser population. There were long periods of stationary growth, that is, no growth, until around the time of Christ, when the world's population numbered approximately 250 million (Biraben, 2003). The population did not double again until about the year AD 1600. The annual rate of growth then was a mere 0.04 percent. To be sure, the growth patterns were uneven. The population would grow fairly rapidly for a few years, and this was followed by epidemics or plagues, and the population would decline in size. Indeed, the size of the world population apparently declined a little between 1300 and 1400 because of the Black Death (see our discussion in Chapter 12). Overall, death rates were very high, and birth rates had to be at least as high if the population was to grow even very slowly.

These stationary conditions of near zero to very low population growth rates continued until the period of around 1650 to 1700, when the population of the world numbered around 650 million. During these many thousands of years, the world's population was kept small in size by the various **Malthusian checks** we mentioned earlier in Chapter 2. Death rates were high because of the positive checks of plagues, famines, and poor living conditions. Generally, populations had high birth rates to

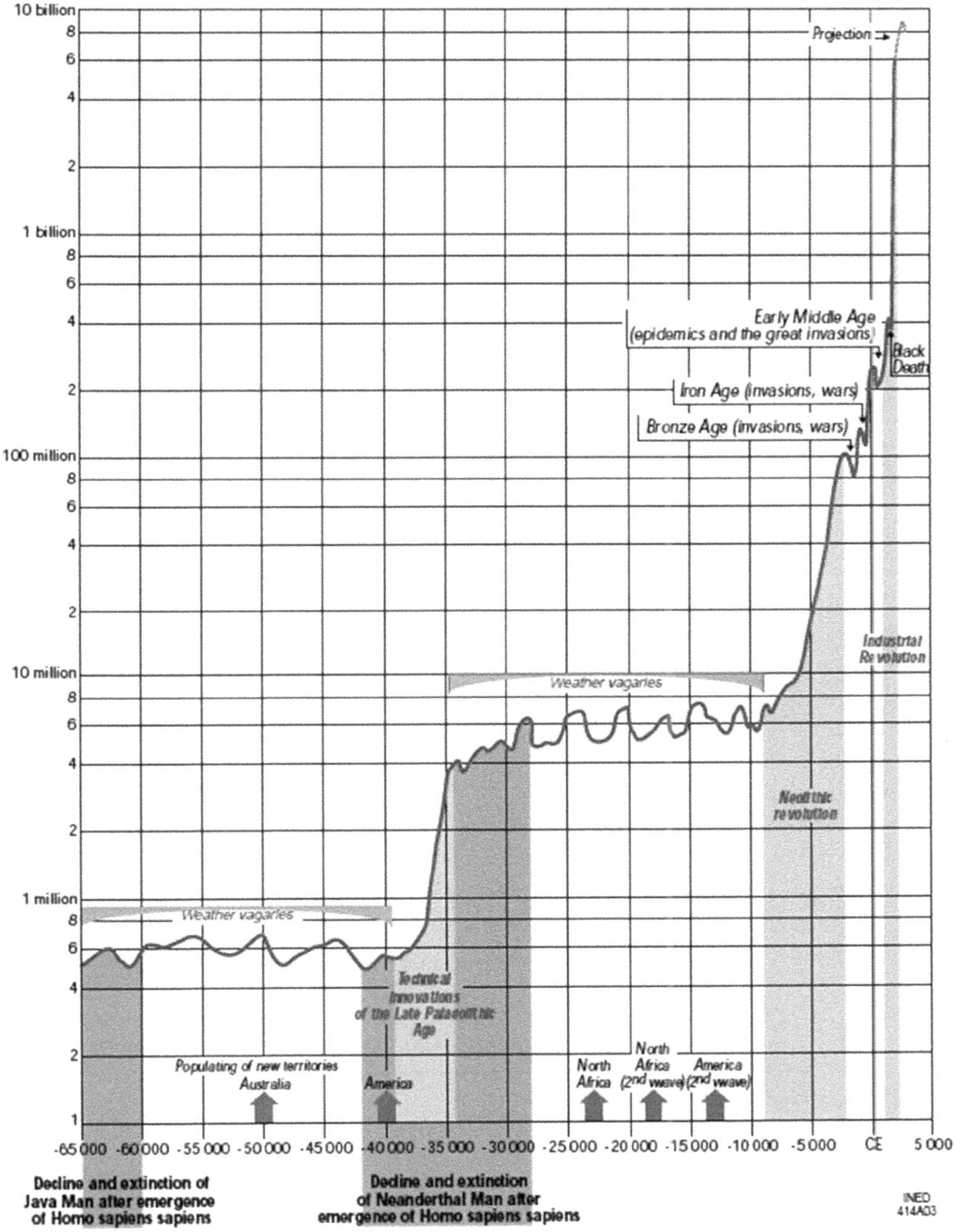

FIGURE 16.2 World population growth over 65,000 years

Source: Jean-Noel Biraben, "The Rising Numbers of Humankind," *Population & Societies*, 394 (2003): 1–4 (reprinted with permission).

compensate for the high death rates. If the birth rates were not high, the human population would likely have become extinct.

Population Change since 1650

The world's population grew from around 650 million in 1650 to 1 billion by 1804. It then took just over 120 years to reach 2 billion in 1927. As the Agricultural Revolution resulted in more density, so too did the Industrial Revolution. People began to leave their farms and move to cities where factories and mills were humming. An urban revolution occurred along with the Industrial Revolution. This made it possible for density to increase as well.

Table 16.1 shows the years when the world reached each billion from the first billion in 1804 to the eighth billion in 2022; the world is projected to reach 9 billion in around 2035 and 10 billion in around 2055.

It took most of human history for the world to reach its first billion; it took more than another 120 years to reach 2 billion, then thirty-three years to get to 3 billion. It took fourteen more years to attain a population of 4 billion, and only thirteen more to reach 5 billion, and then twelve more to get to 6 billion, and twelve more to reach 7 billion. It only took eleven more years for the world to get to 8 billion, reaching this level in 2022. It is projected that it will take thirteen more years to reach 9 billion, and then around twenty more to attain 10 billion. The United Nations projects that the world will not ever reach 11 billion. We discuss some of these issues in later sections of this chapter.

Much of the growth in the world's population is attributable to lower death rates while birth rates remained high. The improved standards of living eventually resulting from industrialization help explain the declining death rates. However, death rates rose slightly before they fell.

The onset of the Industrial Revolution was not especially kind to the individuals who joined the urban labor force. Indeed, their situation was a major concern of Karl Marx, who saw this as an attempt by the bourgeoisie to force the proletariat to accept incredibly poor working conditions (Marx and Engels, [1848] 1935). Only later did conditions improve slightly, and this was accompanied by a lower death rate. With the birth rates

TABLE 16.1 *Years the world reached and is projected to reach billions of populations*

Population in billions	Year reached
1 billion	1804
2 billion	1927
3 billion	1960
4 billion	1974
5 billion	1987
6 billion	1999
7 billion	2011
8 billion	2022
9 billion	2035
10 billion	2055

Source: United Nations, 2024b.

remaining high, the result was massive population growth. A latent function of that growth was international migration away from the highly populated European countries to the underpopulated Americas and elsewhere (see our discussions in Chapter 7).

The rapid population growth during this period was mostly limited to Western Europe. In the other regions of the world, where the Industrial Revolution had not fully taken hold, death rates remained high, as did birth rates. It was only later that the death rates began to fall rapidly in the developing regions.

The decline in mortality in the developed nations was later followed by a decline in fertility. By the 1930s, growth rates were coming down. Whereas throughout most of human history until the eighteenth century, population growth was very slow because of high fertility and high mortality, this time population growth slowed down because of low fertility and low mortality.

The political and economic challenges from these demographic shifts in distribution are considerable. Will the massive numbers of poor people in the developing regions rise up against the far fewer rich in the developed nations? Will it be necessary for the rich to increase their contributions to the poor of the world? The lists of questions are endless.

The declines in both fertility and mortality warrant explanations. As we have already noted, the Industrial Revolution eventually created a healthier society. With better transportation, food supplies were improved and famines occurred less frequently. In Europe new foods were introduced from the colonies in the Americas and elsewhere. Also, better housing was constructed, and better clothing became available as cotton was plentiful. In the nineteenth century, sanitary behavior began to be practiced by the people, and public-health movements were appearing. Medical improvements did not really contribute too much to declining mortality until the twentieth century.

Death rates remained very high in the developing regions. It was not until after World War II that there were significant improvements in longevity in those regions. Then, death rates in many places fell rapidly. These areas benefited from the knowledge learned in the more advanced nations a decade or two earlier. By then, too, medical knowledge had increased, and the residents were the benefactors of this information.

The decline in fertility is not as easily understood as the decline in mortality. Note that individual decisions were not as important when it came to lowering mortality. The social system, for the most part, was the major contributing factor. When it came to fertility, however, individual decisions were necessary if the rates were to be lowered. But even those decisions depended on the social situation. As urbanization and industrialization began to occur, the family became less important as an economic unit of production. When most people resided in rural areas, having large families was important. The children, as they grew up, participated in the daily household chores. Having another child was economically feasible since families lived mainly off the land. With the move to the city, impersonal systems like the factory took over the allocation of jobs. Families moving from the farm to the city often found themselves living in tenement houses, often with only one or two bedrooms. It was soon concluded that children who were useful as a cheap supply of labor in farming families were not as useful in industrial working-class urban families. Furthermore, child labor laws were soon passed and formal education became mandatory. Hence, children did not contribute as much to the family economy as they did prior to the initiation of these changes.

Another factor in the process of declining fertility was the fall in infant mortality. Along with overall mortality declines, there was also a decrease in infant deaths. Prior to the Industrial Revolution, some families would have as many as nine or ten or more children, perhaps subconsciously realizing that only three or four would survive to adulthood. Now, most survived; the solution, thus, was to limit fertility.

Returning to our earlier point, individual decisions had to be made with reference to limiting family size. (We have already discussed birth prevention measures in Chapter 11.) Such decisions were long in the making. For centuries, the culture virtually dictated that women should have as many offspring as possible. Consider how dramatic this shift in sexual behavior was for those couples. It was not at all surprising that it took more than one generation for smaller families to become the norm. This was a major cultural change in familial behavior.

The decline in fertility among people in the developing regions has been very slow. With mortality falling swiftly, this slow decline in fertility began in the 1960s and resulted in large increases in the size of the population. This, in turn, led to a growing concern about overpopulation (Connelly, 2008).

The fairly esoteric topic of demographic growth took on a new meaning in the United States and elsewhere with the publication in the 1960s of several high-profile books: Frederick Osborn's *This Crowded World* was written in 1960; it was followed in 1967 by William and Paul Paddock's *Famine, 1975*, and in 1968 by Paul R. Ehrlich's best-seller, *The Population Bomb*, which sold over 2 million copies and was translated into many languages. These treatises, sometimes referred to as **neo-Malthusian**, "were designed to be alarmist in tone, and Ehrlich and his wife Ann went on to advocate the need for incentives bordering on coercion to induce couples to have fewer children" (Bouvier and Bertrand, 1999: 64; see also Connelly, 2008).

Since then, however, there have been several success stories among the countries of the developing world that were not predicted by the neo-Malthusians. Bangladesh, one of the poorest countries, has seen its total fertility rate fall from 7 births per woman in 1970 to 2.2 births per woman in 2024. Iran's fertility rate declined from 6.4 in 1970 to 1.8 in 2013 to 1.7 in 2024. Mexico's rate has fallen significantly, from 6.7 in 1970 to 1.6 in 2024. And India, the country that Paul Ehrlich highlighted in *The Population Bomb* as the place where he first began to experience "the feel of overpopulation" (Ehrlich, 1968: 16), dropped its fertility rate from 5.5 in 1970 to 2.4 in 2013 to 2.0 in 2024. There are many, many other examples of evolving success. Indeed pretty much the only countries today with high birth rates are in sub-Saharan Africa, but even some of these are beginning to show evidence of fertility declines (Population Reference Bureau, 2014, 2024). The alarmist predictions of the neo-Malthusians, for most of the world, were somewhat off the mark.

Ehrlich noted in his autobiography published in 2023 that *The Population Bomb*, despite its exaggerations and the many criticisms directed against its alarmist arguments, helped launch a worldwide debate that continues to today about "the fundamental issue of the Earth's finite capacity to sustain human civilization; ... it still provides a useful lens through which to view the environmental, energy, pandemic, and food crises of the present time" (Ehrlich, 2023: 285). We do not disagree with Ehrlich's recent statement and appraisal.

Let us finally mention the demographic situation in sub-Saharan Africa. In many countries in Western and in Middle Africa and in some countries in Eastern Africa, fertility rates remain above five births per woman, and above six births in a few countries. For example, in 2024, the Central African Republic reported a total fertility rate of 6.4, and Chad, Somalia, Niger, and the Democratic Republic of the Congo all reported total fertility rates (TFRs) of 6.1 (Population Reference Bureau, 2024). But the fertility rates of many sub-Saharan African countries have been declining in recent years. Will their fertility rates continue to fall to lower levels? Projections of the United Nations (see our discussion below) assume they will. So do we.

The Future Population of the Earth

Before gazing into the future, allow us to reexamine world population growth of the last few decades. Recent demographic trends can be described without exaggeration as revolutionary, a virtual discontinuity with all of human history. It was not until about 1804 that world population reached the first billion, and it is now over 8 billion. It is clear that for most of the time that *Homo sapiens* has been on this planet, growth has been infinitesimal. This point is made most clearly in Figure 16.2. The population projections we now present suggest that such a demographic balance will necessarily take place again in the not-too-distant future as population approaches the ultimate carrying size of the planet.

Note that we have used here and elsewhere in this textbook the word projection rather than "prediction" or "forecast." Predictions of things to come are best left to seers and psychics. Forecasts are best left to meteorologists. Demographers usually do not make population forecasts or population predictions. They make population projections. A **population projection** refers to the number of people who will comprise the population of an area at some future point in time according to clearly stated demographic assumptions about the demographic variables.

A population projection is intended to answer the question, "What if…?" It need not necessarily be realistic. In fact, population projections are sometimes used to demonstrate the impossibility of maintaining certain rates of growth. For example, Ansley Coale (1974) once stated that if the then-current rate of world population growth continued indefinitely, in less than 700 years there would be one person for every square yard of the earth's surface. Coale's calculation was definitely not intended to be a prediction. Rather, it was meant to illustrate rather vividly that the planet cannot maintain such a rate of population growth indefinitely.

Such examples are extreme, yet they demonstrate what the esteemed demographer Peter Morrison (1977: 12) meant when he wrote that "the purpose of projecting population is not exclusively, or even primarily, to make accurate predictions. Rather, it is to identify and chart the likely effects of influences and contingencies that will determine future population size."

Most projections, however, are intended to be realistic. The assumptions generally reflect what appears to be reasonable at a given point in time. Populations rise and fall because of shifts in fertility, mortality, and migration. Assumptions are made about the future levels of such demographic behavior. The person making the assumptions must be clear about the intent of the effort. Are the projections realistic, or are they intended to show the absurdity of the assumptions? Far too many projections are reified. Looking for quick and easy answers, analysts who are not well versed in demographic research too often ignore the assumptions and only emphasize the projections.

In this chapter, we use world population projections prepared recently by the Population Division of the United Nations (2024b). It is our view that these reflect reasonable assumptions about future demographic behavior. Nevertheless, they are just that, namely, projections that indicate what the population of the world will be according to stated assumptions. In no way should they be seen as predictions, nor should they be considered the final word. The UN is continuously revising its assumptions based on the latest data available.

Another issue with projections is the length of time for which they are made. The longer the period, the less reliable the projection. Short-term projections are usually grounded in a detailed analysis of current trends. These projections amount to statements of a sort about the near-term future, as long as the underlying trends do not change substantially. Of course, these trends can affect the future, and ultimately falsify themselves, by alerting policymakers to the need for policies to thwart an undesirable future.

Fluctuations have occurred and will continue to occur in the future. The projections that we set forth here extend to the year 2100. Confidence in the first several decades is far greater than in the latter part of the century.

What do the numbers tell us? The world population was estimated to number 8.1 billion in 2024. UN demographers believe that there is a high likelihood that the size of the population of the world will peak at around 10.3 billion in the 2080s and then start to slowly decline, reaching 10.2 billion in 2100 (United Nations, 2024b).

You may be asking about the assumptions that the UN demographers used to arrive at these figures, and you are correct in asking such a question. Whether it is the United Nations or the US Census Bureau making the projections, alternate projections are usually prepared, namely, a high one, a low one, and one in the middle. In this chapter, we are using the middle projection set out by the United Nations that assumes fertility declines for countries with large families, and very slight fertility increases for countries with small families, that is, fewer than two children per woman. As for mortality, the UN middle range projections are based on gradual improvements in life expectancy, and this is expected to occur especially in developing countries. Since we are considering here the projected population numbers for the entire world, there is obviously no need to make assumptions about migration.

We show in Figure 16.3 a population growth chart for the world from 1950 to 2023, with projections to 2100. You will notice from 2027 until 2100 a 95 percent prediction interval that indicates possible variations about the center prediction line. The projections are based on the medium variant, as already discussed.

The middle or medium scenario projects that the population of the world will continue to grow after 2023, peaking in the 2080s and then experiencing a slight decline to 2100.

How large can a population grow? Or, to borrow the question from the title of Cohen's (1995) book, *How Many People Can the Earth Support?* Unfortunately,

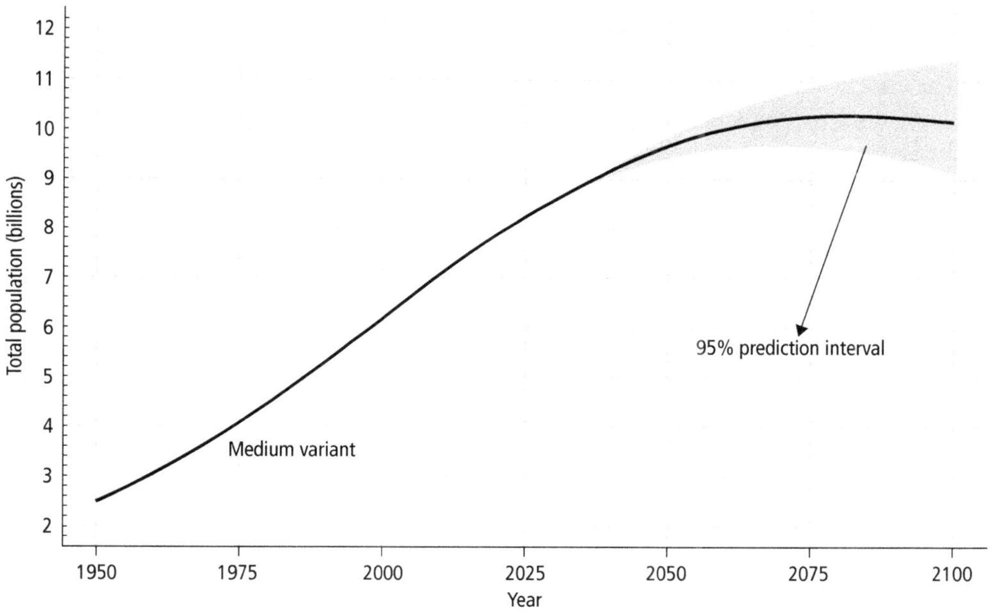

FIGURE 16.3. Total population of the world in billions from 1950 to 2023, with projections to 2100 (based on the medium variant)
Source: United Nations, 2024b.

Cohen did not provide a direct answer, but he did identify the variables that must be considered before arriving at one. For example, at what standard of living will the people of the earth live? Will it be that of the United States, France, or Nigeria? He stated the following:

> The human population of the Earth now travels in the zone when a substantial fraction of scholars have estimated upper limits on human population size. These estimates are no better than present understanding of humankind's cultural, economic, and environmental choices and constraints. Nevertheless, the possibility must be considered seriously that the number of people on the Earth has reached, or will reach within a half century, the maximum number the Earth can support in modes of life that we and our children and their children will choose to want. (Cohen, 1995: 76)

It may seem contradictory to project such momentous increases while the growth rate itself is falling. Three factors account for this apparent anomaly. First, the population itself is expanding. Even though the growth rate is falling, it is based on an ever-growing population. Consider the parallel situation in banking, where one's bank account continues to grow in size despite falling interest rates.

Second, infant and childhood mortality rates have fallen rapidly in many developing countries during the past few decades. The result is a sort of baby boom attributable not to higher fertility, as occurred in the United States, but rather to lower mortality. This baby boom has contributed to a third factor. In any young population, there is a built-in momentum for growth. Looking at the world, and particularly its developing regions, the numbers of young people are enormous, proportionally speaking. Even if these people all decide to lower their fertility, the number of births will increase because there are more and more women of reproductive age who are available to have children. This is called *population momentum*. (See our earlier discussion in Chapter 4.)

The conclusion is apparent. Despite recent declines in fertility, population growth is likely in store for the world for the foreseeable future, but it is projected to peak in the mid-2080s, with a slight decline for the remaining years of the century. However, different regions and countries will exhibit different demographic behaviors, resulting in a growing proportion of the world's population residing in the developing areas.

Today, major portions of Malthus' line of reasoning are suspect, particularly his doubts concerning people's ability (and willingness) to practice "moral restraint." His rejection of contraception and abortion as immoral (although the latter view is still held today by some) is clearly not in line with the thinking of a majority of the inhabitants of the world. Yet, his concern about a sufficient supply of food for a growing population remains an issue to this very day. We will have more to say on this issue of available resources in Chapter 20.

SUMMARY

Through most of the human time on earth, the population has grown very slowly. High birth rates and high death rates prevailed. It was not until about 1650 or so that population growth began to accelerate when death rates fell faster than birth rates. By the early twentieth century, births had fallen; growth in the developed regions, especially in much of Europe, began to fall and has recently reached a situation of "no-growth." This has not been the case with developing nations, particularly those in sub-Saharan Africa. There, the death rates did not fall until the twentieth century and birth rates in some countries are still fairly high, although there are many examples of lower birth rates in some of these African countries.

The world continues to grow at about 0.9 percent annually, but this has declined in recent years. The population of the world will likely be over 10 billion by the end of this century, but world growth is projected to have peaked by the mid-2080s. However, growth will continue in many developing countries, contributing to several problems such as massive malnutrition, pressures on nonrenewable resources, and low standards of living.

We believe that one of the most important points made in this chapter is that the population of the world is expected to stop growing. We inhabit a finite space, so we cannot continue to grow forever. UN demographers project that by 2100 the population of the world will have stopped growing and will start declining. This will likely occur almost three centuries after the world first attained a total population of one billion.

DISCUSSION QUESTIONS

1. This chapter traces the history of the growth of the population of the world. For thousands of years, the population of the world grew slowly. About 35,000 BC, world population numbered around 4 million. It reached around 650 million by 1650. It increased to 1 billion in the early 1800s and to 8 billion in 2022. World

population is projected to reach 9 billion in around 2035 and 10 billion in around 2055. Given what you have learned, do you believe there is a maximum number of people who can live on this planet? How many? Be sure to give reasons for your answer.

2. In demographic history, why were Malthusian checks particularly important? Now in the modern era, the Malthusian checks are less important. Various features of modern societies have greatly reduced the effects of Malthusian checks and helped to extend life. List the various Malthusian checks and indicate which one you deem to have been the most influential. Then list the various features of modern societies that have reduced the effects of the Malthusian checks and indicate which one you deem to be the most influential. Be sure to give reasons for your answer.
3. Explain what is meant by the Rule of 69.3. Why, when, and how is it used? In your answer be sure and use the three concepts of "doubling time," "halving time," and the "natural log of 2." What, in your opinion, is the major feature or focus of doubling time? Answer the same question with regard to halving time.

17

Population Change in the United States

INTRODUCTION

The United States is the third most populous country in the world after the two demographic billionaires, India and China. In 2024, the population of the United States numbered 336.6 million inhabitants, compared to 1.44 billion in India and 1.41 billion in China (Population Reference Bureau, 2024). When the first census was conducted in the United States in 1790, the population size of the country (as then defined geographically) was just above 3.9 million, which is near the size today of the metropolitan area of Seattle, Washington. In 234 years, the United States has increased tremendously in size, from 3.9 million inhabitants in 1790 to more than 331 million in 2020 (Figure 17.1) and to almost 337 million in 2024. In this chapter, we trace the patterns of growth of the United States from colonial times to the present and then examine some projections of the US population for the future.

HISTORY OF POPULATION CHANGE IN THE UNITED STATES

The Precolonial Period

Estimates for the precolonial period of the size of the population in the land now known as the United States are not easy to obtain, and they vary considerably: "There is probably no single figure that can be accepted as the 'best' estimate of the late fifteenth century North American population" (Snipp, 1989: 9). According to Howard Zinn,

> The Indian population of [around] 10 million that lived north of Mexico when Columbus came would ultimately be reduced to less than a million. Huge numbers of Indians would die from diseases introduced by the whites. A Dutch traveler in New England wrote in 1656 that "the Indians ... affirm, that before the arrival of the Christians and before the smallpox broke out amongst them, they were ten times as numerous as they now are, and that their population had been melted down by this disease, whereof nine-tenths of them have died" (2003: 16)

The number of American Indians (or Native Americans) continued to decline over the next centuries and by 1900 totaled only between 125,000 and 150,000 (Thornton, 1990: 42). This decline resulted in part from attrition during the continual warfare in

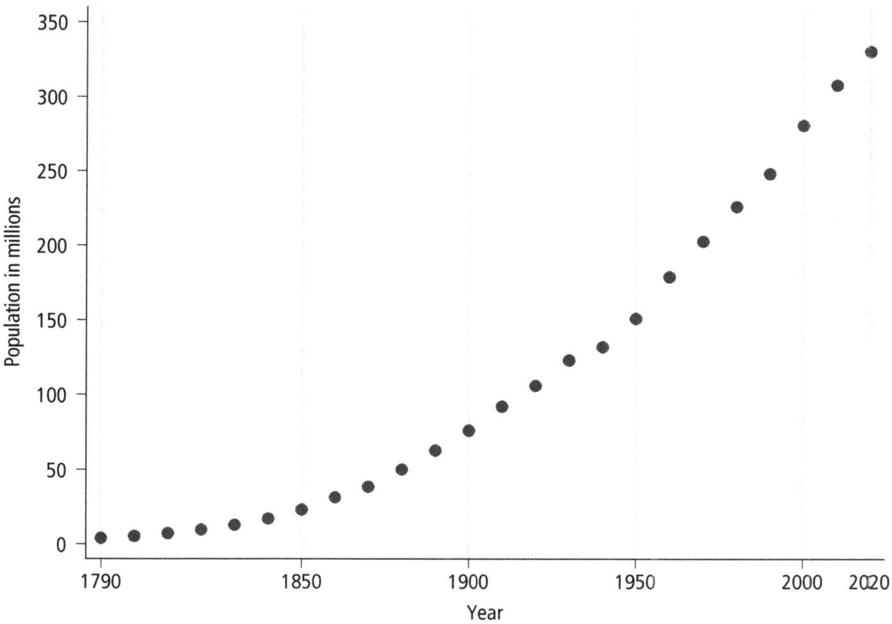

FIGURE 17.1 US population in millions from 1790 to 2020
Source: US Census Bureau.

which they participated in the defense of their tribal lands, as well as from unusual hardships imposed and, as just noted, from diseases introduced by the European settlers. At the beginning of the twentieth century, "there were so few Indians left in America that it was widely believed that they would eventually disappear" (Snipp, 1989: 23).

For many decades up through the 1950s, the American Indian population hardly grew at all, reaching just over 500,000 according to the 1960 census. But by 2020, the number of persons in the United States self-identifying as American Indians or Alaska Natives was roughly 8 million. This growth from just over 500,000 to around 8 million is demographically impossible without a massive amount of immigration or without a change in the manner the data were collected. It is the latter factor that has been largely responsible for this extraordinary growth.

Beginning in the 1970 decennial census, population counts of the American Indian and Alaska Native populations have been based on self-identification. The demographer Jeffrey Passel has noted that

> [P]ersons answering the census choose their response to the race question. A person choosing the American Indian racial response did not have to provide any substantiation or documentation of this identification. There was no requirement that an "American Indian" be enrolled as a member of a recognized tribe or that any tribal group recognize the respondent as a member, and there was no "blood quantum" requirement. This method of identification differs from that of previous censuses, in which a person's racial identification tended to be assigned by an enumerator, usually based on observation, local knowledge, or custom. (Passel, 1996: 80)

Demographers and other social scientists have undertaken considerable research on the phenomenal growth since 1970 of the American Indian population (Eschbach, 1993; Gilligan, 2022; Ostler, 2019; Passel, 1976, 1996; Passel and Berman, 1986;

Sanchez-Rivera et al., 2023; Snipp, 1989; Wilson and Martin, 2024). They have shown that at least through the 1990s, the extraordinary growth of the American Indian population "was achieved through changing patterns of racial self-identification on the part of people with only partial or distant American Indian ancestry, coupled with relatively high fertility and improving mortality" (Passel, 1996: 79).

Of the roughly 8 million persons identifying themselves as American Indians or Alaska Natives in 2020, nearly one-half are multiracial; that is, they selected two or more races. (See our discussions in Chapter 15 of the multirace option on the census and ACS.) Compared to results of the 2010 census, in the 2020 census, multiple-race American Indian and Alaska Native (AIAN) responses increased by 240.6 percent, "while single-race AIAN responses [AIAN alone] increased 37.2 percent. According to the Census Bureau, the increase in multiple-race AIAN responses is largely due to redesigned questions for race and ethnicity, which included a write-in option with examples of corresponding national origins for each racial or ethnic category" (Wilson and Martin, 2024).

The Colonial Period: 1607–1790

On May 14, 2007, the town of Jamestown, Virginia, celebrated the four hundredth anniversary of its first settlement. At its founding in 1607, Jamestown had just over a hundred colonists. By 1610, Virginia counted 350 settlers. The non–Native American population of the colonies numbered more than 2,000 in 1620 and is estimated to have reached 50,000 by 1650. By 1790, when the first census of the United States was conducted, almost 4 million people were enumerated. The eightyfold increase from 1650 to 1790 is surely one of the most spectacular examples of population growth in human history (Weller and Bouvier, 1981: 52–53).

Immigration was the main contributor to growth in the decades immediately following settlement. Later in the colonial period, natural increase became as important as, if not more important than, immigration. The pattern of population growth in that era follows closely the phases of the demographic equation. At the end of the eighteenth century, the crude birth rate (CBR) was estimated at about 55 per 1,000 and the crude death rate (CDR) at about 25 per 1,000 (Thompson and Whelpton, 1933). This rate of growth alone would increase the population by 3 percent annually. Massive immigration compounded this growth.

The first population census in the United States was conducted in 1790; the official census day was August 1st. The "1790 Census Act" authorizing the first census was signed into law on March 1, 1790. We show in Figure 17.2 the bottom page of the 1790 Census Act with the names of George Washington, the President of the United States, and John Adams, the Vice-President of the United States and President of the Senate, among others. The Marshalls of the US Judicial Districts were responsible for conducting the census. They were required to visit every household; moreover, census schedules were to be posted in "two of the most public places within [each jurisdiction], there to remain for the inspection of all concerned ..." and that "the aggregate amount of each description of persons" for every district be transmitted to the president (US Bureau of the Census, 2015a: 1).

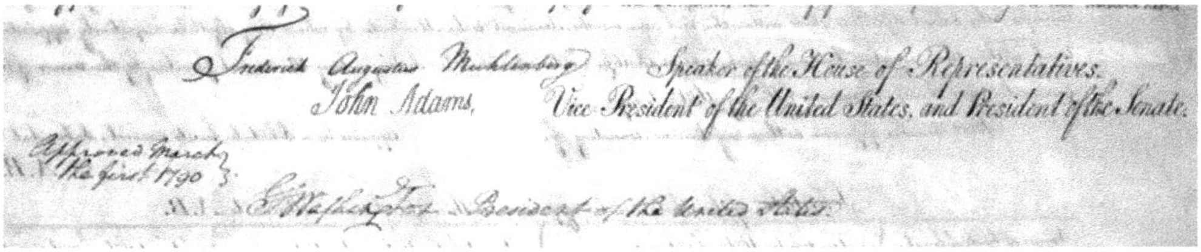

FIGURE 17.2 The bottom page of the 1790 Census Act
Source: US Bureau of the Census, 2015a.

As we stated at the start of this chapter, the population of the United States was just under 4 million at the time of the first census in 1790. However, the census count included only the populations of the original thirteen states, along with the districts of Kentucky, Maine, and Vermont, as well as the so-called Southwest Territory, that is, what is now the state of Tennessee (Gauthier, 2002: 5). The actual census questionnaire was short. We noted in Chapter 3 that the first census only counted people according to whether they were free White males 16 years and older, free White males younger than 16 years of age, free White females, slaves, and "other" persons. Most of the Native American population was not included in the enumeration. About 80 percent of those counted were White. Most were of either English or Scotch-Irish ancestry; others came from Holland, Sweden, Spain, and France. The bulk of the remaining 20 percent of the population was Black. Most were slaves who had involuntarily immigrated to the United States from Africa. Their forced migration began slowly in the seventeenth century and increased in the eighteenth and early nineteenth centuries. The settlement of Blacks was concentrated in the South (Taeuber and Taeuber, 1971: 5).

The Nineteenth Century

The United States grew rapidly between 1790 and 1860. The US population numbered 3.9 million in 1790, 5.3 million in 1800, 12.9 million in 1830, and 31.4 million in 1860. The size of the population increased approximately 30 percent per decade from 1790 to 1860, which was amazing considering that the growth rate in Europe at the same time was less than half as much. The numbers of the US population more than quadrupled between 1800 and 1850 (Figure 17.1). The combination of high levels of immigration and a high rate of natural increase explains this phenomenal growth in just a half-century. For example, the total fertility rate (TFR) in 1800 was more than 7.0 and had dropped only to 5.4 by 1850 (US Bureau of the Census, 1975).

We just mentioned that in addition to high fertility, the other component of this population increase was immigration (Hughes and Cain, 2010). Before 1830, the contribution of immigration to population growth in the United States was small. Between 1821 and 1825, for example, the average number of immigrants every year totaled only about 8,000. This number increased to almost 21,000 each year between 1826 and 1830. From 1841 to 1845, immigrants to the United States each year numbered more than 86,000. In the eight years between 1850 and 1857, the number of immigrants was 2.2 million. In sum, between 1790 and 1860, the total number of immigrants to the United States was almost 5 million, and most of them were from Europe (Taeuber and Taeuber, 1958).

Of course, we need also to mention that the country grew geographically as well as demographically. The land area of the United States, according to the first census in 1790, comprised only 889,000 square miles. The Louisiana Purchase of 1803 nearly doubled the land area. The accession of Florida in 1819 added still more land. Between 1840 and 1850, the territory of the United States was increased by two-thirds through the annexation of Texas in 1845, and Oregon in 1846, as well as the cession by Mexico in 1848 (Taeuber and Taeuber, 1958). The addition of these new states brought with them vast increases in the numbers of people.

Most of the population growth between 1800 and 1850 occurred on the Atlantic seaboard. Yet, despite the geographic growth to encompass the forty-eight contiguous states, the population density (the number of persons per unit of land) actually grew from 6.1 persons per square mile in 1800 to 7.9 persons per square mile in 1850. The newly acquired western part of the United States remained relatively underpopulated, except for the Native Americans, who were not counted in the decennial censuses until 1890. After 1850, the rate of population growth slowed down somewhat, although the population still managed to triple in size by 1900 when the 1900 census counted about 76 million inhabitants (Figure 17.1). By then, the population density was 25.6 persons per square mile.

The first major slowdown in the population growth rate in the United States occurred in the 1860s during the Civil War. Compared with a 32 to 36 percent increase in each decade between 1790 and 1860, the increase from 1860 to 1890 was around 26 to 27 percent per decade.

Despite this decline in the rate of population growth, the Industrial Revolution had a major impact on the American population during the second half of the nineteenth century. Urbanization intensified, and the CBRs and CDRs both fell. By 1900 the CBR was 32.2 and the CDR was 17.2. Here again we see the demographic transition in action.

By the beginning of the twentieth century, almost 40 percent of the people lived in urban areas, compared to only 15 percent in 1850. The nation was also becoming increasingly heterogeneous. Until the middle of the nineteenth century, most of the population was of White Anglo-Saxon ancestry. These people, along with the African Americans and the Native Americans, comprised the bulk of the nation's population. However, during the second half of the century, new waves of immigration brought people from southern Europe and from Asia, particularly China and Japan. By 1900, the nation could no longer be classified as predominantly White, Anglo-Saxon, and Protestant (WASP).

The African American population increased from around 1 million in 1800 to 8.8 million in 1900. Yet the percentage of the total population that was African American fell from almost 19 to 12 percent during the period. One reason for the decline was that the mortality rate for African Americans was higher than that for Whites. Another reason was that large numbers of Whites immigrated to the United States from Europe, while few Blacks immigrated from Africa, particularly after the slave trade was abolished in 1808 (Taeuber and Taeuber, 1958).

The Twentieth Century

We noted above that the first major decline in the population growth rate of the United States occurred during and after the years of the Civil War. The second decline occurred between 1890 to 1910, when the rate of population growth dropped to about 20 percent per decade. The third major decline was in the decade between 1910 and 1920, when the growth rate dropped to about 15 percent, largely due to World War I. During the war years, immigrant flows were interrupted, fertility rates declined, and death rates rose. The increase in death rates was also due to the influenza epidemic of 1918–1919 (Barry, 2004; Crosby, 2003), a topic we already discussed in Chapter 12. Although there was a little rebound in the next decade, the population growth rate in the 1930s dropped to a new record low of 7.2 percent, which was less than half of the lowest decennial increase in earlier decades (Taeuber and Taeuber, 1958). This very low rate of increase resulted mainly from the Great Depression of the 1930s, which caused a sharp decline in births (Kahn, 1974). The decline of the 1930s did not continue into the 1940s and 1950s, however. The baby boom after World War II ended in the late 1950s, and the population growth rate began to decline, dropping to almost 10 percent in the 1980s.

Although the size of the US population increased by more than four times in the next 110 years, from 76 million in 1900 to almost 309 million in 2010 (Figure 17.1), the rate of population growth slowed slightly. The population merely doubled between 1900 (76 million) and 1950 (151 million).

Two demographic events greatly affected the growth of the population. First, the baby boom began around 1947. Fertility rates rose to levels unanticipated in any industrialized nation. In the late 1950s, at the height of the baby boom era, the TFR reached its peak of more than 3.7 children per woman. This high fertility following World War II was promoted by the need to compensate for population losses during the war, as well as to rehabilitate the economy and production. The demographic effects were startling. About 30 million people were added to the population between 1950 and 1960, compared to only 19 million during the 1940s.

The second demographic surprise came in the late 1960s and early 1970s when fertility declined sharply (the **baby bust**). Many factors came together to influence the decline, such as increases in living expenses, the extension of education, increases in voluntary childlessness, and more women employed in the labor force. Cheap and easily accessible contraceptives and abortions, permitting greater control over births, were an added factor. In 1972, the country's TFR dropped for the first time below the replacement level of 2.1. Total population increase in 1972 was only 0.7 percent, almost half of the average annual increase during the 1960s (Kahn, 1974). US fertility kept declining, although not as rapidly as in earlier years. Since 1990, the TFR each year has been right at around 2.0 to 2.1, some years slightly below and other years slightly above. We note later in this chapter that it dropped below 2.0 to 1.9 in 2009, and to 1.6 in 2024.

People continued to settle in and around cities during the first half of the century. By the time of World War II, about two-thirds of the population lived in urban areas, compared to only 40 percent in 1900. Immigration had dwindled after World War I, slowing the pace of heterogeneity. However, as we mentioned in Chapter 7, immigration soared after World War II, reaching its largest levels ever. Once again, heterogeneity became a part of American society.

THE US POPULATION: TODAY AND TOMORROW

The 2020 census counted more than 331 million residents. This absolute numerical increase in the US population between 2010 and 2020 of 22 million people was a little less than the 27.3 million increase between 2000 and 2010, and was quite a bit less than the 32.7 million increase between 1990 and 2000.

In 2024, the estimated US population was almost 337 million. More than 86 percent of the people resided in 2023 in one of the nation's 387 metropolitan areas, and around 8 percent of them in one of the country's 538 micropolitan areas. Although the population living in metropolitan areas, on average, has grown more rapidly than the populations residing in micropolitan areas and in areas neither metropolitan nor micropolitan (Mackun and Wilson, 2011), the inner cities of many of the larger metropolitan areas have been losing population. We will cover these issues in greater detail in Chapter 18.

Two important phenomena warrant noting here. First, heterogeneity has been on the increase. According to the 2020 census, the non-Hispanic White (i.e., Anglo) population represented less than 58 percent of the nation's population – the lowest ever recorded. African Americans comprised 14 percent and Hispanics almost 19 percent. Early in 2003, the Hispanic percentage became larger than the African American percentage, so that Hispanics are now the nation's largest minority group. The Anglo share of the US population has been dropping, from under 90 percent in 1950 to under 58 percent in 2020. If current trends continue, we project that the Anglo population will drop below 50 percent in around 2044 (Poston and Saenz, 2019).

Second, the United States has become an older population. In 2010, more than 40 million elderly (defined as anyone age 65 and over) were enumerated; the 2020 census counted more almost 56 million elders. This is the largest number of elders ever recorded in the United States. As with growing heterogeneity, aging in America is just beginning.

The US Census Bureau prepares projections of the nation's population every few years. We discuss here their recently developed 2020–2060 projections (Vespa et al., 2020). We noted earlier in Chapter 16 that a population projection is a systematic calculation of the future population size of an area using certain assumptions about fertility, mortality, and migration. The projections discussed here were calculated using a cohort-component method approach, "which projects the three components of population change – fertility, mortality, and international migration – separately for each birth cohort based on historical trends. The base population is advanced each year using projected survival rates and net international migration. New birth cohorts are added to the population by applying the annual projected age-specific fertility rates to the female population" (Vespa et al., 2020: 2).

By 2060, there are projected to be almost 405 million people living in the United States, that is, around 67 million more than the 337 million in 2024. The foreign-born population of the country is projected to increase from 46.2 million in 2022 to 69.3

million in 2060, an increase from 13.9 percent of the population in 2022 to 17.1 percent in 2060. The projected foreign-born percentage of 17.1 percent would be the highest ever foreign-born percentage for the country.

Regarding race and ethnicity, by 2060, the United States is projected to become more racially and ethnically diverse compared to the present. The Non-Hispanic White (Anglo) proportion of the US population is the "majority" race–ethnic group in the United States at 58 percent in 2020; it was slightly under 90 percent in 1950 and is projected to fall gradually to 44.3 of the population in 2060. "The point at which the non-Hispanic White population will comprise less than 50 percent of the nation's total population [is the point at which the country] ... becomes a majority-minority nation" (Colby and Ortman, 2015: 9). As noted above (Poston and Saenz, 2019), we have projected this to occur in 2044. At that time, no race–ethnic group in the United States will have a majority share of the population, and the country will have become a "plurality of racial and ethnic groups" (Colby and Ortman, 2015: 9).

The Asian share is projected to increase, from over 7 percent in 2022 to 9.1 percent by 2060. The African American population, while increasing numerically, will see its share grow very little – from 14 percent in 2020 to 15.3 percent in 2060. Persons identifying themselves with two or more races will increase from 3 percent in 2020 to over 7 percent by 2060. The Hispanic population is projected to grow from 19 percent in 2020 to over 25 percent in 2060. The minority population of the United States, that is, all race–ethnic groups except for NH-Whites, is projected to comprise well over one-half of the total population in 2060. The nation can thus expect major shifts in its population composition between now and 2060.

The aging of America is another major challenge for today and for the future. The data in Table 17.1 inform us that in 2020 there were 56.1 million elderly (persons of age 65 and older) in the United States, representing 17 percent of the population. By 2030, there are projected to be over 73 million elders (around 21 percent of the population). By 2060, the projected number of elderly will be just under 95 million (around 23 percent of the population). By 2060, almost one in four inhabitants of the United States is projected to be 65 years of age or older. Between 2020 and 2060, the total US population is projected to increase by almost 22 percent; the elderly population is expected to increase by almost 69 percent. Younger persons (under 18 years of age), by contrast, are projected to increase their size between 2020 and 2060 by just over 8 percent.

TABLE 17.1 *Projections of the older-age (65+) population, 2020 to 2060*

Year	Frequency (millions)	Percentage of total US population
2020	56.1	17
2030	73.1	21
2040	80.8	22
2050	85.7	22
2060	94.7	23

Source: Vespa et al., 2020: 1.

What is causing this enormous growth? Life expectancy among the older citizens is increasing; that is, more people are living longer. More important is the effect of the baby boom. Babies born during the peak years of the boom, between 1950 and 1960, started/will start reaching retirement age in 2020/2030. The huge baby boom cohort of the population that has "haunted" the United States since the late 1940s remains with us and will continue to be with us for some time to come, culminating in, as these data show, a gigantic **senior boom.**

The rather dramatic changes that we have noted are the result of variations in demographic behavior. Indeed, any change in the basic demographic processes will affect population size as well as population composition. There have been significant changes in fertility and mortality, and these have contributed to the size and composition of the nation. We now consider some of these changes.

FERTILITY

Fertility was high during the colonial period. Women averaged eight to ten births, resulting in a crude birth rate (CBR) of about 55 per 1,000. Fertility then began to decline slowly. By 1850, when the CBR was 44.3, women were averaging 5.5 live births. In 1900, the CBR was 29.8; the total fertility rate (TFR) was 3.6. This drop in fertility continued until after the Great Depression in the 1930s. In 1937, the CBR was 17.4 and the TFR was 2.2. This change in fertility mostly mirrors the demographic transition theory (DTT) model we discussed in Chapter 2 and elsewhere in this book.

The birth rate began to increase during the early 1940s. The period after World War II was characterized by rather large increases in fertility; this was expected. Historically, fertility has always increased at the conclusion of a war during demobilization when the men return home and renew the process of family formation interrupted during wartime. However, the fertility rate was not expected to remain high for so long a period. Instead of dropping just a few years after the war ended, the US fertility rate climbed steadily for more than a decade. The TFR in 1957 was 3.7, a figure 60 percent higher than the rate in 1940. The CBR of 25.3 in 1957 was the highest recorded in the United States since 1924. What caused this unexpected baby boom?

It can be partially explained by the "catching up" of veterans after World War II; it can be partially explained by the end of the severe economic conditions during the 1930s. But other factors were also at work. Weller and Bouvier (1981: 57) suggested the following factors as instrumental: (1) The proportion of women in their childbearing years was greater than normal; this resulted from the high fertility of the 1920s relative to that of the 1930s. (2) The percentage of women who remained single dropped significantly during this period. (3) Voluntary childlessness declined to a new low. (4) The three- or four-child family became the norm, as people moved to the suburbs and had more space, time, and money to raise children. (5) The prosperous postwar economic situation encouraged parents to have an extra child. (6) The average age at marriage decreased, and people began having their children sooner after marriage and closer together.

Together, all these factors contributed to the baby boom. The people born in that period have represented and will continue to represent a bulge in the age and sex composition of the nation's population throughout their lives. This is now starting to happen and will continue to happen as the baby boomers become part of the senior boom (Carlson, 2008).

Fertility fell rapidly after the baby boom. By 1961, the CBR was 23.5; by 1968, it was 17.6. By the 1970s, the United States was experiencing a baby bust, and the CBR reached a new low of 14.8 in 1975; in 1978, it was 17.8. The CBR was 13 in 2010, it reached 12.2 in 2016, and 11 in 2024. The TFR also fell spectacularly from its high level of 3.7 in 1957. By 1968, it had fallen to 2.5 and reached 2.1 in 1972. It dropped further to 2.0 in 1972. It then hovered around 2.1 and 2.2 for many years, and then declined to 1.9 in 2009; it reached 1.6 in 2020, and in 2024 remained at 1.6 (Osterman et al., 2024; Population Reference Bureau, 2024).

The rapid shift in behavior from the baby-boom period to the baby-bust period was amazing. Admittedly, fertility could not stay high. Sooner or later, it was bound to fall. However, it only took a short time to accomplish this shift. What are some of the causes of such a change in behavior?

Perhaps the unsettled economic conditions that began in the late 1960s were a factor that led people to postpone marriage or childbearing. Perhaps people felt that they could not afford another baby. Morgan and Rybinska (2019: 323) have noted that "the factors include 'structural' changes in the way we live and work that make children costly, in economic terms and in terms of foregone opportunities. Secular forces also include ideologies of self-actualization and individualism that could become even more powerful and pervasive antinatalist ideologies." In a word, the declines in fertility that occurred in the United States, Europe, and Japan may be explained by "modernity."

Predicting the future course of fertility is difficult, if not impossible. Norms could change; economic booms and busts could occur. Conversely, it is quite likely that we will continue our current pattern of low fertility, and that the two-child (or smaller) family norm will continue as modernity becomes ever more meaningful in the twenty-first century. In Chapter 2 we discussed some of these issues in the context of what demographers refer to as "the second demographic transition."

MORTALITY

Death data for the early years of the United States are scant at best. Nonetheless, Irene and Conrad Taeuber (1971: 495) have written that "the mortality of the early American population was low in comparison with that in many areas of the world at that time." It is estimated that the CDR averaged about 25 per 1,000 between 1800 and 1820. From that high level, the rate dropped steadily, and by 1900 it was 17.2 per 1,000. Americans born in 1900 could expect to live on average for about forty-seven years. In 1940, the CDR was 10.8, it dropped to 8.8 in 1980, and to 8.0 in 2010; in 2024 it was 9.0 (Table 17.2).

A better measure of mortality is life expectancy. When Poston was born in 1940, a newborn male could expect to live, on average, 60.8 years; when Sullivan was born in 1949, a newborn female could expect to live, on average, 70.7 years. In 1950, the life expectancies for males and females were 65.6 years and 71.1 years. And as we show in Table 17.2, since then life expectancy has continued to increase. Data for 2024 indicate

TABLE 17.2 *Mortality in the United States, 1940 to 2024*

Year	CDR	Life expectancy at birth	
		Male	Female
2024	9.0	75.0	80.0
2020	10.3	74.2	79.9
2010	8.0	76.2	81.0
2000	8.5	74.1	79.3
1990	8.6	71.8	78.8
1980	8.8	70.0	77.4
1970	9.5	67.1	74.7
1960	9.5	66.6	73.1
1950	9.6	65.6	71.1
1940	10.8	60.8	65.2

Sources: Murphy et al., 2024; Population Reference Bureau, 2024.

that men can expect to live 75 years from their birth, and women 80 years. Yes, it is true: Women live longer than men! We discussed in earlier chapters the main reasons for the female advantage.

Some molecular biologists have written that we are on the verge of major new discoveries that will increase life expectancy to more than a hundred years in the not-too-distant future, and this has been a topic of discussion for many years (Endres, 1975). No one can say for certain that this will not occur. Some argue it will not. First, there is little evidence that dramatic improvements in disease elimination will come to pass. Heart disease and cancer remain high, and we now have the tragedies of AIDS and COVID to consider. Second, the demographic effects of the elimination of a specific disease will be rather small. For example, the demographer Nathan Keyfitz (1977b: 411–418), estimated that totally eliminating cancer deaths would only increase life expectancy at birth by just about 3 percent. This is because deaths from other causes would increase, and the major causes of death are clustered largely in the same age groups. We mentioned this already in Chapter 5.

INTERNATIONAL MIGRATION

Admittedly, there is a lot of guesswork and conjecturing involved when examining data on international migration. The US Citizenship and Immigration Services (USCIS), formerly the Immigration and Naturalization Service (INS), did not begin gathering immigration data until a few decades into the nineteenth century. These data revealed nothing about undocumented immigration because for all practical purposes, there was no undocumented immigration at that time; there were not then even any immigration laws in existence. Moreover, there are few reliable estimates about emigration, that is, the number of people leaving the United States to live elsewhere.

Since the early 1840s, there have been three main waves of immigrants to the United States, numbering over 104 million people. The first wave occurred between 1840 and 1889 and came mainly from Northern and Western Europe and numbered over 14.3 million. The second wave, from 1890 to 1919, originated in Southern and Eastern

Europe and numbered over 18.2 million. The third wave, from 1965 to 2024, came from Latin America, South/East Asia, Europe, Africa/Middle East and Canada, and numbered over 72 million (Moslimani and Passel, 2024).

The first wave of immigrants was mainly from England, Ireland, and Germany. By the time of the second wave, starting in 1890, the emphasis had shifted from Northern and Western Europe to Southern and Eastern Europe, particularly Italy, Poland, and Greece. It was at that time, too, that immigration from Asia, especially from China and Japan, began to rise. Tensions arose between the older immigrants (mostly WASPs) and these newer immigrants, who were less likely to speak English and were more likely to be Catholic or Jewish rather than Protestant.

The volume of immigration reached what was then a historic peak in the second decade of the twentieth century. Immigration then dropped sharply, in part because of World War I and the Great Depression of the 1930s. Only about 100,000 came during the 1930s. In some years, more people left the country than entered (Taeuber and Taeuber, 1971: 97).

After the Great Depression and World War II, immigration began to increase to levels not seen previously. With the start of the third wave, 4 million came during the latter 1960s, and almost 5 million in the 1970s. During the 1990s and to this day, more than 1 million immigrants enter the United States most every year. "The United States received a historical high of over 1 million legal immigrants annually in the 2000s . . ." (Iceland, 2014: 112). Again, there has been a shift in the sending countries. About one-half of all immigrants to the United States from 1965 to 2023 have been from Latin America. Mexico is the top country of birth. In 2022, about 10.6 million, 23 percent of all immigrants, were born in Mexico. "The next largest origin groups were those from India (6%), China (5%), the Philippines (4%) and El Salvador (3%)" (Moslimani and Passel, 2024).

Figure 17.3 presents data on the numbers of foreign-born persons living in the United States from 1850 to 2010, and projected from 2020 to 2060. Recall our above discussion of the three immigration waves: the first from 1840 to 1889, mainly from Northern Europe; the second from 1890 to 1919, mainly from Southern and Eastern Europe; and the third from 1965 to 2024, from many countries, but mainly Latin America. Compare the size of the much larger third wave with those of the first two waves. Figure 17.3 also gives data projecting the numbers of immigrants in the United States to the year 2060. The projections indicate around 60.2 million immigrants (16.1 percent of the US population) in 2040 and 69.3 million (17.1 percent) in 2060 (Vespa et al, 2020). Recent data indicate that in 2023, the number of US residents born in another country reached a record high of 47.8 million, accounting for 14.3 percent of the total population. "The immigrant share of the population today is the highest since 1910 but remains below the record of 14.8 percent in 1890" (Moslimani and Passel, 2024). But if the projected percentages shown in Figure 17.3 turn out to be correct, they will easily surpass the record-high 14.8 percentage mark that was attained in 1890.

Undocumented (also referred to as *unauthorized* or *irregular*) immigration movements, especially across the country's southern border with Mexico, are significant, although it is difficult to be precise about the numbers. There were perhaps as many as 11.2 million undocumented immigrants residing in the United States in 2012, with 5.9

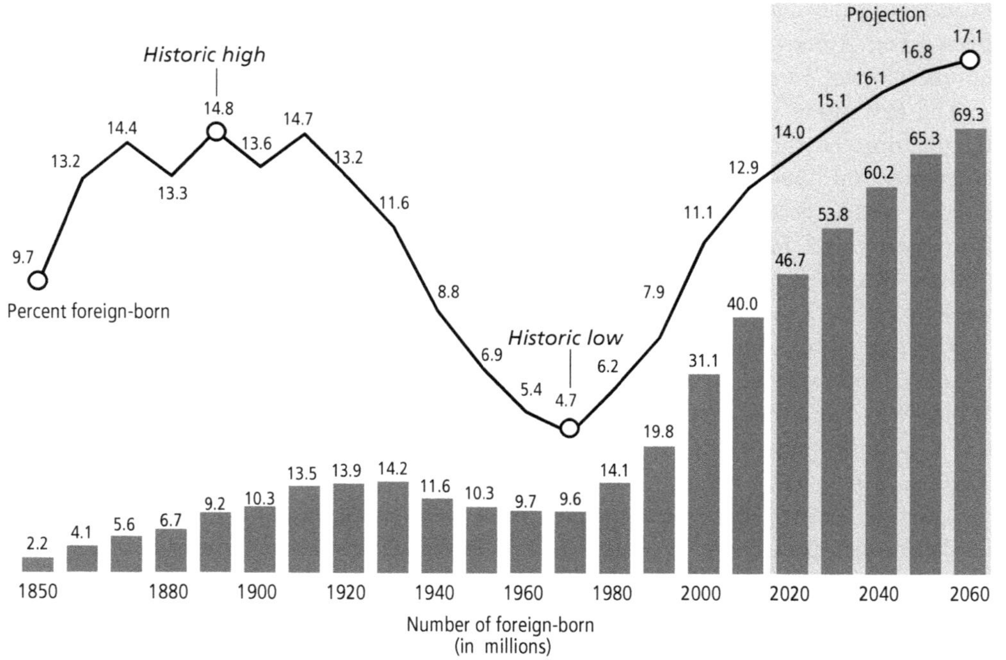

FIGURE 17.3 Foreign-born people living in the United States, 1850 to 2010, and projected numbers from 2020 to 2060. By 2028, the foreign-born share of the US population is projected to be higher than at any time since 1850.
Source: Vespa et al., 2020.

hailing from Mexico (Passel and Cohn, 2014), and around 11 million in the 2020s. We noted in Chapter 7 that undocumented immigrants usually consist of two groups, visa overstayers and persons who entered the country without inspection. Presently, the two groups are about equal in size. Visa overstayers are persons who "entered the US with legal passports and legal visas but either stayed past their visa expiration dates or otherwise violated the terms of their admission into the US, perhaps by accepting employment ... Most flew in legally from Asia, Europe and other continents, and entered at major airports in San Francisco, New York, Los Angeles, Houston and elsewhere" (Poston, 2025). The other group, persons who entered the United States without inspection, are often referred to as EWIs; their entry into the United States occurred "without detection or [they] used fraudulent documents when crossing the border. Almost all of them entered at the US–Mexico border, and until recently most of them were from Mexico. Now, most are from Central America" (Poston, 2025). We reported in Chapter 7 that as of the year 2022, there were roughly 11 million undocumented immigrants in the United States; one-half were visa overstayers and one-half were EWIs.

Future levels of immigration are difficult to forecast. The levels depend on economic conditions in the sending country, as well as those in the United States. More importantly, they depend to a considerable extent on legislation passed by Congress determining the number of immigrants who will be allowed to enter in any given year and the countries from which these immigrants may come.

SUMMARY

Since the first census was taken in 1790, the population of the United States has increased from just less than 4 million to more than 336 million as of 2024 (Figure 17.1). The proportion that is urban has grown from 5 percent to over 80 percent. The US population has aged during the years and will continue to do so in future decades. The population is increasingly heterogeneous and is projected to become more heterogeneous in future years. The twenty-first century will be an era of major shifts. Americans need to be aware of these changes and prepared to adapt to them.

Birth rates and death rates fell steadily during the nineteenth and twentieth centuries. The death rate is unlikely to fall too much more; the birth rate is another story. As we have shown, it has fluctuated wildly during the twentieth century, highlighted by the baby boom and the baby bust. Currently, the TFR is just at about 1.6.

The population of the United States will continue to grow during the twenty-first century but likely at rates below those of the 1950s and 1960s. How large the population will be in 2100 depends on the demographic behavior not only of Americans born in the US but also of immigrants entering the country.

DISCUSSION QUESTIONS

1. In this chapter on population change in the United States, attention is given to the overall impacts of international migration on the size of the US population and its social characteristics. Consider and discuss several of these impacts. Given their effects, do you believe the US should have an international migration policy? Should the policy restrict the numbers of international migrants, or should it have no restrictions, or should there be a middle position? Tell us what the policy should include and be sure and defend your reasons and arguments.
2. Following the end of World War II, the US experienced a baby boom, and it was then followed by a baby bust. Write a paragraph about the boom and then write one about the bust. What factors led to the baby boom? Which factor was the most important one for the boom? Justify your selection. What factors led to the baby bust? Which factor was the most important for the bust? Justify your selection.

18

Population Distribution

INTRODUCTION

Whether one is looking at the planet Earth or at Africa or at the United States or at Texas, it is clear that the population is far from being equally distributed. Fossett and Crowell have written that "structured patterns in spatial distribution are evident from the highest levels of macrospatial scale. . .to fine-grained patterns in metropolitan areas" (2019: 555).

Most know that China's population is more than 1.4 billion, and that the population of the United States is around 340 million. However, many may not be aware that China and the United States are very close in geographic size. China has 9.6 million square kilometers of surface area compared to the United States with 9.8 million square kilometers. But the populations in both countries are not distributed randomly. Most of the people in both countries live in the eastern sections. However, the distribution in China is far more concentrated in the eastern half of the country, where 90 percent of the population resides. A nighttime satellite map of the United States (Figure 18.1) shows that much more than 10 percent of the US population resides in the western half of the country, unlike the situation in China.

In some countries, people are more likely to be rural than urban dwellers. Generally, however, there is an **urbanization** movement throughout the world: "Without question, the dominant feature of spatial distribution in the United States and other developed countries is the concentration of population in densely settled urban areas" (Fossett and Crowell, 2019: 555). For that matter, the way in which cities have evolved is a quite interesting phenomenon. In this chapter, we examine how the inhabitants of the world are distributed, and how most of us have become city dwellers rather than cave dwellers, as was the case thousands of years ago.

DISTRIBUTION OF THE POPULATION OF THE WORLD

Only about one-third of the earth's land is permanently inhabited. Areas such as the Arctic and the Antarctic, as well as the vast deserts such as the Sahara, have very few people. The situation is similar where rugged mountains make it almost impossible for

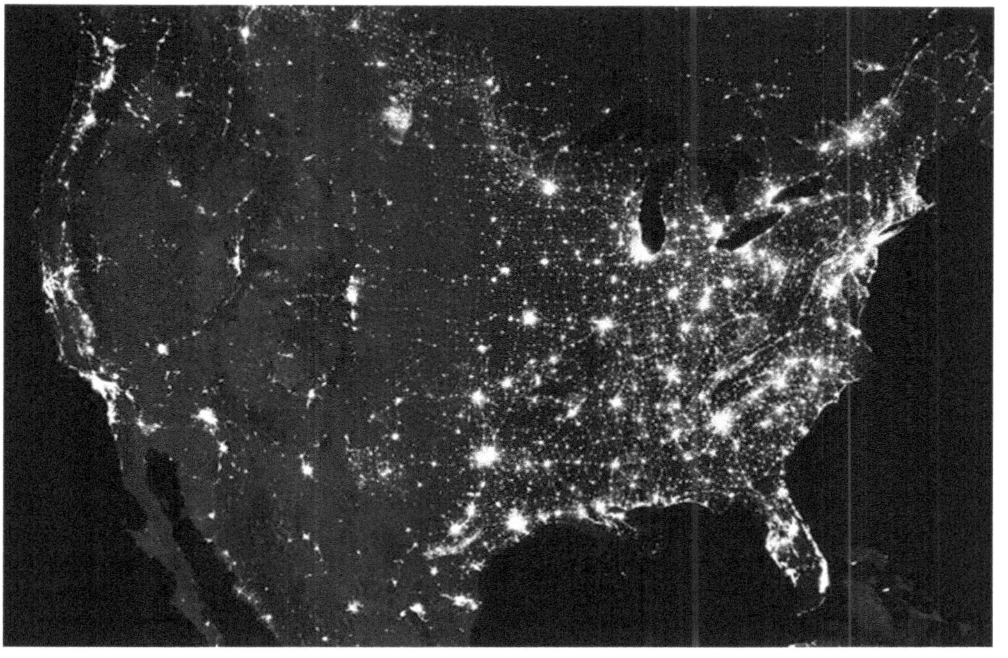

FIGURE 18.1 Nighttime satellite map of the United States
Source: National Aeronautics and Space Administration, available at: https://earthobservatory.nasa.gov/images/79800/city-lights-of-the-united-states-2012

humans to survive. The geographic distribution of the global population is shown in Table 18.1. South Asia (mainly India) and East Asia (mainly China) are the most populated of the world regions. Oceania (primarily Australia) is the least.

Today, four countries have populations that exceed 200 million, and they are led by India and China. Table 18.2 lists the top ten countries by current population size, as of 2024, and projected to 2050.

Back in 1930, Great Britain, France, Germany, and Italy were among the ten largest nations in the world. Changes that have occurred in past decades reflect the rapid growth in developing nations and the slow and even declining growth in many of the developed nations. For several centuries China was the most populous country in the world. In 2022, China registered more deaths in the year than births, and the following year India surpassed China as the most populous. Peering into the future, Table 18.2 informs us that between 2024 and 2050, India is projected to grow by 373 million people, and China is projected to decline by 113 million people. This will mainly be the result of the much lower fertility rate in China (total fertility rates in 2024 in China of 1.0 and in India of 2.0) and the fact that India's current rate of natural increase (RNI) is 1.0 percent and China's is -0.1 percent (Population Reference Bureau, 2024). If present demographic trends in China continue, the country is likely to decline in population to around 800 million by the year 2100 (Poston, 2023a).

Note also the two countries projected to be newcomers to the list of the ten most populated countries in 2050: the Democratic Republic of the Congo (formerly Zaire) and Ethiopia, replacing Japan and Russia. Again, their entry into the top ten is a

TABLE 18.1 *Distribution of the world's population by major area and region, 2024 (in millions)*

Major areas and regions	Estimated midyear population	
WORLD		8,083
Africa		1,478
Northern Africa	261	
Western Africa	444	
Eastern Africa	490	
Middle Africa	212	
Southern Africa	72	
Americas		1,040
Northern America	378	
Central America	181	
Caribbean	44	
South America	437	
Asia		4,773
Western Asia	306	
Central Asia	82	
South Asia	2,046	
Southeast Asia	693	
East Asia	1,646	
Europe		747
Western Europe	200	
Northern Europe	109	
Eastern Europe	286	
Southern Europe	152	
Oceania		46

Source: Population Reference Bureau, 2024.

TABLE 18.2 *The world's ten most populous countries in 2024 and in 2050 (in millions)*

2024		2050	
Country	Population	Country	Population
China	1,364	India	1,669
India	1,296	China	1,251
United States	318	United States	361
Indonesia	252	Pakistan	360
Brazil	203	Nigeria	352
Pakistan	194	Indonesia	319
Nigeria	178	Congo, Dem. Rep.	218
Bangladesh	159	Brazil	218
Russia	144	Ethiopia	215
Japan	127	Bangladesh	215

Source: Population Reference Bureau, 2024.

reflection of the major population increases projected for the African continent and the very low fertility rates in most of the developed nations.

Earlier, we noted that China and the United States are quite similar in areal size, although the former is four times larger in population. Thus, regional or national population figures do not fully take into account differences in the number of people living in the areas. Demographers often use another measure, **population density**, defined as the number of persons per square mile (or square kilometer; a mile equals about 1.6 kilometers). This is a crude measure because it divides the number of persons in the population by the size of the area of the country. An alternative and more meaningful and accurate measure uses the amount of arable land area as the denominator. It is calculated by dividing the number of persons by the area's quantity of arable land (in square kilometers or miles) (Getis, Getis, and Fellmann, 2008; Plane, 2004: 96).

The world's population density in 2023 was 2,203 persons per square kilometer of arable land. The density of the United States was 212, and China's was 1,296. Countries with the highest population densities per square kilometer of arable land in 2023 include the two city states of Singapore and Hong Kong with density values of 1,035,714 and 365,000, respectively. Other countries with high population densities per square kilometer of arable land include Bahrain at 76,190, Seychelles at 66,667, Kuwait at 55,000, and Djibouti at 36,667 (Population Reference Bureau, 2023).

Western Asia is much more densely settled than Western Europe, with population densities of 3,468 and 808, respectively, and Western Asia has a population size that is 100 million larger than that of Western Europe (see Table 18.1). Southeast Asia is the most densely settled, and the third most populated (behind South Asia and East Asia), of all the regions in the world.

Of course, considerable variation in population density exists among countries in the same region, and even greater differences exist within any particular country. In the United States, for instance, vast portions of the Mountain states are sparsely inhabited compared to the Northeast and parts of the West Coast (Map 18.1).

Many factors influence the distribution of the population. These include geographic factors (climate, terrain and soils, and natural resources); economic, social, and political factors (the type of economic activity and the form of social organization); and demographic factors (mainly the rates of population change due to the three demographic processes of fertility, mortality, and migration). These factors continue to contribute to the distribution of the world's population, some more than others. In the sections that follow, some of these factors are considered and their impacts addressed.

RESIDENTIAL DISTRIBUTION AND URBANIZATION

When demographers are discussing population distribution, whether for the world or for a country such as the United States, it is customary for them to examine the percentages of the populations living in rural and urban areas. More than simple numbers are involved here. The economy of rural areas tends to be overwhelmingly agricultural. The economy of an **urban area** is more likely to be diversified and nonagricultural. Sociologists have long pointed out that lifestyles differ in rural and **urban places**. For example, the sociologist Emile Durkheim ([1893] 1984) labeled the lifestyles

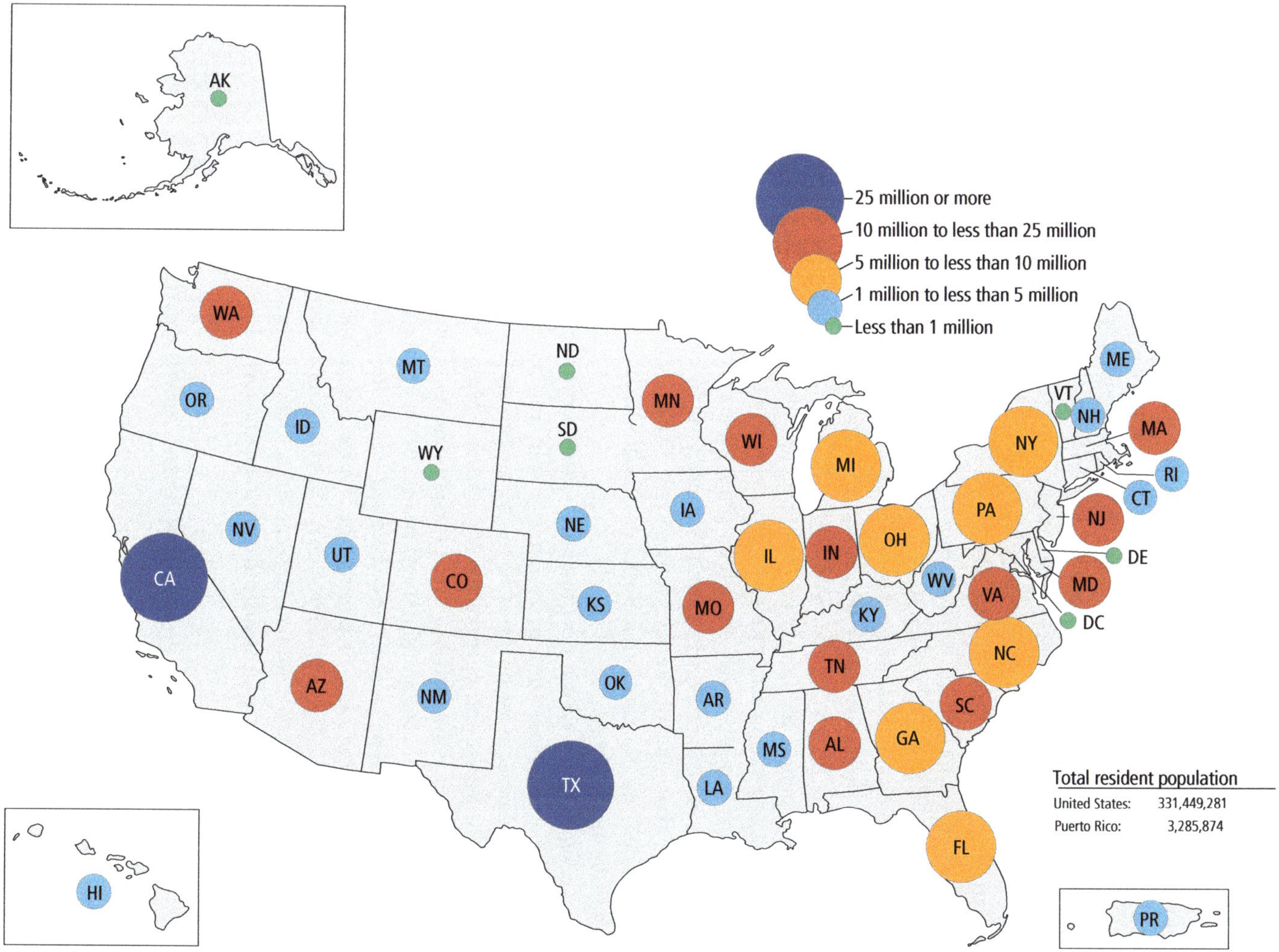

MAP 18.1 Population size in five categories (25 million or more, 10–25 million, 5–10 million, 1–5 million, less than 1 million), of the resident population of each of the fifty states, the District of Columbia, and Puerto Rico, 2020
Source: US Census Bureau.

as mechanical and organic, respectively. That is, in rural areas, behavior and relationships more or less follow mechanical rules and approaches. Roles are not as complex and are few in number. In contrast, in urban areas the roles are many, and there is a division of labor leading to an "organic" lifestyle, that is, one with increasing complexities and differences.

Typically, there are also sharp demographic differences between rural and urban areas. For example, fertility has usually been higher in rural than in urban areas. Educational attainment has been lower. But in industrialized nations, many of these differences have been reduced, largely through the pervasiveness of the modern media, namely, the Internet, cell phones, TV, the radio, and other forms of social media. As a result of these means of rapid communication, distinctions between rural and urban areas have become blurred. The differences, however, are still apparent in most of the developing nations of the world.

Throughout much of history, humans were rural dwellers. Even after the Industrial Revolution, many people were still "living on the farm." They had simply stopped wandering in search of food and shelter. It was really not until the Industrial Revolution that true urbanization began to occur, especially in the countries of Western Europe and their colonies. True, there were exceptions, like the ancient cities of Chang'an in China (now known as Xi'an), Rome, Athens, and several others. These housed governments and religious headquarters but were not urban in the modern meaning of the word. Thus, large-scale **urbanization** – or changes in the proportion of people that dwells in cities – is a modern development. It should not be confused with **urbanism**, which is a reflection of lifestyle and is a sociological, not a demographic, term.

China is the country with the longest urban tradition of any country in the world. Cities made their first appearance in China more than 2,000 years ago. By AD 100, the city of Luoyang had reached a population size of 650,000, a number equal at the time to that of Rome, another **metropolis** (United Nations, 1980: 6). Ancient Chang'an (the present city of Xi'an, the capital of Shaanxi Province) attained a population size of 1 million residents in AD 700, the first million-plus city on record in all of Asia (Chandler and Fox, 1974: 291). Indeed, between 600 and 900, no capital in the Western world would compete with Chang'an "in size and grandeur" (Fairbank and Goldman, 2006: 78). For most of the thousand years between 800 and 1800, China was unsurpassed by any country in the world in both the number and size distribution of its cities (Poston and Gu, 1989).

Three conditions must always be present for cities to develop. First, there must be a surplus of farm products. That is, farmers must produce more than is needed for their own subsistence. Second, there must be a means of transporting these products to the urban areas, where they may be processed into items of food, clothing, and shelter. Third, there must be a sufficiently developed technology in the urban areas to use the farm products and to provide employment for the urban dweller. The mills and factories thus emerge in the urban areas where the products coming from the farms are developed into cotton, machinery, and the like.

The United States serves as an example of how the impacts of the Industrial Revolution contributed to the growth of cities. It is especially important to concentrate on the mode of transportation available at any point in time. Here, we are assuming that the farm regions of the nation are producing a sufficient amount of goods for export to the cities. We are also assuming that the mills and factories are being developed to handle such products. How do they get there? Early in the nineteenth century, water was the main source of transportation. Horses and wagons are not really capable of moving large amounts of material.

The first large and important cities in the United States, thus, were all water based, namely, Boston, New York, Baltimore, and Charleston, South Carolina. The latter was one of the ten largest cities in the nation in 1800, due primarily to the cotton industry and the slave trade. A little later, Chicago and Detroit emerged, mainly because of their locations on the Great Lakes. New Orleans was another early city, the result of its location near the mouth of the Mississippi River.

Then came the railroad era in the nineteenth century, opening up more areas for **urban growth**. Atlanta, Denver, and Indianapolis, among others, emerged as major urban centers. The automobile and the construction of the interstate highway system also contributed to this urban growth. Another recent contributor is the airline system with its hubs. On a smaller dimension, consider that wherever two interstate highways intersect, fast-food restaurants and hotel chains open for business and more residents move in. These may not be particularly great in number but, nevertheless, are examples of how growth follows the transportation modes. Indeed, Garreau (1991) has written about the so-called **edge cities**. These are new "cities" that are actually formed at the edges of metropolitan areas to better serve those residing more remotely from the central cities. (A **central city** is the largest city in a metropolitan area.)

Returning to our discussion of world urbanization, in 1800 only 3 percent of the population of the world was classified as urban. Later, as technological and economic changes made possible large agricultural surpluses, people began moving to the cities in search of jobs in the factories. Consequently, massive urbanization was soon underway. By 1950, 29 percent of all the residents in the world lived in urban places. In 2024, 58 percent of all the world's inhabitants was classified as urban. The United Nations projects this figure to be 70 percent in 2050 (United Nations, 2024b).

Recent urbanization has been especially marked in the developing regions of the world. Some concern has been expressed over this growth as faceless migrants multiply in and near metropolitan areas such as Mexico City and Mumbai (in India, formerly known as Bombay). There, millions of homeless migrants from rural areas live in slum conditions with little hope of securing employment. This is also true of other large cities such as Lagos in Nigeria and Harare in Zimbabwe.

Is this phenomenon urbanization, or is it simply urban growth? We will distinguish between the two. As mentioned earlier, *urbanization* refers to an increase in the percentage of a region's or country's population living in urban areas; *urban growth* refers to an increase in the number of people living in urban areas. This is not to minimize the problems exhibited in today's large cities in developing countries; however, it may well be that the rural populations are also growing.

The enormous growth of large urban areas is a recent development. Large cities existed in ancient times. We already mentioned Chang'an, Rome, and a few others. But such cities were not common. In 1800, only one city in the world, London, had more than a million residents (LeGates, 2006).

TABLE 18.3 *World's ten largest cities in 2018 and 2030 (in thousands)*

City size rank	City	Population in 2018	City	Population in 2030
1	Tokyo, Japan	37,468	Delhi, India	38,939
2	Delhi, India	28,514	Tokyo, Japan	36,574
3	Shanghai, China	25,582	Shanghai, China	32,869
4	São Paulo, Brazil	21,650	Dhaka, Bangladesh	28,076
5	Mexico City, Mexico	21,581	Cairo, Egypt	25,517
6	Cairo, Egypt	20,076	Mumbai, India	24,572
7	Mumbai, India	19,980	Beijing, China	24,282
8	Beijing, China	19,618	Mexico City, Mexico	24,111
9	Dhaka, Bangladesh	19,578	São Paulo, Brazil	23,824
10	Osaka, Japan	19,281	Kinshasa, DR Congo	21,914

Source: United Nations, 2019.

Starting in 1900, however, a very rapid urbanization began in many parts of the world.

> Globally, more people live in urban areas than in rural areas. In 2007, for the first time in history, the global urban population exceeded the global rural population, and the world population has remained predominantly urban thereafter. The planet has gone through a process of rapid urbanization over the past six decades. In 1950 ... 70 per cent of people worldwide lived in rural settlements and ... 30 per cent in urban settlements. In 2014, 54 per cent of the world's population is urban. The urban population is expected to continue to grow, so that by 2050, the world will be one third rural ... and two-thirds urban ..., roughly the reverse of the global rural-urban population distribution of the mid-twentieth century. (United Nations, 2014b: 7)

Table 18.3 presents population data for the ten largest cities in 2018 and the ten cities projected to be the largest in 2030. All have populations larger than 19 million. With almost 37.5 million residents in 2018, Tokyo is the most populous of the world's cities. Tokyo in 2018 had more residents than the countries of Malaysia (34.2 million), Peru (34 million), and Nepal (30 million) in 2024. Delhi and Shanghai with 28.5 million and 25.6 million residents, respectively, follow Tokyo. Next come São Paulo and Mexico City, each with 21.6 million. By 2030, Delhi is projected to have overpassed Tokyo, with a population size of almost 39 million compared to Tokyo's 36.6 million (United Nations, 2019).

ECONOMIC DISTRIBUTION

Another way to consider the distribution of the world's population is to classify people according to the level of **economic development** of their country of residence. Economic development is not an easily defined concept. Two common measures are (1) per capita income, and (2) per capita energy consumption. Each yields similar results with respect to population distribution. The World Bank (2024) distinguishes countries economically according to their per capita gross national incomes (GNI). Countries with a GNI per capita of $1,145 or less in 2023 are classified as "low-income economies," whereas countries with a GNI per capita of more than $14,005 are classified as "high-income economies." In 2024, 15.6 percent of the population of the world resided in countries with high-income economies, and 9.2 percent of the population in countries with low-income economies. North America and Europe contain most of the richest countries, and Africa contains most of the poorest countries.

DISTRIBUTION OF THE UNITED STATES POPULATION

Over history, several trends have occurred to shape the distribution of the population of the United States. Generally, there has been a longtime movement westward. After the end of the Civil War, a migration out of the South also occurred. However, in more recent decades, there has been a resurgence of population movement into the South. Table 18.4 shows population data for each of the four geographic regions of the United States for 1970, 2010, and 2024. (Map 6.1 in Chapter 6 shows the four census regions, as well as their divisions.) In the fifty-four years since 1970, the percentage shares of the US population living in the South and the West have increased, and they have declined in the Northeast and the Midwest.

The United States is divided into four regions and nine divisions (Map 6.1). The nation's population is concentrated in the eastern third of the land area. Vast proportions of the land remain sparsely populated (see Map 18.1). Nevertheless, the long-term trend in geographic distribution has been westward.

Map 18.2 shows the approximate center of the US population for each decade from 1790 to 2020. The **center of population** "is determined as the place where an imaginary, flat, weightless, and rigid map of the United States would balance perfectly if all residents were of identical weight" (US Bureau of the Census, 2007: 11). In 1790, the center of population was located in the upper portion of the Chesapeake Bay. A gradual movement westward followed. By about 1820, the entire middle section of the United States started its growth as agricultural and grazing lands were developed west of the Mississippi. The West began to grow around 1850 as the frontier became more accessible to settlers, rich ore deposits were located, and cheap land became scarcer in the East. As a result of this expansion, the center of population moved farther west with each census. By 1970, the center was located in St. Clair County, Illinois. Since then, the center has continued its movement west and, by 1980, it had crossed the Mississippi River for the first time. As the map illustrates, by the time of the most recent census in

TABLE 18.4 *Population (in thousands) of the United States, by region, 1970, 2010, and 2024*

Region	Population 1970	% 1970	Population 2010	% 2010	Population 2024	% 2024
Northeast	49,041	24.1	55,317	17.9	57,833	17.0
Midwest	56,572	27.8	66,927	21.7	69,597	20.5
South	62,795	30.9	114,556	37.1	132,666	39.0
West	34,804	17.1	71,946	23.3	80,016	23.5

Sources: US Bureau of the Census, 1994, 2024; Mackun and Wilson, 2011.

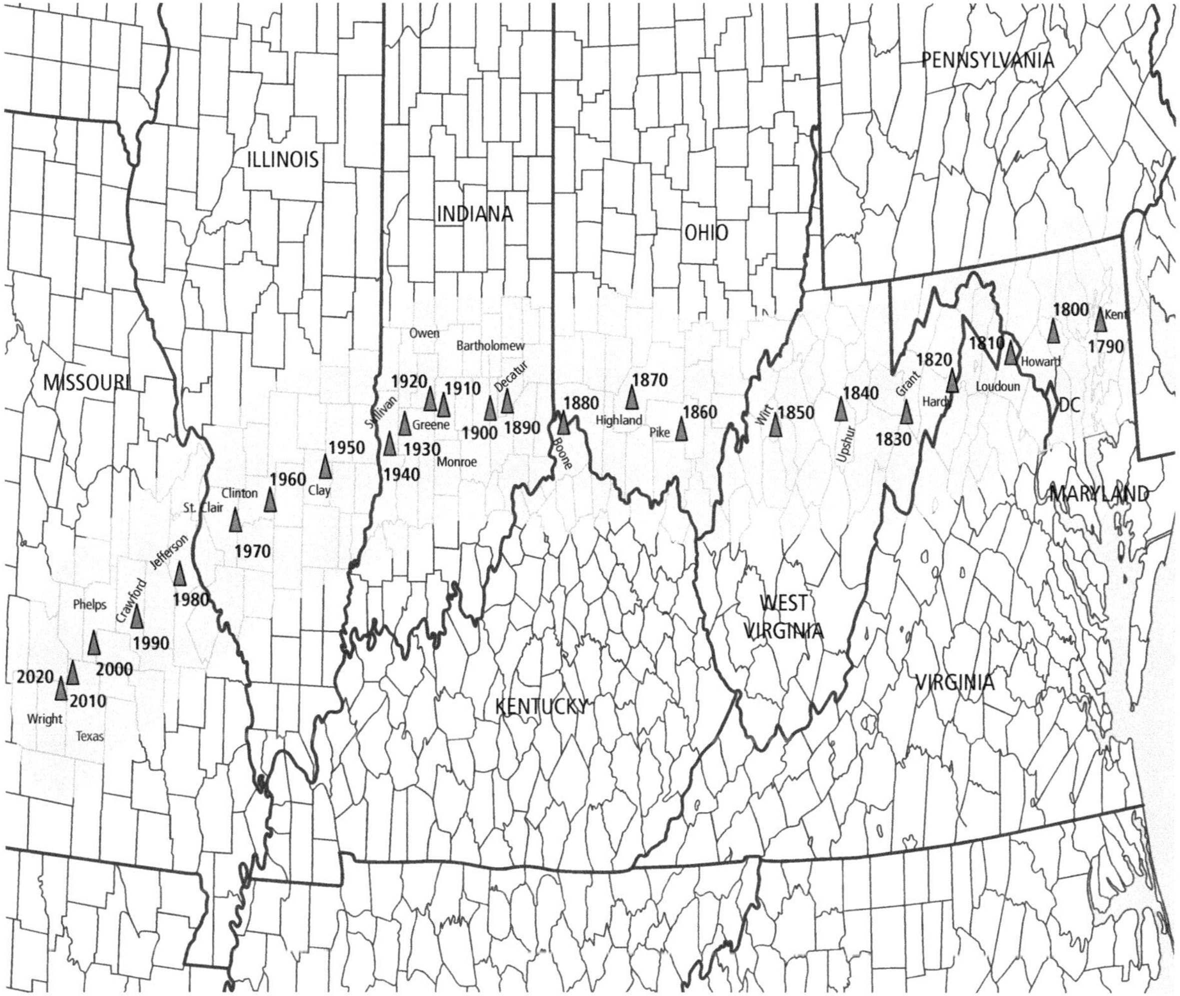

MAP 18.2 Centers of the US population, 1790–2020
Source: US Census Bureau.

2020, the center of the population of the United States was in Wright County, Missouri, near the city of Hartville.

In the past, most changes in US population distribution resulted from migration movements from one part of the country to another. Historically, there has been a movement out of the South into the East, then the Middle West, and finally the Far West. In more recent decades, people have been more likely to move into the South from other regions. Especially notable has been the massive migration of retirees into the states of Florida, Arizona, and Texas. As a result, there is a **concentration** of elderly in these states.

In Chapter 1, we mentioned the situation of an urban area in Florida, The Villages. Despite the fact that deaths outnumbered births, The Villages was one of the fastest growing areas in the United States between 2020 and 2021. Since about 1970, however, the United States has witnessed a substantial increase in international migration, especially from Latin America and Asia. Many of these newcomers have settled in a few states, namely, Florida, California, New York, and Texas. This, too, has contributed to shifts in population distribution. (See our earlier discussions in Chapters 6, 7, and 17.)

METROPOLITANIZATION AND MICROPOLITANIZATION

Even more important than the western and southern shifts in the nation's population has been the rapid concentration in urban areas, or **metropolitanization**. First, we need to define an **urban area**. In the United States, one type of urban area is an **urbanized area** (UA); it consists of a densely settled core of census blocks and block groups that meet minimum population-density requirements, along with adjacent, densely settled surrounding census blocks that together encompass a population of 50,000 people, at least 35,000 of whom live in an area that is not part of a military installation. In contrast, an **urban cluster** (UC) consists of a densely settled core of blocks and block groups, along with adjacent densely settled surrounding blocks that together encompass a population of at least 2,500 people, but fewer than 50,000 people, or greater than 50,000 people if fewer that 35,000 of them live in an area that is not part of a military installation. Strictly speaking, any place that is not in an urban area or urban cluster is defined as *rural*.

Within these broadly defined urban areas, we now consider the concepts of a **metropolitan area** and a **micropolitan area**. The Census Bureau defines them as follows: Metropolitan and micropolitan areas are

> collectively known as core based statistical areas (CBSAs). A metropolitan area contains a core urban area population of 50,000 or more. A micropolitan area contains a core urban area population of at least 10,000 (but less than 50,000). Each metropolitan or micropolitan area consists of one or more counties and includes the counties containing the core urban area, as well as any adjacent counties that have a high degree of social and economic integration (as measured by commuting to work) with the urban core. (Mackun and Wilson, 2011: 4)

In 1900, there were sixty-one areas that would qualify under the above metropolitan area definition. By 1970, the number had grown to 202. The proportion of the US population living in such areas increased from about one-third in 1900 to two-thirds in 1970. This increase was caused both by actual population increase and redefinitions of

TABLE 18.5 *Population size (in thousands), ten largest and the five smallest metropolitan statistical areas, United States, 2023 and 2020, and percentage change, 2020–2023*

MSA	Population 2023	Population 2020	% change
Ten largest			
New York-Newark-Jersey City	19,498	20,082	-2.91
Los Angeles-Long Beach-Anaheim	12,799	13,201	-3.04
Chicago-Naperville-Elgin	9,263	9,449	-1.97
Dallas-Fort Worth-Arlington	8,100	7,637	−6.06
Houston-Pasadena-The Woodlands	7,510	7,145	−5.04
Atlanta-Sandy Springs-Roswell	6,307	6,105	−3.32
Washington, DC-Arlington-Alexandria	6,305	6,279	−0.42
Philadelphia-Camden-Wilmington	6,246	6,245	−0.02
Miami-Fort Lauderdale-West Palm Beach	6,183	6,138	−0.73
Phoenix-Mesa-Chandler	5,070	4,846	−4.63
Five smallest			
Lewiston, ID-WA	66	64	−1.80
Enid, OK	62	63	-1.31
Walla Walla, WA	62	63	-1.62
Carson City, NV	58	59	-1.03
Eagle Pass, TX	58	58	-0.22

Source: US Census Bureau, www.census.gov/data/tables/time-series/demo/popest/2020s-total-metro-and-micro-statistical-areas.html#v2023

these areas as urban living styles spread beyond what had been the traditional city borders. By the 1990s, there were 331 metropolitan areas in the United States, and they contained around 83 percent of the nation's population. By 2023 there were 387 metropolitan areas, containing almost 86 percent of the US population.

The micropolitan area is a new spatial concept that was introduced in 2003. In 2023, there were 538 micropolitan areas in the United States, and they contained 8.4 percent of the country's population. The US Census Bureau has produced a map of the metropolitan and micropolitan areas of the United States as of July 2023. It is too detailed to produce here in this chapter. We suggest that you download the map at this link: (www2.census.gov/geo/maps/metroarea/us_wall/Jul2023/CBSA_WallMap_Jul2023.pdf), enlarge it and then look at the distribution of the metro and micro areas in the United States and in your state.

Table 18.5 presents data on population size in 2023 and in 2020 in the ten largest metropolitan areas of the United States, and in the five smallest. Note that the three largest metro areas, New York, Los Angeles, and Chicago, experienced slight declines in their populations between 2020 and 2023, whereas the next seven largest areas all increased in population size. The fastest-growing metro areas in the United States are all in the West and the South. Sixty or so years ago, the big cities in the Northeast and Midwest would have been included.

What about the micropolitan areas of the United States? Many of the fastest-growing micro areas tend to be located near fast-growing metro areas. Likewise, many that were slow-growing or declining tend to be near metro areas with slower or no growth in their populations.

MEGALOPOLIS

A new community form has been emerging in recent decades, namely, the **megalopolis**. The term is taken from the Greek words *mega* (μέγα), meaning "large," and *polis* (πόλις), meaning "city," for "great (or large) city." The geographic term was first introduced by Patrick Geddes (1915), then by Oswald Spengler ([1918] 1991), and then by Lewis Mumford ([1938] 1970). The French geographer Jean Gottmann (1961) used the term to refer specifically to the chain of metropolitan areas extending along the northeastern coast of the United States. Generally, the term describes any densely populated social and economic entity encompassing two or more cities and the increasingly urbanized space between them.

One can often drive the entire area of a megalopolis, going from one city to another, with barely any break in nongreen spaces. This vast concentration of people, goods, and services functions as an "economic hinge" for the country. It links the North American continent with the foreign markets accessible via the Atlantic.

In particular, this urban phenomenon came to describe the urbanized region of the northeastern United States that arose in the second half of the twentieth century. *Boswash* is a well-known megalopolis, with over 50 million people in 2022. Stretching between the metropolitan areas of Boston on the northeast side to Washington, DC, on the southwest side, it includes the metropolitan areas of New York City, Philadelphia, Baltimore, and the District of Columbia. Boswash starts with the northern suburbs of Boston, which extend into southern New Hampshire. To the south, the Boston suburbs extend toward the northern suburbs of Providence, Rhode Island. Then it follows to New London–New Haven, Connecticut, and the large cities that approach New York. It continues through New Jersey to Philadelphia, Baltimore, and Washington, and then into the southern suburbs of Washington into northern Virginia. Indeed, as suburbs continue to grow, one could make a case that Boswash extends to Richmond, Virginia, and its suburbs.

There are other *megalopolitan areas* in the United States, such as the *Chi-Pitts* megalopolis, with over 59 million people. It is located in the Great Lakes area and comprises the metropolitan areas of Chicago, Pittsburgh, Detroit, Cleveland, Milwaukee, Buffalo, and some others.

The *Texas Triangle* is yet another megalopolis, so named because its three main metro areas of Dallas–Fort Worth, San Antonio, and Houston are connected by interstate highways 45, 10, and 35, which, when connected, form a triangle. Other metro areas in the Texas Triangle are College Station–Bryan, Killeen–Temple, Waco, and Austin–Round Rock–San Marcos. The Texas Triangle contains five of the twenty largest cities in the United States (Houston, San Antonio, Dallas, Austin, and Fort Worth) and is home to over 70 percent of the population of the state of Texas.

The largest megalopolis in the world is the Taiheiyo Belt in Japan, with over 83 million residents, consisting mainly of Tokyo, Okayama, Hiroshima, Osaka, and some other large cities in Japan. It extends from the Ibaraki Prefecture in the northeast to Fukuoka Prefecture in the southwest; it is almost 750 miles long.

However, does a megalopolis have the essential characteristics of a community? It has one such characteristic, namely, a common geographic area that is distinguishable from other areas. To be a community, its people must be linked in a system characterized by a division of labor, increased differentiation of economic activity, and functional interdependence. Without such a pattern of interaction, it is difficult to conceive of a megalopolis as anything other than a grouping of contiguous metropolitan areas sharing a common, heavily populated geographic area.

TRENDS TOWARD DECONCENTRATION

At the same time that the population has become concentrated into metropolitan areas, there has also occurred a **deconcentration** in metropolitan areas. **Suburbanization** has taken place. This represents a shift from the higher-density central cities to the lower-density areas beyond the traditional city limits. Another form of deconcentration is the shift from metropolitan to nonmetropolitan areas.

Since 1900, the proportion of the United States population living in metropolitan areas has increased and, by 2023, around 86 percent of the US population was residing in metropolitan areas. However, since 1930, the proportion living in the central cities of the metropolitan areas has been falling. Thus, while most metropolitan areas have seen population growth, much of that growth has been taking place in the suburban portions. This does not mean that the population of central cities has necessarily declined. Rather, it means that it has grown more slowly than the suburban portions.

Indeed, some of the growth that has occurred in central cities in past decades can be explained by *annexation*, that is, by placing outlying areas under the jurisdiction of the central cities for one reason or another. Jacksonville, Florida, annexed all of Duval County, much of which is actually quite rural. Similarly, Nashville, Tennessee, has annexed all of Davidson County. Houston, Texas, is an example of a city that has grown by leaps and bounds, partly by gradually annexing all of Harris County: "The city of Houston grew by 29 percent during the 1970s – one of the most rapidly growing large cities in the country. But the city also annexed a quarter of a million people. Without the annexation, the city would have grown only modestly" (Miller, 2004: 31).

A number of older US cities have shown population declines in recent decades. For example, Detroit's population has been reduced by over 60 percent since 1950. The US Census Bureau estimated the population of Detroit in 2013 to be less than 700,000 persons, and just over 633,000 in 2023. Detroit had a population in 1950 of over 1.8 million. These older cities are unable to annex contiguous lands because those territories are already incorporated; there are no more unincorporated sections ready to be grabbed by the larger central cities.

The city of San Francisco – the hometown of Poston, one of the coauthors of this book – increased its population from just over 715,000 in 1970 to more than 805,000 in 2010, and to almost 809,000 in 2023. The rate of growth has slowed down in recent years, mainly due to residents out-migrating. But none of the population changes occurred through annexation. San Francisco is bounded on the west by the Pacific Ocean, and on the north and east by the San Francisco Bay, and on the south by the small cities of Daly City and Brisbane. There is no available contiguous territory anywhere for San Francisco to annex, a situation not unlike that of many other older US cities. San Francisco is not too much larger in population today than it was when

Poston was growing up there in the 1940s and 1950s; its population size in 1950 was just over 775,000.

Social reasons also help explain the declining populations of many central cities. One is the so-called **White flight**. The large movement of poorer, often nonwhite, residents into the central cities has contributed to the massive out-migration to the suburbs of the mostly White middle and upper classes. The very fact that large, relatively moderate housing developments were being produced in the suburbs after the end of World War II also contributed to this movement away from the cities. Admittedly, some of the White flight is a matter of out-and-out racism and takes place to avoid sending children to the same schools as people of color or living in the same neighborhoods with them. But the attractiveness of living in the suburbs – that is, owning a piece of land, having a yard, and leading a middle-class life – is difficult to overcome. More recently, middle-class minority families have also taken advantage of such benefits. Indeed, the declining population of the central cities cannot be ascribed solely to racial fears inasmuch as to the fact that Black migration to the suburbs has been accelerating for many years. The negative side of this movement is that the central cities have often been left to the poor and to the underclass.

International migration should also be considered when discussing population distribution. Whether from Europe or Asia, in the late nineteenth and early twentieth centuries, immigrants to the United States were most likely to settle in the poor downtown areas of the big cities. Later, these immigrants, and their children, started moving to the suburbs. A recent upsurge in immigration, some of which is undocumented, represents a new growth for many downtown areas. It is difficult to determine the exact contribution made by such movements, and some undocumented residents are not counted in the census enumerations. It is clear, however, that these newcomers tend to reside near and in close contact with one another, usually in the bigger cities.

However, there are exceptions. For example, certain middle-size cities with a need for low-wage workers often attract undocumented workers. This has been especially true in some sections of North Carolina and Alabama, such as Winston–Salem and Huntsville.

There was a time when internal migration was overwhelmingly from nonmetropolitan to metropolitan areas. This has changed. Today, people are more likely to move from the suburb of one area to the suburb of another. In other words, the traditional move "to the city" is now being bypassed. Those who move within a metropolitan area are often likely to move from the city to the suburbs, and increasingly to the **exurbs**. Furthermore, those who make these moves are apt to be young adults, along with their children. Thus, an area experiencing net in-migration gains population in two ways: (1) through the net number of movers, and (2) through the number of children born to those movers after the migration has occurred.

Summing up our discussion of population deconcentration in the United States, there was first a movement from rural to urban areas. This was followed by a movement from the urban centers to the inner suburbs. Now there is beginning to be movement even farther away from the historic downtowns into the exurbs. This, in turn, leads to the development of **edge cities**, which then typically contribute to growth ever farther from the "downtown."

The New England Patriots of the National Football League (NFL) are an interesting example of what has been happening in recent decades with population distribution and redistribution. Originally, they were called the Boston Patriots. When the size of the population of Boston and, hence, the fan base declined while the suburbs grew rapidly, the team moved from Boston to Foxboro, Massachusetts. But Foxboro is not just a suburb of Boston. It lies in the center of a triangle composed of Boston, Worcester, and Providence. Since other New England states are geographically close to this area, the team decided in 1971 to choose "New England" as its official name, a truly regional name for a professional football team. Similar statements may be made about the regional appeal, and names, of another NFL team, the Tennessee Titans, as well as at least two Major League Baseball teams, the Texas Rangers and the Colorado Rockies.

CONSEQUENCES OF POPULATION DISTRIBUTION

We have briefly alluded to some of the problems related to the geographical movements of people. One consequence is that particular types of economic activities have also relocated to the ring, that is, the outside portions of metropolitan areas. This tends to remove important sources of tax revenues and jobs from the central city. Also, the composition of the population of central cities has changed radically. The out-migrating middle class has been replaced by relatively disadvantaged segments of the population, often poor minority groups, the chronically unemployed, the aged, and the socially disadvantaged.

The significance of this concentration of economically and socially disadvantaged persons in the central cities is twofold. First, the increasing proportion of such persons has added to the demand for related social services, namely, welfare, health, public housing, sanitation, and police protection, to name but a few. At the same time, the economic status of the resident population is lowered because more families tend to move out of the central cities than move in, and because the average income of the out-migrants tends to be higher than that of the in-migrants. The lowered economic status of the resident population and the loss of industry and business activity through deconcentration combine to reduce the tax base. This subsequently leads to declines in the financial ability of the central-city governments to support the increased need for services brought about by the spatial concentration of the disadvantaged. Thus, many central cities, especially the older ones, are confronted with a financial crisis. Demands for services are increasing at the same time that taxable resources are diminishing. To meet the demands, the central city often responds by greatly increasing the property tax rate, which has the effect of forcing more homeowners and industries to move out of the central city, further lowering the tax base. It is a vicious circle.

In recent years, **gentrification**, that is, the migration of middle-class and affluent people into the once poorer areas of cities, has been taking place in some older central cities. People have begun to move back "downtown" from the outer suburbs as the cities offer new opportunities. New condominiums are being built in many of the areas in the city that were once considered depleted. Other rundown sections have been renovated. New office towers have sprung up as businesses begin to realize that there is much to say about being downtown. These movements back into the cities usually involve older, and sometimes retired, Whites, as well as gay men and lesbians, many of them without children (Bradley and Longino, 2009). Whether this will result in sustained population growth in central cities remains to be seen.

SUMMARY

The terms **population explosion** and **population implosion** appear contradictory. Yet they are both occurring these days throughout the world. We have already written about the population growth that occurred during the twentieth century. (See especially our discussions of world population growth in Chapter 16.) But, as an earlier table illustrates, the growth of metropolitan areas has been enormous, while rural areas have lost population. The demographers Avery Guest and Susan Brown have given us an example of this double phenomenon in a very interesting statement that they wrote in 2019 about population distribution in the United States. They noted that "the Las Vegas metropolitan area quadrupled its population between 1980 and the early 2000s, while 43 of the 65 counties in the state of North Dakota lost population" (2019: 51). We can only speculate as to whether this will be the direction of population distribution in the twenty-first century, not only in Nevada and North Dakota, but all over the world.

DISCUSSION QUESTIONS

1. Economic development is usually measured by per capita income or by per capita energy consumption. Define each of these per capita measures. Which one would you argue is best used to measure economic development. Why? Justify demographically and sociologically your preference for one of the two indicators.
2. We showed in this chapter that the center of population in the United States has moved westward with every decennial census since 1790 up to 2020. What would need to happen to the distribution of the US population for the center of the US population to begin moving eastward? Set forth one or more examples of what would need to happen to population distribution in the United States to experience an eastward shift by the 2040 census. In your answer, explain how this would occur.

19

Population Policy

INTRODUCTION

A **population policy** is a deliberately constructed arrangement or program "through which governments influence, directly or indirectly, demographic change" (Demeny, 2003: 752). These arrangements, typically, are "legislative measures, administrative programs, and other governmental actions intended to alter or modify existing population trends in the interest of national survival and welfare" (Eldridge, 1968: 381). The demographer John May has written that "population policies are designed to regulate and, if possible, mitigate the problems [of too rapid growth or decline] by adjusting population size and structure to the needs and aspirations of the people" (2019: 876–877; May, 2012).

Population policies usually represent strategies for governments or sometimes, albeit less frequently, nongovernmental organizations (NGOs) to attain specific goals. The procedures or programs are put into place to ensure that the goals of the policy are attained. A policy is generally intended to either reduce or increase population levels. Policies are developed in the interest of the greater good "to address imbalances between demographic changes, on the one hand, and social, economic, environmental and political goals, on the other" (May, 2019: 877).

We noted in earlier chapters that some countries in the world today have high rates of population growth, that some have negative or near-negative rates of growth, and that many have fertility rates below replacement levels. In 2024, for instance, 107 countries had total fertility rates below 2.1; in 1970 there were only ten such countries (Population Reference Bureau, 2014, 2024). Countries exhibiting demographic conditions of too-high growth or too-low growth sometimes develop policies whose goals are to try to restore the demographic balance.

Whether the issue is severe or minor, demographic behavior is of interest to all governments. In the United States, the onset of the baby boom in the mid-1940s resulted in major changes in governmental action in many areas. And, of course, some governments installed stated government policies, several of which we will review in this chapter.

As we have noted time and time again in earlier chapters, there are only three ways to change the size of a population, namely, through births, deaths, and migrations.

Therefore, any policies aimed at restoring demographic balance must be oriented toward one, two, or all three of these demographic processes. But not all of the options are used as the bases for policies.

To illustrate, a policy with the goal of increasing mortality to lower population growth would be unethical and not considered to be a viable means for solving an issue of population growth. This is not to say that governments have not developed policies to explicitly raise the mortality levels of groups or subgroups in their countries. One need only recall the explicit policies in the not-too-distant past of the Nazi government in Germany and the Khmer Rouge government in Cambodia to raise the mortality levels of certain subgroups in their populations.

Population policies dealing with mortality are usually intended to reduce, not increase, its levels. Reducing mortality, however, is not as popular, nor as prominent, a strategy of population policies. Most policies focus on manipulating fertility and/or migration. Accordingly, they will receive most of our attention in this chapter.

How do governments affect the demographic processes? Generally, they influence the demographic behavior indirectly. Governments typically find ways to persuade people to act voluntarily in a "desired" manner. But oftentimes, mere legislation and propaganda are insufficient to attain the intended goal. Then governments act directly, say, to either raise or lower fertility levels, or to force people to move or not to move.

The task of formulating a population policy is complicated by the fact that sometimes there is no consensus on the appropriate size of the population and/or its fertility or migration rates. There may be some disagreement as to the magnitude of the problem, if, indeed, there is a problem, of population growth or decline. More frequently, there evolves a "laissez-faire" attitude as opposed to a "let's do something about it now" position. For example, today in the United States, there is widespread disagreement as to whether levels of immigration should be reduced or increased. Most groups argue for the former, and a few others the latter.

Furthermore, not everyone agrees on the true meaning of a population policy. Here are some questions pointing to possible issues of disagreement among demographers as well as nondemographers:

1. Must there be an explicit statement by a government that a policy exists? The United States has no official population policy. Nevertheless, the US government finances and sponsors programs designed to eliminate unwanted childbearing and to make contraception available to certain target populations.
2. Does there have to be a planned course of action or program? Sometimes doing nothing is a policy. In 2024, the US total fertility rate (TFR) was 1.6 children per woman, which is below the replacement level of 2.1 children per woman. But the US government does not appear to be much concerned about raising its level of fertility, or lowering it, to compensate for increases to the population via immigration.
3. Must the goals of a policy be demographic, or may they be social and economic? In other words, do the goals have to be direct or indirect? For example, it is well known that, on average, increased educational attainment of women results in lower fertility; the higher the education of women, the fewer, on average, the

number of children they will have born to them. If a developing country decides to improve the educational levels of its female youth, is this a population policy? Yes, but only indirectly. Similarly, opening job opportunities for women tends to result in lower fertility. This is another example of an indirect population policy.

Our point in raising these questions is to illustrate that there are often no "correct" answers. Governments may differ in their definitions and in the formulation of population policies, and it is sometimes difficult to decide whether a specific country has a population policy. Our concern in this chapter is not to make judgments about objectives. Our purpose is to address the question: In what ways may a government influence levels of fertility, mortality, and migration?

THE WORLD POPULATION CONFERENCES AND SESSIONS

The issue of human population growth as a problem or concern is really a twentieth-century phenomenon. However, as we mentioned in Chapter 16, the concern with overpopulation is not new. Indeed, during the eighteenth century, Malthus declared that overpopulation was bound by nature to occur. He and others wrote about population growth and its problems. (See our discussions of Malthus and others in Chapter 2.) But it was not until the 1960s and the early 1970s that the public became acutely aware of them. Several high-profile books – such as *The Population Bomb* (Ehrlich, 1968), *The Limits to Growth* (Meadows et al., 1974), and *Small is Beautiful* (Schumacher, 1975) – brought the issue of overpopulation to the attention of millions of readers. Unlike Malthus, however, many of these authors gave special attention to the degradation of the environment by larger and larger numbers of humans (Poston, DeSalvo, and Meyer, 2009; Russell and Poston, 2008). To this day, there is still some discussion of the issue of overpopulation (Herrington, 2021; Cafaro et al., 2022). Friedman (2005) has noted, for instance, that aspects of these themes of overpopulation and environmental degradation are reflected in the contemporary anti-globalization movement.

Starting in the 1970s, there was considerable debate in academic circles with many advocating voluntary family planning. The position among the so-called birth controllers and many population specialists was that inducing women in developing countries to practice contraception would simultaneously improve their social and economic situation and alleviate the societal problems of their countries (Connelly, 2008; Hodgson and Watkins, 1997). Affluent countries such as the United States, along with private foundations and other organizations, provided large amounts of financial assistance to the population-control movement and the worldwide endeavor to limit population growth.

In 1965, President Lyndon Johnson established an Office of Population in the Department of State and the US Agency for International Development (USAID). The goal of USAID was to convince governments in developing countries to foster contraceptive usage among its citizens. In many instances, this was a politically charged issue that ran counter to traditional **pronatalist** cultural norms, namely, those advocating increases in fertility. The USAID sent teams of demographers and other specialists to countries all over the world to inform their leaders and officials about the impacts of continued rapid population growth. Our deceased colleague and coauthor of the first edition of this book, Leon Bouvier, made such presentations in several Francophone African countries in the early 1980s.

We are writing this chapter in March 2025. At this very time, President Donald Trump is working to dismantle USAID. The Congressional Research Service has estimated that in 2023 the total USAID funding amounted to $40 billion, representing less than 1 percent of the US federal budget. The Trump administration noted in late February of 2025 that it was cutting more than 90 percent of the agency's aid contracts for humanitarian and development work around the world. The Trump administration then notified nearly all the USAID federal employees and told them to resign or be fired. The USAID has been the world's foremost development and foreign assistance agency, and their programs were responsible for saving many millions of lives worldwide (Kutz, 2025). Only time will tell whether the existence and the goals of USAID will be maintained.

The attempts by the United States to promote family planning overseas in countries not yet "ready" for this message sometimes met with cries of imperialism. Officials in the host countries often asked why the United States was promoting family planning instead of addressing, according to their way of thinking, more pressing needs like assistance in relieving the millions of people suffering from malaria (Connelly, 2008). In part to defuse this issue, the United States worked with the United Nations to help create in 1969 the **United Nations Fund for Population Activities (UNFPA)**. UNFPA has served as a major source of funds for population initiatives in developing countries.

Since the United Nations came into existence in 1945, it has sponsored and conducted three world population conferences that were held in 1974, 1984, and 1994; and it has conducted two special sessions of the UN General Assembly in 1999 and 2014 to review, discuss, and assess the implementation of the actions generated at the 1994 conference. And in 2019, the UN Conference on Population and Development was organized in Nairobi to discuss further and assess actions decided at previous meetings. These conferences and assemblies pretty much framed the story of international family planning that has unfolded since the 1970s.

The first World Population Conference was held in Bucharest, Romania, in 1974. It was an attempt to bring together government officials from around the world and to illustrate the facts and consequences of rapid population growth. It was expected by the developed nations attending the conference that the rest of the world would recognize the so-called population problem and join the growing movement to curb population growth. To the surprise of many, there was no such endorsement. Rather, most developing nations stressed their preoccupation with the importance of socioeconomic development, both in its own right and as a catalyst for lowering fertility. They called for a "New Economic Order," whose position was encapsulated in the expression "Development is the best contraceptive."

The second conference was held in Mexico City in 1984. During the ten years since the first conference, many developing countries had changed their opinions about population growth and were now interested in assistance directed toward their fledgling family planning programs. (A **family planning program** is a systematic effort to promote modern fertility control.) African countries, especially, were seeing the benefits of more widespread family planning programs, if not for demographic reasons, then at least for the health of women and children. However, by this time, the political atmosphere in the United States had changed dramatically. The official US delegation under the administration of President Ronald Reagan asserted that "population is a neutral phenomenon" in the development process, and that excessive state control of the economy was more responsible for economic stagnation than population growth (Hodgson and Watkins, 1997). James Buckley, the brother of the late conservative scholar, editor, and journalist William F. Buckley, headed the US delegation.

This unexpected US position stunned the delegates. Instead of rallying the world community behind population issues, the United States introduced to the world its controversial Mexico City policy. The US administration, over strong Congressional objection, decided to police the actions of developing countries with respect to abortion services by refusing to fund the family planning activities of local organizations that also provided abortion, even if abortion was legal in that country and paid for by private funds (Bouvier and Bertrand, 1999).

We note here that one of the first acts of President Bill Clinton's administration when he took office in 1993 was to reverse this policy of President Reagan. But when the administration of George W. Bush came into power in 2001, the Reagan policy was once again restored. With the inauguration of Barack Obama in 2009, the Bush–Reagan policy was changed back to the policy of the Clinton administration regarding the providing of funds for family planning. When President Obama reversed the Bush–Reagan policy on January 23, 2009, he remarked that "for the past eight years [the Bush–Reagan restrictions] have undermined efforts to promote safe and effective voluntary family planning in developing countries. For these reasons it is right for us to rescind this policy and restore critical efforts to protect and empower women and promote global economic development" (Filteau, 2009: 1).

The 1994 International Conference on Population and Development (ICPD) was held in Cairo, Egypt. This conference radically altered the international population movement. Its major outcome was a new definition of population policy, giving prominence to reproductive health and downplaying the demographic rationale for population policy (McIntosh and Finkle, 1995). Two radically diverse groups, feminists and neo-Malthusians, joined forces to create a new manifesto that included the following stipulations: (1) population stabilization is a desirable, ultimate goal, although not one warranting the use of compulsion; (2) national programs enhancing access to contraception are justified in terms of individual human rights, not in terms of their development advantages for populations; and (3) the empowerment of women is a prerequisite for the enduring low fertility that population stabilization requires (Hodgson and Watkins, 1997).

The Cairo conference was considered to be very successful, mainly because it allowed historically opposed and oppressed groups to identify a unified position. Later, however, many officials and scholars working on population matters were surprised that, apparently, discussions of aggregate demographic concerns were being seen as politically incorrect. Indeed, some argued that "programs that are demographically-driven, and are intended to act directly on fertility, are inherently abusive of women's rights to choose the number and timing of their children" (MacIntosh and Finkle, 1995: 260).

Others argued that there is nothing inherently abusive or intrusive about demographically driven population policy (Presser, 1997).

In sum, Cairo "stressed the importance of individual choices and the necessity to further empower women" (May, 2019: 878). An action program was prepared with the consensus and support of 179 governments that "individual human rights and dignity, including the equal rights of women and girls and universal access to sexual and reproductive health and rights, are a necessary precondition for sustainable development" (UNFPA, 2014: iii). More recent international conferences have agreed largely with this preoccupation.

From June 30 to July 2, 1999, a special session of the UN General Assembly met in New York to review and assess the implementation of the program of action agreed to in Cairo in 1994. Governments were encouraged to implement measures to promote the human rights of women; they were further encouraged to strengthen reproductive and sexual health, as well as the reproductive rights features of the population and development policies and programs.

Five years later in 2004, when a fourth world population conference should have occurred, there was no conference. After three conferences in 1974, 1984, and 1994, a conference was indeed planned for 2004. But when the United States, under the administration of President George W. Bush, withdrew its funding of the UNFPA, it was decided to simply incorporate the goals of earlier conferences for the present and the immediate future.

In 2014, twenty years after the Cairo conference, at another special session of the UN General Assembly in New York, the United Nations reviewed the action programs just mentioned and stated that achievements since 1994 have been remarkable. Noted in particular were the worldwide "gains in women's equality, population health and life expectancy, educational attainment, and human rights protection systems" along with the fact that "an estimated 1 billion people [have been moved] out of extreme poverty" (UNFPA, 2014: iii). Also emphasized was the improvement around the world in the dignity of women and adolescent girls, especially the empowering of them "to exercise their reproductive rights." Moreover, it was stressed that "sexual and reproductive health and rights and understanding the implications of population dynamics are foundational to sustainable development" (UNFPA, 2014: iii).

Twenty-five years after the Cairo conference that was held in 1994 (noted above), the United Nations convened on November 12–14, 2019 the Nairobi Summit, known formally as the International Conference on Population and Development +25 (ICPD +25). It also celebrated the 25th anniversary of the Cairo conference. ICPD+25 was held in Nairobi, Kenya. The United Nations Population Fund (UNFPA) and the Kenya government hosted the Nairobi Summit.

The countries attending the Nairobi Summit committed $1 billion for programs in support of gender equality and sexual and reproductive health. An additional $8 billion was pledged to support work on achieving "zero preventable maternal deaths, zero unmet need for family planning, and zero gender-based violence and harmful practices by 2030" (UNFPA, 2019: 57). A large group of participants, from companies and foundations involved in health care, along with technology companies and international NGOs, discussed "the rights of young people and adolescents ... [as well as] reproductive technology, family planning, low fertility, demographic shifts such as ageing societies, sexual and reproductive health and rights of people living with disabilities" (UNFPA, 2019: 12). All pledged to work toward accomplishing the three zeros: "Zero preventable maternal mortality, Zero unmet need for family planning, [and] Zero gender-based violence and harmful practices" (UNFPA, 2019: 17; also see WHO, 2015).

POLICIES AFFECTING FERTILITY

It is interesting to note that in the world population conferences and assemblies just discussed, fertility was a major topic on the agenda. Reductions in maternal mortality were discussed in the Nairobi Summit. But in the other conferences the only attention to mortality occurred in the context of providing assistance in combating malaria. Issues of international migration were never mentioned. Yet immigration has become an important phenomenon in recent decades in many parts of the world, including the United States. In this section of the chapter, we turn attention to actual policies affecting fertility behavior, whether direct or indirect, that is, whether to raise or lower its levels. Mortality and immigration policies will be covered in later sections.

A Brief History

Prior to the twentieth century, most fertility policies were concerned with increasing population growth, that is, they were pronatalist. These policies usually were of three types: pronatalist propaganda; measures related to the family, such as family allowance programs; and restrictions on the distribution and use of contraceptives and abortion.

Some of the earliest-known population policies were those of the Roman Emperor Augustus, enacted between 18 BC and AD 9. Inheritance laws and rules concerning eligibility for office penalized the childless and favored parents. During the medieval period, high mortality caused by plague, especially the Black Death (see Chapter 5), encouraged the development of pronatalist views and policies. In France in the latter part of the thirteenth century, tax exemptions and other privileges were used to encourage fertility. A Spanish edict in 1623 granted tax exemptions to those who married young and who raised large families (Glass, 1940).

It is important to recall that Marxist leaders long believed that population problems in their countries were social and economic rather than demographic. They believed that if matters deteriorated, a social revolution would occur. Thus, in their view, population growth was seen as a spur for the revolution necessary to achieve social, economic, and political change. We later discuss this issue in the context of our discussions of fertility policies in China.

In the twentieth century during the years between World War I and World War II, the pronatalist movement reached its peak in Germany, Italy, and Japan. Intensive pronatalist propaganda, cash payments to families with children, the restriction of access to contraceptives, and the enactment of so-called eugenic laws aimed at encouraging the reproduction of some genetic traits and discouraging others, reflected the attempts of governments to have larger and racially "pure" populations. Such measures were adopted because power and prosperity were equated with large numbers of people (Eldridge, 1968: 382; Teitelbaum, 2019).

France and Romania and a few other countries adopted pronatalist policies at various times after World War I. These policies represented a reaction to the low fertility that accompanied modernization. These nations feared that their national economic and political wellbeing would decline unless their populations continued to grow.

Sometimes countries' policies have both pronatalist and antinatalist effects. France is a good example. In 1920, France prohibited the distribution of birth-control propaganda and devices. The Law of 1920 stipulated that it was illegal to distribute contraceptives or information on fertility control, not unlike the Comstock Act in the United States, which was passed in 1873 and overturned by the US Congress in 1971. In 1932 in France, laws prohibiting abortion were tightened. In 1939, the French government adopted a *Code de la famille*, which incorporated existing family-welfare and pronatalist measures. Allowances were extended to all economically active persons. Marriage loans, premiums on the birth of a first child, and other forms of aid for parents were provided (Glass, 1940). The code was strengthened after 1945 when the crude birth rate (CBR) in France was less than 15/1,000 (Thevenon, 2016).

However, in 1967, France legalized the distribution of contraceptives in response to public demand. By 1974, a new statute was passed that provided for the distribution of free contraceptives, and another law lifted the prohibition on abortion. These measures were adopted to achieve the social goal of voluntary parenthood, but they also illustrate how social policies with antinatalist effects can exist in countries with pronatalist population policies (Bouvier and Bertrand, 1999: 139–140).

It does not appear that pronatalist measures in industrialized countries have ever been very effective. In 1979, the CBR in France was still under 15/1,000; it is even lower today. Total fertility rates (TFRs) in 2024 in all but two of the countries of Europe were below the 2.1 level needed to replace the population. Only Monaco and Kosovo have TFRs of 2.1; all the other countries have TFRs below 2.0, with fifteen below 1.4 (Population Reference Bureau, 2024). Pronatalist policies have not been sufficient to offset the antinatalist aspects of social and economic policies.

Two countries in particularly difficult demographic straits are China with a TFR in 2024 of 1.0, and South Korea, with a TFR in 2024 of 0.7, the lowest fertility rate in the world. In the 1960s and 1970s both had policies to decrease their fertility rates; now, decades later, both have policies to increase their fertility rates. We discuss both of these countries and their fertility policies later in this chapter.

As programs began to develop in France, their administrators were cautious in the face of legal barriers. Indeed, their Law of 1920 (just discussed) proved to be a serious impediment to the reduction of fertility in Francophone African countries. Most African countries successfully removed the law from their statutes by the late 1980s. However, this law unquestionably has had a dampening effect on family planning promotion.

Singapore is another example of a country reversing its population growth policies. Its determination to reduce growth through lowered fertility was very successful. These efforts included indirect measures such as better facilities for health and education. "The initial effort on family planning combined with demographic investments ... and other productive investments have probably accelerated the transformation of Singapore into a new industrialized country; fertility ... dropped to sub replacement levels in 1986" (May, 2019: 890). Its rate of population growth fell from 2.3 to 1.3 percent in the ten-year period between 1968 and 1978 (Jones and Hamid, 2015). In 2024, its TFR was 1.0.

Recently, the government of Singapore expressed grave concerns over this small country's very low fertility and encouraged certain groups, especially Singapore citizens of Chinese ancestry, to elevate their fertility. Indeed, the government organized a commission to devise ways to bring single adults together (Crosette, 1997). A back-to-work program was also introduced to support the goals and activities of women. These days the Singapore government spends over $1 billion annually in programs to raise its moribund birth rate. One program set aside an evening known as "National night" for citizens to specifically allow their patriotism to "explode" and in so doing help raise the birth rate. The government has also limited the number of small one-bedroom flats. Moreover, a couple receives $15,000 for each child along with tax incentives and extended maternity leave. In 2012 the government of Singapore enhanced the country's Marriage and Parenthood Package to "(a) enable couples to get housing faster and more easily, so that they can marry and start families earlier; (b) provide support for conception and delivery costs; (c) further defray child-raising costs, including healthcare costs; (d) enhance work-life measures to help working couples balance work and family commitments; and (e) signal to fathers to play a bigger role through paternity and shared parental leave" (National Population and Talent Division, 2013: 4). Yet, as we noted in the previous paragraph, Singapore's TFR remains very low at 1.0, and is one of the lowest in the world.

Similarly, South Korea and Taiwan have both adopted incentive programs to increase the number of children per household. To this day, however, there is little evidence of any success in raising fertility, and TFRs remain much below the replacement level. In 2024, South Korea's TFR was 0.7 and Taiwan's 0.9 (Population Reference Bureau, 2024).

Focusing specifically on South Korea, the country's government has been providing financial incentives to couples to encourage them to have more children. It has boosted the monthly allowance already in place for married couples to become parents. And in 2023 a new government team was set up to develop new policies to increase the birth rate. To date, programs to increase the low fertility rate have had virtually no effect. Since 2006, the South Korean government has spent well over $200 billion in programs to increase the Korean birth rate. But despite this very sizable investment, Korea's total fertility rate has continued to drop from 1.1 in 2006 to 1.0 in 2017, to 0.9 in 2019, to 0.7 in 2024 (Poston, 2023b). We discuss later the difficulties involved in developing successful programs to increase a country's fertility rate once it has fallen to low levels.

Abortion has long been a method used in some countries to reduce fertility. Restricting access to abortion may result in a sharp increase in fertility. Such was the case in Romania in the 1950s. By 1956, the birth rate had fallen to 24 births per 1,000 population, primarily due to the widespread use of illegal abortion (David and Wright, 1971). In 1957, the government of Romania legalized abortion to allow women to decide whether and when to have children, as well as to reduce the incidence of illegal abortion (Mehlan, 1965). However, the government did not encourage the use of contraception. As a result, induced abortion became the socially accepted means of birth prevention. The CBR fell from 23 in 1957 to 14 in 1966 (Teitelbaum, 1972: 405).

The Romanian government became concerned about its low birth rate and in November 1966 revised its abortion policy. It restricted legal abortion only to cases involving risk to the mother's life, risk of congenital malformation, evidence of rape, pregnancy to women older than 45 years of age, women supporting four or more living children, and a rigorously defined set of physiological conditions, as well as several other limiting social and economic circumstances (Teitelbaum, 1972).

The results of this dramatic change in Romanian population policy were astounding. The CBR tripled in only nine months from 13 per 1,000 in December 1966 to 40 in September 1967. Since then, it has declined steadily, and fertility is now well below replacement; the TFR in Romania in 2013 was 1.3 and was still 1.3 in 2024. Apparently, the decline has occurred because of a strong preference for small families. However, it took a little time for Romanian couples to make the sudden transition from a primary reliance on legal abortion to other methods of birth prevention, including the use of coitus interruptus, condoms, illegally imported contraceptives, and illegal abortion (David and Wright, 1971). In that interval, the birth rate increased substantially.

Thus far, we have concentrated on policies aimed at increasing fertility, although in some instances, the policies have tended to be redirected as the situation demanded. Now we will examine a few antinatalist policies, both direct and indirect. The two basic approaches are government-sponsored family planning programs and various non–family planning approaches.

Antinatalist Policies

Mexico is an example of a country in which the two approaches have been pursued simultaneously. In the early 1970s, the Mexican government engaged in a historic reversal of its pronatalist policies, embarking on an aggressive family planning initiative. Four branches of the public sector were enlisted to implement this strategy. The program also received additional and important support from two private-sector organizations: MEXFAM (the Mexican affiliate of the International Planned Parenthood Federation) and FEMAP (the Mexican Federation of Private Health Assocations and Community Development). Between the early 1970s and 2000, the TFR fell from 6.5 to 2.8. In 2013, the TFR in Mexico was 2.2, just slightly above the replacement level, and in 2024 it was 1.6 (Population Reference Bureau, 2024).

There have been other family planning successes leading to dramatic reductions in population growth. Bangladesh, despite its incredible poverty, finances a large part of the costs of its very active family planning program (Bouvier and Bertrand, 1999: 109). Other countries with active family planning programs include Colombia, the Dominican Republic, Egypt, El Salvador, India, Indonesia, Jamaica, Peru, Tunisia, and Vietnam. Several countries in sub-Saharan Africa – for instance, Ethiopia, Rwanda, and Kenya – have recently implemented fertility control programs, with modest results; their TFRs in 2024 were 4.0, 3.6, and 3.4, respectively (National Academies of Sciences, 2016).

We have been concentrating much of our attention to this point on family planning efforts to reduce population growth, with some mention of policies intended to increase fertility. We need to go "beyond family planning" to get a more complete picture of population policies intended to reduce growth. Generally speaking, increased education and increased labor force participation for females contribute to lowering fertility, albeit, as noted earlier, indirectly. But there are other less opaque methods that have been used to achieve this purpose. India provides a good example.

In the 1950s, India was the first country to introduce incentives to influence childbearing behavior. They were targeted at three groups: (1) acceptors, that is, women and men complying with the government family planning policy; (2) providers, that is, physicians and other healthcare personnel; and (3) promoters, that is, individuals in the community who influenced the acceptors to adopt family planning. Payment was usually in the form of cash to the providers, and cash, services, or gifts to the acceptors and promoters (Freedman and Isaacs, 1993). For example, men received gifts such as radios, traditional garments, and money for undergoing sterilization. However, it should be noted that such incentives are sometimes linked to abuses of human rights. For example, in the 1970s, India not only provided incentives to individuals but also penalized local officials for not reaching assigned quotas. Problems arose when public officials allegedly used force on low-status individuals to meet their quotas. This, in turn, created a backlash, contributing to the defeat of Indira Gandhi's government in 1977, as well as setbacks for family planning in India (Perkins et al., 2013).

China undoubtedly has had one of the most stringent population policies in human history (Poston and Yaukey, 1992: 397–398). Indeed, one reason why China is such an interesting and intriguing country for demographers to study is precisely its fertility policies. Another reason, as noted by Keyfitz (1984: 45), is that in China the political leaders in the past were "able to control the annual number of births with considerable precision." An important point to make in this regard is that family planning in a socialist country like China differs dramatically from family planning as we know it in Western countries. In China, "births are planned by the state to bring the production of human beings in line with the production of material goods" (Greenhalgh, 2008: 46). The numbers of babies produced are heavily controlled by the country.

In the period between 1949, when Mao Zedong and the Chinese Communists assumed control of the country and established the People's Republic of China (PRC), and the early 1970s, China's fertility policy was characterized as "on-again-and-off-again." During the early years of the PRC, there was very little attention given to the size of the population. But when the 1953 census data were made public, many leaders expressed anxiety about the size and growth trends of the country. Accordingly, by the summer of 1956, a birth control campaign was underway. However, this fledgling campaign lost its momentum and importance with the introduction in 1958 of communes and the nationalized movement in the country known as the Great Leap Forward, which was intended to move China to the status of an industrialized society. The Leap proved to be a disaster and, as we have already noted in Chapter 5, there was a tremendous increase in mortality; an estimated 30 to 40 million people died as a result of famine (Ashton et al., 1984; Dikotter, 2010; Yang, 2012). China soon recovered and the fertility rate skyrocketed to a TFR in the early 1960s of more than 6.0. In early 1962, China resumed its family planning program, mainly via the publication of propaganda encouraging family size limitation. But this second campaign lasted only until the beginning of the Great Proletarian Cultural Revolution in 1966, at which time all birth-control efforts in the country were interrupted.

In 1971, China introduced its third family program, the so-called *wan-xi-shao* program, a campaign stressing *later* marriages (*wan*), *longer* intervals between children (*xi*), and *fewer* children (*shao*). However, the large numbers of children born during China's baby boom in the early 1960s caused government leaders and officials in the middle to late 1970s to be concerned about demographic momentum and the concomitant growth potential of this huge cohort. Population projections for China developed by two scientists, Song Jian and Yu Jingyuan, and their associates, showed that under the *wan-xi-shao* program, China would greatly exceed its goal of a population size of 1.2 billion by the year 2000 (Song, Tuan, and Yu, 1985; Song and Yu, 1988). Hence, with arguments and data from Song and his colleagues (Greenhalgh, 2008), the government of Deng Xiaoping approved the "one child is best" norm and intensified its already strong family planning program by launching, in 1979, the so-called One-Child Campaign. Its principal goal was to eliminate births above or equal to three per family, and to encourage families to have no more than one child, especially those in the urban areas. In practice, because of the many exceptions to the policy allowing some couples to have more than one child (Scharping, 2003), China's fertility policy became to be best defined as a one-and-a-half child policy, usually one child allowed for urban dwellers, and sometimes two for rural dwellers and also for members of many of China's minority nationalities. China's total fertility rate dropped from over 6.0 in the early 1970s to significantly below-replacement levels; as we already noted, in 2024 China's TFR was 1.0.

It would be a mistake, however, to attribute the dramatic reduction in China's fertility rate solely to the policies. Yes, the *wan-xi-shao* and the one-child policies likely had impacts in the 1970s and 1980s. But the policies were in force while China was modernizing and moving toward becoming an industrial and urbanized society. Societal modernization has many components, not the least of which are increased and enhanced educational and occupational opportunities for women. Demographers have argued now for almost four decades that China's socioeconomic development must not be overlooked when appraising its remarkable fertility reduction (Poston and Gu, 1987; Poston, 2000; Cai, 2010; Wang, Cai and Gu, 2013; Wang, 2015). As demographer Yong Cai noted several years ago, "structural changes brought about by socioeconomic development and ideational shifts accompanying the new wave of globalization played a key role in China's fertility reduction" (Cai, 2010: 419).

On October 29, 2015, the government abandoned the one-child policy, permitting all couples in China to have two children. The "announcement of the new policy came on the last day of a meeting of top party leaders known as the Fifth Plenum, where they charted out China's economic and social plan for the next five years" (Burkitt, 2015). The government was concerned about its increasing numbers of elderly and small numbers of children. Many leaders believed that "an aging population with fewer young people could drain resources" (Burkitt, 2015), making more difficult the intended shift in the country toward economic policies focusing more so on consumer spending and services. And in May 2021, the two-child policy was abandoned in favor of a three-child policy. The hope was these changes would result in sizable increases in the national fertility rate, which at the time stood at 1.2 – well below the level of 2.1 children per woman of childbearing age that is needed to replace the population.

But these policy changes have not led to fertility increases in China, and there is little reason to think they will result in any fertility uptick in the years ahead. This is because most of China's fertility reduction, especially since the 1990s, has been voluntary and more a result of modernization than fertility control policies. Chinese couples are having fewer children owing to the higher living costs and educational expenses involved in having more than one child (Poston, 2023a).

We do not expect that these policy changes will result in any dramatic increases in China's fertility rate. The total fertility rate in China might go up over the next decade by 0.1 or 0.2 at best, in our opinion. But demographers largely agree that it will never go up by one child or more per woman, the kind of increases needed if China is to reach the replacement level.

One factor to take into consideration is what demographers refer to as the "low fertility trap." This hypothesis, advanced by demographers in the 2000s (Lutz, 2006), holds that once a country's fertility rate drops below 1.5 or 1.4 – and China's is now at 1.0 – it is very difficult to increase it by a significant amount. The argument goes that fertility declines to these low levels are largely the result of changes in living standards and increasing opportunities for women. Accordingly, it is most unlikely that China's three-child policy will have any influence at all on raising the fertility rate.

China's past fertility policies – the antinatalist ones – have been characterized by some as especially coercive. For instance, Aird (1990) wrote that the policy followed a cycles-of-coercion model of family planning: The Chinese central authorities enforced an unpopular birth-control policy by exerting the local authorities to coerce the people and to force them to accept the program's mandates. The pressures continued until opposition became so strong that a relaxation of the policy occurred, which led to more new births than can be allowed, thus leading to another wave of coercion. This caused the kinds of fluctuations one sees in China's vacillating fertility rates, especially in the 1980s and early 1990s.

An alternate view espouses a linear model in which, over time, the mandates of an unpopular policy are more and more relaxed, and the mechanisms for enforcing the regulations are weakened; increasing numbers of couples, especially rural ones, are permitted to have more children. A linear model does not necessarily assume that all of the political directives in China are top-to-bottom in direction, but that cadres, who are the approximate equivalent in China of civil servants, at the local level have considerable influence in not only enforcing but also developing fertility plans and policies (Greenhalgh, 1986; 1990a; 2008).

Pronatalist Policies

We now move away from countries that were once characterized by fertility policies designed to reduce population growth, and direct attention to countries with policies encouraging population growth. Some of the countries mentioned above with antinatalist policies now have pronatalist policies; we'll mention two of them in this section, once again China, as well as South Korea. The current situation in many of the countries in the world is one with fertility rates well below the level needed to replace the population. We noted earlier that as of 2024, 107 countries of the world had total fertility rates below 2.1. Such low rates over a long period of time have many consequences, not the least of which is a dramatic aging of the population and, later, a reduction in the size of the population. Thus, there is much concern about below-replacement fertility in many countries. The concern is not solely about population decline but also about the aging of the population owing to the very low fertility. This kind of ramification of a below-replacement fertility rate in place for several decades will challenge social security and healthcare systems and may even hinder productivity and global competitiveness (Lutz, O'Neil, and Scherbov, 2003).

Development of pronatalist policies in countries these days is difficult to promote. Today, family policies seem to be based on an equal-opportunities rationale and aim to help women combine childrearing with employment (Lutz, O'Neil, and Scherbov, 2003). Different countries have developed different types of policies to encourage increased fertility. We have already mentioned France. In recent years, France has employed numerous policies with two purposes, namely, reconciling family life with work and reversing declining fertility. According to the Rand Corporation,

> To accomplish the first goal, France instituted generous child-care subsidies. To accomplish the second goal, families have been rewarded for having at least three children. Sweden, by contrast, reversed the fertility declines it experienced in the 1970s through a different mix of policies, none of which had the specific objective of raising fertility. Its parental work policies during the 1980s allowed many women to raise children while remaining in the workforce. The mechanisms for doing so were flexible work schedules, quality childcare, and extensive parental leave on reasonable economic terms. (Rand Corporation, 1995: 1–4; Thevenon, 2016)

Other countries have implemented fertility policies involving financial remittances for each child born, liberal parental-leave benefits, and guaranteed childcare and schooling for children. One of the most expansive and generous fertility policies has been enacted in Australia, where remittances per child per year exceeded US $3,000 (Balter, 2006). The efforts to increase the country's fertility rate have been extensive. The TFR actually increased between 2001 and 2008 from 1.73 to 1.96. An appraisal of the effects of the policies on this small increase suggest that components of the program known as the "Baby Bonus" and the "Child Care Rebate" have had only a slight effect. Most of the small fertility increase has been attributed to indirect effects, such as increased levels of education and income (Parr and Guest, 2011; McDonald, 2015).

In Russia, efforts to increase fertility have focused on an aggressive pronatalist policy involving financial incentives, medals for "baby-making," and an array of other awards (Rodriguez, 2009; see also Eberstadt, 2009). However, the effectiveness of these fertility incentives is hotly debated. Some argue that incentives are beneficial in easing the financial burdens caused by additional children, making families more willing to increase their childbearing. Others emphasize that any increases due to these policies will be small, as was the case in Australia. While financial resources may make it easier for families to pay for the children they already want to have, they are unlikely to raise fertility to the level necessary to stave off population decline (Howden and Poston, 2008).

We have already mentioned China and South Korea. Let us look at them again, this time focusing on some of the implications of their extremely low fertility rates. In 2024

China's TFR stood at 1.0, and South Korea's at 0.7. China's leaders have become very concerned about the country's extremely low fertility rate and its effect on the age distribution. The country has stopped growing and in 2022, for the first time in a long time, experienced more deaths than births. China's future is one of declining population, with an enormous increase in the numbers of elderly. Compounding the problem, China has long been hostile to the idea of supplementing its native-born population with persons born elsewhere; just 0.1 percent of China's population is foreign-born; this is the smallest percentage of any major country in the world.

Thus, in late July 2024, China's ruling Communist Party adopted a resolution that would see the country's statutory retirement age gradually rise over the next five years. The final retirement age has not been specified, but it is likely to end up at around 65 years. This would put China more in line with other large countries, including the United States. In 2024 China had one of the lowest retirement ages in the world, at 60 for men, and 55 for women in white-collar jobs or 50 if they are in blue-collar jobs. Party leaders have mulled reforming China's retirement plan for several years. But the apparent urgency in 2024 reflected a growing concern over the impact that a shrinking and aging population would have on the country's dwindling pension resources. In 2019 the Chinese Academy of Social Sciences projected that funds set aside to cover retirement costs in China could be completely used up by 2035 (Poston, 2024b).

Population projections developed by the United Nations (2024b) suggest that if current trends continue China's population will fall below 1 billion in 2070, below 800 million in 2086 and down to 633 million by 2100. This would represent a loss in around 75 years of more than half its current population of 1.4 billion. A population decline that drastic would wreak havoc on its labor force, causing untold economic problems. Furthermore, there would be large increases in the numbers of elderly. In 2023, 20 percent of China's population was in the current retirement bracket of 60 and over. But by 2100, according to the UN projections, this is projected to increase to an astounding high of over 52 percent.

China needs immigrants. But as we noted earlier in Chapter 10, changing immigration policies will likely require a change in mindset. China's current immigration policies are characterized by a deep-rooted belief in racial purity. The best way to maintain this racial purity, many in China believe, is to limit or prohibit migration into China. Were the Chinese to relax their immigration policies, it would not only boost the numbers of people, but it would also bring in more younger people. Immigrants are typically of prime working age and productive, and they also tend to have more younger children than native-born residents (Poston, 2023a).

South Korea is in a similar situation, with an even lower fertility rate. In the more than sixty-year period from 1960 to 2024, South Korea has undergone the most rapid fertility decline in recorded human history. In 1960, the country's total fertility rate stood at just under six children per woman. In 2024, it had declined to 0.7 children per woman. With its extremely low fertility rate, in recent years South Korea has been seeing population decline; since 2020 the country has been experiencing more deaths than births. This once-vibrant nation is on the way to becoming a country with lots of elderly people and few workers. If this trend continues, and if South Korea does not start welcoming millions of immigrants, its population in 2024 of 52 million is likely to decline to under 38 million in the next four or five decades (Poston, 2023b).

To be sure, even if successful, these are long-term goals in China and South Korea and some other countries that will take decades to come to fruition. While international migration may be beneficial in the redistribution of national populations, immigration policies encouraging migration from developing countries remain the least-favored policies of countries experiencing population declines (Howden and Poston, 2008). We will focus on immigration policy in a later section.

In sum, fertility policies vary across the world, and they have for decades. In some regions, birth rates are high; in others, they are low. Both governmental and nongovernmental agencies have been and are involved in attempting to restore some demographic balance in their respective societies.

POLICIES AFFECTING MORTALITY

Some demographers hold that mortality-related policies should not be considered to be direct population policies. The reduction of mortality should be the goal of governments, even those wishing to reduce their rates of population growth. Thus, measures taken by governments that deal with mortality may only be viewed as indirect population policies as long as they have a demographic effect. For example, most industrialized countries subsidize medical care. Often, medical clinics provide free healthcare to the public. While these can be said to be examples of health care policies, their overall effect is to increase life expectancy. We look now at some examples of how indirect policies can affect mortality by causing either increases or decreases in the number of deaths.

Mortality policies receiving the most attention are those supporting the development of medical knowledge with the potential to expand life expectancy, as, for example, through the development of new wonder drugs or the facilitation of organ transplants. Beginning in the eighteenth century, there was considerable scientific work in this area of medical knowledge. The work of scientists such as Edward Jenner (1749–1823), Louis Pasteur (1822–1895), and Alexander Fleming (1881–1955) all contributed to the reduction of mortality in Western Europe and elsewhere. Before World War II, "colonial powers as well as independent governments in Latin American and Asia had enacted public health measures, launched sanitation and disease vector control programs, and organized targeted campaigns to bring down high mortality levels, notably in cities" (May, 2019: 885).

The demographer Massimo Livi-Bacci (2012) has noted that programs to eradicate malaria in Sri Lanka (then known as Ceylon) were successful as early as in the 1940s, and the successes were mainly attributable to the use of DDT (dichloro-diphenyl-trichloroethane). For centuries, mosquitoes had been major killers in Ceylon and elsewhere, where the malaria parasite would afflict "more than half of the population with anemia and chronic fatigue" (Connelly, 2008: 116). In the mid-1940s, public health officials sprayed more than half a million homes in Ceylon with DDT: "Within two years the total number of malaria cases had been cut by three-quarters, and six years later life expectancy had increased from 46 years to 60, largely because of the decline in infant mortality" (Connelly, 2008: 116).

Government policies can directly contribute to lower mortality. Almost every developed country in the world offers free or subsidized healthcare to all its citizens. This is reflected in comparative levels of life expectancy, as we discussed earlier in Chapter 5. Government policies aimed at reducing the incidence of specific diseases are clearly related to mortality. In 1972, then-President Richard Nixon declared a "War on Cancer," and millions of dollars were spent for this purpose with much success. Thousands of lives are saved each year as a result of government regulations requiring installation of safety features, such as seat belts in new vehicles.

Perhaps the most publicized health policy that affects mortality relates to the use of tobacco. The US National Institutes of Health have for many years cited studies showing a strong positive relationship between smoking and the risk of lung cancer and certain cardiovascular diseases. Even second-hand smoke is detrimental. Today in the United States, smoking is banned in virtually all public buildings, including restaurants and bars in most states. Again, these efforts were not directly intended to increase life expectancy; their intent was to improve health.

If we accept the fact that some existing government measures or policies contribute to declining mortality, we must also accept the fact that some government policies can lead to increased mortality. Measures that endanger health, although unintentionally, will eventually raise mortality. Just as there are policies that decrease mortality, there are also policies that raise it.

International warfare is the most obvious mortality-related governmental policy. Hundreds of millions of people have been killed as a result of humans declaring war on one another. We noted earlier in Chapter 5 that the greatest number of deaths due to wars occurred during the first part of the last century: "Plausible sizes of the military and civilian death toll would be around 8.5 million in World War I and 40 million in World War II" (Etherington, 2003: 964). The number of civilian deaths due to wars usually exceeds the number of military deaths. For instance, it is likely that during World War II in Russia, 60 percent of the deaths were to civilians (Petersen, 1975: 269). The Civil War resulted in the greatest number of American deaths of any war ever experienced by the United States, before or after. Around 620,000 men died during the four years of fighting between 1861 and 1865 (Faust, 2008).

Government policies are sometimes deliberately aimed at increasing mortality. We discussed earlier the practice of genocide in Nazi Germany as an example. Sadly, the world has witnessed more and more genocides in recent decades, for example, in Rwanda where Hutus tried to eliminate Tutsis, and in the Darfur region of Sudan where religious hatred led to millions of deaths.

In far less revolting ways, governments frequently, albeit indirectly, affect mortality. Even while state and federal agencies are speaking out against smoking, they continue to subsidize tobacco growers and benefit from cigarette tax revenues. Indeed, cigarette advertising is still allowed in many media, except in broadcasting. Cigarette smoking, however, is but a minor contributor to air pollution; its main lethal effects are in the lungs and other organs of smokers.

For decades, the growth policies of most developed countries have resulted in increased degrees of smog and dangerous chemicals, which infect the environment, both air and water. Epidemiologists have found relationships between polluted air and water and the prevalence of certain respiratory and gastrointestinal diseases. Nicholson (1976) found in the mid-1970s that asbestos and textile workers with twenty years of working in the industry had more than four times greater risk of cancer of the respiratory system than the general population.

Perhaps the strongest example of failure on the part of the US government to do everything possible to improve health and longevity is its policy on medical assistance. For at least a half-century, there has been a growing demand for a national health program. According to an observation written more than seventy years ago but still applicable today, the United States remains "the only great industrial country without a compulsory nationwide program for health insurance or sickness benefits. ...There is ample evidence, however, of a shift of public opinion toward handling medical care as a predictable and insurable risk and responsibility" (Woytinsky and Woytinsky, 1953: 238). Note that this statement was made more than seventy years ago!

The United States has instituted the Medicare and Medicaid programs to help the poor and the aged. Assistance has been provided to the elderly for pharmaceutical expenses. An almost nationwide program of health insurance in the United States known as the Affordable Care Act, colloquially as Obamacare, was signed into law by President Barack Obama on March 23, 2010, and upheld by the US Supreme Court on June 28, 2012, and again on June 22, 2015. But it continues to be challenged. In January 2025 the court heard yet another case involving the Affordable Care Act. This lawsuit followed many prior and unsuccessful efforts by some conservative litigants to abolish the Affordable Care Act. Yes, the Act has surely raised the insurance coverage levels of the population, but, still, not everyone is covered.

For its degree of modernization, the United States has a poor showing on various health indices, such as life expectancy and infant mortality, an issue that we already discussed in Chapter 5. Perhaps the failure to institute a national health program that would provide subsidized medical care to everyone explains in part this poor showing.

Thus far, we have concentrated on policies related to natural population change. We now turn to policies related to immigration.

POLICIES AFFECTING INTERNATIONAL MIGRATION

Throughout most of human history, people have been free to move about in search of a better life. We noted in Chapter 7 that human populations began their migrations out of Africa around 50,000 to 60,000 years ago, first going to southern Asia, China, and Java, and later to Europe. There were no legal encumbrances then that made such moves difficult or impossible. To a considerable extent, however, such freedom of international movement has been significantly restricted since late in the nineteenth century. Many countries have introduced laws that infringe on the freedom to engage in international migration. In some instances, people have not been permitted to enter a country, and, in other instances, people have not been allowed to enter certain parts of a country.

Policies regarding international migration are much more common and pervasive than those pertaining to internal migration. Nevertheless, some governments have taken measures to encourage movement into some areas and out of others. There have been instances of policies involving both nations and areas within a nation. An example of the latter is China's prohibition of many rural residents to migrate legally to urban areas, an issue we discussed in Chapter 6. In this section, we restrict our discussions to policies related to international migration.

Some countries encourage immigration in order to increase the size of their population. This was true of the United States during the eighteenth and nineteenth centuries. Immigration from other countries was necessary for the United States to grow in population. Canada, Australia, and New Zealand also fall into this category. Indeed, most of the current residents of these countries are immigrants or the descendants of immigrants. In the United States in 2023, less than 3 percent of the US resident population, around 8.8 million people, identified as American Indian/Alaskan Native alone or in combination with one or more other races. This means that more than 97 percent of the US population is comprised of persons with no American Indian / Alaskan Native ancestry. Thus, more than 97 percent of the US population consists of immigrants or the descendants of immigrants. But the United States, Canada, Australia, and New Zealand, all of which owe their heritage to immigration, are no longer encouraging large numbers of people to immigrate there.

Today, Israel is one of the few countries that actively seeks immigrants. We noted earlier in this chapter that more countries should be seeking immigrants, but few are doing so. In Israel immigration is considered the lifeblood of the country. Other nations, faced with rapid population growth, view **emigration** (movement out of a country) as a safety valve to relieve population pressures; some of the Caribbean countries are examples. In actuality, there are no countries in the world today without some sort of immigration policy, for or against. Some encourage immigration, and others, such as Japan (Tsuya, 2015), allow little if any immigration. In the few countries that permit modest amounts of immigration, such as the United States, there is often considerable discussion, and even disagreement, about the numbers and the policies, and how those policies should be enforced.

In the developed world today, there are three main types of national immigration regimes. The first is the so-called traditional immigration regime. The United States, Canada, and Australia are the three most important and sizable traditional immigration countries: "Founded by European settlers, they have long experiences with immigration and [to this day] allow the acquisition of citizenship through naturalization or birth within their territory" (Freeman, 2003: 515). The numbers of people legally admitted into these three countries are categorized in terms of family unification, economic needs of the country, and refugees. The United States admits most of their immigrants under the family unification category, whereas Canada and Australia admit most of their immigrants under the skilled worker category. These three countries used to restrict immigrants on the basis of their national origins; persons from certain European countries were usually preferred. But "all three countries ceased to discriminate on the basis of national origin by the early 1970s" (Freeman, 2003: 515).

The second type of national immigration regime includes countries that mainly allow immigrants to enter as guest workers. In past decades these were primarily "European countries that recruited temporary labor, i.e., guest workers, or received substantial colonial migration during the post–World War II economic expansions" (Freeman, 2003: 516). The immigrants came from Southern Europe, Eastern Europe, North

Africa, Turkey, South Asia, and the West Indies, for the most part. The receiving countries were mainly in Northern and Western Europe, particularly Germany, Great Britain, France, and the Netherlands. These immigrations stopped in the early 1970s, but not many of the guest workers ever returned to their home countries. Indeed, most of the workers brought members of their families into their new host destinations. Consequently, by the 1980s, most of the countries in Northern and Western European had large immigrant and foreign-born populations, as well as second-generation immigrants, many of whom were not citizens of these host countries. Today, many Gulf countries, for example, Qatar, the United Arab Emirates (UAE), and Kuwait, among others, fall into this second category. Recall Figure 10.3 that we presented in Chapter 10 showing the huge imbalances in the UAE in the working-age population of males from other countries.

The third type of immigration regime is mainly in the group of Southern and Southeastern European countries "more likely to receive than to send immigrants" (Freeman, 2003: 516). The four countries most prominent in this category are Greece, Spain, Portugal, and Italy. These countries serve as entry points for undocumented immigrants from other countries who are seeking to enter the European Union (EU). As a consequence, in early 2022, almost 24 million non-EU citizens had immigrated to EU countries, representing over 5 percent of the EU's 447 million inhabitants. Over 75 percent of them reside in Germany, Spain, France, and Italy (United Nations, Regional Information Center, 2023). When one adds in the children of these immigrants, the foreign population becomes larger. Freeman (2003) has remarked about the difficulties that these countries have experienced in embracing multiculturalism. Their difficulties may be compared with the less difficult and problematic experiences of the United States, Canada, and Australia. To get an idea of the many and varied types of immigration policies, we turn in the next section to a discussion of the history of immigration policies in the United States.

US IMMIGRATION POLICIES

Immigration was not a concern in early America, and there were no formal laws or policies regulating immigration on a national level. But the new *US Constitution* dealt with the issue of naturalization, that is, the process by which an individual becomes a citizen (Purcell, 1995). The *Articles of Confederation* allowed aliens to naturalize as American citizens after two years residence in the United States, something that was not previously permitted under British rule (Gabaccia, 2002). These policies, however, did not apply to White indentured servants or to Blacks. The restrictions were particularly reflected in the Aliens Acts of 1798, which required aliens to register and allowed the president to deport any individuals deemed dangerous. The laws expired in 1801 when Thomas Jefferson became president, and the citizenship waiting period increased to five years (Cortes and Poston, 2008; Purcell, 1995).

One of the most notable laws restricting immigration to the United States was the Chinese Exclusion Act of May 6, 1882, which reflected the public concern about the large numbers of Chinese who had come to the country to provide inexpensive labor for the construction of the transcontinental railroad. This law suspended the immigration of

Chinese laborers for ten years; it permitted Chinese who were in the United States as of November 17, 1880, to stay, travel abroad, and return; it prohibited the naturalization of Chinese; and it created the so-called Section 6 exempt status for Chinese teachers, students, merchants, and travelers who were admitted on the presentation of certificates from the Chinese government (Cortes and Poston, 2008).

The next significant exclusionary legislation was the Act to Prohibit the Coming of Chinese Persons into the United States of May 1892, better known as the Geary Act, and discussed earlier in more detail in Chapter 7. It allowed Chinese laborers to travel home to China and reenter the United States, but its provisions were very restrictive. Other restrictive immigration Acts affecting citizens of Chinese ancestry followed (King and Locke, 1980). The Chinese Exclusion Act and later exclusionary laws were the first to use the concept of an illegal **alien** (Pedraza and Rumbaut, 1996).

The next major immigration policy was the 1917 Immigration Act that increased the head tax on immigrants to $8.00 and required incoming migrants to pass literacy tests. The Immigration Act also "established several new categories for exclusion, including vagrants, alcoholics, and the psychopathically inferior" (Purcell, 1995: 82). This law required the potential immigrant to be able to read a passage in English or in another language. It also extended the exclusion of Chinese and Japanese to all Asians (Cortes and Poston, 2008).

In 1921, further restrictions were passed that set quotas based on nation of origin. In 1924, Congress took this one step further by passing the National Origins Act, which restricted the total number of immigrants to 150,000; the division of the quotas reflected the American population enumerated in the 1890 census. This was done in an attempt to accept mainly immigrants from Great Britain, Scandinavia, and Germany, while reducing immigration from all Asian countries and severely restricting the immigration of Italians, Slavs, Jews, Greeks, and other Southern and Eastern Europeans (Purcell, 1995).

From the 1920s to the 1950s, immigration in the United States changed significantly. The Great Depression and World War II resulted in a period of slow and sometimes negative immigration, culminating in net losses in population size due to international migration. The only significant immigration was from Mexico under the *bracero* program, which admitted Mexican male workers while Americans were overseas (see Chapter 7). In 1952, the Immigration and Nationality Act of 1952, also known as the McCarran–Walter Act was passed, maintaining most of the quotas set forth in the National Origins Act of 1924 (Hay, 2001). It was introduced by Representative Francis E. Walter of Pennsylvania and Representative Pat McCarran of Nevada.

The next major US immigration policy was the Immigration and Nationality Act of 1965, also known as the Hart–Cellar Act; it became law in 1968. It was proposed by Representative Emanuel Cellar of New York and cosponsored by Senator Philip Hart of Michigan. This Act, signed by President Lyndon B. Johnson, ended the national origins quota system and allowed the immigration of family members of those already living in the United States, as well as individuals in certain occupations. It also ended the restrictions on Asian immigration, and it limited immigration from the Western Hemisphere as a whole to 120,000 (Hay, 2001). Iceland has noted that the most significant effect of the 1965 law "was that it spurred immigration from countries that had little recent history of sending immigrants to the United States, especially Asia and later Africa" (2014: 111).

Total permanent immigration to the United States has undergone many changes in recent years. The numbers increased from about 600,000 in 1986 and 1987 to over 1.8 million in 1991, and then back to around 660,000 in 1998. The number of immigrants increased to over 1 million in 2001 and 2002, dropped to under 1 million in 2003 and 2004, and then rose to over 1 million in the years up to 2012, falling back to just under 1 million in 2013 (US Department of Homeland Security, 2014: table 1).

Since 2014, the numbers of persons immigrating to the United States have vacillated around 1 million per year. Starting after 2020 the number increased to nearly 1.7 million in the 2021–2022 period and to 2.8 million in the 2023–2024 period; this surge accounted for more than four-fifths of the country's population growth for the period (Frey, 2025).

The rise in the total number from 1987 to 1991 may be attributed in part to the Immigration Reform and Control Act (IRCA) of 1986 that granted legal status to undocumented immigrants who had been in the United States continuously since 1982. This Act has also been cited as a reason for the increased number of pending "adjustment of status" applications and the subsequent reduction in the number of approved applications. "Immigration continues to invoke heated debates, particularly in light of the ... Trump administration's proposed policies regarding immigration control and deportations, which could sharply reduce immigrant gains for the U.S. population" (Frey, 2025).

Changes in the numbers of permanent immigrants to the United States from all countries in the world are also explained in part by the impact of the Immigration Act of 1990, which revised the annual ceiling on immigration and the preference categories used to regulate immigration. This Act, which became effective on October 1, 1991, increased the levels of employment-based immigration and allotted a higher proportion of visas to highly skilled immigrants.

The numbers of permanent immigrants from China to the United States have fluctuated since 1989. The IRCA, a one-time-only amnesty, does not appear to have had as dramatic an impact on Chinese permanent immigration as it had on total permanent immigration. Indeed, the Chinese immigration rate to the United States has been relatively stable since 1980, except for increases in 1993 and 1994. They were due in part to the influence of the Immigration Act of 1990 but, more importantly, to the Chinese Student Protection Act of 1992, a bill sponsored by Representative Nancy Pelosi of California, which granted permanent resident status to Chinese immigrants who were in the United States after June 4, 1989, and before April 11, 1990. Its stated purpose was to prevent the political persecution of Chinese students in the aftermath of the Tiananmen demonstrations and protests of 1989. One of its provisions was that permanent residency status slots granted to Chinese nationals under the Act would be subtracted from the immigration spaces available in later years. But, ironically, the primary beneficiaries of this Act were reported to be undocumented immigrants from Fujian Province, China, who were not students at all (Poston and Luo, 2007).

From 2004 to 2013, the numbers of Chinese immigrants to the United States ranged from 55,000 to 72,000 per year, resulting in China being one of the three countries sending the largest numbers of immigrants each year to the United States (US Department of Homeland Security, 2014: table 3). In 2023 there were over 2.4 million immigrants living in the United States who hailed from China. Immigrants from China are the third largest immigrant group in the United States, after Mexico and India (Greene and Batalova, 2025).

In 1996, two laws were passed that impacted the levels of permanent immigration to the United States, namely, the Welfare Reform Act of 1996 and the Illegal Immigration Reform and Immigrant Responsibility Act of 1996. One eliminated the entitlement of support for poor families, requiring able-bodied persons who received government assistance to work (Espenshade, Baraka, and Huber, 1997). The other circumscribed the eligibility of immigrants for public benefit programs by creating a four-tier system. Espenshade and his colleagues have noted that "the broadest eligibility is reserved for U.S. citizens; next come refugees and asylees; newly limited access is imposed on legal immigrants; and illegal immigrants remain ineligible for almost all social programs" (1997: 771–772). Prior to its enactment, US citizens, legal immigrants, and refugees were all equally eligible for most public benefit programs. (An **asylee** is a person forced to leave home to seek legal refugee status in another country.)

The Illegal Immigration Reform and Immigrant Responsibility Act of 1996 was passed to strengthen the effects of the Welfare Reform Act that year by combating illegal immigration and creating higher standards of financial self-sufficiency for the admission of sponsored legal immigrants. This Act focused in particular on immigrant access to public benefits: (1) it established measures to control US borders, protect legal workers through worksite enforcement, and remove criminal and other deportable aliens; (2) it placed added restrictions on benefits for aliens; and (3) it introduced miscellaneous limitation provisions, such as a limit on the ability of F-1 students to attend public schools without reimbursing those institutions.

Espenshade, Baraka, and Huber (1997) have argued that the combined effects of these two laws of 1996 have had important consequences. The welfare reforms of 1996 led to a larger number of eligible legal immigrants becoming naturalized so that the actual cost savings attributable to benefits for immigrants were smaller than expected. In addition, the 1996 immigration and welfare reforms were expected to reduce the future volume of US legal immigration and to produce a legal immigrant stream with higher skill and income levels.

In 1998, the US Congress passed the American Competitiveness and Workforce Improvement Act. It was a response, in part, to the belief in the Congress that the United States was facing a severe shortage of workers qualified to perform skilled jobs in information technology, even though the evidence of a shortage was inconclusive. Under this Act, the annual ceiling of certain petitions valid for initial employment was increased from 65,000 to 115,000 in fiscal years 1999 and 2000 and to 107,500 in 2001.

The stated purpose of the Act was to protect native-born American workers by preventing employers from hiring low-skilled aliens instead of native-born workers. Employers are required to take good-faith steps to recruit American workers for jobs potentially performed by certain immigrants, and to offer the jobs to American workers who are equally or better qualified than the aliens.

The Enhanced Border Security and Visa Entry Reform Act of 2002 dealt with entry documents and data sharing among government agencies. It was passed by the Congress and signed into law by President George W. Bush on May 14, 2002, around eight months after the terrorist attacks of 9/11. It represented "the most comprehensive immigration-related response to the continuing terrorist threat" faced by the United States (Jenks, 2002:1).

The Real ID Act of 2005 modified several federal laws pertaining to the issuance standards of drivers' licenses and identification cards accepted by the federal government for official purposes, such as entering federal buildings and boarding national and international air flights.

The preceding is a summary of many of the immigration and immigration-based laws passed in the United States since the late 1800s. The immigration laws, especially the more recent ones, are numerous and very complex in their meaning and interpretation. Attorneys specializing in immigration law are needed these days to facilitate the entry of immigrants into the United States, and this process, if it is successful, usually takes not months but years. Compare this long-drawn-out and complicated process of entering the country with that of many of our ancestors who entered the United States after undergoing a screening at Ellis Island of, at best, a few days (see Chapter 7).

REPLACEMENT MIGRATION

We noted earlier that in this new era of declining fertility and reductions in population size, countries might consider turning to immigration as a means for redressing the population losses occurring through fertility. In other words, migration could be used as a means for replacing the population lost through fertility. In this last section, we consider the concept of **replacement migration** (Keeley, 2009), how it works and how it would be applied. We do so within the context of South Korea, a country with an extremely low fertility rate in 2024 of 0.7 children per woman.

US Census Bureau population projections prepared for South Korea for the next several decades indicate that if the country does not welcome several millions of immigrants into the country, its present population of 52 million will drop to under 38 million by 2070 or so, and a growing proportion of the Korean society will be over the age of 65.

South Korea's population aged 65 and over comprised under 7 percent of the population in 2000. By 2050 the country is projected to be comprised of lots of older people. Elders now comprise around one-fifth of the country's population and could reach an unprecedented and astoundingly high 43 percent in 2050. South Korea's working-age population will then be just a few million larger in size than its population of elders.

By 2050, South Korea is projected to have made the transition to a top-heavy and demographically very old country. What are some of the implications of the aging of South Korea's population? One effect is the tremendous change that will occur in the extent to which the older members of the population will be able to be supported economically and emotionally by the younger members. To appraise quantitatively the extent of this age-structure imbalance, the United Nations (2001) developed a measure of elderly support, known as the **potential support ratio** (PSR). It represents "the extent that persons of working age [15 to 64] can be seen as supporting the older population [65 years or older], and is the ratio between the two" (United Nations, 2001: 7). The PSR value represents the number of persons in the population who "support" each old person in the population.

Please do not confuse the potential support ratio (PSR) with another PSR measure we discussed in Chapter 13, namely, the parent support ratio (PSR). It takes the number of persons 80 years old and older, per 100 persons of aged 50–64; it represents the relative burden that the oldest-old population, that is, the elderly parents, has on the population aged 50–64, that is, the children of the elderly parents.

To illustrate, we show in Table 19.1 that in 1950 in South Korea, there were 11.26 million persons of aged 15–64 and 610,000 persons 65+. Dividing the former by the latter indicates the number of persons in the population who are available to support every one old person. In 1950, the PSR for South Korea was 18.5. The United States had a PSR in 1950 of 8.0, less than half that of South Korea, mainly because the US fertility rate at the time was considerably lower than South Korea's. The values of the PSR for South Korea and for the United States for 1950, 2025, and 2050 are shown in Table 19.1.

In the last few decades in South Korea, "life expectancy at birth for both sexes combined increased from 47.5 years in 1950–55 to 70.9 years in 1990–95" (United Nations, 2001: 59). In 2024, life expectancy at birth for males was 80 years, and it was 86 years for females (Population Reference Bureau, 2024). Increasing levels of life expectancy, along with a rapidly declining fertility rate, have resulted in the pace of population aging in South Korea being one of the fastest in the world. The proportion of

TABLE 19.1 *Total population and population in broad age groups (in millions), potential support ratios (PSR), South Korea and the United States, 1950, 2025, and 2050*

	1950	2025	2050
South Korea			
Total population	20.34	51.49	45.65
Age group 0–14	8.48	5.23	2.35
Age group 15–64	11.26	35.54	23.78
Age group 65+	0.61	10.72	19.52
Potential support ratio (15–64 / 65+)	18.46	3.32	1.22
United States			
Total population	152.27	338.02	360.64
Age group 0–14	41.00	58.02	54.83
Age group 15–64	98.88	216.67	223.68
Age group 65+	12.40	63.32	82.13
Potential support ratio (15–64 / 65+)	7.97	3.42	2.72

Source: 2025 and 2050 projection data from International Database of the US Census Bureau. www.census.gov/data-tools/demo/idb/.
Calculations by DLP.

persons age 65 and older in South Korea's population increased from 3.0 percent in 1950 to 4.0 percent in 1960 to 5.6 percent in 1995 (United Nations, 2001: 59) to 11 percent in 2010, and it is projected to be 43 percent in 2050.

Of even greater interest is the change in the PSRs. The PSR dropped from 18.5 in 1950 to 6.6 in 2010. Whereas in 1950 there were more than eighteen "supporting" persons in the South Korean population for every one old person, this ratio declined in 2010 to less than seven supporters for every one old person. During this sixty-year period, the PSR also decreased in the United States from 8 to 5. In 2010, the PSR of the United States was a little less than that of South Korea.

By 2025, however, the PSR in South Korea is projected to plummet to 3.3, and in 2050 to 1.2. That is, in South Korea in 2050, there will be just over one supporting person available per every one South Korean elder. The United States is projected to have a PSR in 2050 of 2.7, more than twice that of South Korea. The process of population aging in the United States has been less rapid than the aging process in South Korea.

Given the projected PSR of 1.2 for South Korea for 2050, one might ask what could be done to return to a higher PSR. Specifically, what would South Korea have to do demographically to have a PSR of 12 in 2050 instead of the projected PSR of 1.2? (We selected a PSR of 12 because it is midway between South Korea's PSRs of 18 in 1950 and 6 in 2010.) In other words, what would South Korea have to do to alter its demographic destiny of a highly imbalanced PSR of 1.2 for 2050? How could South Korea obtain more persons in the supporting population so as to offset its very low projected PSR for 2050?

One way would be to increase the fertility rate. South Korea's TFR of 0.7 in 2024 is the lowest in the world. Some countries have introduced population policies to raise their fertility rates, and we reviewed some of these earlier in this chapter. Although this is one approach, it would be demographically inefficient because even if it worked, and we suspect it would not work, it takes many years before a newborn becomes a supporting member of the population. Plus, the "low fertility trap" works very much against a country's raising its fertility rate once it falls below 1.5 or 1.4.

A quicker approach would be international migration, a strategy that would permit South Korea to bring supporting members into its population directly and immediately. How many international migrants would South Korea require if the end result would be to maintain, from 2025 through the year of 2050, a PSR of around 12? That is, between the years of 2025 and 2050, how many immigrants would South Korea need to admit into the country if it wished to maintain a PSR of 12?

The answer is an astonishingly high number of 4.7 billion immigrants! That is, for South Korea to maintain between 2025 and 2050 a PSR of 12 supporters for every one elderly, it would require a total of 4,749,382,000 immigrants (United Nations, 2001: 57), or an average of almost 189 million immigrants each year. The UN reports that this "number is enormous because the initial level of the PSR ... is relatively high" (2001: 60). This number of immigrants into South Korea required between 2025 and 2050 would be almost 60 percent of the current total population of the world.

A less drastic scenario would be to ask how many immigrants would South Korea need if the end result was to keep the PSR in future years at 3.0. We have shown in Table

19.1 that South Korea's PSR in 2025 was expected to be 3.3 and projected to be 1.2 in 2050. If South Korea's policymakers wished to not allow the PSR to reach the projected level of 1.2, but to stabilize at 3.0, how many immigrants would be needed?

To attain this objective, "no immigrants would be needed until 2035, and 11.6 million immigrants would be needed between 2035 and 2050, an average of 0.8 million" new immigrants per year (United Nations, 2001: 60). Under this scenario, South Korea would have a total population in 2050 of 65.7 million, of which "14 million, or 21 percent, would be post-1995 immigrants or their descendants" (United Nations, 2001: 60).

The provision of elder care in South Korea will be a major concern between now and the year of 2050 and beyond. As we have mentioned above, Korea's PSR was over 18 in 1950 and is projected to drop precipitously to 1.2 by 2050. One way for South Korea to offset this dramatic decline in its PSR would be to develop population policies encouraging persons to immigrate to South Korea, that is, to turn to international migration for demographic replacement. Although replacement migration is a more efficient strategy than increasing fertility, the number of replacement immigrants needed is so large that this approach may not be quite as easy as one might suspect. Nevertheless, we agree with Keeley that "replacement migration will probably continue to be a topic that is redressed from time to time as the demography of the last century and the demographic behaviors of the 21st century play out in a variety of social settings. ... Its salience, however, is unlikely to become very high" (2009: 403).

SUMMARY

Populations change in size, composition, and distribution via fertility, mortality, and migration. But these changes do not occur randomly. Many governments have passed laws and regulations that deal with their levels of fertility, mortality, and migration, particularly migration. Many of the laws represent direct effects to influence national rates of population change, and others involve indirect effects.

Regarding policies intended to influence levels of fertility, there are two main approaches. One is to provide birth-control knowledge and services and related enhancements through massive government-sponsored family and family planning programs. The other is to change the social and economic environments so that people are motivated to have fewer, or more, children. Examples of these nonprogram efforts include modernization, payments for having or not having children, increased opportunities for the employment of women, population education, and maternal and paternal employment leaves. The two approaches are often viewed as complementing each other.

Governments influence mortality mainly through their attempts to improve the health levels of the population. But there are several government practices, for instance, wars, that serve to increase mortality rather than lower it. The failure of governments to enact remedial laws and programs, say, regarding health insurance coverage, has also been shown to increase mortality.

Governments also have laws and policies influencing the numbers of people coming across their borders, and some have laws related to persons departing. The United States receives the largest number of immigrants of any country of the world and, consequently, has a wealth of laws dealing with immigration, many of which we reviewed and commented on in this chapter. At times, countries have expressed a concern in their immigration laws about the "quality" of the population. This was particularly the case with immigration laws invoked in many countries, including the United States, in the last two centuries, regarding the national origins of the immigrants. Such concerns, along with laws to address them continue to this day. Quality restrictions are still found in the immigration laws of many countries regarding the labor-force, educational, and economic qualifications of potential immigrants.

With the increasing number of countries in the world today with below-replacement fertility – 107 countries in 2024 had fertility rates below the replacement level of 2.1 children per woman – we can expect to see more countries writing and implementing policies in an attempt to increase the numbers of babies born. With the growing socioeconomic gap between countries and the desires of persons from the poorer countries to move to the better-off countries, we can expect the receiving countries to continue to prepare policies and laws in an attempt to regulate and balance these streams of migrants from abroad. But the policies, whatever their intention and reason for their genesis, will never be successful unless they take into account the social, cultural, and economic milieu in which demographic behavior occurs, and unless they consider the indirect as well as the direct effects.

DISCUSSION QUESTIONS

1. Imagine you are the legislative aide to a US Senator. The Senator asks you to write a memo outlining which population policy or policies the United States should undertake in the next ten years. In the policy area/areas you decide to focus on, first discuss the existing policy/policies and why it/they should be changed. Then provide detailed justification, demographic and social, about why the policy area/areas should be developed or expanded. You may also consider whether there are existing policies that should be expanded or eliminated.
2. What do demographers mean by "replacement migration"? In your opinion, is replacement migration a more efficient strategy for maintaining a balanced population than would be increasing fertility? Why or why not?

20

The Earth in the Twenty-First and Twenty-Second Centuries

INTRODUCTION

You now know more demography than you did when you first started to read this book. You have learned a good deal about population and demography and the world in which we live. There is much more to learn, but even at this point you have probably acquired a good bit of demographic literacy. We hope that this knowledge will benefit you no matter what your future career path might be. In this chapter, we provide a quick summary and then imagine with you how the human population could change and develop as far as the next century.

We have discussed the three demographic processes: fertility, mortality, and migration. We have discussed the basic population characteristics, especially age and sex, as well as the family and race/ethnicity. We have discussed population growth and population decline. Although we have included information on many other countries in the preceding chapters, our principal focus has been on the United States. In this final chapter, we look specifically at the population of the Earth, the number of inhabitants on our planet now and in the future. We will inquire how the world population now and in the 2100s may be related to other major factors of life on Earth. This last chapter has less to do with demography per se and more to do with the influence of population in several other arenas.

POPULATION SIZE

A good place to start is with population size. Box 20.1 is a summary of world population size from the United Nations. When Poston and Sullivan first began to study demography, the critical issues that preoccupied demographers were high fertility rates and an accompanying fear of world overpopulation. As the United Nations notes, fertility rates have declined. Indeed, many countries are now facing or have already entered a situation of natural decrease. As a result, today there are multiple concerns among demographers as they look to the future: rapid growth in some areas and declines in others.

As the United Nations mentions, there is still high fertility in sub-Saharan Africa, so there is concern about their potentially rapid population growth, and the negative

Box 20.1 The United Nations on Population Growth

The world's population is more than three times larger than it was in the mid-twentieth century. The global human population reached 8.0 billion in mid-November 2022 from an estimated 2.5 billion people in 1950, adding 1 billion people since 2010 and 2 billion since 1998. The world's population is expected to increase by nearly 2 billion persons in the next thirty years, from the current 8 billion to 9.7 billion in 2050 and could peak at nearly 10.4 billion in the mid-2080s.

This dramatic growth has been driven largely by increasing numbers of people surviving to reproductive age, the gradual increase in human lifespan, increasing urbanization, and accelerating migration. Major changes in the fertility rate have accompanied this growth. These trends will have far-reaching implications for generations to come.

> On 15 November 2022, the world's population reached 8 billion people, a milestone in human development. While it took the global population 12 years to grow from 7 to 8 billion, it will take approximately 15 years – until 2037 – for it to reach 9 billion, a sign that the overall growth rate of the global population is slowing. Yet levels of fertility remain high in some countries. Countries with the highest fertility levels tend to be those with the lowest income per capita. Global population growth has therefore over time become increasingly concentrated among the world's poorest countries, most of which are in sub-Saharan Africa.
>
> *Source:* United Nations, 2025.

effects that such growth has on providing food, shelter, education, and income to all of the people in those countries.

Balancing the high fertility, there has also been rising mortality in parts of Africa. Indeed, neo-Malthusians see in Africa the potential for the positive checks that Malthus forecast (see Chapter 2). Crowding into cities provides a setting for some infectious diseases to spread. In more rural areas, infectious diseases have also increased because of new transfers of infectious agents from wildlife to humans (Fenollar and Mediannikov, 2018). There has also been an increase in mortality from noncommunicable diseases, such as cancer. The impact of these diseases has apparently been amplified by a lack of prevention, detection, and adequate health care (World Health Organization, 2022a; 2022b). Finally, there has been a significant and often underreported increase in mortality from civil unrest and violence (Gang et al., 2023).

Nevertheless, the recent high fertility means that there is population momentum because the younger age cohorts are large. Even if the *rates* decline, the *numbers* may increase when today's children grow up to have children of their own.

POPULATION PROJECTIONS

In Chapter 16, we considered several different scenarios with respect to the size of the population of our world in the year 2100. We present here as Figure 20.1 the same figure we presented earlier as Figure 16.3. Let us review the different scenarios to get an idea of what the size of the world's population might be in 2100.

In Chapter 16, we used world population projections prepared recently by the Population Division of the United Nations (2024b). We preferred them over projections

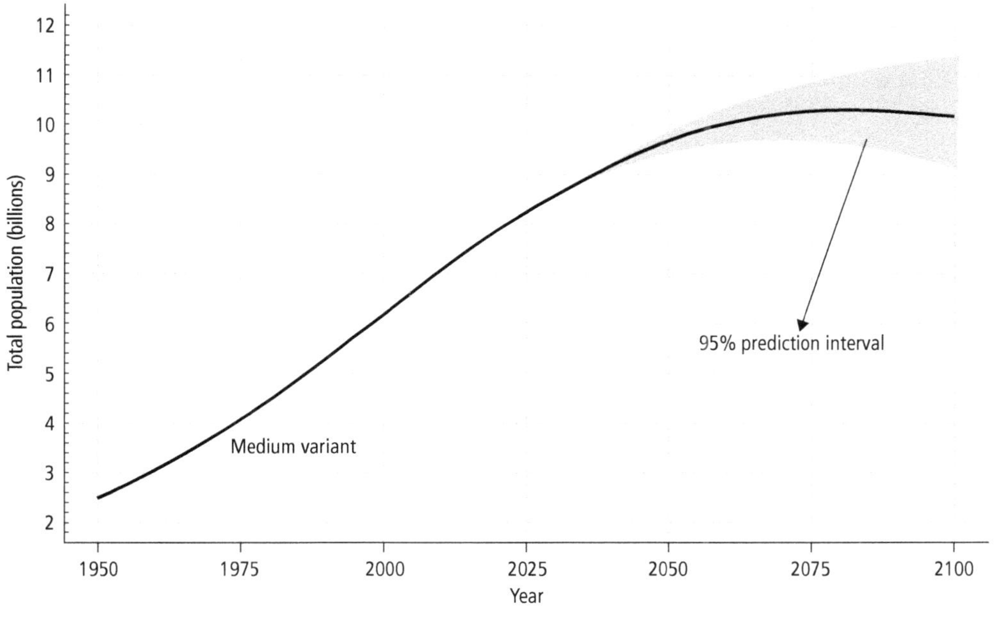

FIGURE 20.1 Population of the world, 1950 to 2023, with projections to 2100 (based on medium variant)
Source: United Nations, 2024b.

prepared by other organizations because, in our view, the UN projections reflect the most reasonable assumptions about future demographic behavior. However, as we have reminded you before, these projections are made using assumptions. In no way should they be seen as *predictions,* nor should they be considered the final word. Figure 20.1 uses the medium variant of the UN projections. (Please look back at Chapter 16 for our discussion of the assumptions that guided the development of these UN projections.)

What do the trend data in Figure 20.1 tell us? Observe first the single line in the figure showing the population growth of the world from 1950 to about 2027; then there is a shaded area extending out from the main line for the period between approximately 2027 and 2100. This shaded area represents uncertainty. The population of the world was 2.5 billion in 1950, 4.4 billion in 1980, and around 8 billion in 2025. It is from this point in time that the UN then set out projections about the future size of the world population through the year 2100.

The solid line curves slightly downward as it approaches 2100. This curve reflects assumptions that between now and 2100 a fertility decline will occur in those countries where large families are now prevalent. The area of uncertainty indicates that by 2100, world population could range between around 9 billion and nearly 11.5 billion. This is a wide range ; it is equivalent to the entire population of the Earth in 1950, when both of your coauthors were young children.

The lower bound, around 9 billion, anticipates a rapid and sustained fertility decline; the upper bound anticipates a growth rate that is similar to today's growth rate. This range of possibilities, of course, assumes there will be no major cataclysmic events such as catastrophic global warming, fresh-water shortages, a nuclear war, ever more deadly pandemics, and so forth.

What do these numbers mean, and what are their implications?

POPULATION DISTRIBUTION

Africa is projected to receive more than half of global population growth by 2050. The United Nations projects that the population of sub-Saharan Africa will double by 2050, even if there are reduced fertility levels (United Nations, 2025). Some of the countries that are most likely to be affected by this rapid growth are Mali, Niger, Uganda, and the Democratic Republic of Congo (Population Reference Bureau, 2024).

On the other hand, the United Nations projects that the populations of 61 countries will decrease by 2050, and 26 of them could be reduced by at least 10 percent. Europe will be affected in particular because the European countries are below replacement fertility (TFR< 2.1), some of them for a number of years. Just as there can be rapid population growth in spite of fertility decline because of **population momentum**, successive small cohorts of children can result in a different sort of momentum – more rapid decline. The United Nations projects that there are countries expected to experience a population decline of more than 15 percent by 2050 (United Nations, 2025). These countries are mostly in Europe: Bosnia and Herzegovina, Bulgaria, Croatia, Hungary, Latvia, Lithuania, Republic of Moldova, Romania, Serbia, and Ukraine. In Asia, Japan is expected to experience a similar decline.

As you learned in Chapter 18, shifts in the distribution of the world's population have been underway for centuries, affected by the differing times some countries entered the demographic transition, the openness to immigration, and progress toward extending longevity. However, the changes projected for the rest of the twenty-first century are happening fairly rapidly, often without much attention from policymakers.

ECONOMIC EFFECTS OF THE DEMOGRAPHIC TRANSITION

Africa's slowly dropping fertility rates and unstable mortality rates raise the issue of how far along the demographic transition might be in Africa. Both fertility and mortality rates are lower than the rates in the same countries a generation ago. These declines offer hope that the demographic transition is underway. As we learned when we studied the demographic transition (Chapter 2), when fertility begins to decline there is potential for the demographic dividend. If the growing cohorts of young African adults can be successfully incorporated into the labor force, there is a good prospect for economic growth and higher standards of living. There is not, however, always the economic infrastructure available to provide the education, training, and jobs that enable the demographic dividend. Securing financing to build new industries is difficult when so much investment needs to be made just to keep up with the large numbers of young dependents.

Meanwhile, in the higher-income countries of the world (Europe, the Americas, Australia and New Zealand, much of Asia, and some of the Middle East), low fertility rates have begun to alarm some policymakers. China and India have worked hard to reduce their birth rates, to the point that Chinese policymakers are now worried about China's rapidly growing old age dependency ratio. An aging population potentially reverses the demographic dividend; although there are fewer young dependents, there are more older dependents, and the larger cohorts that were part of the dividend become part of the aging population.

Japan is currently the world's oldest society. In Japan, one in every ten persons is over the age of 80, and in 2022 its TFR was 1.2 (Population Reference Bureau, 2024). Japan's adjustment to an older population and population decline forms a potential case study. In 2015 the Japanese government proposed a Smart Platinum Society in which many Japanese persons could live to be one hundred years old (Voegele, 2022). An important part of this plan is to encourage older people to stay healthy. Traditional healthcare is costly, and so the government was looking for alternatives to provide healthy aging-in-place. The experiment with Carebots (robots to provide elder care) has so far had mixed results at best. Other initiatives to create elder living arrangements look promising.

In terms of the labor force, Japan seeks to raise its retirement age and to encourage employers to create alternative work schedules and other accommodations to retain older workers past the usual retirement age. There is also interest in using artificial intelligence and other technological solutions to reduce the dependence on human workers. The market power of older persons will grow along with their share of the population, and their spending patterns will change the demand for goods and services, and presumably affect what jobs are available.

Japan, which is a heavily urbanized society, has also rethought its urban infrastructure to be more friendly to the needs of an older population. This includes the redesign of public transport and the accessibility of buildings. Voegele (2022) has written that the Japanese initiatives have "included asset recycling of schools turned into care facilities for older persons, repurposing community facilities to meet both day-to-day multi-generational gatherings and disaster response centers in emergency situations, renovating vacant housing by attracting young students and artists to create momentum for community-led area-based regeneration efforts, among others." Barrier-free design has been adopted in many Japanese cities to improve mobility, especially for older and disabled persons. An example is the widespread use of Braille to supplement printed language.

TWO ALTERNATIVE ROUTES TO THE UNEQUAL DEMOGRAPHIC SCENARIOS

Africa, parts of the Middle East, and parts of Asia now look very different, demographically, from North and South America, Europe, Australia, and much of Asia. The results of these differences are that the former group of countries are young and have lower incomes; the latter group of countries are much older with higher incomes. Policymakers in many countries are conscious of the very different demographic situations in the world and they are interested in the best path forward for their own country. Many also have altruistic interests in achieving a better standard of living everywhere.

One solution is increased immigration from high-fertility places to low-fertility places. Because of the pending shortages of young workers in low-fertility countries, there could be an opportunity for young people in higher-fertility countries, such as sub-Saharan African countries, to immigrate to take jobs. This movement of young people would also aid the economic growth in their home countries through their remittances and just through the simple fact that the home countries no longer need to feed, clothe, and shelter their emigrants. In addition, the indirect effect of immigration (see Chapter 7) would mean that the children of the young immigrants would be born in the host country, adding to the fertility rate of that country.

As attractive an alternative as immigration might seem to be, strong anti-immigration sentiments have broken out in many higher-income countries. Some countries have historically resisted all immigration, believing that a homogeneous population is more harmonious. Japan, for example, has shown little interest in revising its restrictive immigration policy. Some countries have a history of receiving immigrants but would now like to control the size and composition of the migration stream. To take two examples, both Australia and Canada remain open to immigration, but they use a point system to reward desirable characteristics such as skill levels, language proficiency, and ability to create jobs or invest in the host society. The point-system approach is attractive to the host country and to the lucky persons chosen to be immigrants; to the home country, it may represent a brain drain of their most skilled young workers. There are basically no longer any countries that are willing to accept all potential immigrants, although some countries are willing to receive groups of refugees, often for specific time periods.

What are the objections to receiving more immigrants? (See our earlier discussions in Chapter 7.) One objection is that immigrants may be personally undesirable because of ill health, terrorist orientation, or criminal intent. A second objection is that unskilled immigrants take jobs from native-born citizens, even though immigrants often find themselves relegated to the lowest-paid, most dangerous and dirty jobs – jobs that many citizens do not want to take. The mirror image of this objection is that highly skilled immigrants (e.g., technology specialists) will take the most desirable jobs. Thus, whether or not highly skilled, immigrants are not favored. A third objection is that the immigrants will not "fit in," especially if their culture, language, and religion are markedly different from the host country's. Although immigrant communities have added to the cosmopolitan sparkle of cities such as Toronto, London, and New York, reservations about immigrants' "otherness" remain.

A different alternative to immigration is to raise the fertility rate of the high-income countries. **Pronatalism** is the umbrella term for policies that encourage higher birth rates. These policies are usually governmental, although private employers may also have pronatalist policies. There are aspects of pronatalism in the United States, where public education is free no matter how many children are in the family, or employee health insurance must cover all children under the age of 26 without penalizing large families. Much more far-reaching government policies are in place in other countries that include cash allowances, mandatory paternity and maternity leaves, subsidized childcare, and free medical care. European countries are devoting as much as 4 percent of their GDP to family-friendly policies. Most economists agree, however, that these measures make relatively slight differences in terms of raising fertility rates.

ECOLOGICAL CONSIDERATIONS

What might be the impact of 10 billion or more inhabitants of the Earth were we to take an *ecological* view of the population? We will use here what demographers and human ecologists refer to as the ecological complex, that is, the interaction of population, organization, environment, and technology (POET) (Duncan, 1959; Hawley, 1950, 1968; Poston, 2015; Poston and Frisbie, 2019).

The world's population in 2100 could number around 10 billion and could be higher (see Figure 20.1). But an ever-growing proportion of that population will reside in the developing (that is, lower-income) regions of the world. Around 1.3 billion of the world's population in 2100 will likely be in the developed countries. The developed or high-income countries are the United States, Canada, all of Europe, Japan, Australia, and New Zealand, and by 2100 some additional countries could be included in this group. Thus, as much as 85 percent of the world's population in 2100 will be in countries we classify today as developing. Most of the projected growth in the world population before 2100 is expected to occur in developing countries. And much of this population growth will come disproportionately from people on the margins, those with limited resources and life opportunities.

The US population now stands at 347 million and is likely to reach around 366 million by 2100 (US Bureau of the Census, 2023c, middle series of projections). As with the world's population in general, the subpopulations in the United States that are increasing disproportionately are mainly those with limited resources and life opportunities.

Let us use these numbers and consider how they are related to resources, pollution, and technology. We first look at resources, specifically oil and water. To maintain any kind of ecological balance in a social system, there must be sufficient resources for the system to maintain itself. While it is not our intention here to delve deeply into resource issues, it is appropriate to point out that today the world is very much concerned with respect to the availability of petroleum (Deffeyes, 2005; Juvkam-Wold and Dessler, 2009). A worldwide energy crisis is not beyond reason, and we already are aware of the growing tensions in the Middle East and elsewhere, in large part because of the need for oil.

But there is a problem with respect to distinguishing between resources and reserves (US Energy Information Administration, 2023). It is believed that the world has sufficient petroleum reserves to last until 2050. We have a fairly good idea of the extent of reserves, but reserves are not necessarily available as resources. The costs of mining them may be so high as to make them uneconomic; in addition, alternate sources of energy (e.g., wind, solar) could reduce the demand for converting reserves to resources.

A cause for optimism is the determination on the part of many countries both to foster limitations on petroleum use and to find alternative sources of energy. The 1997 Kyoto Protocol is an international treaty intended to bring countries together to reduce global warming and to call on nations to stabilize greenhouse gases in the atmosphere. Most of the developed countries of the world support the protocol; the United States and Canada are among the few that do not.

Another resource is water. To most readers of this book, water is probably taken for granted. Yes, we know of polluted water but, overall, "What's the problem?" First of all, water is a far more unreliable resource than oil. It is fundamental to life, whether human, animal, or plant. Indeed, water is a prerequisite for all living things. Second, there are no substitutes for most of its uses, unlike oil, which can be replaced with other forms of energy. Finally, while water is a renewable resource, it is also finite. In the twenty-first century, the scarcity of water may be the single greatest threat to global food production.

The United Nations Sustainable Development Goal 6 (clean water and sanitation) is for universal access to clean water and sanitation by 2030. It is estimated in 2025, when we are writing this chapter, that 10 percent of the world's population does not have access to clean water. An even larger proportion does not have access to adequate sanitation. A major cause of infant mortality in the low-income countries is water-borne diseases from polluted water; although adults may be able to survive the water, children are more susceptible to infections and the dehydrating effects of the resulting diarrhea.

A lack of water also has important consequences for agriculture. Changing climate patterns, such as droughts or the melting of glaciers, can reduce the amount of fresh water available. And a growing population puts more pressure on the available water supplies. In some parts of the world, water conflicts have broken out between countries that share a river or lake as part of their boundaries.

Sandra Postel, a leading authority on water resources, has noted the following in her book about water and sustainability. Although she wrote this paragraph in the early 1990s, its insights are still considerable today:

> We are entering an unprecedented period of water stress globally. In 2015, nearly 3 billion people – 40 percent of the projected world population – will live in countries that find it difficult or impossible to mobilize enough water to satisfy the food, industrial, and domestic needs of their citizens. How nations respond to this dilemma individually and collectively will have serious implications for food security, for the health of the aquatic environment, and for social and political stability. A new mindset for water policy and management is required if we are to meet the needs of 9 billion people while protecting the health of the aquatic environment that our economies and all life depend upon. (Postel, 1992: 12)

Aquifers are crucial to our water supplies. Consider aquifers as huge water-storage reservoirs. Whereas groundwater is a renewable source, the reserves replenish slowly. We put water in, and we take water out. "Falling water tables have already curtailed irrigation from some aquifers, and the competition for water between irrigated agriculture and urban population growth has already led to a systematic diversion of water from agriculture to cities in Arizona and California" (Bouvier and Grant, 1994: 15). Increasing numbers of cities are beginning to experience water shortages: "Cities like San Antonio, El Paso and Phoenix could run out of water in 10 to 20 years. San Diego's water company has resorted to a once-unthinkable option, namely, recycling toilet water for drinking" (Rubenstein, 2008/2009: 5). Today in the United States, groundwater is utilized about four times faster than it is replaced naturally. The great Ogallala Aquifer that covers parts of eight states is gradually being depleted but remains a primary source of water for much of the Great Plains. It is so important that attempts have been made by billionaire industrialists to purchase much of the land that covers the aquifer. The end result is more expensive water for ordinary users.

In his usual pithy manner, Benjamin Franklin said it best: "When the well runs dry, we know the worth of water" (cited in Bartlett, 1968). If there were a billion or so fewer inhabitants in the world in 2100, it would at least postpone the water crisis that will likely be felt eventually. We should not take out more water than enters the system, although we already are doing just that. We should not see our aquifers dry up and disappear, but we do face that prospect. The water wars of the nineteenth century made famous, or infamous, by western movies could return to haunt us in the twenty-first century, if population growth continues unabated. This could, in turn, lead to food shortages and significant increases in the cost of food.

We turn next to considerations of the environment. What do we mean by environment? The term is extremely broad and vague. Hawley defined it as "whatever is external to and potentially or actually influential on a phenomenon under investigation" (1968: 330). Schnore wrote that it is "a set of limiting conditions, which may be narrow or broad, depending on the technological devices and modes of organization that prevail in a given population" (1958: 628). These definitions are useful in limiting the term. For our purposes here, however, we will limit our discussion to the physical environment, specifically global warming and pollution, and the related problem of waste. These are environmental issues that are significantly related to the human population.

Global warming is the evidence of a rise in the Earth's temperature. It is sometimes referred to as climate change. There is an almost unanimous agreement among scientists that global warming is taking place. Furthermore, "most of the observed increase in globally averaged temperatures since the mid-20th century is very likely due to the observed increase in anthropogenic greenhouse gas concentrations" (Intergovernmental Panel on Climate Change, 2007: 8).

To be sure, other factors are involved, but greenhouse gases seem to be the primary cause of this momentous change in the Earth's temperature. There is already evidence near the Arctic Circle where Greenland is losing some of its ice foundation, causing massive increases in oceanic water – sea level rise – to be sent in a southward direction.

Our primary concern here is the contribution of population to the problem, as opposed to an in-depth discussion of climate change. Carbon dioxide is a major contributor to greenhouse gases. Motor vehicles are a major contributor to carbon dioxide. As a general rule of thumb, we can add 700 motor vehicles for every 1,000 people added to a population. This is true in developed nations, including China and India, although less so in the other regions of the world. Now let us add a billion or more inhabitants to the planet. You do the math and see what the result will be. So, once again, although reductions in population growth will not solve all these problems, they would be alleviated if such reductions were at least discussed. In an otherwise excellent article several years ago in the *American Prospect*, Gelbspan (2007) failed to even mention population limitation as a possible aid to solving the planet's problems. He cited a report from the insurance giant Swiss Re in which it was noted that "there is a danger that human intervention will accelerate and intensify climate change to such a point that it will become impossible to adapt our socio-economic systems in time" (Gelbspan, 2007: 47). One wonders what he meant by the phrase "human intervention."

Pollution is closely related to global warming. There are, of course, numerous types of pollution, such as air, water, soil, and noise. Here, we will concentrate on air pollution that involves the release of chemicals into the atmosphere. Examples are carbon monoxide and nitrogen oxide, both of which are produced by industry and motor vehicles. Motor vehicle emissions are among the leading causes of air pollution. For decades, we have lamented the dense smog over such cities as London, Los Angeles, and Houston and, more recently, some of the major cities in China, particularly Beijing. Although complicated by local weather conditions such as fog, the primary cause has been too many vehicles, along with some industrial air pollution. In Mexico City and some other cities, the widespread use of charcoal for cooking and heating can also produce smog. Limiting population growth could well reduce many of our problems; this time, it is pollution.

Of all the problems associated with continued rapid population growth, garbage and waste disposal may be among the most visible. Cities today in the developed world produce more solid waste than they did in the 1960s (Bouvier and Grant, 1994: 15). The problems associated with waste disposal are critical: "Because they were polluting, or simply full, the number of landfills has declined ... Cities have unsuccessfully tried to unload the waste on third world countries. ... Eastern cities [in the United States] have been negotiating with rural counties as far away as New Mexico and Texas to accept the stuff. The nation is on a treadmill" (Bouvier and Grant, 1994: 16). The challenge of waste disposal continues, and some states today, for example, Virginia, are questioning the wisdom of accepting waste from northern cities.

The overall environmental problems faced by the planet include "encroaching deserts, rising sea levels, deforestation, acid precipitation, resultant forest dieback, toxic contamination of food supplies, soil oxidation and pollution of water tables, ozone depletion, greenhouse gas buildup and climatic change" (Rees, 2004: 12). Population growth is a contributor, direct or indirect, to all of these challenges for our planet.

SOCIOLOGICAL CONSIDERATIONS

Thus far, we have presented a rather dismal picture of population growth and its impact on the world. Allow us to present here a less dismal point of view, indeed an optimistic one, from two economists, Ester Boserup and Julian Simon.

Boserup, a Danish economist, argued in her book *The Conditions of Agricultural Growth* (1965) that population growth was a stimulus to social change. To illustrate, it was population growth that contributed to the move from an agricultural to an industrial society. She also wrote that a society with a growing population is more likely to experience economic development than one where growth is limited or even nonexistent (Boserup, 1981).

Simon, the late American economist, was also demographically optimistic. Politically conservative, he was a major proponent for the argument that "population growth is neutral." This was the basis for the US position at the Second World Population conference in Mexico City. See our discussion in Chapter 19.) Simon argued in his influential and very interesting book *The Ultimate Resource* (1981) that population growth and the ability to innovate go together. Indeed, the "ultimate resource" referred to more people. People innovate, and the more people there are, the more likely innovation will occur. In his later years, Simon paid less attention to population growth and more to the commercial market: "Misplaced attention to population growth has resulted in disastrously unsound advice being given to developing nations" (1992: xiii).

While the views of optimists such as Boserup and Simon may have had merit in the past, it is more difficult for such arguments to hold significant sway in a world with more than 8 billion inhabitants that according to projections will grow to more than 10 billion by 2100.

Perhaps technology is one area where optimists and pessimists can agree. The great spurt in agricultural productivity, which Malthus did not foresee, helped to forestall one of the positive checks he theorized. Technology assisted increased agricultural yields and continues to do so. The technological changes in the developed and developing countries, especially during the last half of the twentieth century, have been remarkable. One immediately thinks of the computer and the Internet. The computer chip has made communications incredibly rapid. A person in New York can contact a person in Beijing in seconds. The interstate highway system increased our ability to get almost anywhere in the United States faster than previously possible. Now we have more speed in our communications and in our travel capabilities. What will the future bring? What technological changes will take place in this century that might affect our lifestyles even more than have been observed in recent decades?

If one thinks that the recent advancements in technology were amazing, sociologists with an evolutionary perspective on humanity believe we have seen only the beginnings. Auguste Comte (1853), generally considered to be the father of sociology, believed that humanity progressed through three stages of thought and development: theological, metaphysical, and positivist. Emile Durkheim ([1893] 1984) saw a gradual evolving of society from what he called "mechanical" to "organic." Herbert Spencer believed there to be "an inexorable tendency toward differentiation both in the case of organisms into species and in the case of societies into more differentiated structures" (Wallace and Wolf, 2005: 160).

Anthony Giddens (2002: 7) remarked:

> [W]e live in a world of transformations, affecting almost every aspect of what we do. For better or worse, we are being propelled into a global order that no one understands, but which is making its effects felt upon all of us. Globalization may not be a particularly attractive or elegant word, but absolutely no one who wants to understand our prospects ... can ignore it. ... The global spread of the term is evidence of the very developments to which it refers. ... [E]ven in the late 1980s the term was hardly used. ... It has come from nowhere to be almost everywhere.

Two of Pulitzer-prize-winner Thomas Friedman's books, *The World Is Flat* (2005) and *Hot, Flat, and Crowded* (2008), provide additional examples of the rapid changes that are occurring as globalization intensifies and as Friedman finds himself communicating instantly from Boston to Bangalore and elsewhere.

PHILOSOPHICAL CONSIDERATIONS

Humankind is evolving. We see it in our behavior, in our changing activities, in the globalization of knowledge, and in our relationships. When do we stop evolving? One of our favorite theologians, the Jesuit priest and scientist, Pierre Teilhard de Chardin (1959, 1969a, 1969b), argued that reaching the noosphere (or the Omega point) will mark the end of human evolution. Indeed, the noosphere could be easily interpreted as heaven for believers, although Teilhard made no such assertion. For others, perhaps

Karl Marx's dictum, namely, "From each according to his abilities to each according to his needs," will mark the end of social evolution.

In the process of human evolution, our numbers have increased at an ever-increasing rate. We have made this point several times in earlier chapters in this book. Now let us bring back a term we used earlier, **exponential growth**. Important to bear in mind is the fact that the number of "items" doubles in size in every doubling time. Two exponential concepts will concern us as we look at the future of the world, namely, population, that is, human exponentialism, and noetic (i.e., thought and intellectual) exponentialism.

We have already discussed **population exponentialism**; we referred to this in Chapter 16 as **doubling time**. We noted in Chapter 16 that in 2024 the world population was growing at a rate of 0.8 percent annually. At a rate of increase of 0.8 percent per year, a population doubles its size about every 87 years, that is, 69.3 / 0.8 = 86.6 (see our discussions in Chapter 16). If this world population growth rate continues into the future, the world would number 16.2 billion people in 2111, that is, 2024 plus 87 years; the twenty-second century would see twice as many people as we have today. We cannot double the size of the world population for very much longer, given the earlier discussion about resources: "Human society is presently breaching the biophysical limits to growth, but this time on a global scale. As a result, the very qualities that once assured humanity's remarkable evolutionary success are threatening to do us in" (Rees, 2004: 11).

Exponentialism is present in many areas of human life. "Thought" is such an area. Our knowledge, be it technical, medical, philosophical, or scientific, grows exponentially. This is a result of human thinking. Consider all that has developed over recent generations, not only with regard to computers and the Internet but also with respect to artificial intelligence, medicine, the genome project, and stem-cell research. Indeed, more has happened in the last forty years than in the last several centuries. This, too, is exponentialism.

We might, however, consider here the remarks made in 1981 by the biologist Lewis Thomas, namely, that "the greatest single achievement of science in this most scientifically productive of centuries is the discovery that we are profoundly ignorant; we know very little about nature and we understand even less ... There is no limit to the ingenuity of the nature of this planet" (quoted in Gellerman, 2003: 1). This suggests that care is necessary in integrating human technologies with those of the natural world. It warns us about the challenges of noetic exponentialism.

Humans rely on the knowledge acquired in previous generations and build on it. What, then, might transpire in the next generation? Our consciousness may improve, but one wonders about the growing complexity that will also occur. Will humankind be able to adapt to an exponentially growing availability of knowledge? With increasing complexity, will we be able to adjust to these rapidly growing challenges? Many of us elders are aware of a generational gap in computer knowledge, with children of elementary and high school age often knowing more about the basics than their parents and grandparents. When we or our spouses need help with our iPhones or iPads, we ask younger family members for assistance.

As both numbers and thoughts grow exponentially, what will happen to social interactions? We are already witnessing a significant decrease in the number of our actual face-to-face interactions, especially as a result of the computer and, more recently, email, the cell phone, and social media. COVID-19 lockdowns also revealed how much of daily life could be carried on virtually. On the pessimistic side, does this mean an end to social interactions? Will we lose the capability to simply "talk" to one another face-to-face? Will college professors, for example, be replaced by computerized lessons? On the more optimistic side, improved technology should allow us to communicate with more people, although much of that communication will be "artificial." Perhaps we are entering a new phase in the evolutionary process of humanity in which, increasingly, social interactions will take place through ever-improving technologies. If so, we must all adapt to a new paradigm of communication.

Population exponentialism is also related to human evolution. For example, how are increasing numbers related to human interaction? Perhaps surprising to some demographers, Pierre Teilhard de Chardin was seriously concerned about population growth. In his remarkable book *The Future of Man* he wrote:

> [A]fter rising slowly until the seventeenth century when it reached about 400 million, the Earth's population began to shoot up again in an alarming fashion. It was 800 million by the end of the eighteenth century, 1.6 billion by 1900 and over 2 billion by 1940. At the present rate of increase, regardless of war and famine, we must expect a further 500 million in the next 25 years. This demographic explosion is closely connected with the development of a relatively unified and industrial Earth. Clearly it gives rise to entirely new necessities and problems, both quantitative and qualitative. (Teilhard de Chardin, 1969a: 242–243)

He then asked, "[H]ow are we to prevent this compression of mankind on the closed surface of the planet from passing the critical point beyond which any increase in numbers will mean famine and suffocation?" (Teilhard de Chardin, 1969a: 243). Teilhard was clear in his concern about population growth interfering with the ultimate evolution of humankind. He anticipated the writings of the neo-Malthusians, some of whom we have mentioned in Chapter 2 and elsewhere in this book.

So here we are now in the third decade of the twenty-first century, faced with the challenge of adapting to both evolution and exponentialism. Will we be able to support 2.5 billion or more additional inhabitants on this small planet? These questions face us today, questions of which we must be aware if we are to handle the increasing complexity that comes with these types of exponentialism.

Furthermore, increasing complexity can be directly related to social interaction. What kind of social interaction can be expected in the kind of world foreseen for the twenty-first and twenty-second centuries? Virtually all sociologists note that without human social interaction, any group, or any nation for that matter, is bound to fail. Yet, as we continue into the twenty-first century and move toward the twenty-second, it is clear that actual face-to-face human interaction is declining. Electronic technology has contributed to this dangerous decline. This is not to say that these new technologies are not beneficial. The sociologist Robert Merton (1968) pointed out many years ago that there are manifest functions and there are latent functions. We know the manifest functions of these technologies, most of which are positive. But a latent function of them has been a serious decline in the real face-to-face interactions that must occur if the society is to coalesce.

All of us must develop a "self" if we are to maintain some sort of identity. More than a hundred years ago, the social psychologist Charles Horton Cooley (1902) coined the term "looking glass self." To a certain extent, we develop a personal self by looking at how others react to us through social interaction. How will one develop a self if there is no longer a "looking glass"?

We cannot turn back the clock and bar all new technology. But perhaps we can all try just a little harder to talk more to friends and even strangers and, yes, even enemies. How much more difficult might this be with 10 or more billion people inhabiting the Earth, rather than 8 billion?

In Chapter 1, we mentioned the phrase "demography is destiny." While journalists occasionally use it, some demographers tend to shy away from it. Upon reflection, however, there may be some truth to "demography is destiny," at least in the short term. For example, the world population is projected to grow to over 10 billion by the year 2100. The actual number may prove to be a little more or less, but the population of the world will grow. Here in the United States, we can forecast the problems associated with the baby boom now reaching retirement age. In that sense, demography *is* destiny. In his book *The Post-American World* (2008) the noted journalist Fareed Zakaria concluded that "as the industrial world ages, India will continue to have lots of young people – in other words, workers. China faces a youth gap because of its successful 'one-child' policies. India faces a youth bulge because, ironically, its own family planning policies of the past failed. If demography is destiny, India's future is secure" (2008: 132).

SUMMARY

Demographers do not have crystal balls, nor do we pretend to be able to tell the future. We can, however, describe demographic trends and the possible scenarios to which they could lead. In this final chapter, we have looked very broadly at the remaining years of the twenty-first century and the start of the twenty-second. In so doing, we have considered the implications of a world population in 2100 that approaches or exceeds 10 billion. Some, if not all, of these musings may appear dismal to many readers. Certainly, we are facing monumental population and environmental challenges. We have addressed some of them in this chapter, but a little thought will show you that there are also demographic implications for governance and civil society, national security, human rights, and international relations (Hayutin, 2022: 355ff.).

We are witnessing enormous advances in technology. Both population and noetic exponentialism are becoming even more problematic. The era of the Industrial Revolution is long over. Now we are experiencing the Information Revolution. Indeed, we are at the onset of dramatic transformations never before imagined. Population size and change are in the middle of this incredible phenomenon. In this looming era of globalization, we once again ask the question, "Will we all get along?" The answer depends on how we adapt to one another in this twenty-first century.

DISCUSSION QUESTIONS

1. Two themes discussed throughout this book are "population is neutral," and "demography is destiny." Describe what demographers mean by each theme.

Next, choose the one you believe is more applicable and relevant for the future development of a society. Justify your selection; and make sure you define what you mean by "applicable" and "relevant."

2. Describe some of the ecological, sociological, and philosophical impacts if the world population reaches a size of 10 billion inhabitants by the year 2100. Which of the three sets of impacts do you hold would be the most detrimental for the world? Justify your arguments, and make sure you define what you mean by "detrimental."

Glossary

Abortion: termination of a pregnancy after the implantation of the fertilized egg in the uterine wall, but before the fetus is viable; includes both spontaneous and induced abortions.

Adolescent fertility: the fertility of adolescents, usually referred to as people aged 15–19.

Adolescent fertility rate: the age-specific fertility rate for people aged 15–19.

Adrenogenital syndrome (AGS): an intersex trait of an XX fetus or an XY fetus that receives an excessive amount of androgens; also known as congenital adrenal hyperplasia; classic CAH is recognized at birth; late-onset CAH is at puberty or early adulthood.

Age composition: the composition of a population with respect to age (i.e., the distribution of a population among age categories).

Age curve of mortality: a plot reflecting the changing mortality rates of over the life course, best reflected with data from the full schedule of age-specific death rates (ASDRs); most often the age curve is a "U" form.

Age dependency ratio: within a population, the ratio of persons aged 0–14 and 65 years and older to persons aged 15–64, multiplied by 100; assumed to show the burden of economic dependency on working-age adults.

Age distribution: see **age composition**.

Age grading: the social expectations of persons of a given age, such as the expectations that children will receive schooling.

Age heaping: irregularities or inconsistencies in the age data for a population due to an overreporting of certain ages (e.g., those ending in 0 or 5) at the expense of others.

Aged dependency ratio (ADR or aged-DR): the ratio of persons 65 years and older to the working-age population (i.e., persons aged 15–64 years), multiplied by 100; also known as the old-age dependency ratio.

Agent: a factor, such as a microorganism, whose presence or excessive presence, is causative in a disease.

Age-specific death rate (ASDR): deaths to persons in a specific age group per 1,000 persons in that age group; also known as the "M" rate.

Age-specific fertility rate (ASFR): births to women according to their age. ASFRs are usually calculated per 1,000 women in each of the five-year age groups of 15–19, 20–24, and so forth to 45–49.

Age-specific rates: a rate referring to the demographic behavior (e.g., births or deaths) of a subset of the population categorized by age.

Aging: the process of growing older.

Aging population: a population in which the average age is increasing.

Alien: a person living in a country who is not a citizen of that country.

Androgen insensitivity syndrome (AIS): an intersex trait of fetuses that are chromosomally male with genitals that are ambiguous or look more like a clitoris than a penis.

Area of destination: in the context of migration, the place where the migration ended.

Area of origin: in the context of migration, the place where the migration began.

Ascribed characteristic: an attribute – such as race, sex, or age – that an individual is born into or involuntarily assigned to, and over which they have little to no control.

At-risk population: the set of people who could have produced a specified type of demographic event (e.g., a birth, death, or migration); the at-risk population is usually the denominator of a rate.

Asylee: a person forced to leave their country of birth or nationality and move to another country seeking legal refugee status.

Baby boom: the increase in fertility that occurred after World War II during the late 1940s and 1950s in most developed nations; more generally, a baby boom is any dramatic and extended increase in the birth rate.

Baby bust: the decrease in fertility that occurred during the 1970s in most developed nations; more generally, a baby bust is any dramatic extended decline in the birth rate.

Basal body temperature (BBT): the lowest body temperature measured in the morning before walking and eating.

Billings ovulation method: a fertility awareness method based on the woman's knowledge of the presence or absence of cervical secretions associated with ovulation.

Birth: "the complete expulsion or extraction from its mother of a product of conception, irrespective of the duration of pregnancy, which, after such separation, breathes or shows any other evidence of life, such as the beating of the heart, pulsation of the umbilical cord, or definite movement of voluntary muscles, whether or not the umbilical cord has been cut or the placenta is attached" (Shryock, Siegel, and Associates, 1976: 221).

Birth control: deliberate measures taken to delay or avoid a birth, including contraception, sterilization, or induced abortion.

Birth order: the numerical order in which a person is born (e.g., first born, third born); also known as parity.

Birthright citizenship: the right of a person to be a citizen in the country of the person's birth.

Bracero program: an immigrant guest worker program established from 1942 to 1964, allowing laborers from Mexico to work temporarily in the United States.

Calendar method: see **rhythm method.**

Cervical cap: a small, thimble-shaped cup used to prevent conception by blocking the cervix.

Census: a periodic complete count of every inhabitant in a given geographic entity at a specific point in time; censuses are typically conducted once every five or ten years.

Center of population: the geographical point or location in a country at which an imaginary flat, weightless, and rigid map of the country would balance perfectly if all persons distributed in the population were of identical physical weight.

Central city: the largest city in a metropolis or a metropolitan area.

Childbearing ages: the age range 15–49 that typically marks the biological limits of childbearing for women; sometimes in developed countries the age range is 15–44 because so few births occur to women older than 44.

Childlessness: the status of having no children, either voluntarily or involuntarily.

Class of worker: a categorization of workers by the characteristics of the employing organization or self-employment.

Closed population: a population in which migration across its borders does not occur.

Cohort: a group of people who experience a major demographic event in the same time period; e.g., a birth cohort consists of people born in the same year or the same five-year period.

Cohort analysis: examination of a cohort's demographic behavior over time (e.g., children ever born to a particular birth cohort of women); this is in contrast to an examination of a demographic event at one point in time (i.e., a period or cross-sectional analysis).

Coitus reservatus: the behavior in which the male enters his partner, does not ejaculate, and endeavors to remain at the plateau phase of sexual intercourse and excitement; also known as *amplexus reservatus*.

Combined oral contraceptive: a hormonally based contraceptive containing estrogen and progestin.

Concentration: the clustering of the population in areas of high population density surrounded by areas of low population density.

Conception: the fertilization of an ovum by a sperm, marking the beginning of a pregnancy, or gestation.

Congenital adrenal hyperplasia (CAH): see **adrenogenital syndrome (AGS)**.

Contraception: measures taken to prevent coitus from resulting in conception.

Contraceptive implant: a small plastic rod inserted under the skin of a woman's arm to prevent pregnancy by releasing the hormone progestogen, stopping the release of an egg from the ovaries.

Contraceptive injection: an injection containing hormones to prevent pregnancy; typically administered once every three months in the arm, buttocks, upper thigh, or abdomen.

Contraceptive patch: an adhesive device placed on the buttocks, arms, or stomach to release estrogen and progestin at a constant and continuous level each day to prevent pregnancy.

Contraceptive sponge: a vaginal spermicide designed for a single use to prevent pregnancy.

Cross-sectional: refers to a one-point-in-time measurement, such as the size, composition, or distribution of a population, such as would be obtained in a census. Also see **cohort analysis.**

Crude birth rate (CBR): the number of live births in a given year per 1,000 total population at the midpoint of the given year.

Crude death rate (CDR): the number of deaths in a given year per 1,000 total population at the midpoint of the given year.

Death: "the permanent disappearance of all evidence of life at any time after a live birth has taken place; a death can occur only after a live birth has occurred" (Shryock, Siegel, and Associates, 1976: 221).

Deconcentration: a shift in population distribution from the higher-density central cities to the lower-density areas located beyond the traditional city limits; or a shift from metropolitan to nonmetropolitan areas.

De facto population: the population physically present in an area at a given moment in time, such as the time the census was undertaken.

De jure population: the population that usually, habitually, or legally lives in an area.

Demographic dividend: the change in age composition after fertility rates drop such that more of the population is in the working ages of 15–64 and fewer are in the young dependent ages of 0–14.

Demographic equation, demographic balancing equation, population equation: the equation that states that the size of area's population can change because of only three types of events; births, deaths, and migration. It is also known as the accounting equation.

Demographic processes: the three processes of fertility, mortality, and migration that account for any changes in the size of a population.

Demographic transition theory (DTT): the theory that describes the change from a situation in which a population has high fertility and high mortality rates to one in which fertility and mortality rates are low.

Demography: the scientific study of the size, composition, and distribution of human populations, and their changes resulting from fertility, mortality, and migration.

Denominator: the bottom number in a fraction; the number below the line; the divisor.

Dependent variable: a variable whose value depends upon one or more other variables known as independent variables; also known as the outcome variable or the Y variable.

Diaphragm: a contraceptive device consisting of a flexible disk that covers the uterine cervix.

Differential fertility: differences in fertility behavior that are associated with demographic, social, or economic characteristics of the population.

Differential migration: differences in migration behavior that are associated with demographic, social, or economic characteristics of population; also known as **migration selectivity.**

Differential mortality: differences in mortality rates that are associated with demographic, social, or economic characteristics of the population.

Discouraged workers: potential workers who are not employed, not looking for work, and who are willing and able to work but believe that no work is available.

Division of labor: differences among members of a population in their work activities; the more complex the division of labor in a society, the more differentiated the members are in their work activities.

Doubling time: the number of years required for a population to double its size were it to maintain its current rate of natural growth (as long as the growth rate is positive); at a +1.0 percent rate of growth, the doubling time is 69.3 years; the numerator of the doubling formula is the natural log of 2 x 100, i.e., 69.3; the denominator is the rate of natural increase (RNI); if the growth rate is negative, see **halving time**.

Dual labor market theory: the theory that argues that economic structure leads to jobs that can be classified as better or worse; given the reluctance of the local population to accept the worse jobs, the dual labor market is a stimulus to migration.

Echo effect: the tendency toward repetition, one generation hence, of any span of abnormally high or low fertility, which is caused by the effect of the initial fertility level on the age structure.

Economic dependency ratio: the ratio of the population aged 0–14 plus the population aged 65 and over plus the nonworking adults aged 15–64, divided by the members of the labor force aged 15–64, multiplied by 100. It is interpreted as the number of dependents each worker supports.

Economic development: the level of economic activity in a population; two common measures are (1) per capita income and (2) per capita energy consumption. The higher these measures are, the more developed the population is considered to be.

Edge cities: new cities formed at the edges of metropolitan areas.

Effectiveness (of family planning methods): how well a specific family planning method works in preventing pregnancy. There are two types of effectiveness: **theoretical effectiveness** and **use effectiveness**; theoretical effectiveness refers to the efficaciousness of the method when it is used exactly as prescribed; use effectiveness refers to the effectiveness of the method taking into account the fact that some users do not follow the directions perfectly; thus representing how effective the method is in typical use.

Emergency contraceptive pill (ECP): a contraceptive medication taken after unprotected intercourse; designed to prevent pregnancy by interfering with implanation of the fertilized ovum in the uterine lining; also known as the **morning-after pill.**

Emigrant: one who migrates away from a country with the intention of establishing a permanent residence in another country.

Emigration: the permanent departure of people from one country to establish permanent residence in another country.

Employment-population ratio: the ratio of the number of employed persons to the number of adults of working age (16–64 years) within a population, usually multiplied by 100.

Endemic: refers to a disease that regularly occurs within a population or a territory.

Endogenous causes: a cause of death that originates from within the body or its genetic makeup; in the case of infant death, endogenous causes of death include congenital malformations, chromosome abnormalities, complications of delivery, and low birthweight (Pebley, 2003: 534.)

Endometrium: lining of the uterus.

Entries without inspection (EWIs): international migrants who during the process of migrating to the host country "avoid inspection by crossing borders clandestinely or ... traveling with fraudulent documents, e.g., a falsified visa or counterfeit passport" (Armbrister, 2003: 512).

Epidemic: an infectious disease that spreads and then disappears within a fairly short time, if it can be controlled. Where it appears in a large number of countries, it may be called a **pandemic**. The term is sometimes used for a cause of death that is increasing in a population even if the disease is not infectious, such as "an epidemic of diabetes."

Epidemiological paradox: the empirical finding that Mexican Americans have death rates of about the same magnitude and sometimes lower than Anglos despite what appear to be adverse circumstances; also known as the **Latino mortality paradox** or **Hispanic paradox.**

Epidemiological transition theory (ETT): the theory that focuses on the society-wide decline of infectious disease and the rise of chronic degenerative causes of death.

Essentialism: the essentialist view with regard to sexuality is dimorphism; that is, there is an "essential" biological or psychological characteristic or attribute that is common to all persons of one sexuality and that distinguishes them from the other sexuality.

Ethnic enclave: a community with distinctive cultural characteristics that can help migrants transition into life as immigrants by providing support and environments much like those in their mother countries.

Exogenous causes of death: a cause of death that is external to the body or genetic makeup; exogenous causes of death include infectious diseases, accidents, and injuries.

Exponential growth: a constant rate of growth applied to a continuously growing population.

Exurbs: geographic residential areas beyond the beltways that encircle the metropolitan areas.

Failure rate (of a contraceptive): the number of pregnancies per 100 person years of use of a birth control method.

Family planning: attempts by couples to regulate the number and spacing of births.

Family planning program: a systematic effort, often government sponsored, to provide the information, supplies, and services for modern fertility control.

Fecund: capable of giving birth.

Fecundity: the biological capacity or capability of a man, a woman, or a couple to produce a live birth.

Fecundity indeterminate: referring to couples who meet the criteria for being semifecund, except that the wife sometimes reports douching "for cleanness only" soon after intercourse.

Female condom: a female-initiated barrier to conception and disease. The female condom is a sheath about the same length as a male condom (around 16.5 centimeters [6.5 inches]) with a flexible ring at each end; the inner ring at the closed end of the condom is inserted into the vagina and remains in place behind the pubic bone; the outer ring at the open end is soft and remains outside the vagina during intercourse.

Fertility: the frequency with which a birth of either sex occurs within a population; i.e., the actual production of female or male births.

Fertility awareness methods: several "natural" family planning methods such as the Standard Days Method, the Billings ovulation method, and others.

Fetal death: the disappearance of life prior to a live birth.

Floating migrant: in China, an internal migrant who moves from one place to another without government authorization.

Flow: for a given time, the movement of international migrants both into and from a specific country.

Forced migration: in modern context, a form of migration in which individuals are compelled by government authorities to move; includes flight, displacement, and the creation of refugees (see **refugee**); historically, it would also include migration for slavery and involuntary indentured servitude. Contemporary human trafficking is also forced migration but does not usually involve government coercion.

General fertility rate (GFR): the number of live births per 1,000 women aged 15–44 (or 15–49) in a given year.

Generation: all of the people who were born and live at about the same time; an example is the **baby boom** generation.

Gentrification: a process in which a poor urban area is changed because more affluent people move in, improve the housing, and attract new businesses. The process often raises the cost of housing, so that the previous inhabitants are dislocated.

Geographic information system: mapping of areas used to analyze data.

Gestation: the carrying of a fetus within the uterus from conception to delivery. The average time for human gestation is 280 days, measured from the first day of the last menstrual period.

Great Migration: refers to the several decades after the Civil War in the United States when large numbers of Black persons migrated from the South to the North and the West, and especially to cities in those areas.

Green card: an identification card documenting that the holder is a legal permanent resident of the United States. Known officially as a United States Permanent Resident Card, the green card is so called because its color was green between 1946 and 1964; although it was not green for almost fifty years, its color once again became green in 2010.

Gross migration: the sum of the number of in-migrants to an area and out-migrants from the area, usually measured for a given year or range of years.

Gross migration rate (GMR): the sum of the number of in-migrants to an area and out-migrants from the area, per 1,000 members of the population.

Gross reproduction rate (GRR): the average number of daughters that would be born to a hypothetical group of 1,000 women if they completed their childbearing years following the age-specific fertility rates for a given year; similar to the total fertility rate but restricted to female births.

Halving time: the number of years for a population to reach half its present size were it to maintain its current rate of growth; this will occur if the growth rate is negative; at a –1.0 percent growth rate, the halving time is 69.3 years. If the growth rate is positive, see **doubling time.**

Healthy migrant effect: the hypothesis that states that the longevity advantage of Latinos compared with other minority groups (e.g., African Americans, American

Indians) occurs because many Latinos in the United States were born elsewhere, and migration is known to be selective of persons in better physical and mental health.

Histogram: a graphical representation of tabulated data frequencies shown as bars.

Hispanic paradox: see **epidemiological paradox**.

Host: a human who harbors a pathogen, allowing it to reproduce, and playing a critical role in disease transmission; the host often contracts the disease. Also, an animal that harbors a pathogen.

Household: a group of individuals who reside together, whether or not they are related to one another.

Human ecological theory: a macro-level explanation of population growth and decline.

Hypothetical cohort: an imaginary set of people traced through a series of specified risks to detail the cumulative effects of those risks.

Hysterectomy: the surgical removal of the uterus.

Hysteroscopic sterilization: a minimally invasive procedure that creates sterilization by permanently blocking the Fallopian tubes.

Immigrant: a person who enters a country with the intention of residing there permanently.

Immigration: the migration of people into a new country from any other country with the intention of establishing residence there.

Independent variable: a variable that is believed to have an effect on the dependent variable; also known as an X variable and as a covariate.

Induced abortion: a pregnancy that has been terminated by human intervention with an intent other than to produce a live birth; an induced early fetal death, legal or illegal, specifically, the deliberate premature expulsion of the fetus before it is capable of sustaining life.

Industry: the product or service produced by the employer of a worker.

Industry sector: a grouping of industries into a small number of groups, typically extractive, transformational, and service.

Infant mortality: the mortality of infants, i.e., persons less than one year of age.

Infant mortality rate (IMR): the number of deaths among infants under one year of age per 1,000 live births in the same year.

Infectious diseases: disorders caused by organisms, usually microscopic, that can then be passed directly or indirectly to other persons.

Infecundity: the physiological inability to produce a live birth.

Infertility: the production of no children, also known as childlessness; may be voluntary or involuntary.

In-migration: the residential migration of persons into a specific political subdivision (e.g., a county or state) from another subdivision of the same country.

In-migration rate (IMR): the number of persons migrating into an area usually during a one- or five-year time interval, divided by the population of the area at the beginning of the interval, times 1,000.

Internal migration: the geographical movement within a country for a permanent change of residence that involves the crossing of a county boundary.

International Classification of Diseases (ICD): the classification of diseases developed by the World Health Organization; the present classification (the eleventh revision) was adopted in 2022 and categorizes causes of death under twenty-one major headings.

International migration: migration between countries.
Intersex: referring to people with atypical combinations of the physical attributes (e.g., chromosomes, gonads, genitalia) that are commonly used to distinguish males from females.
Intrauterine device (IUD): A small device that is inserted directly into the uterus to prevent conception.
***In vitro* fertility:** the process whereby an ovum is fertilized by a sperm outside the body.
Jacob's syndrome: characteristic of person born with an extra (i.e., third) sex chromosome, in the configuration XYY.
Keyhole vasectomy: alternate term for no-scalpel vasectomy, a male sterilization procedure.
Klinefelter's syndrome: characteristic of person born with an extra (i.e., third) sex chromosome, in the configuration XXY.
Labor force: the proportion of the adult population that is employed or actively looking for work. In the United States, refers only to the civilian population aged 16 and older.
Labor force participation rate (LFPR): for a given point in time, the number of people employed plus those looking for work divided by the population aged 16 and over, times 100.
Laparoscopic sterilization: a female sterilization procedure that uses a laparoscope to view and then close the Fallopian tubes.
Least-developed countries (LDCs): countries with the lowest indicators of socioeconomic development, as defined by the United Nations.
Less developed countries: countries with low indicators of socioeconomic development, although not the lowest indicators.
Life expectancy: the average number of years of life yet to be lived by people attaining a given age, according to a given life table; it is the value of the function "e," usually the last function in a life table.
Life span: the maximum number of years a person can expect to live; the numerical age limit of human life.
Life table: a statistical table used for tracing the cumulative effect of a schedule of age-specific death rates over a life cycle for a hypothetical cohort.
Live birth: "the complete expulsion or extraction from its mother of a product of conception, irrespective of the duration of pregnancy, which, after such separation, breathes or shows any other evidence of life, such as beating of the heart; pulsation of the umbilical cord; or definite movement of voluntary muscles, whether or not the umbilical cord has been cut or the placenta is attached" (Shryock, Siegel, and Associates, 1976: 221).
Local movement: a short-distance change of residence within the same community that does not involve crossing a county jurisdictional boundary.
Longevity: the length of an individual life; collectively, average length of life of a cohort.
Long-term immigration: the movement of a person from one country to another for the purpose of establishing residence in the receiving country for at least one year.
Lucky Few: the birth cohort born in the United States between 1929 and 1944. This cohort enjoyed higher employment rates and a greater variety of social opportunities

than Americans in the preceding or in the following generations, and much of that was due to their small population size.

Macroanalysis: the study of the behavior of large population groups, such as countries.

Male condom: a thin, soft sheath worn over the penis during intercourse to prevent pregnancy and sexually transmitted infections (STIs).

Male fertility: the production of children due to the sperm of a male individual.

Malthusian checks: two kinds of controls, preventive and positive, that Thomas Malthus argued would limit population growth. The preventive checks were moral restraint, including late marriage; the positive checks were war, famine, and pestilence.

Masculinity proportion: the proportion of a population that is male, times 100.

Maternal death: "the death of a woman while pregnant or within 42 days of the termination of pregnancy, irrespective of the duration or site of pregnancy, from any cause related to or aggravated by the pregnancy or its management, but not from accidental or incidental causes" (Maine and Stamas, 2003: 628).

Maternal mortality ratio (MMR): deaths in a year occurring to women dying as a result of complications of pregnancy, childbirth, and the puerperium (the condition immediately following childbirth), per 100,000 live births occurring in the year.

Mean: the arithmetic average of numbers (e.g., ages, incomes) within a population or a subset of a population.

Median: the number that divides a distribution into two equal halves; the median age is the age at which half the population or population subset is older, and half is younger.

Megalopolis: a term referring to any densely populated social and economic area encompassing two or more contiguous metropolitan areas and the increasingly urbanized space between them.

Menarche: the beginning of the female reproductive or childbearing life cycle stage signified by the first menstrual flow, i.e., menstrual period.

Menopause: the end of the female reproductive or childbearing life cycle stage characterized by the termination of menstruation.

Mercantilism: an economic practice by which a country or population attempts to grow economically by trading with other countries and exporting more materials and goods than importing them.

Metropolitan: refers to a large concentration of population usually consisting of one or more central cities of at least 50,000 people and the surrounding settlements.

Metropolitanization: the relative growth of the metropolitan area population compared with other populations.

Microanalysis: the study of the behavior of individuals.

Micropolitan area: a geographic area that contains at least one urban cluster of between 10,000 and 49,999 people.

Micropolitanization: the relative growth of micropolitan populations compared with other populations.

Migrant: a person who changes residence with the change involving crossing a political boundary, such as a county.

Migration: the spatial movement of people resulting in their permanent change of residence; if the movement is within a country, it is referred to as **internal migration**; if it is between countries, it is known as **international migration**.

Migration counterstream: a body of migrants, smaller in size than its corresponding migration stream, going in the opposite direction during the same time interval.
Migration efficiency: an area's net migration divided by its gross migration.
Migration efficiency ratio (MER): the number of gross migrants divided by the number of net migrants, multiplied by 100.
Migration interval: the time period, usually expressed in the number of years, in which migration occurs.
Migration network theory: the theory of migration that focuses on networks, such as interpersonal ties that connect migrants, former migrants, potential migrants, and nonmigrants in the origin and destination countries.
Migration selectivity: the fact that migrants are selected from the sending population on the basis of age, race, sex, socioeconomic status, health, and other characteristics; in other words, some people are more likely to migrate than others.
Migration stream: a body of immigrants departing from a common area of origin and arriving at a common area of destination during a specified time interval; compare with **migration counterstream.**
Minipill: oral contraceptive containing only progestin.
Miscarriage: the spontaneous or accidental termination of fetal life that occurs during pregnancy, often early in the pregnancy.
Mode: in a collection of numbers or values, the one that occurs most frequently.
Morbidity: the prevalence of sickness within a population.
More developed countries: countries with higher indicators of socioeconomic development, as defined by the United Nations
Mortality: the frequency with which deaths occur in a population.
Mortality reversals: the increase in mortality after a population has experienced a decrease in mortality.
Mover: a person who changes residence.
Mulatto: a racial classification that was used at one time (e.g., in the 1890 US census) to refer to a person born of one Black parent and one White parent, or to persons with two Mulatto parents.
Natural decrease: a negative change between two points in time between the number of births minus the number of deaths in a population.
Natural increase: a positive change between two points in time between the number of births minus the number of deaths in a population.
Natural log: the natural logarithm of a number is the power to which *e* (an irrational constant equal to approximately 2.71821) would have to be raised to equal the desired number; thus, the natural log of 2 is 0.693, i.e., $e^{0.693}$, or $2.718210^{0.693} = 2$.
Neoclassical economic theory of international migration: the theory that migration is based on individual cost-benefit decisions to maximize expected incomes through geographic movement.
Neo-Malthusianism: the belief according to Thomas Malthus in the tendency of populations, if left unchecked, to outgrow the means of subsistence; also, advocacy (but not by Malthus) of the promotion of birth control as a solution to this dilemma.
Neonatal mortality rate (NMR): deaths to babies of 28 days of age or less, per 1,000 live births.

Net migration: the migration balance of an area, consisting of the number of in-migrants minus the number of out-migrants; the balance may be positive or negative.
Net migration rate (NMR): for a given time period, the number of persons moving into an area minus the number of people moving from the area, divided by the population size of the area, times 1,000.
Net reproduction rate (NRR): the average number of daughters that would be born to a female birth cohort if the mothers completed their childbearing years subject to the schedules of age-specific fertility and mortality rates of a give place and time.
New economics theory of migration: the theory that migration decisions are made not only by isolated individuals, but also by larger units, such as families and households.
Nonmarital fertility: the fertility of women who are not married.
Nosologists: people who study the classification and categorization of diseases and causes of death.
Nulliparous women: women who have not given birth.
Obituary: an announcement, or story, in a newspaper or online source of a person's death that usually includes a brief biographical sketch.
Occupation: a classification of the actual work that a worker does on the job (e.g., nurse, mechanic.)
Occupational segregation: the expectation that certain jobs are filled by people with certain demographic characteristics, followed by hiring practices that reinforce the expectation.
Octoroon: a racial classification that was used at one time (e.g., the 1890 US census) to refer to a person with one Black great-grandparent and seven White great-grandparents.
Old-age dependency ratio (ADR or Aged-DR): the ratio of persons 65 years of age or older to the working-age population (i.e., persons aged 15–64 years), multiplied by 100.
Out-migration: the residential migration of persons out of a specific political subdivision (e.g., a country or state) into another subdivision of the same country.
Outmigration rate (OMR): the number of persons migrating from an area usually during a one- or five-year time interval, divided by the population size at the start of the time interval, times 1,000.
Pandemic: an epidemic spreading throughout a very large area, such as a continent, or even the world, and affecting a very large portion of the population.
Parent support ratio: the ratio of the number of persons aged 80 years and older per 100 people aged 50–64; meant to represent the relative burden of the oldest-old population, i.e., the elderly parents, on the population aged 50–64, i.e., the children of the elderly parents.
Parity: the number of times a woman has given birth; also refers to birth order of the children.
Parous women: women who have had one or more births.
Parturition: the act or process of giving birth.
Period perspective: the viewing or studying of a population process cross-sectionally as the combined experience of population groups in a specified short period of time, normally one year.

Period rate: a rate based on behavior occurring at a particular point or period in time, such as one year; also known as a cross-sectional rate.

Political economic theory of fertility: an investigative framework used to study fertility in which several fields of knowledge are used, such as economics, politics, anthropology, sociology, and psychology; the analysis combines both microlevel and macrolevel perspectives.

Polygyny: the marital union of a male to two or more females simultaneously.

Population: a set of people residing in a given area at a specific time.

Population density: the relationship between the size of a population and the size of the area in which it lives, usually expressed as the number of persons per square mile or kilometer of land.

Population explosion: a dramatic increase in population size.

Population exponentialism: see **doubling time.**

Population implosion: a dramatic decrease in population size.

Population momentum: the growth of a population attributable to the high proportion of people in the childbearing years; the growth continues to occur even after replacement-level fertility has been attained. A negative version appears when the proportion of people in their childbearing years is proportionally small,

Population projection: a systematic calculation of the future population size of an area based on an assumed level of population growth and/or the assumed levels of fertility, mortality, and migration.

Population pyramid: a conventional form of bar graph representing the age–sex structure of the population at a particular point in time.

Population register: the continuous recording of population events for individual members of a population.

Population replacement: replacing a group of females who have completed their childbearing ages with a new group of females beginning their childbearing ages; this occurs via the production of female births, known as reproduction.

Postneonatal mortality rate (PMR): deaths to babies between the ages of 29 days and 1 year, per 1,000 live births.

Postpartum infecundability: "Following a pregnancy a woman remains infecundable (i.e., unable to conceive) until the normal pattern of ovulation and menstruation is restored. The duration of the period of infecundability is a function of the duration and intensity of lactation" (Bongaarts, 1978: 107).

Potential support ratio (PSR): a measure that represents the extent to which the people of working age can support the older population, calculated by dividing the number of persons of working age (15–64 years) by the number of older persons (65 years old or older). Also see **old-age dependency ratio.**

Progestin-only pill: a hormonally based contraceptive pill containing only progestin; see **mini-pill.**

Pronatalism: attitudes, customs, tradition, and policies directed toward increasing fertility.

Pronatalist: referring to advocating an increase in fertility.

Prospective age: based on life-table values, the average number of years an individual of a given chronological age can be expected to live, focusing on remaining life span rather than years lived. Prospective age assumes that the underlying age-specific death rates of the life table do not change.

Proximate determinants: the most immediate causes of a population process such as fertility; those biological and behavioral variables that are "intermediate" or "between" the broad social factors that influence fertility and fertility per se.

Push and pull factors of migration: the combination of factors pushing or not pushing the person from the area of origin and pulling or not pulling the person toward the area of destination.

Quadroon: a racial classification term that was used at one time, e.g., in the 1890 US census, to refer to a person born of a Mulatto parent and a White parent.

Racial mortality crossover: the demographic finding that at the very oldest ages the death rates for Blacks become lower than those for Whites and in some cases lower than those for Hispanics.

Rate of natural increase (RNI): the percentage rate of change in a population due to births and deaths; usually calculated as (crude birth rate – crude death rate)/1,000.

Ratio of the excess or deficit of males: the excess or deficit of males is calculated by subtracting the number of males from the number of females and dividing by the total population, times 100.

Refugee: a person who has immigrated into a new country in response to strong pressure in the home country arising from natural disaster, war, or persecution.

Registration: the recording of events in a register of population on a continuous basis for all members of a population.

Registration system: a continuous recording of a population's demographic events (births and deaths and in some cases, migration) as they occur.

Remigrant: an international migrant who moves back to and reestablishes permanent residence in the original country of origin.

Remigration: the international migration of persons back to their country of origin at some time after their emigration from that country.

Remittance: a transfer of money by a foreign immigrant worker from the host country to an individual in the home country.

Replacement level fertility: the level of fertility at which a cohort of women, on average, has only enough children to replace themselves in the population, at current mortality levels; in low-mortality populations, replacement fertility equals around 2.1 children per woman.

Replacement migration: the international migration needed by a country to offset population decline and aging resulting from low fertility and mortality rates, aiming to maintain a stable population size and workforce.

Reproduction: the production of female births (there is no demographic term to refer to the production of only male births); analogous to fertility, but limited to female births.

Residence: the location with which an individual is affiliated and habitually lives.

Residential mobility: the movement within and across geographic units that includes not only migration, but also residential moves not involving migration (e.g., a residential move within a county); all migrations are residential movements, but not all residential movements are migrations.

Return migrant effect: the hypothesis that states that the longevity of Latinos compared with other minority groups (e.g., African Americans) occurs because Latinos in poor physical health often return to their home country at old ages to live out the rest of their lives and thus, their deaths are not counted in US statistics.

Return migration: the migration within a country of persons back to their area of origin at some time after their initial out-migration.

Rhythm method: also known as periodic abstinence or continence; it is based on the idea that a woman can avoid pregnancy if she refrains from intercourse around the time of ovulation, when the egg is produced, usually determined by a calendar charting menstrual cycles.

Rule of 69.3: a formula based on the **natural logarithm** of 2 to determine the length of time before the size of a population would become twice as large, or one-half as large, if birth and death rates did not change; if the difference between the two is positive, it results in a doubling of the size of the population; if the difference is negative, a halving; the numerator of the doubling time/halving time formula is the natural log of 2 × 100, i.e., 69.3; the denominator is the rate of natural increase (RNI).

Salmon bias: see **return migrant effect.**

Second demographic transition (SDT): further fertility declines in a population after reaching the fourth stage of the (first) demographic transition; the demographic behaviors observed in the SDT include, but are not limited to, increasing the age at first marriage, increases in cohabitation, increases in divorce, the emergence of same-sex partnerships and marriages, increasing rates of nonmarital childbearing, and voluntary childlessness.

Semifecund: descriptive of couples who have married or cohabited for a relatively long time without using contraception but have not conceived.

Senior boom: a large increase in the number of seniors resulting from the aging of the baby boom cohort born between the late 1940s and 1960.

Sex composition: the composition of a population with regard to sex.

Sex ratio (SR): the number of males in a population divided by the number of females in the population, times 100.

Sex ratio at birth (SRB): the number of males of age 0 divided by the number of females of age 0, times 100.

Social constructionism: with respect to sexuality, this view argues against essentialism and the notion of binary categories; instead, it argues for a continuum with varying degrees of the categories of sexuality.

Stable population theory: the theory stating that a population closed to migration that experiences constant schedules of age-specific fertility and mortality rates will develop a constant age distribution and will grow at a constant rate, irrespective of initial age distribution.

Standard Days Method: the contraceptive method based on the principle that "women with regular menstrual cycles lasting 26–32 days can prevent pregnancy by avoiding unprotected intercourse on days eight through 19" (Gribble, 2003: 188).

Standardized death rate (SDR): a death rate that has been adjusted for age composition and, perhaps, other factors such as race and sex. If the death rates for two populations with different age structures are being compared, death rates standardized for age need to be used rather than crude death rates.

Stationary population: a stable population in which the birth rate equals the death rate, resulting in no change in the size of the population, in the absence of migration.

Stem pessary: antecedent form of the modern IUD, developed in the late 1860s.

Sterility: infecundity.

Sterilization: an operation or procedure performed on either a male or a female to prevent conception.

Stillbirth: a late fetal death at 20–28 weeks or more of gestation.

Stock: the number of foreign-born persons in a country at a particular point in time.

Subfecund: whereas fecund couples are capable of giving birth, subfecund couples have impairments of one sort or another making it difficult for them to produce children.

Suburbanization: the process of population movement from the core city to the fringe area around and nearby the core city.

Symptothermal method: the most effective of the fertility awareness methods of contraception; it uses both cervical secretions along with basal body temperatures to identify the times when conception is most likely.

Taeuber paradox: the paradox attributed to demographer Conrad Taueber that a cure found for one degenerative disease will provide the opportunity for death to occur from another.

Taxonomy: the branch of science concerned with classification.

Theoretical effectiveness of a contraceptive: degree of effectiveness that would occur with "perfect" use of the contraceptive.

Third demographic transition: the tendency, indeed perhaps the need, for countries with very low levels of fertility to rely on immigration to replenish their populations.

Total dependency ratio (Total DR): aged-dependency ratio plus youth-dependency ratio.

Tourist: a person who travels to another country for a short-term visit; a visitor.

Transgender: an umbrella term referring roughly to all persons whose gender identity, expression, or behavior does not conform to the sex they were assigned at birth.

Trisomy X: characteristic of a person born with an extra (i.e., third) sex chromosome, in the configuration XXX; also called Triple X syndrome.

Turner's syndrome: a chromosomal abnormality that occurs when the fertilizing sperm has been produced with neither an X nor a Y chromosome. If this sperm fertilizes a normal egg, the offspring will have only one X chromosome.

Unauthorized immigrant / undocumented immigrant: an international migrant residing in the host country of destination who is not a citizen of the host country and has not been admitted for permanent residence, nor is "in a set of specific authorized temporary statuses permitting longer-term residence and work" (Passel, 2006: 1).

Unemployment rate: for a specific time and geographic area, the number of people actively looking for work (or waiting for results of such a search) plus people waiting to report to a job within thirty days, divided by the total number of people in the labor force (employed plus unemployed), times 100.

Urban area: beginning with the 2020 census, an urban area comprises a densely settled core of census blocks that meet minimum housing unit density and/or population density requirements. This includes adjacent territory containing non-residential urban land uses. To qualify as an urban area, the territory identified according to criteria must encompass at least 2,000 housing units or have a population of at least 5,000.

Urban cluster (UC): a densely settled core of blocks and block groups, along with adjacent densely settled surrounding blocks, that together encompass a population of at least 2,500 but fewer than 50,000 people.

Urban growth: an increase in the number of people living in urban areas.

Urbanism: a lifestyle characteristic of urban places.

Urbanization: the process of increasing the proportion of the total population living in urban places.

Urbanized area (UA): in the United States, this term referred to a densely settled core of census blocks and block groups that met minimum population density requirements, along with adjacent densely settled surrounding census blocks that together encompassed a population of 50,000 people. Beginning with the 2020 census, this term was no longer used by the Census Bureau.

Urban place: densely populated places; in the United States, incorporated and unincorporated places of 2,500 or more inhabitants.

Use effectiveness of a contraceptive: measure of the effectiveness of a method, taking into account the fact that some users do not follow directions perfectly or carefully, or may not use the method all the time. Use effectiveness data reflect how effective the method is in "typical" use.

Utopianism: the goal of creating the perfect society in which all people are treated equally and with respect.

Vaginal contraception: foams, jellies, or pastes that are inserted into the vagina to prevent contraception by chemically immobilizing or destroying the sperm.

Vaginal ring: a thin, transparent, flexible device similar in content to the combined oral contraceptive pill, which contains both estrogen and progestin that are released on a continuous basis into the woman's body to prevent conception.

Vasectomy: male sterilization involving the surgical excision of a part of the vas deferens.

Vector: an organism that can transmit infectious pathogens between humans, or from animals to humans.

Vital statistics: the processed results of registrations of vital events; strictly speaking, vital events are births and deaths only, but the term is often broadened to include other population events such as marriages and divorce.

Wealth Flows Theory: a theory that explains fertility decline as a rational decision by parents based on how intergenerational transfers of wealth flow. In a high-fertility context, children produce more than they consume and provide net wealth to parents. In a low-fertility context, children are expensive to rear and educate, causing net wealth to flow to the children.

Whipple's method (MW): an index of age data of a population designed to reflect preference for the terminal digits of "0" and "5."

White flight: the massive out-migration to the suburbs from the core cities by the mostly White middle and upper classes.

Withdrawal: a birth control method that consists of removing the penis from the vagina before ejaculation; also know as coitus interruptus.

World systems theory of migration: the theory arguing that international migration is the natural result of the globalization of the market economy.

Youth dependency ratio (YDR or Youth-DR): the number of persons under 14 years of age, divided by the number of persons aged 15–64, multiplied by 100.

Zero net international migration: the equal number of persons immigrating into a country compared with the number emigrating from the country.

Zygote: a fertilized egg produced when the sperm of a male and an egg of a female are united.

References

Aaronson, S., T. Cajner, B. Fallick, F. Galbis-Reig, C. Smith, and W. Wascher. 2014. "Labor Force Participation: Recent Developments and Future Prospects." *Brookings Papers on Economic Activity*, 197–255.

Abma, Joyce C., and Gladys M. Martinez. 2006. "Childlessness among Older Women in the United States: Trends and Profiles." *Journal of Marriage and Family* 68: 1045–1056.

2023. "Teenagers in the United States: Sexual Activity, Contraceptive Use, and Childbearing, 2015–2019." *National Health Statistics Reports* 196 (December 14). www.cdc.gov/nchs/data/nhsr/nhsr196.pdf

Abraido-Lanza, A. F., B. P. Dohrenwend, D. S. Ng-Mak, and J. B. Turner. 1999. "The Latino Mortality Paradox: A Test of the 'Salmon Bias' and Healthy Migrant Hypotheses." *American Journal of Public Health* 89: 1543–1548.

Acock, Alan C. 2023. *A Gentle Introduction to Stata*, 6th ed. rev. College Station, TX: Stata Corporation.

Aird, John S. 1972. "Population Policy and Demographic Prospects in the People's Republic of China." In *People's Republic of China: An Economic Assessment, a Compendium of Papers Submitted to the Joint Economic Committee, Congress of the United States, 18 May (92nd Congress, 2nd Session)*. Washington, DC: US Government Printing Office.

1990. *Slaughter of the Innocents: Coercive Birth Control in China*. Washington, DC: AEI Press.

"All About Adam." 2013. *The Economist*. November 23.

Alvira-Hammond, Marta. 2019. "Hispanic Women Are Helping Drive the Recent Decline in the U.S. Fertility Rate." National Research Center on Hispanic Children & Families. March 19. www.hispanicresearchcenter.org/research-resources/hispanic-women-are-helping-drive-the-recent-decline-in-the-us-fertility-rate

Amigo, Ignacio. 2024. "Shades of Blue: Blue Zones, Supposed Havens of Longevity, Have Become a Global Brand. But Skeptics Think They Rest on Shaky Science." www.science.org/content/article/do-blue-zones-supposed-havens-longevity-rest-shaky-science

Anderson, Margo. 2003. "Census." In Paul Demeny and Geoffrey McNicoll (eds.), *Encyclopedia of Population*, I: 122–126. New York: Macmillan Reference USA.

2015. *The American Census: A Social History*, 2nd ed. New Haven, CT: Yale University Press.

Annie E. Casey Foundation. 2024. "Pandemic Learning Loss and COVID-19: Education Impacts." www.aecf.org/blog/pandemic-learning-loss-impacting-young-peoples-futures

Arévalo, Marcos, Irit Sinai, and Victoria Jennings. 1999. "A Fixed Formula to Define the Fertile Window of the Menstrual Cycle as the Basis of a Simple Method of Natural Family Planning." *Contraception* 60: 357–360.

Arias, Elizabeth. 2014. "United States Life Tables, 2010." *National Vital Statistics Reports* 63 (7).

Arias, Elizabeth, Melonie Heron, and Betzaida Tejada-Vera. 2013. "United States Life Tables Eliminating Certain Causes of Death, 1999–2001." *National Vital Statistics Reports* 61 (9).

Arias, Elizabeth, Jianquan Xu, and Kenneth Kochanek. 2023. "United States Life Tables, 2021." *National Vital Statistics Reports* 72 (12). November 7.

Armbrister, Adria N. 2003. "Immigration, Unauthorized." In Paul Demeny and Geoffrey McNicoll (eds.), *Encyclopedia of Population*, II: 512–515. New York: Macmillan Reference USA.

Arnold, F., and Z. Liu. 1986. "Sex Preference, Fertility, and Family Planning in China." *Population and Development Review* 12: 221–246.

Arriaga, Eduardo E., and Associates. 1994. *Population Analysis with Microcomputer*, Vol. 1: *Presentation of Techniques*. Washington, DC: US Bureau of the Census.

Ashford, Lori S. 2006. "How HIV and AIDS Affect Populations." *Population Reference Bureau BRIDGE Policy Briefs* (July).

Ashton, Basil, Kenneth Hill, Alan Piazza, and Robin Zeitz. 1984. "Famine in China, 1958–1961." *Population and Development Review* 10: 613–645.

Aubrey, John. 1898. *Brief Lives, Chiefly of Contemporaries, set down by John Aubrey in 1669–1696*, Andrew Clark (ed.). Oxford: Clarendon Press.

Bachi, R. 1951. "The Tendency to Round Off Age Returns: Measurement and Correction." *Bulletin of the International Statistical Institute (Proceedings of the 27th Session, Calcutta)* 33: 195–221.

Badenhorst, L. T., and Edward Higgins. 1962. "Fecundity of White Women in Johannesburg." *Population Studies* 15: 279–290.

Baker-Hughes, Sharon Wiederstein. 2019. "Sexual Minority Status: A Call for Standard Measures." Ph.D. diss., Texas A&M University, Department of Sociology.

Balinski, Michael L., and H. Peyton Young. 1982. *Fair Representation: Meeting the Ideal of One Man, One Vote*. New Haven, CT: Yale University Press.

Balter, Michael. 2006. "The Baby Deficit." *Science* 312 (5782): 1894–1897.

Banister, Judith. 1992. "China's Changing Mortality." In Dudley L. Poston, Jr., and David Yaukey (eds.), *The Population of Modern China*, 163–223. New York: Plenum.

2004. "Shortage of Girls in China Today." *Journal of Population Research* 21: 19–34.

Barrett, R. E. 1994. *Using the 1990 U.S. Census for Research*. Thousand Oaks, CA: Sage.

Barry, John M. 2004. *The Great Influenza: The Epic Story of the Deadliest Plague in History*. New York: Viking.

Bartlett, John. 1968. *Bartlett's Familiar Quotations*, 14th ed. Boston, MA: Little, Brown.

Bartz, Deborah, and Alisa B. Goldberg. 2011. "Injectable Contraceptives." In Robert A. Hatcher, James Trussell, Anita L. Nelson, Willard Cates, Jr., Deborah Kowal, and Michael S. Policar (eds.), *Contraceptive Technology*, 20th rev. ed., 209–236. New York: Ardent Media, Inc.

Bauer, J. 1990. "Demographic Change and Asian Labor Markets in the 1990s." *Population and Development Review* 16 (4): 615–645.

Baumle, Amanda K., D'Lane R. Compton, and Dudley L. Poston, Jr. 2009. *Same Sex Partners: The Demography of Sexual Orientation*. Albany, NY: SUNY Press.

Baumle, Amanda K., and Dudley L. Poston, Jr. 2004. "Apportioning the House of Representatives in 2000: The Effects of Alternative Policy Scenarios." *Social Science Quarterly* 85: 578–603.

Bean, Frank D., and Teresa A. Sullivan. 1987. "Immigration and Its Consequences: Confronting the Problem." In R. C. Rist (ed.), *Policy Studies Review Annual*, 8: 76–71. New Brunswick, NJ: Transaction.

Bean, Frank D., Edward E. Telles, and B. Lindsay Lowell. 1987. "Undocumented Migration to the United States: Perceptions and Evidence." *Population and Development Review* 13: 671–690.

Bean, Frank D., and Marta Tienda. 1987. *The Hispanic Population of the United States*. New York: Russell Sage Foundation.

"Before the Exodus." 2008. *The Economist*. April 26: 101.

Belkin, Lisa. 2008. "70 Year-old Woman Gives Birth." *New York Times*. December 9.

Bell, F. C., and M. L. Miller. 2005. *Life Tables for the United States Social Security Area, 1900–2010*. Washington, DC: Social Security Administration.

Bener'ia, L. 1999. "The Enduring Debate Over Unpaid Labour." *International Labour Review* 138 (3): 287–309.

Benetsky, Megan J., Charlynn Burd, and Melanie Rapino. 2015. "Young Adult Migration: 2007–2009 to 2010–2012." *American Community Survey Reports*, ACS-31. Washington, DC: US Census Bureau.

Benjamin, Harry. 1966. *The Transsexual Phenomenon*. New York: Ace Books.

Berglund, Agnethe, Marie J. Ornstrup, Marie Lind-Holst, Morten Dunø, Marie Bækvad-Hansen, Anders Juul, Luise Borch, Niels Jørgensen, Åse K. Rasmussen, Marianne Andersen, Katharina M. Main, Dorte Hansen, and Claus H. Gravholtb. 2023. "Epidemiology and Diagnostic Trends of Congenital Adrenal Hyperplasia in Denmark: A Retrospective, Population-Based Study." *The Lancet* 28 (May): 1–12. https://pmc.ncbi.nlm.nih.gov/articles/PMC9986638/pdf/main.pdf

Bernard, Aude, Martin Bell, and Elin Charles-Edwards. 2014. "Life-Course Transitions and the Age Profile of Internal Migration." *Population and Development Review* 40: 213–239.

Bernstein, E. L. 1940. "Who Was Condom?" *Human Fertility* 5: 172–175, 186.

Besamusca, K. L., K. Tijdens, M. Keune, M., and S. Steinmetz. 2015. "Working Women Worldwide: Age Effects in Female Labor Force Participation in 117 Countries." *World Development* 74: 123–141.

Biggar, Jeanne C. 1979. "The Sunning of America: Migration to the Sunbelt." *Population Bulletin* 34 (March).

Billings, Evelyn, John J. Billings, J. B. Brown, and H. G. Burger. 1972. "Symptoms and Hormonal Changes Accompanying Ovulation." *Lancet* 1: 282–284.

Billings, Evelyn, and Ann Westmore. 2000. *The Billings Method: Controlling Fertility without Drugs or Devices*. Toronto: Life Cycle Books.

Billings, John J. 1984. *The Ovulation Method: Natural Family Planning*, 5th ed. Collegeville, MN: Liturgical Press.

Biraben, Jean-Noel. 2003. "The Rising Numbers of Humankind." *Population & Societies* 394: 1–4.

Black, Dan A., Gary Gates, Seth G. Sanders, and Lowell J. Taylor. 2000. "Demographics of the Gay and Lesbian Population in the United States: Evidence from Available Systematic Data Sources." *Demography* 37: 139–154.

Black, Isabella. 1963. "American Labour and Chinese Immigration." *Past and Present* 25: 59–76.

Blackless, Melanie, Anthony Charuvastra, Amanda Derryck, Anne Fausto-Sterling, Karl Lauzanne, and Ellen Lee. 2000. "How Sexually Dimorphic Are We? Review and Synthesis." *American Journal of Human Biology* 12: 151–166.

Blake, Judith. 1974. "Can We Believe the Recent Data on Birth Expectations in the United States?" *Demography* 11: 25–44.

Blank, Hanne. 2012. *Straight: The Surprisingly Short History of Heterosexuality*. Boston, MA: Beacon Press.

Blow, Charles M. 2015. "Black Dads Are Doing Best of All." *New York Times*. June 8, A21.

Blumenbach, Johann. [1775, 1776] 1969. *On the Natural Varieties of Mankind*. New York: Bergman.

Bogaert, Anthony F. 2004. "Asexuality: Prevalence and Associated Factors in a National Probability Sample." *Journal of Sex Research* 41: 279–87.

2012. *Understanding Asexuality*. Lanham, MD: Rowman and Littlefield.

2013. "The Demography of Asexuality." In Amanda K. Baumle (ed.), *International Handbook on the Demography of Sexuality*, 275–88. Dordrecht: Springer Netherlands.

Bogue, Donald J. 1969. *Principles of Demography*. New York: Wiley.

1985. *The Population of the United States*. New York: The Free Press.

Bogue, Donald J., and James A. Palmore. 1964. "Some Empirical and Analytic Relations among Demographic Fertility Measures, with Regression Models for Fertility Estimation." *Demography* 1: 316–338.

Bongaarts, John. 1978. "A Framework for the Proximate Determinants of Fertility." *Population and Development Review* **4**: 105–132.

1982. "The Fertility-Inhibiting Effects of the Intermediate Fertility Variables." *Studies in Family Planning* **13**: 179–189.

2006. "How Long Will We Live?" *Population and Development Review* **32**: 605–628.

Bongaarts, John, and Robert G. Potter. 1983. *Biology and Fertility Behavior: An Analysis of the Proximate Determinants*. New York: Academic Press.

Bonilla-Silva, Eduardo. 2013. *Racism without Racists: Color-Blind Racism and the Persistence of Racial Inequality in the United States*, 4th ed. Lanham, MD: Rowman & Littlefield.

Borjas, George J. 2003. "Benefits and Cost of Immigration." In Paul Demeny and Geoffrey McNicoll (eds.), *Encyclopedia of Population*, II: 509–512. New York: Macmillan Reference USA.

Borjas, George J., Richard B. Freeman, and Lawrence F. Katz. 1997. "How Much Do Immigration and Trade Affect Labor Market Outcomes?" *Brookings Papers on Economic Activity* **28** (1): 1–67.

Borjas, George J., and Marta Tienda. 1993. "The Employment and Wages of Legalized Immigrants." *International Migration Review* **27** (4): 712–747.

Borrie, W. D. 1973. "The Place of Demography in the Development of the Social Sciences." In *International Population Conference, Liège*, 73–93. Liège, Belgium: International Union for the Scientific Study of Population.

Boserup, Ester. 1965. *The Conditions of Agricultural Growth*. Chicago: Aldine.

1981. *Population and Technological Change: A Story of Long-Term Trends*. Chicago: University of Chicago Press.

2005. *The Conditions of Agricultural Growth: The Economics of Agrarian Change under Population Pressure*. New Brunswick, NJ: Aldine Transaction.

Bouvier, Leon F. 1965. "A Genealogical Approach to the Study of French-Canadian Fertility." *Sociological Analysis* **26**: 148–156.

Bouvier, Leon F., and Jane T. Bertrand. 1999. *World Population: Challenges for the 21st Century*. Santa Ana, CA: Seven Locks.

Bouvier, Leon F., and Lindsey Grant. 1994. *How Many Americans? Population, Immigration and the Environment*. San Francisco, CA: Sierra Club Books.

Bouvier, Leon F., John J. Macisco, and Alvan Zarate. 1976. "Toward a Framework for the Analysis of Differential Migration: The Case of Education." In Anthony H. Richmond and Daniel Kubat (eds.), *Internal Migration: The New World and the Third World*, 24–36. Beverly Hills, CA: Sage.

Bouvier, Leon F., Dudley L. Poston, Jr., and Nan Bin Zhai. 1997. "The Population Growth Impacts of Zero Net International Migration." *International Migration Review* **31**: 294–311.

Bouvier, Leon F., Henry S. Shryock, and Harry W. Henderson. 1977. "International Migration, Yesterday, Today, and Tomorrow." *Population Bulletin* 30 (September).

Bouvier, Leon F., and Jean van der Tak. 1976. "Infant Mortality: Progress and Problems." *Population Bulletin* 31 (April).

Boyd, Nan Alamilla. 2003. *Wide Open Town: A History of Queer San Francisco to 1965*. Berkeley: University of California Press.

Bradley, Don E., and Charles F. Longino. 2009. "Geographic Mobility and Aging in Place." In Peter Uhlenberg (ed.), *International Handbook of Population Aging*, 319–339. Newark, NJ: Springer.

Brewster, K. L. and R. R. Rindfuss. 2000. "Fertility and Women's Employment in Industrialized Nations." *Annual Review of Sociology* **26**: 271–296.

British Broadcasting Corporation (BBC). 2008. "Woman in India 'Has Twins at 70.'" *BBC News*. http://news.bbc.co.uk/1/hi/world/south_asia/7491782.stm

Brokaw, Tom. 1998. *The Greatest Generation*. New York: Random House.

Brotto, Lori A., Gail Knudson, Jess Inskip, Katherine Rhodes, and Yvonne Erskine. 2010. "Asexuality: A Mixed-Methods Approach." *Archives of Sexual Behavior* 39: 599–618.

Brown, Susan K., Frank D. Bean, and Sabrina Nasir. 2019. "International Migration." In Dudley L. Poston, Jr. (ed.), *Handbook of Population*, 2nd ed., 421–455. New York: Springer.

Browning, Harley L., and Dudley L. Poston, Jr. 1980. "The Demographic Transition." In Rochelle N. Shain and Carl J. Pauerstein (eds.), *Fertility Control*, 197–203. New York: Harper and Row.

Brucker, H. 2002. "Can International Migration Solve the Problems of European Labour Markets?" Paper presented at the UNECE Economic Analysis Division's Spring Seminar: Labour Market Challenges in the ECE Region, Geneva.

Bryan, Thomas. 2004. "Basic Sources of Statistics." In Jacob S. Siegel and David A. Swanson (eds.), *The Methods and Materials of Demography*, 2nd ed., 9–41. San Diego, CA: Elsevier Academic.

Bryn, Mary and Morgan Holcomb. 2012. "Same Sex Divorce in a DOMA State." *Family Court Review* 50: 214–221.

Budiman, Abby and Neil G. Ruiz. 2021. "Key Facts about Asian Americans, a Diverse and Growing Population." *Short Reads*. April 29. Washington, DC: Pew Research Center.

Buettner, Dan. 2012. *The Blue Zones, Second Edition: 9 Lessons for Living Longer From the People Who've Lived the Longest*. Washington, DC: National Geographic.

Burch, Thomas K. 2003. "Demography in a New Key: A Theory of Population Theory." *Demographic Research* 9: 263–284.

Burnett, Kristin D. 2011. "Census Apportionment." *2010 Census Briefs,* C2010BR-08 (November): 1–7.

Burkitt, Laurie. 2015. "China Abandons One Child Policy." *Wall Street Journal*. October 30.

Busby, George. 2016. "Here's How Genetics Helped Crack the History of Human Migration." *The Conversation*. January 13. https://theconversation.com/heres-how-genetics-helped-crack-the-history-of-human-migration-52918

Buss, T. F., and Redburn, F. S. 1988. *Hidden Unemployment: Discouraged Workers and Public Policy*. New York: Praeger.

Cafaro, Philip, Pernilla Hansson, and Frank Götmark. 2022. "Overpopulation Is a Major Cause of Biodiversity Loss and Smaller Human Populations are Necessary to Preserve What is Left." *Biological Conversation* 272.

Cafferty, Pastora San Juan, Barry R. Chiswick, Andrew M. Greeley, and Teresa A. Sullivan. 1983. *The Dilemma of American Immigration: Beyond the Golden Door*. New Brunswick, NJ: Transaction Books.

Cai, Yong. 2010. "Social Forces behind China's below Replacement Fertility: Government Policy or Socioeconomic Development." *Population and Development Review* 36: 419–440.

Caldwell, John C. 1976. "Toward a Restatement of Demographic Transition Theory." *Population and Development Review* 2: 321–366.

2006. "Epidemics." In David Lucas and Others (eds.), *Beginning Australian Population Studies*, ch. 3a. Canberra: Australian National University. http://demography.anu.edu.au/Publications/Books/BAPS.php

Callen, Tim. 2022. "Gross Domestic Product: An Economy's All." *Finance and Development Magazine* (August): 14–15. www.imf.org/en/Publications/fandd/issues/Series/Back-to-Basics/gross-domestic-product-GDP

Carey, Arlen D., and Joseph Lopreato. 1995. "The Biocultural Evolution of the Male-Female Mortality Differential." *The Mankind Quarterly* 36: 3–28.

Carey, James R. 1997. "What Demographers Can Learn from Fruit Fly Actuarial Models and Biology." *Demography* 34: 17–50.

2003. *Longevity: The Biology and Demography of Life Span*. Princeton, NJ: Princeton University Press.

Carey James R., P. Liedo, D. Orozco, and James W. Vaupel. 1992. "Slowing of Mortality Rates at Older Ages in Large Medfly Cohorts." *Science* **258**: 457–461.

Carey, James R., and James W. Vaupel. 2019. "Biodemography." In Dudley L. Poston, Jr. (ed.), *Handbook of Population*, 2nd ed., 713–745. New York: Springer.

Carlson, Elwood. 2008. *The Lucky Few: Between the Greatest Generation and the Baby Boom*. New York: Springer.

Carlson, Marcia, Sara McLanahan, and Paula England. 2004. "Union Formation in Fragile Families." *Demography* **41**: 237–261.

Carrier, N. H. 1959. "A Note on the Measurement of Digital Preference in Age Recordings." *Journal of the Institute of Actuaries* **85**: 71–85.

Case, Anne, and Angus Deaton. 2020. *Deaths of Despair and the Future of Capitalism*. Princeton, NJ: Princeton University Press.

Castells, Manuel. 1989. *The Information City: Information Technology, Economic Restructuring, and the Urban-Regional Process*. Oxford: Basil Blackwell.

Castor, Helen. 2015. *Joan of Arc: A History*. New York: HarperCollins.

Cates, Willard, Jr., and Byrna Harwood. 2011. "Vaginal Barriers and Spermicides." In Robert A. Hatcher, James Trussell, Anita L. Nelson, Willard Cates, Jr., Deborah Kowal, and Michael S. Policar (eds.), *Contraceptive Technology*, 20th rev. ed., 391–408. New York: Ardent Media, Inc.

Centers for Disease Control and Prevention (CDC). 2014. "Contraception Effectiveness, Recommendations and Reports." *Morbidity and Mortality Weekly Report* 63 (RR04) (April 25): 47. www.cdc.gov/mmwr/preview/mmwrhtml/rr6304a5.htm

2023. "*QuickStats:* Life Expectancy at Birth, by Sex – National Vital Statistics System, United States, 2019–2021." *Morbidity and Mortality Weekly Report* **72**: 775. http://dx.doi.org/10.15585/mmwr.mm7228a5

2024a. "About Smallpox." October. www.cdc.gov/smallpox/about/index.html

2024b. "Infant Mortality." September 16. www.cdc.gov/maternal-infant-health/infant-mortality/index.html

2024c. "Maternal Mortality Prevention." September 25. www.cdc.gov/maternal-mortality/preventing-pregnancy-related-deaths/index.html

2024d. "Stillbirths." May 15. www.cdc.gov/stillbirth/data-research/index.html

2024e. "Tobacco Product Use Among Adults – United States, 2021." May 15. www.cdc.gov/tobacco/data-statistics/mmwr/2023-mm7218a1.html

2024f. "COVID Data Tracker": www.cdc.gov/covid-data-tracker

Central Intelligence Agency (CIA). 2015. *The World Factbook*. Washington, DC: Central Intelligence Agency.

2024. *The World Factbook*. www.cia.gov/the-world-factbook/

2025. *The World Factbook*. Washington, DC: Central Intelligence Agency.

Central Statistical Office, Zambia, and the DHS Program, ICF International. 2014. *Zambia Demographic and Health Survey, 2013-2014, Preliminary Report*. Lusaka, Zambia: Central Statistical Office.

Chamie, Joseph. 2025. "America's Single-Parent Households and Missing Fathers." *N-IUSSP, the News Magazine of the International Union for the Scientific Study of Population*. January 13.

Chan, Kam Wing. 2021. "China's Hukou Reform Remains a Major Challenge to Domestic Migrants in Cities." *People Move*. December 17. Washington, DC: The World Bank.

Chandler, Tertius, and Gerald Fox. 1974. *3000 Years of Urban Growth*. New York: Academic Press.

Chandra, Anjani, William D. Mosher, and Casey E. Copen. 2011. "Sexual Behavior, Sexual Attraction, and Sexual Identity in the United States: Data from the 2006–2008 National Survey of Family Growth." National Center for Health Statistics, *National Health Statistics Reports* 36 (March 3).

Charles, M. 1992. "Cross-national Variation in Occupational Sex Segregation." *American Sociological Review* 57: 48–502.

Charmantier, Isabelle. 2020. "Linnaeus and Race." The Linnean Society of London. www.linnean.org/learning/who-was-linnaeus/linnaeus-and-race

Child Trends. 2015. "Births to Unmarried Women." *Child Trends Data Bank* (March). Washington, DC: Child Trends.

China Daily. 2004. "China Bans Selective Abortion to Fix Imbalance." www. chinadaily.com.cn/english/doc/2004-07/16/content_349051.htm

Chu, J. 2001. "Prenatal Sex Determination and Sex-Selective Abortion in Rural Central China." *Population and Development Review* 27: 259–281.

Clarke, J. I. 2000. *The Human Dichotomy: The Changing Numbers of Males and Females*. Amsterdam: Pergamon.

Cleland, John. 1996. "Demographic Data Collection in the Less Developed Countries." *Population Studies* 50: 433–450.

Cleland, John, and J. Hobcroft. 1985. *Reproductive Change in Developing Countries: Insights from the World Fertility Survey*. New York: Oxford University Press.

Cleland, John, and C. Scott. 1987. *The World Fertility Survey: An Assessment*. New York: Oxford University Press.

Coale, Ansley J. 1957. "How the Distribution of Human Population Is Determined." *Cold Spring Harbor Symposium on Quantitative Biology* 22: 83–89.

1971. "Age Patterns of Marriage." *Population Studies* 25: 193–214.

1972. *The Growth and Structure of Human Populations*. Princeton, NJ: Princeton University Press.

1974. "The History of the Human Population." *Scientific American* 231: 51.

1987. "Stable Populations." In J. Eatwell, M. Milgate, and P. K. Newman (eds.), *The New Palgrave: A Dictionary of Economics*, IV: 466–469. London: Macmillan.

Coale, Ansley J., and Paul Demeny. 1983. *Regional Model Life Tables and Stable Populations*, 2nd ed. New York: Academic Press.

Coale, Ansley J., and Susan Cotts Watkins (eds.). 1986. *The Decline of Fertility in Europe*. Princeton, NJ: Princeton University Press.

Coan, Peter Morton. 2004. *Ellis Island Interviews: Immigrants Tell Their Stories in Their Own Words*. New York: Fall River.

Cohen, Joel. 1995. *How Many People Can the Earth Support?* New York: W. W. Norton.

Cohen, Stephanie. 2009. "Retire to the Bedroom." *New York Post*. January 25.

Colby, Sandra L., and Jennifer M. Ortman. 2015. "Projections of the Size and Composition of the U.S. Population: 2014 to 2060." *Current Population Reports* P25–114 (March). Washington, DC: US Census Bureau.

Coleman, David A. 2000. "Male Fertility Trends in Industrial Countries: Theories in Search of Some Evidence." In Caroline Bledsoe, Susana Lerner, and Jane I. Guyer (eds.), *Fertility and the Male Life-Cycle in the Era of Fertility Decline*, 29–60. Oxford and New York: Oxford University Press.

2006. "Immigration and Ethnic Change in Low-fertility Countries: A Third Demographic Transition." *Population and Development Review* 32: 401–446.

College Transitions. 2024. "101 Largest High Schools in the United States 2024." May 17. www.collegetransitions.com/blog/largest-high-schools-in-the-united-states

Compton, D'Lane R., D. Nicole Farris, and Yu-ting Chang. 2015. "Patterns of Bisexuality in America." *Journal of Bisexuality* 15: 1–17.

Comte, Auguste. 1853. *The Positive Philosophy of Auguste Comte*. Tr. Harriet Martineau. New York: Calvin Blanchard.

Conceptus, Inc. 2010. *When Your Family Is Complete, Choose Essure*. Mountain View, CA: Conceptus, Inc.

Congressional Budget Office. 2023. "The Foreign-Born Population, the U.S. Economy, and the Federal Budget." April. www.cbo.gov/publication/59046

Connelly, Matthew. 2008. *Fatal Misconception: The Struggle to Control World Population*. Cambridge, MA: Harvard University Press.

Connor, Phillip, D'Vera Cohn, Ana Gonzalez-Barrerra, and Russ Oates. 2013. "Changing Patterns of Global Migration and Remittances." Washington, DC: Pew Research Center.

Cooley, Charles Horton. 1902. *Human Nature and the Social Order*. New York: C. Scribner's Sons.

Coontz, Stephanie. 2000. *The Way We Never Were: American Families and the Nostalgia Trap*. New York: Basic Books.

2005. *Marriage, A History: From Obedience to Intimacy or How Love Conquered Marriage*. New York: Viking.

Corijn, Martine, and Erik Klijzing. 2001. *Transitions to Adulthood in Europe*. New York: Kluwer Academic.

Cortes, Rachel Traut, and Dudley L. Poston, Jr. 2008. "Immigrants to North America." In William A. Darity (ed. in chief), *International Encyclopedia of the Social Sciences*, 2nd ed., III: 576–580. Detroit: Macmillan Reference USA.

Corti, Maria-Chiara, Jack M. Guralnik, Luigi Ferrucci, Grant Izmirlian, Suzanne G. Leveille, Marco Pahor, Harvey J. Cohen, Carl Pieper, and Richard J. Havlik. 1999. "Evidence for a Black-White Crossover in All-Cause and Coronary Heart Disease Mortality in an Older Population: The North Carolina EPESE." *American Journal of Public Health* **89**: 308–314.

Costagliola, A. 2021. "Labor Participation and Gender Inequalities in India: Traditional Gender Norms in India and the Decline in the Labor Force Participation Rate (LFPR)." *Indian Journal of Labour Economics* **64**: 531–542. https://doi.org/10.1007/s41027-021-00329-7

Couzin-Frankel, Jennifer. 2011. "A Pitched Battle over Life Span." *Science* 333 (July 29): 549–550.

Couch, K., and R. Fairlie. 2010. "Last Hired, First Fired? Black-White Unemployment and the Business Cycle." *Demography*, **47**(1): 227–247.

Cox, T. K., and G. Pendell. 2007. "Attitudes about Childlessness in the United States: Correlates of Positive, Neutral, and Negative Responses." *Journal of Family Issues* 28: 1054–1082.

Crosby, Alfred W. 2003. *America's Forgotten Epidemic: The Influenza of 1918*, 2nd ed. New York: Cambridge University Press.

Crosby, Molly Caldwell. 2007. *The American Plague: The Untold Story of Yellow Fever, the Epidemic that Shaped Our History*. Reprint ed. New York: Berkley Books.

Crosette, Barbara. 1997. "How to Fix a Crowded World." *New York Times*, November 2.

Cui, Xiaoxiao, Yazhou Cui, Liang Shi, Jing Luan, Xiaoyan Zhou, and Jinxiang Han. 2018. "A Basic Understanding of Turner Syndrome: Incidence, Complications, Diagnosis, and Treatment." *Intractable & Rare Diseases Research* 7(4): 223–228.

Curtin, Philip. 1969. *The Atlantic Slave Trade*. Madison, WI: University of Wisconsin Press.

Curtin, Sally C., Stephanie J. Ventura, and Gladys M. Martinez. 2014. "Recent Declines in Nonmarital Childbearing in the United States." *NCHS Data Brief* **162** (August). Hyattsville, MD: National Center for Health Statistics.

Dahl, Melissa. 2015. "5 Ways to Better Understand Asexuality." *New York Magazine*. August 10.

Daily Mail. 1903. September 10. London.

Darwin, Charles. [1887] 1958. *Autobiography and Selected Letters*, Francis Darwin (ed.). New York: Dover.

Darwin, John. 2008. *After Tamerlane: The Global History of Empire Since 1405*. New York: Bloomsbury USA.

David, Henry P., and Nicholas H. Wright. 1971. "Abortion Legislation: The Romanian Experience." *Studies in Family Planning* **2**: 205–210.

David J. Senser CDC Museum. 2024. "CDC Museum COVID-19 Timeline." www.cdc.gov/museum/timeline/covid19.html

Davis, Georgiann. 2015. *Contesting Intersex: The Dubious Diagnosis*. New York: New York University Press.

Davis, Kingsley. 1963. "The Theory of Change and Response in Modern Demographic History." *Population Index* **29**: 345–366.

1974. "The Migrations of Human Populations." *Scientific American* 231: 92–105.

Davis, Kingsley, and Judith Blake. 1956. "Social Structure and Fertility: An Analytical Framework." *Economic Development and Cultural Change* 5: 211–235.

Davis, Mary Ann. 2008. *Alzheimer's Disease Mortality: A Demographic Analysis of Alzheimer's Disease Deaths in the United States from 1998 to 2002*. Saarbrücken, Germany: VDM Verlag.

Davis, Mary Ann, D'Lane R. Compton, and Dudley L. Poston, Jr. 2025. "Socioeconomic Inequalities in the Transgender and Nonbinary Populations." In Joachim Singelmann and Dudley L. Poston, Jr. (eds.), *International Handbook of the Demography of Poverty and Inequality*, ch. 8. Cham, Switzerland: Springer Nature.

Dean, Gillian, and Eleanor Bimla Schwarz. 2011. "Intrauterine Contraceptives (IUCs)." In Robert A. Hatcher, James Trussell, Anita L. Nelson, Willard Cates, Jr., Deborah Kowal, and Michael S. Policar (eds.), *Contraceptive Technology*, 20th rev. ed., 147–191. New York: Ardent Media, Inc.

Decker, Julie Sondra. 2014. *The Invisible Orientation: An Introduction to Asexuality*. New York: Carrel Books.

Deffeyes, Kenneth. 2005. *Beyond Oil: The View from Hubbert's Peak*. New York: Hill and Wang.

Demeny, Paul. 2003. "Population Policy." In Paul Demeny and Geoffrey McNicoll (eds.), *Encyclopedia of Population*, II: 752–763. New York: Macmillan Reference USA.

de Zwarte, I. J. J., P. Ekamper, and L. H. Lumey. 2024. "Infant and Child Mortality in the Netherlands 1935-1947 and Changes related to the Dutch Famine of 1944–1945: A Population-based Analysis." *Population Studies* (Camb) 78(3): 483–501. doi: 10.1080/00324728.2023.2243913. Epub 2023 Sep 12. PMID: 37698237; PMCID: PMC10927613.

Diamond, Lisa. 2003. "What Does Sexual Orientation Orient? A Biobehavioral Model Distinguishing Romantic Love and Sexual Desire." *Psychological Review* 110 (1): 173–192.

Dikotter, Frank. 2010. *Mao's Great Famine: The History of China's Most Devastating Catastrophe, 1958–1962*. New York: Walker and Company.

Djerassi, Carl. 1992. *The Pill, Pygmy Chimps, and Degas' Horse: The Autobiography of Carl Djerassi*. New York: Basic Books.

Dols, M. J. L., and D. J. A. M. van Arcken. 1946. "Food Supply and Nutrition in the Netherlands during and Immediately after World War II." *The Milbank Memorial Fund Quarterly* 24(4): 319–358.

Dominguez, Kenneth, Ana Penman-Aguilar, Man-Huei Chang, Ramal Moonesinghe, Ted Castellanos, Alfonso Rodriguez-Lainz, and Richard Schieber. 2015. "Leading Causes of Death, Prevalence of Diseases and Risk Factors, and Use of Health Services among Hispanics in the United States – 2009–2013." *Morbidity and Mortality Weekly Report* 64: 469–478.

Donato, Katharine M. 1994. "U.S. Policy and Mexican Migration to the United States, 1942–1992." *Social Science Quarterly* 75: 705–729.

Dreger, Alice Domurat. 1998. *Hermaphrodites and the Medical Intervention of Sex*. Cambridge, MA: Harvard University Press.

Dreyer, Edward L. 2007. *Zheng He: China and the Oceans in the Early Ming Dynasty, 1405–1433*. New York: Pearson Longman.

Dublin, Louis, Alfred J. Lotka, and Mortimer Spiegelman. 1949. *Length of Life*, rev. ed. New York: Ronald Press.

Duncan, Otis Dudley. 1959. "Human Ecology and Population Studies." In Philip M. Hauser and Otis Dudley Duncan (eds.), *The Study of Population*, 678–716. Chicago: University of Chicago Press.

Dunn, Megan, Stephen E. Haugen, and Janie-Lynn Kang. 2018. "The Current Population Survey – Tracking Unemployment in the United States for Over 75 Years." *Monthly Labor Review*. January. www.bls.gov/opub/mlr/2018/article/the-current-population-survey-tracking-unemployment.htm

Dupre, Matthew E., Alexis T. Franzese, and Emilio A. Parrado. 2006. "Religious Attendance and Mortality: Implications for the Black-White Mortality Crossover." *Demography* **43**: 141–164.

Durand, Jorge, Douglas S. Massey, and Emilio A. Parrado. 1999. "The New Era of Migration to the United States." *Journal of American History* **86**: 518–536.

Durkheim, Emile. [1893] 1984. *The Division of Labour in Society*, trans. W. D. Halls. London: Macmillan.

Dwyer-Lindgren, Laura, Matthew M. Baumann, Zhuochen Li, Yekaterina O Kelly, Chris Schmidt, Chloe Searchinger, Wichada Lamott-Kerr, Ali H Mokdad, and Christopher J. L. Murray. 2024. "Ten Americas: A Systematic Analysis of Life Expectancy Disparities in the USA." *The Lancet*, **404** (10469): 2299–2313.

Easterlin, Richard A. 2008. "Introduction." In Elwood Carlson, *The Lucky Few: Between the Greatest Generation and the Baby Boom*, xvii–xx. New York: Springer.

Eberstadt, Nicholas. 2000. *Prosperous Paupers & Other Population Problems*. New Brunswick, NJ: Transaction Publishers.

2009. "Drunken Nation: Russia's Depopulation Bomb." *World Affairs* **171** (Spring): 51–62.

Eberstein Isaac W., Charles B. Nam, and K. M. Heyman. 2008. "Causes of Death and Mortality Crossovers by Race." *Biodemography and Social Biology* **54**: 214–228.

Eckenstein, Lina. 1896. *Women Under Monasticism*. Cambridge, UK: Cambridge University Press.

Edin, Kathryn, and Maria Kefalas. 2007. *Promises I Can Keep: Why Poor Women Put Motherhood before Marriage*, 2nd ed. Oakland, CA: University of California Press.

Ehrlich, Paul R. 1968. *The Population Bomb*. New York: Ballantine Books.

2023. *Life: A Journey Through Science and Politics*. New Haven, CT: Yale University Press.

Eig, Jonathan. 2014. *The Birth of the Pill: How Four Crusaders Reinvented Sex and Launched a Revolution*. New York: W. W. Norton.

Eldridge, Hope T. 1968. "Population Policies." In David L. Sills (ed.), *International Encyclopedia of the Social Sciences*, XII: 380–388. New York: Macmillan.

Ellis, Havelock. 1897–1928. *Studies in the Psychology of Sex*, 7 volumes. Watford, UK: London University Press.

Elsayed A., A. de Grip, D. Fouarge, and R. Montizaan. 2018. "Gradual Retirement, Financial Incentives, and Labour Supply of Older Workers: Evidence from a stated preference analysis." *Journal of Economic Behavior and Organization* **150**: 277–294.

Endres, Michael E. 1975. *On Diffusing the Population Bomb*. New York: John Wiley and Sons.

England, Paula, Jonathan Bearak, Michelle J. Budig, and Melissa J. Hodges. 2016. "Do Highly Paid, Highly Skilled Women Experience the Largest Motherhood Penalty?" *American Sociological Review* **81** (6): 1161–1189.

Epstein, Helen. 2007a. "Death by the Numbers." *New York Review*. June 28: 41–43.

2007b. *The Invisible Cure: Africa, the West, and the Fight Against AIDS*. New York: Farrar, Straus and Giroux.

Epstein, Randi Hutter. 2015. "Howard W. Jones Jr., a Pioneer of Reproductive Medicine Dies at 104." *New York Times*. July 31.

Eschbach, Karl. 1993. "Changing Identification among American Indians and Alaska Natives." *Demography* 30: 635–652.

Escourrou, Emile, Sarah Laurent, Jacques Leroux, et al. 2022. "The Shift from Old Age to Very Old Age: An Analysis of the Perception of Aging among Older People." *BMC Primary Care* **23** (3). https://doi.org/10.1186/s12875-021-01616-4

Espenshade, Thomas J., J. L. Baraka, and G. A. Huber. 1997. "Implications of the 1996 Welfare and Immigration Reform Acts for US Immigration." *Population and Development Review* **23**: 769–801.

Espenshade, Thomas J., Leon F. Bouvier, and W. Brian Arthur. 1982. "Immigration and the Stable Population Model." *Demography* **19**: 125–133.

Espenshade, Thomas J., and Katherine Hempstead. 1996. "Contemporary American Attitudes toward U.S. Migration." *International Migration Review* 30: 535–570.

Espenshade, Thomas J. and Wenzhen Ye. 1994. "Differential Fertility Within an Ethnic Minority: The Effect of 'Trying Harder' Among Chinese-American Women." *Social Problem* 41(1): 97113. https://doi.org/10.2307/3096844

Espey, David. 2014. "Spanish Influenza in San Francisco 1918–1919: A Case Study." Unpublished Senior Thesis, Kenyon College, Gambier, OH.

Etherington, Norman. 2003. "War." In Paul Demeny and Geoffrey McNicoll (eds.), *Encyclopedia of Population*, II: 963–966. New York: Macmillan Reference USA.

Euler, Leonhard. [1760] 1970. "General Research on Mortality and Multiplication," trans. Nathan Keyfitz and B. Keyfitz. *Theoretical Population Biology* 1: 307–314.

Eversley, D. E. C. 1959. *Social Theories of Fertility and the Malthusian Debate*. Oxford, England: Clarendon Press.

Ewing, Walter A, Daniel E. Martínez, and Rubén G. Rumbaut. 2015. *The Criminalization of Immigration in the United States*. Washington, DC: American Immigration Council.

Fagundes, Nelson J. R., Nicolas Ray, Mark Beaumont, Samuel Neuenschwander, Francisco M. Salzano, Sandro L. Bonatto, and Laurent Excoffier. 2007. "Statistical Evaluation of Alternative Models of Human Evolution." *PNAS* 104 (November 6): 17614–17619

Fairbank, John K., and Merle Goldman. 2006. *China: A New History*, 2nd enlarged ed. Cambridge, MA: Belknap Press.

Fallon, K. M., A. Mazar, and L. Swiss. 2017. "The Development Benefits of Maternity Leave." *World Development* 96: 102–118.

Farris, Demetrea Nicole. 2016. *Boomerang Kids: The Demography of Previously Launched Adults*. New York: Springer.

Farris, Demetrea Nicole, and Dudley L. Poston, Jr. 2014. "Family Issues in Taiwan and China." In Dudley L. Poston, Jr., Wen Shan Yang, and D. Nicole Farris (eds.), *The Family and Social Change in Chinese Societies*, vii–xviii. New York: Springer.

Faust, Drew Gilpin. 2008. *This Republic of Suffering: Death and the American Civil War*. New York: Alfred A. Knopf.

Fausto-Sterling, Anne. 2000. *Sexing the Body: Gender Politics and the Construction of Sexuality*. New York: Basic Books.

Feagin, Joe R. 2006. *Systemic Racism: A Theory of Oppression*. New York: Routledge.

2014. *Racist America: Roots, Current Realities, and Future Reparations*, 3rd ed. New York: Routledge.

Federal Interagency Forum on Child and Family Statistics. 2007. *America's Children: Key National Indicators of Well Being, 2007*. Washington, DC: US Government Printing Office.

Feinstein, James A., Peter J. Gill, and Brett R. Anderson. 2023 "Preparing for the International Classification of Diseases, 11th Revision (ICD-11) in the US Health Care System." *JAMA Health Forum* 4 (7): e232253 https://jamanetwork.com/journals/jama-health-forum/fullarticle/2807690

Fenollar, F., and O. Mediannikov. 2018. "Emerging Infectious Diseases in Africa in the 21st Century." *New Microbes New Infections* 26: S10–S18. doi: 10.1016/j.nmni.2018.09.004

Field, Layton, and Dudley L. Poston, Jr. 2013. "Subnational Depopulation via Natural Decrease in the Countries of Europe and in the States of the United States in the Early Twenty-first Century." Paper presented at the XXVII International Population Conference, International Union for the Scientific Study of Population, Busan, South Korea, 26–31 August.

Filteau, Jerry. 2009. "Obama Rescinds Family-Planning Aid Restrictions." *National Catholic Reporter* 45 (February 6): 1, 12–13.

Finer, L. B. 2007. "Trends in Premarital Sex in the United States, 1954–2003." *Public Health Reports* 122: 73-78.

Fingerhut, Lois A. 2003. "Accidents." In Paul Demeny and Geoffrey McNicoll (eds.), *Encyclopedia of Population*, I: 2–6. New York: Macmillan Reference USA.

Fischer, Peter A., Reiner Martin, and Thomas Straubhaar. 1997. "Should I Stay or Should I Go?" In Thomas Hammar, Grete Brochmann, and Kristof Tamas (eds.), *International Migration, Immobility and Development*, 49–90. Oxford, UK: Berg.

Flatau, E., Z. Josefsberg, S. H. Reisner, O. Bialik, and Z. Laron. 1975. "Penis Size in the Newborn Infant." *Journal of Pediatrics* 87: 663–664.

Fossett, Mark, and Amber R. Crowell. 2019. "Urban and Spatial Demography." In Dudley L. Poston, Jr. (ed.), *Handbook of Population*, 2nd ed., 555–598. New York: Springer.

Foster, R. F. 1988. *Modern Ireland: 1600–1972*. New York: Penguin Books.

Foucault, Michel. 1978. *The History of Sexuality: An Introduction*, Vol. 1. New York: Vintage Books.

Freedman, Lynn P., and Stephen L. Isaacs. 1993. "Human Rights and Reproductive Choice." *Studies in Family Planning* 24: 18–30.

Freedman, Mary Anne, and James A. Weed. 2003. "Vital Statistics." In Paul Demeny and Geoffrey McNicoll (eds.), *Encyclopedia of Population*, II: 960–962. New York: Macmillan Reference USA.

Freeman, Gary P. 2003. "Immigration Policies." In Paul Demeny and Geoffrey McNicoll (eds.), *Encyclopedia of Population*, II: 515–519. New York: Macmillan Reference USA.

Frejka, Tomas. 2011. "Long-Term Trends of Differential Racial Fertility in the United States." www.humanfertility.org/File/GetDocument/Docs/Symposium/Frejka_Tomas.pdf

2017. "Half the World's Population Reaching Below Replacement Fertility." www.niussp.org/fertility-and-reproduction/half-the-worlds-population-reaching-below-replacement-fertility/

Frey, William H. 2003. "Internal Migration." In Paul Demeny and Geoffrey McNicoll (eds.), *Encyclopedia of Population*, II: 545–548. New York: Macmillan Reference USA.

2015. *Diversity Explosion: How New Racial Demographics Are Remaking America*. Washington, DC: Brookings Institution Press.

2025. "Immigration Drives the Nation's Healthy Post-Pandemic Population Growth, New Census Data Show." *Brookings Metro*. January 6. Washington, DC: Brookings Institution. www.brookings.edu/articles/immigration-drives-the-nations-healthy-post-pandemic-population-growth-new-census-data-show/

Friedman, Benjamin M. 2005. *The Moral Consequences of Economic Growth*. New York: Knopf.

Friedman, Thomas L. 2005. *The World Is Flat: A Brief History of the Twenty-First Century*. New York: Farrar, Straus and Giroux.

2008. *Hot, Flat, and Crowded: Why We Need A Green Revolution, and How It Can Renew America*. New York: Farrar, Straus and Giroux.

Fries, James F. 1980. "Aging, Natural Death, and the Compression of Morbidity." *New England Journal of Medicine* 303: 130–136.

1983. "The Compression of Morbidity." *Milbank Memorial Fund Quarterly* 61: 397–419.

2000. "Compression of Morbidity in the Elderly." *Vaccine* 18: 1584–1589.

Frisbie, W. Parker. 2005. "Infant Mortality." In Dudley L. Poston, Jr., and Michael Micklin (eds.), *Handbook of Population*, 251–282. New York: Kluwer Academic/Plenum.

Fry, Richard. 2023. "A Record-High Share of 40-Year-Olds in the US Have Never Been Married." *Short Reads*. June 28. Washington, DC: Pew Research Center.

Funk, Carey, and Mark Hugo Lopez. 2022. "A Brief Statistical Portrait of U.S. Hispanics." Pew Research Center. www.pewresearch.org/science/2022/06/14/a-brief-statistical-portrait-of-u-s-hispanics/

Gang, Karume Baderha Augustin, Jennifer O'Keeffe, Anonymous, and Les Roberts. 2023. "Cross-sectional Survey in Central African Republic Finds Mortality 4-Times Higher than UN Statistics: How Can We Not Know the Central African Republic Is in Such an Acute Humanitarian Crisis?" *Conflict and Health* 17: 21. https://doi.org/10.1186/s13031-023-00514-z

Gabaccia, Donna R. 2002. *Immigration and American Diversity: A Social and Cultural History*. Malden, MA: Blackwell.

Garcia, Ginny E. 2011. *Mexican American and Immigrant Poverty in the United States*. New York: Springer.

Garner, Lesley. 1991. "Lesley Garner Meets the Legendary Actress as She Prepares for This Week's Unicef Gala Performance." *The Sunday Telegraph*. May 26. https://web archive .org/web/20050117094236/http://ahepburn.com/article6.html

Garreau, Joel. 1991. *Edge City: Life on the New Frontier*. New York: Doubleday.

Gates, Gary J. 2013. "Geography of the LGBT Population." In Amanda K. Baumle (ed.), *International Handbook on the Demography of Sexuality*, 229–242. New York: Springer.

Gates, Gary J., and J. Ost. 2004. *The Gay and Lesbian Atlas*. Washington, DC: The Urban Institute Press.

Gauthier, Jason G. 2002. *Measuring America: The Decennial Censuses from 1790 to 2000*. Washington, DC: US Census Bureau.

Geddes, Patrick. 1915. *Cities in Evolution*. London: Williams and Norgate.

Gelbspan, Ross. 2007. "Two Paths for the Planet." *The American Prospect* (August): 45–47.

Gellerman, Jo. 2003. "Medical Ignorance Conference to Explore Timely Challenges and Questions." http://uanews.org/node/8144

Getis, Arthur, Judith Getis, and Jerome D. Fellmann. 2008. *Human Geography*, 12th ed. New York: McGraw-Hill.

Ghosh, Bimal. 2005. "Economic Effects of International Migration: A Synoptic Overview." In Irena Omelaniuk (ed.), *World Migration, 2005: Costs and Benefits on International Migration*, 163–184. Geneva: International Organization for Migration.

Gianchecchi, Elena, Virginia Cianchi, Alessandro Torelli, and Emanuele Montomoli. 2022. "Yellow Fever: Origin, Epidemiology, Preventive Strategies and Future Prospects." *Vaccines*, 10 (3): 372. https://doi.org/10.3390/vaccines10030372

Gibson, Campbell, and Kay Jung. 2006. "Historical Census Statistics on the Foreign-born Population of the United States: 1850 to 2000."Population Division, Working Paper 81. Washington, DC: US Census Bureau.

Giddens, Anthony. 2002. *Runaway World: How Globalization Is Reshaping Our Lives*. London: Macmillan.

Gill, Richard T., Nathan Glazer, and Stephen A. Thernstrom. 1992. *Our Changing Population*. Englewood Cliffs, NJ: Prentice Hall.

Gilligan, Chris. 2022. "Facts and Figures: The Native American Population at a Glance." *U.S. News and World Report*. November 22. www.usnews.com/news/health-news/articles/2022-11-22/the-native-american-and-alaska-native-population-at-a-glance

Gimenez, Martha E. 1971. "The Population Issue: Marx vs. Malthus." Revised version of a paper presented at the annual meeting of the Pacific Sociological Association, Honolulu.

Glass, David V. 1940. *Population Policies and Movements in Europe*. New York: Augustus M. Kelley.

(ed.). 1953. *Introduction to Malthus*. New York: John Wiley.

Glover, James W. 1921. *United States Life Tables, 1890, 1901, 1910, and 1901–1910*. Washington, DC: US Government Printing Office.

Goebel, Ted. 2007. "The Missing Years for Modern Humans." *Science* 315: 194–196.

Goebel, Ted, Michael R. Waters, and Dennis H. O'Rourke. 2008. "The Late Pleistocene Dispersal of Modern Humans in the Americas." *Science* 319: 1497–1502.

Goldscheider, Calvin. 1971. *Population, Modernization and Social Structure*. Boston: Little, Brown.

Goodkind, Daniel. 1996. "On Substituting Sex Preference Strategies in East Asia: Does Prenatal Sex Selection Reduce Postnatal Discrimination?" *Population Research and Policy Review* 22: 111–125.

2011. "Child Underreporting, Fertility, and Sex Ratio Imbalance in China." *Demography* 48: 291–316.

Gordon, Mary. 2000. *Joan of Arc*. New York: Penguin Putnam.

Gottmann, Jean. 1961. *Megalopolis: The Urbanized Northeastern Seaboard of the United States*. Cambridge, MA: MIT Press.

Graf, Nikki. 2019. "Key Findings on Marriage and Cohabitation in the U.S." *Short Reads*. November 6. Washington, DC: Pew Research Center.

Graunt, John. [1662] 1939. *Natural and Political Observations Made Upon the Bills of Mortality*. American ed. with Introduction by Walter F. Willcox. Ed. Jacob B. Hollander. Baltimore, MD: Johns Hopkins University Press.

Greene, Madeleine, and Jeanne Batalova. 2025. "Chinese Immigrants to the United States." January 15. Washington, DC: Migration Policy Institute: www.migrationpolicy.org/article/chinese-immigrants-united-states

Greene, Margaret E., and Ann E. Biddlecom. 2000. "Absent and Problematic Men: Demographic Accounts of Male Reproductive Roles." *Population and Development Review* **26**: 81–115.

Greenhalgh, Susan. 1986. "Shifts in China's Population Policy." *Population and Development Review* **12**: 491–515.

1990a. "The Evolution of the One-Child Policy in Shaanxi, 1979–1988." *China Quarterly* **122**: 191–229.

1990b. "Toward a Political Economy of Fertility: Anthropological Contributions." *Population and Development Review* **16**: 85–106.

1994. "Controlling Births and Bodies in Village China." *American Ethnologist* **21**: 3–30.

2008. *Just One Child: Science and Policy in Deng's China*. Berkeley: University of California Press.

Greenwood, Michael J. 1975. "Research on Internal Migration in the United States: A Survey." *Journal of Economic Literature* **13**: 397–433.

Gribble, James M. 2003. "The Standard Days Method of Family Planning: A Response to Cairo." *International Family Planning Perspectives* **29**: 188–191.

Grieco, Elizabeth M., and Monica Boyd. 1998. "Women and Migration: Incorporating Gender into International Migration Theory." Working Paper WPS98–139. Tallahassee: Florida State University, Center for the Study of Population.

Griffith, J. 1973. "Social Pressures on Family Size Intentions." *Family Planning Perspectives* **5**: 237–242.

Gu, Baochang, and Krishna Roy. 1995. "Sex Ratio at Birth in China, with Reference to Other Areas in East Asia: What We Know." *Asia-Pacific Population Journal*. **10**: 17–42.

Guest, Avery M., and Susan K. Brown. 2019. "Population Distribution and Suburbanization." In Dudley L. Poston, Jr. (ed.), *Handbook of Population*, 2nd ed., 51–77. New York: Springer.

Gugliotta, Guy. 2008. 'The Great Human Migration: Why Humans Left Their African Homeland 80,000 Years Ago to Colonize the World." *Smithsonian Magazine* (July). www.smithsonianmag.com/history/the-great-human-migration-13561/

Guillard, Achille. [1835] 2010. *Éléments de statistique humaine ou démographie comparée*. Charleston, SC: Nabu Press.

Guillebaud, John. 2005. *The Pill and Other Hormonal Contraceptives*, 6th ed. New York: Oxford University Press.

Guttmacher Institute. 2008. "Facts on Induced Abortion in the United States." New York: Guttmacher Institute.

2012. "Facts on Induced Abortion Worldwide." *In Brief: Fact Sheet* (January). New York: Guttmacher Institute.

2014a. "American Teens' Sexual and Reproductive Health." *Fact Sheet* (May). New York: Guttmacher Institute.

2014b. "Induced Abortion in the United States." *Fact Sheet* (July). New York: Guttmacher Institute.

2021. "Contraceptive Use in the United States by Method." *Fact Sheet*. New York: Guttmacher Institute.

2022. "Unintended Pregnancy and Abortion Worldwide." *Fact Sheet.* New York: Guttmacher Institute.

Haaga, John. 2000. "Alfred Lotka, Mathematical Demographer". Population Reference Bureau. www.prb.org/resources/alfred-lotka-mathematical-demographer/

Haines, Michael R. 2003. "Trans-Atlantic Migration." In Paul Demeny and Geoffrey McNicoll (eds.), *Encyclopedia of Population*, II: 942–946. New York: Macmillan Reference USA.

2007. "Fertility and Mortality in the United States." https://eh.net/encyclopedia/fertility-and-mortality-in-the-united-states/

Haines, Michael R., and Avery M. Guest. 2008. "Fertility in New York State in the Pre-Civil War Era." *Demography* 45: 345–361.

Hajnal, J. 1965. "European Marriage Patterns in Perspective." In D. V. Glass and D. E. C. Eversley (eds.), *Population in History*, 101–143. London: Edward Arnold.

Hamilton, Brady E., Joyce A. Martin, and Michelle J. K. Osterman. 2024. "Births, Provisional Data for 2023." *NVSS Vital Statistics Rapid Release* 35 (April). www.cdc.gov/nchs/data/vsrr/vsrr035.pdf

Hamilton, Brady E., Joyce A. Martin, and Stephanie J. Ventura. 2007. "Births: Preliminary Data for 2005." *National Vital Statistics Reports* 55 (11). Hyattsville, MD: National Center for Health Statistics.

Hamilton, C. Horace. 1964. "The Negro Leaves the South." *Demography* 1: 273–295.

Harris, J. R., and Michael P. Todaro. 1970. "Migration, Unemployment, and Development: A Two-Sector Analysis." *American Economic Review* 60: 126–142.

Hart, N. 1993. Famine, Maternal Nutrition and Infant Mortality: A Re-Examination of the Dutch Hunger Winter. *Population Studies*, 47(1), 27–46.

Haskell, Molly. 2013. *My Brother, My Sister: Story of a Transformation.* New York: Penguin Books.

Hassold, T., S. D. Quillen, and J. A. Yamane. 1983. "Sex Ratio in Spontaneous Abortions." *Annals of Human Genetics* 47: 39-47.

Haub, Carl. 2011. "How Many People Have Ever Lived on Earth?" Washington, DC: Population Reference Bureau.

Haub, Carl, and Machiko Yanagishita. 1991. "Infant Mortality: Who's Number One?" *Population Today* 19: 6–8.

Hauser, Philip M. 1949. "The Labor Force and Gainful Workers: Concept, Measurement, and Comparability." *American Journal of Sociology* 54 (4), 338–355.

1964. "Labor Force." In R. E. L. Faris (ed.), *Handbook of Modern Sociology*. Chicago: Rand McNally.

Hauser, Philip M., and Otis Dudley Duncan (eds.). 1959. *The Study of Population: An Inventory and Appraisal.* Chicago: University of Chicago Press.

Hawley, Amos H. 1950. *Human Ecology: A Theory of Community Structure*. New York: Ronald Press.

1968. "Human Ecology." In David L. Sills (ed.), *International Encyclopedia of the Social Sciences*, 328–337. New York: Crowell, Collier, and Macmillan.

Hay, Jeff (ed.). 2001. *Immigration.* San Diego, CA: Greenhaven.

Hayford, Sarah R., and S. Philip Morgan. 2008. "Religiosity and Fertility in the United States: The Role of Fertility Intentions." *Social Forces* 86: 1163–1188.

Hayutin, Adele. 2022. *New Landscapes of Population Change: A Demographic World Tour.* Stanford, CA: Hoover Institution Press.

Healy, Bernadine. 2006. "Beyond the Baby Count." *U.S. News and World Report*. September 24.

Henesy, Alex. 2021. "ESRI's Economic Dependency Ratio." June 30. www.esri.com/arcgis-blog/products/esri-demographics/analytics/an-alternative-portrait-of-dependency-esris-economic-dependency-ratio/

Henry, Louis. 1961. "Some Data on Natural Fertility." *Eugenics Quarterly* 8: 81–91.

Henshaw, Stanley K. 2003. "Induced Abortion, Prevalence." In Paul Demeny and Geoffrey McNicoll (eds.), *Encyclopedia of Population*, II: 529–531. New York: Macmillan Reference USA.

Heo, Nayoung, Hsin-Chieh Chang, and Guy J. Abel. 2023. "Investigating the Distribution of University Alumni Populations within South Korea and Taiwan Based on Data from the LinkedIn Advertising Platform." *Cities* 137. https://doi.org/10.1016/j.cities.2023.104315

Herlihy, David. 1997. *The Black Death and the Transformation of the West*. Cambridge, MA: Harvard University Press.

Herrington, Gaya. 2021. "Update to Limits to Growth: Comparing the World3 Model with Empirical Data." *Journal of Industrial Ecology* **25**: 614–626.

Hill, E. T. 1995. "Labor Market Effects of Women's Post-School-Age Training." *Industrial and Labor Relations Review* **49**: 138–149.

Hill, Reuben, J. Mayone Stycos, and Kurt Back. 1959. *The Family and Population Control: A Puerto Rican Experiment in Social Change*. Chapel Hill: University of North Carolina Press.

Hillygus, D. Sunshine, Norman H. Nie, Kenneth Prewitt, and Heili Pals. 2006. *The Hard Count: The Political and Social Challenges of Census Mobilization*. New York: Russell Sage Foundation.

Himes, Norman E. [1936] 1970. *Medical History of Contraception*. New York: Schocken Books.

Hinde, Andrew. 1998. *Demographic Methods*. London: Arnold.

Hipple, Stephen F. 2015. "People Who Are Not in the Labor Force: Why Aren't They Working?" *Beyond the Numbers: Employment & Unemployment*. December 4. www.bls.gov/opub/btn/volume-4/people-who-are-not-in-the-labor-force-why-arent-they-working.htm

Hipple, Steven F. 2016. "Labor Force Participation: What Has Happened since the Peak?" *Monthly Labor Review*. September. https://doi.org/10.21916/mlr.2016.43

Hirschman, Charles. 1994. "Why Fertility Changes." *Annual Review of Sociology* **20**: 203–233.

HIV.gov. 2023. "A Timeline of AIDS and HIV." www.hiv.gov/hiv-basics/overview/history/hiv-and-aids-timeline#year-1981.

Hobbs, Frank. 2004. "Age and Sex Composition." In Jacob S. Siegel and David A. Swanson (eds.), *The Methods and Materials of Demography*, 2nd ed., ch. 7, 125–173. San Diego, CA: Elsevier Academic.

Hochschild, Jennifer L., and Brenna Marea Powell. 2008. "Racial Reorganization and the United States Census, 1850–1930: Mulattoes, Half-breeds, Mixed Parentage, Hindoos, and the Mexican Race." *Studies in American Political Development* **22**: 59–96.

Hodson, Randy, and Teresa A. Sullivan. 2012. *The Social Organization of Work*, 5th ed. Belmont, CA: Wadsworth Cengage Learning.

Hodgson, Dennis, and Susan Watkins. 1997. "Feminists and Neo-Malthusians: Past and Present Alliances." *Population and Development Review* **23**: 469–523.

Hollinger, David. 2006. *Postethnic America: Beyond Multiculturalism*. New York: Basic Books.

Holzer, Harry J. 2011. "Immigration Policy and Less-Skilled Workers in the United States: Reflections on Future Directions for Reform." Washington, DC: Migration Policy Institute.

Hopcroft, Rosemary L. 2015. "Sex Differences in the Relationship between Status and Number of Offspring in the Contemporary U.S." *Evolution and Human Behavior* **36**: 146–151.

Hopcroft, Rosemary L., Martin Fielder, and Susanne Huber. 2024. *Not So Weird After All: The Changing Relationship Between Status and Fertility*. New York: Routledge.

Horton, Hayward Derrick. 1999. "Critical Demography: The Paradigm of the Future?" *Sociological Forum* **14**: 363–367.

Howden, Lindsay, and Dudley L. Poston, Jr. 2008. "Depopulation." In William A. Darity (ed. in chief), *International Encyclopedia of the Social Sciences*, 2nd ed., II: 301–302. Detroit: Macmillan Reference USA.

Hoyer, Niels. [1933] 2004. *Man into Woman: The First Sex Change*. Ashburn, VA: Blue Boat Books.

Hoyert Donna L. 2012. "75 Years of Mortality in the United States, 1935–2010." NCHS data brief, No. 88. Hyattsville, MD: National Center for Health Statistics.

Hoyert, Donna L. 2023. " Maternal Mortality Rates in the United States, 2021." www.cdc.gov/nchs/data/hestat/maternal-mortality/2021/maternal-mortality-rates-2021

Hudson, Valerie M., and Andrea M. den Boer. 2004. *Bare Branches: Security Implications of Asia's Surplus Male Population*. Cambridge, MA: MIT Press.

Hughes, Ieuan A., John D. Davies, Trevor I. Bunch, Vickie Pasterski, Kiki Mastroyannopoulos, and Jane MacDougall. 2012. "Androgen Insensitivity Syndrome." *The Lancet* 380 (October 20): 1419–1428.

Hughes, Jonathan, and Louis P. Cain. 2010. *American Economic History*, 8th ed. New York: Pearson Publishing.

Humes, Karen R., Nicholas A. Jones, and Roberto R. Ramirez. 2011. "Overview of Race and Hispanic Origin, 2010." *2010 Census Briefs*, C2010BR-02 (March). Washington, DC: US Census Bureau.

Hummer, Robert A., and Elaine M. Hernandez. 2013. "The Effect of Educational Attainment on Adult Mortality in the United States." *Population Bulletin* 68 (1): 1–15.

Iceland, John. 2014. *A Portrait of America: The Demographic Perspective*. Oakland, CA: University of California Press.

Ihrke, David K. 2014. "Reasons for Moving, 2012–2013." *Population Characteristics* P20–574. Washington, DC: US Census Bureau.

Ihrke, David K., and Carol S. Faber. 2012. "Geographic Mobility, 2005–2010." *Population Characteristics* P20–567. Washington, DC: US Census Bureau.

Ihrke, David K., Carol S. Faber, and William K. Koerber. 2011. "Geographical Mobility, 2008–2009." *Population Characteristics* P20–565. Washington, DC: US Census Bureau.

Intergovernmental Panel on Climate Change. 2007. *Climate Change, 2007: The Physical Science Basis*. Geneva: IPCC.

International Organization for Migration (IOM). 2010. *World Migration Report 2010*. Geneva: International Organization for Migration.

International Organization for Migration (IOM). 2024. *World Migration Report 2024*. https://worldmigrationreport.iom.int/msite/wmr-2024-interactive

Iredale, Robyn. 2005. "Balancing the Benefits and Costs of Skilled Migration in the Asia-Pacific Region." In Irena Omelaniuk (ed.), *World Migration, 2005: Costs and Benefits on International Migration*, ch. 11, 221–237. Geneva: International Organization for Migration.

Ismail, Mehreen S. 2023. "Number and Percentage of State-to-State Movers Increased Between 2021 and 2022." *America Counts: Stories Behind the Numbers*, November 21. Washington, DC: US Census Bureau. www.census.gov›stories›state-to-state-migration

Issawi, C. 1987. *An Arab Philosophy of History: Selections from the Prolegomena of Ibn Khaldun of Tunis (1332–1406)*. Princeton, NJ: Princeton University Press.

Jacobstein, Roy, and Chelsea B. Polis. 2014. "Progestin-only Contraception: Injectables and Implants."*Best Practice & Research Clinical Obstetrics and Gynaecology* 28: 795–806.

Jaffe, A. J. 1959. "Working Force." In P. M. Hauser and O. D. Duncan (eds), *The Study of Population*, 604–619. Chicago: University of Chicago Press.

Jedwab, Remi, Noel D. Johnson, and Mark Koyama. 2022. "The Economic Impact of the Black Death." *Journal of Economic Literature* 60 (1): 132–178.

Jenks, Rosemary. 2002. "The Enhanced Border Security and Visa Entry Reform Act of 2002: A Summary of HR 3525." *Backgrounder 5–02*. Washington, DC: Center for Immigration Studies.

Jennings, Victoria H., and Anne E. Burke. 2011. "Fertility Awareness-Based Methods." In Robert A. Hatcher, James Trussell, Anita L. Nelson, Willard Cates, Jr., Deborah Kowal, and Michael S. Policar (eds.), *Contraceptive Technology*, 20th rev. ed., 417–434. New York: Ardent Media, Inc.

Jensen, Eric, Andrew Roberts, and Luke Rogers. 2023. "Age Heaping in the 2020 Census Demographic and Housing Characteristics File (DHC)." May 25. US Census Random Samplings Blog. www.census.gov/newsroom/blogs/random-samplings/2023/05/age-heaping-2020-census-dhc.html

Jha, P., R. Kumar, P. Vasa, N. Dhingra, D. Thiruchelvam, and R. Moineddin. 2006. "Low Male-to-Female Sex Ratio of Children Born in India: National Survey of 1.1 Million Households." *Lancet* 367 (9506): 211–218.

Johansson, S. Ryan. 2003. "Epidemics." In Paul Demeny and Geoffrey McNicoll (eds.), *Encyclopedia of Population*, I: 302–307. New York: Macmillan Reference USA.

Johnson, Kenneth M. 2023. "Three Years of Record High Mortality and Low Fertility Leave Many States with More Deaths than Births." *Data Snapshot*. June 27. Durham, NH: University of New Hampshire, Carsey School of Public Policy.

Johnson, Kenneth M., Layton Field, and Dudley L. Poston, Jr. 2015. "More Deaths than Births: Subnational Natural Decrease in Europe and the United States. *Population and Development Review* 41: 651–680.

Johnson, Kenneth M, and Daniel T. Lichter. 2008. "Natural Increase: A New Source of Population Growth in Emerging Hispanic Destinations." *Population and Development Review* 34: 327–346.

2010. "Growing Diversity among America's Children and Youth: Spatial and Temporal Dimensions." *Population and Development Review* 36: 151–175.

Johnson, Nan E. 2000. "The Racial Crossover in Comorbidity, Disability, and Mortality." *Demography* 37: 267–283.

Johnson, Niall, and Juergen Mueller. 2002. "Updating the Accounts: Global Mortality of the 1918–1920 'Spanish Influenza Pandemic.'" *Bulletin of the History of Medicine* **76**: 105–115.

Johnson, Peter D. 2000. "Population Censuses: Observations on the Past 50 Years and a Peek at the New Century." Paper presented at the Workshop on Gridding Population Data, Columbia University, New York.

Johnson, Steven. 2006. *The Ghost Map: The Story of London's Most Terrifying Epidemic, and How It Changed Science, Cities, and the Modern World*. New York: Riverhead Books.

Jones, Gavin W., and Wajinah Hamid. 2015. "Singapore's Pronatalist Policies: To What Extent Have They Worked?" In Ronald R. Rindfuss and Minja Kim Choe (eds.), *Low and Lower Fertility Variations Across Developed Countries*, 33–61. Cham, Switzerland: Springer.

Jones, Jeffrey M. 2024. "Sharply More Americans Want to Curb Immigration to the U.S." July 12. https://news.gallup.com/poll/647123/sharply-americans=curb=immigration.aspx

Jones, Nicholas A., and Jungmiwha Bullock. 2012. "The Two or More Races Population: 2010." *2010 Census Briefs*, C2010BR-13 (September). Washington, DC: US Census Bureau.

Jones-Myers, Amara, and Lydia Anderson. 2024. "Where Do Male and Female Same-Sex Couples Live?" www.census.gov/library/stories/2024/08/same-sex-couples-geographic-variation.html

Jorgensen, Christine. 1967. *Christine Jorgensen: A Personal Autobiography*. New York: Paul S. Eriksson.

Jutte, Robert. 2008. *Contraception: A History*, trans.Vicky Russell. Malden, MA: Polity.

Juvkam-Wold, H. C., and A. J. Dessler. 2009. "Using the Hubbert Equation to Estimate Oil Reserves." *World Oil* (April): 107–115.

Kahn, E. J. 1974. *The American People: The Findings of the 1970 Census*. New York: Weybright and Talley.

Kalben, Barbara Blatt. 2003. *Why Men Die Younger: Causes of Mortality Differences by Sex*. Society of Actuaries (SOA) Monograph M-LI101. Schaumburg, IL: Society of Actuaries.

Kalleberg, Arne L. 2000. "Nonstandard Employment Relations: Part-time, Temporary, and Contract Work." *Annual Review of Sociology* **26**: 341–65.

2011. *Good Jobs, Bad Jobs: The Rise of Polarized and Precarious Employment Systems in the United States, 1970s to 2000s*. New York: Russell Sage Foundation.

Kalton, Graham. 2021. *Introduction to Survey Sampling*. Thousand Oaks, CA: Sage Publications.

Kasarda, John D. 1971. "Economic Structure and Fertility: A Comparative Analysis." *Demography* 8: 307–317.

Keeley, Charles B. 2009. "Replacement Migration." In Peter Uhlenberg (ed.), *International Handbook of Population Aging*, 395–403. Newark, NJ: Springer.

Kent, Tyler V. Kent, Daniel R. Schrider, and Daniel R. Matute. 2024. "Demographic History and the Efficacy of Selection in the Globally Invasive Mosquito *Aedes aegypti*". *bioRxiv: The Preprint Server for Biology*. https://doi.org/10.1101/2024.03.07.584008

Kerns-D'Amore, Kristin. 2023. "Change in Marital Status Became More Common Reason for Moving from 2021 to 2022, Housing/Neighborhood Improvement Reasons Declined." *America Counts: Stories Behind the Number*. September 19. Washington, DC: US Bureau of the Census. www.census.gov/library/stories/2023/09/why-people-move.html

Kerns-D'Amore, Kristina. Brian McKenzie, and L. Slagan Locklear. 2023. "Migration in the United States: 2006 to 2019." *American Community Survey Reports*, ACS 53 (July). Washington, DC: US Bureau of the Census.

Kertzer, David I., and Dennis P. Hogan. 1989. *Family, Political Economy, and Demographic Change: The Transformation of Life in Casalecchio, Italy, 1861–1921*. Madison: University of Wisconsin Press.

Keyfitz, Nathan. 1977a. *Applied Mathematical Demography*. New York: John Wiley.

1977b. "What Difference Would It Make if Cancer Were Eliminated? An Examination of the Taeuber Paradox." *Demography* 14: 411–418.

1984. "The Population of China." *Scientific American* **250** (February): 38–47.

Keyfitz, Nathan, and W. Flieger. 1971. *Population: Facts and Methods of Demography*. San Francisco: W. H. Freeman.

Kim, D. 1997. "The Pattern of Changing Trends and the Regional Difference in the Sex Ratio at Birth: Evidence from Korea and Jilin Province, China." *Korea Journal of Population and Development* **26**: 19–24.

Kimmel, Michael S. 2016. *The Gendered Society*, 6th ed. New York: Oxford University Press.

King, Helen. 2025. *Immaculate Forms: A History of the Female Body in Four Parts*. New York: Basic Books.

King, H., and F. B. Locke. 1980. "Chinese in the United States: A Century of Occupational Transition." *International Migration Review* **14**: 15–42.

Kingsland, Sharon. 2015. "Alfred J. Lotka and the Origins of Theoretical Population Ecology". *PNAS* **112**: 9493-9495. https://doi.org/10.1073/pnas.1512317112

Kinsey, Alfred C., Wardell B. Pomeroy, and Clyde E. Martin. 1948. *Sexual Behavior in the Human Male*. Philadelphia, PA: Saunders.

Kinsey, Alfred C., Wardell B. Pomeroy, Clyde E. Martin, and Paul H. Gebhard. 1953. *Sexual Behavior in the Human Female*. Philadelphia, PA: Saunders.

Kintner, Hallie J. 2004. "The Life Table." In Jacob S. Siegel and David A. Swanson (eds.), *The Methods and Materials of Demography*, 2nd ed., 301–340. San Diego, CA: Elsevier Academic.

Kinugasa, T. 2018. "Demographic Dividends." In Z. Zhao and A. C. Hayes (eds), *Routledge Handbook of Asian Demography*, 456–471. New York: Routledge.

Kipley, Sheila K., and John F. Kipley. 1996. *The Art of Natural Family Planning*, 4th ed. Cincinnati, OH: Couple to Couple League International.

Kiser, Clyde V. 1953. "The Indianapolis Fertility Study: An Example of Planned Observational Research." *Public Opinion Quarterly* **17**: 496–510.

Kiser, Clyde V., and Pascal K. Whelpton. 1953. "Resume of the Indianapolis Study of Social and Psychological Factors Affecting Fertility." *Population Studies* **7**: 95–110.

Kitagawa, Evelyn, and Philip M. Hauser. 1973. *Differential Mortality in the United States*. Cambridge, MA: Harvard University Press.

Knodel, John, Aphichat Chamratrithirong, and Nibhon Debavalya. 1987. *Thailand's Reproductive Revolution: Rapid Fertility Decline in a Third-World Setting*. Madison: University of Wisconsin Press.

Knodel, John, and Etienne van de Walle. 1979. "Lessons from the Past: Policy Implications of Historical Fertility Studies." *Population and Development Review* **5**: 217–245.

Knoll, Spencer, Jordan Lloyd, Blynda Metcalf, Joseph Quinn, and Tristan St. Onge. 2024. "NAICS Changes Will Begin to Be Reflected in Census Bureau's Economic Surveys and Programs." November 30. www.census.gov/library/stories/2024/11/naics-changes.html_

Kolata, Gina. 1999. *Flu: The Story of the Great Influenza Pandemic of 1918 and the Search for the Virus That Caused It*. New York: Farrar, Straus and Giroux.

Kost, Kathryn, Susheela Singh, Barbara Vaughan, James Trussell, and Akinrinola Bankole. 2008. "Estimates of Contraceptive Failure from the 2002 National Survey of Family Growth." *Contraception* 77: 10–21.

Kowal, Deborah. 2011. "Coitus Interruptus (Withdrawal)." In Robert A. Hatcher, James Trussell, Anita L. Nelson, Willard Cates, Jr., Deborah Kowal, and Michael S. Policar (eds.), *Contraceptive Technology*, 20th rev. ed., 409–415. New York: Ardent Media, Inc.

Kraeger, Philip. 1988. "New Light on Graunt." *Population Studies* 42: 129–140.

Krieger, N., D. Rowley, A. Herman, B. Avery, and M. Phillips. 1993. "Racism, Sexism and Social Class: Implications for Studies of Health, Disease and Well-Being." *American Journal of Preventive Medicine* 9 (Suppl.): 82–122.

Kwong, Peter. 1988. *The New Chinatown*. New York: Hill and Wang.

Kutz, Jessica. 2025. "USAID's Reproductive Health Funding Has Saved Millions of Lives. Now It's Gone." *The 19th News Network* (February 7). https://19thnews.org/2025/02/usaid-women-lgbtq-reproductive-health-funding-pause/

Laczko, Frank. 2005. "Enhancing the Benefits of Return Migration for Development." In Irena Omelaniuk (ed.), *World Migration, 2005: Costs and Benefits on International Migration*, ch. 16, 287–295. Geneva: International Organization for Migration.

Lamb, Vicki L., and Jacob S. Siegel. 2004. "Health Demography." In Jacob S. Siegel and David A. Swanson (eds.), *The Methods and Materials of Demography*, 2nd ed., 341–370. San Diego, CA: Elsevier Academic.

Lamptey, Peter R., Jami L. Johnson, and Marya Khan. 2006. "The Global Challenge of HIV and AIDS." *Population Bulletin* 61 (1): 1–28.

Landry, Adolphe. 1945. *Traité de démographie*. Paris: Payot.

Laub, John H., and Robert J. Sampson. 2006. *Shared Beginnings, Divergent Lives: Delinquent Boys to Age 70*. Cambridge, MA: Harvard University Press.

Laumann, Edward O., John H. Gagnon, Robert T. Michael, and Stuart Michaels. 1994. *The Social Organization of Sexuality: Sexual Practices in the United States*. Chicago: University of Chicago Press.

Laurino, Mauria. 2024. *The Price of Children: Stolen Lives in a Land Without Choice*. New York: Open Road Integrated Media, Inc.

Lawrence, D. H. [1928] 1962. *Collected Letters*, ed. H. T. Moore. New York: Viking Press.

LeClere, Felicia, Richard G. Rogers, and Kimberley Peters. 1997. "Ethnicity and Mortality in the United States: Individual and Community Correlates." *Social Forces* 76: 169–198.

Lee, Everett S. 1966. "A Theory of Migration." *Demography* 3: 47–57.

Lee, S. B., J. H. Oh, J. H. Park, S. P. Choi, and J. H. Wee. 2018. "Differences in Youngest-Old, Middle-Old, and Oldest-Old Patients Who Visit the Emergency Department." *Clinical and Experimental Emergency Medicine* 5: 249–255. https://doi.org/10.15441/ceem.17.261

LeGates, Richard. 2006. "Visualizing World Urbanization with GIS and Data Graphics." Paper presented at the annual meeting of the Association of American Geographers, Chicago.

Legrain, Philippe. 2006. *Immigrants: Your Country Needs Them*. Princeton, NJ: Princeton University Press.

Lesthaeghe, Ron J. 1995. "The Second Demographic Transition in Western Countries: An Interpretation." In Karen O. Mason and A. M. Jensen (eds.), *Gender and Family Change in Industrialized Countries*, 17–62. Oxford: Clarendon Press.

2010. "The Unfolding Story of the Second Demographic Transition." *Population and Development Review* 36: 211–251.

Lesthaeghe, Ron J., and Lisa Neidert. 2006. "The "Second Demographic Transition" in the U.S.: Spatial Patterns and Correlates." *Population Studies Center Research Report* No. 06-592 (March). Ann Arbor, MI: University of Michigan.

2009. "U.S. Presidential Elections and the Spatial Pattern of the American Second Demographic Transition." *Population and Development Review* 35: 391–400.

Liang, Zai. 2001. "Demography of Illicit Emigration from China: A Sending Country's Perspective." *Sociological Forum* 16: 677–701.

Liang, Zai, Zhen Li, and Zhongdong Ma. 2014. "Changing Patterns of the Floating Population in China, 2000– 2010." *Population and Development Review* 40: 695–716.

Liang, Zai, and Zhongdong Ma. 2004. "China's Floating Population: New Evidence from the 2000 Census." *Population and Development Review* 30: 467–488.

Lichter, Daniel T. 2013. "Integration or Fragmentation: Racial Diversity and the American Future." *Demography* 50: 359–391.

Linnaeus, Carolus. 1735. *Systema Naturae*, 1st ed. Leiden: Haak.

Lipset, Seymour Martin. 1997. *American Exceptionalism: A Double-Edged Sword*. New York: W.W. Norton & Company.

Livi-Bacci, Massimo. 2012. *A Concise History of World Population*. Malden, MA: Wiley-Blackwell.

London, Bruce. 1987. "Ending Ecology's Ethnocentrism: Thai Replications and Extensions of Ecological research." *Rural Sociology* 52: 483–500.

London, Bruce, and Kenneth P. Hadden. 1989. "The Spread of Education and Fertility Decline: A Thai Province Level Test of Caldwell's 'Wealth Flows' Theory." *Rural Sociology* 54: 17–36.

Lotka, Alfred J. 1907. "Relation Between Birth Rates and Death Rates." *Science, New Series* 26 (653): 21–22.

[1934] 1998. *Analytical Theory of Biological Populations*, trans. David P. Smith and Helene Rossert. New York: Plenum.

Loudon, Irvine. 1992. *Death in Childbirth: An International Study of Maternal Care and Maternal Mortality, 1800–1950*. Oxford: Clarendon.

2000. "Maternal Mortality in the Past and Its Relevance to Developing Countries Today." *American Journal of Clinical Nutrition* 72 (Suppl.): 241S–246S.

Lopez, Mark Hugo, Jens Manuel Krogstad, and Jeffrey S. Passel. 2024. "Who is Hispanic?" September 24. www.pewresearch.org/short-reads/2024/09/12/who-is-hispanic/

Lumey, L. H., and F. W. Van Poppel. 1994. "The Dutch Famine of 1944–1945: Mortality and Morbidity in Past and Present Generations." *Social History of Medicine* 7(2): 229–246. doi: 10.1093/shm/7.2.229. PMID: 11639327

Lutz, Wolfgang. 2006. "Fertility Rates and Future Population Trends: Will Europe's Birth Rate Recover or Continue to Decline?" *International Journal of Andrology* 29: 25–33.

Lutz, Wolfgang, Brian C. O'Neil, and Sergei Scherbov. 2003. "Europe's Population at a Turning Point." *Science* 299 (March 29): 1991–1992.

Ma, Li. 2016. "Female Labor Force Participation and Second Birth Rates in South Korea". *Journal of Population Research* 33 (2), 173–195.

MacDonald, Alphonse L. 2003. "Famine in China." In Paul Demeny and Geoffrey McNicoll (eds.), *Encyclopedia of Population*, I: 388–390. New York: Macmillan Reference USA.

Macisco, John J., Jr., Leon F. Bouvier, and Robert H. Weller. 1970. "The Effect of Labor Force Participation on the Relation between Migration Status and Fertility." *Milbank Memorial Fund Quarterly* 48: 51–69.

MacKellar, F. Landis. 2003. "Homicide and Suicide." In Paul Demeny and Geoffrey McNicoll (eds.), *Encyclopedia of Population*, I: 496–499. New York: Macmillan Reference USA.

Mackun, Paul, and Steven Wilson. 2011. "Population Distribution and Change, 2000 to 2010." *2010 Census Briefs*, C2010BR-01(March). Washington, DC: US Census Bureau.

Madigan, Francis C. 1957. "Are Sex Mortality Differentials Biologically Caused?" *Milbank Memorial Fund Quarterly* 35: 202–223.

Madsen, Elizabeth Leahy. 2018. "Three Takeaways on the Four Dividends: How Age Structure Change Can Benefit Development." www.prb.org/resources/three-takeaways-on-the-four-dividends-how-age-structure-change-can-benefit-development/

Maine, Deborah, and Katrina Stamas. 2003. "Maternal Mortality." In Paul Demeny and Geoffrey McNicoll (eds.), *Encyclopedia of Population*, II: 628–631. New York: Macmillan Reference USA.

Malthus, Thomas R. [1803] 1989. *An Essay on the Principle of Population (with the Variora of 1806, 1807, 1817, 1826)*, 2 vols. Ed. Patricia James. Cambridge: Cambridge University Press.

Mann, Donald. [1992] 2015. "Why We Need a Smaller U.S. Population and How We Can Achieve It." *A Negative Population Growth Position Paper.* July 3. Alexandria, VA: Negative Population Growth.

Manning, Wendy, and Lisa Carlson. 2021. "Trends in Cohabitation Prior to Marriage." National Center for Family and Marriage Research, *Family Profile* FP 21-04. Bowling Green, OH: Bowling Green State University.

Manton, Kenneth G., Sharon Sandomirsky Poss, and Steven Wing. 1979. "The Black/White Mortality Crossover: Investigation from the Perspective of the Components of Aging." *The Gerontologist* 19: 291–300.

Manton, Kenneth G., and Eric Stallard. 1997. "Health and Disability Differences among Racial and Ethnic Groups." In Linda G. Martin and Beth J. Soldo (eds.), *Racial and Ethnic Differences in the Health of Older Americans*, 43–105. Washington D.C.: National Academy Press.

March of Dimes. 2024. "Births." www.marchofdimes.org

Markel, Howard. 2004. *When Germs Travel.* New York: Pantheon.

Markides, Kyriakos S., and Jeannine Coreil. 1986. "The Health of Hispanics in the Southwestern United States: An Epidemiologic Paradox." *Public Health Reports* 101: 253–265.

Markides, Kyriakos S., and Karl Eschbach. 2011. "Hispanic Paradox in Adult Mortality in the United States." In Richard G. Rogers and Eileen M. Crimmins (eds.), *International Handbook of Adult Mortality*, 225–238. New York: Springer.

Marks, Lara V. 2001. *Sexual Chemistry: A History of the Contraceptive Pill.* New Haven, CT: Yale University Press.

Marsh, Margaret, and Wanda Ronner. 2008. *The Fertility Doctor: John Rock and the Reproductive Revolution.* Baltimore, MD: Johns Hopkins University Press.

Martin, Philip. 2013. "The Global Challenge of Managing Migration." *Population Bulletin* 68 (November): 1–16.

Martin, Philip, and Gottfried Zurcher. 2008. "Managing Migration: The Global Challenge." *Population Bulletin* 63 (March): 1–20.

Martin, Sean. 2007. *The Black Death.* Edison, NJ: Chartwell Books.

Martin, Susan F. 2001. "Global Migration Trends and Asylum." UNHCR, The UN Refugee Agency, Evaluation and Policy Analysis Unit Working Paper 41, April 30.

Martinez, Gladys, Kimberly Daniels, and Anjani Chandra. 2012. "Fertility of Men and Women Aged 15–44 Years in the United States: National Survey of Family Growth, 2006–2010. " *National Health Statistics Reports* 51 (April 12).

Martinez, Grace, and Jeffrey Passel. 2025. "Facts about the U.S. Black Population." www.pewresearch.org/race-and-ethnicity/fact-sheet/facts-about-the-us-black-population/

Martinez, Ramiro, Jr. 2010. "Policy Essay: Economic Conditions and Racial/ethnic Variations in Violence: Immigration, the Latino Paradox and Future Research." *Criminology & Public Policy* 9: 707–713.

2014. *Latino Homicide: Immigration, Violence and Community*, 2nd ed. New York: Routledge.

Martinez, Ramiro, Jr., and Abel Valenzuela. 2006. *Immigration and Crime: Race, Ethnicity, and Violence.* New York: NYU Press.

Marx, Karl, and Friedrich Engels. [1848] 1935. "The Communist Manifesto." *Selected Works*, Vol. 1. London: Lawrence and Wishart.

Mason, Karen Oppenheim. 1997. "Explaining Fertility Transitions." *Demography* 34: 443–454.

Massey, Douglas S. 1988. "International Migration and Economic Development in Comprehensive Perspective." *Population and Development Review* 14: 383–414.

1995. "The New Immigration and Ethnicity in the United States." *Population and Development Review* 21: 631–652.

2003. "International Migration." In Paul Demeny and Geoffrey McNicoll (eds.), *Encyclopedia of Population*, II: 548–553. New York: Macmillan Reference USA.

Massey, Douglas S., Joaquin Arango, Graeme Hugo, Ali Kouaouci, Adela Pellegrino, and J. Edward Taylor. 1993. "Theories of International Migration: A Review and Appraisal." *Population and Development Review* **19**: 431–466.

1994. "An Evaluation of International Migration Theory: The North American Case." *Population and Development Review* **20**: 699–751.

2005. *Worlds in Motion: Understanding International Migration at the End of the Millennium.* Oxford: Oxford University Press.

Masters, William H., and Virginia E. Johnson. 1966. *Human Sexual Response.* New York: Bantam Books.

1970. *Human Sexual Inadequacy.* New York: Bantam Books.

Mateyka, Peter J. 2015. "Desire to Move and Residential Mobility, 2010 – 2011." *Household Economic Studies* P70–140. Washington, DC: US Census Bureau.

Mathews, T. J., and Marian F. MacDorman. 2013. "Infant Mortality Statistics from the 2010 Period Linked Birth/Infant Death Data Set." *National Vital Statistics Reports* **62** (December 18). Hyattsville, MD: National Center for Health Statistics.

Matthiessen, P. C., and M. E. Matthiessen. 1977. "Sex Ratio in a Sample of Human Fetuses in Denmark, 1962–1973." *Annals of Human Biology* 4: 183–185.

Matysiak, A., and D. Vignoli. 2008. "Fertility and Women's Employment: A Meta-analysis." *European Journal of Population* **24** (4): 363–384.

May, John F. 2012. *World Population Policies: Their Origin, Evolution and Impact.* New York: Springer.

2019. "Population Policy." In Dudley L. Poston, Jr. (ed.), *Handbook of Population*, 2nd ed., 875–899. New York: Springer.

McCann, Allison, and Amy Schoenfeld Walter. 2025. "Tracking Abortion Bans Across the Country." *The New York Times* (March 6). www.nytimes.com/interactive/2024/us/abortion-laws-roev-wade.html

McClory, Robert. 1995. *Turning Point: The Inside Story of the Papal Birth Control Commission, and how Humanae Vitae Changed the Life of Patty Crowley and the Future of the Church.* New York: Crossroad.

McDonald, Peter. 2015. "The Evolution of Population and Family Policy in Australia." In Ronald R. Rindfuss and Minja Kim Choe (eds.), *Low and Lower Fertility Variations Across Developed Countries*, 143–159. Cham, Switzerland: Springer.

McFalls, Joseph A., Jr. 2007. "Population: A Lively Introduction." *Population Bulletin* **62** (1): 1–31.

McFalls, Joseph A., Jr., Bernard Gallagher, and Brian Jones. 1986. "The Social Tunnel Versus the Python: A New Way to Understand the Impact of Baby Booms and Baby Busts on a Society." *Teaching Sociology* **14**: 129–132.

McGehee, Mary A. 2004. "Mortality." In Jacob S. Siegel and David A. Swanson (eds.), *The Methods and Materials of Demography*, 2nd ed., 265–300. San Diego, CA: Elsevier Academic.

McIntosh, C. Alison, and Jason L. Finkle. 1995. "The Cairo Conference on Population and Development: A New Paradigm." *Population and Development Review* 21: 223–260

McKeown, Thomas. 1976. *The Modern Rise of Population.* New York: Academic Press.

McLaren, Angus. 1992. *History of Contraception: From Antiquity to the Present Day.* New York: Wiley-Blackwell.

McNeill, William H. 1976. *Plagues and People.* Garden City, NY: Anchor Books.

McNicoll, Geoffrey. 2003. "Population." In Paul Demeny and Geoffrey McNicoll (eds.), *Encyclopedia of Population*, II: 730–732. New York: Macmillan Reference USA.

Meadows, Donella H., Dennis L. Meadows, Jorgen Randers, and William W. Behrens, III. 1974. *The Limits to Growth: A Report for the Club of Rome's Project on the Predicament of Mankind*, 2nd ed. New York: Universe.

Meadows, Donella, Jorgen Randers, and Dennis L. Meadows. 2004. *Limits to Growth: The Thirty-Year Update*. White River Junction, VT: Chelsea Green.

Mehlan, K. H. 1965. "Legal Abortions in Romania." *Journal of Sex Research* 1: 31–38.

Meltzer, David J. 2009. *First Peoples in a New World: Colonizing Ice Age America*. Berkeley: University of California Press.

Menzies, Gavin. 2003. *1421: The Year China Discovered the World*. New York: William Morrow.

Merke, D., and M. Kabbani. 2001. "Congenital Adrenal Hyperplasia: Epidemiology, Management and Practical Drug Treatment." *Paediatric Drugs* 3 (8): 599–611.

Merton, Robert K. 1968. *Social Theory and Social Structure*. New York: Simon and Schuster.

Mikles, Natasha L. 2024. *Shattered Grief: How the Pandemic Transformed the Spirituality of Death in America*. New York: Columbia University Press.

Mill, John Stuart. [1848] 1965. *Principles of Political Economy with Some Applications to Social Philosophy*, 2 vols., eds. V. W. Bladen and J. M. Robson. Toronto: University of Toronto Press.

Miller, G. Tyler. 2004. *Living in the Environment: Principles, Connections, and Solutions*, 13th ed. Belmont, CA: Brooks/Cole Thomson Leaning.

Miller, Kerby A. 1985. *Emigrants and Exiles: Ireland and the Irish Exodus to North America*. New York: Oxford University Press.

Minino, Arialdi M. 2013. "Death in the United States, 2011." *NCHS Data Brief* 115 (March).

Minino, Arialdi M., Jian Quan Xu, Kenneth D. Kochanek, and Betzaida Tejada-Vera. 2009. "Death in the United States, 2007." *NCHS Data Brief* 26 (December).

Money, John, and Anke Ehrhardt. 1972. *Man and Woman, Boy and Girl*. Baltimore, MD: Johns Hopkins University Press.

Monte, Lindsay M., and Renee R. Ellis. 2014. "Fertility of Women in the United States: June 2012." *Current Population Reports* P20–575. Washington, DC: U.S. Census Bureau.

Morgan, S. Philip. 1991. "Late Nineteenth- and Early Twentieth-Century Childlessness." *American Journal of Sociology* 97: 779-807.

Morgan, S. Philip, and R. Chen. 1992. "Predicting Childlessness for Recent Cohorts of American Women." *International Journal of Forecasting* 8: 477–493.

Morgan, S. Philip, and Anna Rybinska. 2019. "Fertility." In Dudley L. Poston, Jr. (ed.), *Handbook of Population*, 2nd ed., 319–342. New York: Springer.

Morrison, Peter. 1977. *Forecasting Population of Small Areas: An Overview*. Santa Monica, CA: Rand Corporation.

Morrissey, T. 2017. "Childcare and Parent Labor Force Participation: A Review of the Research Literature." *Review of the Economics of the Household* 15 (1): 1–24.

Mosher, William D., Anjani Chandra, and Jo Jones. 2005. "Sexual Behavior and Selected Health Measures: Men and Women 15–44 Years of Age, United States, 2002." *Advance Data from Vital and Health Statistics* 362: 1–56.

Moslimani, Mohamad, and Luis Noe-Bustamante. 2023. "Facts on Latinos in the U.S." Pew Research Center. August 16. www.pewresearch.org/race-and-ethnicity/fact-sheet/latinos-in-the-us-fact-sheet/

Moslimani, Mohamad, and Jeffrey S. Passel. 2024. "What the Data Says About Immigrants in the U.S." Pew Research Center. September 27. www.pewresearch.org/short-reads/2024/09/27/key-findings-about-us-immigrants/

Mumford, Lewis. [1938] 1970. *The Culture of Cities*. New York: Harcourt Brace.

Münz, Rainer. 2003. "Immigration Trends in Major Destination Countries." In Paul Demeny and Geoffrey McNicoll (eds.), *Encyclopedia of Population*, II: 519–523. New York: Macmillan Reference USA.

Murphy, Sherry L., Kenneth D. Kochanek, Jiaquan Xu, and Elizabeth Arias. 2024. "Deaths: Final Data for 2021." *National Vital Statistics Reports* 73 (8).

Myers, Robert J. 1940. "Errors and Bias in the Reporting of Ages in Census Data." *Transactions of the Actuarial Society of America* 41 (Part 2): 411–415.

1941. "The Validity and Significance of Male Net Reproduction Rates." *Journal of the American Statistical Association* 36: 275–282.

Nam, Charles B. 1995. "Another Look at Mortality Crossovers." *Social Biology* 42: 133–142

Nam, Charles B., Norman L. Weatherby, and Kathleen A. Ockay. 1978. "Causes of Death Which Contribute to the Mortality Crossover Effect." *Social Biology* 25: 306–314.

Nam, Charles B., William J. Serow, and David F. Sly (eds.). 1990. *International Handbook on Internal Migration*. New York: Greenwood.

Nanda, Kavita. 2011. "Contraceptive Patch and Vaginal Contraceptive Ring." In Robert A. Hatcher, James Trussell, Anita L. Nelson, Willard Cates, Jr., Deborah Kowal, and Michael S. Policar (eds.), *Contraceptive Technology*, 20th rev. ed., 343–369. New York: Ardent Media, Inc.

National Academies of Sciences, Engineering and Medicine. 2016. *Recent Fertility Trends in Sub Saharan Africa*. Washington, DC: National Academies Press.

National Academies of Sciences, Engineering, and Medicine: Division of Behavioral and Social Sciences and Education; Committee on National Statistics; Committee on Measuring Sex, Gender Identity, and Sexual Orientation. 2022. *Measuring Sex, Gender Identity, and Sexual Orientation*. Washington, DC: National Academies Press.

National Center for Health Statistics. 2009. "The U.S. Vital Statistics System: A National Perspective." www.ncbi.nlm.nih.gov/books/NBK219884

2015. "About the National Survey of Family Growth." Hyattsville, MD: National Center for Health Statistics.

2021. National Survey of Family Growth. *NCHS Fact Sheet* (May). www.cdc.gov/nchs/data/factsheets/factsheet-nsfg.pdf

2022. "Life Expectancy in the U.S. Dropped for the Second Year in a Row in 2021." www.cdc.gov/nchs/pressroom/nchs_press_releases/2022/20220831.htm

2024. "Alzheimer Disease." November. www.cdc.gov/nchs/fastats/alzheimers.htm

National Commission on Employment and Unemployment Statistics. 1979. *Counting the Labor Force*. Washington, DC: Government Printing Office.

National Park Service. 2015. "Fact Sheet." www.nps.gov/npnh/learn/news/fact-sheet-elis.htm

National Population and Talent Division (Singapore). 2013. *A Sustainable Population for a Dynamic Singapore: Population White Paper*. Singapore: National Population and Talent Division.

Nelson, Anita L., and Carrie Cwiak. 2011. "Combined Oral Contraceptives (COCs)." In Robert A. Hatcher, James Trussell, Anita L. Nelson, Willard Cates, Jr., Deborah Kowal, and Michael S. Policar (eds.), *Contraceptive Technology*, 20th rev. ed., 249–341. New York: Ardent Media, Inc.

Newman, Saul Justin. 2024. "Supercentenarian and Remarkable Age Records Exhibit Patterns Indicative of Clerical Errors and Pension Fraud." *bioRxiv*. www.biorxiv.org/content/10.1101/704080v3

Nicholson, W. J. 1976. "Case Study I, Asbestos – The TLV Approach." *Annals of the New York Academy of Science, Occupational Carcinogenesis* 271 (May 28): 152–159.

Nielsen, J., and M. Wohlert. 1991. "Chromosome Abnormalities Found among 34,910 Newborn Children: Results from a 13-Year Incidence Study in Arhus, Denmark." *Human Genetics* 87(1): 81–83.

Nolan, Peter. 1991. "Petty Commodity Production in a Socialist Economy: Chinese Rural Development Post-Mao." In Jan Breman and Sudipto Mundle (eds.), *Rural Transformation in Asia*, 218–255. Delhi, India: Oxford University Press.

Noonan, John T., Jr. 1966. *Contraception: A History of Its Treatment by the Catholic Theologians and Canonists*. Cambridge, MA: Harvard University Press.

Notestein, Frank W. 1945. "Population – The Long View." In Theodore W. Schultz (ed.), *Food for the World*, 36–57. Chicago: University of Chicago Press.

Obregon, Misael. 2015. "Extending the Latino Paradox: Comparative Findings of STIs among Birth Giving Mexican Origin, Black and White Women." Ph.D. diss., Texas A&M University, College Station.

Odland, J. 2001. "Intermetropolitan Variations in Labour Force Participation Rates of White and Black men in the United States." *Urban Studies* 38: 2327–2349.

Oeppen, Jim, and James W. Vaupel. 2002. "Broken Limits to Life Expectancy." *Science* **296**: 1029–1031.

Office of Child Support Services, Office of the Administration for Children and Families. 2023. "Exploring Tribal Demographic Data: Part Three." March 1. https://acf.gov/css/ocsedata blog/2023/03/exploring-tribal-demographic-data-part-three/

O'Grada, Cormac. 1999. *Black '47 and Beyond: The Great Irish Famine in History, Economy and Memory*. Princeton, NJ: Princeton University Press.

2001. "Markets and Famines: Evidence from Nineteenth Century Finland." *Economic Development and Cultural Change* **49**: 575–590.

2003a. "Famine, Concepts and Causes of." In Paul Demeny and Geoffrey McNicoll (eds.), *Encyclopedia of Population*, I: 382–385. New York: Macmillan Reference USA.

2003b. "Famine in Ireland." In Paul Demeny and Geoffrey McNicoll (eds.), *Encyclopedia of Population*, I: 390–392. New York: Macmillan Reference USA.

Oi, Jean C. 1999. *Rural China Takes Off: Institutional Foundations of Economic Reform*. Berkeley: University of California Press.

Oi, Mariko. 2024. "Japan Nappy Maker Shifts from Babies to Adults." *BBC News*. March 27. www.bbc.co.uk/news/business-68672186

Olshansky, S. Jay, and Brian Ault. 1986. "The Fourth Stage of Epidemiologic Transition: The Age of Delayed Degenerative Diseases." *Milbank Quarterly* **64**: 355–391.

Olshansky, S. Jay, and Bruce A. Carnes. 2001. *The Quest for Immortality*. New York: W. W. Norton.

Olshansky, S. Jay, Douglas J. Passaro, Ronald C. Hershow, Jennifer Layden, Bruce A. Carnes, Jacob Brady, Leonard Hayflick, Robert N. Butler, David B. Allison, and David S. Ludwig. 2005. "A Potential Decline in Life Expectancy in the United States in the Twenty-first Century." *New England Journal of Medicine* **352**: 1138–1145.

Olshansky, S. J., B. J. Willcox, L. Demetrius, et al. 2024. "Implausibility of Radical Life Extension in Humans in the Twenty-First Century." *Natural Aging* **4**: 1635–1642. https://doi.org/10.1038/s43587-024-00702-3

Omran, Abdel R. 1971. "The Epidemiologic Transition: A Theory of the Epidemiology of Population Change." *Milbank Quarterly* **49**: 509–553.

Öner, Ceyda. 2010. "Unemployment: The Curse of Joblessness." *Global Employment Trends*. January. www.imf.org/external/pubs/ft/fandd/basics/unemploy.htm

Orzack, Steven Hecht, J. William Stubblefield, Viatcheslav R. Akmaev, Pere Colls, Santiago Munné, Thomas Scholl, David Steinsaltz, and James E. Zuckerman. 2015. "The Human Sex Ratio from Conception to Birth." *PNAS* (March 30): E2102–E2111.

Osborn, Frederick. 1960. *This Crowded World*. New York: Public Affairs Committee.

Ostby, Lars. 2003. "Population Registers." In Paul Demeny and Geoffrey McNicoll (eds.), *Encyclopedia of Population*, II: 763–765. New York: Macmillan Reference USA.

Osterman, Michelle J. K., Brady E. Hamilton, Joyce A. Martin, Anne K. Driscoll, and Claudia P. Valenzuela. 2023. "Births: Final Data for 2021." *National Vital Statistics Reports* **72** (1). Hyattsville, MD: National Center for Health Statistics.

2024. "Births: Final Data for 2022." *National Vital Statistics Reports* **73** (2). Hyattsville, MD: National Center for Health Statistics.

Ostler, Jeffrey. 2019. *Surviving Genocide: Native Nations and the United States from the American Revolution to Bleeding Kansas*. New Haven, CT: Yale University Press.

Oxford English Dictionary. 2000. 2nd ed. Oxford: Oxford University Press.

Oyez. "Obergefell v. Hodges". 2015. www.oyez.org/cases/2014/14-556

Paddock, William, and Paul Paddock. 1967. *Famine, 1975*. Boston: Little, Brown.

Paget, W. John, and Ian M. Timaeus. 1994. "A Relational Gompertz Model of Male Fertility: Development and Assessment." *Population Studies* **48**: 333–340.

Palloni, Alberto, and Elizabeth Arias. 2004. "Paradox Lost: Explaining the Hispanic Adult Mortality Advantage." *Demography* **41**: 385–415.

Palloni, Alberto, and Jeffrey D. Morenoff. 2001. "Interpreting the Paradoxical in the 'Hispanic Paradox': Demographic and Epidemiological Approaches." In M. Weinstein, A. Hermalin, and M. Stoto (eds.), *Population Health and Aging*, 140–174. New York: New York Academy of Sciences.

Palmore, James A., and Robert W. Gardner. 1994. *Measuring Mortality, Fertility and Natural Increase*, 5th ed. Honolulu: East-West Center.

Pampel, Fred C., and H. Elizabeth Peters. 1995. "The Easterlin Effect." *Annual Review of Sociology* **21**: 163–194. https://doi.org/10.1146/annurev.so.21.080195.001115

Papademetriou, Demetrios G. 2003. "International Labor Migration." In Paul Demeny and Geoffrey McNicoll (eds.), *Encyclopedia of Population*, II: 570–574. New York: Macmillan Reference USA.

Parish, W. L., E. O. Laumann, M. S. Cohen, S. M. Pan, H. Y. Zheng, I. Hoffman, T. F. Wang, and K. H. Ng. 2003. "Population-Based Study of Chlamydial Infection in China: A Hidden Epidemic." *Journal of the American Medical Association* **289**: 1265–1273.

Parr, Nick, and Ross Guest. 2011. "The Contribution of Increases in Family Benefits to Australia's Early 21st Century Fertility Increase: An Empirical Analysis." *Demographic Research* **25**: 215–244.

Parrado, Emilio A., and Chenoa A. Flippen. 2012. "Hispanic Fertility, Immigration, and Race in the Twenty-First Century." *Race and Social Problem* **4** (1): 18–30. https://doi.org/10.1007/s12552-012-9063-9

Passel, Jeffrey S. 1976. "Provisional Evaluation of the 1970 Census Count of American Indians." *Demography* 13: 397–409.

1996. "The Growing American Indian Population, 1960-1990: Beyond Demography." In Gary D. Sandefur, Ronald R. Rindfuss, and Barney Cohen (eds.), *Changing Numbers, Changing Needs: American Indian Demography and Public Health*, 79–102. Washington, DC: National Academy Press.

2006. "The Size and Characteristics of the Unauthorized Migrant Population in the U.S.: Estimates Based on the March 2005 Current Population Survey." Research Report. March 7. Washington, DC: Pew Hispanic Center.

Passel, Jeffrey S., and Patricia A. Berman. 1986. "Quality of 1980 Census Data for American Indians." *Social Biology* 33: 163–182.

Passel, Jeffrey S., and D'Vera Cohn. 2014. "Unauthorized Immigrant Totals Rise in 7 States, Fall in 14." Research Report. November 14. Washington, DC: Pew Research Center.

Passel, Jeffrey S., Jennifer Van Hook, and Frank D. Bean. 2004. "*Estimates of Legal and Unauthorized Foreign Born Population for the United States and Selected States, Based on Census 2000.*" Washington, DC: Urban Institute.

Patrick, Erin. 2003. "Demography of Refugees." In Paul Demeny and Geoffrey McNicoll (eds.), *Encyclopedia of Population*, II: 825–830. New York: Macmillan Reference USA.

Patterson, K. David. 1992. "Yellow Fever Epidemics and Mortality in the United States, 1693–1905." *Social Science & Medicine* **34**: 855–865. https://doi.org/10.1016/0277-9536(92)90255-0

Patterson, Kristine B., and Thomas Runge. 2002. "Smallpox and the Native American." *The American Journal of the Medical Science* **323** (4): 216–222. https://doi.org/10.1097/00000441-200204000-00009

Paul, Maureen, and Tara Stein. 2011. "Abortion." In Robert A. Hatcher, James Trussell, Anita L. Nelson, Willard Cates, Jr., Deborah Kowal, and Michael S. Policar (eds.), *Contraceptive Technology*, 20th rev. ed., 695–736. New York: Ardent Media, Inc.

Pauli, Julia. 2023. "Almost Married: Two Generations of Single Mothers in Namibia." In Joanna Davidson and Dinah Hannaford (eds.), *Opting Out: Women Messing with Marriage Around the World*. New Brunswick, NJ: Rutgers University Press.

Pebley, Anne R. 2003. "Infant and Child Mortality." In Paul Demeny and Geoffrey McNicoll (eds.), *Encyclopedia of Population*, II: 533–536. New York: Macmillan Reference USA.

Pedraza, Sylvia, and Ruben G. Rumbaut. 1996. *Origins and Destinies: Immigration, Race and Ethnicity in America*. Belmont, CA: Wadsworth.

Peel, John, and Malcolm Potts. 1969. *Textbook of Contraceptive Practice*. New York: Cambridge University Press.

Peng, Xizhe. 1987. "Demographic Consequences of the Great Leap Forward in China's Provinces." *Population and Development Review* 13: 639–670.

Perez-Patron, Maria, and Bethany DeSalvo. 2019. "Infant Mortality." In Dudley L. Poston, Jr. (ed.), *Handbook of Population*, 2nd ed., 343–354. Cham, Switzerland: Springer.

Perkins, Dwight H., Steven Radelet, and David L. Lindauer. 2013. *Economics of Development*, 7th ed. New York: W. W. Norton.

Perloff, H. S., E. S. Dunn, Jr., E .E. Lampard, and R. F. Muth. 1960. *Regions, Resources, and Economic Growth*. Baltimore, MD: John Hopkins University Press.

Petersen, William. 1975. *Population*, 3rd ed. New York: Macmillan.

1979. *Malthus*. Cambridge, MA: Harvard University Press.

Pew Research Center. 2024. "Chinese Americans: A Survey Data Snapshot." www.pewresearch.org/2024/08/06/chinese-americans-a-survey-data-snapshot/

Piore, Michael J. 1979. *Birds of Passage: Migrant Labor in Industrial Societies*. Cambridge: Cambridge University Press.

Pison, Gilles. 2004. "Fewer Births, but a Boy at All Costs: Selective Female Abortion in Asia." *Population and Societies* 404 (September).

Pison, Gilles, and Laurent Toulemon. 2025. "Is the French Population on a Path to Decline?" *Population and Societies* 631 (March): 1–4. https://doi.org/10.3917/popsoc.631.0001

Plane, David A. 2004. "Population Distribution: Geographic Areas." In Jacob S. Siegel and David A. Swanson (eds.), *The Methods and Materials of Demography*, 2nd ed., ch. 5. San Diego, CA: Elsevier Academic.

Plankey Videla, Nancy. 2008. "Maquiladoras." In William A. Darity (ed. in chief), *International Encyclopedia of the Social Sciences*, 2nd ed., IV: 591–594. Detroit, MI: Macmillan Reference USA.

Pollard, A. H., Farhat Yusuf, and G. N. Pollard. 1981. *Demographic Techniques*, 2nd ed. Sydney: Pergamon.

1990. *Demographic Techniques*, 3rd ed. Sydney: Pergamon.

Popoff, Carole, and Dean H. Judson. 2004. "Some Methods of Estimation for Statistically Underdeveloped Areas." In Jacob S. Siegel and David A. Swanson (eds.), *The Methods and Materials of Demography*, 2nd ed., 603–641. San Diego, CA: Elsevier Academic.

Population Reference Bureau. 2014. *2014 World Population Data Sheet*. Washington, DC: Population Reference Bureau.

2019. *Family Planning Data Sheet, 2019 Data Sheet*. Washington, DC: Population Reference Bureau.

World Population Data Sheet. Washington, DC: Population Reference Bureau.

World Population Data Sheet. Washington, DC: Population Reference Bureau.

Porter, Katherine Anne. 1939. *Pale Horse, Pale Rider*. New York: Harcourt Brace & Company.

Portes, Alejandro, and Ruben G. Rumbaut. 1990. *Immigrant America: A Portrait*. Berkley: University of California Press.

Portes, Alejandro, and John Walton. 1981. *Labor, Class, and the International System*. New York: Academic Press.

Postel, Sandra. 1992. *Water and Sustainability: Dimensions of the Global Challenge*. Amherst, MA: World Watch Institute.

Poston, Dudley L., Jr. 1974. "Income and Childlessness in the United States: Is the Relationship Always Inverse?" *Social Biology* 21: 296–307.

2000. "Social and Economic Development and the Fertility Transition in Mainland China and Taiwan." *Population and Development Review* 26 (Suppl.): 40–60.

2002. "South Korea's Demographic Destiny: Marriage Market and Elderly Support Implications for the 21st Century." In *International Conference on the Longevity and*

Social, Medical Environment of the Elderly, 69–83. Taegu, South Korea: Institute of Gerontology, Yeungnam University.

2006a. "John Graunt." In Bryan Turner (ed.), *The Cambridge Dictionary of Sociology*, 254. Cambridge: Cambridge University Press.

2006b. "Malthus." In Bryan Turner (ed.), *The Cambridge Dictionary of Sociology*, 347–348. Cambridge: Cambridge University Press.

2015. "Human Ecology." In James D. Wright (editor-in-chief), *International Encyclopedia of the Social and Behavioral Sciences*, 2nd ed., Vol. 11, 283–288. Oxford: Elsevier.

2019. "Age and Sex." In Dudley L. Poston, Jr. (ed.), *Handbook of Population*, 2nd ed., 19–50. New York: Springer.

2020a. "The Contemporary Family." In D. Nicole Farris and A. J. J. Bourque (eds.), *International Handbook on the Demography of Marriage and the Family*, 295–305. Cham, Switzerland: Springer Nature.

2020b. "The Decennial Census and Congressional Apportionment." *Harvard Data Science Review* **2** (1). https://hdsr.mitpress.mit.edu/pub/molpwb4x

2023a. "China Needs Immigrants." *The Conversation*. July 18. https://theconversation.com/china-needs-immigrants-208911

2023b. "South Korea Has the Lowest Fertility Rate in the World – and That Doesn't Bode Well for Its Economy." *The Conversation*. June 27. https://theconversation.com/south-korea-has-the-lowest-fertility-rate-in-the-world-and-that-doesnt-bode-well-for-its-economy-207107

2023c. "韓 미혼남 20년간 한인 여성 배우자 못 찾는다 [더들리 포스턴의 韓 인구문제 고찰]" ("Unmarried Korean Boys Will Not Be Able to Find Korean Female Spouses for the Next 20 Years"). *Korea Herald Busines*. October 31. https://urldefense.com/v3/__https://biz.heraldcorp.com/insight/__

2024a. "A Demographer Does the Math for Heaven." *San Antonio Express News*. April 19, p. 22. www.expressnews.com/opinion/commentary/article/demography-heaven-global-population-19459439.php

2024b. "Raising the Retirement Age Won't Defuse China's Demographic Time Bomb, But Mass Immigration Might." *The Conversation*. August 15. https://theconversation.com/raising-the-retirement-age-wont-defuse-chinas-demographic-time-bomb-but-mass-immigration-might-236041

2025 "Why Donald Trump's Border Wall Won't Work." *Newsweek*. January 26. www.newsweek.com/trump-border-wall-wont-work-2019654

Poston, Dudley L., Jr., and Amanda K. Baumle. 2010. "Patterns of Asexuality in the United States." *Demographic Research* **23**: 509–530.

Poston, Dudley L., Jr., and Yu-Ting Chang. 2013. "Patterns of Gay Male and Lesbian Partnering in the Metropolitan Areas of the United States in 2010." Paper presented at the XXVII International Population Conference, International Union for the Scientific Study of Population, Busan, South Korea, 26–31 August.

2015. "The Conceptualization and Measurement of the Homosexual, Heterosexual and Bisexual Populations in the United States." In M. Nazrul Hoque and Lloyd B. Potter (eds.), *Emerging Techniques in Applied Demography*, 359–378. New York: Springer.

Poston, Dudley L., Jr., Eugenia Conde, and Bethany DeSalvo. 2011. "China's Unbalanced Sex Ratio at Birth: Millions of Excess Bachelors and Societal Implications." *Vulnerable Children and Youth Studies* **6**: 314–320.

Poston, Dudley L., Jr., and Cristina Elizabeth Cruz. 2016. "Voluntary, Involuntary and Temporary Childlessness in the United States. *Quetelet Journal / Revue Quetelet* **4**: 73–99.

Poston, Dudley L., Jr., Mary Ann Davis, and Chris Lewinski. 2006. "Fertility." In Bryan Turner (ed.), *The Cambridge Dictionary of Sociology*, 403–405. Cambridge: Cambridge University Press.

Poston, Dudley L., Jr., Bethany S. DeSalvo, and Heather Terrell Kincannon. 2009. "Sex and Sex Structure." In Zeng Yi (ed.), *Demography, Encyclopedia of Life Support Systems (EOLSS)*. Oxford, UK: UNESCO, Eolss Publishers.

Poston, Dudley L., Jr., Bethany S. DeSalvo, and Leslie D. Meyer. 2009. "Malthusian Theory of Population Growth." In Dennis L. Peck and Clifton D. Bryant (eds.), *Encyclopedia of Death and the Human Experience*, 684–687. Thousand Oaks, CA: Sage.

Poston, Dudley L., Jr., and Charles Chengrong Duan. 2000. "Nonagricultural Unemployment in Beijing: A Multilevel Analysis." *Research in Community Sociology* 10: 287–301.

Poston, Dudley L., Jr., Ceylan Engin, and Yağmur Çağatay. 2022. "Obesity Prevalence and Trends in the Asexual and Sexual Populations." In Ginny Garcia-Alexander and Dudley L. Poston, Jr. (eds.), *International Handbook of the Demography of Obesity*, 257–272. Cham, Switzerland: Springer Nature.

Poston, Dudley L., Jr., and W. Parker Frisbie. 1998. "Human Ecology, Sociology, and Demography." In Michael Micklin and Dudley L. Poston, Jr. (eds.), *Continuities in Sociological Human Ecology*, 27–50. New York: Plenum.

2019. "Ecological Demography." In Dudley L. Poston, Jr. (ed.), *Handbook of Population*, 2nd ed., 697–712. New York: Springer.

Poston, Dudley L., Jr., and Karen S. Glover. 2005. "Too Many Males: Marriage Market Implications of Gender Imbalances in China." *Genus* 61: 119–140.

Poston, Dudley L., Jr., and Baochang Gu. 1987. "Socioeconomic Development, Family Planning and Fertility in the People's Republic of China: A Subregional Analysis." *Demography* 24: 531–551.

Poston, Dudley L., Jr., and Baochang Gu. 1989. "China's Super-large Cities: Dominance and Integration." *Chinese Journal of Population Science* (English Language Edition, Beijing) 1 (2): 199–207.

Poston, Dudley L., Jr., Baochang Gu, Peihang Liu, and Terra McDaniel. 1997. "Son Preference and the Sex Ratio at Birth in China." *Social Biology* 44: 55–76.

Poston, Dudley L., Jr., Kenneth M. Johnson, and Layton Field. 2015. "Natural Decrease in the Countries and Counties of Europe in the Context of the Second Demographic Transition." Paper presented at the XXVI Congress of the European Society for Rural Sociology, Aberdeen, Scotland, August 18–21.

Poston, Dudley L. Jr., Kenneth Johnson, and Layton Field. 2016 "Deaths Exceed Births in Most of Europe, but Not in the U.S., and Not in Texas." *N-IUSSP, the News Magazine of the International Union for the Scientific Study of Population*. February 15.

Poston, Dudley L., Jr., and Kathryn B. Kramer. 1983. "Voluntary and Involuntary Childlessness in the United States, 1955–1973." *Social Biology* 30: 290–306.

Poston, Dudley L., Jr., and Hua Luo. 2007. "Chinese Student and Labor Migration to the United States: Trends and Policies since the 1980s." *Asian and Pacific Migration Journal* 16 (3): 323–355.

Poston, Dudley L., Jr., Hua Luo, and Li Zhang. 2006. "Migration." In Bryan Turner (ed.), *The Cambridge Dictionary of Sociology*, 384–386. Cambridge: Cambridge University Press.

Poston, Dudley L., Jr., and Michael Xinxiang Mao. 1998. "Interprovincial Migration in China, 1985–1990." *Research in Rural Sociology and Development* 7: 227–250.

Poston, Dudley L., Jr., Michael X. Mao, and Mei-Yu Yu. 1994. "The Global Distribution of the Overseas Chinese Around 1990." *Population and Development Review* 20: 631–645.

Poston, Dudley L., Jr., and Michael Micklin. 2019. "Prologue." In Dudley L. Poston, Jr. (ed.), *Handbook of Population*, 2nd ed., 1–15. New York: Springer.

Poston, Dudley L., Jr., and Peter A. Morrison. 2005. "China: Bachelor Bomb." *International Herald Tribune*. September 14.

2011. "Chinese Workers Could Replace Mexican Immigrants." *Houston Chronicle*. August 13.

Poston, Dudley L., Jr., and Richard G. Rogers. 1985. "Toward a Reformulation of the Neonatal Mortality Rate." *Social Biology* 32: 1–12.

Poston, Dudley L., Jr., and Rogelio Saenz. 2019. "The U.S. White Majority Will Soon Disappear Forever." *The Conversation*. April 30. http://theconversation.com/the-us-white-majority-will-soon-disappear-forever-115894

Poston, Dudley L., Jr., and Heather K. M. Terrell. 2006. "Fertility." In Bryan Turner (ed.), *The Cambridge Dictionary of Sociology*, 201–203. Cambridge: Cambridge University Press.

Poston, Dudley L., Jr., and David Yaukey (eds.). 1992. *The Population of Modern China*. New York: Plenum.

Poston, Dudley L., Jr., and Li Zhang. 2008. "Ecological Analyses of Permanent and Temporary Migration Streams in China in the 1990s." *Population Research and Policy Review* **27**: 689–712.

2009. "China's Unbalanced Sex Ratio at Birth: How Many Surplus Boys Have Been Born since the 1980s?" In Joseph Tucker, Dudley L. Poston, Qiang Ren, Baochang Gu, Xiaoying Zheng, Stephanie Wang, and Chris Russell (eds.), *Gender Policy and HIV in China: Catalyzing Policy Change*, 57–69. New York: Springer.

Poston, Dudley L., Jr., Li Zhang, and Heather K. M. Terrell. 2008. "Fertility." In William A. Darity (ed. in chief), *International Encyclopedia of the Social Sciences*, 2nd ed., 126–130. Detroit, MI: Macmillan Reference USA.

Potts, David Malcolm. 2003. "Birth Control, History of." In Paul Demeny and Geoffrey McNicoll (eds.), *Encyclopedia of Population*, I: 93–98. New York: Macmillan Reference USA.

Potts, David Malcolm, and Martha Campbell. 2002. "History of Contraception." *Gynecology and Obstetrics* **6**: Chapter 8.

Potts, David Malcolm, Peter Diggory, and John Peel. 1977. *Abortion*. New York: Cambridge University Press.

Poulain, Michel, Giovanni Mario Pes, Claude Grasland, Ciriaco Carru, et al. 2004. "Identification of a Geographic Area Characterized by Extreme Longevity in the Sardinia Island: The AKEA Study." *Experimental Gerontology* **39**: 1423–1429. www.sciencedirect.com/science/article/abs/pii/S0531556504002141

Presser, Harriet B. 1997. "Demography, Feminism, and the Science-Policy Nexus." *Population and Development Review* **23**: 295–331.

Presser, Harriet B., and J. C. Gornick. 2005. "The Female Share of Weekend Employment: A Study of 16 Countries." *Monthly Labor Review* **128** (8): 41.

Preston, Samuel H. 1987. "The Social Sciences and the Population Problem." *Sociological Forum* **2**: 619–644.

Preston, Samuel H., and Michael R. Haines. 1991. *Fatal Years: Child Mortality in Late Nineteenth-Century America*. Princeton, NJ: Princeton University Press.

Preston, Samuel H., Patrick Heuveline, and Michel Guillot. 2001. *Demography: Measuring and Modeling Population Processes*. Malden, MA: Blackwell.

Prewitt, Kenneth. 2013. *What Is Your Race? The Census and Our Flawed Efforts to Classify Americans*. Princeton, NJ: Princeton University Press.

Purcell, L. Edward. 1995. *Immigration: Social Issues in American History*. Phoenix, AZ: The Oryx Press.

Ramachandran, K. V. 1967. "An Index to Measure Digit Preference Error in Age Data." *World Population Conference, 1965, Belgrade*, III: 202–203.

Ramchandran, Deepa, and Ushma D. Upadhyay. 2007. "Implants: The Next Generation." *Population Reports*, Series K, No. 7. Baltimore, MD: INFO Project, Johns Hopkins Bloomberg School of Public Health.

Ramer S., A. T. Nguyen, L. M. Hollier, J. Rodenhizer, L. Warner, and M. K. Whiteman. 2024. "Abortion Surveillance – United States, 2022." *Morbidity and Mortality Weekly Report, Surveillance Summaries* 73 (7): 1–28. http://dx.doi.org/10.15585/mmwr.ss7307a1

Ramirez D., and S. A. Haas. 2022. "Windows of Vulnerability: Consequences of Exposure Timing during the Dutch Hunger Winter." *Population and Development Review* **48** (4): 959–989. doi: 10.1111/padr.12513. Epub 2022 Sep 14. PMID: 37063488; PMCID: PMC1008747

Rand Corporation. 1995. *Low Fertility and Population Ageing: Causes, Consequences, and Policy Options*. Santa Monica, CA: Rand.

Ravenstein, E. G. 1885. "The Laws of Migration." *Journal of the Royal Statistical Society* **48**: 167–277.

1889. "The Laws of Migration, Part II." *Journal of the Royal Statistical Society* **52**: 241–301.

Raymond, Elizabeth G. 2011a. "Contraceptive Implants." In Robert A. Hatcher, James Trussell, Anita L. Nelson, Willard Cates, Jr., Deborah Kowal and Michael S. Policar (eds.), *Contraceptive Technology*, 20th rev. ed., 193–207. New York: Ardent Media, Inc.

2011b. "Progestin-Only Pills." In Robert A. Hatcher, James Trussell, Anita L. Nelson, Willard Cates, Jr., Deborah Kowal, and Michael S. Policar (eds.), *Contraceptive Technology*, 20th rev. ed., 237–247. New York: Ardent Media, Inc.

Rebhum, U. 2008. "A Double Disadvantage? Immigration, Gender, and Employment Status in Israel." *European Journal of Population* **24** (1): 87–113.

Rees, William. 2004. "Sustainable Development and the Ecosphere." In Arthur Fabel and Donald St. John (eds.), *Teilhard in the 21st Century*, 1–12. Maryknoll, NY: Maryknoll Publications.

Reichert, Josh, and Douglas S. Massey. 1980. "History and Trends in U.S. Bound Migration from a Mexican Town." *International Migration Review* **14**: 475–491.

Renzetti, Claire M., Daniel J. Curran, and Shana L Maier. 2012. *Women, Men, and Society*, 6th ed. New York: Pearson Publishing.

Riddle, John M. 1999. *Eve's Herbs: A History of Contraception and Abortion in the West.* Cambridge, MA: Harvard University Press.

Riley, Nancy E. 1998. "Research on Gender in Demography: Limitations and Constraints." *Population Research and Policy Review* **17**: 521–538.

2019. "Demography of Gender." In Dudley L. Poston, Jr. (ed.), *Handbook of Population*, 107–142. New York: Springer.

Riley, Nancy E., and James McCarthy. 2003. *Demography in the Age of the Postmodern.* Cambridge: Cambridge University Press.

Rindfuss, Ronald R., S. Philip Morgan, and Gray Swicegood. 1988. *First Births in America: Changes in the Timing of Parenthood.* Berkeley, CA: University of California Press.

Rindfuss, Ronald R., Karen Benjamin Guzzo, and S. Philip Morgan. 2003. "The Changing Institutional Context of Low Fertility." *Population Research and Policy Review* **22** (5–6): 411–438.

Riosmena, Fernando, Bethany G. Everett, Richard G. Rogers, and Jeff A. Dennis. 2015. "Negative Acculturation and Nothing More? Cumulative Disadvantage and Mortality during the Immigrant Adaptation Process among Latinos in the United States." *International Migration Review* 49: 443–478

Ritchey, P. Neal. 1976. "Explanations of Migration." *Annual Review of Sociology* **2**: 363–404.

Ritchie, Hannah, and Edouard Mathieu. 2023 "How Many People Die and How Many Are Born Each Year?" OurWorldinData.org. https://ourworldindata.org/births-and-deaths

Roberts, Kenneth D. 1997. "China's 'Tidal Wave' of Migrant Labor: What Can We Learn from Mexican Undocumented Migration to the United States?" *International Migration Review* **31**: 249–293.

Roberts, Sam. 2010. "New Figure for 2010 Census: $1.6 Billion Under Budget." *New York Times*, August 10.

Robine, Jean-Marie. 2003. "Epidemiological Transition." In Paul Demeny and Geoffrey McNicoll (eds.), *Encyclopedia of Population*, I: 307–310. New York: Macmillan Reference USA.

Rock, John. 1963. *The Time Has Come: A Catholic Doctor's Proposals to End the Battle over Birth Control.* New York: Alfred A. Knopf.

Rodriguez, Alex. 2009. "'Parental Glory' Counts in Russia." *Houston Chronicle*. January 29.

Rogers, Andrei. 1975. *Introduction to Multiregional Mathematical Demography.* London: Wiley.

Rogers, Richard G., and Robert Hackenberg. 1987. "Extending Epidemiologic Transition Theory: A New Stage." *Social Biology* **34**: 234–243.

Rogers, Richard G., Robert A. Hummer, and Patrick M. Krueger. 2005. "Adult Mortality." In Dudley L. Poston, Jr., and Michael Micklin (eds.), *Handbook of Population*, 283–309. New York: Kluwer Academic/Plenum.

Rogers, Richard G., Robert A. Hummer, Patrick M. Krueger, and Justin M. Vinneau. 2019. "Adult Mortality." In Dudley L. Poston, Jr. (ed.), *Handbook of Population*, 2nd ed., 355–381. New York: Springer.

Rogers, Richard G., Robert A. Hummer, Elizabeth M. Lawrence, Trent G. S. Davidson, and Samuel H. Fishman. 2022. "Dying Young in the United States: What's Driving High Death Rates among Americans under Age 25 and What Can Be Done?" *Population Bulletin* 76 (2): 1–31.

Rogers, Richard G., Robert A. Hummer, and Charles B. Nam. 2000. *Living and Dying in the USA*. San Diego, CA: Academic Press.

Rogers, Richard G., Robert A. Hummer, Charles B. Nam, and Kimberley Peters. 1996. "Demographic, Socioeconomic, and Behavioral Factors Affecting Ethnic Mortality by Cause." *Social Forces* **74**: 1419–1438.

Rogers, Richard G., Elizabeth M. Lawrence, and Robert A. Hummer. 2018. "A Twenty-First Century Demographic Challenge: Comparatively Low Life Expectancy in the United States." In Dudley L. Poston, Jr., Samsik Lee, and Han Gon Kim (eds.), *Low Fertility Regimes and Demographic and Societal Change*, 49–71. Cham, Switzerland: Springer International Publishing.

Romero, Fabian. 2014. "The Residential Segregation of Latino Immigrants in the U.S.: Exposure to Crime and the Effects of Place of Destination." Ph.D. diss., Texas A&M University, College Station.

Roncari, Danielle, and Melody Y. Hou. 2011. "Female and Male Sterilization." In Robert A. Hatcher, James Trussell, Anita L. Nelson, Willard Cates, Jr., Deborah Kowal, and Michael S. Policar (eds.), *Contraceptive Technology*, 20th rev. ed., 435–482. New York: Ardent Media, Inc.

Rosen, R., C. Brown, J. Heiman, S. Leiblum, C. Meston, R. Shabsigh, D. Ferguson, and R. D'Agostino Jr. 2000. "The Female Sexual Function Index (FSFI): A Multidimensional Self-Report Instrument for the Assessment of Female Sexual Function." *Journal of Sex and Marital Therapy* **26**: 191–208.

Rosenberg, H. M., J. D. Maurer, P. D. Sorrie, N. J. Johnson, M. F. MacDonald, D. L. Hoyert, J. F. Spitler, and C. Scott. 1999. "Quality of Death Rates by Race and Hispanic Origin: A Summary of Current Research, 1999." *Vital Health Statistics* **2** (128): 1–13.

Rosenwaike, Ira. 1991. *Mortality of Hispanic Populations*. Westport, CT: Greenwood.

Rosenwaike, Ira, and Samuel H. Preston. 1983. "Age Overstatement and Puerto Rican Longevity." *Human Biology* **56**: 503–525.

Roser, Max. 2023. "Demographic Transition: Why Is Rapid Population Growth a Temporary Phenomenon?" OurWorldinData.org. https://ourworldindata.org/demographic-transition

Roser, Max and Hannah Ritchie. 2023. "How Has World Population Growth Changed over Time?" OurWorldinData.org. https://ourworldindata.org/population-growth-over-time

Rostron, Brian L., John L. Boies, and Elizabeth Arias. 2010. "Education Reporting and Classification on Death Certificates in the United States." *Vital and Health Statistics* **2** (151): 1–14.

Rothblum, E. D., and K. A. Brehony. 1993. "Why Focus on Romantic but Asexual Relationships among Lesbians?" In E. D. Rothblum and K. A. Brehony (eds.), *Boston Marriages: Romantic but Asexual Relationships among Contemporary Lesbians*, 3–14. Boston: University of Massachusetts Press.

Rowland, Donald T. 2003. *Demographic Methods and Concepts*. New York: Oxford University Press.

Rubenstein, Edwin S. 2008/2009. "The Twin Crises." *The Social Contract* **19**: 3–83.

Rudacille, Deborah. 2005. *The Riddle of Gender: Science, Activism, and Transgender Rights*. New York: Pantheon Books.

Russell, Chris, and Dudley L. Poston, Jr. 2008. "Overpopulation." In William A. Darity (ed. in chief), *International Encyclopedia of the Social Sciences*, 2nd ed., VI: 95–96. Detroit, MI: Macmillan Reference USA.

Ryder, Norman B. 1959. "Fertility." In Philip M. Hauser and Otis Dudley Duncan (eds.), *The Study of Population*, 400–436. Chicago: University of Chicago Press.

1964. "Notes on the Concept of a Population." *American Journal of Sociology* **69**: 447–463.

Ryder, Robert E. J. 1993. "Natural Family Planning: Effective Birth Control Supported by the Catholic Church." *British Medical Journal* **307** (September 18): 723–726.

Sabagh, Georges. 1942. "The Fertility of French Canadian Women during the 17th Century." *American Journal of Sociology* **47**: 680–689.

Saenz, Rogelio. 2010. "Latinos in the United States 2010." *Population Reference Bureau Bulletin Update* (December). Washington, DC: Population Reference Bureau.

Saenz, Rogelio, and E. Colberg. 1988. "Sustenance Organization and Net Migration in Small Texas Nonmetropolitan Communities, 1960–1980." *Rural Sociology* **53**: 334–345.

Saenz, Rogelio, and Maria Cristina Morales. 2019. "Demography of Race and Ethnicity." in Dudley L. Poston, Jr. (ed.), *Handbook of Population*, 2nd ed., 163–207. Cham, Switzerland: Springer.

Sampson, Robert J., and John H. Laub. 1990. "Crime and Deviance over the Life Course: The Salience of Adult Social Bonds." *American Sociological Review* **55**: 609–627.

Sánchez-Rivera, Ana, Paul Jacobs, and Cody Spence. 2023. "A Look at the Largest American Indian and Alaska Native Tribes and Villages in the Nation, Tribal Areas and States." October 3. www.census.gov/library/stories/2023/10/2020-census-dhc-a-aian-population.html

Sanderson, Warren C. 1979. "Quantitative Aspects of Marriage, Fertility and Family Limitation in Nineteenth Century America: Another Application of the Coale Specification." *Demography* **16**: 339–358.

Sanderson, Warren C., and Sergei Scherbov. 2005. "Average Remaining Lifetimes Can Increase As Human Populations Age." *Nature* 435 (7043): 811–813.

2010. "Remeasuring Aging." *Science* , 329 (5997): 1287–1288.

2019. *Prospective Longevity: A New Vision of Population Aging*. Cambridge, MA: Harvard University Press.

Sane, K., and O. H. Pescovitz. 1992. "The Clitoral Index: A Determination of Clitoral Size in Normal Girls and in Girls with Abnormal Sexual Development." *Journal of Pediatrics* **120**: 264–266.

Sassen, Saskia. 1988. *The Mobility of Labor and Capital: A Study in International Investment and Labor Flow*. Cambridge: Cambridge University Press.

Sautter, Jessica M., Patricia A. Thomas, Matthew E. Dupre, and Linda K. George. 2012. "Socioeconomic Status and the Black-White Mortality Crossover." *American Journal of Public Health* **102**: 1566–1571.

Sax, Leonard. 2002. "How Common Is Intersex? A Response to Anne Fausto-Sterling." *Journal of Sex Research* **39**: 174–178.

Scharping, Thomas. 2003. *Birth Control in China 1949–2000: Population Policy and Demographic Development*. London: Routledge Curzon.

Scheidel, Walter. 2003. "Ancient World, Demography of." In Paul Demeny and Geoffrey McNicoll (eds.), *Encyclopedia of Population*, I: 44–48. New York: Macmillan Reference USA.

Schmeckebier, Laurence F. 1941. *Congressional Apportionment*. Washington, DC: The Brookings Institution.

Schnore, Leo F. 1958. "Social Morphology and Human Ecology." *American Journal of Sociology* **63**: 620–634.

Schoen, Robert. 1988. *Modeling Multigroup Populations*. New York: Plenum.

Schumacher, E. F. 1975. *Small Is Beautiful: A Study of Economics as if People Mattered*. New York: Harper Colophon.

Scommegna, Paola, Mark Mather, and Diana Elliott. 2024. "More than a Feeling: How Social Connection Protects Health in Later Life." *Today's Research on Aging* **44**. www.prb.org/resources/Todays-research-on-aging-44-more-than-a-feeling-how-social-connection-protects-health-in-later-life/

Scribner, Richard S. 1996. "Paradox as Paradigm: The Health Outcomes of Mexican Americans." *American Journal of Public Health* 86: 303–304.

Scribner, Richard S., and James H. Dwyer. 1989. "Acculturation and Low Birthweight Among Latinos in the Hispanic HANES." *American Journal of Public Health* 79: 1263–1267.

Segal, Sheldon J. 2003. "Modern Methods of Contraception." In Paul Demeny and Geoffrey McNicoll (eds.), *Encyclopedia of Population*, I: 170–174. New York: Macmillan Reference USA.

Segal, Sheldon, and Olivia S. Nordberg. 1977. "Fertility Regulation Technology: Status and Prospects." *Population Bulletin* 31 (March): 1–25.

Sharpe, F. R., and Alfred J. Lotka. 1911. "A Problem in Age Distribution." *Philosophical Magazine* 21: 435–438.

Shepard, Marguerite K. 1980. "Nonsurgical Methods of Contraception." In Rochelle N. Shain and Carl J. Pauerstein (eds.), *Fertility Control: Biological and Behavioral Aspects*, ch. 6, 71–84. New York: Harper and Row.

Shilts, Randy. 1987. *And the Band Played On: Politics, People and the AIDS Epidemic*. New York: St. Martin's.

Shkolnikov, Vladimir M. 2003. "Mortality Reversals." In Paul Demeny and Geoffrey McNicoll (eds.), *Encyclopedia of Population*, II: 676–679. New York: Macmillan Reference USA.

Shkolnikov, Vladimir M., D. A. Jdanov, E. M. Andreev, and James W. Vaupel. 2011. "Steep Increases in Best-Practice Cohort Life Expectancy." *Population and Development Review* 37: 419–434.

Short, Susan E., and Meghan Zacher. 2022. "Women's Health: Population Patterns and Social Determinants." *Annual Review of Sociology*. 48: 277–298. doi: 10.1146/annurev-soc-030320-034200

Shrestha, Laura B. 2006. "Life Expectancy in the United States." *CRS Report for Congress*, RL 32792. Washington, DC: Congressional Research Service.

Shryock, Henry S. 1964. *Population Mobility within the United States*. Chicago: Community and Family Study Center.

Shryock, Henry S., Jacob S. Siegel, and Associates. 1976. *The Methods and Materials of Demography*. Condensed edition by Edward G. Stockwell. New York: Academic Press.

1980. *The Methods and Materials of Demography*, 2 vols., 4th printing. Washington, DC: the Census Bureau.

Shultz, Jackson Wright. 2015. *Trans/Portraits: Voices from the Transgender Communities*. Hanover, NH: Dartmouth College Press.

Simon, Julian L. 1981. *The Ultimate Resource*. Princeton, NJ: Princeton University Press.

1992. *Population and Development in Poor Countries: Selected Essays*. Princeton, NJ: Princeton University Press.

Singelmann, Joachim. 1978. "The Sectoral Transformation of the Labor Force in Seven Industrialized Countries, 1920–1970." *American Journal of Sociology* 83 (5), 1224–1234. www.jstor.org/stable/2778192

Sivin, Irving, Harold Nash, and Sandra Waldman. 2002. *Jadelle Levonorgestrel Rod Implants: A Summary of Scientific Data and Lessons Learned from Orogrammatic Experience*. New York: Population Council.

Skeldon, Ronald. 2005. "Migration and Poverty: Some Issues in the Context of Asia." In Irena Omelaniuk (ed.), *World Migration, 2005: Costs and Benefits on International Migration*, 253–268. Geneva: International Organization for Migration.

Smith, David P. 1992. *Formal Demography*. New York: Plenum.

Snipp, C. Matthew. 1989. *American Indians: The First of This Land*. New York: Russell Sage Foundation.

Soby, S. D. 2017. "Thomas Malthus, Ester Boserup, and Agricultural Development Models in the Age of Limits." *Journal of Agricultural & Environmental Ethics* 30: 87–98. https://link.springer.com/article/10.1007/s10806-017-9655-x

Solinger, Dorothy J. 1999. *Contesting Citizenship in Urban China: Peasant Migrants, the State, and the Logic of the Market*. Berkeley: University of California Press

Song, Jian, Chi-Hsien Tuan, and Jingyuan Yu. 1985. *Population Control in China: Theory and Applications*. New York: Praeger.

Song, Jian, and Jingyuan Yu. 1988. *Population System Control*. Berlin: Springer-Verlag.

Sonnega, Amanda. 2006. "The Future of Human Life Expectancy: Have We Reached the Ceiling or Is the Sky the Limit?" *Research Highlights in the Demography and Economics of Aging* 8 (March): 1–4.

Spengler, Oswald. [1918] 1991. *The Decline of the West*. New York: Oxford University Press.

Spinney, Laura. 2017. *Pale Rider: The Spanish Flu of 1918 and How It Changed the World*. New York: Public Affairs, Hachette Book Group.

Spitz, I. M., C. W. Bardin, L. Benton, and A. Robbins. 1998. "Early Pregnancy Termination with Mifepristone and Misoprostol in the United States." *New England Journal of Medicine* 338 (18): 1241–1247.

Stark, Oded. 1984. "Migration Decision Making: A Review Article." *Journal of Development Economics* 14: 251–259.

1991. *The Migration of Labor*. Cambridge: Basil Blackwell.

StataCorp. 2021. *Stata Survey Data Reference Manual, Release 17*. College Station, TX: Stata Corporation.

State of Wyoming Economic Analysis Division. 2024. "U.S. Decennial Census Population: 1790 to 2020." https://ai.wyo.gov/divisions/economic-analysis/demographic-information/u-s-census-population-1790-to-2020

Stein, Zena, Mervyn Susser, Gerhard Saenger, and Francis Marolla. 1975. *Famine and Human Development: The Dutch Hunger Winter of 1944–1945*. New York: Oxford University Press.

Sternlieb, George, and James W. Hughes. 1978. *Current Population Trends in the United States*. New Brunswick, NJ: Center for Urban Policy Research.

Stier, H., and Marta Tienda. 1992. "Family, Work, and Women: The Labor Supply of Hispanic Immigrant Wives." *International Migration Review* 26: 1291–1313.

Stock, Kathleen. 2021. *Material Girls: Why Reality Matters for Feminism*. London: Fleet Publishers.

Stockwell, Edward G., Jerry W. Wicks, and Donald J. Adamchak. 1978. "Research Needed on Socioeconomic Differentials in U.S. Mortality." *Public Health Reports* 93: 666–672.

Stone, L. O. 1978. *The Frequency of Geographic Mobility in the Population of Canada*. Ottawa: Statistics Canada.

Stover, John. 1998. "Revising the Proximate Determinants Framework of Fertility. What Have We Learned in the Past 20 Years? *Studies in Family Planning* 29: 255–267.

Stycos, J. Mayone. 1955. *Family and Fertility in Puerto Rico: A Study of the Lower Income Group*. New York: Columbia University Press.

Suárez, Mario I., Guadalupe Marquez-Velarde, D'Lane R. Compton, and Dudley L. Poston, Jr. 2022. "Demographic and Socioeconomic Characteristics of the Transgender and Cisgender Populations in the U.S." In Amanda K. Baumle and Sonny Nord Marken (eds.), *Demography of Transgender, Non-Binary, and Gender Minority Populations*, 73–90. Cham, Switzerland: Springer Nature.

Sullivan, Teresa A. 2019. "Demography of the Labor Force." In Dudley L. Poston, Jr. (ed.), *Handbook of Population*, 2nd ed., 263–278. Cham, Switzerland: Springer.

2020a. *Census 2020: Understanding the Issues*. Cham, Switzerland: Springer.

2020b. "Coming to Our Census: How Social Statistics Underpin Our Democracy (and Republic)." *Harvard Data Science Review* 2 (1). https://hdsr.mitpress.mit.edu/pub/1g1cbvkv/release/3

2020c. "The US African-American Population Experienced a COVID-19 Double Disadvantage: Unemployment and Illness" In Glenn Muschert, Kristen Budd, Michelle Christian, David Lane, and Jason Smith, (eds.), *Social Problems in the Age of COVID-19*, Vol. 1: *US Perspectives*. Bristol, UK: Bristol University Press.

Sullivan, Teresa A., and Daniel Cork (eds.) 2023. *Assessing the 2020 Census*. Washington, DC: National Academies Press. https://doi.org/10.17226/27150

Sullivan, Teresa A., and Sarah M. Panuska. 2020. "Philip M. Hauser, Innovator." In P. Atkinson, S. Delamont, A. Cernat, J. W. Sakshaug, and R. A. Williams (eds.), *SAGE Research Methods Foundations*. https://methods.sagepub.com/foundations/hauser-philip-m

Swanson, David A., and G. Edward Stephan. 2004. "A Demography Time Line." In Jacob S. Siegel and David A. Swanson (eds.), *The Methods and Materials of Demography*, 2nd ed., 779–786. San Diego, CA: Elsevier Academic.

Szreter, Simon. 2007. "The Right of Registration: Development, Identity Registration, and Social Security: A Historical Perspective." *World Development* 35: 67–86.

Taeuber, Conrad, and Irene B. Taeuber. 1958. *The Changing Population of the United States*. New York: John Wiley.

Taeuber, Cynthia M. 2006. *American Community Survey Data for Community Planning*. Victoria, BC, Canada: Trafford.

Taueber, Irene B. 1959. "Demographic Research in the Pacific." In Philip M. Hauser and Otis Dudley Duncan (eds.), *The Study of Population: An Inventory and Appraisal*, 259–285. Chicago: University of Chicago Press.

Taeuber, Irene B., and Conrad Taeuber. 1971. *People of the United States in the 20th Century*. Washington, DC: US Government Printing Office.

Tang, Mengjun, and Jiawei Hou. 2024. "Changes of Sex Ratio at Birth and Son Preferences in China: A Mixed Method Study." *China Population and Development Studies* 8: 1–27.

Tavris, Carol, and Carole Wade. 1984. *The Longest War: Sex Differences in Perspective*, 2nd ed. New York: Harcourt Brace Jovanovich.

Taylor, Danielle, and Caren A. Arbeit. 2024. "The STEM Labor Force: Scientists, Engineers, and Skilled Technical Workers." National Science Board, *Science and Engineering Indicators* (May). https://ncses.nsf.gov/pubs/nsb20245/foreign-born-stem-workers

Teilhard de Chardin, Pierre. 1959. *The Phenomenon of Man*. New York: Harper and Row.

1969a. *The Future of Man*. New York: Harper and Row.

1969b. *The God of Evolution*. Orlando, FL: Harcourt.

Teitelbaum, Michael S. 1972. "Fertility Effects of the Abolition of Legal Abortion in Romania." *Population Studies* 26: 405–417.

2019. "Political Demography." In Dudley L. Poston, Jr. (ed.), *Handbook of Population*, 2nd ed., 775–792. New York: Springer.

Tentler, Leslie Woodcock. 2008. "Bitter Pill." *Commonweal* 135 (20): 22–24.

Thevenon, Olivier. 2016. "The Influence of Family Policies on Fertility in France: Lessons from the Past and Prospects for the Future." In Ronald R. Rindfuss and Minja Kim Choe (eds), *Low Fertility Institutions and Their Policies: Variations Across Industrialized Countries*, 49–76. Cham, Switzerland: Springer.

Thomas, Dorothy Swaine. 1941. *Social and Economic Aspects of Swedish Population Movement, 1750–1933*. New York: Macmillan.

Thompson, Kenneth. 1975. *August Comte: The Foundation of Sociology*. New York: Halsted Press.

Thompson, Warren S. 1929. "Population." *American Journal of Sociology* 34: 959–975.

Thompson, Warren S., and David Lewis. 1965. *Population Problems*. New York: McGraw Hill.

Thompson, Warren S., and Pascal K. Whelpton. 1933. *Population Trends in the United States*. New York: McGraw Hill.

Thornton, Arland, and Tom E. Fricke. 1989. "Social Change and the Family: Comparative Perspectives from the West, China and South Asia." In J. Mayone Stycos (ed.), *Demography as an Interdiscipline*, 128–161. New Brunswick, NJ: Transaction.

Thornton, Russell. 1990. *American Holocaust and Survival*. Norman: University of Oklahoma Press.

Thuy, T. T. Le, David Mendez, and Kenneth E. Warner. 2024. "New Estimates of Smoking-Attributable Mortality in the U.S. from 2020 Through 2035." *American Journal of Preventive Medicine* 66 (5). www.ajpmonline.org/article/S0749-3797(23)00515-9/fulltext

Tienda, Marta. 2002. "Demography and the Social Contract." *Demography* 39: 587–616.

Tietze, Christopher. 1965. "History of Contraceptive Methods." *Journal of Sex Research* 1: 69–85.

Tobler, Waldo. 1995. "Migration: Ravenstein, Thornthwaite, and Beyond." *Urban Geography* 16: 327–343.

Tomes, Nancy. 2010. "'Destroyer and Teacher': Managing the Masses during the 1918–1919 Influenza Pandemic." *Public Health Reports* 125 (Suppl. 3): 48–62. https://doi.org/10.1177/00333549101250S308

Trussell, James. 2004. "Contraceptive Failure in the United States." *Contraception* 70: 89–96.

2011. "Contraceptive Efficacy." In Robert A. Hatcher, James Trussell, Anita L. Nelson, Willard Cates, Jr., Deborah Kowal, and Michael S. Policar (eds.), *Contraceptive Technology*, 20th rev. ed., 779–863. New York: Ardent Media, Inc.

Trussell, James, and Katherine A. Guthrie. 2011. "Choosing a Contraceptive: Efficacy, Safety, and Personal Considerations." In Robert A. Hatcher, James Trussell, Anita L. Nelson, Willard Cates, Jr., Deborah Kowal, and Michael S. Policar (eds.), *Contraceptive Technology*, 20th rev. ed., 45–74. New York: Ardent Media, Inc.

Trussell, James, and Eleanor Bimla Schwarz. 2011. "Emergency Contraception." In Robert A. Hatcher, James Trussell, Anita L. Nelson, Willard Cates, Jr., Deborah Kowal and Michael S. Policar (eds.), *Contraceptive Technology*, 20th rev. ed., 113–145. New York: Ardent Media, Inc.

Tsuya, Noriko O. 2015. "Below-Replacement Fertility in Japan: Patterns, Factors and Policy Implications." In Ronald R. Rindfuss and Minja Kim Choe (eds.), *Low and Lower Fertility Variations Across Developed Countries*, 87–106. Cham, Switzerland: Springer.

Tucker, Joseph D., Gail E. Henderson, T. F. Wang, Y. Y. Huang, William Parish, S. M. Pan, X. S. Chen, and M. S. Cohen. 2005. "Surplus Men, Sex Work, and the Spread of HIV in China." *AIDS* 19: 539–547.

Tucker, Joseph D., Dudley L. Poston, Jr., Qiang Ren, Baochang Gu, Xiaoying Zheng, Stephanie Wang, and Chris Russell (eds.). 2009. *Gender Policy and HIV in China: Catalyzing Policy Change*. New York: Springer.

Turra, Casio M., and Irma T. Elo. 2008. "The Impact of Salmon Bias on the Hispanic Mortality Advantage." *Population Research and Policy Review* 27: 515–530.

United Nations. 1958. *Principles and Recommendations for National Population Censuses*. New York: United Nations.

1973. *The Determinants and Consequences of Population Change*, Vol. 1. New York: United Nations.

1980. *Patterns of Urban and Rural Population Growth*. New York: United Nations.

1990. *1988 Demographic Yearbook*. New York: United Nations.

1998. "Principles and Recommendations for Population and Housing Censuses, Revision 1." *Statistical Papers*, Series M, No. 67/Rev. 1. New York: United Nations.

2001. *Replacement Migration: Is It a Solution to Declining and Ageing Populations?* New York: United Nations.

2007. *World Population Prospects, The 2006 Revision: Highlights*. New York: United Nations.

2013a. *Adolescent Fertility since the International Conference on Population and Development (ICPD) in Cairo*. New York: United Nations:

2013b. *International Migration Report 2013*. New York: United Nations.

2013c. *International Migration Wall Chart 2013*. New York: United Nations.

2013d. *World Population Prospects: The 2012 Revision. Highlights and Advance Tables*. New York: United Nations.

2014a. *World Fertility Patterns Wall Chart, 2013*. New York: United Nations.

2014b. *World Urbanization Prospects, Highlights. 2014 Revision*. New York: United Nations.

2024a. *The Least Developed Countries in Facts and Figures*. New York: United Nations. www.un.org/ohrlls/sites/www.un.org.ohrlls/files/ldcs_facts_and_figures_2024.pdf

2024b. *World Population Prospects 2024*. New York: United Nations.

2025. "Population." www.un.org/en/global-issues/population

United Nations Department of Economic and Social Affairs (UNDESA), Population Division. 2015. *World Population Ageing 2015 – Highlights* (ST/ESA/SER.A/368) www.un.org/en/development/desa/population/publications/pdf/ageing/WPA2015_Highlights.pdf

2019. "Contraceptive Use by Method, 2019." Data booklet. New York: United Nations.

2020. *International Migration 2020 Highlights* (ST/ESA/SER.A/452). www.un.org/en/desa/international-migration-2020-highlights

United Nations Department of Economic and Social and Affairs (UNDESA). 2021. "Policy Implications of the Disruption of the Implementation of the 2020 World Population and Housing Census Programme Due to the COVID-19 pandemic." Policy Brief #118. www.un.org/development/desa/dpad/publication/un-desa-policy-brief-118-policy-implications-of-the-disruption-of-the-implementation-of-the-2020-world-population-and-housing-census-programme-due-to-the-covid-19-pandemic

United Nations Department of Economic and Social Affairs (UNDESA). 2022. *World Family Planning 2022: Meeting the Changing Needs for Family Planning, Contraceptive Use by Age and Method*. New York: United Nations.

United Nations Fund for Population Activities (UNFPA). 2014. *Framework of Actions to the Follow-up to the Programme of Action of the International Conference on Population and Development, Beyond 2014*. New York: United Nations Fund for Population Activities.

2019. *Accelerating the Promise: The Report on the Nairobi Summit on ICPD25*. New York: United Nations Fund for Population Activities.

United Nations High Commission for Refugees (UNHCR). 2023. *Global Trends: Forced Displacement in 2023*. www.unhcr.org/global-trends-report-2023

2024. *Global Focus: Afghanistan*. https://reporting.unhcr.org/operational/operations/afghanistan

United Nations International Children's Emergency Fund (UNICEF). 2002. *Birth Registration Right from the Start*. Florence: UNICEF.

2014. *Every Child's Birth Right: Inequities and Trends in Birth Registration*. New York: UNICEF.

2019. "Despite Significant Increase in Birth Registration, a Quarter of the World's Children Remain 'Invisible'." 10 December. www.unicef.org/press-releases/despite-significant-increase-birth-registration-quarter-worlds-children-remain

2023. *Stillbirths* (January). https://data.unicef.org/topic/child-survival/stillbirths/

2024. *Neonatal Mortality* (March). https://data.unicef.org/topic/child-survival/neonatal-mortality/

United Nations Office of the High Commissioner for Human Rights (UNOHCHR). 2019. *Born Free and Equal: Sexual Orientation, Gender Identity and Sex Characteristics in International Human Rights Law*, 2nd ed. New York: UNOHCHR.

United Nations, Regional Information Center. 2023. "Migration to the EU: Facts, Not Perceptions." (December 14). Brussels: United Nations Regional Information Center. https://unric.org/en/migration-to-the-eu-facts-not-perceptions/

United Nations Statistics Division (UNSD). 2013. "2010 World Population and Housing Census Programme (2005–2014)." *Newsletter* 14 (March).

United Nations Trade and Development (UNCTAD). 2022. "Now 8 Billion and Counting: Where the World's Population Has Grown Most and Why That Matters." November 15. https://unctad.org/data-visualization/now-8-billion-and-counting-where-worlds-population-has-grown-most-and-why

US Bureau of the Census. 1975. *Historical Statistics of the United States*. Washington, DC: US Government Printing Office.

2006. *American Community Survey, Design and Methodology*. Technical Paper 67. Washington, DC: US Government Printing Office.

2007. *Census Atlas of the United States*. Series CENSR-29. Washington, DC: US Bureau of the Census.

2014. “Through the Decades, History: Index of Questions.” Washington, DC: US Bureau of the Census.

2015a. “1790 Overview.” www.census.gov/history/www/through_the_decades/overview/1790.html

2015b. “Calculating Migration Expectancy Using ACS Data.” *Migration/Geographic Mobility, Main Page* (April 1). Washington, DC: US Bureau of the Census.

2017. “American Community Survey: Information Guide.” www.census.gov/content/dam/Census/programs-surveys/acs/about/ACS_Information_Guide.pdf

2021. “2020 Census Apportionment Results.” www.census.gov/data/tables/2020/dec/2020-apportionment-data/

2023a. “German-American Day: October 6, 2023.” Press Release Number: CB23-SFS.147. www.census.gov/newsroom/tories/german-american-day.html

2023b. “Percent Childless, Women Aged 30–44: Selected Years, 1976–2022.” Washington, DC: US Bureau of the Census. www.census.gov/content/dam/Census/library/visualizations/time-series/demo/fertility/figure1.pdf

2023c. “U.S. Population Projected to Begin Declining in Second Half of Century.” Press Release. November 9. www.census.gov/newsroom/press-releases/2023/population-projections/

2024a. “Annual and Cumulative Estimates of the Components of Resident Population Change for Metropolitan Statistical Areas in the United States: April 1, 2020 to July 1, 2023.” Table (CBSA-MET-EST2023-COMP). www.census.gov/data/datasets/time-series/demo/popest/2020s-total-metro-and-micro-statistical-areas/

2024b. “Nearly Two-thirds of U.S. Households are Family Households.” Press Release CB24-TPS-110. November 12.

2024c. “Net International Migration Drives Highest U.S. Population Growth in Decades.” Press Release CB24–213. December 19. www.census.gov/newsroom/press-releases/2024/population-estimates-international-migration.html

2024d. “State to State Migration Flows: 2022.” American Community Survey, 1-Year Estimates. www.census.gov/data/tables/time-series/demo/geographic-mobility/state-to-state-migration/

2024e. “World Population Clock.” www.census.gov/popclock/

2024f. “Historical Living Arrangements of Children.” www.census.gov/library/visualizations/time-series/demo/children-historical-time-series.html

US Bureau of Labor Statistics. 2015. *How the Government Measures Unemployment*. www.bls.gov/cps/cps_htgm.htm

2024a. “Concepts and Definitions – CPS.” www.bls.gov/cps/definitions.htm

2024b. “Occupational Employment and Wage Statistics (OEWS) Tables.” May.

2024c. “35 Percent of Employed People Did Some or All of Their Work at Home on Days They Worked in 2023.” *The Economics Daily*. July 15. www.bls.gov/opub/ted/2024/35-percent-of-employed-people-did-some-or-all-of-their-work-at-home-on-days-they-worked-in-2023.htm

2025a. “Employment Status of the Civilian Population by Sex and Age.” www.bls.gov/news.release/empsit.t01.htm

2025b. “Labor Force Statistics from the Current Population Survey.” www.bls.gov/web/empsit/cpsee_e16.htm

2025c. “The Employment Situation – December 2024.” www.bls.gov/news.release/pdf/empsit.pdf

US Department of Commerce. 1921. *United States Life Tables, 1890, 1901, 1910, and 1901–1910*. Washington, DC: US Government Printing Office.

US Department of Health and Human Services, Office of Population Affairs. 2022. *Trends in Teen Pregnancy and Childbearing*. Washington, DC: US Department of Health and Human Services. https://opa.hhs.gov/adolescent-health/reproductive-health-and-teen-pregnancy/trends-teen-pregnancy-and-childbearing

US Department of Homeland Security. 2014. *Yearbook of Immigration Statistics, 2013*. Washington, DC.: US Department of Homeland Security.

US Energy Information Administration. 2023. "Does the World Have Enough Oil to Meet Our Future Needs?" www.eia.gov/tools/faqs/faq.php?id=38&t=6

US Government Accountability Office (GAO). 2023. "2020 Census: A More Complete Lessons Learned Process for Cost and Schedule Would Help the Next Decennial." GAO-23-105819. March 2. www.gao.gov/products/gao-23-105819

US Supreme Court. 2015. *Obergefell v. Hodges* 576 U.S. 644 (2015).

van de Kaa, Dirk J. 1987. "Europe's Second Demographic Transition." *Population Bulletin* 42. Washington, DC: Population Reference Bureau.

van de Walle, Etienne, and John Knodel. 1970. "Teaching Population Dynamics with a Simulation Exercise." *Demography* 7: 433–448.

van der Zee, Henri A. 1998. *The Hunger Winter: Occupied Holland 1944–1945*. Lincoln: University of Nebraska Press.

van Imhoff, Evert. 2003. "Cohort Analysis." In Paul Demeny and Geoffrey McNicoll (eds.), *Encyclopedia of Population*, II: 155–157. New York: Macmillan Reference USA.

Veevers, J. E. 1973. "Voluntarily Childless Wives: An Exploratory Study." *Sociology and Social Research* 57: 356–366.

Ventura, Stephanie J., Brady E. Hamilton, and T. J. Mathews. 2014. "National and State Patterns of Teen Births in the United States, 1940–2013." *National Vital Statistics Reports* 63 (August 20).

Vespa, Jonathan, Lauren Medina, and David M. Armstrong. 2020. "Demographic Turning Points for the United States: Population Projections for 2020 to 2060." *Current Population Reports* P25–1144 (February). Washington, DC: US Census Bureau.

Voegele, Juergen. 2022. "Rethinking Silver: Lessons from Japan's Age-ready Cities." July 15. https://blogs.worldbank.org/en/voices/rethinking-silver-lessons-japans-age-ready-cities

Vu, Michellle H., Anh-Tho Nguyen, and Snigdha Alur-Gupta. 2021. "Asian Americans and Infertility: Genetic Susceptibilities, Sociocultural Stigma, and Access to Care." *F&S reports*, 3 (2 Suppl.): 40–45. https://doi.org/10.1016/j.xfre.2021.12.004

Waite, Linda J. 2005. "Marriage and Family." In Dudley L. Poston, Jr., and Michael Micklin (eds.), *Handbook of Population*, 87–108. New York: Kluwer Academic/Plenum.

Wallace, Ruth, and Alison Wolf. 2005. *Contemporary Sociological Theory*. Upper Saddle River, NJ: Prentice Hall.

Wang, Feng. 2015. "China's Long Road toward Recognition of Below Replacement Fertility." In Ronald R. Rindfuss and Minja Kim Choe (eds.), *Low and Lower Fertility Variations Across Developed Countries*, 15–31. Cham, Switzerland: Springer.

Wang, Feng, Yong Cai, and Baochang Gu. 2013. "Population, Policy, and Politics: How Will History Judge China's One-Child Policy?" *Population and Development Review* 38 (Suppl.): 115–129.

Warner, Lee, and Markus J. Steiner. 2011. "Male Condoms." In Robert A. Hatcher, James Trussell, Anita L. Nelson, Willard Cates, Jr., Deborah Kowal, and Michael S. Policar (eds.), *Contraceptive Technology*, 20th rev. ed., 371–389. New York: Ardent Media, Inc.

Warren, Robert, and Jeffrey S. Passel. 1987. "A Count of the Uncountable: Estimates of the Undocumented Aliens in the United States 1980 Census." *Demography* **24**: 375–393.

Waters, Mary C. 2002. "The Social Construction of Race and Ethnicity: Some Examples from Demography." In Nancy A. Denton and Stewart E. Tolnay (eds.), *American Diversity: A Demographic Challenge for the Twentieth-first Century,* 25–49. Albany, NY: State University of New York Press.

Weiss, Martin A., and Andrew P. Scott. 2023. "Remittances: Background and Issues for the 118th Congress." Report R4321. May 10. https://crsreports.congress.gov/product/pdf/R/R43217

Weller, Robert H., and Leon F. Bouvier. 1981. *Population: Demography and Policy*. New York: St. Martin's.

Westoff, Charles F., Robert G. Potter, and Phillip C. Sagi. 1963. *The Third Child: A Study in the Prediction of Fertility*. Princeton, NJ: Princeton University Press.

Westoff, Charles F., Robert G. Potter, Philip C. Sagi, and Elliot G. Mishler. 1961. *Family Growth in Metropolitan America*. Princeton, NJ: Princeton University Press.

Whelpton, Pascal K., Arthur A. Campbell, and John E. Patterson. 1966. *Fertility and Family Planning in the United States*. Princeton, NJ: Princeton University Press.

White, Michael J., Frank D. Bean, and Thomas J. Espenshade. 1990. "The U.S. 1986 Immigration Reform and Control Act and Undocumented Migration to the United States." *Population Research and Policy Review* **9**: 93–116.

Whitney, Craig R. 1997. "Jeanne Calment, World's Elder, Dies at 122." *New York Times*. August 5.

Wilkinson, David O. 1980. *Deadly Quarrels: Lewis F. Richardson and the Statistical Study of War*. Berkeley: University of California Press.

Williams, David R., and Chiquita Collins. 1995. "U.S. Socioeconomic and Racial Differences in Health: Patterns and Explanations." *Annual Review of Sociology* **21**: 349–386.

Wilmoth, Janet. 2004. "Population Size." In Jacob S. Siegel and David A. Swanson (eds.), *The Methods and Materials of Demography*, 2nd ed., 65–80. San Diego, CA: Elsevier Academic.

Wilson, Valerie and Stevie Martin. 2024. "How Trends in American Indian and Alaska Native Population Growth Impact Employment Data." Working Economics Blog. November 2. Washington, DC: Economic Policy Institute. www.epi.org/blog/how-trends-in-american-indian-and-alaska-native-population-growth-impact-employment-data/

Winch, Donald. 2003. "Malthus, Thomas Robert." In Paul Demeny and Geoffrey McNicoll (eds.), *Encyclopedia of Population*, II: 619–621. New York: Macmillan Reference USA.

Wing, Steven, Kenneth G. Manton, Eric Stallard, Curtis G. Hames, and H. A. Tryoler. 1985. "The Black/White Mortality Crossover: Investigation in a Community-Based Study." *Journal of Gerontology* **40**: 78-84.

Wolfenden, Hugh H. 1954. *Population Statistics and Their Compilation*. Chicago: University of Chicago Press.

Woodham-Smith, Cecil Blanche. 1992. *The Great Hunger: Ireland 1845–1849*. New York: Penguin.

World Bank. 1997. *China 2020: Sharing Rising Incomes: Disparities in China*. Washington, DC: The World Bank.

World Bank. 2024. "GNI (current US$)." Washington, DC: The World Bank. https://data.worldbank.org/indicator/NY.GNP.MKTP.CD

World Health Organization (WHO). 2004. *Maternal Mortality in 2000*. Geneva: World Health Organization.

2006. *Neonatal and Perinatal Mortality: Country, Regional and Global Estimates*. Geneva: World Health Organization.

2014. "HIV-AIDS." *Fact Sheet* (360). Geneva: World Health Organization.

2015. *Trends in Maternal Mortality, 1990 to 2015*. Geneva: World Health Organization.

2022a. "14.9 Million Excess Deaths Associated with the COVID-19 Pandemic in 2020 and 2021." News release. May 5. www.who.int/news/item/05-05-2022-14.9-million-excess-deaths-were-associated-with-the-covid-19-pandemic-in-2020-and-2021

2022b. "Deaths from Noncommunicable Diseases on the Rise in Africa." News release. April 11. www.afro.who.int/news/deaths-noncommunicable-diseases-rise-africa

2022c. "Plague." Fact Sheet. www.who.int/news-room/fact-sheets/detail/plague

2023. "Trends in Maternal Mortality 2000 to 2020: Estimates by WHO, UNICEF, UNFPA, World Bank Group and UNDESA/Population Division." 23 February. www.who.int/publications/i/item/9789240068759

2024a. *Adolescent Pregnancy*. Geneva: World Health Organization:

2024b. "Ageing and Health." Fact Sheet. www.who.int/news-room/fact-sheets/detail/ageing-and-health

2024c. "Civil Registration and Vital Statistics." Fact Sheet. February 27. www.who.int/news-room/fact-sheets/detail/civil-registration-and-vital-statistics

2024d. "HIV." www.who.int/data/gho/data/themes/hiv-aids

2024e. "ICD-11 for Mortality and Morbidity Statistics." https://icd.who.int/browse/2024-01/mms/en#1596590595

2024f. "International Statistical Classification of Diseases and Related Health Problems (ICD)." May. www.who.int/standards/classifications/classification-of-diseases

2024g. "Maternal Mortality." Fact Sheet. April 26. www.who.int/news-room/fact-sheets/detail/maternal-mortality

2024h. "Newborn Mortality." Fact Sheet. March 14. www.who.int/news-room/fact-sheets/detail/newborn-mortality

2024i. "The Top 10 Causes of Death." Fact Sheet. August 7. www.who.int/news-room/fact-sheets/detail/the-top-10-causes-of-death

Worldometer. 2024. "Life Expectancy of the World Population." www.worldometers.info/demographics/life-expectancy

Worldostats. 2025. "Median Age by Country, 2025." https://worldostats.com/median-age-by-country-2025/

World Population Review. 2024. "Death Rates by Country 2024." https://worldpopulationreview.com/country-rankings/death-rate-by-country

Wortman, Judith. 1976. "The Diaphragm and Other Intravaginal Barriers: A Review." *Population Reports*, Series H, No. 7. Baltimore, MD: INFO Project, Johns Hopkins School of Public Health.

Woytinsky, Wladimir S., and Emma S. Woytinsky. 1953. *World Population and Production.* New York: Twentieth Century Fund.

Wu, Cangping, and Lin Wang. 2004. "Contribution of Population Control in Creating Opportunities for China Arising from Fertility Decline Should Not Be Neglected." Paper presented at the International Symposium on the 2000 Population Census of China, Beijing.

Yang, Jisheng. 2012. *Tombstone: The Great Chinese Famine, 1958–1962.* New York: Farrar, Straus and Giroux.

Yang, Xiushi. 1994. "Urban Temporary Out-migration under Economic Reforms: Who Moves and for What Reasons?" *Population Research and Policy Review* 13: 83–100.

1996. "Labor Force Characteristics and Labor Force Migration in China." In *Changes in China's Labor Market: Implications for the Future*, 13–44. Washington, DC: US Department of Labor.

Young, Paul. 2002. *L. A. Exposed: Strange Myths and Curious Legends in the City of Angels.* New York: St. Martin's Griffin.

Yusuf, Farhat, Jo. M. Martins, and David A. Swanson. 2014. *Methods of Demographic Analysis.* New York: Springer.

Zaba, Basia. 2003. "AIDS." In Paul Demeny and Geoffrey McNicoll (eds.), *Encyclopedia of Population*, I: 37–43. New York: Macmillan Reference USA.

Zakaria, Fareed. 2008. *The Post-American World.* New York: W. W. Norton.

Zelnik, Melvin, and John F. Kantner. 1980. "Sexual Activity, Contraceptive Use and Pregnancy Among Metropolitan-Area Teenagers: 1971–1979." *Family Planning Perspectives* 12 (September/October): 230–231, 233–237.

Zeng, Yi, Ping Tu, Baochang Gu, Y. Xu, B. Li, and Y. Li. 1993. "Causes and Implications of the Recent Increase in the Reported Sex Ratio at Birth in China." *Population and Development Review* 19: 283–302.

Zhang, Li. 2013. *Male Fertility Patterns and Determinants.* New York: Springer.

Zhang, Li, Dudley L. Poston, Jr., and Chiung-Fang Chang. 2014. "Male and Female Fertility in Taiwan." In Dudley L. Poston, Jr., Wen Shan Yang, and D. Nicole Farris (eds.), *The Family and Social Change in Chinese Societies*, 151–161. New York: Springer.

Zhou, Bo, and Yumeng Zhong. 2022. "Young Floating Population in the City: How Outsiderness Influences Self-Esteem of Rural-to-Urban Migrant Children in China." *International Journal of Environmental Research and Public Health* 19: 1863. www.ncbi.nlm.nih.gov/pmc/articles/PMC8835061/

Zhou, Min. 1992. *Chinatown: The Socioeconomic Potential of an Urban Enclave*. Philadelphia, PA: Temple University Press.
Zinn, Howard. 2003. *A People's History of the United States*. New York: HarperCollins.
Zuehlke, Eric. 2008. "The 'Lucky Few' Reveal the Lifelong Impact of Generation." Washington, DC: Population Reference Bureau.

Name Index

Subject Index

For EU product safety concerns, contact us at Calle de José Abascal, 56–1°,
28003 Madrid, Spain or eugpsr@cambridge.org.

www.ingramcontent.com/pod-product-compliance
Ingram Content Group UK Ltd.
Pitfield, Milton Keynes, MK11 3LW, UK
UKHW052242170526
471087UK00012B/744

* 9 7 8 1 0 0 9 6 9 6 9 1 3 *